UNITED

THE FIRST 100 YEARS

CENTENARY

NEWCASTLE UNITED

1892-1992

Joe Harvey receiving the FA Cup from Prime minister Winston Churchill.

UNITED
THE FIRST 100 YEARS
The Official Centenary History of Newcastle United

By Paul Joannou

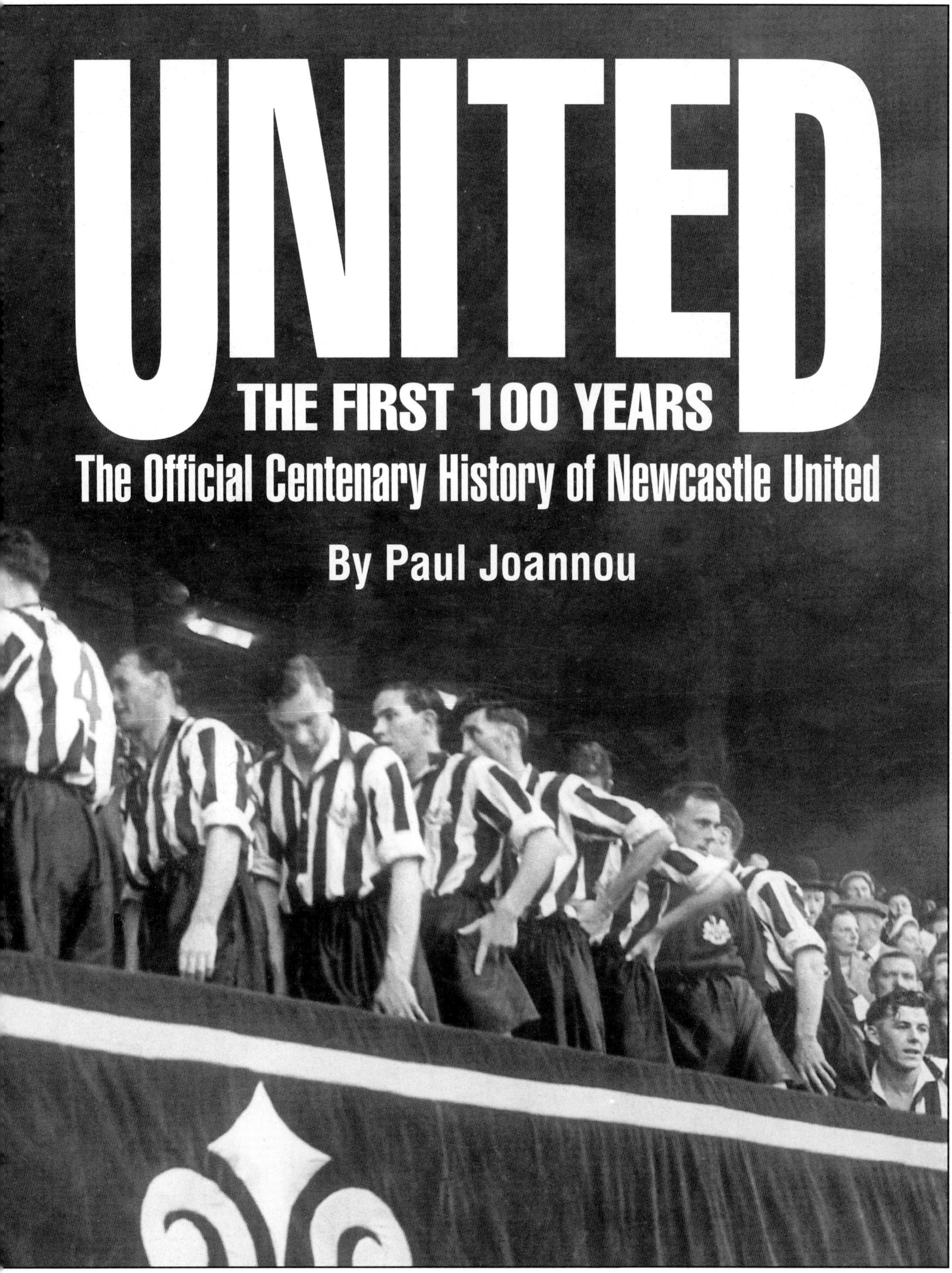

Dedication

To Newcastle United's loyal supporters
- without doubt the best there are.

A LAZY FIT.

THE MAGPIE:—" Bother the League. I wish the 25th was here."

The Magpie, a regular feature in the local press during the 1900's, dreams of United's forthcoming FA Cup final appointment on April 25th, 1908.

First published in Great Britain by
ACL Colour Print & Polar Publishing (UK) Ltd
2 Uxbridge Road, Leicester LE4 7ST, England

ISBN 0 9514862 4 1

Dust Cover Design
Eamon C. Heighway

Edited by
Julian Baskcomb & Julia Byrne

Designed and Printed by
ACL Colour Print & Polar Publishing (UK) Ltd
2 Uxbridge Road, Leicester LE4 7ST, England
Telephone: (0533) 610800

FRONT DUST COVER ILLUSTRATIONS
Newcastle memorabilia throughout the century.
United's No. 9 shirts past and present as worn by Hughie Gallacher and Mick Quinn.
Scotland international cap won by Sandy Higgins in 1911, England badge awarded to Colin Veitch together with the 1927 Championship (left) and 1951 FA Cup (right) medals won by Roddie McKenzie and Charlie Crowe.

REAR DUST COVER ILLUSTRATIONS
Left to right, top; Cigarette cards featuring Jackie Milburn and Joe Harvey, a souvenir card from United's pioneers East End, Mick Quinn and Paul Gascoigne.
Middle; Promotion celebrations in 1965.
Bottom; Sam Weaver, Colin Veitch, Alec Gardner, Kevin Keegan and Hughie Gallacher.

CONTENTS

AUTHOR'S INTRODUCTION & ACKNOWLEDGEMENTS

As the Club's Historian, Newcastle United's Centenary is an event I have been looking forward to for several years. With two, or even three, significant years to choose from, the Club nearly celebrated their 100th birthday ten years ago, in 1982, marking the formation of Newcastle East End as the start of it all. As it turned out the decision was made to wait another decade and celebrate the event when two historic moments reached their century. Firstly, the move by East End from Heaton across the city in May 1892 to take-over the lease of St James Park following the winding up of their rivals West End. Then seven months later, in December 1892, the change in name to Newcastle United. By the end of that year Newcastle United Football Club had developed from its embryo state into a club ready to set forth on a century of incident.

Research of United's absolutely unique story has taken on and off all of a decade. My aim has been to be thorough with an historian's eye, and to represent the many events that have taken place in a balanced way, giving as much emphasis on Edwardian years to those of, say, the seventies. And the club's bad times are given equal ranking with the glory days. This book fully chronicles the Magpies 'First 100 Years' together with their equally eventful formative period on Victorian Tyneside.

Appreciation has to be noted to many people in the compilation of this Centenary History. First a special thanks to the staff of Newcastle United. To Chairman George Forbes and Vice Chairman Peter Mallinger who have both been as enthusiastic as the author in seeing this volume take shape. To Assistant Secretary Ken Slater and Office Manager Tony Toward, who I have continually pestered for information over the past ten years. And also to Secretary & General Manager Russell Cushing and Commercial Manager Grahame McDonnell who have assisted in their different ways. Former Chairman and life long supporter, Gordon McKeag has been an invaluable source of information, both on his father's involvement with the club and his own time at St James Park.

Many former players have passed on their memories over the period of research, too many to mention here. But special thanks to Charlie Crowe, whose humorous anecdotes and knowledge were a rare source. And to Bobby Cowell, Albert Stubbins, Tommy Craig, Bob Moncur, David Craig and Jimmy Scoular to name a few of many. Posthumous thanks to Joe Harvey and Jackie Milburn whose extensive interviews before their death were invaluable. Many former stars have also given or loaned photographs, most unpublished before.

The newspaper men of the Newcastle Chronicle and Journal have sometimes been a much criticised bunch, however to any historian's research their columns have been the most important point of reference. The saturation, minute by minute coverage of the activities at St James Park since very early days has been a marvellous diary of events. The men who followed United's fortunes over the years, from pre-war gents 'Hereward' and 'Novocastrian', to Stan Bell, Ken McKenzie and more recent personalities, John Gibson, Alan Oliver and Brian McNally, a special thank you. Editor Graeme Stanton and journalist Paul Tully, have also been of special help at Thomson House.

Over the period of research - especially so in the last twelve months - many individuals and organisations have helped in their various ways. Several members of the Association of Football Statisticians have passed on information since its formation in 1978, and thanks to the help over the years of veteran historian Douglas Lamming, whose enthusiasm and thoroughness I have tried to match. The comprehensive collection of documents and newspapers at the Local Studies department of Newcastle Central Library has been an important source too. United supporters Bill Swann and Steve Corke require acknowledgement for their past work on my previous book Newcastle United : A Complete Record - the central point of reference to this history. Thanks also to the following around the country, my apologies if anyone has been inadvertently missed.

D Brownlow (Newcastle), TM Clark (Stockton),
A Candlish (Newcastle), M Dix (Newcastle),
I Dobson Photography (Newcastle), G Davies (Holyhead),
T Frost (Bradford), A Fiddes (Newcastle),
H Gallacher Junior (Gateshead), R Golding (Newcastle),
A Higgins Junior (Newcastle), D Hallwood (Ryton),
A Hardisty (Sunday Express, Newcastle), M Kirkup (Newbiggin),
A Lodge (Edinburgh), A Mitchell (Edinburgh),
Northumberland FA (Newcastle),
National Library of Scotland (Edinburgh), N Parker (Amersham),
A Rippon (Breedon Books, Derby), P Ratcliffe (Newcastle),
Rev. N Sands (Crystal Palace FC),
A Wilson (Newcastle Museums Service),
John Wardle Agency (Newcastle).

Acute care has been taken to check the text for errors, both factual and typographical, however in a volume of this size it is perhaps inevitable that some will occur. My apologies if they have. In summary, as a self confessed Newcastle United fanatic this book has been a pleasure to compile, a story with never a dull moment and packed with Tyneside fervour. As Malcolm Macdonald remarked, "It is impossible to appreciate the passion and pride football generates at St James Park until you have actually lived through it". Most readers will know exactly what he means.

Paul Joannou
Edinburgh
September 1991

PHOTOGRAPHIC ACKNOWLEDGMENTS
Newcastle United FC, Newcastle Chronicle & Journal,
TE Bainbridge, C Crowe, L Craig, A Rippon, R Stokoe,
A Fiddes, Newcastle Central Library, J Scoular, C Willoughby,
G McKeag, M Dix, G Dickson, R Golding, AllSport,
Colorsport, P Joannou Collection.

FOREWORD

By Kevin Keegan OBE

It was my privilege to be part of Newcastle United's 100 year history for just two seasons. But I do count those final games of my career as a privilege.

I was fortunate enough to play football at great clubs like Liverpool and Hamburg. There was the thrill and pride of 63 England caps and the honour of being voted Footballer of the Year both in this country and in Europe.

But nothing gave me greater pleasure than helping Newcastle to climb back into the First Division in 1984. It was the culmination of the dream I shared with the best fans I ever played for - the Geordies backed me to the hilt when I joined Newcastle from Southampton in the summer of 1982.

Together we saw that First Division dream come true. Now it hurts me to see them outside the top flight again. It hurts me because Newcastle United do have, beyond question, the most loyal fans in football. In fact the fans are the Club's biggest success and the basic reason why I would always have to be optimistic about the future at St James Park. No matter how disappointing the results may be and how bleak the overall picture may look, Geordie supporters have a thread of optimism running through them that is unique in football.

How else could you possibly explain why the support has been so good for so long when honours have been so thin on the ground? It is more than 60 years since the First Division title was won and you have to be a tidy age to remember those fabulous FA Cup triumphs of the 1950s.

In recent years, a great club - and Newcastle is a great club - has spent too many frustrating seasons in the Second Division. They are there now and it hurts all of us who love the place. But through all the disappointments the fans have never lost the belief that one day the golden era will dawn again. I believe it too.

There is a passion about Tyneside that only those who have lived there can possibly understand. I had been told about it before my debut against Queen's Park Rangers at the start of the 1982/83 season. I had sampled it as a visiting player, most notably with Liverpool and most memorably on Malcolm Macdonald's home debut in 1971. Supermac's hat-trick that day and the joy and noise of a special Tyneside occasion are still vivid memories for me. But not until I began to play regularly for those supporters did I come to appreciate just how special they are. The biggest compliment I paid them was choosing to retire as a Newcastle player.

If I could make a wish for football in general it would be to have a successful Newcastle United. What a tonic that would be for our national game. My wish for those men, women and children who go on supporting their Club through thick and thin is that they get the team on the pitch that their loyalty richly deserves. If that wish were to come true then Newcastle United would be the most successful Club of them all.

This Centenary History of United represents one man's love affair with that Club. The fans will love it as much as they love everything to do with what is, in essence, the very heartbeat of a great city.

PREFACE

By George Forbes
Chairman, Newcastle United Football Club

Newcastle United is a club steeped in history and tradition. Over the last hundred years it has also been packed with character, controversy, colour and comedy. Boredom is one commodity not on sale at St James Park.

Newcastle United has lived in the spotlight and existed in headlines ever since the city's East End team took over St James' in 1892. Now a century on, the club survives as one of the most famous and passionate centres of football in Britain. Our supporters have ensured that through their fanatical devotion to every minute detail of club affairs. If somebody sneezes here, it's news. Those same fans may have accused the club of many indiscretions over the past hundred years. But boring..never!

The famous black'n'whites invoke a feeling rarely matched in other parts of the country. That is why, as Chairman of Newcastle United, it is my pleasure and privilege to introduce this history as the club enters its second century. If the next hundred years proves as exciting and incident packed as the first, then future generations are in for a treat.

I am well aware of the special place the Football Club holds in the affairs of Tyneside. They used to say that if the team won on Saturday, production in the shipyards or down the mines went up 50 per cent on Monday. Equally, a bad defeat meant that Monday in the workplace was a dismal and depressing place to be. These days the jobs may have changed, but the message is the same. We know that we can put smiles on people's faces. It is a responsibility that we don't shirk.

A CENTURY OF INCIDENT

Success, failure, famous players, larger-than-life characters, goals ...all this and more is woven into the fabric of a club that has never lacked charisma. Newcastle, for example, has been the home for some of the game's most exciting personalities. The names of players like Hughie Gallacher, Jackie Milburn, Malcolm Macdonald and Kevin Keegan would be on everybody's lips. Some of them were born and bred in the north east. Others came here to make their reputations and secure a place in history. Whatever their backgrounds they all had one thing in common. They were larger-than-life figures, elevated to cult status by a public that still believes in heroes. Newcastle always was a club that hung its hat on a star. 'Keegan to Newcastle? What a joke', suggested some. But he came. 'The first Brazilian in the Football League? Forget it', said others. But Mirandinha turned up none the less.

Now it's Ossie Ardiles' turn. 'Ossie for Tyneside?' Why not. This club has never been afraid to aim for the best, and in Ardiles we have a man who stands to become just as famous throughout the world as a manager as he was as a World Cup winner with Argentina. His arrival simply adds a little bit more to the universal appeal of the club. There has always been somebody or something to capture the imagination at St James Park. That's what, over the years, has made the club interesting, vibrant, alive. Now we've got Ossie and a young team that I believe can write its own headlines during the coming decade.

My own family involvement with Newcastle United goes back to the 1930s when my uncle James Johnston was on the playing staff at Gallowgate. I still have his contract - £2 in the winter, £1 in the summer - as a keepsake. But my love affair with the club really flourished around 30 years ago when, as a teenager, I would make the 120 mile round trip with some friends from the Border country where I lived to see my idols in action. I'd stand in the Centre-Paddock and drool over the skills of Jinky Jimmy Smith. He was my own particular favourite player, and along with thousands of others I remember watching his come-back in a reserve game after he'd been out for a year with injury.

Newcastle demanded that sort of passion and commitment from its fans and still does. People need heroes - particularly at this club. And they've rewarded them with a love and affection that can never be diminished. Ask Malcolm Macdonald how he felt when, with the rest of the United players, he returned to a hero's welcome after losing the FA Cup final at Wembley in 1974. The experience reduced him to tears. And those who lined the streets to pay homage to Wor Jackie Milburn when he died in October 1988 were mourning more than the passing of a great player - they were saying a personal thank-you to a legend.

Big hearts, big emotions. They are all part of the Geordie character and over a hundred years the club has had players to match. Great games - such as the three FA Cup final victories in the 1950s. Great occasions - like the Fairs Cup triumph over Ujpesti Dozsa. Great goals. Who, for example, could forget the marvellous 30 yard goal that Milburn scored from Ernie Taylor's backheel to win the FA Cup against Blackpool in 1951? Or Len Shackleton's achievement in scoring six goals on his debut against Newport County in a 13-0 win in 1946...still the club's record victory.

But with the highs have come lows - coupled with controversy. Newcastle and controversy have never been far apart. More than once over the years we have shot ourselves in the foot. Fans have criticised the club, with some justification, for lacking ambition. It used to be said that Newcastle took their supporters for granted - that fans would turn up just to see the grass grow. Unseemly boardroom squabbles have also done little to promote the club's image. United over the years has had an unfortunate habit of airing its dirty linen in public. At times you couldn't turn to the back pages of the newspapers without one Newcastle row or another hitting you between the eyes.

Now we don't want to make the same mistakes again. We are aware of supporters' needs and aim to do something about them. I personally have resented criticism of directors that they are not as ambitious or as passionate as the fans. Nobody is more ambitious than I am to see this club back where it belongs. I know how the fans feel. I used to shout at directors myself when things went wrong! Everything stems from success on the field. People talk about potential - but I want success now. I hope we have learned the lessons of the past - both good and bad - to build a better club. The goodwill is out there. There is a new mood about. I can feel it. People want to help and I believe that everybody from the general public to local business has a part to play.

It is our aim to march into our second century with a magnificent stadium and a team to match. If we get there I hope people will look back to read this history of the 'First Hundred Years' and say 'that's how they did it'.

A WORD FROM. .

I look forward to many more years of success and echo the cheer of 'Haway the Lads'.

CLUB SPONSORS
THE NEWCASTLE BREWERIES LTD

Haydn Biddle, Managing Director

The close relationship which joins the two great North East institutions of Newcastle Breweries and Newcastle United Football Club is one which has spanned the decades and given pleasure to millions of people.

As neighbours in the heart of Newcastle Upon Tyne, the association between the two is a popular marriage held in affection by Newcastle folk everywhere. It has long been established that along with the Tyne Bridge, the Blue Star and the Magpie are symbols of a proud North East region.

Individually, both organisations have over the years established a strong community involvement programme drawing on their own resources to set up activities and events for local people. But by acting together and combining their efforts, the two have produced many memorable moments which will go down in local history.

That momentous occasion during the glorious summer of 1982, which heralded the arrival of Kevin Keegan, was one such event. It was that professional partnership of Brewery and Football Club which secured the signature of the footballing star and provided enormous benefits for the region.

The immediate impact was felt on the terraces of St James Park as fans young and old turned up in their thousands to see the England captain pull on a black'n'white strip. But Kevin also wanted to meet and chat with the local people and by working together, the two organisations made this possible. Visits to schools, hospitals and clubs throughout the North East were arranged giving Kevin that important opportunity to meet the fans. A series of soccer days were also held where youngsters could pit their wits and skills against Kevin and his team members. Again, this was set up and organised by volunteers from both camps.

More recently, Newcastle Breweries were the first company to step in to launch a fund to erect a statue in memory of Jackie Milburn, one of Newcastle United's most famous players. And during the period of the Gulf War, Newcastle United and Newcastle Breweries were at the forefront of North East companies to forward parcels to the Geordie troops involved in the conflict.

As a trademark of Tyneside, it is fitting that the Blue Star should once again be returned to the famous Black & White strip. Both organisations have enthusiastic followers around the globe and have a history which is rich in tradition and local folklore.

Newcastle Breweries celebrated its Centenary during 1990 and now it is the history of Newcastle United which will be honoured at the 100 year celebration. We wish the Newcastle United Directors, their staff and the team our warmest congratulations and hope that success and prosperity will follow

THE LORD MAYOR
OF NEWCASTLE UPON TYNE

Councillor Thomas J Marr

Having served the community of Byker now for more than 18 years, it gives me enormous pleasure to contribute a personal view for United's Centenary, very proud of the fact that the club's early beginnings grew of course from the grass roots of Byker in the form of the East End Football Club.

It's amazing to look back at those early days, with huge rivalry between the club and another in the West End of the City which started in Leazes Park. The East End team soon moved to Chillingham Road in Heaton and boasted a growing band of enthusiasts aiming to make the club Tyneside's best.

And they succeeded, after ten years of strong competition with West End (by then resident at St James Park) an historic meeting between the two clubs resulted in the West End team folding and the East End team moving to what we now know as the home ground for Newcastle United.

Over the years the name of Newcastle United became synonymous with exciting football. Even when the tide of fortune turned occasionally against them there was always a keen desire on the part of other clubs to play United home and away.

From a host of excellent players who dares mention but a few without running the risk of offending many fans. Mention must be made however of such stalwarts as Colin Veitch who combined great artistry on the field with superb acting at the People's Theatre now celebrating its 80th birthday.

Other most memorable stars were of course the heroic Scot, Hughie Gallacher and our very own brilliant, Jackie Milburn who was not only a terrific player but a superb ambassador for the region and of course was given the Freedom of the City in 1980.

Strong links with the City Council have been evident throughout the club's development. St James Park is leased to the Football Club jointly by the City Council and the Freemen.

As Lord Mayor of this fine City in celebration of Newcastle United's Centenary, and indeed as a supporter of good football,

" THE BLAYDON RACES"

Aw went to Blaydon Races,
'twas on the ninth of Joon,
Eiteen hundred an' sixty-two,
on a summer's efternoon;
Aw tyuk the bus frae Balmbra's,
an' she wis heavy laden,
Away we went alang Collingwood Street,
that's on the road to Blaydon.
Chorus:
O lads ye shud only see us gannin'
Passin' the foaks upon the road just as
they wor stannin';
Thor wes lots o' lads an' lasses there,
all wi' smilin' faces,
Gannin alang the Scotswood Road,
to see the Blaydon Races.

We flew past Aimstrong's factory,
and up to the "Robin Adair",
Just gannin' doon te the railway bridge,
the bus wheel flew off there.
The lasses lost their crinolines off,
an' the veils that hide their faces,
An' aw got two black eyes an' a
broken nose in gan te Blaydon Races.
Chorus
Noo when we gat to Paradise
thor wes bonny gam begun,
Thor wes fower and twenty on the bus, man,
hoo they danced an' sung;
They called on me to sing a sang,
aw sung them "Paddy Fagan",
Aw danced a jig an' swung me twig,
that day aw went to Blaydon.
Chorus
When we gat the wheel put on away we went agyen,
But them that had their noses broke, they came back ower hyem;
Sum went to the Dispensary, an' sum to Doctor Gibbs,
An' sum to the Infirmary, to mend their broken ribs.
Chorus
We flew across the Chain Bridge reet into Blaydon toon,
the bellman he was callin' there - they call him Jacky Brown,
Aw saw him talking to sum cheps, an' them he was persuadin'
To gan an' see Geordy Ridley's concert in the Mechanic's Hall at Blaydon.
Chorus
The rain it pour'd aw the day an' myed the groond quite muddy,
Coffy Johnny had a white hat on - they wor shootin' "Whe stole the cuddy?"
There wes spice stalls an' munkey shows, an' aud wives selling ciders,
An' a chep wiv a happeny roond aboot shootin' "Noo, me lads, for riders".
Chorus

The Blaydon Races was composed by Tynesider George Ridley in 1862, and was first sung in John Balmbra's Royal Music Saloon on the 5th June 1862, four days before the actual races began. It soon became Newcastle United's anthem, a rousing battle song.

1 VICTORIAN PIONEERS

1881-1892

• ROMANS TO VICTORIANS • BYKER BIRTHPLACE • ST JAMES PARK RIVALS • EAST VERSUS WEST •

"Rather a friendlie kinde of fyghte than a play or recreation - a bloody and murthering practise than a fellowly sport or pastime"

Philip Stubbs, 1583

IT WAS PERHAPS THE ROMANS **who first brought the game of football to Tyneside, albeit a crude contortion of the sport. In the days when Hadrian's Wall was in its glory and Pons Aelius was astride the Tyne, Romans and local Brits, the Geordie forefathers of old, played the game of harpastum.**

Fought out on a rectangle of land it was a sort of football match that engaged two teams with each endeavouring to take a ball - by any means - to the opposing base line. Following the Romans' departure, the Normans arrived and brought to Tyneside their early form of soccer, La Soule, another rough contest. And a wild game it was. It is recorded that in 1280 at Ulgham near Ashington, Henry son of William de Ellington was killed when playing football with a large number of friends. In the course of play he ran fatally against David le Kell's dagger!

Football, in its modern form, arouses passions on Tyneside like no other sport or pastime. Yet the region was one of the country's late developers and not until around 1890 did Tyneside see rapid progress made, several years after other parts of the country. Even then support was a trickle compared to the 60,000 crowds that were to roar encouragement to Newcastle United in their heyday.

Football had been around the north-east in various forms throughout history as an undisciplined game. Following on from the cohorts of Rome and the early Normans, the game developed in a crude way and was actually banned by Royal decree on several occasions. In 1579 a certain John Winkell of County Durham was sent to prison for a week and had to pay a public penance for playing football, while in the same year Sir Thomas Elyot wrote that the sport was a "game giving no pleasure but beastlie furie and violence", and Philip Stubbs recorded in 1583 that football was, "Rather a friendlie kinde of fyghte than a play or recreation - a bloody and murthering practise than a fellowly sport or pastime".

Macaulay's History of England noted in May 1690 that, "letters from Newcastle give an account of a great match at football, which had been played in Northumberland, and was suspected to have been a pretext for a large gathering of the disaffected, ie Jacobites". The legendary record of England went on, "In the crowd, it was said, were 150 horsemen well mounted and armed, of whom many were Papists".

Early such games were played between rural villages, on sports or carnival days, at places like Alnwick and Chester-le-Street. But it was only during the mid-19th Century that the medieval brawl game evolved in a form that can be recognised as the sport of today. The first rules were drawn up in 1848 at Cambridge University. Notts County were the first senior club to be formed, in 1862, followed by Sheffield Wednesday and Nottingham Forest. The Football Association was set up in 1863 and the game flourished rapidly thereafter.

In the north-east football's advance lagged some way behind. It was more than a decade before any semblance of a football club saw the light of day. The first recorded game on Tyneside took place on 3rd March 1877 at the Elswick Rugby Club when a few keen enthusiasts formed two scratch teams - eight against nine - the nine winning 2-0. Shortly after Newcastle's, and the region's, first club was born. Tyne Association was formed in 1877 composed largely of public school men and keen rugby and cricket players. They played at the Northumberland Cricket Club's ground on Bath Road, then on a pitch in Jesmond at Brandling Village on the site of the present Royal Grammar School playing field. Tyne was the north-east's first entry into the FA Cup, as early as November 1879 when they lost 5-1 at Blackburn before a lowly crowd of 300 souls.

Other fledgling sides took to the game. Newcastle Rangers were formed in 1878 and first played on the Drill Field, Alexandria Road in Gateshead because they couldn't find a pitch in their native town. They eventually moved across the Tyne taking over an enclosed ground close to Leazes Terrace in September 1880. The pitch was immediately referred to as St James Park. The following month the Newcastle Journal noted that the Rangers club had, "inaugurated their new ground close to Leazes Terrace on Saturday by a match between the first team against 15 of others. After a pleasant game of two hours it was found the captain's team was victorious over his numerous but less experienced opponents to the extent of 6 goals to 1".

St James Park was on the map. The local press concluded, "The new ground is very nicely situated and is close to the centre of town. It is 120 yards x 60 yards broad and is completely level". In spite of the latter statement the pitch in fact had a notorious slope, a drop of fully 18 feet from the north to south goal.

The first controlling body was set up on 23rd January 1880 when the Northumberland and Durham Football Association was formed at a meeting in the Turk's Head Hotel. Ten clubs were in membership and from the outset the new association began to form a network of local teams. Football prospered enormously and new teams took to the field all over the region. By 1881 Tyneside had approximately 1,700 men and boys playing both association and rugby forms of the game, and 12 months later the Daily Journal recorded that in Northumberland and Durham, "there are now between 50 and 60 association clubs".

The year 1882 was an important 12 months in the history of Newcastle United Football Club as two of those new clubs who arrived on the scene eventually led to the present-day Magpies. Queen Victoria was on the throne and Gladstone was housed in Downing Street ruling an upstairs-downstairs society. The nation was very much locked in Victorian ideals with the British Empire dominating the world. Tyneside was in the throes of tremendous growth. There was a huge influx of Irish and Scots and the sprawling suburbs of Elswick, Byker and Benwell were just starting to take shape. Gosforth was still a village while Jesmond and Heaton housed the town's upper classes.

Industry developed in a dramatic way with coal-pits expanding and the great factories of Armstrong, Parsons and Palmer becoming larger by the day. Huge manufacturing works sprung up all over the district as Tyneside rose to unparalleled peaks of prosperity. The city became a regional centre with a thriving port and large banking institutions. The department stores of Fenwick and Bainbridge sold goods from all over the world.

Horse-drawn trams ran through the elegant streets of Grainger and Dobson, while a half-penny toll was charged for crossing the High Level Bridge. The nearby Swing Bridge had recently been constructed, the now famous arched Tyne Bridge not even thought about. There was still much poverty though, and people worked long arduous hours. Their leisure time was taken up with gambling - on wrestling, whippets and horse-racing, the Blaydon Races included - on drinking, music-halls and some took part in cycling and rowing, then hugely popular sports.

On the football field in 1882, England had defeated Ireland 13-0 but had been crushed 5-1 by Scotland. The England eleven was made up of players from the likes of the Old Carthusians, Clapham Rovers and The Pilgrims. The Old Etonians won the FA Cup toppling Blackburn Rovers at Kennington Oval. The Football League had yet to be formed and, on Tyneside, in the working class suburb of Byker two clubs were starting to play the emerging game with enthusiasm.

Newcastle United's origins are to be found with two minor football clubs on the east of the city, Stanley and Rosewood. Stanley had originated from a cricket team, formed on 15th November 1881 - the rudimentary start of Newcastle United, although the Northumberland Football Association's records note that the club were playing an unorganised game a year earlier.

Following the cricket club's AGM in the house of a certain Mr Allen of Shields Road in Byker, it was decided to form a sister football club. The new Stanley FC had almost identical membership as the cricket side. The name originated as recorded by William Findlay, the founder, because, "they played on vacant land near Stanley Street in South Byker". They kicked off their first match on 26th November 1881 against Elswick Leather Works 2nd XI and won 5-0.

As they progressed Stanley were often confused with two other local clubs, Stanley Nops and Stanley Albion, both of County Durham, so they decided, at the request of the area's FA to change their name, in October 1882, to Newcastle East End. The Daily Chronicle noted the event with a two line report almost hidden in the mass of teams for the following weekend's programme, "At a meeting of the Stanley Association Football Club, Byker, held lately, it was resolved to change the name to the East End".

Rosewood had been formed a couple of months earlier under their captain R. Marr and secretary R. Murray, but later in the year joined forces with East End to form a stronger outfit - their side being integrated as East End's reserve eleven.

The new club was to play in several colours over their formative years. Records indicate they turned out in dark blue, chocolate and blue stripes, on occasion black and white, as well as red, or red and white striped shirts. The latter became their regular attire while they also wore navy blue jerseys with an orange stripe !

FIRST DIRECTORS' LIST

Newcastle East End's first Board of Directors listed in the club's Articles of Association of February 1890 were:

J. Birkett, J. Armstrong, W. Hudson, W. Henry, J.E. Peel, A.H. White, T. Liddle, W. Woodman, W. Richardson, J. Steele, J. Dixon, M.H. Hiscock. All resided in the city and several were also players. The qualification of a director was that 'he shall be a shareholder to the amount of £2 10s at least.' Their occupations varied from that of a clerk to a pattern-maker and ironfounder.

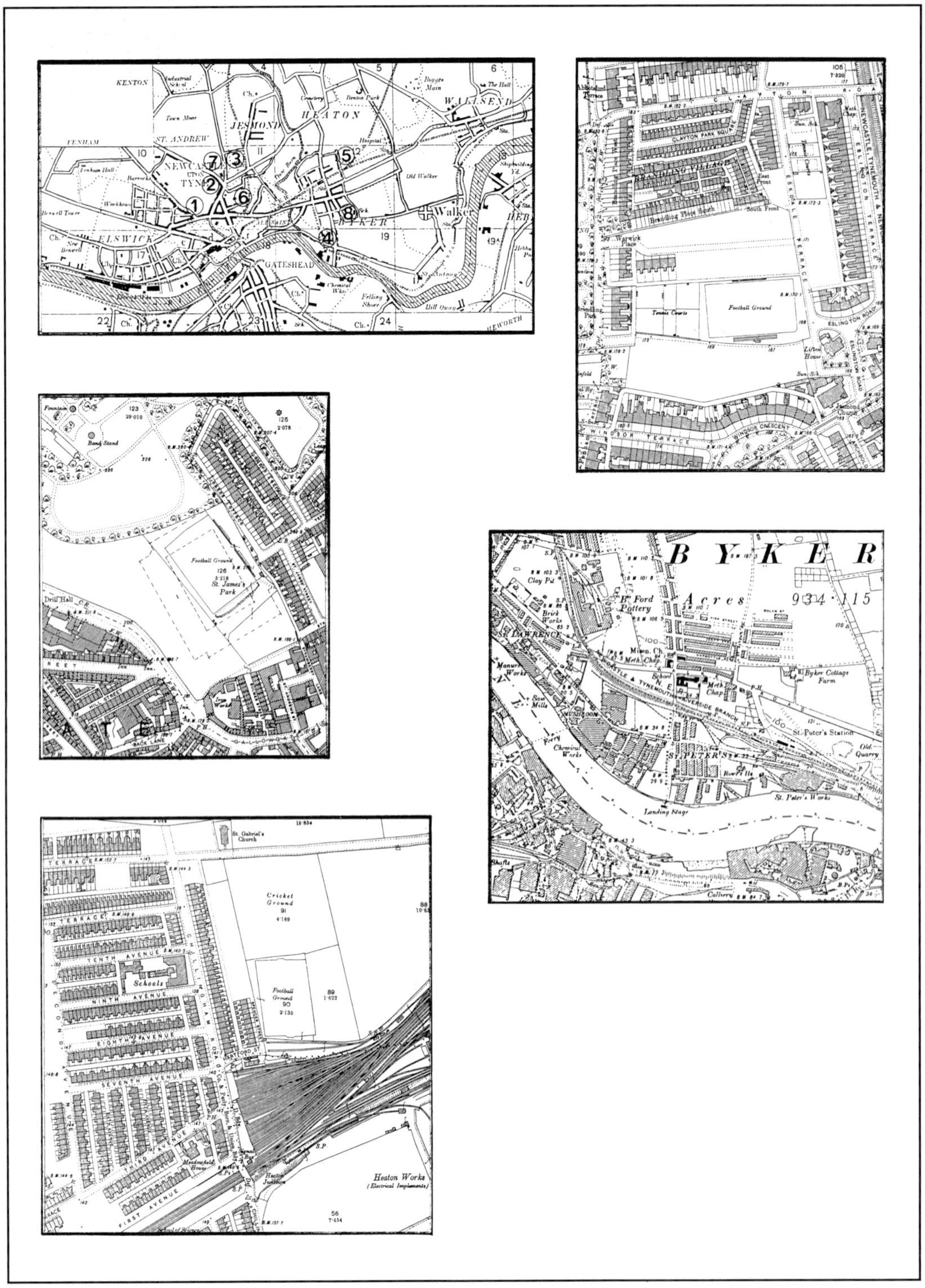

Top left: Football locations on Victorian Tyneside:-
1 - St. James Park,
2 - Leazes Park,
3 - Eskdale Terrace,
4 - St. Peters,
5 - Chillingham Road,
6 - Bath Road,
7 - North Terrace,
8 - Dalton Street.
Top right: Eskdale Terrace 1898, home for a period of West End.
Middle left: St. James Park 1898 showing the outline of the current stadium dotted.
Middle right: The St. Peters area of Byker where Stanley - and Newcastle United - first kicked a football.
Bottom: Chillingham Road 1898 showing East End's ground off Spencer Street and the masssive Heaton railway junction.
Middle right: The St. Peters area of Byker where Stanley - and Newcastle United - first kicked a football.

In the summer of 1884 East End moved the short distance from Stanley Street to a new pitch close by, then again two years later to Chillingham Road, near to the sprawling railway network on the Byker and Heaton border. It was to be known as the Heaton Junction Ground and was next door to another club's pitch, that of North Eastern. It had a bumpy surface when fair and was muddy when wet.

On the other side of the city at the same time East End were taking shape, another club was born which had much to do with the evolution of Newcastle United. Again their origins lay in the bat and ball game of cricket. At the West End Cricket Club more enthusiasts with, by all accounts, Billy Tiffen, - the prime instigator - decided also to switch to football when the cricket season closed. In August 1882 West End FC was set up, almost a year after Stanley had first kicked off. They played in red and black jerseys and white shorts.

West End played on a cricket field on the Town Moor, off Claremont Road and close to Spital Tongues. It was near to the site where the vast complex of the Royal Victoria Infirmary now stands. They moved though, in the summer of 1885 when ball games were banned from the Town Moor for a period, to a pitch off the Great North Road in

Jesmond. A year later, in May 1886, they moved again taking over the lease of St James Park - formerly the pitch of Newcastle Rangers - from the Town's Freemen. It had previously been a piece of common ground granted to the town by Edward III in 1357 and was on the spot where the Scots had used the high ground to besiege and bombard Newcastle's walls at St Andrews. It was also virtually on the site where public hangings had taken place, the last one barely 40 years before in 1844. Some of the gatherings for hangings were as big as many of Newcastle United's football matches. In 1829 a notorious female murderer was led to the gallows watched by 20,000 people - over half of them women!

The ground was bounded by Leazes Park and the Georgian Leazes Terrace, built to house some of the elegant ladies and gents of Tyneside. The surface was rough, latterly used as grazing land for cattle, and still had a pronounced slope. To improve facilities West End employed a number of men to enclose the field behind a substantial eight foot high fence. With East End and West End on the football map the first stage in the development of Newcastle United was complete.

The men who made the club on their respective sides of the city were a mixed bunch - professionals, businessmen, shop-keepers and tradesmen. Many both played and administered the game as it took root. The personalities who stood by East End's fortunes included W.A.Coulson, captain and William Findlay, secretary, both from Byker. Schoolmaster Alex White became very much the leading figure on the playing field and later off it too. Born in the shadows of Glamis Castle near Dundee, he started to play the game with Newcastle Rangers and had appeared in two successful Northumberland FA Cup finals. White later became captain and secretary of East End, a tireless performer and a regular for the County side. He also once appeared for the illustrious Corinthians. Afterwards Alex held a long association with the Northumberland FA and was treasurer from 1913 to 1938. He was a member up to his death in 1940.

Walter Heathcote Golding was another noted figure. Born in Newcastle, Walter was named after a certain Colonel Heathcote who had saved the life of his father during the Crimean War. Golding became East End's secretary succeeding Findlay. Robert Crawford - brother of David Crawford who was later to become a Newcastle United director - trained the players, while other early stalwarts at Heaton were James Peel, who acted as treasurer for a long period, Adam Gilchrist, Daniel Cameron and Alex Turnbull, as well as James Neylon and Joseph Bell. Charles Tinlin became match secretary after his own club, Cheviot, came under East End's control.

Holding West End's flag aloft were William Neasham and John Black. Neasham was a wealthy local dignitary, a merchant who resided in Leazes Terrace and amongst whose land holdings was the lease of St James Park. He was also a highly respected cricketer and, probably along with Tiffen, came up with the idea of forming a football XI at West End Cricket Club. Neasham later became President of the Northumberland FA.

John Black, one of West End's foremost enthusiasts

John Black was also a well known Tynesider, a broadly built innkeeper with a prominent black moustache. He loaned his Lord Hill public-house, situated close to St James Park, as a changing and meeting room. Black lived in Buckingham Street and became a Newcastle United director until 1899. Both men were to spend a small fortune out of their own pockets helping to keep West End afloat in the coming years.

The St James Park club also had Tom Watson working for them, a man who was to become one of early soccer's most prominent secretary-managers. He had played football for Rosehill, later renamed Willington Athletic, and joined West End around 1882. Born in Heaton, Watson was a brilliant administrator, silver tongued and, as he was to prove later, had a golden touch. After helping West End become established, he switched camps to East End and moved to Wearside in 1889. With Sunderland he led the Reds to three titles in four years and in 1896 his success was addressed to Liverpool where he guided the newly promoted Merseysiders to another two Championships. He remained at Anfield for 19 years until his death in 1915.

(left) Tom Watson, who did much to put both East and West End on the football map.

William Tiffen, West End's founder and later an F.A. Council member.

The founder, William Tiffen was another prominent official, secretary and treasurer during his time with West End. Always cheerful and optimistic he played the game too, and was good enough to represent Northumberland in 1886. He became secretary of the Northumberland FA and later was a member of the FA Council. Yet another noted personality in West End's camp was A.Henderson who was eventually elected President of the local FA. After the union of East and West End he drifted out of football to take up a career as a Member of Parliament and later Privy Councillor.

West End's first game was on 7th October 1882 against Rosewood - a 2-0 defeat; this just before the Byker side were to amalgamate with the newly-titled East End. A mile across the city, East End kicked off on the same day, against Hamsterley Rangers at Byker and faired better, winning 1-0. The East Enders though, unlike their rivals, had at least a feel for the new game having played several games under the banner of Stanley. Following these inaugural matches both clubs arranged several more friendlies - league competition being still some years off - and, while both clubs won games, their status in the region was put into perspective when East End met Tyne, the strongest side. They lost 8-0 while West End lost 3-0 to East End's reserve side! Both teams had a long way to go and, as they developed, an intense rivalry built up between the two clubs.

Football of course was very different in those pioneering days. There were no club sponsors or restaurants; no private-boxes or sophisticated tactical plans and no highly paid mega-stars. Players were initially amateurs - although they did receive illegal payments - then became part-timers employed in the many local industries. Matt Hiscock was a shipwright, John Armstrong a joiner and Peter O'Brien a painter. The 'dribbling game' was the norm at first. When a player got the ball he simply ran with it, until he scored or was dispossessed. Tactics and combination play evolved slowly. Pitch markings were different too, with a goal box of two semi-circular areas for many years. Goal nets had not been invented and in many places tapes still acted as a cross-bar, while free-kicks and penalties were just being thought about.

WAGES VICTORIAN STYLE

The advent of professionalism - legally in 1885 and illegally before - saw top players receive up to 7s 6d a week with a 2s 6d win bonus. By 1890 East and West End were paying their stars as much as, "ten shillings each win and 7s 6d a draw or loss". The official umpire received, "2s 6d per match plus 9d per hour for lost time and travelling expenses". Twelve months later East End's wages had risen to, "£1 per match for win or draw". Additionally, virtually all footballers had a job outside football, many of which were fixed up by the club.

Clubs wore a varied collection of strips. One side's outfit consisted of, "blue and red horizontal jerseys with blue knickerbockers". Caps and head cowls were popular before 1890 and shin-pads were strapped outside the socks while boots were ankle length. Braces were even sometimes worn too and they played with a large, heavy leather ball. A referee stood on the touch-line acting as timekeeper and arbitrating whenever the two pitch umpires - each nominated by the clubs - could not agree on decisions. As could be expected arguments were frequent and it was not unheard of for a brawl to develop after debatable verdicts were reached. Both East End and West End were involved in several disputed scorelines.

The majority of supporters were working class and stood without cover on earth mounds, if any, around a primitive roped off pitch. If lucky a small wooden stand housed the club's officials and the odd Victorian gent with, surprisingly, a sprinkling of ladies too. It was said that the first woman to watch a game of football at St James Park was Mrs Watson, wife of the club's secretary.

Apart from the FA Cup, which East End and West End had yet to enter, competitive football had arrived in the region with the Northumberland and Durham Challenge Cup - first played for in 1880/81 and dominated in its formative years by Newcastle Rangers and Tyne Association. Other clubs to take part in that first year of local competition were; Haughton le Skerne, from near Darlington, Bishop Middleham, North Eastern, Corbridge, Burnopfield, Ferryhill, Chester-le-Street, Darlington Grammar School and Sunderland. East End felt they were strong enough to compete in the Challenge Cup in 1882/83 and played their first game in a competitive tournament of any importance during January 1883. They met Elswick Leather Works but were eliminated 2-1 at Byker.

In the spring of that year the local association split into two separate bodies and with it two cup competitions, the Durham Challenge Cup and the Northumberland Challenge Cup. The first tournament took place in the season of 1883/84 and both East and West End took part. In the First Round East End met North Eastern and went out 3-2 while West End were lucky enough to get a bye, but then met Tyne and, like East End in the previous season, were crushed 7-0. Tyne went on to the final in March and lifted the trophy at the expense of Newcastle Rangers.

The first derby meeting between East and West took place that season too. On 10th November East End entertained their city rivals in Byker and a 1-1 draw took place. The return game went West End's way with a 3-0 victory.

Another early competition both clubs took part in was the local Temperance Festival Cup which was part of an immense summer gathering held on the Town Moor. During the era it was a hugely popular event - very much Tyneside's own party - and in 1883 the Northern Athlete magazine noted the attendance in excess of 200,000. Cricket, racing, cycling and tennis contests were played for and, of course, football. East End's under 18 side won the Festival Cup in that year, defeating Marlborough by a single goal and receiving a handsome cup valued at all of 90 shillings.

SUNDERLAND FIRST

When Newcastle Rangers were housed at St James Park they played Sunderland in the semi-final of the Northumberland & Durham Challenge Cup in February 1881. This was almost two years before West End played there. Sunderland therefore played at St James Park before Newcastle United did! The Wearsiders incidentally lost that game by 5-0.

In the year when Arbroath thrashed the canny men from Bon Accord 36-0 and professionalism began to tear British football apart, Newcastle East End won their first senior trophy. In the Northumberland Challenge Cup of 1885, Newcastle United's pioneers defeated Elswick Leather Works, Brunswick Villa Athletic and then, in the semi-final, met West End. Before a crowd of 600 on Tyne's ground they won 5-0 in a replay. One of the goals featured a magnificent solo effort by Alex White. In the final during March they engaged Sleekburn Wanderers and, whilst half-time arrived goal-less, a strike by Gorman after the interval won the cup for the Byker club.

The 1884/85 season marked the emergence of the new East and West End clubs to Tyneside's footballing scene; especially East End who had swept all before them. Not only had they lifted the Challenge Cup, but they had also won the local Charity Shield walloping Newcastle FA by all of 10-0. Press reports noted East End's display as a, "fine combined game and every man in the team worked vigorously". The close of the football year also saw the decline of Tyne and Rangers who had reigned supreme in the years before.

The following season of 1885/86 saw West End emulate their rivals and reach the Challenge Cup final. After a Cup run which saw East End and Benwell club, Rendall, both eliminated, Shankhouse Black Watch faced the West Enders. But, in a close game, they lost by the odd goal in five. To emphasise the strange game it was then, Shankhouse actually shared the trophy - not with West End - but with Morpeth Harriers who had, after five undecided games in the semi-final, lost the toss with Black Watch for a place in the final. East End meanwhile could boast they had thrashed their rivals from St James Park by 6-1.

Apart from White, Coulson and Findlay among the early stars of East End were the Hiscock and Muir brothers - two of several families to appear for the club - and the 6'0" J.P.Cook, a forward of high repute. J. Fenwick was a prominent player too, as was John Armstrong. Several East Enders were honoured by the County in representative games - contests which meant a lot in those Victorian days. E.Hiscock, C.Gorman and William Blackett all appeared, as did Muir, Scott, Alex McDougal, Campbell and J.Raylstone, a tough and uncompromising half-back. So too did Tommy Hoban, ex Hibernians and Newcastle Rangers. Alex White skippered the County side but they rarely won a game against the other associations, highlighting that there was still a gap to close in the region's football development.

Rob McDermidd, the former Renton player.

West End also featured two sets of brothers, the Waggotts and Mathers, as well as J.Angus and Billy Tiffen. Later Harry Jeffrey became a noted player at St James Park, as did right-back Rob McDermidd, ex Renton. Both went on to appear for Newcastle United.

By the middle of the decade one or two prominent names headed for Tyneside as the transfer system began to be used on a wider scale. Both clubs began advertising for players, in Athletic News and, north of the border, in Scottish Sport. West End's management had big ideas and attracted many stars to the region.

Scottish international Ralph Aitken came south from Dumbarton as the 1886/87 season got under way. At outside-left he was a sturdy little player with a penchant for trickery as well as for shoulder-charging. On his debut he scored twice before a 2,000 crowd in the 3-2 derby victory against East End - West End's first match at St James Park. However, Aitken didn't stay long on Tyneside, returning to Scotland under controversial circumstances before the season was out. He rejoined the staff three years later for an equally brief period.

Another famous Scot was to appear in West End's colours too, albeit a single appearance against Shankhouse. Right-back Wattie Arnott, then with Queen's Park and 14 times a player for his country, guested for the club in the hope that he would sign up. He didn't and had to leave the game early to catch a train home. Other early transfer dealings at St James Park included Coleman from Hibernians and William Figures from Small Heath in Birmingham.

The signings at first gave the West End club a boost and saw them outstrip their Heaton rivals. They reached the Challenge Cup final again but once more lost to Shankhouse, by 5-1 at neutral Chillingham Road. 4,000 spectators turned up. West End also began to have FA Cup ambitions. The competition in which Newcastle United was to carve a special niche started to create an interest at St James Park for the first time in 1886. Formed as far back as 1871, West End was the first of the two rivals to appear in the famous tournament.

On 30th October 1886, in the First Round, they were drawn against Sunderland. Before 4,000 on Wearside Newcastle forced their neighbours to extra-time at 1-1 but the home side grabbed a winning goal as the daylight deteriorated - or so they thought. Conditions were so bad that West End protested and earned a replay at St James Park, a game they won 1-0 with a goal from centre-forward Angus ten minutes from the end. Gainsborough Trinity made the trip north in Round Two but were far too good for the West Enders, beating them 6-2.

Twelve months later East End made their debut. On 15th October 1887 they played South Bank on Tees-side - in essence Newcastle United's

Tyneside Harry Jeffrey who played for both East and West End, and later for Newcastle too.

SENIOR CUP ARRIVES

The Northumberland Challenge Cup, later the Senior Cup, was first competed for in season 1883/84. The 22 pioneer clubs who entered were: Prudhoe Rovers, Mickley Rangers, Alnwick, Hastings Rovers, North Eastern, Tyne Association, Newcastle 'A', Newcastle 'B', Jesmond, Newcastle Rangers, Heaton, Bedlington, Rothbury, Elswick Leather Works, All Saints, Newton, Ovingham, St Cuthberts, Marlborough, Ovington, Newcastle East End and Newcastle West End.

Goalkeeper William Jardine, joined West End from Scotland.

John Armstrong, an early star of East End.

very first FA Cup fixture. It was a game that also went into extra-time, the scores being level 2-2 after 90 minutes with one of the Muir brothers scoring both goals. It was South Bank who grabbed the winner though and went through to the next round with a score of 3-2. East End travelled back to Heaton with 6s 9d profit after expenses.

West End's second run in the FA Cup in 1887/88 proved as uninspiring as their first. They defeated Redcar easily, 5-1 at St James Park, then met up once more with Sunderland, a repeat of the previous season's tie. At the Newcastle Road ground on Wearside, the match ended in extra-time after West End had led 1-0 at the interval. Sunderland then wrapped up the game by scoring three times.

Other teams in the FA Cup tournament in those years included several Scottish sides, Third Lanark, Hearts and Rangers among them. Local clubs such as Morpeth Harriers and Tyne Association as well as the likes of the First Surrey Rifles and the Old Foresters also took part. Those First Round games took place on the same day as the famous 26-0 demolition of Hyde by Preston North End. In the years that followed both East End and West End had to qualify through preliminary rounds before they reached the First Round proper.

Although West End could not make any impact on the FA Cup they enjoyed some degree of comfort that season by at last winning the Northumberland Cup - their third successive appearance in the final. Shankhouse were their opponents again and this time West End took a 4-0 lead at the break. The result was never in doubt and the St James Park side won 6-3 at the close.

In the same year's competition, East End recorded an amazing scoreline against minor side Point Pleasant at Heaton Junction. After 20 minutes there was no score, but then a deluge began which ended when East End ran out winners at 19-0, the biggest scoreline Newcastle United, or their pioneers, have recorded. Scott notched the first, then E.Hiscock grabbed two more. Wakefield and White further increased the lead and Hiscock completed his hat-trick to make it 6-0 at half-time. After the interval Alex White went on the rampage. The Scot scored six more goals - seven altogether - A. Muir got five and Scott two more.

SHORT VICTORY

In December 1886 Newcastle West End played Bishop Auckland Church Institute at St James Park and won 1-0, but in a game that lasted only 30 minutes. The Durham club were held up by travel delays and arrived late. It was agreed to play out the game with 15 minutes each way!

It was West End who now began to show as the stronger of the two rivals as both clubs started to dominate the game in the region. They made headlines during the summer months of 1888 by attracting their third Scottish international, Bob Kelso, to St James Park. He was the biggest personality by far to regularly appear for a Tyneside club, having made a name for himself as a right-half with Renton, then a prominent force north of the border. Kelso had won two Scottish Cup medals and was noted as having, "a hard, gritty style". Later the wing-half moved to Everton and Preston winning the League title and reaching the English Cup final. Also to arrive from Scotland were Jardine and McKechnie, two further skilled players.

East End knew though that they had to make changes. In the summer of 1888 they lured Tom Watson from St James Park and underwent drastic surgery of both players and officials, modifications that were to eventually revive their fortunes. Several new faces arrived who were to make a big difference. McCurdie came from Clydebank, as did Mack, ex Hibernian. Joseph Coupe arrived from Blackburn Olympic while James Collins, Robert Crielly and Joe McKane all came from Scotland, three players who were all to play for Newcastle United.

In April 1888 the Football League was set up in Manchester at an old Piccadilly coaching inn. Twelve clubs agreed to try the new venture. Newcastle clubs of course were not part of it, although Wearside teams Sunderland and Sunderland Albion were soon to apply for membership. Tyneside's clubs had no such thoughts. The Football League, however, acted as a catalyst in the development of the game. Regional leagues started to spring up around the country, including the Northern League. Before this major step forward had occurred West End and East End continued a season playing friendlies and cup matches.

In 1888/89 it was East End's turn to lift the Challenge Cup, beating Elswick Rangers 3-2 in a

Scottish international Bob Kelso, Tyneside's biggest personality.

third meeting at neutral St James Park. In the FA Cup, the Chillingham Road club played Sunderland - the first East End verses Sunderland derby in senior competition as such. On Wearside they succumbed to second-half goals by Davison and Jobling, but acquitted themselves well against a club then a few months away from Football League status. West End also went out to Wearside opposition, falling to Sunderland Albion after a disputed scoreline and a replayed tie.

In March 1889, at a meeting at the Three Tuns Hotel in Durham, steps were taken to inaugurate the region's first league competition. Newcastle West End were in attendance along with Darlington, Middlesbrough, Stockton and the two Wearside clubs. A second meeting was arranged in the North Eastern Hotel, Darlington, and this time East End were also in attendance. Sunderland had, by now, moved up a grade into the Football League.

It was agreed to form the Northern League with the ten founder members, a mix of professionals and amateurs, made up of East End and West End, Bishop Auckland, Darlington, Elswick Rangers, Middlesbrough, Stockton, Birtley, Darlington St Augustine and South Bank. Serious football had at last arrived in the north-east. Other leagues quickly followed. The North East Counties League -later the Northern Alliance - and the Wearside League were operating within a short period.

The new competition kicked-off the 1889/90 season on 7th September. Newcastle East End met Darlington at their Heaton ground. A crowd of 1,500 were kept waiting for three-quarters of an hour as the visitors were late, but were happy with the 2-1 scoreline in East End's favour. West End's first game was a week later, against their Heaton rivals at St James Park. Almost 4,000 turned up to see the derby clash and goals from McDonald and McKay gave West End a 2-0 victory.

SEASON 1889-1890
NORTHERN LEAGUE TABLE

	P	W	D	L	F	A	Pts
Darlington St.Augustine's	18	12	2	4	39	17	26
Newcastle West End	18	12	2	4	44	24	26
Stockton	18	10	4	4	41	18	24
Newcastle East End	18	9	3	6	32	28	21
Darlington	18	7	6	5	46	20	20
Middlesbrough	18	8	3	7	42	37	19
South Bank	18	6	2	10	33	60	14
Auckland Town	18	4	4	10	41	49	12
Birtley	18	3	3	12	28	48	9
Elswick Rangers	18	2	5	11	21	66	9

First champions of the Northern League were Darlington St Augustine but West End, the favourites at the outset, pushed them hard in an enthralling finale to the competition when St Augustine's nipped ahead of the Tyne outfit at the last moment. The two rivals met at the end of April and, with home advantage, the Saints won 4-1 at their pleasantly named Chestnut Grove arena. Despite this setback the West Enders still had a good chance of lifting the championship. They had two games to play and needed three points. First

Influential Scot, James Collins.

Joe McKane, another from north of the border.

they thrashed South Bank 6-2 at St James Park and then, requiring only a draw away to the Quakers' other team, Darlington, they lost 3-0. Amazingly West End turned up a man short! St Augustine's won the title on goal average with West End runners-up. Meanwhile East End finished in fourth spot, five points behind.

West End were the first of the two city rivals to win through to the FA Cup Proper when they met Grimsby Town of the Football Alliance, then a rival competition to the Football League. The St James Park club had toppled local sides Port Clarence - by 9-1 - Birtley, South Bank and Stockton to reach the First Round.

Grimsby travelled to Tyneside in confident mood, having little respect for the Novocastrians. The difference in class showed too as, at the end of the first 45 minutes, the visitors headed for the break 2-0 in front. West End showed good cup fighting spirit in the second period and pulled a goal back through McColl but, in spite of a sterling effort, could not grab an equaliser. St James Park was still a long way from witnessing FA Cup glory.

Two rare team groups of East End, unfortunately without a record of the players. The bottom illustration is almost certainly the successful Northumberland Cup squad from 1885 or 1889 pictured at Chillingham Road.

OFF IN DISGUST

Scottish wing-half, Bob Crielly was a forthright character and did not take kindly to poor displays. He was once so incensed at his East End colleagues' inadequacies against Sheffield United that he stormed off the field in disgust. The match on Boxing Day 1891 had been a close affair but he had witnessed team-mate Wilson at full-back give away two goals through shocking play. East End continued with ten men and eventually lost 2-1.

West End also won the Northumberland Challenge Cup for the second time thrashing Rendall 5-0 in the final. However, the competition from now on was to be of secondary importance to the Northern League and FA Cup, and soon Football League. Both East and West End, and later Newcastle United, fielded reserve sides in the renamed Senior Cup, although they still managed to dominate the tournament.

As the Nineties decade opened football was progressing quickly. Goal nets arrived and a team game replaced the solo free-for-all. St James Park was being developed in a small way too. John Black offered to erect a stand and West End requested permission from the Town Moor Management Committee. Timber boards were laid to prevent spectators getting their feet wet while a timber contraption housed three to four press men - a notorious vantage point in those days.

At this time Newcastle East End took a bold and huge leap forward in a bid to oust West End from prominence. They decided to become a Limited Company with an issue of 2,000 shares at 10 shillings each, nominal capital of £1,000. At a Public Meeting in the Leighton School, Byker during February 1890, the folk of Tyneside were given "the opportunity of taking up shares in the new company". It proved a successful evening with about 50 shares purchased. In May the first Annual General Meeting took place and Adam Gilchrist was elected East End's first Chairman. An effort was also made to sell season-tickets for the new season. That was hard going; East End sold £45 3s 6d worth of 6s 0d tickets.

Not wanting to be left behind West End quickly followed suit and, in July 1890, the Newcastle West End Football & Athletic Co Ltd elected twelve directors with William Neasham as Chairman. In the months to follow the city was canvassed for support and eventually enough enthusiasts had taken up much of the shareholding of both clubs. The venture was not to prove an instant recipe for success but within 18 months East End, and not West End, had become Tyneside's top club.

A Share Certificate from the original holding in Newcastle United F.C. The shareholder, William Hudson had purchased his quota in the East End company, subsequently transferred on the club's change of name.

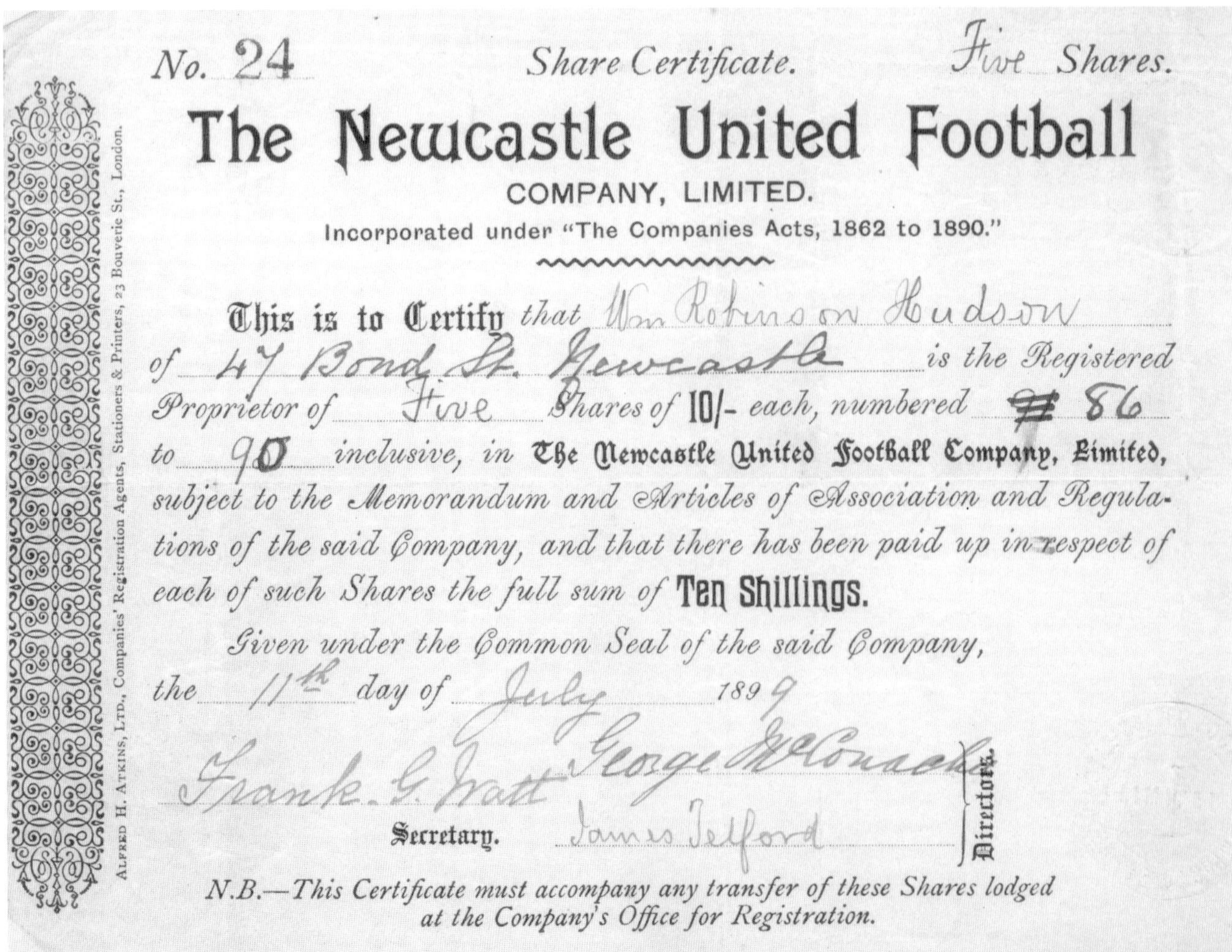

No. 24 Share Certificate. Five Shares.

The Newcastle United Football

COMPANY, LIMITED.

Incorporated under "The Companies Acts, 1862 to 1890."

This is to Certify that Wm Robinson Hudson of 47 Bond St. Newcastle is the Registered Proprietor of Five Shares of 10/- each, numbered 86 to 90 inclusive, in The Newcastle United Football Company, Limited, subject to the Memorandum and Articles of Association and Regulations of the said Company, and that there has been paid up in respect of each of such Shares the full sum of Ten Shillings.

Given under the Common Seal of the said Company, the 11th day of July 1899

Frank G. Watt, Secretary.

George McConachie, James Telford, Directors.

N.B.—This Certificate must accompany any transfer of these Shares lodged at the Company's Office for Registration.

Alfred H. Atkins, Ltd., Companies' Registration Agents, Stationers & Printers, 23 Bouverie St., London.

Public Meeting
Leighton School
Wednesday Feb 17th/90

Chairman. Mr Councillor Jas. Birkett

(1) This Meeting was called for the purpose of allowing the Public the — opportunity of taking up Shares in the new Company in accordance with a circular which was sent out by post

(2) The chairman gave a few suitable remarks setting forth the objects and Benefits that would be derived, by the New Company

(3) Mr W. Henry moved
"That this meeting pledges itself to support the New venture of transforming the "East End Football Club" into a Limited Liability Co"

Mr T. Liddle seconded the resolution and Mr W J. Richardson supported it.

The chairman put the resolution to the meeting. There being no amendment, and it was carried unanimously.

The meeting was then declared open, and the Secretary was ready to Book Shareholders, in response to which about 50 Shares were taken up.

A Vote of Thanks to the chairman terminated the meeting

Extracts from East End's minute book dated Wednesday 17th February 1890 when a public meeting was called at Leighton School, Byker to sell shares in the new company.

REFEREE'S HOWLER

In a Northern League contest between East End and Darlington St Augustine in November 1889 a remarkable refereeing decision robbed the Tynesiders of a point. Referee Phillips disallowed an East End goal, as the press reported "because he was too far away to see it"! The referee was quoted afterwards as saying, "I disallowed the goal in the gathering gloom and gave a goal-kick". The decision astonished everyone at the ground, players and fans alike. East End lost by a single goal.

It was to be a disappointing season for both Newcastle clubs in 1890/91 and, in particular, it marked the sharp decline in West End's fortunes. Both sides finished the season down in the bottom three places of the Northern League along with the previous year's title-holders, St Augustine's. East End had been beaten 8-0 by champions-to-be Ironopolis, and also 7-0 by Sunderland Albion at the Blue House Field. And that was not all. The following day the Heaton side were also demolished 6-0 by Middlesbrough. West End's results were little better. As a measure of their performance East End actually thrashed their rivals 7-1 at Chillingham Road! The Heaton club were to continue their re-organisation, recovering well during the close-season, and the 1891/92 campaign proved to be a significant one for north-east football.

In that year, Sunderland were to win the League Championship for the first time while the deadly rivalry between East and West End was to be resolved in a sudden and definitive way. The season saw East End finish fourth in the Northern League and reach the First Round of the FA Cup. In the qualifying games they comfortably disposed of Tow Law Town, West End, Shankhouse Black Watch and Bishop Auckland Town before facing Nottingham Forest on January 16th. The Trent Club were members of the Football Alliance and included several well known players.

Forest were 1-0 up at half-time and won the tie 2-1 in front of a small crowd at their old Town Ground near the River Trent. Both home goals were netted by Sandy Higgins, father of Newcastle United's future Scottish international of Edwardian years. East End's goal came from the Forest ranks too, - an own-goal by Brown. The tie saw East End wear black'n'white stripes after a colour clash - perhaps the first occasion in a senior game when the famous shirts were worn. East End's amateur second eleven played in black'n'white on a regular basis by this time.

With East End heading up the table and West End down it, the battle for prominence between the two camps continued. The Chillingham Road club was much the stronger now. They possessed more talented players, displayed the better football, could attract larger gates - although still pitifully small - and had a much more enterprising management. West End, a gritty lot, battled for their side of the community with bravado as the season drew to a close.

FOOTBALL LESSONS

Newcastle West End played West Bromwich Albion, winners of the FA Cup, in a friendly during April 1888 - a big attraction at St James Park. The Throstles won easily 5-1 and gave a football lesson to the Novocastrians. West End played Albion again, as well as Wolverhampton Wanderers on Tyneside the following year. Wolves, then Cup finalists, hammered West End 9-2.

East End, not wishing to be in the shadows, entertained FA Cup winners and League Champions Preston North End in the same month. The double holders won 4-1, thanks largely to a hat-trick from England regular John Goodall.

There was a vast difference in footballing ability. Several other top sides visited both East End and West End over these formative years - and usually gave the Tynesiders further lessons in the game of football.

William Neasham, who did much to make sure the game flourished on Tyneside.

One underlying fact remained abundantly clear. The city was not big enough for two football clubs. There was only enough support to ensure the development of the association game for one set-up. If football was to progress further, one club had to go.

THE MEN WHO MADE UNITED

The 83 individuals who supported Newcastle East End's initial share offer during the spring and summer of 1890 are listed opposite, as taken from the original Share Ledger. These are the men - and one woman - who, with their financial backing, made sure East End survived and prospered to become Newcastle United. They all paid a deposit of 2s 6d for each ten shilling share.

Walter Golding, his family still retain shares in the club a century later.

The shares of Walter Dix, purchased in 1890, are now held by his grandson Malcolm Dix.

Name	Address	Occupation	Shares
Armstrong,John Snr	Harbottle St, Byker	Joiner	4
Armstrong,John Jnr	Harbottle St, Byker	Joiner	4
Birkett,John	Heaton Park Rd, Heaton	Ironfounder	1
Bell,Joseph	Rothbury Tce, Heaton	Grocer	3
Brown,Jacob	Heaton Grove, Heaton	Cashier	5
Brown,Thomas	Manor Chare,	Keeper	1
Barrow,Thomas	Chillingham Rd, Heaton	Teacher	1
Cameron,John	Jesmond Vale Tce, Heaton	Traveller	10
Cameron,Daniel	Holmside Pl, Heaton	Clothier	5
Cameron,James	Jesmond Vale Tce, Heaton	Clothier	5
Cranston,James	Norfolk Rd, Byker	Porter	2
Coburn,James	Shields Rd, Byker	Painter	2
Crawford,David	Holly Ave, Jesmond	Chemical Mnfr	4
Cathey,George	Kirk St, Byker	Plater	1
Chambers,William	Seventh Ave, Heaton	Agent	1
Campbell,George G	Mowbray St, Heaton	Joiner	1
Crawford,Robert	Roger St	Foreman	2
Cunningham,J	Wilfrid St, Byker	Telegraphist	1
Chambers,John	Seventh Ave, Heaton	Agent	1
Deuchar,Robert	Portland Hotel,New Bridge St	Wine Merchant	10
Deuchar,Farquhar	Carlisle Hotel,Westgate Rd	Wine Merchant	5
Dawson,John	Clifford St, Byker	Tobacconist	2
Dixon,John	Addison St, Heaton	Compositor	1
Dix,Walter	Tynemouth Rd, Heaton	Engineer	2
Dixon,Joseph	Ouseburn Board School	Joiner	1
Donald,AT	Northumberland St	Hosier	2
Dellow,Richard	Dean St	Printer	2
Foggo,John	Langhorn St, Heaton	Baker	4
Gent,Charles F	Shields Rd, Byker	Tobacconist	2
Golding,Walter H	Chillingham Rd, Heaton	Clerk	1
Gilchrist,Adam	Harbottle St, Byker	Ferryman	5
Grishwood,Robert	Heaton Park Rd, Heaton	Grocer	2
Gilhespy,Graham	Clarence Pl, Gosforth	Clerk	2
Gourlay,John	Kissop St, Jesmond	Plater	1
Harvis,Henry	Albion Rd, Byker	Glassmaker	1
Hudson,William R	Mowbray St, Heaton	Clerk	5
Hiscock,Matthew K	Janet St, Byker	Shipwright	2
Harbottle,Robert	Gosforth Hotel	Wine Merchant	10
Horn,James	Heatherlea, Heaton	Builder	5
Hoy,Robert J	Stratford Grove, Heaton	Agent	2
Johnson,Robert	Hadrian Rd, Wallsend	Joiner	5
Liddle,Thomas	Ouseburn Glass Works	Glassmaker	6
Liddle,John W	Heaton Grove, Heaton	Glassmaker	2
Lindsay,William	Kirk St, Byker	Caulker	2
Laing,Christopher	Regent Tce, Shieldfield	Engineer	10
Laing,Mary A	Regent Tce, Shieldfield	Spinster	2
Lakey,William	Maling St	Innkeeper	2
Large,William L	Shields Rd, Byker	Printer	1
Laing,Alexander	Heaton Park Road South	Agent	2
Marsh,John H	Warwick St, Heaton	Agent	1
McEwan,James	Chester Hotel, Shieldfield	Manager	1
McKenzie,Thomas	Burton St, Byker	Builder	2
March,William F	Heaton Park Rd, Heaton	Clerk	4

Name	Address	Occupation	Shares
McIntosh,William D	Heaton Park Rd, Heaton	Milkman	1
Matthews,George R	Temperance Row, Shieldfield	Grocer	5
McDougal,Alexander	Glasshouse St, Byker	Plater	2
Murray,Samuel	Shields Rd, Byker	Doctor	5
Murton,Henry A	Grey St	Waterproofer	5
Neylon,James J	Wilfred St, Byker	Manager	5
Nevin,John	South View, Heaton	Clerk	2
O'Brien,Peter	Corbridge St, Byker	Painter	1
Peel,James E	Cardigan Tce, Heaton	Clerk	4
Richardson,William J	Addison St, Heaton	Patternmaker	1
Robson,John	Raby St, Byker	Caulker	2
Roche,Thomas	Glendale Inn, Potts St,Byker	Publican	2
Robson,Isaac	Stratford Rd, Heaton	Joiner	1
Russell,Frank	Heaton Rd, Heaton	Surgeon	5
Steel,John	Malcolm St, Heaton	School Officer	5
Spence,Henry G	Chillingham Rd, Heaton	Plater	2
Stewart,John	Northumberland Arms	Wine Merchant	5
Scott,Arthur	Heaton Rd, Heaton	Plumber	5
Spittle,Henry	Gibson St	Draper	4
Taylor,William	Keelman's Hospital	Bookbinder	6
Telfer,David M	Rede St, Byker	Tobacconist	2
Turnbull,Alexander	Rothbury Tce, Heaton	Traveller	5
Turnbull,William	Meadowfield House, Heaton	Wine Merchant	10
Turnbull,Adam	Meadowfield House, Heaton	Builder	10
Turnbull,Joseph	Meadowfield House, Heaton	Builder	10
White,Alex H	Mowbray St, Heaton	Schoolmaster	1
Waters,James	Buxton St, Shieldfield	Compositor	1
Weir,William	Brinkburn St, Byker	Confectioner	4
Wilson,William	Raby St, Byker	Confectioner	5
Woodman,William	Cardigan Tce, Heaton	Clerk	2

Note the prominence of residents of Heaton and Byker, East End's heartland of course. Only a handful of the original shareholders are still on the club's register today. Walter Golding, a solicitor's clerk, and later a solicitor himself, died during World War One, but he had as secretary "laboured long and successfully on behalf of the club". On leaving St James Park he was given a "gold purse" to the value of £16. The shares are still with the family a century later.

Walter Dix is another shareholder whose holding has passed from generation to generation. A Norfolk man, he was the son of an engineer and progressed into the same profession with Hawthorn Leslie on Tyneside. He later founded his own company in Walker and was a noted sportsman, including, of course, football. He died in 1926. His grandson, Malcolm Dix, is a current shareholder and longtime adversary to Newcastle United's board.

Several of the shareholders also played football for East End, including prominent stars like Alex White and Matt Hiscock, while Peter O'Brien later played for Newcastle United. Many of the committee men are also there, personalities like Joe Bell senior, John Cameron and Alex Turnbull who all were later members of the United directorate. The Turnbull family had the largest holding by far.

Also included were members of the Deuchar family, noted Wine and Spirit Merchants in the city whose company eventually formed part of Newcastle Breweries.

2 EAST MEETS WEST

1892-1895

• HISTORIC UNION • APATHY & STRUGGLE • UNITED WE STAND • INTO THE LEAGUE • RECORD DEFEATS •

"On the vote being taken, there was a large majority in favour of Newcastle United"

Newcastle Daily Journal, December 1892

THE YEAR OF 1892 WAS TO BE **a crucial and historic twelve months in the development of Newcastle United Football Club - in essence the first year of the side's centenary. Two important events took place. First the union of East End and West End and then a change in name to that of Newcastle United. Afterwards progression of the club moved rapidly, although at times the Tynesiders came very close to bankruptcy and liquidation.**

By the end of the 1891/92 season Newcastle West End's position, both on the field and at the bank, had become perilous. Their Northern League results were dreadful, finishing second bottom of the table with only eight points. They had recorded some alarming results including a 10-0 reverse at Stockton, although that game was replayed after a West End protest because of the state of the pitch. East End had thrashed their rivals on all of five occasions, including a humiliating 7-1 league defeat at Chillingham Road. The Heaton club were miles ahead of their neighbours.

At the end of April 1892 the St James Park club was on the brink of insolvency and extinction. Gates dipped and revenue had been reduced to a pittance. West End's chief committee men, John Black and William Neasham approached their counterparts from the other side of the city. They offered, as East End's minutes record, "the West End ground for the rest of the lease and would give us (East End) £100". After discussions at East End's headquarters in the Viaduct Hotel in Byker, their board sent James Peel and Walter Golding to continue negotiations and to, "accept West End's ground on the best terms".

Within a week a deal had been agreed. On the 8th May 1892 a full East End committee meeting took place and they "unanimously accepted the West End ground for the residue of the term of the lease". That was for a further twelve years. One condition requested by West End officials was accepted, that East End would use John Black's pub as dressing rooms. This in return for subscribing, "£50 to £75" in shares.

A meeting with West End's men was held at the home of East End's Joseph Bell in Rothbury Terrace, Heaton to finalise the take-over and to conclude plans for moving the club, with all its possessions down to the last bar of soap and paperclip, to St James Park. West End would cease operation as a football club, their players and officials being given the chance to join East End's ranks. Present in Bell's house were, from East End, Messrs Alex Turnbull, T.Carmichael, John Graham, John Cameron, James Neylon and host Bell. West End were represented by William Neasham, John Black, George Milne, James Telford, George McConachie and William Bramwell.

The local newspaper recorded the historical event in some detail. It noted;

"For the last two seasons Newcastle West End has had anything but a prosperous career and a heavy financial loss has been incurred. Dr Neasham and Mr John Black, who have had control of affairs, have done everything in their power for the success

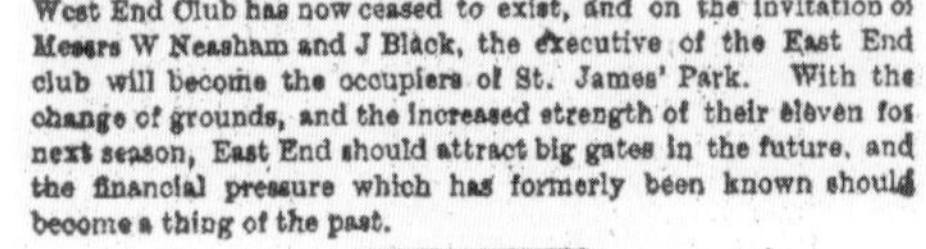

FOOTBALL.

ASSOCIATION.

GOODBYE TO WEST END.—We are informed that the Newcastle West End Club has now ceased to exist, and on the invitation of Messrs W Neasham and J Black, the executive of the East End club will become the occupiers of St. James' Park. With the change of grounds, and the increased strength of their eleven for next season, East End should attract big gates in the future, and the financial pressure which has formerly been known should become a thing of the past.

How the Newcastle Daily Journal reported the demise of West End in May 1892.

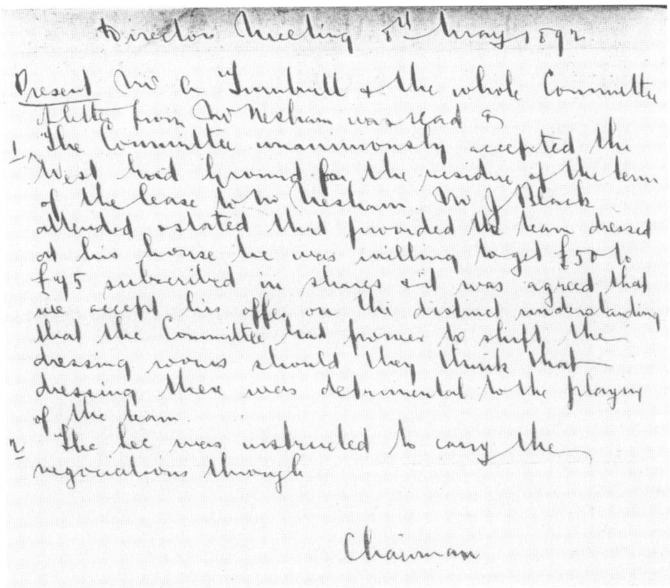

Director Meeting 5th May 1892
Present Mr A Turnbull & the whole Committee
A letter from Mr Neasham was read &
1 The Committee unanimously accepted the West End ground for the residue of the term of the lease to Mr Neasham. Mr J Black attended & stated that provided the team dressed at his house he was willing to get £50 to £75 subscribed in shares & it was agreed that we accept his offer on the distinct understanding that the Committee had power to shift the dressing rooms should they think that dressing there was detrimental to the playing of the team.
2 The Sec was instructed to carry the negociations through
Chairman

Newcastle East End's minute book dated May 1892 detailing the agreement to move to St. James Park.

of the venture, but they have had the worst of luck and now annouce their intention of severing their connection with the club. In sportsmanlike manner however, they have made known their intentions to the executive of the East End club, whose directors have accepted the offer of the lease of the West End field. We regretfully therefore, bid farewell to West End. We shall have only the East End as our representative club in Newcastle. The East Enders will take possesion of the St James Park having a team of the strongest possible description and we look forward to an eventful season"

East End's home at Chillingham Road was left to the East End Wednesday club, although the timber stand was dismantled and moved to St James Park only for the Town Corporation to later order its removal "owing to it having been erected without the permission of the council".

Before the start of the new 1892/93 season, East End's new set-up attempted to gain entry into the Football League, at a time when the competition had only a single division. At the annual meeting held at The Queen's Hotel in Sunderland - in honour of the Wearsiders' Championship victory - East End were refused entry to the First Division after polling a mere one vote. They were not alone though. Applications from Liverpool and both Middlesbrough and Ironopolis were also rejected. However, the Tynesiders were admitted to a newly formed Second Division as one of the largely unknown and untried beginners.

The club's officials though, did not relish the thought of the Second Division as few clubs possessed the drawing power for which East End were looking. They wanted the likes of Preston, Everton, Sunderland and Aston Villa at St James Park and with them much increased gates, and of course revenue. They saw Second Division clubs like Bootle, Lincoln City and Crewe as being no better than the past season's Northern League opposition and, as an added disadvantage, the club would have to fork out increased expenses to travel south. So East End declined the invitation and remained members of the Northern League. It was observed that "they live in expectation that they will be admitted into the charmed circle at some future date". Newcastle officials were dejected at the rebuff but, importantly, were determined to build a club to be recognised.

First evidence of East End's new resolve was an offer of the then huge sum of £80 to attract Glasgow Celtic, holders of the Scottish Cup and Runners-Up in the Scottish League, to St James Park for a pre-season friendly. It was to be East End's - and Newcastle United's - first game at St James Park. On 3rd September the Glaswegians arrived, albeit half an hour late, to a warm welcome from a 6,000 plus attendance. The local press claimed the match as, "The greatest event known in the local history of the game". Little first class opposition had visited Tyneside over previous years and for the inexperienced Newcastle line-up the Celtic formation proved quite a handful at first. The Scots had most of the first-half and went ahead on the half-hour with a controversial goal. Campbell sent in a cross, Newcastle 'keeper, Dave Whitton went to punch clear only to be bundled over the line rugby style by Madden with the ball following him into the net.

Newcastle came back strongly in the second period and, by all accounts, were unfortunate not to defeat their much respected opponents. Celtic's 'keeper, Cullen, however kept East End at bay with a series of punched clearances. Celtic won1-0, but only through that hotly disputed goal. Afterwards the referee, Mr R. Campbell of Sunderland, privately conceded the goal should not have been allowed. Receipts were £147 which was enough to record a small profit.

However, as the season progressed the standard of opposition in the Northern League did not meet the box office attraction of Celtic. Gates were usually under the 5,000 figure, at best approaching

ST JAMES PARK DEBUT

After moving from Heaton, Newcastle East End's first game was against Scottish Cup holders Celtic.
3 September 1892
Newcastle East End v Glasgow Celtic
Lost 0-1(0-1) Scorers: Campbell
Attendance: 6,000

EAST END:	CELTIC:
Whitton	Cullen
Jeffery	Dunbar
Miller	Doyle
Crielly	Maley
Graham	Kelly
McKane	Clifford
Collins	Murray
Crate	Blessing
Thompson	Madden
Wallace	McMahon
Sorley.	Campbell.

goals to one by the Rovers, and in the second half they added other three goals, the game ending:—Rangers, six goals; Rovers, one.

NEWCASTLE EAST END v. CELTIC.

(BY "CUSTOS.")

The football season has come round once more, and on Saturday afternoon the sport-loving portion of the public of this city were to be seen proceeding towards St. James's Park, a field in which have been buried the hopes of many enthusiasts and the reputation of not a few players. For several years past this ground was occupied by the West End Club, but so much money was lost in the concern that the shareholders decided to engage no more players, and the club practically ceased to exist at the end of last season. As St. James's Park is more easily reached by dwellers in the town than the ground of East End at Heaton, the committees of the latter club have become the tenants of Mr W. Nesham, and Saturday's match opened both their season and their new ground. The Celtic eleven were engaged to perform the opening ceremony, and the visit of this famous team created a great amount of interest in local football circles, particularly as the Celts were playing their full strength. A fine morning was followed by a showery afternoon; yet those interested in the sport turned out in large numbers, fully 7,000 spectators being present at 3.30 p.m., the time fixed for the kick off. However, the visitors were half an hour late in putting in an appearance, so that Mr B. McAnulty did not start the ball until on the point of 4 o'clock.

"Captain" Kelly won the toss, and decided to begin with the wind and hill in his favour. Consequently East End kicked off up hill. The early exchanges gave promise of fast and exciting play, as, before the game was a couple of minutes old, both Whitton and Cullen had long shots to deal with, the Celt scooping his out in rather a slovenly fashion. This was followed by even play, the tricky passing of the visitors being counterbalanced by the quick rushes of the home forwards; and the backs on each side were kept fairly busy. Gradually the Celtic left wing worked down, McMahon taking the bulk of the work. After Whitton had saved two or three warm shots, McMahon dodged about with the ball in front of goal, but, not being able to get an opening, passed it out to Campbell, who, from near the corner flag, sent in a beauty, which Whitton, who was hampered by Madden, was not able to stop. Thus the visitors drew first blood after exactly half an hour's play. Crate, Sorley, and Collins were each prominent in turn near the higher goal, the first-named grazing the top side of the crossbar with a very fast shot, which Cullen could not have reached had it been six inches lower, while the goalkeeper cleared the danger from Sorley's attempt, and Doyle attended to Collins. A couple of corners fell to Celtic. Though there were some scrambling work in front of goal from each of them, they were got away, and just before the first whistle blew Sorley was given the easiest of chances, as he was within half a dozen yards of the uprights with an open goal. His shot was a shocking one, as he screwed the ball round towards the corner flag, and ends were changed with the Celtic leading by one goal to none.

On resuming Crate quickly took a shy, and Cullen cleared. By some neat work on the part of Madden, McMahon, and Campbell, play was transferred to midfield. At length Sorley and Wallace made a rush along the left wing, Thompson racing ahead to make the most of any chance which might present itself. When well down Sorley centred, and Thompson shot through, though, as he was offside, the point was not allowed. Right up to the finish East End forced the game, and were continually taking shots at the Celtic goal. The play of Cullen, and the tackling and kicking of Dunbar and Doyle, however, were of the safest kind, and none of the home team managed to score, though several times they experienced the hardest of luck, missing their mark with lightning-like shots by only a few inches. Once the visitors managed to get well up the field, and, taking a forwarded pass from McMahon, Madden banged the ball past Whitton, but the Celt was given offside. As the call of time approached, corner after corner fell to East End. Still they were not able to get the ball through, and when the whistle blew the score stood:—

Celtic ....1 goal.
East End ....None.

East End: Whitton, goal; Jeffrey and Miller, backs; Crielly, Graham, and McKane, half backs; Collins, Crate, Thompson, Sorley, and Wallace, forwards.

Celtic: Cullen, goal; Dunbar and Doyle, backs; Maley, Kelly, and Clifford, half backs; Murray, Blessington, Madden, McMahon, and Campbell, forwards.

Linesmen, Mr J Allison of Ardwick and P Watson.

Referee, Mr R Campbell, Sunderland.

SOUTHWICK v SHANKHOUSE.

The above clubs opened their season on Saturday afternoon by playing their first match—a Northern Alliance one—at Southwick. Shankhouse started and got at once to close quarters, when Bell changed the venue just as the visitors were looking dangerous. Ord then stopped several

Match report from East End's first game at St. James Park, as related by 'Custos' in the Newcastle Daily Journal. Note that ladies were admitted free.

6,000 for the visit of Sheffield United. After paying out heavy guarantees to visiting clubs - the norm then - East End's treasurer had little or nothing left in the kitty. The club's disappointed Chairman said: "If the public want a professional team they must be prepared to pay for it, as those who have hitherto found the funds can no longer do so".

In an attempt to attract more support from Victorian Tyneside it was decided that radical changes had to be implemented. At a meeting during December in the Bath Lane Hall - a goal-kick from St James Park - Chairman Alex Turnbull presided over a large gathering of football enthusiasts, perhaps 200-300 strong. An open discussion took place on the future of football on Tyneside, and one of the points agreed upon was a need to dispose of the title of 'Newcastle East End' in a bid to attract wider support from the city and the region as a whole.

Several names were proposed. Newcastle FC, Newcastle City, Newcastle Rangers, City of Newcastle and Newcastle United were among the favourites. Voting was almost unaminous for Newcastle United, most fans obviously thinking it was the most appropriate title following the union of East and West End.

So, on Friday, December 9th 1892, East End became Newcastle United although the legal title of the club was not altered until several years later. Indeed, that caused problems for the club, as when they attempted to purchase McIntosh of Dundee and forwarded the registration forms to the Football Association, that august body replied, noting that they could not accept the transfer because they had never heard of Newcastle United!

On December 22nd the Football Association agreed to the change, but it took three years. When at a specially convened meeting of shareholders at Locharts Cafe, in St Nicholas Buildings on September 6th 1895, the Newcastle East End Football Co Ltd became the Newcastle United Football Club Ltd. The Board of Trade sanctioned the transfer two months later in November.

The Newcastle Daily Journal made the comment, "The club certainly deserves better support than it is at present receiving and if a change in name will have the effect of bringing up the public, by all means let us have it". One facet of East End's existence remained though. The club, for the time being at any rate, still retained the colours of red and white stripes. The famous black'n'white was still several months away. For Newcastle's debut in the Football League, Athletic News noted the club's colours as "red shirts, white knickers".

Newcastle used the title 'United' for the first time on the following day when Ironopolis from Middlesbrough arrived at St James Park. On a frosty pitch the 'new' United lost 2-1 in front of only 2,500 spectators. During January, United played their first FA Cup tie using the name - a match against Tees-side's other club, Middlesbrough. It was a game which caused much controversy. Fellow Northern Leaguers 'Boro offered United £20 to move the tie to their ground but Newcastle bluntly refused to comply with this and, before a healthy crowd nearing 8,000, the visitors won 3-2 at a drizzly St James Park.

United had got off to a winning start and were 2-1 ahead at half-time. Firstly, Reay crossed for the 'Boro keeper - aptly called Fall - to miss the ball and allow Thompson to net. Two minutes later Reay was back again, bundling over the unfortunate goalie into the net. United

Redpath, half backs; Southern, Purvis, Wood, Henderson, and Brennen, forwards. Linesman, R Forster.

THE EAST END FOOTBALL CLUB.

THE NAME CHANGED.

Last night a meeting of persons interested in Association football in Newcastle and district was held in the Bath Lane Hall, Newcastle, for the purpose of considering the advisability of changing the name of the East End Football Club, which succeeded West End this season at St. James's Park. Mr A. Turnbull presided, and there was a large attendance.

The Chairman expressed his pleasure at seeing so large an audience, and said it augured well for Association football in the future. They would all be aware that they were met to consider the question of changing the name of the East End Football Club. He believed that there was a certain amount of jealousy existing amongst some people regarding the present title of the club, and it was considered that a more general and representative name should be chosen for it. (Hear, hear.) He might tell them that it was understood between the management of East End and West End when the former changed their quarters that the name of the club should be altered at the end of the season, but it had been conveyed to them that the change should be made at once if they wished to obtain the unanimous support of the public. The directorate were quite willing to accede to this request, for all they wanted was a first class team, and to see the game played as it ought to be, and they all knew that to secure a team to do honour to the city they must have the unanimous support of the public. Amongst the new titles that had been suggested were Newcastle, Newcastle United, Newcastle City, and City of Newcastle. It was for them to decide which it should be, and, whichever one they chose, he hoped they would be unanimous upon it. (Hear, hear.)

Councillor Henderson said he attended that meeting to show that he was still in sympathy with one of their manliest sports, and he was glad to see such a large audience, for it proved that the interest in Association football, so far as Newcastle was concerned, was not diminishing. (Hear, hear.) They all regretted the West End Club was extinct, but that was no reason why they should withhold their influence and support from the club which had come to take its place with the best of intentions. (Hear, hear.) He believed the chief desire of the directorate was to place the best team on the field they could, in order to attract the people to witness the game played as it ought to be. (Hear, hear.) The supporters of the East End and the old West End would have to sink any little jealousies they had, and be united. (Hear, hear.) With the support of the whole of the Newcastle sporting public, they ought to have a team second to none in the country. It might be said the ground was not suitable, but if they brought their influence to bear upon the powers that be, they might then make it as they would like to see it. (Hear, hear.) The East End Club was to be complimented on the excellence of their present combination, and he was sure that, if they got rid of their old jealousies, the team would have a prosperous career. (Hear, hear.)

The names of Newcastle, Newcastle City, and Newcastle United were proposed as new titles for the club, and, on the vote being taken, there was a large majority in favour of Newcastle United, and when the latter was put in the form of a substantial motion it was carried with only three dissentients.

The Chairman said the English Association would meet on Monday next, and they would bring the new name of the club before that body.

A vote of thanks to the chairman concluded the proceedings.

RUGBY.

Local press reports on the historic meeting in December 1892 which saw East End change their name to Newcastle United.

3

THE COMPANIES ACTS, 1862 TO 1890.

COMPANY LIMITED BY SHARES.

(COPY)

Special Resolution

(Pursuant to The Companies Act, 1862, s.s. 13 and 51)

OF THE

NEWCASTLE EAST END FOOTBALL COMPANY, LIMITED.

Passed 9th August, 1895. *Confirmed 6th September, 1895.*

At an Extraordinary General Meeting of the Members of the said Company, duly convened, and held, at Lockhart's Cafe, No. 1, Denton Chare, Saint Nicholas Buildings, Newcastle-on-Tyne, in the County of Northumberland, on the 9th day of August, 1895, the following Special Resolution was duly passed; and at a subsequent Extraordinary General Meeting of the Members of the said Company, also duly convened, and held, at the same place, on the 6th day of September, 1895, the following Special Resolution was duly confirmed :—

RESOLVED—

"*That the name of the Company be changed to "NEWCASTLE UNITED FOOTBALL COMPANY, LIMITED.*"

J. S. FERGUSON,

Secretary to the Company.

Filed at the Company's Register Office, on the 31st day of October, 1895.

though, let their advantage slip dramatically in a dreadful second-half performance. The local press printed in clear tone what they thought of the display: "Newcastle United grievously disappointed an enormous attendance; their forwards were useless. The only men in the United ranks to play up to their reputations were Graham and Crielly. The rest were off, distinctly off".

Afterwards there were allegations that Newcastle players had been bribed and were part of a betting ring with Middlesbrough enthusiasts. It was said they had taken it easy after the interval. An Official Inquiry followed and, sensationally, it was concluded that bribery of sorts did, in fact, take place. Two un-named players were disciplined, one who didn't play was sacked and another suspended. The club's trainer was dismissed also. The comment was made: "There is only one feeling prevailing in Newcastle - that of disgust". Secretary Golding resigned under pressure only to be re- instated after certain fresh evidence had been brought to light. A club statement was made: "Although the executive feel their Cup-tie defeat very keenly, they have satisfied themselves that no suspicion rests on any of the players". That was perhaps contradictory to the sackings and suspensions. It was also revealed that United's players' boots contained upwards of 140 nails - inserted to prevent slippage on the wet turf! Newcastle United had started their life in the controversial way they were to continue.

The club's first season ended with the side in Runners-Up spot to Ironopolis in the Northern League table. The team had performed well, winning convincingly several times including 7-0 and 5-0 victories over Darlington. In friendlies, more prestige games were arranged - with Sunderland, Everton and Glasgow Rangers - while Nottingham Forest, Derby County, West Bromwich Albion and Preston all visited St James Park too. All were top-class opposition and only Sunderland - to be a bogey club for several years to come - inflicted heavy defeats, 0-4 and 1-6. United toppled West Brom 7-2 and also won comfortably in the other contests.

(left) The Special Resolution issued by secretary J.S. Ferguson confirming the company's new name.

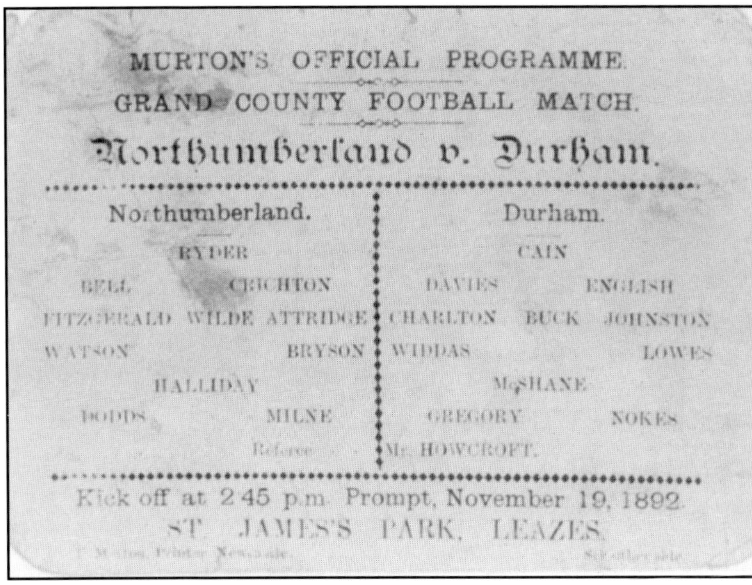

A rare match card from the East End versus Darlington fixture in November 1892 played at St. James Park. East End won 5-0 before 2,000 spectators.

Dave Whitton, Harry Jeffery and John Miller were United's defensive formation. 'Keeper Whitton, a Tynesider, was described in one journal of the period as "a bundle of energy". Former West Ender Jeffery, was a stylist and a "scientific exponent of the game" and very much one of the town's footballing pioneers.

In midfield, three Scots performed boldly for Newcastle and all were East End men. Robert Crielly, capped by Northumberland, played alongside skipper, Willie Graham, and Joe McKane. Signed from Dumbarton, McKane was an aggressive player once fined two weeks' wages for using "most insulting language" against Notts County players.

Up front Wallace and Reay played wide while Willie Thompson, ex-Shankhouse Black Watch, was at centre-forward. He sported a magnificent moustache and was United's earliest goalgetter. He also represented the County XI. Thompson was assisted by Jock Sorley, Tom Crate and James Collins in seeking goals. From Newmilns, near Kilmarnock, Sorley was a popular character and later appeared for Middlesbrough and Blackburn Rovers. Fellow Scot, Collins, was also effective in the club's early sides. Mobile and dangerous, he tragically died of tetanus following an injury when turning out for Chatham.

Newcastle players at this time were a difficult bunch to handle. Crielly, like McKane, was

FOOTBALL LEAGUE DEBUT

2 September 1893
Woolwich Arsenal v Newcastle United
at Manor Ground Drew 2-2(0-1)
Scorers: United; Crate, Sorley.
Arsenal; Shaw, Elliott.
Attendance: 6,000(average)
Arsenal: Williams; Powell, Jeffrey; Devine, Buist, Howat; Gemmell, Henderson, Shaw, Elliott, Booth.
United: Ramsay; Jeffery, Miller; Crielly, Graham, McKane; Bowman, Crate, Thompson, Sorley, Wallace.

The moustached Willie Thompson, he netted 40 goals for the Club.

suspended for bad language; Jeffery was told not to attend the club for two weeks because he was a "non trier", while McKane found himself in trouble again when, for the last game of the league season at Middlesbrough, he failed to turn up. His excuse was that he missed the train and his absence resulted in United having to play with only ten men. They lost 4-0, the player being suspended for a week and fined two weeks' wages for his neglect. He soon left St James Park. There were many other instances too of lax training and frequent reprimands were issued.

Although playing performances were satisfactory, United came close to ending the season in the bankruptcy court. The club had made a loss of £384 8s 9d on the year's trading. Expenditure figures showed that travelling expenses were £134, wages £872 and guarantees to visiting clubs - the financial killer - were £924. An appeal was launched to raise cash. A club official said, "What is wanted for next season is the guarantee from supporters of at least £200 to enable things to be put straight and engage first class men who are known to be anxious to play for Newcastle United".

One supporter offered to give £20, and a canvass resulted in a further £40 being pledged. But the club's directors got nowhere near the target and a terse club statement was made: "The management of the United club do not expect to become millionaires as a result of running a team, but surely they have the right to expect that they would not lose their money in their efforts to provide the masses with sport".

Yet even with such a precarious financial position the Tynesiders attempted to gain entry into the First Division once more - officials maintaining it was the only way to increase gate revenue and develop in stature. Chairman Alex Turnbull and secretary James Neylon were the men to put forward Newcastle's application to the Football League committee. Both were influential figures in the rise of Newcastle United. Turnbull, who lived close to Joseph Bell in Heaton, spoke out for United's cause during those early difficult years with much gusto. Neylon was appointed director-secretary in September 1893. He was a works manager from Byker and had long been associated with East End's prominence.

The Football League again though would not accept United's direct entry into the First Division but, for a second time, offered Turnbull and Neylon the opportunity of Second Division status. Several new places were up for grabs. Bootle had resigned

ENTER THE MAGPIES

By the end of 1895 Newcastle had acquired the nickname of 'The Magpies', the origins of which are somewhat unclear. Some reports indicate that it came about because of a fervent supporter by the name of Father Dalmatius Houtmann. A Dominican priest, resident at Blackfriars Monastery close to St James Park, this Dutchman was often to be seen with the players dressed in a distinctive black and white habit. Perhaps the likeness to a magpie in both the players' strip and fan's attire, pointed some to dub the club 'The Magpies'.

Another legend that has been handed down over the years is the story of a pair of real magpies nesting in the original Victorian stand on Leazes Terrace. It was said that United's players of the time became so attached to the two birds that they decided to call themselves 'The Magpies'.

and Accrington, after being demoted from Division One refused to play in Division Two. Then it was decided that the division was to be extended from twelve to 15 clubs, giving a total of five vacancies.

Seven clubs sought election and United, along with Rotherham Town were given places unopposed. This time Newcastle accepted. Also to be elected were Liverpool, Arsenal and neighbours Ironopolis. The clubs unlucky enough not to succeed were Doncaster Rovers and Loughborough Town. So Newcastle United became a member of the Football League on the same day as Liverpool and Arsenal- a momentus hour in the history of football when three famous names entered the fray in earnest.

The north-east, from having a single League side(Sunderland), now had three clubs. It was an enormous leap forward towards making the region one of football's hotbeds. Among the clubs Newcastle were to face were names which are now lost to the senior game - Northwich Victoria, Burton Swifts and Darwen. Neighbours Sunderland, on the other hand, were League Champions and a most feared side in the world of football. United still had a long way to go to match the status of their local rivals.

Willie Graham, workhorse in midfield.

The club's first ever match as members of the Football League took place on the 2nd September 1893 against Woolwich Arsenal; that team's inaugural fixture also. The match was played at the Londoners' Manor Ground arena in Plumstead, to the south of the capital, unlike their now well-known and more northern base. However, Newcastle United almost never made that historic appointment. The club's cash-box was empty as the Daily Journal noted, "It has been common gossip of late that money was needed". That was an understatement, for it was only after a whip-round at a crisis meeting of

United's 1893-94 line up: Left to right, Back: W. Golding, J. Willis, H. Jeffery, W. Lowery, T. Rodgers, J. Pearce, J.Graham. Middle: R. Crielly, W. Graham, J. McKane. Front: C. Quinn, T. Crate, W. Thompson, J. Wallace, J. Law. The group may look as though they are wearing black and white shirts, however the colour is red.

THE LEAGUE—SECOND DIVISION.
ROYAL ARSENAL v NEWCASTLE UNITED.

At Plumstead, in beautifully fine weather, before fully 6,000 spectators. It is the first League match that has ever been played in London. The ground was in splendid condition. Arsenal won the toss, and had a light wind behind them. They had considerably the best of the play in the first half, which was not of a high order, both showing want of practice. Shaw scored a very soft goal for Arsenal eight minutes after starting, and kept the visitors pressed till just before the change, when Newcastle rallied, and had bad luck in not scoring. With the wind in their favour, Newcastle played better, and twenty minutes later Graham scored out of a scrimmage. Sorley equalised, and play in the last ten minutes was very exciting, but nothing further was scored. Newcastle had decidedly the best of the second half. Score:—

Newcastle United ....2 goals
Royal Arsenal ....2 goals

LIVERPOOL v. IRONOPOLIS.

• At Middlesbrough, before 2,000 spectators. The home team was weak in comparison with that of last season, financial considerations having caused an extensive

Match report from September 4th 1893, United's first Football League game.

directors that enough money was raised to pay for the train journey south. Even then United travelled budget class with no hotel accomodation - through Friday evening, arriving in London early on Saturday, a journey of almost eight hours.

United's weary party spent a few hours' sightseeing. For many it was their first visit to the capital and, by the time United's footballers arrived at the Manor Ground many were exhausted. Some even dozed off on bales of straw which they found close to the dressing-rooms and had to be aroused in time for the kick-off!

On a fine sunny day, Arsenal quickly ran into a 2-0 lead. Shaw netted after a neat bit of football and some poor defending. Then, immediately after the interval, Elliott grabbed another goal with a fierce shot off the crossbar. United though recovered in the last 20 minutes of play to gain a point in a 2-2 draw; no doubt after shaking themselves from their doze. Tom Crate had the distinction of scoring the club's first League goal. He had joined the East End club from local football and later appeared for Blyth Town and Seaton Burn as well as other north-eastern sides. It should be noted that some newspaper accounts credit the goal to Willie Graham. Jock Sorley netted the equaliser with a strong header following a free-kick into the box. The attendance was recorded by several reports of the match as somewhere between 2,000 and 10,000, indicating, as in the goalscorers, the inaccuracies of many early bulletins.

Newcastle had a long break between that opening game and the next Football League match - some three weeks - due to the Football League's inadequacy in compiling fixture cards then. United arranged several friendlies to keep in trim, and both

A caricature by Tom Smiles depicting the Arsenal v United inaugural League fixture.

Middlesbrough and Sunderland faced the Novocastrians. With an urgent need to raise cash this did little to help their financial problems. Attendances of 3,000 and 1,400 against their local rivals made no money. The sporting public's apathy towards the club was extreme. Since moving from the east of the city to St James Park Newcastle United had been

Tom Crate, scored Newcastle's first League goal.

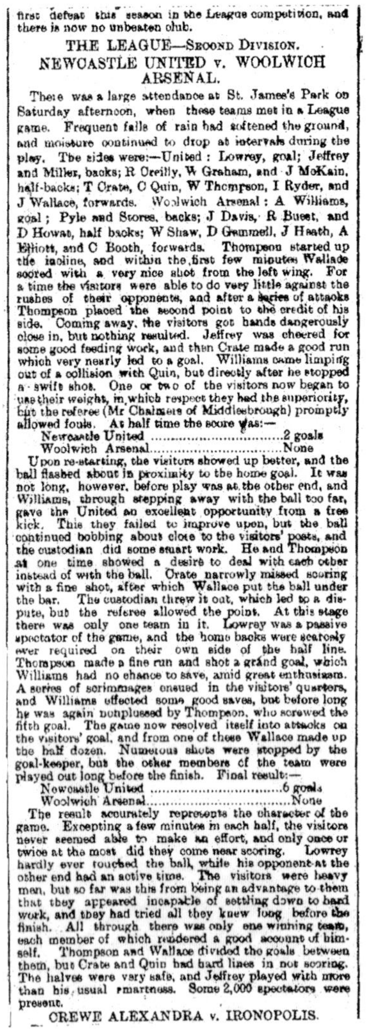

first defeat this season in the League competition, and there is now no unbeaten club.

THE LEAGUE—SECOND DIVISION.

NEWCASTLE UNITED v. WOOLWICH ARSENAL.

There was a large attendance at St. James's Park on Saturday afternoon, when these teams met in a League game. Frequent falls of rain had softened the ground, and moisture continued to drop at intervals during the play. The sides were:—United : Lowrey, goal; Jeffrey and Miller, backs; R Oreilly, W Graham, and J McKain, half-backs; T Crate, C Quin, W Thompson, I Ryder, and J Wallace, forwards. Woolwich Arsenal : A Williams, goal ; Pyle and Stores, backs; J Davis, R Buest, and D Howat, half backs; W Shaw, D Gemmell, J Heath, A Elliott, and C Booth, forwards. Thompson started up the incline, and within the first few minutes Wallace scored with a very nice shot from the left wing. For a time the visitors were able to do very little against the rushes of their opponents, and after a series of attacks Thompson placed the second point to the credit of his side. Coming away, the visitors got hands dangerously close in, but nothing resulted. Jeffrey was cheered for some good feeding work, and then Crate made a good run which very nearly led to a goal. Williams came limping out of a collision with Quin, but directly after he stopped a swift shot. One or two of the visitors now began to use their weight, in which respect they had the superiority, but the referee (Mr Chalmers of Middlesbrough) promptly allowed fouls. At half time the score was:—

Newcastle United ....2 goals
Woolwich Arsenal..............................None

Upon re-starting, the visitors showed up better, and the ball flashed about in proximity to the home goal. It was not long, however, before play was at the other end, and Williams, through stepping away with the ball too far, gave the United an excellent opportunity from a free kick. This they failed to improve upon, but the ball continued bobbing about close to the visitors' posts, and the custodian did some smart work. He and Thompson at one time showed a desire to deal with each other instead of with the ball. Crate narrowly missed scoring with a fine shot, after which Wallace put the ball under the bar. The custodian threw it out, which led to a dispute, but the referee allowed the point. At this stage there was only one team in it. Lowrey was a passive spectator of the game, and the home backs were scarcely ever required on their own side of the half line. Thompson made a fine run and shot a grand goal, which Williams had no chance to save, amid great enthusiasm. A series of scrimmages ensued in the visitors' quarters, and Williams effected some good saves, but before long he was again nonplussed by Thompson, who screwed the fifth goal. The game now resolved itself into attacks on the visitors' goal, and from one of these Wallace made up the half dozen. Numerous shots were stopped by the goal-keeper, but the other members of the team were played out long before the finish. Final result:—

Newcastle United ....6 goals
Woolwich Arsenal..............................None

The result accurately represents the character of the game. Excepting a few minutes in each half, the visitors never seemed able to make an effort, and only once or twice at the most did they come near scoring. Lowrey hardly ever touched the ball, while his opponent at the other end had an active time. The visitors were heavy men, but so far was this from being an advantage to them that they appeared incapable of settling down to hard work, and they had tried all they knew long before the finish. All through there was only one winning team, each member of which rendered a good account of himself. Thompson and Wallace divided the goals between them, but Crate and Quin had hard lines in not scoring. The halves were very safe, and Jeffrey played with more than his usual smartness. Some 2,000 spectators were present.

CREWE ALEXANDRA v. IRONOPOLIS.

The Newcastle Daily Journal's report of the first League contest at St. James Park in September 1893. United won 6-0.

somewhat boycotted by many East End fans who were not happy at travelling to their arch rival's base at Leazes. As if that was not enough West End supporters, incensed at the takeover of their club by the Heaton men, did not rally to the new club's side either. On top of that, the general populus of the city were still many years from being a fervent football community. Few knew anything about the game.

The club was in dire straits. They couldn't sell their meagre hundred or so 10s 6d season-tickets and the side's officials felt betrayed and frustrated at the lack of support. They made a strongly worded statement, "The Newcastle public do not deserve to be catered for so far as professional football is concerned". It made little difference in the short term and it was to take several years before Tyneside recognised the St. James Park club as their own and for it to become a part of the region's lifestyle.

In a bid to put United's financial standing on a better footing, the directors made a plea to their players - to take a cut in wages. They, of course, didn't like it and some departed, including 'keeper Andrew Ramsay, reserves Brown and McFarlane, together with regular inside-forward Jock Sorley. Fund-raising concerts were arranged - one at the People's Palace - and others at venues around the city. With this depressing background United boldly continued their first season as a League force.

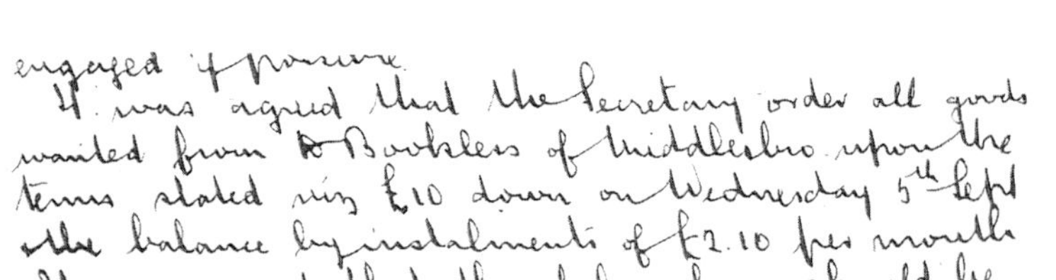

engaged of premises

It was agreed that the Secretary order all goods wanted from R Bookless of Middlesbro upon the terms stated viz £10 down on Wednesday 5th Sept the balance by instalments of £2.10 per month

It was agreed that the clubs colours should be changed from Red Shirts & white knickers to Black & white shirts (2 inch stripe) & dark knickers.

Mr Graham offered to provide a large flag for the flagstaff in the clubs colours & this offer was accepted & a vote of thanks passed to him.

Hidden in the mass of club minutes is a three line statement noting that United had changed colours to black and white; the date, 2nd August 1894.

At the end of September Arsenal made the trip north for United's initial Football League tussle at St James Park, but only a pitiful 2,000 turned up. In that return game, United won handsomely 6-0 with the help of the notorious Gallowgate slope.

78 MINUTE MATCH

An astonishing contest with Walsall Town Swifts took place during the 1894/95 season. Newcastle were kept waiting for fully 20 minutes before their opponents took the field. Arguments had raged in the dressing-room as Walsall players demanded wages which had not been paid. After strike threats, the game eventually started, but so late that bad light forced the referee to abandon the game in the 78th minute. Newcastle were leading 3- 2, with Willis claiming a hat-trick. The Football League ruled that the result should stand - the only incident when United have gained points without completing a match. Swifts ended the season in financial crisis and lost their league status.

Newcastle scored four goals in the second-half when playing downhill. Hat-tricks from Wallace and Thompson registered the goals in a victory that raised several eyebrows.

Newcastle's league results continued to be good and, over New Year, they defeated Lincoln City 5-1 and Ironopolis 7-2 within the space of 24 hours. It was at this time that United began occasionally to wear black and white shirts. The club had found that their red attire often clashed with their opponents' colours. Indeed, on one such occasion they had to tie white handkerchiefs around their arms to differentiate them from the home team. In December the press reported, "Owing to Burslem Port Vale playing in red, Newcastle East End will play in the county colours lent for the occasion". The county colours being black'n'white stripes. It is worth pointing out that although East End had become United, for several months the wider country still referred to the club by its former title.

Newcastle played in white shorts to start with, then dark blue. In fact black did not appear on a regular basis until the late 1900's. Several football annuals and match reports list United's shorts as blue as late as 1912. By the time the new season had kicked off East End's old red shirts had totally disappeared. The club's minutes of 2nd August 1894 record, "It was agreed that the club's colours should be changed from red shirts and white knickers to black and white shirts (two inch stripe) and dark knickers".

United finished the second half of the season with a winning habit. They lost only once after New Year's Day and completed their first Football League programme in an extremely creditable 4th placing. They actually went close to qualifying for the Test Matches - one step from promotion to the club's eventual goal, the First Division.

Sheffield United were the side's Cup opponents in January and the First Division team did not savour the thought of a trip to Tyneside. And it wasn't then for the fear of a partisan gate and a renowned home record. The Yorkshiremen didn't want to play in front of a poor crowd which would hardly cover their expenses and on the much criticised St James Park surface. As Middlesbrough had done in the previous season, they offered

United £100 to play the tie at Bramall Lane, but again Newcastle rejected the offer. United increased their prices hoping to cash in at the turnstile. The admission charge was doubled to one shilling and, on a wet and windy afternoon, a good crowd of 7,000 turned up and paid almost £172 in receipts.

Newcastle won 2-0 on a quagmire of a pitch, both goals being scored by Joe Wallace - one a splendid shot from the ege of the box into the top corner of the net. Wallace, one of the side's many Scots was very much the crowd favourite at the time. It was Newcastle's first victory in the FA Cup competition proper and their opponents were not pleased. They complained about the pitch, and their share of the gate. As the Blade's official history records, "some of the turnstile registers stood at the same number at the finish as they did at the opening of the gates". Suspicion remained that Newcastle had used both foul and fair means to collect as much money as they could from the big attraction.

In the next round Bolton Wanderers, another First Division club, had to face Newcastle on Tyneside and again an offer to switch the venue was refused. The Wanderers then lodged a protest to the Football Association about the state of the pitch in an attempt to get the tie moved to Lancashire. It was, though, to no avail.

Bolton, however, need not have worried. They won 2-1 before a record 10,000 crowd and went on to the final. The game was played out in a gale with goal-kicks hardly reaching 30 yards at best but, in spite of difficult conditions, United were unlucky not to end the game level. Newcastle piled on the pressure in the second-half and time and time again showered the visitors' goal with shots. Yet in defeat the club's officials could contemplate a lucrative gate and that perhaps support would increase if First Division opposition, like Sheffield United and Bolton, arrived on Tyneside on a regular basis.

United had signed a new 'keeper for their debut in league football, a position that was to be a problem for several years to come. Lowery came from Blyth having played for Trafalgar and Gateshead NER. Forwards Quinn and Willis were two other notable signings, while left-back Rogers arrived from north of the border in Perth. Joe Wallace was the club's top scorer with 17 goals.

Trouble continued with players and several minor incidents took place. At one stage the club's reserve side, mostly amateurs, made an audacious stand over money wishing to turn professional. They demanded 1s 6d per match and, when it was not forthcoming, went on strike and held the club to ransom. However, Newcastle directors would stand no nonsense. They promptly disbanded the team, sacking the lot, then re-formed a fresh amateur line-up in time for the new Northern Alliance programme.

By the end of the club's first season in the big-time United may have been a Second Division side, but they had little glamour. Their position off the field was still in an unhealthy state despite the Cup boost to their coffers and their initial fear that Second Division opposition would not attract enough support had been a valid one. Finances continued to be a major problem and had worsened from the early season difficulties. Indeed, after less than twelve months of senior action, Newcastle United were on the brink of collapse. Average support at St James Park was only 4,000, with top gates of 10,000 at the Cup-tie against Bolton and the late season fixture with Crewe when a Test Match place was a possiblity.

Guarantees to visiting clubs were again a burden. United owed large amounts to other clubs for both match receipts and transfer fees. Derby County, Liverpool and West Bromwich Albion were among those teams seeking payment. United operated with an overdraft of £100, but still could not pay their bills and it was left to John Black to send personal cheques to settle some accounts. The situation deteriorated when, as recorded in the club's minutes, the Football Association had, "suspended the club for non payment of the balance of £26 13s 4d due to Derby County". Urgent approaches were then made to the Bank for assistance and an emergency meeting of the directors took place, as it was noted, at the foot of Grey's Monument. The clatter of traffic forced the officials to reconvene in the quieter surroundings of Brunswick Place where they agreed to pay the sums owed out of their own pockets, albeit reduced amounts.

The Football Association was also able to be surprisingly helpful to United's plight. It was reported that Newcastle's reduced offer to the clubs in question had been accepted by both Derby and Liverpool but West Bromwich Albion held out for their, "pound of flesh". It was then that the FA stepped in, "The Association, however, recognise the fact that the United club have acted in a straightforward manner throughout and that seeing that Newcastle had done so much for association football in their district the Association took the matter into their own hands and ultimately decided that the three clubs should receive £18 each - much to the chagrin of the Bromwich delegate".

Players were asked to take a cut in wages again, while one director proposed that board members should pawn their gold watches and give the proceeds to the club. It had been a season of regular crisis, with the raising of sufficient money to pay travelling expenses a weekly headache. There was one occasion when officials were unable to raise, borrow or beg enough money to cover the cost of

CORINTHIAN FRIENDS

On several occasions during Newcastle's early years the club played friendly fixtures with noted amateur outfit, The Corinthians, made up from University and Public School sportsmen. Newcastle were usually too good for the educated part-timers. One match took place on New Year's Eve 1892 and the score in Newcastle's favour was "8 goals, 2 off-side goals and 20 smacks at the crossbar, to one goal"! A crowd of 1,500 witnessed that spectacle.

WATSON'S RUSH TO HELP

On Sunday, 6th March 1892, East End full-back Peter Watson was walking in the vicinity of Byker Bank when he saw a policeman, PC Walton, being attacked by several local ruffians. Peter immediately rushed to the constable's assistance and, after a struggle, the assailants were arrested. An award was made to the player by the Ouseburn Division of the Newcastle Constabulary and PC Walton himself presented Watson with a silver-mounted briar pipe on behalf of the local division.

One of the earliest known team photographs of Newcastle United. Pictured in all probability in Leazes Park. Officials John Graham and John Black are on the right of the back row. Dated 1892/93.

taking the team to Liverpool. And at one stage debts were so bad that one creditor actually sent two of his burly workmen to demand part of the gate money to pay his bill. However, they did not have a Court Warrant and United's staff had them forcibly ejected from the stadium.

More collections and fund-raising activities were urgently organised and adequate resources were found to pull the club through their worst financial crisis. It was only through the support of a hardcore of enthusiasts that Newcastle United Football Club survived to create what was to be a century of headlines.

With some degree of financial security, United continued with their bid for glory, albeit for several years yet, a stuttering one. During the summer months of 1894, United's directorate scoured Scotland for new talent, a raiding party that was to be sent annually north of the border. Bob McDermidd returned to Gallowgate from Dundee Wanderers with a formidable reputation as a full-back, but only after John Black had advanced the club a £7 10s transfer fee. McDermidd was an experienced professional, having played for Renton, Sunderland Albion, Accrington and Burton, as well as having a brief spell at West End.

Forwards Dickson, Rendall and McNee all arrived too. Dickson came from Dundee also, via Football Agent, Peter Allan, then a common way of purchasing new talent. £5 went to Dundee, £5 to the agent and Dickson's wages were negotiated at £2 per week with a £5 bonus. Inside-right Jack Smith was a star newcomer in a much changed line-up. Ayrshire born, Smith returned to Tyneside from Sheffield Wednesday after periods at Liverpool, Sunderland and East End. Another goalkeeper was tried as Ward was signed from Loughborough Town, while United also announced that Harry Kirk, late of Notts County, would act as trainer to the side, although very much as a fitness man and not a tactical coach. Football was not yet a technical game.

The new look black'n'whites eleven took the field against Darwen at their Barley Bank ground with a lot of optimism for the 1894/95 season. But it was soon evident that the defence couldn't knit together at all. In that opening fixture Darwen hit five goals, United's worst ever start to a season. And after a "miserable farce" against Grimsby Town, in which United lost 3-0 at St James Park, two players were suspended. Newcastle's directors made the comment, "When we pay men to play football we expect them to do so".

Against Leicester Fosse, United were 4-0 up but allowed the home side to claw back a point in a 4-4 draw, and then Leicester missed a penalty. Seven

LADIES CONTEST

On 19th April 1895, Newcastle United hosted an exhibition ladies match at St James Park to promote interest in the game from the fairer sex. Under the guidance of Miss Netty Honeyball the British Ladies Football Club took to the field in an eleven-a-side contest between the Reds and the Blues. A big crowd of almost 8,000 turned up - United's average attendance was only a little over half that number - and saw the "tastefully dressed" ladies "supply plenty of fun of the gentlest order". The Reds won 4-3.

days later at St James Park it was Manchester City's turn to run United's defence ragged, - thankfully though Newcastle got the winner in the last minute to record a 5-4 victory. In attack United looked good with Thompson, Willis, Dickson and Smith all grabbing goals. In a spell of three successive home games United netted almost 20 times. Thompson led the way with 18 in the season but, no matter how many they scored, the defence would always let their opponents in. Officials knew the team needed strengthening but had no money to spend. A meeting was even called at the Hotel Metropole to raise £250 which "would enable the club to engage a really first class team". The money never came and United deteriorated. Worse, much worse was to follow. Results became dreadful, bad enough to register not only the club's worst FA Cup defeat but also the heaviest league reverse too. Record scores to stand unchallenged for the next 97 years.

After toppling Burnley 2-1 in the First Round of the FA Cup at St James Park in which the players were offered a huge £5 win bonus, United were paired with Aston Villa, then the most feared side in the country. With a line-up of stars, Villa were five time Champions and four times Cup finalists before the turn of the century. In Birmingham the Novocastrians lost 7-1. Dorrell, Davey and Athersmith - household names then - scored two goals apiece and simply ripped United apart. It could have been even higher. Villa led 6-1 at half-time and eased up after the break.

However, worse was to follow. On the last day of the season United's wavering set of players travelled to the Midlands once again, this time to face Burton Wanderers, one of two Second Division clubs from the Trent community and a club only to compete in league football for three seasons.

United were demolished to the tune of 9-0 with Burton's goalscoring brothers, Art and Andrew Capes, scoring seven of the goals. That dire performance at Burton's Derby Turn ground is the worst recorded in United's history.

Newcastle finished their second season in the Football League in 10th position. Those shattering results at the hands of Aston Villa and Burton Wanderers left the black'n'whites a demoralised side.

ADMISSION 1892/93

United's first season at St James Park

Season-tickets	Ground	7s	6d
	Reserved ground	10s	6d
	Boys	3s	6d
	Ladies	3s	0d
Match-day	Adults		6d
	Boys		3d
	Reserved	(extra)	6d

FINANCE 1893/94

United's first Football League season

Income:			
Season-tickets	£35	17s	10d
Gate receipts	£1978	3s	10d
Donations	£9	9s	8d
Expenditure:			
Printing & post	£82	3s	0d
FL & FA fees	£12	7s	6d
Secretary's exp	£9	17s	6d
Wages	£643	0s	0d
Travelling	£287	9s	6d
Signing-on fees	£76	12s	0d
Rent, rates, tax	£38	13s	9d
Guarantees	£473	3s	7d
Police, gatemen	£102	12s	2d
Outfitting	£22	5s	3d
Ground	£57	6s	3d

Left: The old 'English Cup'.

Jack Smith, an experienced addition to United's ranks.

3 TEST MATCH UPROAR

1895-1904

• TRANSFER ACTIVITY • PROMOTION TEST • FIRST DIVISION STATUS • GOOD FRIDAY RIOT • TALENT DEVELOPS •

"The teams could have done without goalkeepers, so anxious were the forwards not to score"

Athletic News, April 1898
(after the Stoke v Burnley Test Match)

FOLLOWING THE RECORD HAMMERINGS during the previous season much had to be done at St James Park to bring together a team capable of reaching the First Division. The club's directors spent many hours at their Hotel Metropole headquarters discussing the club's future. They put up more funds to pay off debts and to finance the new season and, following a public meeting to discuss the side's plight, they received a moral boost from their loyal, but small band of followers. Encouraged, they went in search of new talent.

Many new players were to arrive on Tyneside in the coming months, several were to play a big part in establishing the club as a first-class team. Scottish international left-back, Bob Foyers cost £100 from Edinburgh St Bernards and was installed as the team's new captain. He was the club's first international signing since the union of East and West End. Jimmy Stott arrived from Grimsby Town with a reputation of being afraid of no man. He was a tough competitor and at one stage Newcastle's selection committee had to caution him, "against his continual fouling of opponents".

Forwards Willie Wardrope and Malcolm Lennox added flair to the attack. Both were from north of the border, United's favourite hunting ground. Lennox was signed from the Glasgow Perthshire side while Wardrope, from Wishaw, became one of the Magpies' most celebrated players before the turn of the century. Operating on both wings and inside positions, he scored regularily - 50 in 141 appearances - and later appeared for the Scottish League. James Collins, another Scot, returned to Tyneside too, this after a spell with Nottingham Forest.

More Scots joined the staff; Willie McKay (Rangers), Jimmy Logan (ex Notts County), Willie Miller (Kilmarnock) and John Henderson (Clyde), a new goalkeeper. Logan had had the distinction of scoring a hat-trick in the FA Cup final of twelve months earlier. Another newcomer introduced for the start of the new season was Andy Aitken, who was secured from Ayr Parkhouse. Just a teenager, the half-back was to develop quickly. In only his third game he netted three goals and was soon to become one of football's most accomplished players.

The other important addition to Newcastle's set-up was the appointment of a new secretary. The club chose a man to play a central role in its forthcoming rise to prominence, Dundee's official Frank George Watt. Newcastle advertised the post on the departure of J.S.Ferguson, following his resignation after a controversial incident when in charge of the team for trips to Liverpool and Newton Heath (Manchester United). Motherwell born, Ferguson had been socialising in the early hours of the morning with some of the team the evening before the match in Manchester. There had also been irregularities in payments to gatemen by Ferguson.

Advertisements for his replacement were placed in the Athletic News and Scottish Referee and the club received several applications. United needed a dedicated man and they certainly picked one. Born on the Royal Mile in the heart of Edinburgh, Frank Watt had been one of the pioneers of Scottish football in the capital. He had helped form Edinburgh Rifles FC and was first secretary of the city's local football association. In his younger days he played for several sides, St Bernards, Dundee and Hearts, as well as officiating at many games. One such match he refereed was the so called

ADMISSION 1898/99

Match-day:	Adults		6d
	Boys		3d
	Reserved	(extra)	6d
Season-tickets			
Grandstand:	Adults	25s	0d
	Ladies	12s	6d
Terracing:	Adults	15s	0d
	Ladies	7s	6d
	Boys	5s	0d

Bob Foyers, Newcastle United's first international player.

Championship of the World in 1888 between Renton and West Bromwich Albion.

Watt took up his post with a salary of £140 per annum on 28th December 1895. From that moment the Magpies never looked back. As soon as the genial, moustached Scot arrived, the club went from strength to strength. He was a brilliant administrator and driving force and his aim was to transform Newcastle into the best club in the country. He was to do just that. Although employed as club secretary, he was also general manager and talent spotter and did much to ensure United's forthcoming grandeur, yet he always shunned the limelight. The club leased a house in Westgate Road and later in St James Street and created a new centre of operations for Watt.

United's new secretary was immediately called upon to look at a serious incidence of misconduct by players after matches at Grimsby and Lincoln over the Christmas holiday period of 1895. According to the club's official minutes no fewer than six players had brought the name of Newcastle United into disrepute. The most serious incident was the alleged theft of two rings by William Millar. He was suspended for 14 days without pay and ordered to refund the value of the rings. Skipper Foyers was stripped of the captaincy and given a similar suspension and Lennox was fined 20 shillings, while McKay, Collins and Andy Aitken were all censored.

The incident was another example of the frequent indiscipline of players during the years upto the turn of the century. Further incidents took place which resulted in fines, suspensions and even sackings. John White and Bob Foyers, again, were rebuked for, "being seen the worse for liquor in the evening". Foyers in fact was in trouble once more soon after and quickly departed back to Scotland. John Campbell was dismissed for taking over the management of the Darnell Hotel, against a club rule that no player was allowed "to have anything to do with licensed premises". Many times players missed training and some even skipped matches.

Newcastle's display in the 1895/96 season was much improved. They found the net frequently; Rotherham Town and Crewe Alexandra conceded six goals to United in successive weeks, while Darwen was thrashed 7-2 and both Lincoln City and Burton Swifts 5-0. Wardrope was the dangerman; he scored 20 goals although operating on the left-wing.

A remarkable contest took place on Tyneside against Burton Wanderers during February. United's opponents arrived late, six players having missed a train connection at Sheffield, and the match kicked off 45 minutes behind schedule. Even then Newcastle faced only eight players and no recognised goalkeeper. Wanderers' 'keeper, Watts, arrived along with the rest of the team 15 minutes later and played the remainder of the half in his trousers. United won the match 4-0.

Never quite getting into the promotion frame, having ended the season in 5th position, Newcastle promised much for the future. Gates rose too, at times even above the 10,000 mark and at last cash was now rolling into the till, albeit slowly. 12,000 saw United topple Manchester City 4-1 during March.

In the FA Cup, United still had the humble task to qualify for the First Round Proper and once they had been given a walkover against Leadgate Exiles after the Durham side scratched in return for a £30 fee, Newcastle thrashed locals, West Hartlepool NER (8-0), Rendal (5-0), Tow Law (4-0) and Middlesbrough (4-1). In the competition proper Chesterfield were no opposition either, United cruising into Round Two with a 4-0 victory in which Willie Thompson netted with one brilliant solo run past several defenders.

First Division Bury were the big prize for the mundane, if not hazardous Cup run. United players spent a week on Cup training at Talking Tarn near Brampton and returned to the Hotel Metropole on Friday to prepare for the big match. In days when United still did not possess decent accommodation, the side stripped in the hotel and made their way to St James Park ready for action by charabanc. Newcastle opened well and took the lead in the first few minutes when Bury's 'keeper couldn't hold a long range Collins effort. Thompson, following up, headed home. The visitors though were too good over 90 minutes. They hit three goals in the second-half in front of a record attendance of 14,250. United had yet to give their fans a taste of Cup glory. That took a while to arrive, the black'n'whites being eliminated early from the competition until the opening years of the 20th Century.

Jimmy Stott, tough and uncompromising at half-back.

New secretary Frank Watt. He stayed at St. James Park for almost 40 years.

Goalkeeper Charlie Watts, one of United's earliest characters.

Over the next twelve months, United continued grooming and adding to a squad of players that would make a strong bid for promotion. Again they finished in 5th place and attendances again rose. The club's average attendance was now 8,399 and the previous year's record gate was overtaken when 16,125 turned up for the league clash with Newton Heath on New Year's Day. United won 2-0 against the future Manchester United eleven. Newcastle though, still had to complement funds by holding variety concerts in the Bath Lane Hall featuring song and dance acts, ventriloquists and comedy sketches.

Veteran centre-forward Willie Thompson moved on, to be replaced by ex Forest striker Dick Smellie who had a good year claiming 15 goals. Aitken was proving a valuable youngster, netting 24 times in his first two seasons. But there was still a vast difference between the Magpies and top opposition. Aston Villa once more overpowered United in another Cup meeting. On their way to lifting the League and Cup double, they gave Newcastle a further lesson, this time by 5-0 at their old Perry Barr ground. The 650 travelling Newcastle fans cheered their side nevertheless and showed that the Geordie support was as noisy as any in the country.

It was a remarkable number of black'n'white followers that made their way to Birmingham. Supporters backing the side on away trips in those days faced long and weary journeys by either train, or horse-driven brakes for shorter trips. The first motor-car journey had just taken place and this mode of transport was still far off. Tyneside saw supporters' 'brake-clubs' set-up to pay a weekly subscription to hire the vehicle for a forthcoming away trip. The wagonettes could seat up to 24 and they were usually gaily decorated in United's colours as the early fanatics followed the team around the country.

Better quality talent was progressively wearing the black'n'white. Newcastle's board signed another 'keeper, Charlie Watts from Burton Wanderers who had taken part in that remarkable game in the previous year. From Middlesbrough, Watts was a jovial character, later in his career becoming famous as a racing tipster and was supposed to have won three fortunes on the turf - and lost them all. He certainly did win £600 in September 1898, then a mammoth sum, on a Sporting Chronicle racing competition. Sadly, Watts committed suicide in 1924 by cutting his throat. Centre-half Jack Ostler, a dominating Scottish personality - not the first or last - was another important addition. He settled on Tyneside in a joint £200 deal from Motherwell which also saw Tom Stewart sign for the Magpies. Full-backs Stewart and John White, ex Clyde, formed a defensive formation with Watts. It was a much improved combination.

Jack Ostler

Tommy Ghee

John Campbell, signed from rivals Sunderland in a joint deal with John Harvey for £40.

John Auld

Jock Peddie

In the summer of 1897 concern was expressed by the board at the sorry finances of the club - and even drastically questioned how Newcastle United could continue for another season. Revenue was still wretched compared to the better wages the club had to pay for their quality players. Newcastle's directors had to come to the rescue again by guaranteeing a loan of £750 to the North East Banking Company. With another lease of life assured another signing quickly took place, one that just about completed United's team plan.

St Mirren right-half, Tommy Ghee joined the club and was said to have signed for the Magpies while having a pint at a Paisley bar. Ghee joined Stott and Ostler in a formidable half-back line. United's new man was a tireless worker and did a first-class job of stopping the opposition through both fair, and at times, foul means. He was also a proficient all-round sportsman, especially in swimming and polo. Captain of the side, he remained at St James Park for many a year as trainer. Stott controlled the left-flank and Ostler, at centre-half, dominated the centre-circle. Ghee, on the right complemented his colleagues perfectly. All three were tenacious and rugged characters and the trio became the midfield force that took Newcastle into Division One for the first time.

Other new faces were to play a part in that taste of success. The Magpies made a swoop on Wearside and took two of Sunderland's famous 'Team of all the Talent'. Although both John Harvey and John Campbell were classed as veterans, they gave United's line-up much needed experience and composure. Both had won honours with the Reds and Newcastle's youngsters, especially 20 year-old Andy Aitken, benefited greatly from their presence. They joined yet another ex-Sunderland stalwart, Scottish cap John Auld, who had crossed the Tyne a few months before. Auld was later appointed to Newcastle's board and his transfer was the first from Wear to Tyne. Also to arrive from Wearside was a new trainer, Tom Dodds, who did much in Sunderland's rise to fame.

John Jackson arrived from Rangers, a steadfast and eyecatching defender, but one final piece in the jig-saw still needed to be put into place, that at centre-forward. Smellie had fallen out of favour and to fill the position United again looked to Scotland and brought Third Lanark's tearaway leader, Jock Peddie, to St James Park for the sum of £135.

From the working-class heartland of Glasgow, the tough looking Scot possessed awesome shooting power and often scored with a piledriver at goal from 25 or 30 yards. Many of his colleagues in that early era reckoned Jock had the hardest drive in football, "a shot like the kick of a mule", as one old-timer described it. Although a moody character, his off days were more than made up for with electric displays. Peddie became the crowd's favourite, the first hero figure and first in a long line of famous dynamic style centre-forwards. He provided, along with Wardrope and Campbell in particular, a dangerous threat up front. The former Third's striker went on to net 18 goals in only 24 games to spearhead the Magpies into the promotion frame.

It was to be an eventful season from the opening day of the programme. United entertained Woolwich Arsenal and won 4-1 before a 10,000 crowd. The Geordie public at last began to appreciate their side and, by previous standards on Victorian Tyneside, they flocked to watch their team. United's attendance figures leapt dramatically with a regular 12,000 crowd and some 700 season-ticket holders. Yet this upsurge in support brought with it various problems. The club received a letter of complaint from the Chief Constable noting the unacceptable situation of "the public committing a nuisance against the wall in front of Leazes Terrace"! United were forced to build more urinals on this side of the ground. Leazes Terrace residents, then upper class citizans of the town, frequently objected to councillors at the inconvenience football caused. In October 1898 the Town Clerk received notice that residents were planning legal proceedings to stop the "intolerable nusiance" of playing football at St James Park. Subsequently the Town Council debated a "stop football" motion, with the outcome, of course, that Newcastle United was allowed to continue. There were also frequent complaints of bad language and the club had to maintain a careful watch, ejecting any fans heard swearing.

AFRICAN VISITORS

In September 1899 United entertained the Kaffirs Touring XI, the first black side to visit Britain. The novice footballers from the Basuto tribe in South Africa opened their nationwide tour at St James Park in front of 6,000 onlookers. As a football match the game was something of a farce with a vast difference in ability between the sides. Newcastle gave the opposition two goals in a 6-3 walkover. The tourists played 36 games altogether and didn't win a single fixture, conceding 235 goals!

Newcastle won their first four fixtures, with Wardrope netting in each game, and the side had moved up the table into 3rd place by the turn of the year. Again the ground's record gate was broken. At the Christmas meeting with Burnley, 24,959 witnessed the Magpies' clash with their main rival for promotion. It was by far the biggest gathering at any football match on Tyneside. United lost 1-0 but chased the Turf Moor club for the rest of the season along with Manchester City. Burnley though went out in front and the race was on for second spot.

As spring approached a fabulous series of results saw United record six wins in a row. They netted 21 goals to only four conceded. The Magpies met Manchester City in one of those games - a deciding tussle - and won 2-0 to give Newcastle a five point lead. United finished Runners-Up, three points behind Burnley. Promotion though was not guaranteed back in 1898 just because a club had finished in the top two places, or indeed lifted the Second Division Championship. A Test Match system operated then, similar to the modern-day Play-Offs.

The top two sides from the Second Division and

WEAR v TEES DERBY

On the 18th April 1903 a crowd of 26,000 saw the Division One meeting between Sunderland and Middlesbrough played, unusually, at St James Park. The game had been switched to Tyneside because Roker Park had been closed due to the stoning of Sheffield Wednesday players by Sunderland supporters. They had also pelted the referee with oranges after a controversial 90 minutes on Wearside. Sunderland won the derby by 2-1.

the bottom pairing from Division One had to compete in a mini-league to decide the relegation and promotion positions. Whoever finished in the leading two places of the table would achieve success. So it was Burnley and Newcastle United from Division Two, against Stoke and Blackburn Rovers from the bottom of the First Division to battle it out over a ten day period.

United kicked off on Tyneside against the old Stoke club, forerunner of the present City outfit. Newcastle began with a victory, by 2-1, but it was a costly success. United lost both Bill Lindsay and the player the Magpies could ill afford to be without, Jock Peddie. Three days later Newcastle travelled to the Potteries and, with Johnny Campbell in for Peddie, the black'n'whites lost by a lone second-half goal converted by centre-forward Maxwell.

They lost again in another close game, at Ewood Park against Blackburn, this time by 4-3. It was quite a match, with Newcastle 3-1 down at half-time but in the second period fighting back and very nearly snatching a valuable point. They made a tremendous assault in the last 15 minutes against a ten man Blackburn side who had Killean carried off on a wooden board. Smith, Aitken and Wardrope claimed the goals in front of 30,000 spectators. United players had been offered a win bonus of £3 each for success in that contest.

On the last day of the Test Match series Burnley and Stoke led the table with four points each. Newcastle and Blackburn each had two. United met Blackburn in the return game at St James Park. In the other match Burnley travelled south to face Stoke. The Turf Moor club had been relegated from Division One the previous season after a Test Match play-off and were determined to succeed this time around.

United had to win, and win well, to stand any chance of catching their rivals. A 13,324 crowd were at Gallowgate to see the crucial meeting and Newcastle did exactly what they had to do - they went for glory and won by four goals to nil. Tommy Ghee put United on their way, then Jackson, Harvey and Campbell completed the rout. Some of the railings, then somewhat primitive, collapsed under the sway of the crowd during a United attack, causing several several injuries including a young fan with a broken ankle and another who had a foot severed. United later paid out gratuities of £50 to the injured.

Newcastle's victory mattered little, as only a draw was needed by Stoke and Burnley to send both clubs into the First Division. They played out the game in such a fashion that a draw was inevitable, a goalless one at that. The match was a farce. No fewer than five balls were used, some wildy kicked out of the ground to waste time, others kept by the fans as a protest at the rigging of the match. The spectators, however partizan, didn't like it and jeered and hooted throughout the game.

An outcry followed claiming that Burnley and Stoke had pre-arranged and 'fixed' their deciding game, giving neither Blackburn nor United a chance. The Official History of the Football League recorded the match was of, "high comedy". The Staffordshire Advertiser reported, "The game proved a complete fiasco", while another report observed, "what was supposed to be a test was a waste of time". Respected sports paper, Athletic News, published a scathing comment on the game, "The teams could have done without goalkeepers, so anxious were the forwards not to score" and, as an added weight behind the outcry, their editor was non other than the Football League's President, J.J.Bentley. Criticisms from such a quarter created considerable sensation. One of the linesmen at the game was also a high ranking official, William Bellamy, a member of the Management Committee.

At the Football League's AGM during May there was much debate on the Test Match system and the Burnley-Stoke controversy. Something had to be done to restore public confidence. The outcome was that the Test Match system was abolished and the First Division extended by two places, but even then Newcastle United's promotion was not automatic. Voting took place to elect the new clubs. The poll revealed;

Blackburn Rovers (27 votes), Newcastle United (18 votes), Manchester City (10 votes), Small Heath (4 votes), Newton Heath (3 votes), Woolwich Arsenal (1 vote). Blackburn and Newcastle United entered the First Division.

Newcastle's Annual Report noted, "The season 1897/98, has proved the most successful since the introduction of the Association Game to the City of

FIRST INTERNATIONAL

England 6
(Bloomer 4, Foster, Needham)
Wales 0
18 March 1901

United's newly found prestige earned the club the right to play host to the England versus Wales, Home International Championship match. Matt Kingsley was capped in that meeting and he had one of the easiest debuts ever. Steve Bloomer of Derby netted four goals as Wales were thrashed 6-0. The popular and gifted amateur, Reginald Foster of The Corinthians, was the star despite Bloomer's goals and the Oxford University man, "delighted the crowd with dribbling". He scored the fifth goal with a solo run. 11,000 were at Gallowgate.

England: Kingsley (Newcastle Utd)
Crabtree (Aston Villa) Oakley (Corinthians)
Wilkes (Aston Villa) Bannister (Burnley)
Needham (Sheffield Utd) Bennett (Sheffield Utd)
Bloomer (Derby County) Beats (Wolves)
Foster (Corinthians) Corbett (Corinthians).

Wales: Roose (London Welsh)
Merideth S. (Chirk) Morris (Derby County)
Parry M. (Liverpool) Jones (Aberdare)
Hughes (Tottenham Hotspur)
Meredith W. (Man City) Pugh (Lincoln City)
Morgan-Owen (Rhyl) Parry T.D. (Oswestry)
Williams (Druids).

INTO THE MODERN AGE

During September 1896 St James Park's facilities entered the modern age. Plans submitted to the City Engineer included for the erection of a, "Bath Room" for players, while refreshment stands for the fans were opened around the ground. The Daily Chronicle erected a telephone, "with a view to facilitate the publicising of reports". Many of those reports though, were not to the liking of the club. Within a few weeks the Chronicle's newsman was in discussion with officials as to the tone of his reporting. Relationships were patched up with the press, and a year later Newcastle United sent a Christmas gift of cigars to the four daily paper reporters.

John Graham in later years. He was associated with East End and Newcastle United for over three decades.

Success may have been achieved in league football but there was no joy yet in the FA Cup. United still had to qualify - to their annoyance - and again they did it easily and afterwards complained bitterly to the FA that the club had now developed far enough to be excluded from the qualifying competition. After no little debate the ruling body eventually accepted that plea and from now on Newcastle gained automatic entry into the Cup proper.

After playing wonderfully well to dispose of Preston North End of the First Division, with Peddie getting the winner and his second goal of the game with a terrific 30 yarder, non-league outfit Southampton St Marys gave the Magpies their first taste of giant-killing by winning 1-0 at the Saint's old County Ground. St Marys, the same club as today's Saints, boasted a Cup fighting tradition and were Southern League champions that year. It was not to be the last cup shock to rock Tyneside, but at the time it mattered little. Newcastle United was now a First Division club.

TRAINING SESSION

In the early 1900's training sessions at St James Park usually started at 10.00am, a time when the mass of the male population had started work some three hours earlier. A session consisted of;

- Weight training with dumb-bells
- Skipping
- Ball punching
- Sprinting
- Eight mile walk at brisk pace
- A bath and rub down

Few actual sessions took place with the ball; perhaps two afternoons a week, with a practise match during the spring and summer evenings.

Newcastle". Off the field a lot of credit was down to James Telford, the power behind United at this time. A Scot of sometimes domineering personality, Telford believed in getting things done. He was a shrewd judge of a player and was involved in virtually all of the club's transfer negotiations. One ex-player recorded, "he more than any other individual was responsible for putting Newcastle United on the football map". A West End man originally, Telford was to remain a prominent figure until a board shake-up in 1904 saw him leave the club - ironically just as the team he built was to embark on a dominating period. His controversial departure left much bad feeling with players close to Telford, then virtual manager as well as Chairman, thinking long about remaining with the club. Future stars Bob McColl and Colin Veitch were two players who considered their positions, the former moving quickly. It was not to be the last occasion board-room rumblings were to affect the team. Another of the club's backstage officials was John Graham, who was on United's board for over 30 years. Before being elected a director he had been a valued supporter since the days of East End.

The unsung heroes of the promotion success were left-back John White and front runner R. Allen. A former Dundee and Preston man, Allen appeared frequently on the right-wing during the campaign and linked well with Peddie and Wardrope. Newcastle's home form was outstanding, a factor to help the club through every year of any success in the future. They won 16 of the 17 games on their Leazes pitch.

Bert Gosnell training with a punch ball. He was one of several star players to shortly become associated with the new First Division force of Newcastle United.

Centenary Highlight

United's promotion squad in 1898. Left to right, Back: Cockburn (groundsman), T. Ghee, J. White, J. Ostler, J. Stott, T. Dodds (trainer). Middle: F. Watt (secretary), C. Watts, J. Jackson, M. Lennox, G. Stewart. Front: R. Allen, J. Harvey, J. Campbell, A. Aitken, W. Wardrope.

BYE-LAWS

OF THE

Newcastle United

FOOTBALL COMPANY LD.

1898-9.

Player J. Harvey

J. B. BOWES, NEWCASTLE-ON-TYNE

BYE-LAWS.

1.—On the field of play, all commands of the Captain must be promptly obeyed.

2.—All articles for the use of Players, are the property of the Company, and the Players will be held responsible for loss or damage sustained through neglect.

3.—Players shall keep themselves in fit and proper condition, and must attend at the Club House at the proper time, or in the event of illness, a message must be sent to the Secretary. Any violation of this Bye-Law will incur a penalty of 2s. 6d for each offence, which will be rigidly enforced.

4.—Hours of Training: On Tuesday Wednesday, Thursday, and Friday, the Hours of Training shall be from 10 a.m. to 12 noon, and from 3 p.m. to 5 p.m. No Player to leave before these hours without permission.

Players must also attend on Monday for Training when required.

5.—Players requiring leave of absence must apply for and receive the permission of the Directors.

6.—The Directors will not be responsible for payment for medical attendance, unless such attendance is necessary through injuries received while engaged Training or Playing.

7.—A Bonus of 5s. for every win will be paid to each Player of the First Team, but such Bonus or any increased Bonus shall not be paid until the end of the Season, but shall be banked on a separate account, in the names of the Chairman, W. Nesham, Esq., and the Hon. Treasurer, W. Bramwell, Esq.

8.—The attention of Players is drawn to the Rules of the Football Association. Any Player ordered off the field by the Referee and suspended by the Council of the Football Association, shall not receive any wages during such term of suspension.

9.—Any infringement of the foregoing Bye-Laws will be dealt with by the Directors, according to the nature of the offence.

10.—Players not signing the Attendance Book by 10.15 a.m. or 3.15 p.m., will be counted as absent.

By order of the Directors,

FRANK G. WATT, SECRETARY.

31st August, 1898.

Club Colours:

BLACK AND WHITE STRIPED SHIRT, BLUE KNICKERS.

Newcastle United's Bye-laws as issued to inside-forward John Harvey in 1898. Note that the club still had not adopted black shorts, wearing blue for several years to follow.

DIVISION TWO 1897-1898	P	W	D	L	F	A	Pts
Burnley	30	20	8	2	80	24	48
Newcastle United	**30**	**21**	**3**	**6**	**64**	**32**	**45**
Manchester City	30	15	9	6	66	36	39
Newton Heath	30	16	6	8	64	35	38
Woolwich Arsenal	30	16	5	9	69	49	37
Small Heath	30	16	4	10	58	50	36
Leicester Fosse	30	13	7	10	46	35	33
Luton Town	30	13	4	13	68	50	30
Gainsborough Trinity	30	12	6	12	50	54	30
Walsall	30	12	5	13	58	58	29
Blackpool	30	10	5	15	49	61	25
Grimsby Town	30	10	4	16	52	62	24
Burton Swifts	30	8	5	17	38	69	21
Lincoln City	30	6	5	19	43	82	17
Darwen	30	6	2	22	31	76	14
Loughborough Town	30	6	2	22	24	87	14

Promotion 1898

REGULAR SIDE

Watts

White - Jackson

Ghee - Ostler - Stott

Allen(R) - Harvey - Peddie or Campbell - Aitken - Wardrope

RESULTS	Home	Away
Woolwich Arsenal	W 4-1	D 0-0
Walsall	W 2-1	W 3-2
Burton Swifts	W 3-1	L 1-3
Lincoln City	W 3-0	W 3-2
Burnley	L 0-1	L 0-3
Newton Heath	W 2-0	W 1-0
Blackpool	W 2-0	W 3-2
Grimsby Town	W 4-0	L 0-2
Small Heath	W 4-0	L 0-1
Gainsborough Trinity	W 5-2	W 3-1
Loughborough Town	W 3-1	W 1-0
Manchester City	W 2-0	D 1-1
Darwen	W 1-0	W 3-1
Leicester Fosse	W 4-2	D 1-1
Luton Town	W 4-1	L 1-3

Test Matches		
Stoke	W 2-1	L 0-1
Blackburn Rovers	W 4-0	L 3-4

CHAIRMAN: William Neasham
MANAGER: Director's Committee
TRAINER-COACH: Tom Dodds
CAPTAIN: Jimmy Stott

Ever-present Charlie Watts does a spot of training watched by directors Bell and Oliver.

LARGEST VICTORY:
4-0 v Small Heath(H), Grimsby Town(H), Blackburn Rovers(H)

HEAVIEST DEFEAT:
0-3 v Burnley(A)

AVERAGE HOME ATTENDANCE:
11,905

TOP GATE:
24,959 v Burnley

LEAGUE APPEARANCES
Including Test Matches
34 Watts, 32 Ghee, 31 Jackson, 30 Ostler, Stott, Wardrope, 27 Harvey, Aitken, 24 Allen(R), Campbell, 21 Peddie, 20 White, 14 Smith, 10 Stewart, 9 Lindsay, 4 Lennox, 2 Carr, Lockey, 1 Allen(J), Milne, Niblo.

LEAGUE GOALS
Including Test Matches
16 Peddie, 13 Wardrope, 10 Campbell, 7 Harvey, 6 Smith, 5 Aitken, 4 Allen(R), Own Goals, 2 Ostler, Stott, 1 Lennox, White, Ghee, Jackson.

Willie Wardrope, invaluable up front with 13 goals.

THERE WAS MUCH TO DO FOR THE club's debut in the First Division. New dressing-rooms were hurriedly built, the teams entering the pitch from the goal behind the Gallowgate End. A small stand was erected and further plans agreed with the Corporation for another stand along the Barrack Road side of the ground. Other improvements for the comfort of spectators were carried out now the club had a new status.

Matt Kingsley, soon to play for England.

The directors found cash to purchase Sandy MacFarlane from Airdrie and Matt Kingsley arrived from Darwen to take over between the posts from Watts. Both players went on to appear for their respective countries, Scotland and England. MacFarlane, a classic schemer, played most of his best football when he returned north, with Dundee, while Kingsley became an efficient 'keeper for United who was noted for his fisted clearances. He was a hefty size too, at over 14 stone and became the first Magpie to be capped by England, playing against Wales in 1901.

Scottish purchase, Sandy MacFarlane.

Experienced forwards Joe Rogers and James Stevenson arrived to play alongside Peddie and Wardrope, who both just missed a Scottish cap, appearing in the trial match along with Tommy Ghee. Rogers was signed from Grimsby Town and before Kingsley's appearance for England, toured with an unofficial national party in November 1899. He played for the FA eleven and netted all of five goals in a 10-1 victory, and seven in the three games played. Stevenson cost £225 from Derby County, a player full of craft who had just appeared in the FA Cup final. A Scot, he was described as, "a wizard of the leather".

William Higgins was another quality acquisition. Having represented the Football League when with Bristol City, he eventually replaced Ostler in United's line-up. In defence and midfield, Newcastle relied largely on their Division Two stars with the exception of another ex-Grimsby player, Billy Lindsay, who appeared at left-back throughout the year after impressing towards the end of the promotion season. His elder brother Jimmy, was also on United's books during the same period.

Joe Rogers who toured Germany with the FA Team in 1899.

The Magpies' first opponents in Division One were Wolverhampton Wanderers, a home fixture on 3rd September 1898. United's players had been offered a bonus of £10 a man if the club finished in the top six and there was much interest on Tyneside, 20,000 turning up to see the better standard of football. Jock Peddie continued where he had left off, scoring the club's historic first goal, but the defence found the First Division's forwards a handful. Despite scoring twice - Peddie getting Newcastle's second also - United let in four goals and fell 4-2.

It was tough going for the club in their early weeks as a First Division force. They lost at Everton, then to Notts County. United picked up their first point at Stoke but it took eleven games before they recorded their first win. That was against Liverpool on 5th November at St James Park. Prolific scorer Peddie netted twice as Newcastle broke their duck in an emphatic 3-0 victory before another packed house of 20,000. With a victory under their belts the tide of misfortune turned. United grew in confidence and pulled away from the bottom of the division.

On Christmas Eve the first Football League meeting with Sunderland took place at the Wearsiders' new ground, Roker Park. A capacity crowd of 25,000 were present and they were treated to what the press later called, "one of the most remarkable games ever witnessed on a football field in the north of England". Sunderland opened the scoring when a mix-up between Jackson, Ostler and Ghee allowed Leslie to pounce. United looked the better side, however, and their deserved equaliser came from Willie Wardrope after good work from Stevenson, Rogers and Andy Aitken. Before the interval, Newcastle went ahead when Jock Peddie chased a huge Jackson clearance and struck home a terrific drive.

The game became physical in the second period, but Wardrope recovered from a heavy challenge to send Aitken away. Peddie finished off the move to put United 3-1 ahead, and although they fell back and allowed Sunderland to score through Leslie, the Magpies held on for their first win over the Wearsiders and their first away victory in the First Division. Indeed they might have increased their lead when Peddie went inches wide in the last minute. Newcastle had good support at Roker with railway bookings alone exceeding 4,000.

Sunderland gained revenge in the return game by winning 1-0 at St James Park. In fact the Reds were to remain a bogey side to United during this era, Newcastle not recording a home victory over their arch rivals until 1903.

The Magpies finished their inaugural season in the top flight in 13th place, a satisfactory conclusion after a devastating start which saw the club bottom of the table. In the FA Cup they fell early again. After dismissing Glossop, Newcastle lost to Liverpool who won 3-1 at Anfield.

Football entered the 20th Century during the following two seasons and saw the club consolidate their newly found First Division place. During 1899/1900 and 1900/01 United's management slowly transformed an emerging organisation into an experienced set-up equipped to challenge the might of soccer at the time - Aston Villa and neighbours Sunderland. The search for talent continued and many of the players to become megastars to Edwardian Tyneside arrived on the scene.

Much was done to the St James Park arena. First to go was the problem pitch which, in spite of much work, still caused concern to an extent that Grimsby officials described it as, "primitive". A new drainage system was installed and the turf completely relaid. A terrace was formed in the grass bank at the Leazes Terrace and Park sides of the ground and levelled with wooden boards, while ropes acted as barriers. Further work was carried out to the dressing-rooms and club facilities. Capacity was increased to 30,000. Newcastle were slowly developing their stadium, although as has occurred throughout the club's history, United faced problems obtaining permission from the Freemen and Corporation landlords. It was even noted at the time that if co-operation was not obtained, United would move from St James Park. The club was also faced with a claim, "requesting compensation for the loss of grazing at the bottom part of the field". St James Park was still classed as common feeding land.

Alec Gardner (left) one of the Magpies' most consistent performers over the next decade.

United finished the 1899/1900 season in a merited 5th place, and 6th the following year, a season when United held second spot for several weeks. Led by Chairman, James Telford and director John Graham, with Frank Watt always evident, United began to put together the side that took the club to its greatest period. Alec Gardner, Jack Carr and Colin Veitch entered the action, three of the black'n'whites' most renowed servants over the next decade. In total the trio appeared over 900 times for the club.

Gardner came from Leith Athletic and was a most versatile player for United, mainly at right-half. Unlucky not to be selected for Scotland - perhaps the best uncapped player in the 1900's - Gardner specialised at the low, precise pass and was to form an almost telepathic understanding with his colleagues. Alec matured quickly in Scotland, a very popular transfer market, even more so than at any time in the future. But, in days before the turn of the century, Newcastle's representatives had to be careful. The Scots resented the continual poaching of their players by English clubs and United scouts were literally thrown out of Leith's stadium and chased out of Edinburgh when they went for Gardner. It was all worth it though, the player was with them.

Jack Carr hailed from Tyneside, one of the few Geordies in United's growing Scottish camp. He appeared for juniors Seaton Burn at half-back and left back, the position he played in for England. Well built and something of a humourist, he was a gentlemanly defender, the ball always being his objective rather than the man - unlike many contemporaries of his era. Colin Veitch, like Carr, arrived from local football having skippered the very first Newcastle Boys' line-up. He was given a run out in a friendly with Hearts, impressed and assisted the black'n'whites as an amateur until being persuaded to turn professional when 17 years of age late in 1899. His first wage was £2 per week.

Other names arrived too. Scottish international full-back, Dave Gardner, no relation to Alec, was also secured. He came from Third Lanark and was something of an extrovert, pleasing the crowd with tricks on and off the ball. Another Scottish back, Charles Burgess was purchased also, one of several full-backs to be tried before the club settled on a trio of names to serve the club for over a decade. Outside-left Jock Fraser came from Notts County, and yes, he too was a Scot, later to be capped by his country. Tommy Niblo, like Fraser a tall and well built winger, graduated from the reserves. He later also played for Scotland.

Newcastle went out of the FA Cup in 1900, once more to Southampton the eventual Cup finalists, and this after narrowly toppling Southern League Reading. Jock Peddie, who had prolonged a leave period, almost missed the game and was subsequently disciplined. Against the Saints, Peddie - the club's top scorer for the third season in succession - was back after suspension and scored the opener only for Southampton to blast four goals to secure victory. The following year was to be no better, United being eliminated in Round One 3-1 by Second Division Middlesbrough on Tees-side.

The major talking point at the turn of the century was an amazing derby meeting with Sunderland that never took place. With the Boer War casting shadows across the nation, United were scheduled to meet their rivals at St James Park on Good Friday 1901. There was unprecedented interest in the holiday match. Sunderland were the division's leaders and United were in 7th position. A huge crowd, estimated at between 50,000 and even as high as 70,000 converged on the Leazes stadium, which then still had only a capacity of 30,000. Club officials and the meagre scattering of about 25 police were swamped by fans trying to get onto the terracing. Three quarters of an hour before the kick-off every part of the ground was packed. The gates were locked and events then rapidly got out of control and a full scale riot took place, one of the worst scenes at a football match in this country.

Full-back Jack Carr, locally born and who went on to appear for England.

The stadium gates were broken down, fencing demolished and, as the local press reported, the fans "clambered over the rails like cats". Hundreds sat precariously on the stand roof, "causing the frightened people underneath to make a hurried departure". Thousands upon thousands spilled onto the pitch and the police were powerless to clear the playing area. The teams and referee attempted to enter the arena at 3.30, but it was impossible to even start the game and the match was abandoned before a ball was even kicked. The effect was to

FINED FOR SPEEDING

At the turn of the century Newcastle's travelling footballers were caught red-handed by police in the act of exceeding the speed limit. On a visit to Blackburn the side was late in catching their return train. In an open coach, driven by four horses, the driver bounced his way towards the railway station at a terrific pace. Police took chase and caught the driver at the station. He was hauled before the local magistrates and fined 40 shillings plus costs for speeding. United's records do not indicate whether the club paid the driver's fine or indeed caught the train.

before a ball was even kicked. The effect was to make matters worse.

Up until then, the crowd had been fairly good humoured, but it quickly changed into an angry mob and the two sets of rival fans clashed in one huge free-for-all. It was noted, "Three or four thousand persons, mostly young fellows with caps formed themselves into one compact body and went on an expedition of wreckage". The goal timbers and nets were ripped down, the Athletic News' correspondent humorously wrote, "the crossbar in falling fetched one or two of the rioters a reverberating smack on the headache department". The club flag was torn to shreds, barriers and fencing were uprooted and used as weapons and missiles and bottles and stones flew through the air. At last wagon loads of police reinforcements arrived. Some came on horseback and several baton charges were ordered in an attempt to quell the riot. It took the overworked police until 5.00pm to clear the ground.

Amazingly only a dozen people were injured and treated at Newcastle Infirmary, including one who had fallen from the grandstand. A disaster had been averted only through good fortune. Only a year later 26 spectators were killed at Ibrox Park. Afterwards an aggrieved Sunderland fan sued United for his wasted admission money together with expenses. It was a Test Case as regards the Law of Contract in football. He lost his litigation and had to fork out legal costs to the extent of £39 17s 6d. The Football Authorities did, however, order that receipts from the replay, which was won 2-0 by the Wearsiders, be given to local charities.

Ronald Orr, one of the growing band of international talent at St. James Park.

With the death of Queen Victoria Newcastle entered the new Edwardian era, continuing with their steady progress. In 1901/02 they finished the season with the best defensive record in the division and it was only in attack, where Peddie had an off season, that the side fell down. But for this lack of penetration up front, Newcastle could well have gone close to lifting the title for the first time. As it turned out United finished 3rd, seven points behind Champions Sunderland. Yet United had put down a mark of their growing stature in the game and results like the record 8-0 victory over Notts County served notice on the team's impending dominance. United were 5-0 ahead at half-time with a scintillating display. New acquisition Ronald Orr registered four goals, while Peddie got three.

Orr headed south from Scotland in May 1901, from St Mirren, and made a big impression. He was a great team player, unselfish and, for such a small man - he was only 5'5" - was proficient in the air too. After several seasons of splendid service, Ron got into the crowd's bad books and he was virtually driven away by the taunts of the St James Park boo-boys.

At last Newcastle had a degree of success in the FA Cup too. The defeat of Arsenal in London by 2-0 earned United a glamour derby with Sunderland. There was again tremendous enthusiasm in the north-east. The game was played on a Wednesday afternoon, due to snow cancelling the scheduled Saturday's fixture, and this in the days when time off work was frowned upon. The region's industries found that the attraction of football was becoming a big problem, as the press recorded, "the workmen in many large factories on Tyne and Wear ceased work at midday, and so large was the exodus from Messrs Hawthorn Leslie, Stephenson and the Elswick Arsenal that operations were seriously affected".

St James Park was packed with 23,000 and at the outset the men from Sunderland were clear favourites, but the black'n'whites shocked everyone by winning 1-0, "outplaying the Wearsiders at every point". Orr netted the important goal in the final minutes, a close-in stab from a Willie Stewart corner. Scottish international Stewart had arrived from Queen's Park in another cheque-book raid north of the Cheviots.

The whole of Tyneside thought it was going to be their year, but mid-table Sheffield United stunned a 20,000 Gallowgate crowd by holding United to a 1-1 draw in the quarter-final. They subsequently won the replay 2-1 and it was the Blades who ended up at the Crystal Palace and not the Geordies. The match at St James Park showed the remarkable way in which the club handled a frosty and ice-bound pitch. In a bid to ensure that the game went ahead, sand and straw were laid across the field and several fires were lit on the pitch to raise the temperature. Unfortunately rain then soaked the protective straw and, mixing with the sand, created quite a mess. It took officials and workmen hours to clear the surface ready for action while afterwards it took groundsmen months to rid the St James Park surface of the straw which, in time, rooted in the pitch.

More transfer activity centred on St James Park as new faces continued to arrive on Tyneside. Winger Dick Roberts came from West Bromwich Albion and impressed many on Tyneside with a straight forward style. His departure to

Middlesbrough in 1904, after netting 17 goals in 55 games, caused dismay and much protest. Alex Caie, a hefty half-back was purchased from Millwall Athletic and was recalled by one colleague as being, "hard as nails". Experienced full-back, Tom Davidson also came from the Londoners and had recently won an FA Cup medal with Bury's noted side. International trialist Bob Bennie travelled across the border in the same deal that brought Orr to Tyneside. He was an honest and solid performer and, after being forced to quit the game by a knee injury, became a United director and successful businessman in the region.

Two other names featured on United's team-sheet; two individuals who were important factors in the rise of the Magpies. Jackie Rutherford made his first appearance as a 17 year-old, the club's youngest debutant at the time, and was eventually to claim the No 11 jersey in the months ahead. Star of Scottish football, Bob McColl, an amateur, turned professional and signed for United in November 1901. Known as 'The Prince of Centre-forwards', The Journal described him as, "the smartest dribbler and goalscorer in Scotland". The Scottish international from Queen's Park didn't stay long at St James Park - only a little over two seasons - but his influence on the side was immense.

McColl was his country's number one personality and had recently netted a hat-trick for the Scots against the English. He stamped his impression on the side, a blend of football that featured short passing and intricate movements for the purist and very much with the ball on the ground. Colin Veitch recorded, "I have no hesitation in saying that McColl set the high standard of football which Newcastle attained shortly afterwards". He was a superb ball-player who also possessed a sharpness in front of goal and the mind of a tactical master.

With Andy Aitken now good enough to appear for Scotland, along with McColl and Orr against England, Newcastle's first masterful line-up was almost complete. Gardner, Carr, Orr, Rutherford and Veitch claimed places along with McColl, while Howie, McWilliam, McCombie and Bill Appleyard were to sign for the club in the next few months. United's supporters, and the football world at large, had only one more year to wait before the name of Newcastle United was to be considered as a serious contender for trophies.

The excellent promise of 1901/02 was not carried on into the 1902/03 season. United slipped to 14th position and the directors were perplexed as to the problem. The Magpies were an enigma. They had started well and were perched at the top of the division with a goals' record of nine for, and nought against. But they had a terrible time after that. Injuries didn't help but, as Colin Veitch recalled in his memoirs, one of the causes was, "a policy of team selection which completely bewildered not only the supporters but the players themselves".

They were crushed by West Bromwich 6-1 and then, seven days later, gave Notts County a similar six goal hiding, while Aston Villa scored seven against United. An important meeting with senior players took place at the club's St James Street office in an effort to solve the team's problems. Chairman James Telford boldly said, "We seem to be making a mess of things. Will you go to the board-room, lock yourselves in, and choose what you consider to be our best team". He gave Aitken, Veitch and Carr the opportunity of rectifying the slide - unprecedented action then, as it would be today. Respected journalist, Ivan Sharpe was to write, "it was the birth-pains of one of the most brilliant teams in the history of the game". Immediately United's players promoted young Scot, Peter McWilliam, who had been signed during the close-season from Inverness Thistle. Within a year he was to become one of football's most popular characters. It was his special talent in midfield that perhaps, more than anything else, made United tick. United defeated Aston Villa 2-0 and won six of the final eight games to climb away from the relegation zone.

Another reason for the loss of form was the lack of a goalscoring replacement for the departed Peddie who had joined Manchester United. Peddie had

Bob McColl, Scotland's centre-forward and a most celebrated player.

Another well known personality of the era, Bobby Templeton who became a huge favourite on Tyneside.

England winger Arthur Turner, signed from Southampton.

become embroiled in several disagreements with United's management. He had been fined, suspended for missing training and, as one entry in the club's minutes record, for "turning out in an unfit state". He had actually refused to play in one game against Wolverhampton Wanderers in 1899. Bob McColl was never an out and out striker and, to counter the weakness, United splashed out late in the season for Grimsby Town's burly leader, Bill Appleyard, who had a big reputation in every sense of the word and who had played an important part in knocking United from the FA Cup that season. It was to be a brilliant coup.

Two more Scottish stars arrived on Tyneside. Yet another full-back, Billy Agnew from Kilmarnock and Aston Villa's Bobby Templeton who cost a massive £400. Both were to be capped by their country. The much travelled Templeton was as graceful as a gazelle on the flank and Scotland's brilliant but, at times, selfish matchwinner. He cost the club a record fee and was one of the characters of the time, always immaculately dressed in the fashion of the day. He was even presented with a gold medal for having the audacity to enter a lion's cage at a circus and place his head between the lion's jaws! He was a wonderful entertainer in whatever he did and for a short while formed a terrific wing with McColl. England forward, Arthur Turner was added to the squad too, remembered by United's officials after good FA Cup displays for his club, Southampton, against the Magpies. But he was soon to be replaced by the up and coming teenager Rutherford.

TRAINER'S REPORT

Tom Dodds' report to the directors in January 1899 consisted of;
"Lindsay - shirking his training"
"Stevenson - worse for liquor at Glossop match and absent from training"
"Niblo - absent from training"
"Watts - does not train"

On the last day of the season Newcastle played a big part in the destiny of the League Championship when United defeated Sunderland 1-0 to deprive the Roker team of the trophy. The Wearsiders were running neck and neck with Sheffield Wednesday and had to win to lift the title. They were confident, too, with a first class record at St James Park, but a goal by Bob McColl gave United their very first Football League success over their rivals on Tyneside. In front of a 26,500 crowd and early in the second-half, Veitch broke away and slipped the ball to Appleyard who played a one-two with Gardner before pushing the ball through a gap for McColl to score. Following a week of rumours that Newcastle would throw the match to Sunderland's advantage, the game was watched by Football League officials to make sure no favours were handed to their close neighbours. McColl's goal sent the title trophy to the Hillsborough sideboard to the delight of 500 Yorkshiremen in the crowd.

In spite of a poor season and several shortsighted calls for a 'sack the lot' policy, Newcastle's directors were happy with their team-building and United now possessed a terrific looking set of players. With a professional staff of 44 for the 1903/04 season, no fewer than eleven of the squad were already, or shortly to become, full internationals for either England or Scotland. Yet more Scots joined the side in the season. Inside-forward Jimmy Howie, who was to become one of the team's most influential players, was purchased from Bristol Rovers while full-back Andy McCombie crossed from Wear to Tyne for £700 after being a regular with Sunderland for several years. It was the biggest transfer fee the game had seen. Also, towards the end of the season, more big names arrived. Irish international Bill McCracken settled on Tyneside after a move from Distillery and winger Albert Gosnell was signed too. All four players were to be regular internationals.

Newcastle could now afford to compete with the best in the transfer market. Gates had grown steadily with a solid support of 19,000 coming through the turnstiles each match-day, and 30,000 for attractive fixtures. Even the club's second string attracted good crowds. Over 9,000 saw the Northern League game with the Sunderland 'A' side. Demand was to reach new levels as more and more stars began to wear the black'n'white jersey.

With revenue constant, the club did not now have to watch thier financial situation quite so carefully as in the past. A capacity crowd saw the Tyne-Wear derby on Boxing Day in which Sunderland again won at St James Park, this time 3-1. Newcastle ended the season in 4th place only five points behind Champions Sheffield Wednesday and they displayed the brand of football that was, in the immediate years, to be United's hallmark - a short passing, possession style to enlighten football audiences.

Much of the team's effectiveness was brought about by the meetings of players on a regular basis

to discuss their performances - as one said, "for the development of method, tactics and general understanding". Coaching and tactical talks had arrived in the St James Park dressing-room.
It worked a treat and results were good that season, derby games excepted. In the second-half of the campaign they lost only three league games. It was to be the springboard to greater achievement.

The only bad patch occured during February and unhappily it was in the FA Cup. Holders of the trophy, Bury, who had defeated Derby by a record 6-0 to win the Cup, were United's First Round opponents. At Gigg Lane Newcastle lost 2-1 and the Magpies' fans had to wait a further season before they tasted a slice of Cup glory.

Following the last match of the year, a convincing 4-0 victory over Sheffield Wednesday, the club embarked on a close-season tour which took the side abroad for the very first time. After a few games in Scotland, United's party sailed to Denmark on board a Neilson & Anderson steamer and played four games in Copenhagen including a match against Southampton. They won them all, netting 19 goals in the process.

On their return St James Park was ready for another season. It was to be a special campaign and the year in which Newcastle United Football Club became League Champions for the very first time. After almost a decade of struggling to survive, the Magpies were to progress into football's elite.

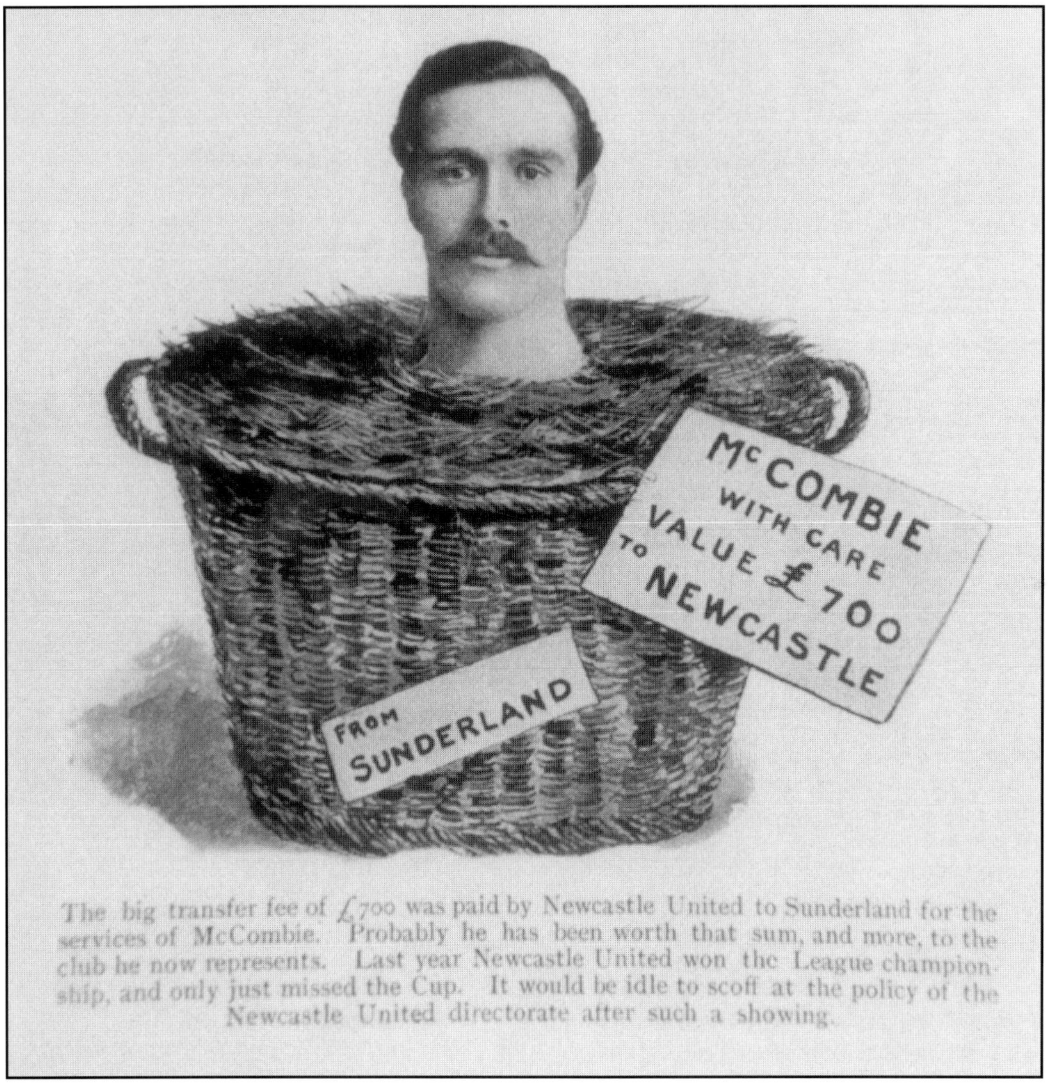

Andy McCombie joined United from Sunderland for a staggering £700, a record at the time. The Scottish international full-back remained on the club's staff until 1950.

Centenary Profile 1

Mr Versatile

"He was a master....a player above the ordinary. A born footballer"

Colin Veitch, 1931

NEWCASTLE UNITED'S HISTORY IS LITTERED with footballers who have brought their skills over the border from Scotland. One of the very first of the Scottish breed to become a big star at St James Park was Andrew Aitken. He was one of their most versatile half-backs as United won promotion to the First Division and afterwards established themselves as a force in the game.

As a mark of his stature in football, Aitken was selected for Scotland's line-up in every one of the Auld Enemy clashes against England - with a single exception - from 1901 to 1911. It was then the only major international fixture, the games against Wales and Ireland being very much secondary affairs. As an added honour Aitken also captained his country.

Those years saw United field internationals literally by the dozen and he was capped on 14 occasions, eight times as a Magpie player - the first ever Scot to be honoured. Aitken played in front of some massive crowds for those days -121,452 at Hampden Park in 1908, 110,000 in 1910 - while he was also on the pitch when 26 people were killed at Ibrox after wooden terracing collapsed during the England v Scotland match of 1902.

From Ayr, Aitken was a half-back who loved to go forward and one who could play in a variety of roles; full-back, inside or centre-forward and on either side of the field, left or right, as well as the central role in midfield. He started with the black'n'whites at inside-left but was capped predominantly at right-half, a position he really did not favour. Along with Colin Veitch, another truly versatile player, United had two men able to fit into any role almost with perfection.

The Scot was prominent in the air, in spite of a small build at 5'8", but his timing in aerial duels was phenomenal and he often out-jumped 6'0" opponents. When operating in a central midfield role, Aitken largely played a defensive game - an anchor man - years ahead of the advent of the stopper centre-half.

Newcastle's directors were first attracted to Aitken's talents in the summer months of 1895 when scouts noted his name whilst he was turning out for Ayr Parkhouse, one of the forerunners of the current Ayr United side. He was born in April 1877 and had joined Parkhouse after appearing for other local clubs Elmbank and Ayr Thistle. Andy also worked as a boy assistant in a grocer's shop.

After interest from both Newton Heath and Preston, Aitken signed for United in July and was immediately thrown into the club's Second Division side for the new 1895/96 season. He was only 18 years old when he made his debut against Loughborough Town - the opening game of the programme - and he scored in the 3-0 victory. Aitken went on to appear just under 350 times for United in a career that spanned twelve seasons. Remarkably, he played in every position except goalkeeper for the club.

Always able to score goals too, he netted 42 when at Gallowgate. Aitken linked well alongside outside-left Willie Wardrope and centre-forward Jock Peddie and the forward trio did much to take the club into the First Division in 1898. He was appointed club skipper shortly after and led the side during their early days of dominance, to the Championship and Cup final in 1905, and to another final appearance twelve months later.

Andy Aitken

AITKEN'S PLAYING RECORD	League		FA Cup		Total	
	App	Gls	App	Gls	App	Gls
1895-96	27	10	5	3	32	13
1896-97	30	11	1	0	31	11
1897-98	27	5	4	4	31	9
1898-99	26	4	2	0	28	4
1899-1900	34	0	2	0	36	0
1900-01	32	1	1	1	33	2
1901-02	30	1	4	0	34	1
1902-03	32	0	1	0	33	0
1903-04	32	0	1	0	33	0
1904-05	28	2	8	0	36	2
1905-06	15	0	4	0	19	0
1906-07	3	0	0	0	3	0
	316	**34**	**33**	**8**	**349**	**42**

Nicknamed, 'Daddler', he was lean and lissom, artistic in method and touch and a silky player to watch. Dropping into midfield, Aitken forged a brilliant half-back line for United alongside Veitch, Gardner or McWilliam. Alec Gardner said of his team-mate, "He may lack physique, but for clever headwork and terrier-like persistence he would be hard to beat".

When Aitken was approaching 30 years of age, at the end of October 1906, he joined Middlesbrough as player-manager. He cost 'Boro £500 and had quite a job in revitalising the Ayresome Park side who were, at the time, bottom of Division One. Under Aitken's influence though, they rallied to finish in 11th place. He was an inspiring example and motivated star forwards Bloomer and Common into action. The following season the Tees club had one of their best ever seasons ending in 6th place, only two points behind runners-up Aston Villa. The following year they did well again and Aitken said his experience at Ayresome Park had given him the most satisfaction of his career. However, he was to leave on a sour note, a clash of personalities with a member of the board ending his stay at Middlesbrough.

The Scot moved south to take charge of Leicester Fosse in February 1909, although initially only as captain. Leicester were newly promoted from Division Two and again Aitken was put in charge of a struggling team. Like Middlesbrough, he arrived to see his new club near the foot of the table, this time however, his talents couldn't save the Midland side and they were relegated. Second Division football didn't bother Aitken, he still performed well, playing on, and was good enough to be selected for Scotland again, although now 34 years old.

He moved back to Dundee in his homeland at the end of the 1910/11 season and concentrated on the playing side of the game once more. Andy joined Kilmarnock the following summer, but was soon sidelined through injury and he retired after a groin problem in 1913. He then returned to Tyneside and managed local North Eastern League side, Gateshead Town, for a period. He also ran several pubs in the area including The Railway Inn in Galashiels. Aitken later resided in Newcastle's west-end and scouted a little, recommending his own son to United during the Twenties.

He remained in the north-east up until his death in Ponteland Hospital in February 1955. Colleague Colin Veitch said of Aitken, "He was a master. He was an individual who could play anywhere, a player above the ordinary. A born footballer".

Centenary Profile 2

The Scholarly Master

"One of the finest footballers in Britain. Veitch's name was synonymous with honesty and good fellowship"

The Guardian, 1938

THE RISE OF NEWCASTLE UNITED in the football world was due to an imposing collection of international talent from defence through to attack. Colin Veitch was one of those immortals and perhaps the most famous of those stars. Veitch, like Andy Aitken, was a most versatile player. He filled every position except left-back, goalkeeper and outside-left for the club and appeared in five FA Cup finals - in four different roles - as well as being part of three Championship victories at St James Park.

Very much a Novocastrian from his first to last day, Colin Campbell McKechnie Veitch, to give his full name, hailed from the east of the city. The open spaces of Heaton Park were his playground and Colin started kicking a football around at an early age. He appeared for Larkspur, Malcolm Rovers and Dalton - three junior clubs - during the years before the turn of the century. He was Newcastle School's first captain in 1895 and took part in the first inter-town game on Tyneside, against Sunderland Boys. Jimmy Stewart, later a colleague of Veitch's in the United side was reserve to that XI. Rarely, if ever, have two future England internationals been in the same city school's team.

Colin's career really took off when he enrolled at Rutherford College and appeared for the soccer team, one of the top amateur outfits on Tyneside. His three elder brothers appeared for the club too and the family started opposing the likes of Bishop Auckland, Crook Town as well as Newcastle United's 'A' side. The Magpies' officials were impressed with the youngest Veitch, so much so that they gave the teenager a run out in a friendly fixture. All went well, he signed amateur forms and, during the summer of 1899, was offered the chance to turn professional.

At a meeting in the now long-gone Hotel Metropole, the Magpies made one of their foremost acquisitions. Colin Veitch signed for a paltry fee. He was just 17 years-old, but had a career that was to unfold into something very special.

The following season, in October 1899, Veitch made his debut against Wolves. He recalled, "I was not a success in the team. We lost 1-0 and I was not too cheerful after the game". There was a spell when Veitch decided to pursue a scholastic career and actually retired from the game, only occasionally appearing under the pseudonym of 'Hamilton'. However, after a spell in the reserves, Colin changed his mind and soon made a place for himself in Newcastle's senior line-up. He prefered the middle half-back role and played most of his football from the centre-half position - then the midfield area of today. But he filled other roles equally well. He was just 5'6" but quite hefty at over 11 stones yet he oozed class. Veitch possessed masterly ease and in action always appeared to have time and space as well as immaculate control of the ball, almost as if it was tied to his toe.

He was to develop into an adroit tactician and his understanding with Bill McCracken was uncanny. Together they formed a famous offside-trap which tormented the football scene for over a decade. Colin was a footballer who pioneered the application of pre-match tactics and it was Veitch more than any other, who developed United's celebrated possession football. Listening and learning from Bob McColl, he forged a marvellous team pattern that quickly started to win honours. They were League Champions in 1905, 1907 and 1909, with Cup final visits in 1905, 1906, 1908, 1910 and 1911 and Veitch was part of them all.

Captain on many occasions during his 15 years as a player, he was the first United skipper to lift the FA Cup. Colin represented England on six occasions, but would have won many more international honours had he held one firm playing position. He was his country's permanent reserve, owing to his marvellous versatility, and was over a dozen times on the sidelines in case of injury. Veitch also skippered both England and the Football League XI.

Colin Veitch

VEITCH'S PLAYING RECORD

	League		FA Cup		Total	
	App	Gls	App	Gls	App	Gls
1899-1900	1	0	0	0	1	0
1900-01	1	0	0	0	1	0
1901-02	10	3	2	1	12	4
1902-03	17	0	1	0	18	0
1903-04	33	1	1	0	34	1
1904-05	24	10	4	0	28	10
1905-06	28	7	8	3	36	10
1906-07	29	7	1	0	30	7
1907-08	25	3	4	0	29	3
1908-09	34	9	7	0	41	9
1909-10	27	1	5	0	32	1
1910-11	26	0	8	1	34	1
1911-12	5	1	1	0	6	1
1912-13	9	1	3	1	12	2
1913-14	6	0	0	0	6	0
1914-15	1	0	0	0	1	0
	276	**43**	**45**	**6**	**321**	**49**

A gent on and off the field, his abilities away from football gave him almost as much distinction. A man of high intellect, Veitch was a lover of the Arts. A scholar, good enough to be offered a post of headmaster with a local public school, he was a playwright, producer, conductor and composer. An actor and musician of enormous talent also, Colin was a key figure in the Newcastle People's Theatre and often rubbed shoulders with the truly greats of the stage world, George Bernard Shaw being among the guests at Veitch's Gosforth home. He was also a leading personality of the Clarion Choir and Newcastle Operatic Society.

Married to a gifted actress, Greta Burke, Veitch amazingly dabbled in politics too. He was once approached to stand as a Labour Member of Parliament and, while very politically aware, he didn't think football and the Commons mixed too well. He did though take his statesman's voice into the world of football being a Players' Union activist and Chairman for a number of years. Having to avert a threatened players' strike in 1909, he held an important role. Veitch was highly respected and one comment on his leadership noted, "The players have never had a man of such vision and suave power".

Veitch appeared for United up until the First World War although, after a dispute with the club in 1911, only sparsely played regular First Division football. He returned to Gallowgate after the hostilities and took a coaching position, suggesting in 1924 the formation of a junior side, the Newcastle Swifts - pioneers of the current junior set-up. Veitch knew the future of the club lay with grooming youngsters and he worked hard to establish, and prove, the point. But, within two years, Colin had been sacked and his break with United was a bitter one. After 27 years with the Magpies, he was given one week's notice to quit.

Not surprisingly many offers came his way and Colin was appointed Bradford City manager in August 1926 when the Valley Parade club were at a low point. They dropped out of Division One as Veitch arrived, but his tactical mind staged a recovery and, during his second season in charge, they just missed promotion. Veitch though moved on and didn't take to football management returning to Tyneside. Instead he turned to journalism and worked as a full-time reporter for the Newcastle Chronicle. He became a bold critic, once banned from the United press-box for his uncensored reviews of Newcastle's dismal efforts in the Thirties.

In 1938 the former United star was laid low for several months with pneumonia. When recuperating in the Swiss Alps, he died suddenly in a Berne hospital at the age of 56. On the news of his death tributes from all over Britain were printed in every newspaper, from The Times to the Nuneaton Tribune. The Guardian noted, "One of the finest footballers in Britain. Veitch's name was synonymous with honesty and good fellowship and the men who played under his leadership would do anything for him". One of those men, Jock Rutherford, said, "Colin Veitch had a great football brain. A brilliant individual in everything he did".

All told Veitch appeared in a black'n'white jersey well over 300 times. He was a player who would have stood out in any era of football, the modern brand included. He was a remarkable Tynesider for many reasons, but most of all a wonderful footballer.

4 EDWARDIAN MASTERS I

1904-1908

• QUEST FOR THE DOUBLE • CUP FINAL FLOP I • CHAMPIONS AGAIN • FA CUP VICTIMS • CUP FINAL FLOP II •

"The best eleven I ever played against was Newcastle United. They had the greatest side that was ever possessed by any club"

Billy Meredith, Manchester City, Manchester United & Wales

FOR ALMOST THE NEXT TEN YEARS Newcastle United was to dominate English football with a brand of artistic play that saw the club achieve recognition as one of the greatest of all teams. They possessed a line-up of internationals throughout the decade and were known in every pub from Berwick in the north, to Brighton in the south. During the history of football few clubs have sustained a period of mastery for such a long spell. During early years Aston Villa maintained a dominance. Huddersfield Town did it in the Twenties, Arsenal the following decade, while of course Liverpool have achieved enduring success in modern day football. Newcastle accomplished that feat during the 1900's.

Edwardian Britain had changed the country's society dramatically with many of Queen Victoria's ideals and values losing esteem. Edward VII came to the throne in 1901. He had a lifestyle very different to his mother; a rich, flamboyant one and the Edwardian era very much followed his lead. It was the age of country-house parties, shooting week-ends and lavish entertainment, whether it be in clubs, hotels or the theatre. The Liberals and Tories vied for power in Downing Street and while many were still living in an impoverished state, levels of comfort were improving rapidly.

In 1903 the first powered flight by Wilbur and Wright took place while in the north-east of England industry continued to boom with coal mining, shipbuilding and engineering developing at an accelerating rate all creating a spiral of expansion and prosperity. Great liners such as the SS Mauritania were launched on the Tyne, steam and electric tramcars started to replace horse drawn vehicles. Newcastle itself developed further as an important centre of commerce, very much the region's capital. Newcastle United Football Club was to follow the city's lead.

United's first trophy-winning season of 1904/05 opened with a home fixture with Woolwich Arsenal, the Gunners' debut in Division One. Newcastle started in a convincing manner cruising to a 3-0 victory in front of a 21,897 attendance. Ronald Orr struck two goals, and Rutherford one with a vicious in-swinger direct from a corner. For the remainder of the season the team was confident in every department, playing their own brand of attacking football of short passes in intricate triangular movements.

The right-wing trio of Howie, Gardner and Rutherford was especially prominent. On the left Bert Gosnell, a capture from Southern League Chatham, was challenging Templeton, perhaps the original enigmatic Scot, who was both a delight and despair to thousands. Gosnell was a big man for a winger, 5'10" and over 12 stone in weight. He was an orthodox player yet an extremely effective team-man. Linking up with Orr and McWilliam they formed a dangerous left attack. Appleyard and Aitken filled the central roles up front and in midfield respectively, while McCombie and Carr commanded defence. Jimmy Lawrence had taken over between the posts following a move from the Glasgow Perthshire club.

As winter approached United collected full points in ten of eleven games played to put them on top of the table for the first time in their history. The run included seven wins in a row, still a club record. By April, the Magpies were separated from Everton and Manchester City at the head of Division One by only two points. With four matches left, City had the toughest programme on paper and crucially Everton met their Manchester

PLAYER'S ROUTINE

A typical Friday pre-match schedule for Newcastle's stars consisted of;

- Light exercise in morning
- Billiards match in the club room
- Train to Monkseaton
- Walk to Tynemouth for lunch
- Tea back in Newcastle
- Pantomime at the Theatre Royal

Lord Beresford, Admiral of the Fleet, kicking off the Tyne & Wear clash of September 1904, a friendly won by Sunderland 2-1 in front of 20,000.

rivals. Newcastle had opened a two point gap when that game was played and the black'n'whites hoped for a draw, but City won 2-0 and the final flurry of action was left between United and the Blues.

The title race was settled on the last day of the season after the Magpies had faltered against Sunderland, losing 3-1 on the last home Saturday of the season, in front of a capacity crowd of 30,000. United still hadn't completely overcome the Wearside jinx, Sunderland also having toppled United by the same scoreline on Christmas Eve. As a double blow, Alec Gardner cried off injured for the remaining games. It was a giant set-back. Newcastle had two away games left, at Sheffield Wednesday and another local derby at Middlesbrough. It was an uphill struggle that faced United. The pressure was on, but Newcastle did it in style, winning both games and scoring three goals in each outing.

Sheffield Wednesday had been close rivals for much of the season and at Owlerton, then in days before the famous Hillsborough stadium was built, blue and white lined up against black and white. Title dreams appeared to fade rapidly as the home side went in front and held their lead until eleven minutes from the end. However, United at last found their form and a rapid three goal flourish turned despondency into anticipation. Out injured for the final show-down though, were McCombie, Veitch and McWilliam.

At Middlesbrough, who struggled to avoid the drop that year, Newcastle were a goal up inside five minutes as Orr's low shot found a corner of the net. Then Jackie Rutherford scored a second, a goal described as, "a magnificent effort". The emerging youngster flashed past two defenders and rounded the goalkeeper with consummate ease. A minute later the powerful physique of Appleyard wrapped up the game - and the title - after more, "brilliant" play opened the 'Boro defence.

Rivals Manchester City, the only side that could catch United, and that only on goal average, lost 3-2 at Aston Villa in a game that saw the club rocked by a bribery and bonus scandal. City players were firstly accused of handing inducements to Villa's men, then the club was found guilty of offering their own players a £100 bonus - then an astronomical sum - totally in contradiction to the game's rules. Afterwards no fewer than 17 players were suspended.

Newcastle had become worthy League Champions by a single point ahead of Everton, who leap-frogged over City. They had scored most goals and conceded least in the division. Four players reached double figures in the goal charts, evidence of a good all-round combination. The title trophy was delivered to Tyneside by President of the League, J.J.Bentley and after a celebration gathering it was displayed in several local shops, including Bainbridge & Company and John Sinclair Ltd, the giant cigarette manufacturer.

As a footnote, during April, just when the Championship race was hotting up, United allowed no fewer than five regulars from their side to join the Scotland and England squads. Newcastle's depleted side faced Blackburn Rovers without Aitken, McCombie, Howie, McWilliam and Colin Veitch, and dropped points in a 2-0 defeat. It was a club or country decision which could have been critical to the season's outcome.

Bert Gosnell, a most useful outside-left capped by England in 1906.

Action from Newcastle v Manchester United on a snow-covered St. James Park. Bill Appleyard goes close with an effort at goal.

Newcastle's success was not restricted to the Football League programme that year, for they also headed for the FA Cup, narrowly missing the coveted double. Southern League Plymouth Argyle were the first to be humbled by the new power in football, but not until the minnows had proved to be torrid opponents. It took United three games to dispose of Argyle, with their 'keeper Titchie Horn stopping everything United's forwards fired at him. On a heavy and greasy pitch at Gallowgate, Plymouth held United to a 1-1 draw, coming from behind after Gosnell had put Newcastle ahead after only three minutes. The following Wednesday another 1-1 draw was played out, this after extra-time, again Gosnell netting. Eventually at Plumstead, home of Arsenal, United settled the tie with a 2-0 victory, but the Magpies did not get their second goal until near the end with a late Ronald Orr penalty. Colin Veitch was later to record, "We were lucky to avoid defeat".

Tottenham Hotspur was next to face the Tynesiders, then also in the Southern League. Once more United could not see off non-league opposition at the first attempt. However they brought Spurs to Tyneside and in the replay promptly won 4-0 before a turn out of 26,755. Orr put the club on course after a fierce Appleyard effort had been blocked, while Jimmy Howie cracked home a superb volley.

In the quarter-final, leading Second Division promotion chasers, Bolton Wanderers held home advantage, but on a soft pitch outside-left Bert Gosnell stamped his authority on the match once more. First he went close by crashing a drive against the post, then he collided with the home 'keeper Davies who had to leave the field with full-back Taylor ending between the posts. It proved a turning point in the tie. Appleyard bustled his way through the middle to give United the lead, then Howie added the decider. Gosnell had by now replaced the popular Templeton on the flank, to the annoyance of many of the St James Park crowd. Gosnell suffered for it, rarely being the crowd's favourite and this despite consistent, if not flamboyant displays up front which earned him an England call up in 1906.

So to the Geordies' first FA Cup semi-final, a tie at Hyde Road, Manchester against Sheffield Wednesday who had lifted the Championship for the last two seasons. Newcastle had already toppled the Yorkshire side 6-2 in league action and were odds on favourites. Playing in white shirts, 40,000

Newcastle's party bound for the F.A. Cup Final. Left to right, Back: A. McCombie, J. Lawrence, J. Carr. Middle: F. Watt (secretary), A. Gardner, A. Aitken, P. McWilliam, J. McPherson (trainer). Front: J. Oliver (Director), J. Rutherford, J. Howie, W. Appleyard, C. Veitch, A. Gosnell, R. Oliver (Director).

saw Jimmy Howie clinch the goal which sent United through to their first FA Cup final. After 18 minutes, Gosnell went past two defenders, crossed for Howie to control the ball and stab home from six yards. Wednesday thought they had a clear penalty when McCombie appeared to handle, but the referee didn't see it their way, a controversial decision talked about in Sheffield for years after. The sturdy and robust Tykes were outclassed in every department, although the touches of their Tyneside born inside-forward, Jimmy Stewart stood out. He was a name United marked down for the future.

In the FA Cup final, United's opponents were three times winners of the trophy, Aston Villa, still the most revered side in the country. The venue was the massive Crystal Palace bowl in Sydenham, the largest sporting venue in the country. The arena staged FA Cup finals and many internationals from 1895 until 1914, while Crystal Palace FC and The Corinthians played there for a while too. The setting was a dynamic one with the backdrop of Prince Albert's giant glass and metal building - The Crystal Palace itself - hovering over the stadium. It was surrounded by trees and vast parkland. The area had become a leisure and holiday focus and attracted tourists from all over Victorian and Edwardian Britain. The spectacular exhibition palace, as well as the football ground, are now long gone - destroyed by fire in 1936 - although the present-day Crystal Palace athletics stadium is now sited on the same spot.

The Crystal Palace was to be a ground Newcastle players never took a liking to. It had a paralysing affect on the team and the very name seemed to shatter their nerves to a thousand pieces.

ERRANT TOURISTS

United were a big attraction for continental sides during the mid 1900's and were frequent visitors to Europe during the close-season gaining lucrative financial guarantees. The Magpies received £240 for four matches arranged by the Karlsruhe club of Germany and there was no end to the offers, even as far afield as Buenos Aires and Australia.

Following on from their first overseas tour in 1904, Newcastle visited Bohemia and played five matches in Prague, returning the following year when they also took in games against Austrian and German sides, while in 1907 another tour of Germany took place. In total United played 20 games, won all of them and scored an impressive 122 goals.

United on tour in Denmark, pictured with the opposition in Copenhagen during 1904.

Centenary Highlight

"Our tactics were wrong. We went for defence when we should have attacked"

Colin Veitch, 1931

ALTHOUGH ASTON VILLA BOASTED UNDOUBTED Cup qualities, the Magpies were favourites and a confident lot. And why not? They had scored a double over the claret and blues winning at both Villa Park and Gallowgate. Newcastle, though started off with their preparations badly.

Firstly, United's side missed the ability of Ronald Orr, out with a broken collar-bone and secondly, the squad's Cup headquarters was only a few hundred yards from the Crystal Palace stadium and it was a wrong move. One official noted, "A tactical error was committed". Many of United's players started to think of the game far too early and suffered from over-confidence and some by nerves. Even skipper Andy Aitken was caught by one journalist sitting out on the hotel lawn days before, learning by heart the speech he was to deliver when he received the Cup.

A huge crowd of 101,117 was attracted to the meeting of the country's finest clubs. It remains the biggest attendance to watch a United game and one of only four finals to top the 100,000 figure. Almost 10,000 Geordies made the trip, a journey to be repeated time and time again in the next few years. Many varied excursions were organised, by train or by bus. Most pubs on Tyneside had parties heading south. One old-timer recorded that they, "set off at midnight after carefully taking on board beer, bottles of whisky and whole hams with loaves of bread and pickled onions in great jars". One trip included a ticket and meals for 22s 6d. For an extra 4 shillings fans could obtain a stand seat. Ground tickets could be purchased for 2 shillings and there was no trouble getting one. Some made their journey by boat too! A 24 hour trip down the North Sea cost either 12s 0d or 8s 0d, and with food, 20s 0d or 15s 0d

There was even a Ladies Outing Club - limited to Newcastle enthusiasts of the fairer sex alone. They had their own lady secretary and paid their own subscriptions and headed for London in a special saloon on the train, and without the assistance of a single male - a rarity in Edwardian Britain. Sight-seeing trips round London were organised too. The mass of Tynesiders rarely travelled far in those days and a journey to the capital was, in most cases, a dream. Newcastle fans went mad with their first taste of a Cup final atmosphere. They had trumpets, drums and rattles. One observer related they, "not only wore their colours of the club on breast and buttonhole, but actually fashioned umbrellas in the colours they love too". They flocked to South London and in the wonderful park setting, happy parties sat in groups under the trees munching sandwiches and drinking beer. The Cup final took the character of a picnic with friendly banter between the two sets of supporters and thousands of neutrals.

By the time the match was ready to get under way everyone was packed into the bowl. The Crystal Palace was a poor stadium to watch from, without much terracing to speak of. Probably only a third of the vast crowd saw the proceedings on the pitch, so inadequate was the eye view from the banking. In an attempt to gain a better vantage point many fans clung precariously to the branches of surrounding trees.

As the game got under way, Aston Villa showed only too well their proven Cup qualities. Those at the picturesque enclosure saw a thrilling match that was talked about for years and that

Newcastle's Team line-up before the 1905 FA Cup Final:
McPherson (Trainer) McWilliam, Rutherford, Howie, Gardner, Aitken, Veitch, Lawrence, Appleyard, McCombie, Carr, Gosnell, Watt (Secretary)

FA CUP RUN				
R1	Plymouth Argyle	H	D	1-1
	Plymouth Argyle	A	D	1-1
	Plymouth Argyle	N	W	2-0
R2	Tottenham Hotspur	A	D	1-1
	Tottenham Hotspur	H	W	4-0
R3	Bolton Wanderers	A	W	2-0
SF	Sheffield Wednesday	N	W	1-0
F	Aston Villa	N	L	0-2

FA Cup Finalists 1905

FACTS & FIGURES	P	W	D	L	F	A
Home	2	1	1	0	5	1
Away	6	3	2	1	7	4
Total	**8**	**4**	**3**	**1**	**12**	**5**

Crystal Palace action:
Left: United fans taste the Cup Final atmosphere for the first time.
Above: Aston Villa get the game under way.
Below: Hampton scores the first of two goals to crush the Magpies. Note that goalkeeper Jimmy Lawrence wears stripes along with the rest of United's side.

Panoramic view of proceedings at the Crystal Palace with Villa attacking United's goal.

lived up to the pre-match hype. Aitken won the toss on a windy but sun-filled day and Villa stormed forward from the kick-off to shock United with an early goal, the worst possible start for the Magpies. Only two minutes had gone when Villa won a midfield tackle and Hall was sent away on the left wing. A quick cross caught United asleep and Bache tried a shot that was blocked only for Hampton to crash the loose ball past Lawrence.

Play swayed from end to end for the next 15 minutes, but then Villa took control and went close on several occasions, Brawn hitting a post. It was something of a miracle they only had a goal advantage and it almost paid off for United, when Howie drove over the bar - when he should have scored - after being put through by Appleyard. The second-half saw Newcastle fight their way back into the game for a period. George saved from Howie and Gosnell went close with a fierce shot. They had the chances to grab an equaliser but the Magpies' finishing was wild and erratic.

Villa's tactics were not to Newcastle's liking. They played a fast long ball game, sweeping passes to the wings and in turn their wingers hit long deep crosses. It caught United flat. They almost went two down when McCombie sliced a clearance, then with 15 minutes remaining the claret and blue's danger-man, Harry Hampton, settled the issue. Villa's outside-left, Hall swerved inside McCombie and fired in a hard shot. Lawrence parried but only to the on-rushing Hampton who whipped the ball into the net opportunist style.

It was a deserved 2-0 victory. Colin Veitch said, "Our tactics were wrong. We went for defence when we should have attacked". The early goal rocked Newcastle's pre-match plan. United had, or so everyone thought, learnt a valuable lesson in their first Cup final. But it was only to be the start of an enigma that appeared to jinx United's performances at the Crystal Palace.

Tyneside's masses took defeat with dignity. One report observed, "When their team lost the fans were not ashamed to show to which team they belonged". Newcastle's return home on Monday saw a huge crowd turn out. One of the players remarked, "If this is the kind of reception we get for losing the Cup, I wouldn't have enjoyed being among the throng if we had won it"! Pandemonium broke out. The players could hardly get off the train and it took hours for the team to end up at a gathering at the People's Theatre. They were scenes to be repeated again and again over the next six years, alas all but one without the actual FA Cup in view.

FA Cup Finalists 1905

FINAL
15 April 1905 at The Crystal Palace
Newcastle United 0 (0) Aston Villa 2 (1)

UNITED:
Lawrence,
McCombie, Carr,
Gardner, Aitken, McWilliam,
Rutherford, Howie, Appleyard, Veitch, Gosnell
ASTON VILLA:
George,
Spencer, Miles,
Pearson, Leake, Windmill,
Brown, Garratty, Hampton, Bache, Hall

GOALS: Hampton(2m), Hampton(76m)
ATTENDANCE; 101,117 (£7,785)
Referee: P.R.Harrower (London)
Guest of Honour; Lord Kinnaird
Cup HQ; Bedford Hotel, Sydenham

CUP GOALGETTERS
4 Orr, Howie, 2 Gosnell, Appleyard

CHAIRMAN: James Cameron
MANAGER: Directors' Committee
TRAINER-COACH: James McPherson
CAPTAIN: Andy Aitken

Top right: A wider view of Hampton's opening goal. Andy McCombie appeals for an infringement.
Above: More defending for the black'n'whites. Lawrence this time clears his lines.
Right: United's 'keeper has no chance at Hampton's second goal.

Centenary Highlight

Football League Champions for the first time. Left to right, back: McCombie, Milne (Director), J.W. Bell (Director), Archibald (Director), Lawrence. Middle: R. Oliver (Director), J. Oliver (Director), Carr, McCracken, Cameron (Chairman), J. Bell (Director), McWilliam, McClarence, Graham (Director), F. Watt Jnr (asst. secretary). Seated: F. Watt (secretary), Aitken, Rutherford, Howie, Appleyard, Orr, Gosnell, McPherson (trainer). On ground: Veitch and Gardner.

United's stars relaxing at Saltburn.

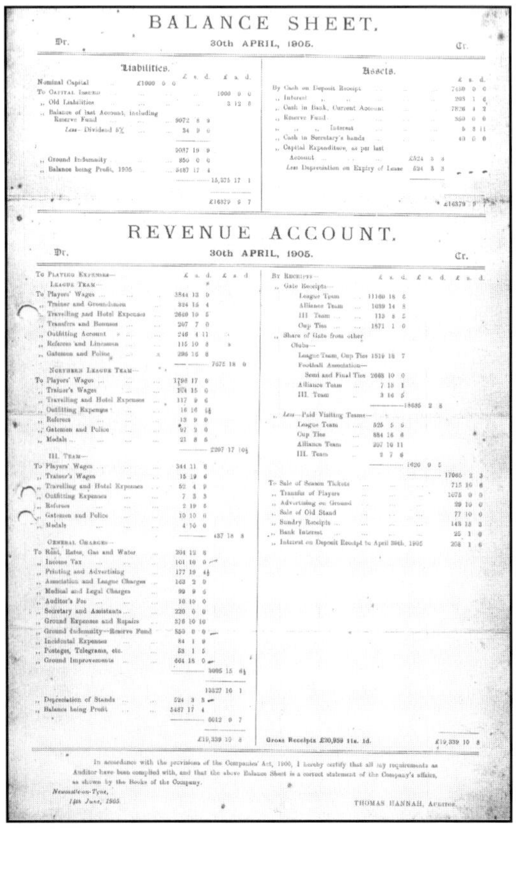

BALANCE SHEET.

Dr. 30th APRIL, 1905. Cr.

Liabilities.	£ s. d.	£ s. d.
Nominal Capital £1000 0 0		
To Capital Issued		1000 0 0
,, Old Liabilities		3 12 8
,, Balance of last Account, including Reserve Fund	9072 8 9	
Less—Dividend 5%	34 9 0	
	9037 19 9	
,, Ground Indemnity	850 0 0	
,, Balance being Profit, 1905	5487 17 4	
		15,375 17 1
		£16379 9 7

Assets.		£ s. d.
By Cash on Deposit Receipt		7450 0 0
,, Interest ,, ,,		208 1 6
,, Cash in Bank, Current Account		7826 4 2
,, Reserve Fund		850 0 0
,, ,, ,, Interest		5 3 11
,, Cash in Secretary's hands		43 0 0
,, Capital Expenditure, as per last Account	£524 3 3	
Less Depreciation on Expiry of Lease	524 3 3	— — —
		£16379 9 7

REVENUE ACCOUNT.

Dr. 30th APRIL, 1905. Cr.

To Playing Expenses—	£ s. d.	£ s. d.
League Team—		
To Players' Wages	3844 13 0	
,, Trainer and Groundsmen	324 15 4	
,, Travelling and Hotel Expenses	2640 10 5	
,, Transfers and Bonuses	207 7 0	
,, Outfitting Account	246 4 11	
,, Referees and Linesmen	115 10 8	
,, Gatemen and Police	296 16 8	
		7675 18 0
Northern League Team—		
To Players' Wages	1798 17 6	
,, Trainer's Wages	104 15 0	
,, Travelling and Hotel Expenses	117 9 6	
,, Outfitting Expenses	16 16 1½	
,, Referees	13 9 0	
,, Gatemen and Police	97 3 0	
,, Medals	21 8 6	
		2207 17 10½
III. Team—		
To Players' Wages	344 11 8	
,, Trainer's Wages	15 19 6	
,, Travelling and Hotel Expenses	52 4 9	
,, Outfitting Expenses	7 3 3	
,, Referees	2 19 5	
,, Gatemen and Police	10 10 0	
,, Medals	4 10 0	
		437 18 8
General Charges—		
To Rent, Rates, Gas and Water	294 12 8	
,, Income Tax	101 10 0	
,, Printing and Advertising	177 19 4½	
,, Association and League Charges	163 2 0	
,, Medical and Legal Charges	99 9 5	
,, Auditor's Fee	10 10 0	
,, Secretary and Assistants	220 0 0	
,, Ground Expenses and Repairs	376 10 10	
,, Ground Indemnity—Reserve Fund	850 0 0	
,, Incidental Expenses	84 1 9	
,, Postages, Telegrams, etc.	53 1 5	
,, Ground Improvements	664 18 0	
		3005 15 6½
		13327 10 1
,, Depreciation of Stands	524 3 3	
,, Balance being Profit	5487 17 4	
		6012 0 7
		£19,339 10 8

By Receipts—	£ s. d.	£ s. d.	£ s. d.
,, Gate Receipts—			
League Team	11160 18 6		
Alliance Team	1039 14 8		
III Team	113 8 5		
Cup Ties	1871 1 0		
,, Share of Gate from other Clubs—			
League Team, Cup Ties	1519 18 7		
Football Association— Semi and Final Ties	2668 10 0		
Alliance Team	7 15 1		
III. Team	3 16 5		
		18685 2 8	
,, *Less*—Paid Visiting Teams—			
League Team	525 5 6		
Cup Ties	884 16 6		
Alliance Team	207 10 11		
III. Team	2 7 6		
		1620 0 5	
			17065 2 3
To Sale of Season Tickets			715 10 6
,, Transfer of Players			1075 0 0
,, Advertising on Ground			29 10 0
,, Sale of Old Stand			77 10 0
,, Sundry Receipts			148 18 3
,, Bank Interest			25 1 0
,, Interest on Deposit Receipt to April 30th, 1905			208 1 6
Gross Receipts £20,959 11s. 1d.			£19,339 10 8

In accordance with the provisions of the Companies' Act, 1900, I hereby certify that all my requirements as Auditor have been complied with, and that the above Balance Sheet is a correct statement of the Company's affairs, as shown by the Books of the Company.

Newcastle-on-Tyne,
14th June, 1905.

THOMAS HANNAH, Auditor.

After struggling financially for so long, Newcastle were now one of the richest clubs in the country. The balance sheet dated 30th April 1905 shows gate receipts totalling £18,685. 2s. 8d.

League Champions 1905

FIRST DIVISION CHAMPIONS 1904-1905	P	W	D	L	F	A	Pts
Newcastle United	**34**	**23**	**2**	**9**	**72**	**33**	**48**
Everton	34	21	5	8	63	36	47
Manchester City	34	20	6	8	66	37	46
Aston Villa	34	19	4	11	63	43	42
Sunderland	34	16	8	10	60	44	40
Sheffield United	34	19	2	13	64	56	40
Small Heath	34	17	5	12	54	38	39
Preston North End	34	13	10	11	42	37	36
Sheffield Wednesday	34	14	5	15	61	57	33
Woolwich Arsenal	34	12	9	13	36	40	33
Derby County	34	12	8	14	37	48	32
Stoke	34	13	4	17	40	58	30
Blackburn Rovers	34	11	5	18	40	51	27
Wolverhampton W.	34	11	4	19	47	73	26
Middlesbrough	34	9	8	17	36	56	26
Nottingham Forest	34	9	7	18	40	61	25
Bury	34	10	4	20	47	67	24
Notts County	34	5	8	21	36	69	18

RESULTS	Home	Away
Woolwich Arsenal	W 3-0	W 2-0
Derby County	W 2-0	D 1-1
Everton	W 3-2	L 1-2
Small Heath	L 0-1	L 1-2
Manchester City	W 2-0	L 2-3
Notts County	W 1-0	W 3-0
Sheffield United	D 1-1	W 3-1
Stoke	W 4-1	L 0-1
Preston North End	W 1-0	L 0-1
Middlesbrough	W 3-0	W 3-0
Wolverhampton Wand	W 3-0	W 3-1
Bury	W 3-1	W 4-2
Aston Villa	W 2-0	W 1-0
Blackburn Rovers	W 1-0	L 0-2
Nottingham Forest	W 5-1	W 3-1
Sheffield Wed	W 6-2	W 3-1
Sunderland	L 1-3	L 1-3

LEAGUE APPEARANCES

Gardner	32
Howie	31
Rutherford	31
McCombie	31
Lawrence	29
Aitken	28
Appleyard	28
Carr	27
McWilliam	26
Gosnell	25
Veitch	24
Orr	20
McCracken	13
Templeton	10
McClarence	6
Watts	4
Graham	3
Wills	2
McIntyre	2
Innerd	1
Crumley	1

LEAGUE GOALS

Howie	14
Appleyard	13
Rutherford	10
Veitch	10
Orr	9
Gosnell	4
McClarence	4
McWilliam	4
Aitken	2
Gardner	1
own-goal.	1

REGULAR SIDE

Lawrence

McCombie - Carr

Gardner - Aitken - McWilliam

Rutherford - Howie - Appleyard - Orr or Veitch - Gosnell

CHAIRMAN: James Cameron
MANAGER: Directors' Committee
TRAINER-COACH: James McPherson
CAPTAIN: Andy Aitken

LARGEST VICTORY:
6-2 v Sheffield Wed(H),
5-1 v Nottingham Forest(H)

HEAVIEST DEFEAT:
1-3 v Sunderland(H) & (A)

AVERAGE HOME ATTENDANCE:
22,411

TOP GATE:
30,000 v Sunderland

Billiards was the players' favourite pastime during the Edwardian era. Pictured are two of the club's stars in a contest.

AFTER AN EARLY SEASON HICCUP, Newcastle continued where they had left off last April for the 1905/06 season. They were in the title race for most of the year, highlighted when the black'n'whites thrashed Wolves 8-0 at Gallowgate. The visitors, destined for relegation that year, were overwhelmed from start to finish. On a gloomy afternoon, United went ahead through Howie after seven minutes following an ingenious passing movement.

The Scot was soon on target again, this time after Bill Appleyard had created space. Ronald Orr gave United a 3-0 lead when Rutherford supplied an immaculate cross, and the fourth arrived after Orr had made a, "magnificent dodgy dribble" and finished off his solo effort with a stunning volley. Before the interval, Appleyard's deadly boot made it 5-0 from a Gosnell centre.

United just kept going, with midfielder Howie outstanding in a team of stars. The classy ball-player created so many chances for his forwards that the North Mail noted, "One would have imagined they had an Armstrong Gun at their toes". Cheekily, Howie, Veitch and Rutherford began to play exhibition football, juggling with the ball to underline their massive superiority. Newcastle eased up considerably after the break, but still the goals came. Appleyard's brace completed his hat-trick and Veitch, after going close all afternoon, netted a last minute penalty.

FIRE ALARM

On the 13th January 1908 United's new West Stand caught fire and a catastrophe was averted only because Leazes Terrace residents had noticed smoke and flames at an early point in the blaze. They raised the alarm during early evening and a big crowd watched the local Fire Brigade with horse drawn tenders tackle the incident. Luckily little damage was done.

United eventually finished in fourth spot behind Liverpool. Again goals came from all sources, five players netting ten or over with Orr top scorer with 21. Appleyard(17) and Howie(14) were both dangerous strikers too. Jimmy Howie had been the side's best player over the last two seasons. Known as 'Gentleman Jim', he was mooted by some judges as the best inside- forward in football during the era. From Ayrshire, Howie possessed a leisurely style and a peculiar hopping action when running which confounded opponents. He wasn't the fastest or with a noted shot - in fact Howie scored more goals with his head than his feet - but he hit the target with expert placement rather than power. Scoring 83 goals for the club in 235 games, Howie's double-edged game of goalmaker and goaltaker was invaluable. He was capped three times for Scotland, and scored two goals in the 1906 Auld Enemy meeting.

Newcastle's finances were now becoming increasingly healthy. No other club could surpass their drawing power at the turnstile in the next few years. The average gate was now 24,954 and receipts for the year amounted to £21,460 13s 8d plus a bonus of reaching the semi-final and FA Cup final of £2,182 9s 1d. And these record figures were soon to be substantially bettered. Much of the money was spent on major ground redevelopment at St James Park. The capacity was more than doubled from 30,000 to 65,000. Prizes had been offered of up to £30 to the local architect who came up with the most innovative and suitable design. The club's directors visited both Celtic Park and Hampden Park as a guideline and in March 1905 new plans had been approved. The construction cost a total of £11,325 plus a later addition of £1,068 and work was carried out by Isaac Bewley and Co after the lowest contractor, W.T. Weir of Howden had refused to sign a contract.

A new stand, seating 4,680 was erected on Barrack Road as well as substantial new terracing on the other sides of the ground. Also built was a vast swimming-pool beneath the structure, a luxury touch and the envy of every club in the Football League. Temporary accommodation was provided during the works and the team, who up to then trained on the St James Park pitch, were kept in trim at Gosforth Park.

The new stadium, 'Greater St James Park', as it was dubbed, was opened by the Lady Mayoress on 6th September when Manchester City were visitors. Although it was only half finished one journalist's comment was, "and now with the immense structures of corrugated iron enclosing the arena, Newcastle United's ground can rank amongst the most perfectly appointed football enclosures in the country". 20,000 were at that game and a new record crowd - not only for St James Park, but for the whole country - of 56,000 was set-up for the Sunderland clash on 30th December.

A pattern began to fall into place during the era that saw the club either be successful in the Championship, or in the FA Cup. In 1906 it was the Cup's turn and Newcastle equalled their feat of the previous season by reaching the final once more.

Jimmy Howie, known throughout the game as 'Gentleman Jim'. He was a potent goalscorer for United.

Action from the 1906 F.A. Cup semi-final with Woolwich Arsenal. Ronald Orr challenges an Arsenal player.

Six goals went past the Grimsby Town goalkeeper, Cartledge in the First Round at St James Park, this after the Magpies had swopped venues for a guaranteed share of the gate of £300, money which helped keep the Grimsby club afloat. The home goal was never threatened especially when the visitors lost outside-left Swarbrick and were reduced to ten men.

United needed a replay to dispose of Derby County though, who proved much more difficult opponents. County had beaten Newcastle the week before in a league fixture but after a 0-0 draw at the Baseball Ground, the Magpies won 2-1. The game featured a picture goal by Rutherford after Gardner's delightful footwork had left a defender dead. He then passed to Gosnell who interchanged with Appleyard before Newcastle's outside-right netted with a scorching cross shot. The Magpies were now on a run and when Blackpool arrived at Gallowgate two goals from Orr helped send the Seasiders back home dejected and well beaten 5-0, although yet again United had the advantage of facing a ten man opposition for most of the match.

A tough meeting followed with Birmingham City at Small Heath and at stake was a place in the semi-final. Over 2,000 travelling black'n'white fans made the trip to St Andrews and were left dejected as Brum went ahead by two goals within eight minutes. A second-half revival though, saw Newcastle outplay the home side and pull the game back level at 2-2 with Colin Veitch leading the recovery. The famous Novocastrian put the ball in the net twice, one an equalising penalty to save the tie. Even in those days players were overcome by the occasion. On netting Veitch was, as the local press reported, "the recipient of a smashing kiss from Orr"! It was a close call however, as 'keeper Jimmy Lawrence made save after save as City rallied. The Scot noted his own performance as, "my best game ever".

On Tyneside, United showed their class by winning 3-0, although they left it late, all the goals coming in the final period of extra-time after the Midland side had proved stern defenders for all of 105 minutes. Appleyard broke the deadlock with a volley that crashed home off the bar. The victory took United into the semi-final to meet Woolwich Arsenal at the Victoria Ground, Stoke. Former favourite, Bob Templeton was in the Gunners' ranks and before a 20,000 crowd it was a game of contrasting styles. Arsenal played the long ball game while United stuck to their short, first- time movements with periods of long possession. It was a close affair, but United's big names had the edge, although before Newcastle's opener found the net, Arsenal centre-forward Bert Freeman hit the bar. The Geordies' forwards pressurised the Arsenal 'keeper for most of the game, but Ashcroft saved everything sent at him - or almost. It was Colin Veitch who cracked open the Londoners' defence with a moment of brilliance. Just before half-time, Howie found Orr who quickly chipped a ball into Veitch's path. United's half-back leaped high and sideways to hit a terrific hook shot that flew into the corner of the net. As the player said, "it was one of the best goals of my career". After that Newcastle toyed with their opponents and Howie and Veitch dribbled between them for fully 30 yards before the Scot rounded the 'keeper and walked the ball into the net.

Everton were to be the Magpies' Cup final opponents this time, again at The Crystal Palace. They had beaten their Merseyside rivals, Liverpool in the other semi-final. The Goodison Park club were also to have a terrific rivalry with United during this period — in both Cup and league contests. Much was expected of the showpiece final.

CLUB MASCOTS

During the Edwardian years Newcastle United possessed a Great Dane dog called Rex as a mascot. In colouring it was patchy black'n'white, of course, and was a special favourite of the players because of its playfulness. During match-days it was to be seen tied next to the players tunnel and once, Rex broke his chain and joined the United forwards in an attack on the opponents' goal to the hilarity of everyone at St James Park!

Another lucky omen was handed to the club in 1908, from the journalists of the North Mail. They described it as, "a beautiful stuffed Magpie which is hoped would prove a mascot". United's directors placed it in the board-room, today it remains at St James Park, in one of the club's display cabinets.

Centenary Highlight

> *"Until Newcastle make up their minds to play an open game with long passing and plenty of dash, I cannot see that they will ever win the English Cup"*
>
> *Athletic News, April 1906*

AGAIN NEWCASTLE WERE FAVOURITES for the trophy and again United had beaten their opponents twice in Football League action. Everton had not yet won the Cup either, but had appeared in two finals before the turn of the century. They included ex-Magpie player, Hugh Bolton, who had appeared once for United earlier in the season.

It was a much awaited contest, a clash between two clubs noted as, "the aristocrats of the world", and between two line-ups of similar style, two refined sides although Everton were hailed as a, "small, nippy team", compared to United's, "elegant giants".

On a bright afternoon a nervous first-half was a total let down for the 75,000 crowd hoping to see the game of the season. Chances were few and when they came, were squandered at both ends. Passes from both sides continually went astray and the game became scrappy and untidy. Lawrence saved well from a Settle header, while Gosnell and Rutherford both fired wide for United when in good scoring positions. Orr went close when he sailed through and cracked a, "hurricane shot just wide of the post".

Early into the second period Everton had the ball in the net when Sharp's cross was fumbled by Lawrence, the ball broke to Settle and was passed across the face of goal for Young to net, but he was ruled offside. Both sides played well below standard with neither team showing an appetite for the game. They were disjointed, with many aimless punts up field being a favourite tactic, a very unproductive and boring one. Goalmouth incident was in short supply and the crowd howled at every misplaced pass.

Newcastle supporters on their way to the Crystal Palace in horse-drawn brakes.

Everton though, got the break every side needs to lift the Cup in a rare moment of danger. Jack Sharp, the Mersey club's international winger, and the only player on the field to play to ability, made the goal that broke the deadlock in the 77th minute. Taylor slipped the ball across field to Sharp. He dribbled up to McWilliam, feinted one way and went the other, then left Carr also for dead. A low cross and centre-forward Sandy Young crashed the ball beyond Lawrence. As one report noted it was, "the only good bit of play in the whole game". Near the end Andy McCombie went close to grabbing an equaliser for United by firing a free-kick narrowly over the bar.

Tyneside's favourites pictured on a contemporary postcard also showing the Crystal Palace arena.

Caricature of the day highlighting the action between United and Everton.

FA Cup Finalists 1906

FA CUP RUN				
R1	Grimsby Town	H	W	6-0
R2	Derby County	A	D	0-0
	Derby County	H	W	2-1
R3	Blackpool	H	W	5-0
R4	Birmingham City	A	D	2-2
	Birmingham City	H	W	3-0
SF	Woolwich Arsenal	N	W	2-0
F	Everton	N	L	0-1

FACTS & FIGURES

	P	W	D	L	F	A
Home	4	4	0	0	16	1
Away	4	1	2	1	4	3
Total	**8**	**5**	**2**	**1**	**20**	**4**

FINAL

21 April 1906 at The Crystal Palace

Newcastle United 0 (0) Everton 1 (0)

UNITED:
Lawrence,
McCombie, Carr ,
Gardner, Aitken, McWilliam,
Rutherford, Howie, Veitch, Orr, Gosnell.

EVERTON:
Scott,
Balmer, Crelley,
Makepeace, Taylor, Abbott,
Sharp, Bolton, Young, Settle, Hardman.

GOALS: Young(77m)
ATTENDANCE: 75,609 (£6,625)
Referee: F.Kirkham (Preston)
Guest of Honour: Lord Kinnaird
Cup HQ: Ivanhoe Hotel, London

CUP GOALGETTERS

6 Appleyard, 4 Orr, 3 Veitch, 2 Rutherford, Howie, 1 Gosnell, Gardner, own- goal.

CHAIRMAN: James Cameron
MANAGER: Directors' Committee
TRAINER-COACH: James McPherson
CAPTAIN: Alec Gardner

United's Cup Final party - ladies included - at the Ivanhoe Hotel in London.

Everton threaten Jimmy Lawrence's goal, but with seven men back United survive this attack.

Andy Aitken was the Tynesider's best man, but as one correspondent wrote, "Newcastle were feeble in the extreme. Their halves and backs could do nothing right - Aitken excepted — and the forwards were slow and their passes went astray with monotonous regularity". Colin Veitch admitted, "I played, along with others, one of the worst games of my career".

The Crystal Palace hoodoo had paralysed United once again. The reason for the Magpies' inability to perform there was increasingly being debated after their second flop. Some pointed to the clinging turf, cut long rather than short as at St James Park, and it held up their passing game. If this was the reason, then why didn't United alter their tactics and use a more direct style many said. Athletic News made the comment that on such a big pitch that did not help a passing game, United needed a different approach, "Until Newcastle make up their minds to play an open game with long passing and plenty of dash, I cannot see that they ever will win the English Cup". 'Nerves' was another reason mooted, yet no fewer than nine of the side were experienced internationals with a tenth, Lawrence, to be capped in the future. Perhaps it was simply the very name - Crystal Palace - that created a problem. The harder they tried to remove the hoodoo the worse they appeared to worry about it. It was a strange anomaly, and one that would become even stranger.

As a sequel to the FA Cup final, both United and Everton were fined £50 each for fielding weak teams in Football League games during the run-up to the big day. Neither club bothered too much, it was more an irritation, but Newcastle United were to find that the authorities were to slap more penalties on the club for similar offences in years to come - and the fines became heavier.

AFTER MANY YEARS OF FRENZIED activity in the transfer market, United kept a somewhat low profile by comparison to before. They didn't need to spend vast amounts on new players now a squad had knitted together almost to perfection. Jimmy Lawrence had proved he was an able 'keeper - despite odd lapses in concentration - and Bill McCracken, Jack Carr and Andy McCombie shared the defenders' duties at full-back. In the middle line, Aitken moved on, to Middlesbrough, but Gardner, McWilliam and Veitch remained at the very heart of the side. On the flanks, Rutherford and Gosnell were unchallenged and Bill Appleyard, ably assisted by Howie and Orr as inside partners, was a terror at centre-forward. He took the weight off the side's pattern-makers, an ideal foil to the many skilled ball players alongside him.

Bill Appleyard. He was big and cumbersome but a marvellous leader.

The ex North Sea fisherman from Cleethorpes was a fierce looking character with short cropped hair and massive shoulders. Appleyard just missed an England cap, being selected as 12th man for his country in a fixture against Scotland.

In reserve, United did bring several new faces to the First Division scene and they ably stepped in for the stars when called upon. Joe McClarence was picked up from Wallsend Park Villa and deputised up front. Harry Hardinge, from Maidstone United, was another forward reserve, he later went on to play for England at both football and cricket. Chris Duffy(Middlesbrough), John Ridley(Willington Athletic) and Alex Hall(St Bernards) were all competent players who filled in too.

Altogether the selection committee could call upon over 40 professionals, an incredible number by modern standards, and the club's reserve side was to dominate the Northern League, and on joining in 1906, the newly formed North Eastern League, they also lifted more often than not the Northumberland Senior Cup. In days before the advent of the Third and Fourth Divisions, Newcastle's second string was as good as modern day lower division clubs. Many of the players eventually graduated to Second Division or other First Division sides.

Finlay Speedie cost £600 when he moved over the border.

Occasionally Newcastle took a liking to one or two players, some bought as a reserve stand-in, others strategic buys to replace an ageing star. In July 1906 Harry Brown was purchased for £380 from Southampton, very much as a reserve forward, but he played so well, scoring a hat-trick on his debut, that he was to claim a place in 22 games in the coming season. Sadly, illness later caused him to go blind. Scottish international, Finlay Speedie arrived from Glasgow Rangers for a big £600 fee as a play anywhere man. A dressing-room joker, he proved a valuable asset operating in seven different positions for the Magpies. He was one of the most versatile players of his time, and in his short stay in north-east England gave many exhibitions of brilliance, wandering through a game with superb nonchalance.

It was to be the Football League's turn for attention in season 1906/07. Sunderland was the big attraction for the opening fixture of the programme. A crowd of 56,375 - a new record - watched Newcastle win 4-2 after a terrific contest played in sweltering heat. It had been the hottest summer for decades and the temperature on the St James Park pitch was all of 91 degrees - the hottest day recorded in British football. United ran out wearing white sun caps with the peaks reversed as protection against sunstroke, while Sunderland's Jimmy Watson collapsed from the tropical heat. Elsewhere in the country, one team finished with only seven men on the field.

AULD ENEMY CLASH

England 1 (Bloomer) Scotland 1 (Crompton og)
6 April 1907

The Football Association rewarded United's dramatic rise to the top of the game, by handing the club the England versus Scotland fixture, then along with the Cup final, the match of the season. Included in the two international line-ups were no less than five players who were already on United's books, or who were shortly to sign for the club; Veitch, Rutherford, McWilliam, Stewart and Wilson. Additionally, Andy Aitken had just joined Middlesbrough. The game ended in a 1-1 draw but most observers felt that the Scots deserved the victory. A crowd of 35,829 saw the game. Steve Bloomer equalised a 90 second Scottish goal. Bloomer and Rutherford were the stars for England, while Aitken shined for Scotland who played in the colours of Lord Roseberry - primrose and pink.

ENGLAND:
Hardy (Liverpool)
Crompton (Blackburn Rovers)
Pennington (WBA)
Warren (Derby Co)
Wedlock (Bristol C)
Veitch (Newcastle Utd)
Rutherford (Newcastle Utd)
Bloomer (Middlesbrough)
Woodward (Tottenham H)
Stewart (Sheffield Wed)
Hardman (Everton).
SCOTLAND:
McBride (Preston NE)
Thomson (Hearts)
Sharp (Arsenal)
Aitken (Middlesbrough)
Raisbeck (Liverpool)
McWilliam (Newcastle Utd)
Stewart (Man City)
Walker (Hearts)
Wilson (Sheffield Wed)
White (Bolton Wandrs)
Wilson (Everton).

The Magpies displayed the same dominating style throughout the season. United were, incredibly, consistent and into New Year occupied either second or third placing. They took over the lead with a fine 5-0 hammering of Manchester United on February 2nd and no club was to remove the black'n'whites from the head of the table for the rest of the campaign.

Sheffield United, Bristol City and Cup final victors, Everton were Newcastle's rivals for the Championship. It was Bristol City, only promoted the previous year, who posed the biggest threat and on the 30th March an important Easter confrontation took place at Gallowgate. The west country club had won at Bolton the previous day, Good Friday, and had to pick up points against Newcastle to give themselves a realistic chance of stopping the Magpie machine from walking away with the title. City were six points behind, but with two games in hand. The black'n'whites would have none of it. They ran off 3-0 winners in front of 40,000.

United were virtually home and dry, yet afterwards slipped up alarmingly in the final four games. They lost at Meadow Lane, home of Notts County, and at Burnden Park, Bolton. On the final home Saturday of the season, against Sheffield United, then one of the Magpies' bogey sides, the winning point was taken in a draw. But Newcastle's crowd was far from happy with the side's latter performances. Expecting an exhibition display from their team, United's faithful were treated to a dull and lifeless 0-0 draw. Celebrations were muted and jeers greeted the new Champions. Peter McWilliam later wrote, "Never a cheer as we trooped off. Instead of well-merited applause, that crowd commenced hooting". It was an astonishing reaction. Several of United's players of that time observed that Newcastle fans were highly critical and they quickly barracked players if things went wrong. Notably Orr and Gosnell felt the taunts of the Geordie crowd.

United had not dropped a single point at St James Park until that game with the Blades, winning 18 league fixtures on the run. Sheffield United were also the only side United had failed to score against. Newcastle finished three points in front of Bristol City, but they could have just crept ahead of Newcastle had it not been for their own poor form. City lost two home fixtures against Bolton and Aston Villa which, in effect handed the title trophy to United.

Japanese visitors to St. James Park. Top: The Japanese Navy docked in the Tyne during April 1906 and a large party took part in an Anglo-Japanese day. Several made the trip to St. James Park and witnessed United's 5-0 victory over Stoke. Above: Another naval visit later in the same month saw more of 'Togo's Heroes' at the United v Blackburn fixture. Again Newcastle won, by 3-0.

Derby action in 1906 between Newcastle and Sunderland at Gallowgate. United are in the white shirts, Sunderland in stripes. In the background the club's new West Stand.

In spite of the disappointing anti-climax to the season, the club's popularity and standing in the game had grown to immense proportions by now. After two convincing Championship victories and two Cup final visits in only three years, Newcastle became recognised as the team of the land. Every player was nationally known and grounds burst at their seams whenever United were the visitors. Ivan Sharpe said of United, "They were an even finer side measured by methods than by results. Newcastle set standards". The former England amateur player and respected Athletic News correspondent also noted, "they gave football craft and cohesion. Newcastle's style was unruffled and almost unrivalled". Another eminent football writer, Geoffrey Green said, "They were great enough then to beat the world. Their prowess was such as to take away the breath and make opponents quiver in their boots when they took the field".

Fame brought with it off-the-field benefits. Newcastle United's players arranged advertising deals with the likes of Oxo and with various clothing manufacturers. They were in demand - shades of the Kevin Keegan or Paul Gascoigne mania to hit Tyneside many years later - albeit at vastly reduced amounts of income. Still, in Edwardian Britain, footballers were well paid. They could earn a basic of £4 per week, with bonus and illegal - in the eyes of the authorities - fringe benefits, perhaps an extra £2. They would also receive £10 as a signing on fee. A carpenter would have earned 42 shillings a week in 1906, a labourer, 28 shillings.

Even great teams are fallible however, and Newcastle United certainly caused a mighty sensation when they played their First Round FA Cup tie on January 12th. United were paired with Crystal Palace of all clubs, then a non-league side near the foot of the Southern League. It seemed a waste of time for the Londoners to travel the long distance north, but the hoodoo of the Palace continued as they sensationally won 1-0.

Their side included several exiled north-easterners, including a trio of former Magpie players which made them fight even harder. In their ranks were Hewitson(ex Morpeth Harriers), Innerd (ex Newcastle United) and Harker(ex Newcastle United). They had Edwards(ex Todds Nook), Astley(ex Middlesbrough), Roberts(ex Newcastle United) and Wallace(born Sunderland). Manager Jack Robson was also local, from Gainford in County Durham.

Palace performed heroics and were reduced to ten men at one stage. The visitors even had the ball in the net only for the effort to be scratched for offside, while Howie also had an offside effort called up. Had that strike been allowed perhaps the floodgates would have opened. Instead the tie turned on that moment. The Londoners' winning goal came four minutes before half-time when

Another marvellous pre-match team group of the Magpies. Left to right, players only: Gosnell, Brown, McWilliam, Lawrence, Appleyard, Howie, Speedie, Gardner, Carr, McCracken, Rutherford.

Trainer Jimmy McPherson puts Jack Carr through a session of weight training inside St. James Park.

Harry Astley was left with a clear run at Lawrence and he made no mistake. Seldom were Newcastle United out of the Palace penalty area in the second-half, but it was one of those days when the ball would not go into the visitors' net.

The victory is probably the biggest FA Cup upset ever - even more so than the much recalled giant-killing feats by Yeovil Town of later years. It was certainly Newcastle's most embarrassing exit in the famous competition, more so than the Hereford United defeat some 65 years later. Newcastle were League Champions elect, had won every game on Tyneside that season and fielded nine internationals in their line-up. The whole country was shocked to the extreme. A United player recalled, "The crowd remained on the terraces for several minutes after the game, as though everything was a dream". United had been leisurely and totally over-confident in front of goal. And they paid for it dearly. It had been no dream.

Newcastle also lifted the Sheriff of London Charity Shield that year, the forerunner of the current Charity Shield competition. At that time the splendid trophy was presented to the winners of the top professional side against the top amateur XI. United defeated the Corinthians 5-2 at Craven Cottage.

Among the backstage personalities of St James Park were four characters who brought life and vitality into the dressing-room. Joe Bell, together with John and James Cameron, were directors who worked their hearts out for the club. Bell, to be nicknamed 'Uncle Joe', took over the leading role after Telford had been deposed. A jovial and well known Tynesider, he was seldom away from the players and at times led the side out of the dressing- room. Bell struck accord with United's men, a unique director-player relationship.

The Camerons hailed from Perthshire. John had been a local preacher in his early days and was later to become a publican in Jarrow. The family had been involved with the club since East End days, like Bell, and were enthusiastic workers in United's cause. Both were Newcastle directors, and John became a member of the Football League Management Committee.

Trainer Jimmy McPherson was the other unsung hero of this era. He had joined the staff in 1903, was a Fifer from Cupar and had a sporting pedigree coming from a family of footballers and athletes, several of international standard. Pipe smoking, Jimmy was a printer by trade, but an expert runner and after a term in charge of Kilmarnock's players took over at St James Park. As contemporary reports noted, McPherson added cheery good humour to the dressing-room and was to the players, "one of the most important people in securing - and maintaining - the prominent position of the club". He remained trainer to United for nigh on 30 years, succeeded, like Watt, by his son.

John Cameron, another dedicated director.

Joe Bell, nicknamed 'Uncle Joe'.

Centenary Highlight

League Champions in 1907 pictured with the title trophy (centre left) as well as the Northumberland Senior Cup (left), Royal Victoria Infirmary Cup (centre), Tynemouth Infirmary Cup (centre right), N.E. League Championship (right) and the massive Sheriff of London Charity Shield.

A damaged, but unusual picture of United's strip being hung out to dry.

Bert Gosnell, a regular at outside-left, pictured training at Rhyl.

League Champions 1907

FIRST DIVISION CHAMPIONS 1906-1907

	P	W	D	L	F	A	Pts
Newcastle United	**38**	**22**	**7**	**9**	**74**	**46**	**51**
Bristol City	38	20	8	10	66	47	48
Everton	38	20	5	13	70	46	45
Sheffield United	38	17	11	10	57	55	45
Aston Villa	38	19	6	13	78	52	44
Bolton Wanderers	38	18	8	12	59	47	44
Woolwich Arsenal	38	20	4	14	66	59	44
Manchester United	38	17	8	13	53	56	42
Birmingham City	38	15	8	15	52	52	38
Sunderland	38	14	9	15	65	66	37
Middlesbrough	38	15	6	17	56	63	36
Blackburn Rovers	38	14	7	17	56	59	35
Sheffield Wednesday	38	12	11	15	49	60	35
Preston North End	38	14	7	17	44	57	35
Liverpool	38	13	7	18	64	65	33
Bury	38	13	6	19	58	68	32
Manchester City	38	10	12	16	53	77	32
Notts County	38	8	15	15	46	50	31
Derby County	38	9	9	20	41	59	27
Stoke	38	8	10	20	41	64	26

REGULAR SIDE

Lawrence
McCombie or McCracken - Carr
Gardner - Veitch - McWilliam
Rutherford - Howie - Appleyard or Speedie - Orr or Brown - Gosnell

CHAIRMAN: James Cameron
MANAGER: Directors' Committee
TRAINER-COACH: James McPherson
CAPTAIN: Alec Gardner

LEAGUE APPEARANCES
34 Rutherford, 33 Lawrence, Gardner, 32 McWilliam, 31 Howie, 29 Veitch, 27 Speedie, 26 Carr, McCombie, Gosnell, 23 Appleyard, 22 Brown, McCracken, 19 Orr, 7 Duffy, 5 McClarence, 4 Dodds, 3 Aitken, Blackburn, Kirkcaldy, Sinclair, 2 Kelsey, 1 Higgins, Jobey, Liddell, Nicholson, Soye.

LEAGUE GOALS
17 Appleyard, 10 Rutherford, Speedie, 8 Brown, 7 Howie, Veitch, 4 Orr, 3 Gosnell, 2 McClarence, McWilliam, 1 Duffy, Gardner, Kirkcaldy, McCracken.

RESULTS	Home	Away
Sunderland	W 4-2	L 0-2
Sheffield Wed	W 5-1	D 2-2
Birmingham City	W 2-0	W 4-2
Everton	W 1-0	L 0-3
Woolwich Arsenal	W 1-0	L 0-2
Bury	W 3-2	L 2-3
Manchester City	W 2-0	D 1-1
Middlesbrough	W 4-0	W 3-0
Preston North End	W 2-1	D 2-2
Derby County	W 2-0	D 0-0
Aston Villa	W 3-2	D 0-0
Liverpool	W 2-0	L 1-4
Bristol City	W 3-0	L 1-2
Notts County	W 4-3	L 0-1
Sheffield United	D 0-0	D 0-0
Bolton Wanderers	W 4-0	L 2-4
Manchester United	W 5-0	W 3-1
Blackburn Rovers	W 3-1	L 0-4
Stoke	W 1-0	W 2-1

LARGEST VICTORY:
5-0 v Manchester Utd(H)

HEAVIEST DEFEAT:
0-4 v Blackburn Rovers(A)

AVERAGE HOME ATTENDANCE:
33,319

TOP GATE:
56,375 v Sunderland

The club's Great Dane mascot, Rex.

More training the Edwardian way. Jimmy Howie and Jack Carr are watched by Jimmy McPherson and director J.P. Oliver.

NEWCASTLE UNITED SUPPORTERS **certainly had a rousing time following the black'n'whites. After the Championship success they proceeded to have another try for the FA Cup in 1907/08, yet the Crystal Palace hoodoo was to once more work its fateful trick on the club. There was plenty for the fans to debate, for the Magpies also created headlines in the transfer market again.**

Newcastle's regular side that season was reinforced by the record purchase of George Wilson, a chunky little outside-left at only 5'5" in height. Small he may have been, but what a handful he was on the football pitch. Born in Scotland, he cost £1,600 from Everton after the winger had fallen out with the Merseyside club. Already an international player, Wilson was a weighty flanker, but one who confounded those who said he hardly looked an athlete by turning in top class performances week after week. He was nicknamed 'Smiler' by his team-mates, a touch temperamental like a lot of Scots, he was a player who added to United's already awesome power up front. Wilson spent eight seasons on Newcastle's wing topping 200 games, scoring 33 goals.

Also to come into the side were Dick Pudan, at left-back, and Dave Willis in the half-back line. Pudan, a Cockney signed from Bristol Rovers for £150, was a very cultured defender, rare for the period. He had been promoted after a season in the North Eastern League and took the place of McCombie who was soon to concentrate on coaching United's reserves. Willis, Byker born and bred, arrived after a brief spell with Sunderland. A gritty and tough character, he was to replace Speedie as the club's 'Mr Versatile'.

George Wilson, another star arrives at St. James Park in a record signing from Everton.

United completed the league campaign in fourth position following a weary start which included a then record 6-1 home defeat by Champions to be, Manchester United. Newcastle recovered though, and did hit spells of outstanding form on occasion. They gave Birmingham City an 8-0 hiding in November, Jackie Rutherford scoring three. Newcastle occupied second position for a long period, but lost any chance of catching the Old Trafford side by drawing too many games - twelve in all. Had the Magpies won some of those fixtures they could well have pinched the title again. They also lacked conviction in the final month, losing five games when the FA Cup took precedence.

ADMISSION 1906/07

With the new, 'Greater St James Park', all completed and looking a picture of grandeur, season-ticket charges had now increased to:

Enclosure & Stand A	15s	0d
Stand B	21s	0d
Stand C	30s	0d
Centre Pavilion	£2 guineas	

It was in the Cup that most of the season's action was to be found and United were in convincing mood all the way to another final. Nottingham Forest were first to be eliminated from the competition. They lost 2-0 on a frost bound pitch at St James Park in front of a near 42,000 attendance. Appleyard and Rutherford set the black'n'whites on what was to be an emphatic Cup run which saw Newcastle score no fewer than 18 goals with only two conceded. That game with Forest was famous for a terrific duel between power men, Dave Willis and 'Knocker' West of the Reds. They clashed all afternoon in furious combat with the result that more than a few bruises were taken home.

West Ham United, not yet in the Football League, were next in line to feel the Geordie force. They were put on the rack and despatched comfortably by 2-0, although Newcastle didn't score their goals until the Hammers had lost 'keeper Kitchen. West Ham were to be frequent Cup opponents at this time, the two clubs faced each other five times in a seven year period. Luck was again on United's side when the Third Round draw was made gaining another home tie, their third in a row.

This time they faced sterner opposition in Liverpool, who were to finish slightly below Newcastle in the Division One table. The Magpies though were supremely confident. They had already won 5-1 at Anfield back in December and were not only clear favourites for this tie, but to lift the FA Cup too.

A 45,987 crowd turned up to see the contest and saw United power their way to a 3-1 victory on a muddy park. Bill Appleyard again found the net; he had scored in every round so far. At 6'0" and over 14 stones he was quite a handful. A cumbersome looking figure, but in spite of his bulk he possessed a surprising turn of speed. This combined with a powerful shot and good positioning sense made him a menace for any defender. It was to be Appleyard's last season in a black'n'white shirt, then 30 years old. He was certainly to go out with a bang.

Newcastle reached the semi-final without playing a tie away from Tyneside with a 5-1 thrashing of Second Division strugglers, Grimsby Town, and Appleyard got three more goals, this against his old club. Surprisingly it was the first hat-trick by a United player in the Cup Proper. One of his efforts was actually recorded as going into the net off his backside! The ball was struck across the box from the left-wing. Both sets of players had thought it had gone out of play and stopped, but Appleyard casually stuck out his behind and the ball ricocheted into the goal. The referee pointed to the centre-circle and Grimsby players were left stunned and somewhat annoyed.

The semi-final was staged at Anfield, Liverpool and Newcastle faced Fulham, giant-killers of the season. The Londoners were in their first season in the Football League and were near the top of the Second Division with the scalps of both Manchester United, the Champions, and their neighbours Manchester City, in the previous rounds. Newcastle spent a week on 'Special Training' at Rhyl in North Wales and there was to be no shock result this time as United destroyed Fulham by 6-0 in the most one sided semi-final in history. And that man Appleyard again had a big part to play.

Big Bill relished giving goalkeepers a hard time in more ways than one. He liked not only to bang the ball into the net frequently, but he also occasionally sent the then unprotected 'keeper flying too. During the course of the match he bundled over Fulham goalie, Leslie Skene, Appleyard planting "a foot between those of his adversary whilst shouldering him at the same time". The Scottish international 'keeper received a bad knock and was only a passenger from that moment.

United by that time were well on course having found the back of the net with two goals in the first period through Appleyard and Howie. After the break it was simply a rout. Fulham, slow and erratic, were punished heavily for mistakes. By the time Jimmy Howie had given United a 5-0 lead, the Magpies were at walking pace. Jackie Rutherford enjoyed a field day on the right-wing and he grabbed his second, and United's sixth when he flew past two defenders and planted the ball in the back of the net. The victory is still a record score for a semi-final meeting and it took Newcastle into their third FA Cup final, this time to face Wolverhampton Wanderers.

Byker born, Dave Willis cost United £100 from Sunderland.

Newcastle pound the Fulham defence during their record-breaking victory over the Londoners in the F.A. Cup semi-final of 1908.
Top: Bill Appleyard opens the scoring from close in.
Middle: Fulham's 'keeper just clears his line.
Bottom: Another anxious moment as a United effort clears the bar.

CHARITABLE UNITED

With the St James Park bank account overflowing, Newcastle United, always generous to local charities, were extra beneficial during Edwardian years. In days before the Welfare State and National Health Service, many social and health organisations received donations from the club. From a long list, the Royal Victoria Infirmary, Blind Asylum, Newcastle and Northumberland Sanatorium and Dr Barnardo's all received sums.

Ex players were often given a helping hand. Former East End forward 'Pat' O'Brien was given £5 guineas, "on account of his illness and destitute circumstances", while £10 guineas was sent to the wife of Robert Crielly who had been, "removed to Coxlodge Hospital". United also received literally hundreds of cash pleas from all and sundry on Tyneside. They were asked to contribute to the strike funds of the Amalgamated Societies of Engineers, to supply cooking apparatus for poor children, while Newcastle United and Glasgow Rangers agreed to play each other, "for the benefit of the unemployed". A total of £198 8s 0 d was raised. Newcastle also agreed to sponsor a baby cot at the RVI — named the 'Newcastle United Cot'. It was probably the first sponsorship deal put in place by the club!

Centenary Highlight

"Never mind. We shall come again and our turn will surely arrive one day"

Alec Gardner, April 1908

JACKIE RUTHERFORD TOOK A CORNER KICK on the right. The Newcastle winger clipped the ball into the Wolves box. It fell to Colin Veitch who steadied himself and fired the ball towards the goal. The ball flew off a defender straight into the path of Jimmy Howie who with a hard shot powered the ball into the net off a post. It was to be Newcastle's first goal in a FA Cup final, yet it mattered little as opponents Wolves had already rattled two past Lawrence at the other end of the field.

On a dismal, wet and cold day, an afternoon when fans found out what a bleak wilderness the Palace ground could be, Newcastle wasted early opportunities as their closely woven passing movements looked good. Rutherford had two chances but he, "failed badly", and Appleyard shot into the side netting from 20 yards. Speedie got in a close range shot too, but Wolves made United pay for the missed opportunities. Within half an hour Newcastle's cultured football was quickly destroyed by the physical, quick-tackling approach of Wolves. One newspaper headline declared, "Speed and determination overcame skill and science".

United had plenty of play, swopping passes in midfield, but rarely penetrating into the penalty area. As soon as the Novocastrians got anywhere near their opponents' box, in came a strong challenge which inevitably broke up United's move.

As half-time approached the Wanderers caught United, not once, but twice. First, Harrison on the wing crossed and Hunt hit a shot from 18 yards that surprised Lawrence. The Magpies' 'keeper fumbled it and the ball spun into the net for the opening goal. Almost immediately Hedley got the better of McCracken to drive a cross shot into the net past Lawrence's outstretched hand. United dejectedly trooped into the tunnel as the referee's whistle brought the first 45 minutes to a close.

Jimmy Howie's interlude for United after 73 minutes gave the Geordie support a brief period of hope. Lunn in the Wolves goal twice made good saves to rob United of an equaliser, but as Newcastle put the pressure on, Wolves broke away and scored their third. Harrison took the ball half the length of the field in a superb solo run to make it 3-1. Second Division Wolves, and their all English XI walked away with the Cup in convincing style - a shock victory that had football folk talking for months.

Above: United's Cup party start their journey to the Crystal Palace in a procession of horse-drawn carriages.
Above right: Action from the contest with Wolves.
Right: Match day ticket for one of the best seats in the stadium, Stand B at 5/-.

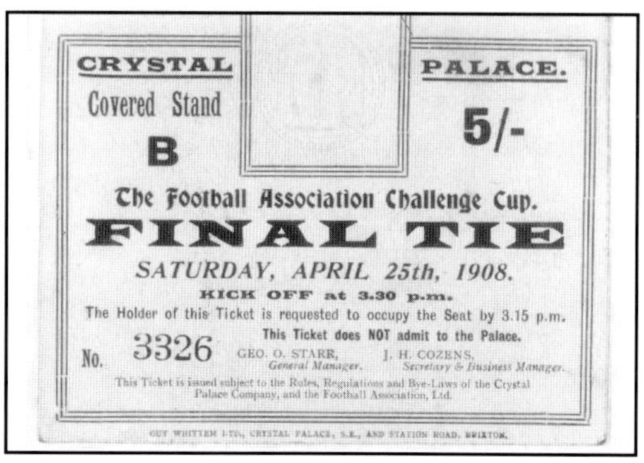

CRYSTAL PALACE.

Covered Stand B 5/-

The Football Association Challenge Cup.

FINAL TIE

SATURDAY, APRIL 25th, 1908.

KICK OFF at 3.30 p.m.

The Holder of this Ticket is requested to occupy the Seat by 3.15 p.m.

This Ticket does NOT admit to the Palace.

No. 3326 GEO. O. STARR, General Manager. J. H. COZENS, Secretary & Business Manager.

This Ticket is issued subject to the Rules, Regulations and Bye-Laws of the Crystal Palace Company, and the Football Association, Ltd.

FA Cup Finalists 1908

FA CUP RUN

R1	Nottingham Forest	H	W	2-0
R2	West Ham United	H	W	2-0
R3	Liverpool	H	W	3-1
R4	Grimsby Town	H	W	5-1
SF	Fulham	N	W	6-0
F	Wolverhampton Wand	N	L	1-3

FACTS & FIGURES

	P	W	D	L	F	A
Home	4	4	0	0	12	2
Away	2	1	0	1	7	3
Total	**6**	**5**	**0**	**1**	**19**	**5**

CHAIRMAN: James Cameron
MANAGER: Directors' Committee
TRAINER-COACH: James McPherson
CAPTAIN: Alec Gardner

CUP GOALGETTERS
8 Appleyard, 4 Rutherford, 3 Howie, 2 Gardner, 1 Speedie, own-goal

An enthusiastic Magpie follower decked out in Cup final suit and top hat.

FINAL

25 April 1908 at The Crystal Palace
Newcastle United 1(0)
Wolverhampton Wanderers 3(2)

UNITED
Lawrence
McCracken, Pudan
Gardner, Veitch, McWilliam
Rutherford, Howie, Appleyard, Speedie, Wilson.

WOLVERHAMPTON WANDERERS
Lunn
Jones, Collins
Hunt, Wooldridge, Bishop
Harrison, Shelton, Hedley, Radford, Pedley.

GOALS: Hunt(40m), Hedley(43m), Howie(73m), Harrison(85m)

ATTENDANCE: 74,967 (£5,988)

Referee: T.P.Campbell (Blackburn)
Guest of Honour: Sir John Bell
Cup HQ: Inns of Court Hotel, London

Newcastle's first goal in a Cup final scored by Jimmy Howie.

It had been an entertaining final, fast and strenuous, full of incident and skilful football. But it had gone all wrong for United for a third time. Newcastle had been the hottest Cup favourites for years and Wolves were never given a chance by anyone, save by their own fans, and even some of those were sceptical. Tactically the Magpies had been toppled again. Not changing their style at all, United's possession football and slow precise build up was swamped by pace and aggression in the white hot den of a Cup final. Wolves skipper, Kenneth Hunt, said to a reporter before the match, "We shall hustle them off their game". Newcastle also paid the penalty for playing both Pudan and McWilliam when only half fit instead of drafting in capable reserves.

There was, as expected, massive disappointment on Tyneside. Rumours spread that two of Newcastle's side, Appleyard and Speedie, had been nobbled by mischief making characters and that some players had been seen, "in an intoxicated condition" the evening before. Allegations were strongly denied. However more spice was added to the bribery controversy when the players in question were transferred to Oldham Athletic in June, only a matter of weeks after the final. It was a deal which left a lot of questions unanswered.

The Cup final defeat was a bitter experience again. But again massive crowds lined the streets of Newcastle to welcome back the players. However only four of the supporters' unsuccessful heroes, Lawrence, McWilliam, Gardner and Willis, had returned north, and Willis had not been in the team. Arrangements had been made for the side to proceed to the Pavilion Theatre, but only Jimmy Lawrence and a few officials turned up! Alec Gardner was determined his side would bring that trophy back to Newcastle. He afterwards maintained, "Never mind. We shall come again and our turn will surely arrive one day". Come again they did and their day would indeed arrive.

Record Servant

"has the approved coolness, insouciance, and resource which are the hall-mark of the heaven-sent 'keeper"

Association Football & The Men Who Made It, 1906

GOALKEEPERS WERE A DIFFERENT BREED IN EDWARDIAN years, far removed from the super-fit and athletic figures of the modern age. Jimmy Lawrence played the game for most of his career in an era when keepers were unprotected by referees and forwards were able to barge them in mid-air without ceremony over the goal-line. And most of them did. As a consequence goalkeeping tactics were not quite as we know them now. 'Keepers learnt to punch the ball in a crowded goalmouth rather than catch it, and if they did gather the ball, quickly got rid of it for fear of an uncompromising charge.

The now familiar green 'keeper's shirt had not taken to the field and Jimmy Lawrence for most of his record service with the Magpies, wore a black'n'white striped jersey like the rest of his colleagues. Up to 1912 he could handle the ball anywhere on the pitch and also, did not have to stand still on his line when facing a penalty kick. Yes it was a different game.

To compare Jimmy Lawrence with recent guardians of United's goal is futile. He was never as fit or agile as the modern footballer, but one fact remains indisputable - a total of 505 senior games over an 18 year period. No other individual in one hundred years has come close to surpassing his record turn-out for United.

A Scot, he was born in Glasgow in 1885 and kept goal for Partick Athletic and Glasgow Perthshire, two strong Clyde teams. He occasionally assisted Hibernians too, as a replacement for Harry Rennie, when the Scottish international and, at the time, Britain's finest goalkeeper, was unavailable for action. Lawrence learnt much from his senior colleague at Easter Road and United took notice of the 5'10" 'keeper on one of their many journeys north. They brought him back to Tyneside in July 1904.

He succeeded the experienced Matt Kingsley and Charlie Watts in the Geordies' goal when given a chance at the beginning of the 1904/05 season. He replaced the injured Watts on the first day of October against Manchester City and never had to stand aside for any cause other than injury, and they were few and far between over the next 14 league campaigns.

Consistency was Lawrence's great asset. He wasn't the flashy type, but a steady last line of defence. Jimmy studied the game long and hard, and worked out goalkeeping positions from every conceivable angle. The valued early text, Association Football & The Men Who Made It, noted Lawrence having, "the approved coolness, insouciance, and resource which are the hall-mark of the heaven-sent 'keeper". Yet the Scot could make mistakes like every other player - even the greats. And being a goalkeeper they were costly. Twice in FA Cup finals Jimmy was at fault having cruel luck. Firstly against Wolves in 1908, he fumbled a shot for the opening goal, then in 1911 against Bradford City misjudged a bouncing ball and conceded one

Jimmy Lawrence

LAWRENCE'S PLAYING RECORD

	League		FA Cup		Total	
	App	Gls	App	Gls	App	Gls
1904-05	29	0	8	0	37	0
1905-06	33	0	8	0	41	0
1906-07	33	0	1	0	34	0
1907-08	38	0	6	0	44	0
1908-09	38	0	7	0	45	0
1909-10	34	0	8	0	42	0
1910-11	36	0	8	0	44	0
1911-12	27	0	0	0	27	0
1912-13	34	0	8	0	42	0
1913-14	21	0	0	0	21	0
1914-15	31	0	5	0	36	0
1919-20	20	0	1	0	21	0
1920-21	42	0	4	0	46	0
1921-22	16	0	0	0	16	0
1918-19 (War Time)					9	0
	432	**0**	**64**	**0**	**505**	**0**

of the softest - and as it turned out - winning goals in the history of the competition. However, along with Colin Veitch and Jock Rutherford, Lawrence appeared in all of United's Edwardian Cup finals and Championship sides.

In 1911 Lawrence also achieved the ambition of every Scot, selection for his country in the top billing fixture against England. After several years of being tipped for a cap, he replaced his great contemporary, John Brownlie, at Goodison Park and took part in Scotland's 1-1 draw. His United colleague Sandy Higgins netted the goal to give the Scots a point in the Home International Championship. Also in the side was Andy Aitken. Jimmy Hay was captain, with Wilf Low alongside him, two other tremendous United competitors.

During his time at St James Park, Lawrence held a reputation of being a prize joker - the life and soul of the dressing-room many said. He was gifted with a keen sense of humour and Jimmy was both a raconteur and mimic of considerable ability. Jokes flowed in a rich Scots dialect without effort and there wasn't a more popular figure in the camp. Colin Veitch said of him, "he was a social asset of the very best type". His wider support among professionals later earned him the Chairmanship of the Players Union in 1921.

When aged 37, Jimmy gave way to Bill Bradley in the Magpies' goal. He departed in May 1922 being appointed South Shields manager. Shields were then a Football League side, in Division Two, but his stay at Horsley Hill didn't last long, resigning less than a year later. In 1923 he moved up a grade to take control of Preston North End and was instrumental in bringing the legendary Alex James to England. Again though he didn't remain long, moving from Deepdale within a couple of years with relegation from the First Division hanging over his head.

Lawrence was one of several eminent home stars of the period who helped develop football on the Continent. In August 1925 he joined German outfit, Karlsruhe as manager and led them to the League Championship at a time when there was an all amateur set-up in that country. After a spell of several years on the Continent, Lawrence returned to Scotland joining the Stranraer club. He became a director, and later Chairman, of the Stair Park side and was associated with them until his demise at a relatively early age in November 1934.

It is unlikely that Jimmy Lawrence's appearance record for Newcastle United will be passed and he will remain at the forefront of the club's history.

Centenary Profile 4

The Newcastle Flier

"One of the side's most influential players. A match-winner for us on dozens of occasions"

Jimmy Howie, 1909

ONLY A HANDFUL OF TYNESIDERS HAVE APPEARED for England when in the ranks of Newcastle United. One of that select group of players was a Percy Main lad called Jackie Rutherford, known as 'The Newcastle Flier' the country over during his era prior to World War One. An outstanding winger, he took part in every one of United's successful sides during that great period and in a long career was rated with the very best, alongside Steve Bloomer and Billy Meredith of those halcyon days. Only Jackie Milburn has played more full games for England as a Newcastle player.

Rutherford came from a large family. He was one of twelve, born in October 1884. The son of a coal trimmer, Jackie was the eldest of the pack, working in the Tyne shipyards as an apprentice plater. In schools football he recorded 88 goals in season 1897/98 and when 16 years of age blossomed as a centre-forward in local soccer netting more goals. Jackie, or as he was often called, Jock, signed for Willington Athletic in 1900 and started to earn a wage in football as a part-timer, getting 7s 6d a match. His younger brothers were starting off too, both Sep and Bob Rutherford had notable Football League careers as well, while a third brother, Andrew, later had a chance at St James Park, appearing in a trial for the club's 'A' side.

Jock's displays in the Northern Alliance against Newcastle, Sunderland and Middlesbrough elevens were outstanding. Local scouts sent rave reports about the starlet, who still was only a kid, thin and wiry, but able to take a lot of rough treatment in that standard of football. He was a durable character, and needed to be. Newcastle snapped up the youngster in January 1902 for all of £75. Jock's wage as a professional was now £2 10s a week.

He quickly made the senior ranks when only 17 years 139 days old, then the club's youngest debutant. And in that first game against Bolton Wanderers during March 1902 he found the net. In the next home fixture with Wolves, Jock scored another two. It was a marvellous start in a black'n'white shirt. He operated initially at inside-left or centre-forward but moved to outside-right for the beginning of the 1903/04 season, a position he made his own for ten years. Not a big man, only 5'9" and of slight build, Rutherford created a reputation of sound, consistent play rather than one of fancy tricks. A partnership with Jimmy Howie proved such a success that many judges noted it as the best right-wing in the business.

Rutherford was also a deadly goalscorer, almost 100 goals came from his shooting boots, and the inch perfect balls he was able to deliver from the touch-line made him a defender's nightmare. United's centre-forwards of the time, Bill Appleyard, and later Albert Shepherd, cashed in on the brilliant service Rutherford offered.

The Tynesider first appeared for England in 1904, in the Scotland clash. He was only 19 years old, certainly United's youngest England player, and one of the youngest of all time to pull on a white shirt. He scored three goals in eleven appearances for his country and also took part in other representative matches throughout the decade. Jackie was a national personality. With a receding hairline at an early age, he was known and feared on every ground he visited. A superstitious character, Rutherford would always be last out and at one stage during his career, at Arsenal, even refused the captaincy because it meant running out first.

When approaching 30 years of age, a few 'set-to's' with Newcastle officials took place which eventually saw the winger

Jackie Rutherford

RUTHERFORD'S PLAYING RECORD

	League		FA Cup		Total	
	App	Gls	App	Gls	App	Gls
1901-02	11	5	0	0	11	5
1902-03	22	6	0	0	22	6
1903-04	33	7	1	0	34	7
1904-05	31	10	5	0	36	10
1905-06	34	9	8	2	42	11
1906-07	34	10	1	0	35	10
1907-08	19	11	6	4	25	15
1908-09	24	5	5	2	29	7
1909-10	24	8	7	4	31	12
1910-11	15	1	5	1	20	2
1911-12	23	4	1	0	24	4
1912-13	20	2	5	1	25	3
	290	**78**	**44**	**14**	**334**	**92**

move on. The close-season of 1911 saw Rutherford, and team-mate Colin Veitch, in dispute with the club's hierarchy over benefit payments. Both were placed on the transfer-list and while disagreements were eventually patched up, the relationship between player and club was never the same again. By the summer of 1913, Jackie was in dispute again and after completing 334 games for Newcastle, he travelled south in October to sign for Arsenal for an £800 fee.

It was anticipated by Arsenal's directors that Rutherford would have a couple more seasons in the Londoners' Second Division promotion bid before hanging up his boots, but amazingly he played on for a further 13 years clocking up over 200 appearances for the Gunners. Balding on top at an alarming rate now, Rutherford became an even bigger character in the game as the well respected veteran.

During the First World War he guested for Chelsea and helped win the Victory Cup in 1919, netting twice in the final against Fulham. Back at Highbury, Jackie was a marvel to Arsenal, an experienced old hand who established the North London club when they retained First Division status in 1919. In March 1923 he tried management with newly relegated Stoke, but it was a brief encounter. Rutherford was appointed as City's first ever boss. However, he remained in charge a matter of only a few weeks before resigning after a row saw him make a quick exit.

Jock scurried back to Highbury and played on for another couple of seasons and at one stage had a rival at outside-right in his own son! Both played for the Gunners in season 1925/26. He called it a day in the summer of 1925, or so he thought. After five months on the retirement list the Tynesider jumped back into action, again with Arsenal, the third time he had signed for the Londoners. In January 1926 Rutherford was seen once more running down the wing, now into his 40th year and more. At the start of the following season he moved to Clapton Orient where he played a year before finally hanging up his well worn boots. That was in the summer of 1927 when aged 42, with almost 600 matches behind him. Jackie spent 25 years in the game as a player, few individuals can boast such service.

He remained in London, an exiled Geordie, becoming a well known licensee, shunning a managerial career in football. He coached local sides like Tufnell Park, while Rutherford occasionally watched his old club Arsenal, and United too when they were in the capital. Jackie Rutherford died in Neasden, a stone's throw from Wembley, the stadium he would have graced so well, in April 1963, a year short of his 80th birthday. Inside partner Jimmy Howie said of Rutherford's contribution to Newcastle, "One of the side's most influential players. A match-winner for us on dozens of occasions". Tyneside has produced many famous names, few though in the sporting world as noted as Jackie Rutherford.

5 EDWARDIAN MASTERS II

1908-1912

• POINTS RECORD • CUP VICTORS AT LAST • INJURY SET-BACK • CHEQUE-BOOK FINALE •

"The Newcastle team of the 1900's would give any modern side a two goal start and beat them, and further more beat them at a trot"

Peter McWilliam, c1920

TO MAINTAIN SUCH A HIGH standard of football for which the club now held a reputation was not an easy task. Every side wanted Newcastle's scalp but United coped with the added pressure and attention impressively. Their set-up was a professional one and much credit was to be given to the directors - many times the public's number one enemy - but during this era a cohesive and effective unit.

They made sure that once a position needed filling the replacement found was an established star, and if need be the club paid a big transfer fee in the process. The directors were determined to keep the name of Newcastle United at the forefront of the game. Messrs Bell, Milne and Alderman James Lunn, the men with power in the boardroom as the decade's end neared, thought big and acted big. Their reward was more prestige and more honours including, at last, the FA Cup.

Albert Shepherd, to become one of Newcastle's greatest centre-forwards.

During the summer months of 1908 United's management was occupied with the task of finding a replacement for Bill Appleyard, at centre-forward a key role. It was a position that was always difficult to fill and with his past success would be even harder.

Scouts searched the country for a new leader but without a lot of success. They went back to Appleyard's old club, Grimsby Town and brought their lanky 6'1" No 9, Bob Blanthorne to Tyneside but very much as a prospect for the future. He had impressed United in the previous season's Cup-tie and cost £350. With no-one else arriving Blanthorne was thrown into First Division action for the opening game of the season against Bradford City, but tragically broke his leg within 26 minutes of the second-half.

It had been a hapless day for United for 13 minutes later they were down to nine men when Jack Carr left the field also injured. Newcastle still won by a single goal although that was of secondary importance.

The black'n'whites were back to square one. A centre-forward was now even more of a necessity. That quickly became an urgent problem when the experiment with reserve half-back turned centre-forward Stan Allan failed. To rectify the crisis United went for one of the best leaders in the country, Bolton Wanderers and England striker, Albert Shepherd. He was a forward of much acclaim and Albert quickly agreed to join the Magpies.

Newcastle paid £800 for his services and it proved a good bit of business, money well spent down to the last half-penny. Shepherd's record was first-class. He had scored an impressive 90 goals in only 123 games for Bolton, many of them in dare-devil style that had fans jumping with excitement. At 5'8" tall and extremely fast he was to display the same thrilling form at St James Park. He could be physical, brushing opponents aside with a shoulder charge and he packed a ferocious shot, according to one old-timer, "so hard that it carried the 'keeper over the line too"!

What a sensational start awaited the England international. At the time several of United's most experienced players were either off form, injured or in dispute over payments. They included McCracken, Rutherford, Stewart, McWilliam, Gardner and Howie, virtually half of the line-up.

With these players missing Shepherd came into a makeshift side for the trip to Nottingham Forest. Opportunities were given to Scott Duncan, reserve captain Bob Liddell, full-backs Tony Whitson and Dick Pudan as well as Dave Willis and Sandy Higgins. Outside-right Duncan developed into a potential international player appearing for the Anglo-Scots in both 1910 and 1911.

Both Whitson and Pudan had a tough undertaking competing with Bill McCracken and Jack Carr for the full-back's position. But with Carr now ageing the opportunity for a regular place was there.

Tony Whitson was born in South Africa but brought up in the terraces of Walker and proved a grand defender. Fast and rarely at fault, he was good enough to appear for the Football League. Sandy Higgins was another youngster who developed into international talent. The son of an ex Scottish national centre-forward, he had arrived from Kilmarnock in 1905 and took time to break into the side. However once established Higgins created a big impression up front with a dazzling array of skills. He later followed his father into Scotland's side and went on to net 41 goals for United.

The Magpies' new look team did extremely well to the surprise of many. They won 4-0 and Shepherd started as he was to continue for the next three seasons - with a goal. But the victory gave a false impression. Forest were a mediocre side, the opposition for the next fixture was to be a different class, Sunderland, still one of the First Division's most consistent teams. Colin Veitch related, "I spent a long time trying to persuade the directors that the retention of the same team was a grave risk". Yet his judgement was ignored and the same eleven faced the Wearsiders.

A crowd of 56,000 crushed into St James Park on a wet afternoon to witness what was to be the most sensational match played at the stadium. The date was December 5th 1908, a day remembered afterwards by every Newcastle supporter, whole generations of them. The fateful day when Sunderland overwhelmed United by all of 9-1,

Sandy Higgins who started to make an impression up front.

Full-back Tony Whitson, born in Cape Town but brought up on Tyneside.

still the biggest away victory of all time in the First Division.

Newcastle were just behind the leaders at the top of the table while Sunderland were a few places back in 6th position. United ran out wearing all white shirts and the first-half saw a fairly even period end one goal each - Shepherd striking home an equaliser a minute from the break with a rocket penalty.

There was nothing to indicate the avalanche of goals to follow. The pitch became increasingly greasy and slippery and United found it difficult to play controlled football. Sunderland though adapted to the worsening conditions. George Holley put the visitors ahead then Hogg made it 3-1. The Roker eleven then went goals crazy and Newcastle collapsed. Inspired by England inside-forward Holley, they netted no fewer than five goals in eight minutes, all in the Leazes End goalmouth, then fired home another three. Their centre-forward Arthur Brown incredibly didn't get onto the scoresheet !

It was afterwards declared that Sunderland's players had been so incensed at the referee's penalty decision just before half-time, that they decided to go all out for victory. True or not, they certainly did that !

United finished the game with only nine men, with Whitson and Duncan - carried off on the back of Jimmy McPherson - in the dressing-room. But injuries aside it had been a dreadful performance during the second-half, a 45 minute nightmare.

UNITED'S BENEFICIARIES

In a neighbourly way the club was quick to come to the aid of several local sides in need of financial assistance. Among the teams to receive, either loans, or donations were;

Carlisle United (£300), Hebburn Argyle (£15), Newcastle City (£100), while Middlesbrough were loaned £1,000 in 1905.

Newcastle City actually applied for Football League membership in 1912 attempting entry into Division Two. They only received one vote. United's records unfortunately do not note if the Magpies voted, for, or against.

Athletic News made the comment, "Veitch was the only man who showed solidity and class", and the Newcastle Evening Chronicle noted, "The defence was absolutely smashed up and the halves were quite run off their feet".

On every ground in the country the result was met with astonishment. It had been United's blackest day ever. Newcastle fans were absolutely stunned with the extraordinary afternoon. And even more so as the Magpies went on to run away with

Jimmy Stewart pictured in England colours. He was capped three times for his country as well as making four appearances for the Football League XI.

the League Championship. Never before, or since, have the Champions elect suffered such a defeat - a home one at that and to such local rivals.

From that moment though Newcastle immediately sorted out the internal feuding. For the next match against Chelsea some of the stars were back and, with Shepherd linking perfectly, Newcastle won 2-1. The Magpies stormed through the rest of the season in rip-roaring fashion. It was as if the 9-1 humiliation had never occurred. Instead of allowing it to humble the club for months, and it could easily have done that, the defeat only served to spur them on to greater heights.

In a spell from that remarkable defeat in December, through to mid April and yet another reverse to their Roker foes, Newcastle lost only a single game. In a sequence into the New Year they won seven in a row and created a club record which still stands of 16 league and cup games unbeaten.

The black'n'whites came to the make or break stage of the season as leaders. Everton were again their main challengers but United had a comfortable points lead as Easter approached. After that second defeat by Sunderland, they faced the Mersey club two days later at St James Park. It was a title decider as Everton had to take full points to stand any chance of catching United. 30,000 saw two goals from Stewart settle the issue. Bill McCracken also netted a penalty as the Magpies won 3-0. One correspondent wrote that Newcastle, "sparkled and scintillated, volleyed and thundered and completely outclassed Everton".

United ended Champions with a new points record of 53 - a massive seven points clear of the Merseysiders. Had it not been for three late defeats when the trophy had been secured, the margin could have been even greater.

Newcastle also failed narrowly to reach the Cup final again, falling in the semi-final and on the way handing out some degree of revenge to Sunderland. After eliminating Clapton Orient 5-0, then both Blackpool and West Ham by 2-1, the Wearsiders arrived at Gallowgate in the quarter-final.

Another big gathering turned up. Fans started queuing from eight in the morning and almost 54,000 were present on a bitterly cold day that saw driving sleet pour down on St James Park. The derby crowd were soon warmed up though with a typical all action local battle that produced goals but nothing like the number of three months earlier.

Rutherford put United ahead after 14 minutes but 60 seconds later all was level when Mordue scored with a long range shot. Then it was Sunderland who took the lead only for an equaliser to be quickly scored by 'Smiler' Wilson. The game ended all square 2-2 and the scene moved to Wearside four days later.

Turnstiles were again closed with 27,512 in the much smaller Roker Park and they saw Newcastle display style, cruising through to a memorable 3-0 victory. The game hinged on a crucial early penalty save by Jimmy Lawrence after Wilson had put United 1-0 in front. Albert Shepherd then netted two wonderful break-away goals in the final ten minutes. First he flashed past two defenders to score, then again he raced half the length of the field to another gem.

The previous season's League Champions Manchester United faced the Tynesiders in the semi-final at Bramall Lane, Sheffield. Newcastle were all set to have a go at the double again. However, a late goal by England forward Harold Halse was enough to knock the Magpies out. United were reduced to ten men in the second-half when Shepherd hobbled off while they also missed

Outside-left Andy Anderson who won a Championship medal in 1909.

Rutherford, sidelined through injury too.

It had been a dour match but a very sporting occasion. At the time Newcastle and Manchester United were a close body of players both giving much support to the Players' Union cause. They held brotherly solidarity for the much criticised organisation led by their respective stars, Billy Meredith and Colin Veitch, two outspoken activists.

Newcastle did however secure a double of sorts. To add to the Championship trophy they also won the FA Charity Shield that year. They defeated Northampton - the top non-league side - by 2-0 at Stamford Bridge.

Jimmy Stewart was another headline signing that season. Although born and bred on Tyneside, he made an name with Sheffield Wednesday as a delicate, skilled and flexible inside-forward able to score plenty of goals. Stewart had already been capped by England by the time he returned to the north-east in 1908. Nicknamed 'Tadger', he became another nationally recognised figure in United's ranks. Andy Anderson was also a new face, signed from St Mirren as competition for Wilson and Gosnell.

Although the club gained the substantial talents of both Shepherd and Stewart, they lost one star player, Alec Gardner who suffered a bad leg fracture in the cup-tie with Blackpool. Gardner was the only one of United's Edwardian stars not to be picked for an international fixture. He did come very close to winning a cap for Scotland, appearing in a trial game during 1904, but the elusive honour passed him by. He was a stalwart player, as one colleague remembered, "a model of consistency". Following his retirement, Alec became a city publican looking after the popular North Terrace to his death, a United supporter to his final day.

INTERNATIONAL GALLERY

During the club's Edwardian supremacy from 1904 to 1912 no fewer than 21 international players wore the black'n'white shirt on a regular basis.

GOALKEEPER:
J Lawrence (Scotland)
DEFENDERS:
J Carr (England)
A McCombie (Scotland)
W McCracken (Ireland)
HALF-BACKS:
C Veitch (England)
A Aitken (Scotland)
J Hay (Scotland)
W Low (Scotland)
P McWilliam (Scotland)
F Speedie (Scotland)
INSIDE-FORWARDS:
A Gosnell (England)
J Stewart (England)
A Higgins (Scotland)
J Howie (Scotland)
R Orr (Scotland)
CENTRE-FORWARDS:
A Shepherd (England)
W Hibbert (England)
R McColl (Scotland)
WINGERS:
J Rutherford (England)
R Templeton (Scotland)
G Wilson (Scotland)

Andy Aitken, Colin Veitch, Jimmy Hay, Bill McCracken and Peter McWilliam all skippered their respective countries.

A contemporary sketch of Wilf Low, one of the club's many internationals.

Three of the Magpies most consistent players of the era, left to right: Bill McCracken, Colin Veitch, Jimmy Howie. All are wearing their respective country's international shirts; Ireland, England and Scotland.

Advertisement for Oxo, according to trainer Jimmy McPherson, a drink that was very much part of Newcastle United's match preparations giving "great staying power to players".

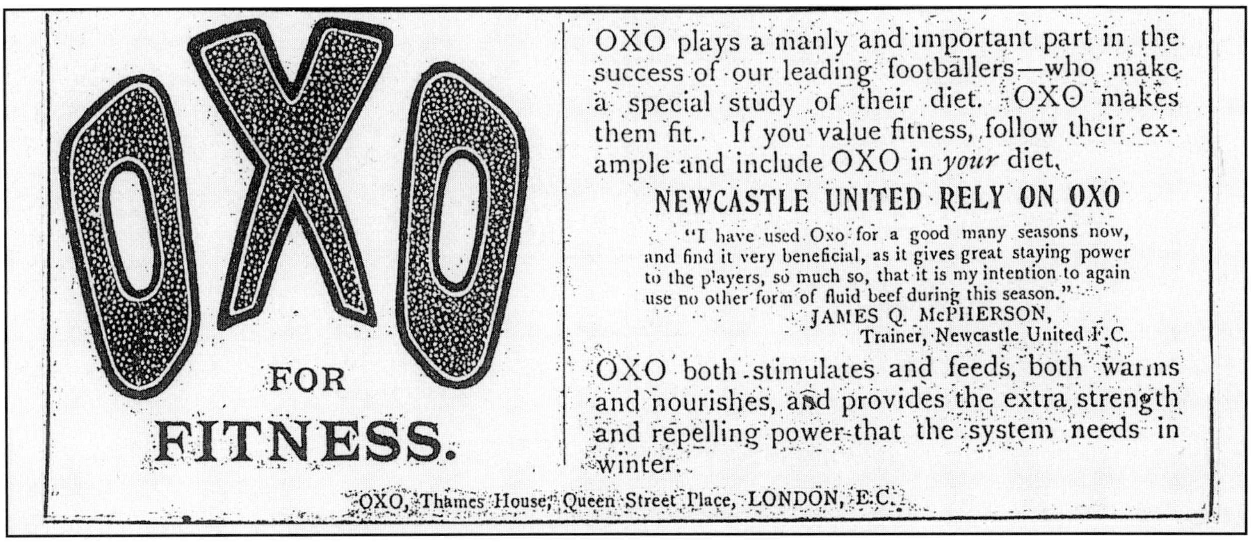

League Champions 1909

FIRST DIVISION CHAMPIONS 1908-1909	P	W	D	L	F	A	Pts
Newcastle United	**38**	**24**	**5**	**9**	**65**	**41**	**53**
Everton	38	18	10	10	82	57	46
Sunderland	38	21	2	15	78	63	44
Blackburn Rovers	38	14	13	11	61	50	41
Sheffield Wednesday	38	17	6	15	67	61	40
Woolwich Arsenal	38	14	10	14	52	49	38
Aston Villa	38	14	10	14	58	56	38
Bristol City	38	13	12	13	45	58	38
Middlesbrough	38	14	9	15	59	53	37
Preston North End	38	13	11	14	48	44	37
Chelsea	38	14	9	15	56	61	37
Sheffield United	38	14	9	15	51	59	37
Manchester United	38	15	7	16	58	68	37
Nottingham Forest	38	14	8	16	66	57	36
Notts County	38	14	8	16	51	48	36
Liverpool	38	15	6	17	57	65	36
Bury	38	14	8	16	63	77	36
Bradford City	38	12	10	16	47	47	34
Manchester City	38	15	4	19	67	69	34
Leicester Fosse	38	8	9	21	54	102	25

REGULAR SIDE

Lawrence
McCracken - Whitson
Willis - Veitch - McWilliam
Rutherford - Howie - Shepherd or Higgins - Stewart - Wilson

CHAIRMAN: Joseph Bell
MANAGER: Directors' committee
TRAINER-COACH: James McPherson
CAPTAIN: Colin Veitch

RESULTS	Home	Away
Bradford City	W 1-0	W 2-1
Leicester Fosse	W 2-0	W 4-0
Bristol City	W 2-1	D 3-3
Woolwich Arsenal	W 3-1	W 2-1
Notts County	W 1-0	W 4-0
Sheffield Wed	W 1-0	L 0-2
Preston North End	W 2-0	W 1-0
Middlesbrough	W 1-0	D 0-0
Manchester City	W 2-0	W 2-0
Liverpool	L 0-1	L 1-2
Bury	W 3-1	D 1-1
Sheffield United	W 4-0	D 1-1
Aston Villa	L 0-2	L 0-3
Nottingham Forest	D 1-1	W 4-0
Sunderland	L 1-9	L 1-3
Chelsea	L 1-3	W 2-1
Blackburn Rovers	W 2-0	W 4-2
Manchester United	W 2-1	L 0-1
Everton	W 3-0	W 1-0

LEAGUE APPEARANCES
38 Lawrence, 34 Veitch, 30 Whitson, McCracken, 28 Wilson, 27 McWilliam, 26 Howie, Higgins, 25 Stewart, 24 Rutherford, 20 Willis, 19 Anderson, 14 Duncan, Shepherd, 12 Gardner, 11 Carr, 10 Jobey, 9 Allan, 5 Ridley, Liddell, Gosnell, 3 Pudan, 1 Blanthorne, McCombie, Randall.

LEAGUE GOALS
11 Shepherd, 9 Veitch, 8 Stewart, 6 Howie, 5 Allan, Higgins, Rutherford, Wilson, 3 Anderson, 2 Duncan, 1 Jobey, Liddell, McCracken, Ridley, Willis, own-goal.

League Champions for a third time in 1909, United's squad and directors pose at the Gallowgate End entrance steps.

LARGEST VICTORY:
4-0 v Sheffield Utd (H), Leicester Fosse (A), Notts County (A), Nottingham Forest (A)

HEAVIEST DEFEAT:
1-9 v Sunderland (H)

AVERAGE HOME ATTENDANCE:
31,508

TOP GATE:
56,000 v Sunderland

NEWCASTLE'S DIRECTORS NOW HAD TO address the problem of adequately replacing Alec Gardner who had served the club so well for a decade. They had selected the right man at centre-forward, and again their judgement was faultless at half-back, bringing Aberdonian Wilf Low to St James Park during May 1909 for £800.

Low became known as 'The Laughing Cavalier', yet was grim in his methods, a robust breaker-up of the opposition. He went on to appear on 367 occasions for United. With a reshuffle in the half-back line, Low fitted in at centre-half with Veitch and McWilliam alongside.

The pattern of previous seasons continued. United ended the campaign in 4th position once more, and also back at the Crystal Palace. They had started the 1909/10 season well, but only after a footballers' strike was narrowly averted, a national controversy with Newcastle United very much involved.

Wearing his Scotland cap and badge, £800 signing Wilf Low who replaced the injured Gardner.

During the close-season a major confrontation had developed between the outlawed Players Union and football's rulers. Manchester United and Newcastle, as well as Middlesbrough players, were the most determined to stick to principles and fight for membership. There was grave danger that the season would have to start on some grounds with a line-up of amateurs. However, while the Old Trafford club's 'outcasts' held firm Newcastle, led by Colin Veitch decided to retract their strike threat and pursue a more conciliatory path to ensure union recognition. Veitch, as one report noted, "exercised a wise restraining influence". His tact in a highly motivated situation gained Colin much respect and he eventually became Union Chairman.

With the season under way a truly remarkable eleven goal thriller took place at Anfield against Liverpool, led by old East and West End boss Tom Watson. Newcastle struck first in the opening minute and then Shepherd netted four splendid goals to put United 5-2 ahead at the interval. Yet United's centre-forward still found himself on the losing side !

Ex Magpie Ronald Orr, now wearing the red of Liverpool, inspired a brilliant come-back for his new side. He hit the target twice including the equaliser, then helped Goddard clinch the points by 6-5.

With attractive fixtures like that United remained top attraction in the country. Indeed the largest attendance in England to watch a league game was recorded when 70,000 turned up to see the Magpies lose 2-1 at Stamford Bridge in December.

Following that defeat the folk of the Potteries were overwhelmed at the visit of mighty Newcastle to face non-league Stoke in the FA Cup. Their footballers were not so intimidated and held United to a 1-1 draw. Newcastle though made amends in the replay winning 2-1 and set course for the Crystal Palace.

GERMAN SIGNED

Newcastle continued to tour the Continent visiting Scandinavia, Germany and Switzerland. On a tour of Denmark in 1909 they spotted Edwin Dutton, a German international born of English parents. With the Prussen Berlin club, he soon joined United and did well in reserve football although never got a chance in the club's league side. Dutton had played once for the German national side, against Hungary in April 1909. Later he was trainer at Ipswich Town while he also married into the family of United mentor Jimmy McPherson.

Fulham attempted to avenge their 1908 semi-final hammering in the next round, but they were promptly crushed for a second time, 4-0. Blackburn Rovers, that season challenging for the title alongside United, could make little impression on the Magpies either. They lost 3-1 on Tyneside watched by a 55,000 crowd.

Yet another very convincing victory followed, this time by 3-0 over Second Division Leicester Fosse. They included Andy Aitken in their line-up and had lost Hubbard with a broken collar bone. It was a success which took United into the semi-final for the third year running.

The four sides in the Cup draw were United, non-league Swindon Town, Barnsley, and consistent rivals Everton. And it was Southern League Swindon who came out of the hat with

Newcastle. Although classed as a minnow, this still before the inauguration of the Third and Fourth Divisions, Swindon were a good, and somewhat feared side. They included in their line-up regular England inside-forward Harry Fleming and finished runners-up in the Southern League that year and Champions the following season.

Newcastle missed the skills of centre-forward Shepherd, Stewart standing in, but the Wiltshire club, even with the advantage of playing in the south - at White Hart Lane - were no match for a Newcastle side brimming with experience and confidence.

Conditions were dry and fast and immediately United pressed with Higgins, Wilson and Howie all going close. Newcastle dominated the first-half with excellent approach play but missed the deadly touch of Albert Shepherd in front of goal. Swindon in fact only forced Lawrence into one save.

The second period started in the same way with Higgins looking a certain scorer with a "cannon-ball like shot". Then United broke the deadlock with two goals in two minutes. From a free-kick Rutherford gained possession, took a snap shot and the ball flew into the net off the underside of the bar. Seconds later the same player darted through on the right, flicked the ball inside and Stewart was on hand to make it 2-0. One newspaper report made the comment, "Newcastle's win was the triumph of footballing science".

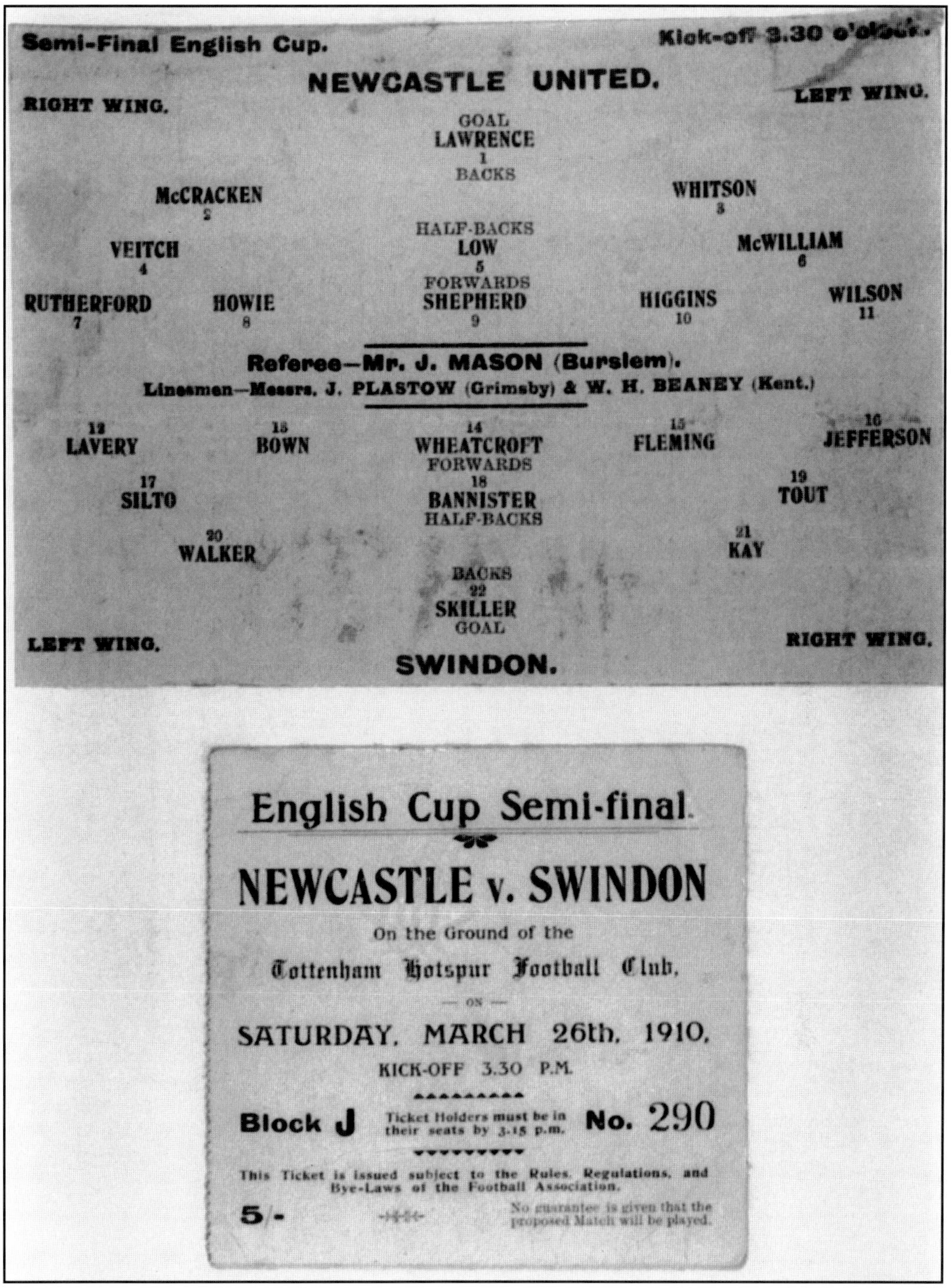

Semi-Final English Cup. Kick-off 3.30 o'clock.

NEWCASTLE UNITED.

RIGHT WING. LEFT WING.

GOAL
LAWRENCE
1

BACKS
McCRACKEN 2 WHITSON 3

HALF-BACKS
VEITCH 4 LOW 5 McWILLIAM 6

FORWARDS
RUTHERFORD 7 HOWIE 8 SHEPHERD 9 HIGGINS 10 WILSON 11

Referee—Mr. J. MASON (Burslem).
Linesmen—Messrs. J. PLASTOW (Grimsby) & W. H. BEANEY (Kent.)

12 LAVERY 13 BOWN 14 WHEATCROFT 15 FLEMING 16 JEFFERSON
FORWARDS
17 SILTO 18 BANNISTER 19 TOUT
HALF-BACKS
20 WALKER 21 KAY
BACKS
22
SKILLER
GOAL

LEFT WING. RIGHT WING.

SWINDON.

English Cup Semi-final.

NEWCASTLE v. SWINDON

On the Ground of the

Tottenham Hotspur Football Club,

— ON —

SATURDAY, MARCH 26th, 1910.

KICK-OFF 3.30 P.M.

Block J Ticket Holders must be in their seats by 3.15 p.m. No. 290

This Ticket is issued subject to the Rules, Regulations, and Bye-Laws of the Football Association.

5/- No guarantee is given that the proposed Match will be played.

Team sheet and match ticket from United's F.A. Cup semi-final with Swindon Town at White Hart Lane in 1910.

Before the season closed and with it the outcome of United's fourth Cup final a series of controversies made headlines. United's committee was very cautious in their team selection, and as in 1906 were carpeted by the Football Association and Football League. Out of the title race, below strength sides were turned out in several league games allowing senior players a rest before the final - and assuring no injuries.

Newcastle's 'reserves' travelled to Bristol City and actually returned with a creditable 3-0 victory. The side was composed of North Eastern League regulars although many were very experienced. Indeed, internationals like Jack Carr and James Stewart were in the line-up.

The game at Ashton Gate, and another at Villa Park, took place between United's drawn Cup final and the pending replay. A directors' meeting took place at the University Hotel in London immediately after the final and it was decided not to risk their Cup side with only a matter of days before the all important re-scheduled meeting.

Everyone, bar football's ruling bodies

FA Cup Semi-final action. Sandy Higgins watches Swindon 'keeper Skiller see his shot go past the post.

Jock Rutherford, lashes the ball home to open the scoring against Swindon Town at White Hart Lane.

Newcastle's second goal. Jimmy Stewart slots the ball into the net to complete United's comfortable victory over the Southern League team.

not see it that way and later severely censored United for deliberately sending out weak combinations. They were fined £100 plus a further £198 for another offence after a postponed game with Bradford City. Newcastle also got a lecture and a further fine for allowing Albert Shepherd to leave the field uninjured and before the end of play against Arsenal, a match only 24 hours before the semi-final.

And that was not all. Football's hierachy disciplined the club for their handling and distribution of Cup final tickets in which many found their way on to the black-market. With all this brewing in the background and before the

Tynesiders headed for the Crystal Palace they took part in another controversial fixture, this time with Middlesbrough at Ayresome Park.

It was a decisive relegation game for the 'Boro, in need of one point for safety. Following a tame 1-1 draw referee Alf Green of Birmingham advised United director, John Oliver, and Middlesbrough Chairman, Colonel Poole, that he considered the match had been rigged. A report went to the Football League and a commission later took up court in Darlington to hear the case. No firm evidence could be found and the commission completely cleared both clubs.

There was more trouble to disrupt the side's plans too. The biggest headline of all was created when Albert Shepherd was accused of bribery only days before the FA Cup semi-final. Rumours spread that he had been 'got at' for the clash with Swindon Town during the side's stay in Saltburn on special training. Fuel was added to the fire when United's centre-forward was left out of the club's squad and actually missed the game at White Hart Lane. His colleagues were incensed, "we were bewildered, stunned", said one.

Shepherd's team-mates demanded his return to the side for the final-tie asserting that the stink had been caused by unscrupulous bookmakers hoping to make a quick profit.

At the time bribery allegations were commonplace in an era when betting on football was totally prohibited. United had to face another enquiry two years later in 1912 following a draw with Liverpool. Again statements were made that the game was fixed, but both clubs were once more completely exonerated. The game's rulers criticised crowd gambling as the cause of stirrings on the terraces. Not all enquiries vindicated the teams concerned. Liverpool were found guilty of pulling off a betting coup just before World War One.

It had been a highly controversial run-up to the Tynesiders' Cup final appointment.

TRAVEL PROBLEMS

During December 1910 United's party were on their way to play Blackburn Rovers and had to change trains at Preston. They were sitting on the train waiting for it to pull out at 1.00pm when someone noticed that it was going to Blackpool, and not Blackburn! Panic reigned as they jumped off with only seconds to spare. They found however, that they had missed the correct train and had to travel to Ewood Park in a convoy of motor cars.

A month later, the Newcastle players and officials almost had a tragic accident en route for Ashbourne for their First Round FA Cup tie at Stoke in January 1910. They travelled by train in an old Pullman carriage and a gas leak occurred as they neared their destination. All of the occupants were taken ill and were almost asphyxiated before they realised their danger.

Cartoon depicting Magpie handing Jimmy Howie his 'bag of gold' for his club benefit, one of several United stars to receive substantial sums for loyal service in this period.

Newcastle were determined to lift the FA Cup in 1910. Magpie is sketched eyeing up The Crystal Palace.

Centenary Highlight

"Newcastle showed clearly that they were a splendid side. They displayed a remarkable control over the wet and slippery ball"

The FA Cup Annual, 1934

Tynesiders' Cup final appointment.

UNITED'S OPPONENTS IN THE CUP FINAL WERE Barnsley, another rugged Second Division outfit and, like Newcastle's 1908 rivals Wolves, not rated as being in the same class as the black'n'whites. Could United at last be successful in the FA Cup the whole country asked ? The answer was yes - but still they couldn't win at the dreaded Crystal Palace.

Newcastle's fans congregated at Sydenham arriving on tramcars, horse-drawn breaks and cycles - some walked to the stadium and a few even came on foot the 280 odd miles from Tyneside ! It was a boisterous all northern gathering, as one observer recorded, "the occasion was one of chaff and hilarious merriment, each side quipping in turn and each wishing the other good luck before parting".

United's directors acceded to the players request of the reinstatement of Shepherd, they had little option with a veiled strike message threatened. And as it turned out United's beleaguered No 9 proved to be the match-winner. But first the Crystal Palace hoodoo quickly hit the Tynesiders as the game got under way.

Barnsley looked the better side. Youthful and fiery, they went into the lead as the interval approached. Their Geordie star, George Lillycrop cleverly jumped over a cross from Bartrop allowing Tufnell space to collect the ball and shoot. Unluckily for Lawrence the ball flicked off Veitch and travelled the opposite way to his dive and into the net. Yes the hoodoo had indeed struck.

For much of the game Newcastle were over cautious and Barnsley frustrated their movements with swift, and sometimes rough, tackles just as Villa, Everton and Wolves had done in past finals. The match was littered with stoppages and United never adapted to a stiff wind, firm ground and lively ball, not to mention the Tykes' aggressive tactics.

It was an uphill struggle with Bill McCracken United's best player in a rearguard action. Newcastle looked a defeated team but suddenly the Magpies took the bit between their teeth in a final 20 minute burst.

It was a stormy last period and at last United received a slice of luck they had up to now never seen at the Palace. With only seven minutes left, and as the wife of Barnsley's manager was tying red ribbons to the trophy, a beautiful long ball from Higgins found Rutherford. He looked yards offside to some, but referee Ibbotson allowed play to continue. Newcastle's outside-right raced clear and headed a dramatic equaliser.

Newcastle rallied and Rutherford was back again very nearly grabbing the winner, just missing another chance from Veitch's free-kick. But in spite of the late come-back it had been another creditless Magpie display. Jimmy Howie said, "We were the same uncertain lot. There was none of that do or die spirit".

At a wet Goodison Park the following Thursday it was to be a different story. Now away from the sinister atmosphere of the Crystal Palace and more at home in the compact northern

At last the F.A. Cup arrives on Tyneside. Crowds mass round United's victory procession in 1910.

FA CUP RUN

R1	Stoke	A	D	1-1
	Stoke	H	W	2-1
R2	Fulham	H	W	4-0
R3	Blackburn Rovers	H	W	3-1
R4	Leicester Fosse	H	W	3-0
SF	Swindon Town	N	W	2-0
F	Barnsley	N	D	1-1
FR	Barnsley	N	W	2-0

FACTS & FIGURES

	P	W	D	L	F	A
Home	4	4	0	0	12	2
Away	4	2	2	0	6	2
Total	**8**	**6**	**2**	**0**	**18**	**4**

FA Cup Winners 1910

CUP GOALGETTERS
4 Higgins, Howie, Rutherford, 3 Shepherd,
1 McCracken, Stewart, Wilson

CHAIRMAN: Joseph Bell
MANAGER: Directors' committee
TRAINER-COACH: James McPherson
CAPTAIN: Colin Veitch

The triumphant side with the 'English Cup'. Left to right, back: McCracken, Low, Shepherd, McWilliam, Carr. Front: Rutherford, Howie, Veitch, Higgins, Wilson, Whitson. On ground: Watt (secretary), Lawrence, McPherson (trainer).

Before the kick-off at The Crystal Palace. Skippers Veitch and Boyle and referee Ibbotson.

surroundings of Liverpool, United got it right.

FINAL

23 April 1910 at The Crystal Palace
Newcastle United 1(0) Barnsley 1(1)

UNITED:
Lawrence
McCracken, Whitson
Veitch, Low, McWilliam
Rutherford, Howie, Shepherd, Higgins, Wilson
BARNSLEY:
Mearns
Downs, Ness
Glendinning, Boyle, Utley
Bartrop, Gadsby, Lillycrop, Tufnell, Forman

GOALS: Tufnell(37m), Rutherford(83m)

ATTENDANCE; 76,980 (£6,898)

Referee; J.T.Ibbotson (Derby)
Guest of Honour; Lord Gladstone

Barnsley 'keeper Mearns saves a Newcastle effort in the first game in London.

United enthusiasts young and old dressed from head to toe in black'n'white.

The gates were closed as almost 70,000 crowded into Everton's ground, and almost 15,000 congregated outside, some of who broke into the stadium and had to be driven back by mounted police. Newcastle had learnt previous lessons and changed their tactics. United's delicate short game was now laced with long balls and swift passes as well as some gutsy and rugged play. Some of the press even labelled the side as, "Dirty Newcastle", and went on to say, "there were cases of deliberate kicking today. It seemed as if some of the players had deliberately gone onto the field to win at all costs". Jimmy Howie's "do or die spirit" was certainly there.

Veteran Jack Carr stepped in for Whitson, out with a thigh strain, and the game kicked off with the sun peering through the rain clouds. Newcastle were all over Barnsley in the first 45 minutes with George Wilson reaping havoc on the left and Jock Rutherford causing trouble on the right. Barnsley's full-backs Downs and Ness received a roasting, yet United couldn't score with 'keeper Mearns stopping everything.

A Higgins shot and a Howie header both went close. Then Wilson, on his old stamping ground, fired just wide. McWilliam had a go and so did Shepherd, while Boyle twice cleared off the line. It was one way traffic - effort after effort but without success. Colin Veitch noted, "Only miracles prevented us from scoring".

It had been an exciting first-half and the same pattern continued after the interval. Newcastle again pressed, Wilson saw a terrific shot heading for the net but Wearsider Mearns dived and made his best save of the afternoon. However the Oakwell club had to crack and it was Albert Shepherd who became the Magpies' hero.

After 51 minutes he put Newcastle 1-0 in front. Higgins pushed an "inch perfect" ball into Shepherd's path. He raced clear and struck a fast ground shot past the 'keeper. Soon after McWilliam made a brilliant run and a Barnsley defender brought down Shepherd in the box after a through pass by Wilson. A penalty ! The first ever in a Cup final. Albert Shepherd coolly stepped up and slotted the ball home. He had scored 31 times that season.

Howie almost made it 3-0 a minute later when a superb shot rocked the upright. Barnsley, as one reporter noted, "degenerated into a mere rabble". The game was over.

United's Cup winning side received a £50 bonus from the directors - then a massive sum. They included nine internationals with the two uncapped players, Lawrence and Low, honoured in the following season. All eleven were capped with the Magpies. It was an imposing line-up.

The victorious team travelled from Goodison to their HQ in Southport then on to Carlisle where the local Shaddongate club (the forerunner to Carlisle United) entertained the squad with a celebration tea. Then it was off to the big gathering back home.

The Magpies on the offensive at The Palace, this attack from a corner kick.

They arrived in the early evening and, as expected after three previous attempts and three losers' welcomes, the scenes were incredible. The Cup was at last on Tyneside, paraded through the densely crowded streets in a procession of eight landaus led by a fan dressed as Cock o'the North followed by a pipe band.

Each player in turn held the small decoratively engraved trophy as they edged their way out of the Central Station along Collingwood Street, up Grey Street and through Grainger Street to Westgate Road. The black'n'white heroes were presented to packed audiences at the Empire and Pavilion Theatres.

Celebrations went on all week and why not. The relief on both players' and supporters' faces told a story as the pent up feeling of previous disappointments was let loose. The FA Cup was at last theirs, for the first, but not last, time.

FA Cup Winners 1910

FINAL REPLAY
28 April 1910 at Goodison Park
Newcastle United 2 (0) Barnsley 0(0)

UNITED:
Lawrence
McCracken, Carr
Veitch, Low, McWilliam
Rutherford, Howie, Shepherd, Higgins, Wilson
BARNSLEY:
Mearns
Downs, Ness
Glendinning, Boyle, Utley
Bartrop, Gadsby, Lillycrop, Tuffnell , Forman

GOALS: Shepherd(51m), Shepherd(65m)

ATTENDANCE; 69,364 (£4,166)

Referee; J.T.Ibbotson (Derby)
Guest of Honour; Lord Derby
Cup HQ; Queen's Hotel, Southport

Newcastle travel back to their Southport HQ with the F.A. Cup safely in their grasp. Inset: Colin Veitch and Wilf Low.

Albert Shepherd's first goal in the replay at Goodison Park - United's centre-forward lashes the ball past the diving Mearns.

theirs, for the first, but not last, time.

THE CUP HOLDERS WERE DETERMINED to keep hold of the trophy they had for so long been close in bringing back to Tyneside. In 1910/11 Newcastle very nearly repeated the success reaching their fifth Cup final in only seven seasons. However they lost after another replay, but had it not been for two unlucky - and very much crucial - injuries to Peter McWilliam and Albert Shepherd, Newcastle may well have retained the FA Cup and in all probability would have.

McWilliam and Shepherd were the two players the side could ill afford to loose, the key playmaker and the ace goalscorer. In the run-up to the final both were dramatically put out of the reckoning.

Firstly Peter McWilliam, when playing for Scotland against Wales at Ninian Park, was crocked in a simple collision, damaging ligaments. Then in a 2-2 draw with Blackburn Rovers at St James Park, Shepherd was carried off after a clash with Rovers' 'keeper Ashcroft - en route for another goal. He sustained torn ligaments as well, just at a time he was on a scoring spree. Albert had fired home 33 goals and ended the season as the highest scorer in the division.

It was a double tragedy Newcastle didn't recover from. Players of that calibre were almost irreplaceable. How United's directors had wished they had put their stars in cotton-wool again - even if it meant once more facing the wrath of football's authorities. A fine, no matter the amount, would have been nothing as compared to having both Shepherd and McWilliam fit and available.

Until the Cup run started in January, Newcastle had gone through an uncharacteristic league programme. Looking jaded at times in the first half of the season, United were off form and inconsistent. They did click occasionally walloping

George Jobey, from Heddon on the Wall, he became more famous as a manager.

Everton 5-1 at Goodison and also both Liverpool and Bradford City 6-1 - with the help of Shepherd hat-tricks.

United's leader also knocked four past Nottingham Forest and, with his free scoring, Shepherd earned a recall to the England side against Ireland. But despite netting in a 2-1 victory, and to the annoyance of Newcastle fans, didn't warrant a regular place for his country.

The Geordies eventually finished in 8th position, perhaps by Newcastle's standards a disappointing placing. But disappointing was not the word when the FA Cup started. Six goals were planted past the Bury goalkeeper as United started their defence of the trophy in style. Shepherd

Another F.A. Cup semi-final contest, this time with Chelsea in 1911. Rutherford is ready to pounce after a colleague knocks the ball into the goalmouth.

Sandy Higgins takes on the Chelsea defence in United's FA Cup semi-final at St. Andrews

claimed another hat-trick in front of his own fans.

Lowly Northampton Town, another club from the Southern League, almost caused a shock in Round Two. The Cobblers held United 1-1 at Gallowgate before a worried 42,000 crowd. Higgins had darted clear to put United ahead, but within a minute the visitors equalised and earned a deserved replay.

The town of Northampton buzzed with anticipation at the visit of Newcastle United, but their much awaited debut never happened - to the fury of the locals. Northampton sold ground rights to United for the sum of £900. Then boss, Herbert Chapman noted that the amount wiped out the club's debts.

In the return match it took a penalty to narrowly take United into a tie with Hull City. The spot-kick was converted by Shepherd who had returned to the side after missing the first match due to the tragic death of his four year-old son.

United went on to despatch Hull, then Derby County travelled to the north-east and, with a record 59,700 Cup mad fans howling their heads off, the Magpies won in glorious manner, by 4-0.

So to the semi-final in Birmingham against Chelsea. The Londoners, then attempting to get out of Division Two, were on the receiving end of another convincing Cup performance. Newcastle were confident in every part of their play. They were devastating and entertaining with it. Passes flowed from man to man in the style that had given the club such a noble reputation. From Veitch to Rutherford, inside to Stewart, back to Higgins and out to Wilson. Chelsea's defenders frantically jumped in with desperate tackles but United's timing was to perfection. The black'n'whites released the ball just at the right moment. It was precision football at its very best.

Newcastle coasted into another Cup final with a 3-0 victory. Wilson opened the scoring and Shepherd made it 2-0 before half-time. Jimmy Stewart scored the third, while Veitch almost made it a 4-0 walk-over when he thudded the ball off the post near the end.

Jock Finlay, a 16 year-old when he made his debut - the club's youngest player at the time.

Once more preparations had to be made for the Crystal Palace. To fill the places of Shepherd and McWilliam, United drafted in Dave Willis and George Jobey. Facing an impossible task of replacing such players of quality, both were to do well. Jobey, born at Heddon-on-the-Wall, spent seven years on the Gallowgate staff starting as a cunning schemer but ending as a tough half-back. He afterwards made a name for himself in a 30 year career as a manager, prominently at Derby County.

Inside-forward Charles Randall, another local lad, from Burnopfield, came into the reckoning that year too, as did Jock Finlay, who had become the club's youngest debutant at only 16 years-old the season before. Finlay had cost a huge fee for such a youngster - £775, when he came south from Airdrie with a big reputation having already played for the Scottish League as a teenager. The left-half, while never living up to his early promise, spent over 20 years on the club's books.

With another colossal amount banked - £27,513 13s 5d - from gate receipts in the season alone, Newcastle headed for London on a well worn path. No-one had to tell United's fans how to get to the Crystal Palace. They could do it just about blindfold by now.

Centenary Highlight

> *"We could not play any sort of game. We could not show any kind of form. We were like a lot of beginners"*
>
> *Peter McWilliam, April 1911*

NEWCASTLE COMPETED FOR A BRAND NEW FA Cup in 1911 - the trophy won at Goodison 12 months ago by this time had been presented to Lord Kinnaird, and a new design had been commissioned. The cup was made by Messrs Fattorini and Sons and they hailed from Bradford - an omen of ill fortune for United as so did their opponents.

The resolute, if unpolished, Yorkshire side were to go through their finest season - not only lifting the Cup but also ending in 5th place in Division One, five points ahead of Newcastle. The Tynesiders, though, had thrashed Bradford City 6-1 at St James Park in December.

Skipper Colin Veitch won the toss and United had the better of the match in a game that saw little good football and lots of midfield endeavour.

Windy conditions were proving an obstacle for both sides and City 'keeper Mark Mellors kept the Magpies at bay when they did get close. United however, squandered their many chances. City on the other hand only had two or three efforts in the whole 90 minutes and Lawrence wasn't tested all afternoon with McCracken and Whitson in complete control ahead of him.

It had been a dreary 0-0 draw at a sun drenched arena. The Daily Mirror headlines noted, "Wretchedly Poor Display by Both Teams". Newcastle had clearly missed an opportunity.

For the fifth time United were spellbound by the Crystal Palace. The injured Peter McWilliam, who watched the game from the stand later said, "We could not play any sort of game. We could not show any kind of form. We were like a lot of beginners and I cannot think of any side that gave such positively wretched displays as we did".

All started again at Old Trafford, Manchester on Wednesday afternoon and, as in 1910, thousands were locked out - as many as 20,000 according to police estimates. Industries had trouble keeping employees at work, notices were sent out to one group of workers stating, "All requests for leave of absence on account of toothache, severe colds and minor ailments, funerals, picnics, church socials and the like must be handed to the Head of Dept before 10.00 am on the morning of the match!" All roads led to Manchester.

With the swirling wind persisting and making good football difficult, United began well with a shoot on sight policy. But after a quarter of an hour and against the run of play it was City who scored.

On their first attack of note Bradford's goal came in bizarre

The 1911 F.A. Cup final in progress showing a glimpse of The Crystal Palace itself in the background and several spectators seemingly uninterested in the match!

FA CUP RUN				
R1	Bury	H	W	6-1
R2	Northampton Town	H	D	1-1
	Northampton Town	H	W	1-0
R3	Hull City	H	W	3-2
R4	Derby County	H	W	4-0
SF	Chelsea	N	W	3-0
F	Bradford City	N	D	0-0
	Bradford City	N	L	0-1

FA Cup Finalists 1911

CUP GOALGETTERS
8 Shepherd, 3 Stewart, 1 Duncan, Higgins, McWilliam, Rutherford, Veitch, Willis, Wilson.

FACTS & FIGURES	P	W	D	L	F	A
Home	5	4	1	0	15	4
Away	3	1	1	1	3	1
Total	**8**	**5**	**2**	**1**	**18**	**5**

CHAIRMAN: J.W.Lunn
MANAGER: Directors' committee
TRAINER-COACH: James McPherson
CAPTAIN: Colin Veitch

FINAL

22 April 1911 at The Crystal Palace
Newcastle United 0 (0) Bradford City 0 (0)

UNITED
Lawrence
McCracken, Whitson
Veitch, Low, Willis
Rutherford, Stewart, Jobey, Higgins, Wilson

BRADFORD CITY
Mellors
Campbell, Taylor
Robinson, Gildea, McDonald
Logan, Speirs, O'Rourke, Devine, Thompson

GOALS; none

ATTENDANCE; 69,800 (£6,512)

Referee; J.H.Pearson (Crewe)
Guest of Honour; Earl of Plymouth
Cup HQ; Endsleigh Palace Hotel, Euston

Newcastle attack the Bradford goal.

An impression of the United v City contest at The Crystal Palace by artist S.J. Dadd. The central picture shows George Wilson centreing the ball into the Bradford goalmouth.

Thompson and Veitch clashed for the ball. It spun to Speirs who gave it a helping nod goalwards. O'Rourke dashed in as Jimmy Lawrence came out and the City forward did enough to distract United's 'keeper and the ball tamely bounced over his shoulder and rolled into the net. It was one of the softest Cup goals in a final on record. It turned out to be the winning goal, credited to Jimmy Speirs, Bradford's captain. The Cup jinx claimed United and once more poor Jimmy Lawrence was its individual victim.

Newcastle attempted to claw their way back and they held territorial advantage. One report noted United forced ten corners while City had only three break-aways in the match. Another observed that, "Newcastle United had chances to win the game rather handsomely". But the Tynesiders could not break down a sturdy Bradford defence. Higgins and Veitch had long range shots saved but rarely was an opportunity created close to goal.

United's cause wasn't helped when Rutherford limped to the by-line with a thigh injury and was a passenger for most of the second-half. The game ended in stalemate, United controlling midfield and City standing firm on the edge of their box.

Appropriately the new FA Cup went to its town of making. In the not too distant future that trophy - still the one played for today - would be heading for St James Park

The Crystal Palace stadium was notoriously bad for viewing the match. Surrounded by trees, many fans took up precarious vantage points in an attempt to see the action.

A wonderful panorama of the Sydenham enclosure with United and City battling it out on the field.

FINAL REPLAY
26 April 1911 at Old Trafford
Newcastle United 0 (0) Bradford City 1 (1)

UNITED:
Lawrence
McCracken, Whitson
Veitch, Low, Willis
Rutherford, Stewart, Jobey, Higgins, Wilson

BRADFORD CITY
Mellors
Campbell, Taylor
Robinson, Torrance, McDonald
Logan, Speirs, O'Rourke, Devine, Thompson.

GOALS; Speirs(15m)

ATTENDANCE; 66,646 (£4,478)

Referee; J.H.Pearson(Crewe)
Guest of Honour; Charles Crump
Cup HQ; Queen's Hotel, Southport

FA Cup Finalists 1911

The fateful moment for Jimmy Lawrence as O'Rourke and Speirs combine to grab the winning goal in the replayed tie at Old Trafford.

Bradford 'keeper Mellors watches the ball go over the bar as Newcastle forwards close in.

THE INJURIES TO McWILLIAM AND Shepherd were a shattering blow to the Magpies. Both players were badly hurt and neither recovered, although Shepherd, following a long lay off, played on but was never the same cunning and fruitful player again.

As a consequence United's cheque book came out. To replace the influential McWilliam, Newcastle lured one of his contemporaries from Scotland, Jimmy Hay, captain of Celtic and latterly Scotland. He cost £1,250 and was described as, "an outstanding capture". In an eight year career at Parkhead, Hay won a considerable array of Scottish medals in a side that ruled football north of the border. He was a naturally gifted individual and quick to support the attack.

Up front Newcastle went for Billy Hibbert, a spritely inside-left or centre-forward who arrived from First Division Bury for a tremendous sum, £1,950 which constituted a new record fee. Not of big build, Hibbert had been capped by England and possessed the instantaneous strikers' touch in and around the box.

He played alongside Sandy Higgins and James Stewart up front, until Higgins was forced onto the treatment table. Rutherford and Wilson remained on the wing while Dave Willis retained a place in the side at the expense of Veitch, now past 30 years of age.

Jimmy Hay, another prominent signing by United's management. He was captain of Celtic and Scotland.

United's expensive buys immediately slipped into the Magpies' system without a hitch. The classic possession style of football continued and by the second month of the new season Newcastle led the table. The turn of the year however, saw Newcastle go through a bad spell winning only two out of nine games played. It was a slip that proved costly in the final reckoning.

A recovery got underway with a 4-1 victory at Notts County and at the start of April, Newcastle were in second place only three points behind leaders Blackburn Rovers. But in the finale to the season, and in the very month that elsewhere in the world saw the Titanic lost in the icy Atlantic, United slipped in the race.

Draws against Bradford City and Liverpool, then a defeat by Aston Villa were expensive lapses. Another draw with rivals Rovers - when a victory was needed - crushed the club's title aspirations. They completed the 1912 season in 3rd position, five points behind and had been foiled by those careless points dropped.

One of the most extraordinary games of the period took place when United faced Manchester City during January at Hyde Road. The scoreline ended 1-1, not too remarkable perhaps, but during the course of play City missed no fewer than three penalties - a record !

Each spot-kick was an opportunity to equalise United's seventh minute goal by reserve Tommy Lowes. First award went City's way after Jobey fouled Young, and Eli Fletcher fired straight at stand-in 'keeper Sid Blake who blocked the shot and then turned aside Hood's follow up effort.

Half-way through the second-half Hudspeth up-ended Dorsett and Fletcher was again entrusted with the penalty. This time he put the kick well out of the Newcastle goalie's reach, but also two yards wide of the left upright to the delight of United's band of travelling fans.

England international Billy Hibbert cost a record £1,950 fee when he moved from Gigg Lane to Tyneside.

Penalty number three was given in the very last minute of the game, for handball. Fletcher - not surprisingly - turned down the chance of a 'hat-trick' so England international centre-forward Irvine Thornley took responsibility. Again Blake saved, but this time George Wynn dashed up and netted the rebound.

Sid Blake, from Whitley Bay, didn't get a game too often for Newcastle's first-team and had incredibly made his debut for the club at outside-left, later being converted to goalkeeper.

For once Newcastle made an early exit in the FA Cup. They fell 3-0 to eventual Second Division champions Derby County at the Baseball Ground and the 1911/12 season saw the end of Newcastle United's heyday draw near.

Edward VII had been replaced on the throne by his son, George V and conflict in Europe was to put an abrupt stop to the club's success. United's performances during these eight years demand the highest praise. Judgement over time has noted the side as one of the game's finest.

Tyneside possessed a collection of footballers second to none. They created a tremendous record that speaks for itself - Champions three times, Cup

CROWD TROUBLE

At the Sunderland v Newcastle derby match at Roker Park in September 1909 an ugly confrontation took place. A pitch invasion held up the match for 15 minutes until baton waving mounted police cleared the playing area. One police-horse was stabbed at the Fulwell goal. The game ended 2-0 in United's favour and the local Chief Constable offered £5 reward to anyone giving information which led to the detection of the person who carried out the knifing.

Crowd trouble at local derby games was not unheard of during Edwardian times. In the Cup-tie of the previous season many spectators and police were injured as free fights raged in the ground and surrounding streets.

finalists on five occasions, winners once and also reaching another semi-final. They were only out of the top four in Division One on a single occasion.

Football critics and historians of the game noted them with superlatives. Tony Pawson in the Official Centenary History of the FA Cup wrote that the side had, "a rhythmic beauty in their forward moves". Eminent manager Herbert Chapman, then just starting on his career and talking about moving to London with Arsenal was quoted, "I would like to build a Newcastle United there". The respected Ivan Sharpe observed, "Each man was an artist".

Maybe Colin Veitch's motto sums up the side's attitude to the game they played so well. "Take the offensive. Take the initiative", he said repeatedly. It worked for most of the time hardly ever allowing the opposition to dominate.

Peter McWilliam said long after he retired, "The Newcastle team of the 1900's would give any modern side a two goal start and beat them, and further more beat them at a trot". Truly it was a magnificent line-up - the best seen in black'n'white colours. And all in spite of the odd and unique influence of the Crystal Palace.

Goalkeeper Sid Blake, reserve to Lawrence, but who had a remarkable day against Manchester City and faced three penalty kicks.

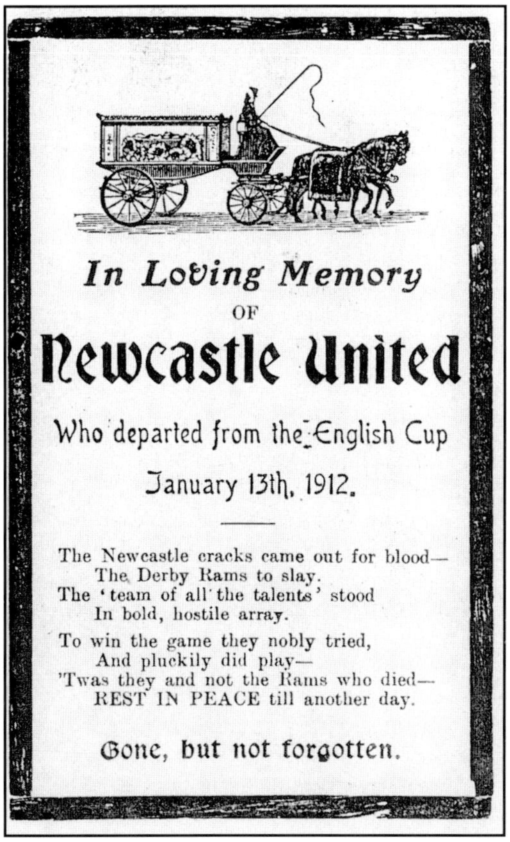

In Loving Memory
OF
Newcastle United
Who departed from the English Cup
January 13th, 1912.

The Newcastle cracks came out for blood—
The Derby Rams to slay.
The 'team of all the talents' stood
In bold, hostile array.

To win the game they nobly tried,
And pluckily did play—
'Twas they and not the Rams who died—
REST IN PEACE till another day.

Gone, but not forgotten.

Funeral card, commonly issued at the time, recording the Magpies' exit from the F.A. Cup at the hands of Derby County.

Centenary Profile 5

The Elegant Playmaker

"He is one of the finest half-backs of all time and was a pleasure to play with"

Colin Veitch, 1931

NEWCASTLE'S HALCYON DAYS AT THE BEGINNING of this century saw many outstanding players at St James Park. A decade of international talent that was a venerable who's who of the game at that time. One player who stood out in the mass of talent was Peter McWilliam, known as 'Peter the Great' throughout football.

At inside-forward or half-back, few were better at the midfield game. McWilliam rivalled Ernest Needham and Hugh Wilson as the best in the business before the First World War, possessing the mark of a master and a famous body wriggle to go with it that deceived and annoyed opponents.

Like so many United players of that era, Peter was a Scot, a Highlander, born in Inverness in 1879. He started his football career with local side Heatherley before joining Inverness Thistle. He was a pal of Andy McCombie, later a distinguished United full-back, but then with arch rivals Sunderland. A former Thistle player too, Andy invited McWilliam down to the north-east with the intention of signing for Sunderland but en route he was nobbled by United directors who heard a whisper of the transfer.

It was said that United officials hauled Peter off the train and whisked him away to St James Park where he quickly became a Newcastle player to the disgust of Wearside's men. But for the fact that trains to Sunderland have to pass through Newcastle Central Station, McWilliam would never have ended up in a black'n'white jersey.

Nicknamed 'Pat', the 22 year-old signed for the Magpies in 1902 and it proved to be a brilliant scoop, but not before an uneasy start to his professional career. Peter went straight into the league side making his first appearance during October at right-half against Middlesbrough, the team he was to later manage. He replaced the injured Alec Gardner but came a cropper against Joe Cassidy who, as McWilliam noted, "had me chasing shadows". He was to say of his debut, "It was torture".

Peter was dropped for the next game and was harshly criticised. After the roasting he received against 'Boro, McWilliam was all set to return to Inverness and pack up the game. But the skilful and elegant Scot was soon to return, with a little help from his colleagues.

McWilliam was not a big man, only 5'9" tall, but he showed up well in Newcastle's reserves and became respected by his fellow team-mates. United went through a disturbing spell which resulted in the selection committee inviting senior professionals to pick the side. Without hesitation they plunged Peter McWilliam back into the team and United never looked back. He was a regular from the opening weeks of season 1904/05 mainly operating on the left side of midfield.

McWilliam possessed an incessant urge to go forward, always on the look-out for openings. A typical Scots ball-player, his passes were usually crisp, precise and along the ground in the style of Newcastle at that time. McWilliam always had a little time to dwell on the ball which players of the modern game certainly do not have. In Edwardian football there wasn't the danger of being overrun in midfield and there were few tackles from behind. The game was slower with skilled players, like McWilliam, allowed time to manipulate the ball.

He rarely got involved in midfield scraps and infrequently tackled. Peter relied on colleagues feeding the ball to him or by gaining possession by clever positioning and timely interventions. In essence he was United's playmaker. He was also a great humourist and compulsive leg-puller too. Rarely downcast and always relaxed, it showed in his football.

Peter became one of the key figures in United's rise to the very top in the next decade. Along with another Scot, Jimmy Howie, and together with Veitch and Gardner, United's midfield had quality the envy of all their rivals. McWilliam was a Championship winner on three occasions and took part in four Cup finals, helping to win the trophy in 1910. It would have been five too, but injury put him out of the 1911 final.

That injury while playing for Scotland was a nasty one. Peter never recovered from damaged lateral ligaments and he was left with a dodgy knee. His marvellous playing career was over. Peter won eight Scottish caps all told in an era when international honours were few and far between. He also captained his country, ironically in his fateful last match.

Peter McWilliam

McWILLIAM'S PLAYING RECORD

	League		FA Cup		Total	
	App	Gls	App	Gls	App	Gls
1902-03	7	0	0	0	7	0
1903-04	5	0	0	0	5	0
1904-05	26	4	8	0	34	4
1905-06	30	2	8	0	38	2
1906-07	32	2	1	0	33	2
1907-08	31	1	5	0	36	1
1908-09	27	0	7	0	34	0
1909-10	23	2	8	0	31	2
1910-11	18	0	4	1	22	1
	199	**11**	**41**	**1**	**240**	**12**

McWilliam clocked up 240 appearances for United, he didn't score many goals - only 12 - but the number he created for his colleagues was phenomenal. Colin Veitch, room-mate to Peter for almost ten years noted, "He is one of the finest half-backs of all time and a pleasure to play football with".

From a glittering playing career McWilliam went straight into a manager's role and became an outstanding figure for the next 30 years. Somewhat a rarity in football to find a great player becoming a great boss, Peter was one of the pioneer managers of football in an era when directors' committees ran the game from both administration and playing aspects.

He was one of a breed of manager who have now disappeared from football - a father figure, highly respected and authoritarian in style. He never wore a track-suit and rarely visited the training ground. McWilliam was a soberly dressed, waistcoat boss. He was addressed as 'Mr McWilliam' or 'Sir'. Although as a player he had a relaxed attitude, as a manager he was a nervous character when it came to match-days. So much so he hardly could stand to watch his team.

But McWilliam made a quick transition to boss. His football philosophy was a simple one. He let the players play the football and all he would do was acquire talented individuals. He was an exceptional judge of a player.

Peter was in charge of Tottenham Hotspur in two spells. Firstly in December 1912 he took over at White Hart Lane as the Londoners' first boss and saw Spurs relegated to the Second Division before war broke out. But Peter had the Midas touch and by 1920 had forged a classic side in North London. They won Division Two's title with a record haul of 70 points, then the FA Cup in 1921. McWilliam became the first man to manage a Cup winning side after having played for one. And that was not all. Within twelve months he came within a whisker of the First Division Championship too, finishing as Runners-up.

The Scot remained in London until 1927 when he was offered what then was described as, "a cabinet minister's salary" to join Middlesbrough. His wage packet was talked about the nation over, £1,500 a year, almost double what he earned at Spurs.

Despite much publicity at his appointment, McWilliam never quite won over 'Boro's fans. He had replaced the most popular Herbert Bamlett and joined the club as they were promoted in 1927. Immediately though they slipped back into Division Two but as at Tottenham, McWilliam took his side quickly to promotion.

The Scot remained on Tees-side until March 1934 when he was sacked after disagreements. McWilliam returned south, firstly to Arsenal as chief scout, then back to White Hart Lane in 1938 when they again needed his guidance in a promotion chase.

Peter McWilliam pictured in the Scotland team to face England in 1906 along with United colleagues Andy Aitken and Jimmy Howie. Left to right, players only. Back: McWilliam, McCleod, McBride, Dunlop, Livingstone, Aitken. Front: Howie, Menzies, Raisbeck, Stewart, Smith.

Peter stayed with Tottenham during the war years and was awarded the Football League's Long Service Medal. He had groomed another fine Spurs line-up by the time he left as peace was restored. Sure enough Tottenham's classic 1950 side eventually materialised.

He then retired and settled down in Redcar - his wife's home town - where he lived until his death in October 1951. Peter McWilliam is remembered with much credit in the corridors of both Tottenham and Newcastle United and he did much to create the tradition both famous clubs now hold.

The Offside King

"A great theorist and a master of tactics - a player who did nothing without thinking"
Peter McWilliam, c1925

BILL McCRACKEN WAS A COLOURFUL CHARACTER, one of the most famous, yet most controversial personalities the game has seen. From Belfast, he angered fans up and down the country like no other has since, only at St James Park was he welcome. Having a superb tactical mind, Bill's perfection of the offside-trap caused blood to boil wherever he played, but he took the taunts and much physical abuse from spectators in his stride, and always with a smile.

McCracken was a typical Irishman in many ways. He possessed a cunning grin, sparkling Irish eyes, was tall and handsome with dark curly hair and of course, as colleague Peter McWilliam said, "was overflowing with Irish wit and was the life and soul of the party".

Born in January 1883, Bill joined the local Belfast Distillery club as a part-timer being employed as an apprentice in the building trade. On the football field, McCracken was soon among the honours. He won Irish league and full caps when only 19 and twice reached the Irish Cup final. English and Scottish clubs took notice and his fast developing talent held the attention of Everton, both Celtic and Rangers, as well as Sunderland and Newcastle United. They chased the right-back for several months with United eventually securing his signature after a somewhat illegal approach from Colin Veitch outside the dressing-room door following an international fixture.

Bill signed for United later in the season, in May 1904 for a £50 fee. It was a controversial transfer as the FA immediately announced that an inquiry would take place to investigate whether McCracken had received illegal payments as part of Newcastle's offer. It was a pattern of notoriety that would follow the defender on his near 20 year career at St James Park. The FA committee as it happened cleared both club and player.

Twenty-one years old, McCracken took the full-back's shirt and easily fitted into United's star-studded formation. Unluckily though he was soon on the sidelines with injury and during his early years at Gallowgate United chose the two defensive places from three international backs...McCracken, Andy McCombie and Jack Carr.

McCracken played his part in three League Championship victories during the Edwardian era and he was also a member of a trio of Cup final teams, picking up a winners medal, like McWilliam in 1910. His organisation at the back proved in many ways the important factor in United's success. With Colin Veitch, these two United masters created an offside-trap which caught opposing forwards almost at will. One of football's most noted judges, Charlie Buchan, said of McCracken, "He brought the system almost to perfection".

Notts County had set the offside game on its course during the early years of the century when Herbert Morley and Jimmy Montgomery started to spring the trap. According to 'keeper Jimmy Lawrence it was during a post- mortem in a railway carriage that McCracken, along with Veitch and McWilliam, United's other two noted tacticians, first evolved the offside system. This after having suffered a dose of it at Meadow Lane.

Veitch recorded, "We had many misgivings in putting the offside-trap into operation but were astounded how easily the forwards fell into it". Bill made a mockery of the law. He had an uncanny anticipation of attacking moves and was ever alert to spring forward arm in the air, yelling, "Offside ! Offside !". Forwards had no answer, they were left stranded as the referee's whistle blew.

Opposing fans had no answer either. Crowds did everything but pull down the stands and throw bits at United's full-back. At Villa Park he was hit on the head by a pipe and had onions thrown his way. At Stamford Bridge his shirt was ripped and he was spat on. At Roker Park he was peppered with oranges, lemons and bananas, while he always collected a fist full of coins thrown in his direction. The attention he received even went to the extent of making a silent celluloid film of his offside-trap. Critics described his performance as, "a delightful surprise performance"! Bill though thrived on the attention. The more the crowd baited him, the more he seemed to annoy them. He would give the howling fans on the terraces an impertinent smile as he went about his disruptive task raising passions even higher. McCracken was an infuriating man to be up against, both as a player and spectator. He once said after a torrent of fans' abuse came his way, "If they knew more about football than we do, there would be 50,000 players and 22 spectators!"

The offside-law was eventually changed in 1925....to its modern format....this after football had become almost unbearable with many clubs copying McCracken's defensive ploy. It was a change thanks largely to Bill. He however said later, "I didn't really change anything. I played the game fair within the existing laws".

Because McCracken was such an expert at the offside game,

Bill McCracken

McCRACKEN'S PLAYING RECORD	League		FA Cup		Total	
	App	Gls	App	Gls	App	Gls
1904-05	13	0	0	0	13	0
1905-06	20	0	0	0	20	0
1906-07	22	1	1	0	23	1
1907-08	21	0	6	0	27	0
1908-09	30	1	6	0	36	1
1909-10	29	0	7	1	36	1
1910-11	30	1	8	0	38	1
1911-12	34	3	1	0	35	3
1912-13	27	0	8	0	35	0
1913-14	20	0	1	0	21	0
1914-15	29	0	7	1	36	1
1919-20	33	0	2	0	35	0
1920-21	30	0	4	0	34	0
1921-22	26	0	2	0	28	0
1922-23	13	0	2	0	15	0
1918-19 (War time)					11	0
	377	**6**	**55**	**2**	**443**	**8**

McCracken tosses a coin with Sunderland captain Charlie Thomson before a St. James Park derby meeting.

many folk lost sight of his brilliance as a defender. Always beaming with tremendous enthusiasm and enjoyment of the game he played, his speed of recovery was excellent and he could use the ball short or long, and kick with either foot. His partner for so long, Colin Veitch, said he was, "the greatest back ever to be associated with the United team. I rate him second to none".

Bill was a born rebel and often found himself in trouble of one sort or another. Even at 16 years of age he was attacked by rival supporters for punching an opponent. He had many differences with referees too. Once after being sent-off for questioning a decision he wrote a four page letter to the official strongly noting a few points about the game of football. Instead of receiving a seven day suspension McCracken was handed a four week ban !

In spite of this somewhat hostile manner, he had two spells as United's skipper in the years immediately before and after World War One. McCracken was a first class motivator, shouting encouragement in a rich Irish accent, so broad at times that his colleagues found it difficult to understand. However, a roar from McCracken on the field meant the same in any language.

He was also at loggerheads for many years with the Irish Football Association. A regular for his country since 1902, Bill would have won a pile of caps but for a personal crusade over payments. During the 1907/08 season he was incensed that while England players, with his Newcastle team- mates, like Jock Rutherford, received £10 a match, Irish caps were worth only £2 2 shillings. He demanded more and when it was not forthcoming quit the party on the eve of a game with England and was banned until differences were patched up much later in 1919. All told McCracken won 17 caps. He also skippered Ireland and was in their side when over 40 years of age in 1923.

Bill's last season in a United shirt was also in that year when he became one of the oldest players to appear for the Magpies. In fact, together with Billy Hampson, who was also over 40, they provided the First Division with the oldest set of full-backs to take the field. McCracken clocked up 432 League and Cup games for United scoring eight goals and holds record service as a player, on United's books for almost two decades. Many critics reckoned Newcastle made a big mistake allowing Bill to depart for Hull City as manager in February 1923. Most viewed that a coaching position should have been found for his undoubted talent.

McCracken's five year appointment at Hull proved to be of mixed fortune. City were a mediocre Second Division outfit and after a few inevitable disagreements with the club's directors, he built a useful side that challenged for promotion in 1926/27. His team included a couple of promising youngsters, both recommended to St James Park, Sammy Weaver and Ron Starling. Both joined United and also later played for England. Bill, not surprisingly, was very much a tactical manager with a keen and penetrating mind.

McCracken took his Anlaby Road side to within a whisker of Wembley, Hull reaching the semi-final in 1930, on the way knocking out his former club. The Tigers play included a previous favourite tactic of his - yes, the offside trap re-emerged, now based on the new laws. Failure to win promotion though, and eventual relegation cost McCracken his job. He resigned in May 1931.

After a brief spell back in the north-east at Gateshead, he was appointed manager of Millwall in May 1933. But at the Den he didn't have a rewarding time. Bill could never get Millwall going and after more rows with directors and another relegation season he departed. McCracken then joined Aldershot in February 1937, another struggling side, this just after the club had to seek re-election to the Football League.

Bill steadily rebuilt the team without cash resources before hostilities disrupted his plans. He remained in charge throughout the Second World War and found much of the cream of Britain's footballers under his control. As guest players on army service, a lot of star names turned up at the Recreation Ground when billeted at the vast Aldershot garrison. McCracken's team did well in wartime football, but as soon as normal soccer resumed league problems followed. In November 1949 he was dismissed from the struggling Surrey club. As ever Bill spoke his mind, he remarked, "The public want a scapegoat, so here I am"!

That was his last experience in the manager's hot-seat. Afterwards McCracken became a talent scout and a very respected one. He was on United's pay-roll again for a few years during the fifties, one of the names he advised the black'n'whites to sign was George Eastham. But it was with Watford when he discovered his greatest talent, a young goalkeeper by the name of Pat Jennings.

Bill was presented with a special medal by the Football Association for long service to the game in 1978 when he was still scouting with vitality into his nineties. He died in a Hull hospital during January 1979, only nine days before his 96th year.
Bill McCracken achieved one of the longest active careers in football....over 80 years in the game.

6 WAR & GLORY

1912-1924

• EDWARDIAN DECLINE • TYNE-WEAR DUEL • CLOUDS OF WAR • MAGPIES IN STORAGE • TITLE CHALLENGE • WEMBLEY MAGIC •

"The feeling as we made our way up to Wembley Stadium was one I never forgot"

Stan Seymour

NEWCASTLE UNITED'S ASCENDANCY **ended as the First World War approached. Many of their Edwardian heroes were fast nearing the veteran stage. The club had to rebuild around the experienced talents of men like McCracken, Rutherford, Hibbert, Lawrence and new skipper Jimmy Hay. After such a pulsating and rewarding period anything that followed was bound to be secondary in contrast.**

Season 1912/13 was United's worst since 1902. They finished the season in 14th position and even briefly flirted with relegation. No single player reached double figures in the goal charts and it was this lack of scoring power that caused United's decline more than anything else. A replacement for Albert Shepherd had not been found and even when he was far from being fit, there was much petitioning for his return.

United had tried to solve the problem by making three big signings in the forward line. John McDonald came from Liverpool, Scottish international, John McTavish arrived from Spurs, but was to leave quickly, while Jack Peart headed north from Stoke. No signing proved a success though. McDonald even failed to turn up for a fixture at Derby during March and was fined a week's wages. Another new name to break into the first-team was Bob Hewison, a local wing-half from Backworth. He graduated from the reserves and went on to have a long career in the game as player and manager.

Even with a lack of scoring prowess in front of goal, Newcastle did begin the season well, going 2nd in the table by November with a 6-0 victory over Everton, a day when the Magpies' forwards for once clicked. It was the FA Cup however, that caused United's league form to dip alarmingly from January to the end of the season. Newcastle began an exciting Cup run with the visit of Bradford City, a much disrupted fixture because of the weather.

Several blizzards swept over Gallowgate during the first-half and the game was abandoned at the interval with the black'n'whites 1-0 ahead. It was a shocking afternoon and the hardy 16,000 crowd, mainly huddled into the corners of the ground were quite happy to rush home to their fireside armchairs. The scheduled replay was postponed because of a waterlogged pitch and at the third attempt, the tie went ahead, but not without its problems. Fog, wind and mud were the conditions for the players to overcome this time, and only 11,953 turned up to witness what was a lottery of a match settled by a fluke goal. United winger George Wilson tried a long range shot that was heading wide, but which caught a gust of wind and altered course viciously, ending in the net. City did anything but enjoy their visit to Tyneside that winter.

Hull City presented United with their next challenge in Round Two. The Magpies completed the task adequately with a 3-0 win after a goalless draw on Humberside in front of a record crowd. Goalkeeper Jimmy Lawrence was the saviour in the next tie at Anfield, home of Liverpool, opposition that had already taken three points off United in league action. United's Scottish international 'keeper saved a penalty which enabled the Geordies to hold on to the equalising goal scored by the now recalled Shepherd. Almost 40,000 saw the replay, a close game decided by a first-half Frank Hudspeth spot-kick. That victory took Newcastle into a series of memorable battles with Sunderland.

The Wearsiders were to become League Champions that season, and went very close to lifting the much hankered after double. But in the first game at Roker Park, United were slightly the better side playing to a tight defensive system. United forced a 0-0 draw in front of a 28,720 crowd, the Roker ground still with a much reduced capacity than St James Park. To increase revenue Sunderland had doubled the admission charges for that game.

Newcastle fans stream out of St. James Park onto Barrack Road and Strawberry Place. Many rush to the awaiting tramcar.

The replay attracted almost 57,000, with another 10,000 reported as locked out. They saw an absorbing contest, a see-saw match that went into extra-time. Newcastle took the lead when McTavish found the net in a goalmouth scramble, then the Roker side hit a couple of goals and were 2-1 in front with time fast running out. Colin Veitch though, netted a dramatic equaliser in the last minute. His 25 yard low shot skidded into the net off defender Gladwin as he miskicked a clearance.

The third tussle, on a Monday, was again at Gallowgate after Frank Watt and Bob Kyle of Sunderland tossed a coin for choice of venue. Once more the rivals lined up before a packed audience and this time the game went Sunderland's way. With snow falling, a heavy pitch suited the Roker eleven who showed why they were to win the title. They cruised home to a 3-0 victory, although they had the luck of playing with the weather behind them and grabbing two goals in the first-half, then on the turnaround seeing the snow and wind subside to their distinct advantage. United not only went out of the FA Cup, but they also faced the wrath of the Football League. Newcastle had rested senior players before this tie, for a game with Blackburn Rovers. The League inflicted a £150 fine on the club.

United ended the season with a short tour of Denmark, the club's favourite destination in those days. However, Newcastle's officials had to be very wary of how it was organised as twelve months earlier they had paid their staff an extra £1 per day on a similar tour and the Football Association carpeted the club for breaking the maximum wage rule. Another hefty £100 fine followed.

Newcastle always used continental tours as a means of testing youngsters and also looking for new faces, even European stars, almost 25 years before United first fielded a foreigner. They brought two Danish players back from Copenhagen for trials, Anton Olsen and Nils Middleboe. Both never showed up too well at St James Park, but Middleboe, 6'2", a past Olympic Games finalist, went on to impress Chelsea and later captained the Stamford Bridge club.

A slight recovery was in store for United's fans in the following season, but not until relegation fears had been averted. Again they struggled in attack. Opportunism in front of goal was severely lacking until Shepherd - still only a shade of the player he was - was again recalled in January. The former England leader fired home ten goals in 14 games and saved the Magpies from remaining in a relegation spot. United recovered from being in 19th position to end in mid-table with a defensive record as good as the attack was poor.

Injuries didn't help either with McCracken, Lawrence and Higgins out for periods, as were Veitch and ex Seaton Delaval winger, Tommy Goodwill. The balance of the team was constantly disrupted. Goodwill, up to his injury, displayed many a fine game on the right flank in his first season.

Injury problems also had a large bearing on the club's exit from the FA Cup. Sheffield United arrived on Tyneside and scored three goals in only four minutes to destroy Newcastle's Cup aspirations. The visitor's winger, Jimmy Revill - something of a speed merchant - gave McCracken a rare hiding, revenge for pre-match remarks made by United's full-back as to the quality of the Blades' line-up. At one stage the black'n'whites were down to eight fit men, a record for the club, including no recognised goalkeeper. Off injured went reserve custodian Jim Wilson(collision), Tom Hall(knee) and Tommy Goodwill(concussion). Hall was a new £425 centre-forward signing from Sunderland's Championship winning squad. The Yorkshire side ran up a 5-0 scoreline in a second-half walk-over. It was a chance result, yet the club's biggest FA Cup defeat at St James Park. All in all it had been a disastrous weekend for United. A fire at the side's

John McDonald, purchased from Liverpool.

The much travelled Jack Peart.

Bill Mellor, arrived as reserve to the ageing Lawrence.

Cup HQ - The Avenue Hotel in Whitley Bay - foiled the team's preparations.

While the Magpies' Cup dreams disappeared, Tyneside could well have hosted the FA Cup final itself that year, this before Wembley Stadium had even been constructed. The Football Association wrote to the club asking about the suitability of using St James Park for the 1914 final, a new venue being required that year. Newcastle's directors though, could foresee problems and replied sympathetically to the FA's dilemma but noted, "as no extensions could be made to our ground, it would be inadequate to accommodate a Final Tie crowd". The final was switched from The Crystal Palace, to firstly Old Trafford, then Stamford Bridge.

Apart from Goodwill and Hall, other notable additions to the squad were Angus Douglas, another Scottish international forward who joined the Magpies for £1,100 with a big reputation from Chelsea. United paid £600 for John King, who was equally respected in Partick Thistle's attack, while £1,300 was spent on right-winger, Ed Cooper of Second Division Glossop. All arrived for, what were then, considerable fees, but all failed to make an impact, although Douglas was compared unfairly to the great Jackie Rutherford, who had moved to Arsenal. Another established international departed in 1913 too. Jimmy Stewart crossed the border to end his career with Glasgow Rangers.

Newcastle also purchased a new right-back, Billy Hampson from Norwich City for £1,250. He was to be groomed into a fine, reliable defender. Hampson's colleague at Southern League Norwich, Bill Mellor headed north as well, to become understudy to Jimmy Lawrence. Newcastle's directors were also interested in Sunderland's Harry Low and made a monster bid of £1,750, but saw the transfer blocked, while an 18 year-old goalkeeper by the name of Elisha Scott appeared at St James Park for Liverpool and made an immediate impression on United officials. They quickly offered a fee of £1,000 for the untried youngster. Again the bid was turned down. Scott went on to become a legend.

The 1913/14 season also saw the clouds of war start to affect life at St James Park. Firstly, United cancelled a planned tour to Denmark, France and Germany, then during the spring the club's training methods began to include military style exercises controlled by the Company Sergeant Major from the local garrison on Barrack Road. The long hot summer of 1914 saw war approach quickly and by August and the start of the new season was underway, Newcastle's stands, gym and dressing-rooms had been commandeered by the government for military use. Over 200 army servicemen from the Royal Field Artillery were now in occupation at St James Park, with at times over 150 horses lodged beneath the stand too in makeshift stables! While the club received compensation - a sum of £44 15s 0d was banked from the Ministry of Defence for rent - there was a real threat to the Magpies commencing the season at all, players and spectators being forbidden to enter the stadium right up to the season's big kick-off. Arrangements were put in place, but frequently games were delayed because of army manoeuvres as the new fixture card began.

The 1914/15 campaign was the strangest of seasons with the entire programme being played as the country became more involved in an horrific war. Football wasn't really on people's minds when the opening game against West Bromwich Albion took place. War had been declared against the Kaiser a month or so earlier following the assassination of Archduke Ferdinand in Sarajevo and this overshadowed everything.

The government of the day, led by Liberal, Asquith, decided that soccer should continue as normal and would in fact provide much needed relaxation for the public who were expected to work extremely long hours for the war effort. It also gave a break to servicemen on leave. The country expected that the war would be over within a few months, but it was to last more than four years and by the time peace was restored over 850,000 British servicemen would have been killed in the trenches of the continent; at Somme, at Ypres and at Passchendale.

At that opening game with Albion, which ended in a 2-1 defeat, a large proportion of the 15,000 crowd were from Lord Kitchener's army, clad in khaki uniforms, allowed into the ground at half-price. As the season progressed, and as war in Europe deteriorated, it was clear that normal football was unable to carry on for long. The club donated cash to the war effort including amounts to supply Indian troops with much need sweaters, while players agreed to take a cut in wages and to subscribe to war funds too. United's stars also continued with further military training after an edict by the authorities. Instead of the normal

Stan Dixon spent almost a decade at St. James Park and was a reserve for England.

trackwork and ball practice on the St James Park turf, they now lined up with rifles at ranges set up in the Gallowgate goalmouth. United had to pay Boer War veteran, Julius Askelund instructor's fees too. The first shooting competition was won by Tony Whitson(43 points), followed closely by Bill McCracken(42 points).

War Minister, Lord Kitchener's call for men at arms received tremendous local response, including several Newcastle United players. Young professionals, Stan Hardy signed up and centre-forward George Pyke left for the Sportsman's Battalion, while George Rivers joined the Army Service Corps. Stan Dixon and Tom Curry entered the Engineer's Corps and all told out of United's playing strength of 40, a total of 27 players joined the forces in the coming months.

The Lord Mayor held rallies at St James Park, recruiting both men and cash for the war effort. One such event coincided with the FA Cup visit of West Ham United during January when collections were made for the Belgian and Serbian Relief Funds. St James Park was also loaned to Tyneside's Scottish Battalion for drill purposes and many of United's fixtures were watched by army casualties from the converted Rutherford College, a makeshift hospital on Bath Lane. They used the directors' enclosure and Centre Pavilion seating areas. These brave young men of Tyneside, many victims of the battle of Mons, saw some thrilling and entertaining games in spite of the gloom of war, especially during a FA Cup run that United embarked on in the New Year.

Two exciting games with then non-league West Ham United took place in which nine goals were scored. The black'n'whites drew 2-2 in London after being ahead 2-0 at the break with Goodwill scoring twice. It was a game that saw four balls used as, one after the other, United kicked them out of the ground when they had their backs to the wall. A midweek ban on football saw the replay take place the following Saturday and on Tyneside new star centre-forward, Bob Pailor, signed from West Bromwich Albion for £1,550, grabbed a brace in a 3-2 victory. Pailor was to be the latest replacement for Albert Shepherd, now departed to Bradford City. Again however, the new man was rarely to wear the centre-forward's jersey with distinction.

Victory over the Cockneys took United to a tie with another Southern League club, Swansea Town. The Welsh side upset the Magpies at St James Park by holding United to a 1-1 draw, and only a Bill McCracken spot-kick saved Newcastle's hide. Goals by Pailor and King though, gave United a 2-0 victory in South Wales and Sheffield Wednesday provided Newcastle with another tough meeting in Round Three.

At Hillsborough, Wednesday battled hard, but so did the black'n'whites, and United returned north with a fine 2-1 win. The prize was a meeting with Chelsea in the quarter-final, but the Pensioners held ground advantage. United again did well away from Tyneside, securing a 1-1 draw after extra-time. In front of a crowd of 58,000, Goodwill scored a deserved equaliser with a long range effort. The Londoners, however, travelled to Gallowgate and toppled Newcastle in front of another big crowd, this time 49,827, again after extra-time. Newcastle fell by a single goal netted by outside-right Ford and threw the game away with poor marksmanship in front of goal. Chelsea marched on to the final that year.

Other notable fixtures that troubled season were a memorable double feast with Sunderland on Christmas Day and Boxing Day. At St James Park, the Wearsiders won 5-2 on an icy pitch, Sunderland also registering United's two efforts through own-goals, while Hudspeth missed a penalty for the Magpies. In the return game it was United's turn in an equally absorbing encounter. They won 4-2 at Roker Park, Billy Hibbert netting twice and 'keeper Mellor saving a spot-kick. Newcastle ended with ten men when Sandy Higgins was led away injured. Former England man, Hibbert, had a good season at inside or centre-forward and ended top scorer with 16 goals.

Another remarkable game took place in this strange season when United met Spurs at White Hart Lane during April. Newcastle officials were thrown into panic when goalkeeper Bill Mellor injured himself saving a shot in the pre-match kick-about. His badly strained back meant he could not take part in the fixture, due to start in only a few minutes. United's management threw their arms up in disbelief - no goalkeeper, and of course no substitute either. Luckily the game hadn't started so travelling reserve Jock Finlay was quickly called into action. But what to do with a goalkeeper was the question? Inside-forward Jock King volunteered to take the 'keeper's jersey, even though he was only 5'7" tall. United started the match with ten men and King played the game of his life in his unaccustomed role as United drew 0-0. It was indeed an odd year for football.

With the season over - United ended in 15th place - football was suspended and players' contracts were cancelled en bloc. Apart from the morals of playing sport for money when so much suffering was unfolding on the fields of France, football could never have survived financially. Revenue fell dramatically at St James Park, from £16,000 in 1913/14 to almost £11,000 in 1914/15. Newcastle United officially all but closed down on 22nd July 1915 - the club in effect being mothballed for the remainder of the war. The St James Park stands and dressing-rooms were insured for £6,500 in case of damage by air raids, but the north east was infrequently affected directly by the war. Rarely did Germany attack the region. However in 1915 a

ST JAMES PARK PURCHASE

Discussion had taken place in October 1921 between the Freemen of the City and United's officials over the possible purchase of St James Park. The club's minutes record that a letter had been received from the Steward's Committee which noted, "they would have no objection whatever to a clause being inserted in the new Bill to Parliament regarding the purchasing of St James Park". The correspondence also made the remark, "The Freemen would sell if a price could be arranged". In time, though, no adjustment to the statute laws was passed allowing the ground to be sold, and St James Park remained outside the club's ownership and ultimate control.

Zeppelin raid did hit the coast but United's arena was not damaged.

St James Park was used continually during the First World War as a military base and while the club received income from the government, much damage was done to both the playing surface and stands. By the time football of sorts returned to Gallowgate, there was a huge repair job to be carried out.

Provincial competitions took the place of Championship and FA Cup matches, but north eastern clubs had little part in this reduced scale of football, mainly because of the geographical difficulties in travelling. United had applied to join the Lancashire Regional League and were admitted, but the club's board withdrew because of travel restrictions. Newcastle United, along with Sunderland and Middlesbrough virtually closed down completely. A local competition did see football continue - The Newcastle District United League - but it was a long way from Division One and opposition like Arsenal, Villa and Everton. Now a scratch United XI played the likes of Aviation Athletic, Brighton West End and Pandon Temperance, and not at St James Park either.

Colin Veitch pictured in uniform during the First World War.

Many United men followed earlier players into the army, while several were engaged on essential work. Frank Hudspeth and Jock Finlay worked in Tyneside's many munition factories and several players ended down the area's coal pits. Many also guested for other clubs while helping the war effort away from the north east. Bill McCracken and Wilf Low turned out for Fulham, Billy Hibbert for Arsenal and Leeds City. The Yorkshire club picked several other United stars too; Hudspeth, Hall, Booth and Hampson, who, along with Hibbert, won a wartime championship medal in 1918.

Several Newcastle players saw action in World War One. Curtis Booth and Alex Higgins served with the Durham Light Infantry, Bill Bradley was in the Tank Corps, while George Wilson entered the Royal Navy. Sadly though, some were not to return. Private Tommy Goodwill was killed in action in 1916 serving with the Northumberland Fusiliers, the only senior player to lose his life. Young reserves, Private George Rivers, Corporal Tom Cairns and Bombardier Richard McGough were all killed too, as were Corporal Dan Dunglinson and Tom Hughes. Angus Douglas was another fatality. He had returned to St James Park following war service to resurrect his career, but was soon to fall ill, a victim of a national flu epidemic. Tragically he died in South Gosforth a month after war ended. Past crowd favourite, Bobby Templeton was another to pass on in this way, as was reserve centre-forward Stan Allen, who died at his home in Wallsend aged 31.

ADMISSION 1919/20

MATCH-DAY

Ground			
	Soldiers, sailors, boys		5d
	Others	1s	0d
Stands	West A & B sections	1s	9d
	West C section	2s	6d
	Centre Pavilion	4s	0d
SEASON TICKETS			
	Ground	25s	0d
	West Stand C	45s	0d
	Centre Pavilion	65s	0d

Two other former Newcastle players lost their lives also. John Fleming, at St James Park from 1911 to 1913 and later at Tottenham, rose to the rank of Major in the East Yorks Regiment but was killed in 1917. Tom Rowlandson, a famed amateur international goalkeeper with Corinthians, fell in battle a year earlier. With the Magpies for two years, he won the Military Cross serving as a Captain, also in the Yorkshire Regiment.

Some returned home disabled and maimed for life. Stan Hardy, a young inside-forward and one of the first United players to sign up, was severely gassed in the trenches when serving in the Machine Gun Corps. He was forced to give up playing and later became Nottingham Forest secretary.

A visit by King George V and Queen Mary to St James Park in 1917 was a sign that war was coming to an end. The monarch was at the ground for the investiture of decorations and medals and over 40,000 attended. World War One ended early into November 1918 and with the signing of the Armistice, it was all systems go to get football back to normal. Being too late for a normal season's calendar to start, a series of Victory Leagues commenced in January 1919. The north east saw all senior clubs back in action, including South Shields, Ashington and Durham City who would all enter the Football League in the immediate post-war years. Middlesbrough won the title of best local side with United finishing in 5th place, although the Magpies hardly fielded a recognisable team with few regulars back to the fold.

Newcastle went ahead with an advertisement campaign to rally Tyneside's public back to football. It included boardmen parading the streets of Newcastle and advertising on the sides of city tramcars. Crowds were healthy with 18,000 turning up for the first fixture at St James Park against Hartlepool United and 40,000 for the 1-1 draw with South Shields.

Ex players started to trickle back to the area and regulars from 1915 to line up for United as a new era commenced were Jimmy Lawrence, entering his 12th season as the side's 'keeper, Wilf Low, Bill

United's professional staff as war approached in 1914. Included on the group are three of the club's players who lost their lives in the hostilities. Goodwill (back row, far left), Dunglinson (back row, far right) and Hughes (second back row, 5th from left).

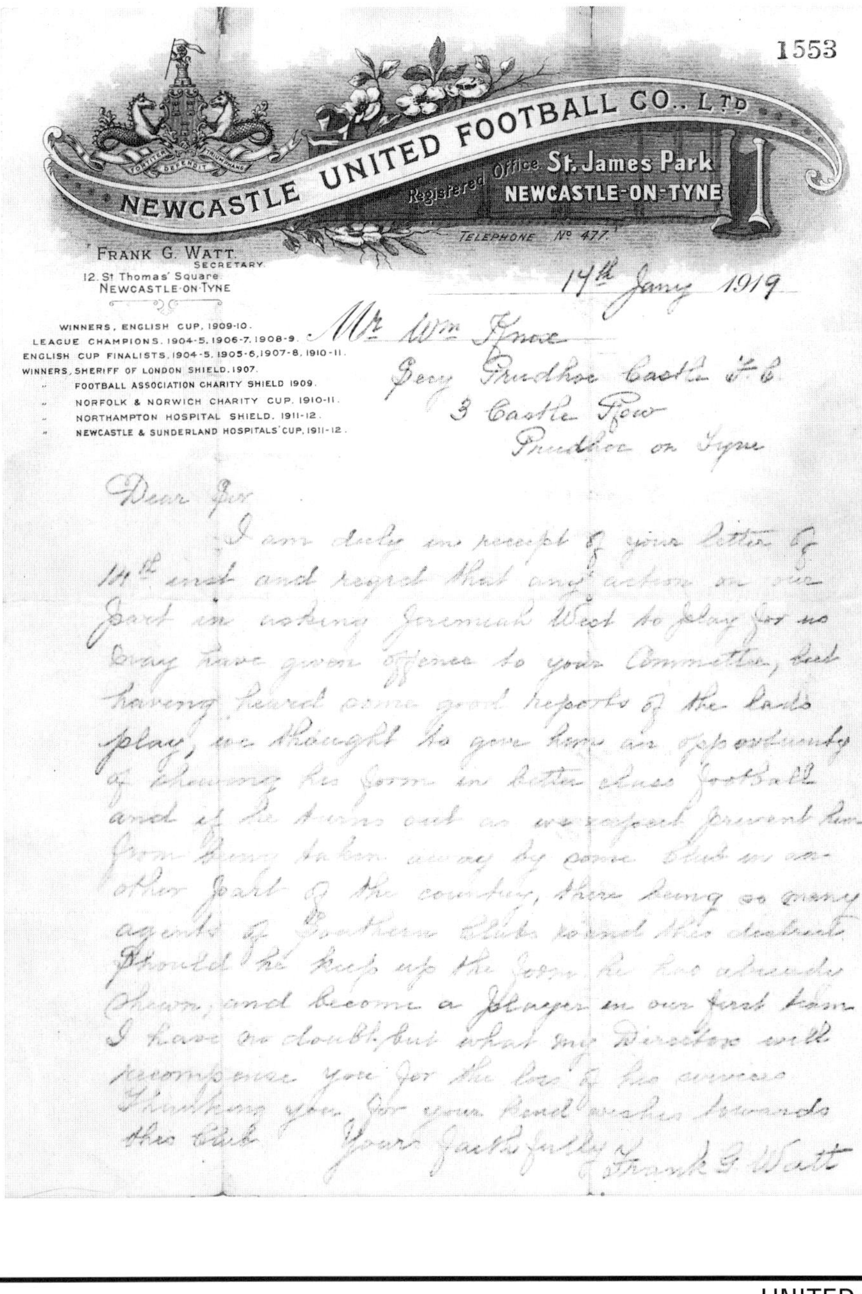

1553

NEWCASTLE UNITED FOOTBALL CO., LTD.
Registered Office St. James Park NEWCASTLE-ON-TYNE
TELEPHONE No 477.

FRANK G. WATT. SECRETARY.
12. St Thomas' Square
NEWCASTLE-ON-TYNE

WINNERS, ENGLISH CUP, 1909-10.
LEAGUE CHAMPIONS, 1904-5, 1906-7, 1908-9.
ENGLISH CUP FINALISTS, 1904-5, 1905-6, 1907-8, 1910-11.
WINNERS, SHERIFF OF LONDON SHIELD, 1907.
" FOOTBALL ASSOCIATION CHARITY SHIELD 1909.
" NORFOLK & NORWICH CHARITY CUP, 1910-11.
" NORTHAMPTON HOSPITAL SHIELD, 1911-12.
" NEWCASTLE & SUNDERLAND HOSPITALS' CUP, 1911-12.

14th Jany 1919

Mr Wm Knox
Secy Prudhoe Castle F.C.
3 Castle Row
Prudhoe on Tyne

Dear Sir

I am duly in receipt of your letter of 14th inst and regret that any action on our part in asking Jeremiah West to play for us may have given offence to your Committee, but having heard some good reports of the lads play, we thought to give him an opportunity of showing his form in better class football and if he turns out as we expect prevent him from being taken away by some club in another part of the country, there being so many agents of Southern Clubs round this district. Should he keep up the form he has already shewn, and become a player in our first team I have no doubt but what my Directors will recompense you for the loss of his services. Thanking you for your kind wishes towards this Club.

Yours faithfully
Frank G. Watt

A letter from secretary Frank Watt to local club Prudhoe Castle dated January 1919, in connection with Jeremiah West, a youngster United wished to give a chance to.

Newcastle v Tottenham just after World War One. Full-back Billy Hampson tackles Arthur Grimsdell.

McCracken, Billy Hibbert and Frank Hudspeth. New faces broke into the side, but with club having adopted, "a definite policy of developing purely local players" no big transfer signings were seen in the immediate post-war months. Local products came into the reckoning, players like goalkeeper Bill Bradley (Jarrow), Stan Dixon (Barrington Albion) and Alex Ramsay (Swalwell) were given chances alongside Andy Smailes (Blyth Spartans), Ray Robinson (Scotswood), Tom Curry (South Shields Parkside) and Tom Phillipson (Scotswood). Billy Hampson, although no youngster, started to break strongly into the side too.

Many old faces did not recommence football. Colin Veitch was one, he hung up his boots and was retained as coach. Another was George Wilson who moved back to Scotland, while skipper Jimmy Hay did likewise. It was a youngster's paradise. Andy Smailes, weighty but a handful up front, impressed many judges and was hailed in 1920 as the best inside-forward in the division by Topical Times. Yet his form slumped dramatically after netting 28 goals in two seasons. He later spent almost 30 years in various capacities with Rotherham United. Tom Curry was to prove an able wing-half, versatile in most positions and went on to appear almost 250 times for the club. He was killed in the Munich Air Disaster in 1958, then Manchester United's trainer. Tom Phillipson was another to have a good career. A former schools' international, he especially starred for Wolves netting a century of goals and afterwards became Lord Mayor of the Midlands town.

Blyth Spartans' forward Andy Smailes joined the Magpies for £300.

United faired well in the seasons that followed war. The new twenties era opened in the capital with a 1-0 victory over Arsenal before 55,000 spectators, the Gunners' first game at their new stadium, Highbury. By November, Newcastle topped the Division One table with a brilliant run of six successive victories. They were in contention for the title until the turn of the year when form deserted them, the Magpies slipping to eventually finish in 8th position, chiefly due to the old weakness up front. In defence though, they were a solid unit, however the combination fielded was

Tom Curry, a long serving United wing-half who was tragically killed in the Munich Air Disaster.

clocking on in years. For several matches United's full-back partnership of McCracken and Hampson became what was thought to be the oldest rearguard in the Football League. Both had passed their 40th birthday. Additionally the last line of defence, with Jimmy Lawrence, and later new signing Sandy Mutch, were fast approaching 40 years of age. When Bill McCracken shortly retired, another veteran, Frank Hudspeth partnered Hampson. He was well past 30!

Bill McCracken shakes hands with Arsenal's captain at Highbury before the start of the first fixture of 1919.

The following year, 1920/21, Newcastle again led the First Division before Christmas, and this time their challenge lasted longer, until into April, being in 2nd or 3rd position to Burnley for much of the season. They slipped though in the last few games and ended in 5th place.

In the FA Cup the black'n'whites didn't allow Crystal Palace to repeat their 1907 sensation. United won 2-0 in the 1920 tie with Dixon and Hall scoring the goals. Big and sturdy, Stan Dixon, at

Newcastle United 1920-21. Left to right, back: McPherson (trainer), Hampson, Lawrence, Harris, Watt (secretary). Middle: Mooney, Curry, McCracken, Low, Hudspeth, King. Front: Aitken, Ward, McIntosh, Finlay, Seymour, Smailes, Pyke.

inside-forward was extremely versatile and was chosen as reserve to the England side in 1919. He afterwards proved a great stalwart for Hull City. Huddersfield Town, then in the Second Division, but just starting their fabulous twenties conquest, met United in the next round. The Terriers won by a single goal at St James Park after an uncharacteristic error by McCracken.

Cup fortune in 1921 was better. Nottingham Forest, low in Division Two and struggling for cash, sold home advantage to United for £500 plus a minimum share of the gate of £1,500. The Reds, with ex United star Sandy Higgins in the side, went on to hold United at St James Park in a controversial match littered with offside decisions. One report noted, "It was monotonous to hear the whistle blown so often". Bill McCracken was then at the height of his offside tactical game. Forest were defeated in the replay, 2-0, at Gallowgate again of course, and the two players who netted on that day were names to appear on the scoresheet time and time again over the coming years, outside-left Stan Seymour and centre-forward Neil Harris.

Seymour returned to his native north east from Morton in a £2,500 deal, perhaps the best piece of transfer business United ever did. He remained associated with the club for almost 50 years. Glaswegian, Harris became Newcastle's record signing, joining the club in 1920 for £3,300. He was a daring leader, not big, but with a quintessence of dash and proved a prolific goalscorer, netting over 100 goals for the Magpies. Harris had his ups and downs at Gallowgate and was once transfer listed only to bounce back and become a Cup hero. The pair at last solved United's goalscoring problem. In 1920/21 they jointly grabbed 29 goals. Frank Watt was to say, "New forwards have come - you'll find us more like the Newcastle of old".

The defeat of Forest took United into battle with Liverpool. A record crowd of 62,073 saw a close contest between clubs 2nd and 3rd in Division One's table. The tie ended in a 1-0 victory with Harris getting the decisive strike with a hook shot. United then had to travel to the other Merseyside giant, Everton, in Round Three. It was probably the toughest draw that was available, Everton had already disposed of the Magpies at Goodison Park in the league. They did it again, this time by three clear goals before 54,205 spectators. Ex favourite, Albert Shepherd, reporting for a local newspaper, noted, "My old team went down with such a wallop! It was an inept display".

New centre-forward Neil Harris caricatured in the club's change strip of the time.

With the war years well and truly over, fans packed into grounds all over the country as men returned from conflict to find relaxation at the football match. A boom occurred now that the country was getting back to normal, just as was to happen immediately after World War Two. United's attendances rose from a pre-war average of 18,000 to over 37,000 in 1919/20 and almost 42,000 a season later. Revenue jumped considerably. Admission charges had doubled - to a minimum of one shilling - and although clubs now had to pay a new government innovation, Entertainment Tax, to help the economy after war, football still proved a lucrative business. Newcastle United's receipts rocketed to an all time high in 1920 of £61,526 19s 4d, while wages remained static at a little over £13,000. Record attendances, and with it record gate receipts, were created throughout the country. In the space of seven days in November 1919 both St James Park and Roker Park crowd figures were broken for derby

YANKS ARRIVE

With the USA entering the First World War, many servicemen found themselves based in England and during June 1918 a Yankee baseball match was staged at St James Park. A crowd of 5,000 watched the new spectacle.

clashes. 47,148 packed into Roker, while 61,761 went through Gallowgate's turnstiles. And that figure was soon to be broken by that Liverpool Cup-tie. Sunderland won both games, although the following year, before more big crowds, United gained revenge by winning 2-0 and 6-1 in close succession. Money kept rolling in to Frank Watt's safe until the country's economy ran into serious difficulties.

The era was a period of marked contrast in Britain. The Roaring Twenties of the jazz phenomenon, the tango, wild parties and the sophisticated comedies of Noel Coward, had in many ways shocked a pre-war establishment. Much had changed since the days of 1914. People were now becoming prosperous and starting to obtain unheard of luxuries. But after economic boom a dramatic slump followed, creating high unemployment which quickly rolled into the Great Depression by the end of the decade....the Wall Street crash and all.

Billy Aitken, crossed the border for Tyneside from Rangers.

Before World War One, Newcastle had been one of the most prominent of industrial cities, however with the depression and major cut backs in heavy industry, Tyneside suffered greatly. By the end of 1921 virtually all shipping orders had dried up and ten years on, it was the same story. The virtual collapse of Armstrongs, the city's biggest single industrial employer, took place as a direct result. Coal prices fell, demand deteriorated and the north east had little share of the new industries of telecommunications and car manufacturing. Inevitably unemployment followed. Those who had been comfortably off now found themselves increasingly poor.

Outside-right Jimmy Low, another ex Ibrox player.

Yet in spite of such problems away from football, the years between the two world wars provided an era rich in character and entertainment. Football was one way to escape from a grey and melancholy state of affairs and the professional game expanded. Both the First and Second Divisions were enlarged and a merger with the Southern League produced the Third Divisions North and South. Newcastle United were one of the top sides in the country along with Aston Villa, Liverpool, Sunderland and the rapidly emerging Huddersfield eleven.

United's next celebrated side was now taking shape. Joining Harris and Seymour, was Tom McDonald, another from Scotland, and he formed a great left-wing partnership with Seymour to last for years. Other Scots arrived too. Billy Aitken came from Rangers during the 1920/21 season in a £2,500 transfer. A forward with clever Scots skills to the fore, he liked to dribble with the ball in the pioneering way. Outside-right Jimmy Low also arrived from Ibrox. He landed on Tyneside

'Peter' Mooney, born in Walker and who never let the side down.

a few months later for a £1,300 fee. Only 5'6" tall, but able to flash past two defenders in a surge forward, he eventually replaced Aitken on the flank.

Dundee provided the talent of Bob McIntosh, a thinly built link-man who appeared 103 times for United, in return for a cheque for £1,250. Newcastle also tried to bring future Scottish international captain, Jimmy McMullan to Tyneside as well. They offered a record £5,000 but couldn't persuade Partick Thistle to part with him.

In spite of a return to the transfer market, there was still time for home grown talent like Tom Mitchell, loyal to the club as Seymour's understudy, Ted Ward, a young forward from Blyth, and Rob Roxburgh, later a noteworthy Blackburn player. Edward Mooney, an unorthodox wing-half, came from Walker Celtic and was more commonly known as 'Peter'. Washington born Charlie Spencer graduated with repute from the reserve side too. Bill Bradley and ex Huddersfield man, Sandy Mutch vied for the goalkeeper's shirt of Jimmy Lawrence who called it a day at the end of the 1921/22 season. Mutch was to become quite a personality at St James Park. Recognised as one of the game's top 'keepers in his prime, he joined United for £850 when almost 38 years of age and ended up groundsman at Gallowgate. His son, Alec junior became United's physio and was an employee for over 60 years, record service with the Magpies.

Seasons 1921/22 and 1922/23 again promised much, but in the end Newcastle perhaps flattered to deceive. Once more they were named in some quarters as potential title contenders and during the latter season made a strong bid during March. However, they suffered having to face no fewer than five away fixtures in succession at a crucial point in

United's goalkeeper Sandy Mutch saves from Manchester City's Johnson.

the title race. United didn't win any of the games and ended up in 4th place, a long way behind the trio in front, Liverpool, the Champions, Sunderland and Huddersfield Town.

In the FA Cup, United were eliminated at an early stage. Firstly, they had given Division Three outfit, Newport County a 6-0 hiding, but then fell to Preston North End 3-1 at Deepdale. The following year Southampton, from the Second Division, and in their first season in that sphere, knocked United out after taking a 0-0 draw from Gallowgate in a muddy battle. The Saints won convincingly 3-1 at the Dell to the joy of their small band of followers, and this after United had taken the lead. That season's competition saw the FA Cup have a new home, The Empire Stadium, Wembley. Newcastle supporters, however, thought little of the new arena and Wembley dreams, as we know them today, were never in anyone's mind. United's Cup form then was nithing to get excited about but that was to change dramatically. The Magpies' love affair with Wembley Stadium was just about to begin.

Bill Bradley was to rival Mutch for the 'keeper's position and win a place at Wembley.

Another notable point in the club's history during the early part of the twenties, was the second visit of Royalty to St James Park in July 1923, when the Prince of Wales, later Edward VIII inspected United's ground. A Royal presence was also seen at the Arsenal versus Newcastle meeting in February 1922, the Duke of York being introduced to United's players and officials. They were two rare instances - other than at Cup finals - when members of the Royal family have been associated with the Magpies.

United also continued to tour the continent on a regular basis. They had visited Denmark, Germany and Austria frequently before World War One, and now ventured further afield. In 1921 they visited Spain and France, recording their first defeat at the hands of a European side. United went down 3-2 to Barcelona, then many years before they were to become one of soccer's giants. Even then though, United's players were impressed with much of the continental set up. Jimmy Low said that facilities, were, "much superior to anything we had previously seen". He also noted that, "referees in most of the games were biased to such an extent that it was impossible to win".

For the 1923/24 season United's directors brought two more Scots over the border, Willie Gibson and Billy Cowan. Both were splendid midfielders and the last piece in the Magpies' team building. Left-half Gibson hailed from a famous soccer family and was valued by his club, Ayr United at £2,500. He was a most able ball-player with near perfect distribution and was on the fringe of international recognition on a number of occasions. Cowan cost the black'n'whites a similar fee, £2,250 from Dundee. Tall, slim and graceful and often able to find the net, he scored 28 goals for United in a short, but very productive spell. Teaming up with McDonald and Mooney, they made Newcastle's midfield tick. Charlie Spencer, to soon be capped by England, displayed the defensive qualities in the middle of the field.

BILL'S DISMISSAL

In September 1922, United full-back Bill McCracken was sent-off against Sheffield United. The referee in his report to the Football League noted that McCracken was dismissed for, "assuming a threatening attitude, disputing his decisions and swearing".

The back three were solid enough with veterans Hampson and Hudspeth in front of Mutch, with one commentator noting the old guard as, "never during their careers having played better". Up front the robust, but sometimes erratic Harris led the line with flankers Seymour and Low always able to score goals too. It was an experienced side, and one getting on in years. Towards the end of the season the line-up's average age was over 32 - the oldest fielded by the club in 100 years - yet it became an FA Cup winning combination.

Nothing sensational had occurred until the start of 1924 except for two defeats by Sunderland just before Christmas. Newcastle had commenced their programme well as in recent seasons. They reached top place at one stage, then slipped to mid-table. The FA Cup however, changed everything as United blended together into a feared outfit to demolish all opposition on a run to the new national stadium at Wembley, although as ever with Newcastle United's story, there were several moments of high drama in the club's path.

The draw for the First Round had paired the Magpies with Portsmouth, in Division Three and eventual

Billy Cowan who developed into a key playmaker in United's coming success.

Talented midfielder, Willie Gibson, (left) related to several star footballers.

WAGES 1923/24

Senior players....£8 per week and £6 per week during the close-season.
Reserve players...£5 per week plus £1 extra for each first-team game.
Bonus agreements were extra, as were international appearances, at £6 per game.
Additionally players who stayed with the club for five years earned a club benefit, a lucrative amount usually in the form of a testimonial fixture or lump sum paid direct from the club.
Tommy Urwin received three benefits during his career, with United, Sunderland and Middlesbrough.

Champions. United crashed to a 2-0 deficit by half-time, but then the 27,000 crowd found themselves in for a football treat. In typical FA Cup tradition goals from Harris, Seymour, Gibson and the underrated Jimmy Low, reversed the score to a 4-2 victory for the Tynesiders. A result to be repeated in the 1952 Cup run, an equally dramatic affair too.

Newcastle were the only local side left in the competition which at that time included Football League sides, South Shields, Ashington and Durham City. United kept the region's flag flying with a match at the Baseball Ground, home of Derby County, one of the top sides in the Second Division. It took Newcastle four thrilling games lasting all of 420 minutes in which 20 goals were scored to climb that hurdle. Eventually United won 5-3 in an epic third replay at St James Park. It was the longest tie in the club's history up to 1989 and the meeting with Watford. Derby, one of the country's leading goalscorers, held their First Division opponents on three occasions - all 2-2 draws - at the Baseball Ground, Gallowgate and at neutral Burnden Park.

United v Watford in the F.A. Cup 3rd Round, 1924. Seymour's goal clinches the tie.

The first meeting on a barren pitch in Derbyshire saw United go 2-0 ahead with a couple of goals from Tom McDonald, one a soft header through the 'keeper's legs, the other a first time drive that roared into the net. But Derby hit back when Newcastle were down to ten men and rattled two late goals from Storer, this after missing a penalty too. The tie went to a replay on Tyneside the following Wednesday and again United were 2-0 up with goals from Harris and a magnificent solo effort past three men from Cowan. With only two minutes left the Rams equalised and in extra-time it was Newcastle's turn to fight to stay in the tie. The third game was held at Bolton and once again classier Newcastle took the lead, this time through a Frank Hudspeth penalty. As the match wore on however, Derby got a deserved leveller and then another to put them in front. It was now United who had to rescue the game in the dying minutes. Stan Seymour was the saviour as he latched on to a free-kick - one hotly disputed by Derby - and hit a first time shot into the net from the edge of the box. The whistle for full-time went a matter of seconds later. Seymour later recorded, "Out of the corner of my eye I saw the referee raise the whistle to his lips so I hit the ball as hard as I have ever hit one". The ball flew past the 'keeper.

Charlie Spencer in a keen contest with Manchester City forward Johnson.

The fourth and decisive battle was held at St James Park after strong protests over a neutral venue and the referee. United won a toss of a coin and staged the game on Tyneside with a new official, John Howcroft taking control of the tie that had seen tempers become increasingly frayed. It turned out to be one of the most memorable 90 minutes of Cup football staged at St James Park. Derby were without their star winger, George Thornewell, but it appeared to matter little as the Rams stormed into a 2-0 lead through Randolph Galloway. Newcastle needed something special - enter centre-forward Neil Harris, who later that year led Scotland's attack. He netted a marvellous first-half hat-trick within the space of 24 minutes to put Newcastle ahead. Eight minutes after the break, Seymour made it 4-2, but Derby were not finished as they had proved in earlier games. England man, Harry Storer pulled a goal back and there were visions of extra-time again and even a fifth meeting as Derby pressed forward for the equaliser. This time though, the pattern was broken when Cowan, also to play for Scotland that season, made the game safe when he shot home the Magpies' fifth goal.

Those stirring ties with Derby had forged United's team into a unit of character and spirit. They progressed from a moderate side to a really potent cut and thrust eleven, one of good all round ability that could go on to win the trophy. In Round Three struggling Watford faced the Tynesiders. In trouble at the foot of Division Three, the southerners were given little chance, but Newcastle were lucky to come back north with a 1-0 victory. The all important goal was netted by Seymour during the first 45 minutes.

A tough meeting followed with Liverpool at St James Park. Over 56,000 witnessed a close encounter between two sides evenly matched and with dangerous forwards. A single goal knocked in with his head by Tom McDonald again took

United through to the next round, this time to the semi-final. United were now 90 minutes away from a visit to Wembley Stadium, in 1924 barely twelve months old and just beginning to possess that irresistible aura that football fans, especially with FA Cup illusions, longed to be part of.

It was on 8th May 1921 when a Football Association committee charged with the responsibility of finding a national stadium and new home for the FA Cup final, signed a 21 year agreement for the lease of the site. Located on the spot of a gigantic steel structure planned to rival the Eiffel Tower that never got past the first stage, Wembley was initially part of the Empire Exhibition, the biggest fair Britain had ever known, sprawling 216 acres over Wembley Park, then a small suburb of London with green fields, hills and a golf course, a virtual unknown dot on the Metropolitan Line to Harrow on the Hill. The Exhibition was a vast advertisement to a declining British Empire, yet still almost 30 million people swarmed to Wembley. They could visit such exhibits as a reconstruction of the tomb of Tutenkhamen and the most popular and enchanting Queen's Doll's House. There was a gigantic fun-fair, a huge market and side shows whichever way visitors turned. There was even a statue of the Prince of Wales made from Canadian butter! It was inspiring yet laughable, but it brought football, Wembley, although it was more majestically known as the Empire Stadium for some time yet.

Early in 1922 the Duke of York, later King George VI, ceremoniously cut a piece of turf and within twelve months the ground took shape. Wembley was ready for the 1923 FA Cup final with only four days to spare. Its focal point was two grandiose twin towers of white stone which dominated the landscape for miles around. It had a capacity of 126,500, but maybe as many as 200,000 crammed through the gates, and over fences, for the West Ham v Bolton FA Cup final and Wembley was immediately in the headlines....white horse, Billie, and Police Constable Storey on the front pages nationwide. From that remarkable beginning, Wembley - its exquisite green surface, its fascinating echo - possessed a special quality of its own unrivalled by any other ground. Newcastle United were to visit that unique Cup final atmosphere on seven occasions in the coming years, most of them triumphant journeys south.

Manchester City stood between United and their first Wembley visit. At St Andrew's, Birmingham, famed City winger Billy Meredith became the oldest player to appear in the FA Cup's senior rounds. He was amazingly three months short of 50 years of age and it was to be his last game, against the club he had made his debut against over 30 years earlier. Newcastle were rarely troubled by City and coasted to the final in a scrappy match. United scrambled a goal in each half, both scored by Neil Harris, on top form and a handful for most defenders. Also to play to his peak was centre-half Charlie Spencer, who with his display in the semi-final earned a call up by England. United, once in front, played a holding game to perfection. United's second goal didn't come until the dying moments, indeed when many of the 50,039 crowd were on their way home.

Before Newcastle headed for the Empire Stadium and special training at Harrow on the Hill, they faced their FA Cup final opponents, Aston Villa in a league meeting only six days before the big day. The Magpies were to take few chances with a risk of injury to their Cup stars, remembering the fate that had befallen the club back in 1911. Only two of the side ran onto the Villa Park turf - 'keeper Sandy Mutch and Willie Gibson - and the home side ran up a 6-1 scoreline, this after United's scratch line-up had gone a goal in front. Ironically it was one of those remaining senior players who was carried off with a nasty injury and was fated to miss the Wembley appointment. Shortly after half-time, Villa sped forward and in a chase for the ball with Teddy York, Sandy Mutch collided with Villa's winger and twisted his knee. Apart from missing the Cup final, it was an injury that caused United's veteran goalie to retire.

DOUBLE TRAINING

After a drab performance against Sunderland at St James Park in November 1919 which resulted in a 3-2 defeat, Newcastle's directors were furious at the team's lack of fitness. They noted that United, "failed to stay the hour and a half and that players in future would train twice a day instead of once a day".

It had not been the first time the club had chosen to rest key players during the Cup run. In all, United decided to field weak sides in seven matches and the Football League was enraged with the Geordies' stance. The game's authority fined United heavily, just as they had done prior to World War One. This time the amount was much larger, £750, then an astronomical sum and a record for many years to follow, in fact until Burnley were fined £1,000 in 1961.

The second goal for United in the 1924 FA Cup semi-final against Manchester City . Neil Harris fires the ball home.

Centenary Highlight

> *"United set about their job in masterly fashion and won by sheer skill and determination"*
>
> *Northern Echo, April 1924*

ON THE MORNING OF THE 1924 CUP FINAL second choice goalkeeper Bill Bradley was called to see trainer Jimmy McPherson. Sandy Mutch had been doubtful all week and had lost his battle for fitness. 31 year-old Bradley stepped in with only hours to go before the kick-off, but the reserve from Gateshead grasped the opportunity and proceeded to make a series of dazzling stops that foiled Aston Villa. It was an inspirational display which made him the hero of Wembley and earned him the freedom of Tyneside. Captain Frank Hudspeth said, "Bradley's brilliant goalkeeping gave us great confidence", while Villa's skipper Frank Moss made the comment, "some of his saves were remarkable".

Newcastle avenged their 1905 Cup final defeat by Aston Villa in 90 minutes that lived up to the show, one of the best since the turn of the century. The Northern Echo noted that, "United gained their victory by superior craftsmanship, an impregnable defence and a complete absence of nerves". Newcastle had the will to win and needed this determination against hot favourites, Villa, just above Newcastle in Division One's table and FA Cup winners in 1920. They possessed a fast and youthful attack to test United's ageing back-line.

After such crowd problems a year earlier in 1923, more adequate arrangements were made this time round. The final was the first all ticket affair and 15,000 Tynesiders made the trip by road, rail, and as in their last invasion of the metropolis, by boat too. About 300 fans sailed to London by the steamer Bernicia. They waved scarfs, hats, banners as well as bells, bugles and rattles. Many were clad in black'n'white from head to foot just like any modern supporter heading for Wembley Stadium. United full-back Billy Hampson created a slice of FA Cup history becoming the oldest player to appear in a final - at 41 years and eight months old.

The weather was wet and on a greasy surface a fast, keen and sporting contest took place. United gave a courageous defensive display in the first-half when Bradley made his mark. Newcastle rode their luck, Villa twice hit the woodwork, but United kept the ball from finding the net through a mix of stern defending and sheer good fortune. Most of the danger in a torrid opening came from Walker and Dorrell as the Midland side concentrated on a short passing style. They weaved through Newcastle's defence but could not get the ball past Bradley. He saved from Kirton, Walker and a wonderful stop from a fierce Moss drive. A storm of cheers greeted a quick succession of thrilling saves. At one stage he faced four Villa forwards on the six yard line and made a magnificent treble stop from point blank range.

United's attack never got going in the first period and any threat came only through individual bursts by Harris and the odd half chance by Seymour - a header wide. In the second 45

Above: United's supporters on their way to Wembley Stadium for the first time.

HRH Duke of York meets Newcastle's players before the kick-off. Bill Bradley, to become the star of the game, exchanges a few words.

Skipper Frank Hudspeth attends to the formalities with his opposite number and referee Russell.

FA Cup Winners 1924

FA CUP RUN

R1	Portsmouth	A	W	4-2
R2	Derby County	A	D	2-2
	Derby County	H	D	2-2
	Derby County	N	D	2-2
	Derby County	H	W	5-3
R3	Watford	A	W	1-0
R4	Liverpool	H	W	1-0
SF	Manchester City	N	W	2-0
F	Aston Villa	N	W	2-0

FACTS & FIGURES

	P	W	D	L	F	A
Home	3	2	1	0	8	5
Away	6	4	2	0	13	6
Total	**9**	**6**	**3**	**0**	**21**	**11**

CUP GOALGETTERS
8 Harris, 5 Seymour, 3 McDonald, 2 Cowan, 1 Gibson, Hudspeth, Low

CHAIRMAN: John P. Oliver
MANAGER: Directors' committee
TRAINER-COACH: James McPherson
CAPTAIN: Frank Hudspeth

Among the thousands of Tynesiders that made the trip south was this group of supporters who travelled by sea on the Bernicia.

Stan Seymour, left, crashes the ball high into the net for United's second goal.

Action in the Villa goalmouth. 'Keeper Jackson attempts to clear with Seymour, McDonald and Harris ready to pounce.

The Magpies' first goal scored by Harris, right.

Centenary Highlight

Right: the packed Geordie end of Wembley Stadium, then open to the elements. Note the same fan and umbrella as on the previous page.

Below: United taste Wembley victory for the first time. Neil Harris receives his medal and F.A. Cup stand from the Duke of York. Inset: Frank Hudspeth is flanked by Spencer (right), Gibson and Cowan (left).

FINAL
27 April 1924 at the Empire Stadium, Wembley
Newcastle United 2 (0) Aston Villa 0 (0)

UNITED:
Bradley
Hampson, Hudspeth
Mooney, Spencer, Gibson
Low, Cowan, Harris, McDonald, Seymour.
ASTON VILLA:
Jackson
Smart, Mort
Moss, Milne, Blackburn
York, Kirton, Capewell, Walker, Dorrell.

GOALS: Harris(83m), Seymour(86m)

ATTENDANCE; 91,695 (£14,280)

Referee; W.E.Russell (Swindon)
Guest of Honour; HRH Duke of York
Cup HQ; Harrow on the Hill

FA Cup Winners 1924

minutes however, Tyneside's men gradually took control and Villa's superiority and chance of lifting the FA Cup faded. Newcastle had opened the game with their half-backs penned back in defensive formation, but now they moved forward to support their forwards in a direct way. Seymour had a couple of opportunities and Harris went close from an acute angle, while Low shot just wide from a good position.

The goals that won the Cup for Tyneside were left to the very end, to the last five minutes as everyone expected extra-time. But in a blaze of glory, United twice netted in as many minutes. A sweeping move, the best of the match, involving Harris and Low, then Seymour and McDonald took an attack down the line. Seymour almost lost the ball, but McDonald, doubtful before the game, picked it up and fired goalwards(although some reports indicate the shot came from Cowan). Villa's 'keeper Jackson was at full stretch and he could only palm the ball clear for Harris to rush forward and fire over the prostrate goalie into the corner of the net.

From the kick-off Newcastle had a lucky escape. Dorrell crossed and Kirton's looping header came down on the top of the bar. Charlie Spencer said, "I was sure the ball was going to fall in the net". It didn't and United stormed forward and within seconds Stan Seymour put Newcastle 2-0 in front and the issue beyond doubt. Jimmy Low(although again some noted the provider as Cowan) received the ball on the flank. The Scottish winger hit a perfect curling pass across the field to Seymour who skipped past Smart. Taking the ball first time he crashed it high into the net off the crossbar. 'Keeper Jackson, who hailed from Benwell, could only look back towards the bulging net. It was a classic goal to complete a fine display. One reporter commented that it was, "a goal for the gods".

Willie Gibson said, "We left it a bit late, but take it from me, we had a bit in hand for the extra-time if there had been any". Newcastle's 2-0 victory was just as Neil Harris had boldly predicted in Saturday morning's newspapers. Apart from goalscorers Harris and Seymour, who did little but find the net, and of course hero Bradley, Gibson and Hudspeth were United's other stars. Gibson especially put on an accomplished display in midfield, while Hudspeth marshalled his defence in a difficult first-half.

The victors returned to Tyneside on Monday evening. A civic reception awaited them amidst dense crowds at the Central Station and then an ever so slow drive through the city with the FA Cup held aloft in open charabancs. To the tune of 'The Conquering Hero' they were led by the Newcastle Tramway's Band and had a mounted police escort. At the Empire Theatre, Stan Seymour was carried shoulder high by cheering fans, special scenes to be repeated time and time again during the next 50 years.

Dense crowds welcome home United's party in Collingwood Street. Hudspeth holds the F.A. Cup for all to see.

A portion of the immense gathering at the foot of Westgate Road.

Centenary Profile 7

Mr Newcastle United

"A magic character. He loved this club and simply lived for football"

Joe Harvey, 1985

HE WAS KNOWN SIMPLY AS 'MR NEWCASTLE'. Stan Seymour was a name respected on every football ground from Aberdeen to Torquay, from Carlisle to Southend. Associated with Newcastle for well over 50 years, he was firstly a brilliant goalscoring winger who won League and Cup medals with United, then after a controversial departure, returned as director and manager to lead the club to more glory. And it all started after being discarded by United as a 16 year old kid.

Seymour was born in south Durham, at Kelloe in 1893. He supported Sunderland of all teams as a small boy and when 13 years old worked as an apprentice joiner in the workshop of one of the many pits in the area. Seymour played for local sides Kelloe Church and Sacriston United, as well as North Eastern League club, Shildon. When only 16 he had a chance of a trial at Roker Park, but being so frightened never plucked up enough courage to make the trip. Another opportunity came his way, this time at St James Park. But after a nervous display at inside-left in borrowed boots, the boyish 5'7" budding footballer was told by a United official, "Come back when you grow up"! Disappointed, Stan returned to local football. However, during the autumn of 1911 he was given another chance, this time by Bradford City, then a strong First Division outfit.

City paid £150 to Shildon for his services and Seymour's first wages were £2 10s a week. His stay in Yorkshire didn't go well. Places in the City first-team were impossible to command for untried youngsters. He made only a single appearance - in 1912 against Manchester City - before moving north, to Scotland and at last the Durham winger made a name for himself.

Joining Greenock Morton in 1913 proved to be a great move. Seymour was a huge success and the folk alongside the Clyde took to his perky displays christening him, 'The Little Englishman'. During the war Seymour worked in the shipyards, and later in a torpedo factory, before concentrating on football again in 1919. He appeared over 200 times for the Greenock club until he headed back to the north east, to St James Park, where he was told ten years earlier that he was too small and too young.

At the time Seymour had been locked in dispute over pay with Morton and had quit the club taking a job back in the shipyard. Newcastle United had to work hard to obtain Seymour's signature. The little lad had grown up and possessed a wise head for figures. After much negotiation, Seymour agreed to move back home. United paid £2,500 in May 1920 for the 26 year old. It was a sizeable fee then and he took over the number eleven shirt for the first time in the clash with West Bromwich Albion at St James Park. Stan scored on his debut and was quickly being tipped for England honours. Seymour became a prodigious goalpoacher from the touchline, hauling almost a century of goals for the Magpies.

Short and thickset, Stan was an instant crowd favourite. In 1924, as United reached Wembley and lifted the FA Cup, Seymour netted five goals in the run. A year later, and after much petitioning, he was called up for England during their tour of Australia. He also played for the Football League side.

Teaming up with Hughie Gallacher and Tom McDonald, he was part of a forward trio that were unstoppable in 1926/27 when United won the Championship. Seymour registered 21 goals that year, the second highest by a United winger of all time. Stan retired two years later, in the close season of 1929. It was a controversial and bitter departure from Gallowgate, as he recorded later, "All I wanted was to complete my ten years service for a second benefit, but instead United gave me a free transfer after nine years". Following his retirement, and with much haggling, the club agreed to an accrued payment and afterwards he ran confectionery and sports outfitters shops opened when a player. He also covered Gateshead's matches for the Evening Chronicle.

	League		FA Cup		Total	
	App	Gls	App	Gls	App	Gls
1920-21	30	9	3	1	33	10
1921-22	18	1	2	1	20	2
1922-23	28	4	1	0	29	4
1923-24	33	16	9	5	42	21
1924-25	35	7	3	0	38	7
1925-26	24	6	2	2	26	8
1926-27	42	18	3	1	45	19
1927-28	29	12	1	1	30	13
1928-29	3	0	0	0	3	0
	242	**73**	**24**	**11**	**266**	**84**

SEYMOUR'S PLAYING RECORD

Stan Seymour

Peter McWilliam tried to lure Seymour to Middlesbrough, but he had no wish to return to football, the Newcastle incident having left a bad feeling. The former United winger did slowly return to the game though. He did a little scouting and out of the blue during the summer of 1938 was sensationally asked to become a Newcastle director at a time of high crisis at the club. United had escaped relegation to the Third Division by a whisker and were after new, young blood to revitalise the club. Rather surprised, as Seymour had been very much a Gallowgate outcast and had been stopped from buying shares, he accepted the post, although he rejected the manager's position also offered. His enthusiasm and inspiration transformed the whole St James Park scene.

Seymour rebuilt the side and led the Magpies back into the First Division. He was a member of the board who didn't appear worlds apart from the players, an official who knew footballers' views and who preferred a pie and a pint to the more traditional boardroom meal. Seymour was very much a working director, full of energy who scouted for the club incessantly, travelling thousands of miles each season. He became a tremendous wheeler-dealer in the transfer market and Seymour alone brought many a famous face to St James Park. Jackie Milburn said, "One of his greatest assets was the ability to make the right decision quickly and without any fuss". Frequently praised, but often criticised too, he had a character it was impossible to ignore and usually dressed smartly in a trilby hat and suit. Seymour was friendly and likeable, but shrewd and tough. He even had the foresight to find out what the fans thought, often standing on the terraces to learn what the punters had to say.

He was director-manager in two periods, from 1939 to 1947, and 1950 to 1954, although between and after had a commanding influence too. It was a spell that saw Seymour lead United to Wembley twice and he was Chairman when the club travelled again in 1955. During the sixties he worked hand in hand with Joe Harvey to bring another fine era to Gallowgate. Harvey said of his colleague, "A magic character. He loved this club and simply lived for football".

There were times of boardroom differences and player disputes, but Seymour always held the respect of the football community. In April 1976 he retired from the board, but still remained associated with United as Vice President, this after almost 50 years active work for United. On Christmas Eve 1978, when 85 years old, Stan Seymour died. His influence and enterprise did much to make Newcastle United a pillar of the game. He was a rarity in football, a terrace hero turned administrator who achieved success in every sphere for United; as a player, director, manager and scout.

Seymour's name lived on within the corridors of St James Park. His son, Stan Junior became Chairman of the club too. It was Jackie Milburn who said. "Newcastle United and their followers owe Stan Seymour a tremendous debt. In every way does he justify his nickname of Mr Newcastle United".

Centenary Profile 8

The First Supermac

"I just picked up the pen without asking any questions and signed on the dotted line"

Tom McDonald, 1921

HUGHIE GALLACHER AND STAN SEYMOUR are the Newcastle stars immediately recalled when the twenties era is remembered. Yet there was another star, a forgotten hero of those glory days, Tom McDonald. He was every bit as important to United's team plans in what many have called, The Golden Age of football. A probing and goalscoring inside-left, McDonald was like Gallacher and Seymour, another 'little 'un', only 5'8" tall, but with the work- rate of a Trojan and the touch of a master on the ball. He was the perfect link-man between Newcastle's defence, Seymour on the wing and Gallacher at centre-forward.

The trio had a marvellous understanding on United's left flank and did much to bring trophies to the St James Park boardroom. In 1924 McDonald missed only one game of the Magpies' FA Cup run and three years on, his contribution to the Championship victory was 41 games and 17 goals. He was deadly in front of the posts and a handy man to have as a secondary goalscorer. In fact, very much the difference between winning or losing a title trophy. During his eleven seasons as a United player, Tom hit the back of the net 113 times, a strike rate which puts him in the club's all time top five goalscorers, behind out and out forwards Milburn, White, Gallacher and Malcolm Macdonald. And that's not bad going for a midfield man. The record book however doesn't note how many times he laid on chances for his colleagues. McDonald was very much a provider too.

Tom McDonald, centre, during a training session at St. James Park. Colleagues Mooney (left) and Hudspeth (right) go through the exercises too.

Tom McDonald

McDONALD'S PLAYING RECORD

	League App	League Gls	FA Cup App	FA Cup Gls	Total App	Total Gls
1920-21	13	2	0	0	13	2
1921-22	39	16	2	2	41	18
1922-23	36	15	2	0	38	15
1923-24	36	9	8	3	44	12
1924-25	33	11	3	2	36	13
1925-26	40	11	3	0	43	11
1926-27	41	17	3	6	44	23
1927-28	41	13	0	0	41	13
1928-29	30	1	0	0	30	1
1929-30	29	5	5	0	34	5
1930-31	3	0	0	0	3	0
	341	**100**	**26**	**13**	**367**	**113**

McDonald signed for the black'n'whites in March 1921 after a spell with Glasgow Rangers. Joining the Blues straight after the war and, although highly thought of, he found a deluge of competition at Ibrox Park. Rangers possessed an all international eleven and Tom was more often than not playing in the Scottish Reserve league. A move was inevitable, McDonald at 25 years of age should have been at his peak and was far too good for that standard of football. Newcastle paid £2,000 to bring the Scot to Tyneside. He had no hesitation in agreeing to the move and said at the time, "I just picked up the pen without asking any questions and signed on the dotted line".

Born in Inverness in 1895, he started playing football with Highland sides but found his youthful zeal taken up by World War One. Soft spoken, with a gentle Highland accent, McDonald was a modest individual on and off the pitch. Stan Seymour related that he possessed, "exceptional unselfishness". Tom was a team-man who left the headlines to others, but an invaluable asset to any successful eleven. He was never gifted with ball skills, of say Gallacher, but as his centre-forward colleague observed, "What he lacked in football craft he more than made up in enthusiasm". Tom kept his game simple, hitting crisp, accurate passes at the right time, and powerful shots at goal.

McDonald was on the fringe of international recognition, but never made the full Scotland team. He was first under the selectors' eye when he appeared in trial games during 1922 and again two years later. McDonald did well in that 1924 run out, part of the Scotland 'B' side that toppled the 'A' combination at Cathkin Park. Gallowgate team-mates, Harris and Cowan, were also in that side, both finding the net. Scotland picked the goalscorers for the full international but ignored McDonald; the closest he came was as travelling reserve. It was a blow McDonald accepted in his stride, yet his United colleagues couldn't understand why he never got a chance. Many observed that he was every bit as good as his rivals for the position, former Rangers' team-mates, Tommy Cairns and Andy Cunningham, United's future boss.

The Scot appeared for Newcastle until he was 35 years old. In his later years McDonald showed much cunning and the craft of the experienced pro, totalling 367 games for the Magpies. Tom joined Third Division York City during May 1931 and by the middle of the decade had called it a day, although he continued in non-league football with Goole Town and, when he returned to Tyneside, with several local sides, notably Usworth Colliery.

McDonald never lost sight of the good times he experienced at St James Park. Like many before, and many since, he settled in the north east, an adopted Geordie. Tom lived in the west end of the city and worked for many years as a timekeeper at the Vickers Works on Scotswood Road. He also kept alive a strong association with the black'n'whites. On every match-day for years and years, Tom McDonald was to be seen as steward in charge of the lofty Gallowgate press-box on top of the old West Stand.

McDonald followed the club with the same enthusiasm as he devoted to United's cause on the field right up to his death in 1969.

7 GALLACHER'S MAGIC FEET

1924-1930

• OFFSIDE CHANGES • RECORD SPENDERS • LEAGUE CHAMPIONS • INTERNAL STRIFE • MANAGER APPOINTED • RELEGATION FIGHT •

"In Hughie Gallacher, their centre-forward and captain, United possess a footballer and leader who stands alone in the matter of skill"

Northern Echo, 1927

FOLLOWING THE CLUB'S FIRST WEMBLEY **success, Newcastle's directors were determined to build on United's glory. The Magpies were led throughout the twenties decade by John Peel Oliver, a wine and spirit merchant who was also a member of the Football League Management Committee during his long Chairmanship of the club. Although he suffered from heart trouble, Oliver enthusiastically made sure United remained at the forefront of the game.**

It took United only a couple of seasons to fashion the FA Cup victors into League Champions. Two factors made United a more powerful outfit, a change in the law of the game and the ability to splash out in a big way in the transfer market due to a hefty bank balance.

Roddie McKenzie, a Highlander, who spent over a decade at St. James Park.

As could be expected, the season after Cup triumph was a good one financially in spite of a deepening recession. A general strike was less than two years away and by the end of the decade almost two million were unemployed. But it did little to dampen the people's craving for soccer. The twenties were halcyon days for football, a galaxy of stars graced the field rich in character with a flamboyant style. The working man idolised the famous on every ground from Gigg Lane to The Dell. And non more so than at St James Park.

Neil Harris and Stan Seymour were the crowd's favourites in season 1924/25, not surprisingly after their Wembley success. Harris, although an erratic finisher, continued to bag the goals netting 20 in that year while Seymour took part in England's summer tour to Australia. United finished the season in sixth position, three places up on the previous campaign. Once more, with a better run-in to the final weeks of the season, they could have lifted the elusive title trophy - now sixteen years since the club had won the honour. Three victories in a row and a point at Birmingham during March saw United go top of the table with only five games remaining. But two home defeats followed, not a Championship performance and Huddersfield Town overtook them in the race.

As FA Cup holders, Newcastle did not produce last year's form to the disappointment of many. They saw off Hartlepool United, newcomers to the Football League and latterly opposition to the Magpies' second eleven. Newcastle won confidently 4-1 in the First Round. In the next tie though, top Second Division side Leicester City were good enough to take a 2-2 draw from St James Park in front of 58,713. Before another big gathering - a record crowd at Filbert Street - City knocked the holders out by a single opportunist goal by George Carr.

Much the same team was utilised that graced Wembley although Roddie McKenzie stepped up from the reserves and new signing Tommy Urwin took over from Low who had run into dispute with the club. He had actually failed to turn up for two league fixtures in December 1925 and was to be suspended by the FA after refusing to play for the reserves three years later.

McKenzie, from Inverness, had joined the Magpies as a youngster a couple of years earlier and became the sides midfield anchor-man in the coming seasons. Small and powerfully built, he was to have a great influence on the team, although more than once was involved in clashes with opponents - frequently being booked or sent off. McKenzie was dour and physical and amassed 256 games for the club as well as several weeks' suspension in his 13 year period on the books.

Tommy Urwin was the first of a series of big purchases in the coming years by United officials. An England international, he joined the staff from Middlesbrough in August 1924 after falling out

England winger Tommy Urwin.

with 'Boro over money. Urwin was all set to join Manchester United before Bill McCracken caught him at Newcastle Central Station and whisked him to St James Park instead. He was to be a great servant to his native north-east, later appearing for Sunderland too and receiving benefits from all three of the region's sides. A crafty winger, capped on both flanks, Tommy was noted for his speed and accurate cross as well as being an accomplished entertainer off the field. One team-mate noted, "his jolly nature kept us cheerful wherever we went".

Urwin was quick to make headlines in a black'n'white jersey. At Liverpool he was sent off along with the home side's brawny centre-half Waddy Wadsworth following a fracas, this in a grudge match after the 1924 FA Cup tie. The Reds' wing-half Jock McNab was ordered off too in an ill tempered 90 minutes that saw the crowd end in very ugly mood. The referee and both linesmen took refuge with the Newcastle party and sneaked away from Anfield in United's char-a-banc. An FA Inquiry followed and all three players were suspended for several weeks.

During the close season St James Park took further steps towards the modern age. Electric lights and heating were installed in the players' dressing rooms replacing the antiquated gas appliances, while a motor car park was laid near the entrance to the West Stand. Horse drawn transport was rapidly becoming a thing of the past. The club also decided to to find a replacement for Neil Harris, now almost 31 years of age. Money was to be no restriction as the directors released cash and Newcastle spent a national record £14,666 on fresh talent.

It was correctly viewed by United's officials that the introduction of a new offside law for the coming 1925/26 season would see revolutionary changes to the game and benefit those clubs with a potent attack. While Harris was still finding the net, he was slower and lacking the sparkle of old. There was also concern at the black'n'whites' defence, also ageing considerably.

Newcastle's scouts hunted the country for new faces. Full-back Albert Chandler was signed from Derby County for £3,250 to inject youth into the defence. United tried to persuade two other youngsters to transfer allegiance to Tyneside. Ralph Dean of Tranmere Rovers was at St James Park, but decided to stay on Merseyside and soon after signed for Everton - very shortly he of course became a footballing legend as Dixie Dean. Another personality of future years, Raith Rovers' inside-forward Alex James was another target. Trainer at Starks Park was ex United man, Dave Willis. A deal had been set up at £2,500 and James was to record his wish to head to Tyneside, "I set my heart on getting there" he said. But the transfer was never completed to James' disappointment and United's eventual loss.

United did sign another Scottish international link-man, Middlesbrough's Joe Harris arrived to compete for the left-half place. Also to join the ranks was Laurie Crown, a tall defender who had made a name for himself in South Shields' Football League side, and Jimmy Boyd, a youngster from Edinburgh St Bernards who was to become a terrace favourite as the thirties decade opened. More new faces were to arrive, including Tyneside's very own footballing legend.

Charlie Spencer (left) and Joe Harris (right), both served the Magpies during the Championship victory in 1927.

Before the revision to the offside law, due largely to the inventiveness of United's Bill McCracken, team formation consisted of a three man defence - the goalkeeper and two full-backs - three midfield workers, the half-backs - and five forwards. The change brought a new pattern, a 3-2-5 outfield formation, with the centre-half, previously a midfielder, now dropping back to become a defensive stopper, or third back to counter an added threat from the centre-forward route. The two inside-forwards now fell back into midfield pushing into attack at every opportunity. Newcastle were one of the leading clubs to show that this new pattern could work and Charlie Spencer became arguably the countries first stopper centre-half.

As clubs changed tactics and became accustomed to this method, a paradise for forwards was unveiled as the season commenced. The offside trap was much harder to spring now and goals, goals and more goals were the order of the day. Newcastle opened the season with the ball finding the net frequently. As yet though a new centre-forward still had to be acquired. They had looked at Falkirk's Puddefoot and Rawlings of Southampton, but by the big kick-off no-one had been signed.

Arsenal fell 7-0, Notts County 6-3, while Spaniards Real Madrid arrived on Tyneside and promptly were thrashed 6-1 in a friendly. In

New goalkeeper Willie Wilson. He had a terrible start for United but developed into a safe custodian.

between though, Newcastle also had a few problems of their own with the new formation. Blackburn Rovers rocked the Magpies 7-1 at St James Park, an afternoon when Ted Harper struck five goals past debutant keeper Willie Wilson. Signed from Peebles Rovers, Wilson was on trial yet still impressed and remained at Gallowgate for four years.

In the success over Arsenal, Newcastle's new team plan worked to perfection - United were 6-0 up at half-time. Bob Clark, a hefty reserve striker, scored a hat-trick but there could have been more than the seven goals that got past the Gunners' keeper. The victory showed the football world that the 3-2-5 line-up worked and Arsenal immediately copied it, as did other sides. Newcastle were the successful pioneers along with other inventive sides like Queen's Park Rangers and Spurs - then managed by ex United tactical genius, Peter McWilliam.

By the end of 1925 United had targeted their new centre-forward, a 5'5" bundle of effervescence by the name of Hughie Gallacher. Newcastle had a problem to overcome however, his side Airdrieonians would not part with his talents. The Broomfield club were Scottish Cup holders and second club to Rangers over the border at the time, and Gallacher was the prime reason for their success having plundered 100 goals for the Diamonds, as well as several for Scotland's national side. Newcastle directors, especially John Graham, Bob McKenzie and secretary Frank Watt were determined to bring the Scot to Gallowgate. Watt said of the Gallacher transfer saga, "It took weeks, aye months of parleying, repeated confabs, almost innumerable rebuffs, and the most painfully fluctuating negotiations before we pulled off the deal". Newcastle were represented at several Airdrie fixtures and everyone knew it. Gallacher recorded, "It was impossible to tell how many times they watched me".

Newcastle decided to have another go at Airdrie's directors and ambushed the Scottish club's midweek board meeting. They received a frosty reception, but in a brisk series of negotiations the mammoth figure of £6,500 offered by United was too big to refuse. At a late hour on Tuesday 8th December 1925 Hughie Gallacher signed for Newcastle United. The Magpies had secured the centre-forward they had tracked for almost six months. It had cost them the biggest fee paid out by the club. Only a week before Bob Kelly moved for £50 more to create a new record transfer. As it turned out Newcastle would have happily paid double the amount to acquire the titch of a Scot with a hunger for goals.

Tyneside's press heralded 22 year-old Gallacher's arrival as the coup of the decade. United were congratulated on the purchase, "Newcastle United Football Club has effected the smartest stroke of football business that has been transacted in modern times" noted one newspaper. Gallacher's debut for United was a Division One encounter at St James Park against Everton during mid December. It turned out to be an exhibition game between two attack minded sides that ended 3-3. Gallowgate bubbled over with expectation before the kick-off. As the players came out Newcastle fans had their first view of their new centre-forward, to become a Geordie hero like no other since. He hardly looked a footballer who was to take the Magpies to honours, but Tyneside's initial disappointment was quickly dispelled. Gallacher immediately got into his stride netting two goals and laying on United's other for Stan Seymour. His first goal in English football came on the half-hour. Willie Gibson sent the ball to the edge of the box. Gallacher collected it with his back to goal. He pivoted, chased between the Everton backs and swept the ball past the 'keeper as he advanced. It was a classic goal.

United should have won the fixture at ease, but ahead 3-1, defensive mistakes let in the Merseysiders. Everton's three goals all came from young England leader Dixie Dean who had interested United and to be Gallacher's great contemporary over the next decade. The Newcastle Evening Chronicle enjoyed Hughie's display, "First impressions of Gallacher were distinctly favourable. No sooner did he touch the ball than one sensed the artistic player. Dwarfed in stature by the Everton backs, he had little or no chance in the air, but on the ground he showed some masterly touches. There were times when he beat three or four men by clear dribbling....Newcastle have found a leader of pure quality".

UNITED'S BENEFICIARIES II

Newcastle, with a healthy bank balance for much of the twenties, continued helping out local clubs with finance arrangements. The club's minutes of meetings summarised the loan situation in 1924 as;

Spennymoor United	£50
Prudhoe Castle	£20
Preston Colliery	£100
South Shields	£1750
Scotswood	£700
West Stanley	£1200

The crowd of 36,000 were also well pleased with the first showing of the Gallacher talent. He had impressed the Geordie public, the Scot noted, "Just before the match ended I realised I had been taken to the hearts of the big crowd. During a lull in play a fog-horn voice roared across the ground ....Haway Wor Hughie". That roar was to be heard over and over again during the next five years.

In his first nine games in a Newcastle United shirt Hughie netted an amazing 15 goals. After the Everton match he scored against Manchester City, then a hat-trick against Liverpool and four opposing Bolton Wanderers including three in the first 25 minutes. Gallacher was rapidly the new idol of

Tyneside. The hero worship was just beginning, it was to grow into the biggest Tyneside has seen, even more fervent perhaps than Jackie Milburn's following 25 years later.

In the FA Cup, Gallacher's addition to United's ranks made the Magpies one of the favourites. Welsh side from Division Three, Aberdare arrived on Tyneside and were toppled 4-1, then neighbours Cardiff City could do little better falling 2-0 on their home soil, although they were down to ten men for most of the tie. But Londoners Clapton Orient - lowly placed in the Second Division - could, and they shocked Newcastle with a 2-0 victory before 31,420 at the O's old Millfields Road ground. It was the first time Orient had overcome top opposition. They continued on a giant-killing run into the quarter-finals.

Gallacher ended the 1925/26 season with a hat-trick over FA Cup finalists Manchester City on Tyneside. It was a crucial game as City needed a point to stay in the First Division. England international Billy Austin struck a penalty-kick and Wilson saved it, City lost 3-2 and were relegated. All told Gallacher grabbed 25 goals in only 22 appearances for his new club. United had netted 90 goals in the season, a campaign in which the offside change had made its mark. Before the alteration a total of just under 1,200 goals had been scored in Division One. Afterwards the goals total rocketed to 1,703 in number. United's directors' wise foresight had paid dividends. They were ready, with Gallacher as the ace, to challenge for the title again, but this time not to slip at the crucial run-in.

On the eve of the 1926/27 season Newcastle made a bold decision. They stripped full-back and veteran of over 400 games, Frank Hudspeth, of the captaincy and appointed the crowd's new hero, yet argumentative import, Hughie Gallacher as the black'n'whites' skipper. The decision raised more than a few eyebrows, "he is too young", some said, "too inexperienced and temperamental" others noted. Gallacher had the perfect answer. His character was such that critics ate their words. He went on to captain United to the Football League Championship, to date the last occasion the Tyneside club has won that distinguished prize.

Hughie Gallacher in the thick of the action against Clapton Orient during February 1926. The Londoners won that F.A. Cup tie in a shock 2-0 victory.

Newburn born, Bob Clark, sends in a drive at goal against Arsenal. A very popular character, he was destined to be in and out of United's team.

The local press had more doubts other than the captaincy controversy. United's potential up front was surprisingly questioned, "Are United's forwards good enough" was the cry ? They certainly were and went on to net almost 100 goals between them, the key to United's success. Gallacher led the line brilliantly and United got off to a tremendous start. In the opening match of the season the Scottish international smashed Aston Villa's defence scoring all four goals in a 4-0 victory.

Newcastle were brought down to earth though with a 5-1 reverse at St James Park four days later. And there were other early season lapses, United missing two penalty kicks against Leicester City. But for the first half of the season United looked good for the majority of the time and were tipped in some quarters for the Championship and Gallacher was the main reason. The magazine All Sports noted, "Gallacher is making Newcastle United a bigger power", while following another four goal strike by the impish leader against Bolton Wanderers it was declared, "What Newcastle owes to Hughie Gallacher can scarcely be overestimated. He simply covered himself with glory". The Daily Journal's scribe, Novocastrian, even wondered that perhaps he was superhuman, "whether he did not possess more than the usual compliment of feet". Gallacher was the matchwinner.

Yet he and Newcastle still had to prove themselves as title challengers to the south - where many of the important media personalities were based. A visit to White Hart Lane during November made them all take notice. United won 3-1, Gallacher netted a brilliant hat-trick, had another three efforts just go wide of the woodwork and a goal disallowed. At this time the forward-line was on a goal feast and Hughie in particular. He banged home seven in four matches and was on the scoresheet in five consecutive games. He was however, not only goal-taker, but also goal provider in chief laying on chances for both McDonald and Seymour who bagged goals by the hatful too. Gallacher possessed the natural touch creating openings for forwards good enough to read his game. McDonald and Seymour could, closing in on the chances from inside-forward and the flank. By December Newcastle were in the leading pack along with Burnley, Huddersfield Town and United's north-east rivals, Sunderland.

As New Year approached the Magpies hit scintillating form. From Christmas Day to the beginning of February, United won six games in a row and moved from the fringe of the title race to take over at the top. Newcastle defeated Cardiff City 5-0, Tom McDonald getting three goals from midfield, then did the double over Leeds United and won at Villa Park. They followed up with two home victories over Bolton and Derby. It was a devastating period of football - a club record - two further victories in the FA Cup meant the team had achieved eight straight wins.

Those Cup triumphs started with an 8-1 thrashing of struggling Second Division outfit Notts County at St James Park. Gallacher claimed a hat-trick within the first 45 minutes even though handicapped with a temperature of 102 degrees just before the kick-off. The duel of Wee Hughie, at 5'5", up against Notts keeper Albert Iremonger, 6'5" and 13 stone was a highlight of the game.

URGENT PLEA

In October 1924 United's board requested that the press issue an urgent appeal to supporters in order, "to suppress the foul language at home matches". Fans caught swearing would be immediately evicted from the ground.

United were declared FA Cup favourites and the Tynesiders continued in fine form defeating famous public school and university combination, The Corinthians, but not before the renowned amateurs almost caused the greatest giant-killing feat of all time. With only a quarter of an hour remaining they were ahead of the First Division leaders by a single goal in front of a crowd of 56,338 who were totally absorbed by the contest. They were deservedly in front too until United staged a late rally. The Times noted, "The professional team turned in their desperation to what the boxers call the rough stuff - some of it fair enough, some of it decidedly not". The Corinthians were reduced to ten men and thankfully Newcastle got a lucky break.

A free-kick was awarded the Geordies' way. Tom McDonald took a crack at goal and the ball found its way into the net for the equaliser via the shoulder of defender Knight. Gallacher was to say, "the shot seemed to be going wide". The Magpies went on to to score two more in the dying minutes to make the result a respectable one, but they hardly deserved it. The game was played at ... yes, The Crystal Palace, and the evil omen of the past very nearly cast its shadow over United again. That 3-1 victory was only the second live radio commentary and the first FA Cup tie to be broadcast.

Spectators eager for a better view of the Corinthians v United Cup tie in 1927.

In the quarter-final Newcastle were paired with Second Division Southampton at the Dell. Frank Hudspeth said, "We hoped for a draw but didn't fancy the small ground". United didn't get a replay, Saints repeated their 1923 feat and surprisingly knocked United out. They had proved quite a bogey club to Newcastle over the years.

This set back only created a keener determination to secure the League Championship. United and Gallacher went on the rampage. Against Everton, 45,000 saw a 7-3 victory, a thrilling contest that saw three goals from the Scotsman, the first of ten in a six match spell which set the Magpies nicely for silverware. Included in those goals was a Gallacher classic, this time at Ewood Park against Blackburn Rovers.

Stan Seymour reckoned it was the greatest Gallacher scored for Newcastle. He recounted the goal, "I remember I passed the ball to Hughie and sent him off on a 30 yard dribble down the wing. I tore down the middle. The goalkeeper came out to narrow the angle expecting, like me, that Hughie would send the ball over as I had a clear shot at goal. That was too simple. Hughie pushed the ball gently through the goalkeeper's legs and into the net". It was typical Gallacher. He would never be afraid to try the unexpected and spectacular. Most times they came off, the mark of his genius.

The title race was now between three clubs. Burnley dropped out and United, Huddersfield Town, winners of the Championship for the previous three seasons, and Sunderland were in competition. United met their north- east foes in a

OLD BAILEY APPEAL

United were involved in a hearing at the Old Bailey in London during February 1927 when they appealed against their Corporation Rates Assessment, One of the club's directors said in court, "the statement that the players' accommodation under the stand was 'palatial' was ridiculous. In fact St James Park is one of the worst equipped grounds in the First Division".

decisive clash during March. A record gate of 67,211 was attracted to St James Park. United were top, Sunderland lay in second place. A goal by Gallacher....who else....was enough to seal the points and by the beginning of April Newcastle were three points clear of the Wearsiders. United then defeated Bury and gave Arsenal a 6-1 mauling, victories which sent the club into Easter's fixtures in confident mood and to an equally crucial double with Huddersfield Town, now the only challengers with games in hand over Sunderland. The Terriers though, were to win only one of their last seven matches and Newcastle surged ahead.

Another massive crowd packed into Gallowgate. 62,500 saw the battle of title challengers versus title holders and once more Hughie Gallacher was the difference between the sides. Just after half-time he grabbed the game's only goal heading into the net, a brilliant neck twisting effort after Seymour had nodded across goal from a move started by McKay. Hughie was challenged by 6'0" Tom Wilson, and to the end of his day the Huddersfield Town centre-half never knew how Gallacher jumped above him. Newcastle defeated Spurs 3-2 the following day and although Huddersfield won the return match, United were almost in a position where they couldn't be caught. They needed all but a point from a trip to West Ham on April 23rd, FA Cup final day. At Upton Park, they gained a 1-1 draw on a bone-hard pitch, Stan Seymour netting the title winning goal in the 17th minute. Newcastle were hailed as Champions at St James Park seven days later when Sheffield Wednesday travelled north. Gallacher netted both goals in a 2-1 victory to bring his tally to 36 in 38 league games, 39 in 41 league and cup outings. A new club record was established, one that still stands over 60 years later.

Gallacher challenges Corinthians' famous goalkeeper Howard Baker in the 1927 Cup tie.

By the end of the season United were a polished line-up displaying football largely played on the deck rather than in the air. It was skilful, yet fast and at times tough and had a big Scots influence. Six of the side hailed from the north and United's mascot then was a kilted Highlander bedecked in black'n'white.

Skipper Gallacher had answered his critics. So too had United's forward line. Apart from Gallacher, Tom McDonald knocked in 23 goals and Seymour 19 while the 96 goals(108 in total) scored in the season is one of the best in a century by United. The Magpies' home form had been outstanding and their 19 victories from 21 matches has been equalled only once, by Liverpool during season 1978/79. All told they registered 25 wins, also the best in the club's history. They possessed a vigorous attack, yet had the shortest forward line in the country. Their average height was a mere 5'6" but they were a handful for opponents.

Newcastle fans with black'n'white berets pose for the camera.

United also had the sternest defensive record too. Deposed captain, Frank Hudspeth marshalled the rearguard alongside Alf Maitland who had been acquired in 1924 from Middlesbrough. Although a Scot by birth he appeared for the Football League side. Hudspeth, notwithstanding that he was almost 36 years-old, was capped by England. Willie Wilson was a safe custodian, Roddie McKenzie and Willie Gibson were two powerful wing-halves while Bob McKay was a new face, another large transfer deal from Rangers after a chase for his signature with Everton. He cost United almost £3,000 and was an expert schemer to be capped by Scotland twelve months later. Only briefly at Gallowgate, his record was a good one - 23 goals in only 66 games - more than an adequate replacement for the departed Cowan. McKay netted a hat-trick on his debut against West Bromwich Albion.

They possessed a wonderful team spirit led by the captivating Gallacher. The Northern Echo summed up, "In Hughie Gallacher, their centre-forward and captain, United possess a footballer and leader who stands alone in the matter of skill. It was largely due to his brilliancy and the support he derived from his colleagues that Newcastle United gained the League honours".

It was a marvellous year for the north-east all round. Apart from United's success, Sunderland finished in third spot while Middlesbrough were Second Division Champions. Everywhere the talk was of football.

Centenary Highlight

The Football League Championship trophy stands in front of captain Gallacher and Chairman John Oliver.

John Peel Oliver, at the helm in the Boardroom for almost 10 years.

One of Hughie Gallacher's record 36 goals - pictured scoring at St. James Park.

Frank Hudspeth taking the field - he marshalled United's defence and earned an England call-up.

League Champions 1927

FIRST DIVISION CHAMPIONS 1926-1927	P	W	D	L	F	A	Pts
Newcastle United	**42**	**25**	**6**	**11**	**96**	**58**	**56**
Huddersfield Town	42	17	17	8	76	60	51
Sunderland	42	21	7	14	98	70	49
Bolton Wanderers	42	19	10	13	84	62	48
Burnley	42	19	9	14	91	80	47
West Ham United	42	19	8	15	86	70	46
Leicester City	42	17	12	13	85	70	46
Sheffield United	42	17	10	15	74	86	44
Liverpool	42	18	7	17	69	61	43
Aston Villa	42	18	7	17	81	83	43
Arsenal	42	17	9	16	77	86	43
Derby County	42	17	7	18	86	73	41
Tottenham Hotspur	42	16	9	17	76	78	41
Cardiff City	42	16	9	17	55	65	41
Manchester United	42	13	14	15	52	64	40
Sheffield Wednesday	42	15	9	18	75	92	39
Birmingham City	42	17	4	21	64	73	38
Blackburn Rovers	42	15	8	19	77	96	38
Bury	42	12	12	18	68	77	36
Everton	42	12	10	20	64	90	34
Leeds United	42	11	8	23	69	88	30
West Bromwich Albion	42	11	8	23	65	86	30

RESULTS	Home	Away
Aston Villa	W 4-0	W 2-1
Burnley	L 1-5	D 3-3
Bolton Wanderers	W 1-0	L 1-2
Manchester United	W 4-2	L 1-3
Derby County	W 3-0	D 1-1
Cardiff City	W 5-0	D 1-1
Sheffield United	W 2-0	L 1-2
Arsenal	W 6-1	D 2-2
Liverpool	W 1-0	W 2-1
Everton	W 7-3	W 3-1
Blackburn Rovers	W 6-1	W 2-1
Sunderland	W 1-0	L 0-2
West Bromwich Albion	W 5-2	L 2-4
Bury	W 3-1	L 2-3
Birmingham City	W 5-1	L 0-2
Tottenham Hotspur	W 3-2	W 3-1
West Ham United	W 2-0	D 1-1
Sheffield Wednesday	W 2-1	L 2-3
Leicester City	D 1-1	L 1-2
Leeds United	W 1-0	W 2-1
Huddersfield Town	W 1-0	L 0-1

LARGEST VICTORY:
6-1 v Blackburn Rovers (H), v Arsenal (H)

HEAVIEST DEFEAT:
1-5 v Burnley (H)

AVERAGE HOME ATTENDANCE:
35,061

TOP GATE:
67,211 v Sunderland

REGULAR SIDE

Wilson
Maitland - Hudspeth
Gibson - Spencer - McKenzie
Urwin - McKay - Gallacher - McDonald - Seymour

CHAIRMAN: John P. Oliver
MANAGER: Directors' committee
TRAINER-COACH: James McPherson
CAPTAIN: Hughie Gallacher

LEAGUE APPEARANCES
42 Wilson, Seymour, Hudspeth, 41 McDonald, 39 Urwin, 38 McKenzie, Gallacher, 36 Maitland, 34 Spencer, 32 Gibson, 25 McKay, 17 Clark, 9 Harris, 5 Curry, Park, 4 Chandler, Loughlin, 3 Mooney, 2 Low, Hampson, Boyd.

LEAGUE GOALS
36 Gallacher, 18 Seymour, 17 McDonald, 10 McKay, 4 Urwin, Clark, 3 Hudspeth, 2 McKenzie, 1 Low, own-goal.

United's heroes at the start of the season. Left to right, back: Watt (secretary), McDonald , Wilson, Cowan (who moved to Manchester City), Graham (director). Middle: Watt Jnr (asst. secretary), Harris, Curry, Gallacher, McDonald, Urwin, McPherson (trainer). Front: Seymour, Oliver (Chairman), Hudspeth, McKenzie, McCombie (trainer).

Newcastle's team ready for a journey to an away fixture, although the picture could easily have been taken outside some Chicago gangsters' club!

ON THE CLUB'S RETURN FROM A TOUR of the Netherlands much was expected of the new Football League Champions. Many United followers thought the Magpies were on the brink of another fine era, one akin to the spell of Edwardian dominance, just as Huddersfield Town were doing at the time. Newcastle started like Champions with a victory over their rivals from Leeds Road and Hughie Gallacher started off where he had finished, with more goals, a hat-trick.

All went well, Manchester United fell by 7-1, Spurs by 4-1 and Newcastle were either 1st or 2nd in the table. But into December the side went through a ruinous period. They didn't win a game for twelve matches and looked more like relegation candidates than reigning Champions. Then, to follow, United were forced to appear without the considerable strikeforce of Gallacher for two months, sidelined through suspension in January. He had been disciplined after an ugly confrontation with Huddersfield Town in somewhat of a grudge match. The impetuous Scot clashed with top referee Bert Fogg in the dressing-room and promptly received a lengthy ban that brought gasps of astonishment throughout the football world.

Newcastle slipped dramatically in the table. From 2nd to 6th by the New Year, to 12th by March and 14th at the end of April. As always though they still managed to entertain, non more so than an amazing 7-5 victory over Aston Villa at Gallowgate, one of the most open and thrilling fixtures played on Tyneside. The local newspaper described the game, "the most sensational ever witnessed at St James Park", it was comparable only with Sunderland's 9-1 victory there.

The contest began in a snowstorm, but bright sunshine interrupted by showers was the pattern for the rest of the afternoon. Both teams ignored the conditions and played marvellous open football. United in particular were on song in attack, Gallacher's replacement, red haired Jonathan Wilkinson led the line brilliantly. From Esh Winning in County Durham, Wilkinson was a popular local player and most unlucky to be understudy to not only Newcastle's great leader, but later at Everton, to Dixie Dean too.

Inside 30 minutes United were 4-0 ahead, Seymour started the goal feast and Tom McDonald made it 2-0. Another reserve forward, Jock McCurley, who like Wilkinson was having an inspired game, netted number three. Nicknamed Monty, Wilkinson grabbed the fourth, but Villa were not totally outplayed and replied with a goal from Cook. Before the interval Pongo Waring scored another for the visitors, but then Newcastle stepped up a gear and by the 77th minute were 7-2 in front through McCurley and Wilkinson, whose hat- trick goal was a superb effort.

United were cruising to a convincing victory when Villa hit them with a devastating spell of football that silenced the terraces. Inside eight minutes the Midlanders scored three fine goals. Waring, Dorrell and York found the net, even though Villa were now down to ten men after keeper Olney had been carried off following a clash with Seymour. Villa pressed for more goals and United were glad to hear the final whistle.

The odd game excepted, it had been a miserable season all round. United also crashed in the FA Cup, 4-1 at Ewood Park to eventual Cup winners Blackburn Rovers. Several new players were tried in an attempt to reverse the trend. Apart from Wilkinson and McCurley, versatile half-back from Darlington, Ossie Park was handed the centre-half jersey for much of the season. Goalkeeper Micky Burns(Chilton Colliery), Stan Barber(Wallsend), Billy Carlton(Washington Colliery) and the elegant Willie Chalmers(Rangers) were all blooded. Burns was to appear between the posts until well after

Micky Burns made his debut in 1927 and proceeded to spend nearly 25 years in the game as a player.

NEW RIVAL

In the summer of 1930, Newcastle United almost had a new rival in the city when South Shields, then a Football League side in the Third Division(North) applied to both the City Corporation and Football League Management Committee for permission to move lock, stock and barrel from Horsley Hill, over the Tyne to set up a new club at Brough Park in Newcastle. United objected and the League would not grant their blessing. Shields still moved nevertheless, to Gateshead and were installed at Redheugh less than a mile from St James Park.

World War Two, notably for Ipswich and Preston. Chalmers was also to have a long career and later assisted Italian club Turin as coach.

Tom Evans(Clapton Orient), John Little(Crook Town) and Billy Gillespie(East Fife) were all tried at full-back. Evans cost £3,650 after standing out in the recent FA Cup tie with United. He became United's first Welsh international player, but was dogged by injury on Tyneside. Scot Tommy Lang was another to break into the side. He played once at outside- left after arriving as a 20 year-old from Scottish junior football and was to soon take over from Seymour on the wing. Small and elusive like his predecessor, Lang was to be an effective forward for the black'n'whites scoring 58 goals in 229 games. He was another who didn't hang up his boots until he was well into his fortieth year.

Tom Evans, the club's first Welsh international.

There were to be more changes the following season as the club's directors discarded the 1927 Championship side and started to build the nucleus of a new eleven - and with it brought revolutionary changes to St James Park.

The 1928/29 season saw the club decide to appoint a manager for the first time. Up to then, like most of football, a directors' committee had picked the team and the board had full control over the side as well as the purchase of players. While total rule was not relinquished for many years - not really until the late 1950s - Newcastle stepped into the modern era by bringing Rangers and Scotland maestro Andy Cunningham to Tyneside. At 38 years-old, Cunningham arrived at St James Park still as a player, but one to be groomed into the club's first boss. He became the oldest debutant in the Football League and later, the first player-manager in Division One. The former Scotland captain displayed much of his talent at inside-forward with precise long passes and fine positional play. By the time he did get the opportunity to pick the side he found that Newcastle's directors still wielded much power. On a few occasions when he sent his team formation to the board-room he received it back promptly altered.

Cunningham's first major task was how to patch up differences between certain members of the directorate and the side's star player Hughie Gallacher. The centre-forward's brush with officialdom - on and off the field - was to continue and caused a serious rift. Always a fiery character, Gallacher was at the centre of several controversial moments, before and after the Fogg incident. Some members of the board were clearly unhappy at the Scot's continual bickering with referees and seemingly uncontrollable temper. They wanted rid of him sources said. Speculation heightened when Arsenal manager, Herbert Chapman turned up at St James Park at the beginning of the season. Rumours circulated rapidly that Gallacher was heading south to Highbury. But the majority of the men in charge insisted that 60 goals netted in two seasons was too valuable to lose. However, Gallacher was stripped of the captaincy before the new season began. Fellow Scottish international, Joe Harris being handed the job, albeit for a short while. Gallacher was in the end reprimanded, he was told to stay out of trouble and concentrate on his job in football....to score goals.

Newcastle had a mediocre season by their standards and come the winter months were struggling at the foot of the table after they had started badly. Against Burnley at St James Park they were sensationally 6-1 down at half-time. All was not well in the Magpie camp with internal strife running through the Gallowgate corridors. The directors had a clear out before New Year, players came and went and it was reported for a second time that Alex James was about to join Newcastle. From Gallacher's birthplace, it was Hughie who nobbled James when the pair met back home in Bellshill. James was then with Preston North End and was keen to move, however United's directors considered the inside-forward too small, an amazing judgement considering Gallacher's contribution. They hesitated again and James signed for Arsenal.

United's first manager, Andy Cunningham, one of Scotland's most celebrated personalities.

While James slipped the net, new players did arrive at St James Park. Apart from Cunningham the most important signing was one of Hughie Gallacher's great antagonists, centre-half Jack Hill, captain of Burnley and England. The pair had clashed many times and the confrontation was one of the most talked about in football at the time. Hill was a fabulous stopper and one of the elite of the twenties. He was one of the few men who could actually tame Gallacher and the Scot was quick to pick the Burnley player when Chairman John Oliver posed the question regarding the club's defensive target, "Who should we buy?".

Immediately the answer came, "Jack Hill". The 6'2" red haired defender joined United for £8,100, a national record transfer after Newcastle just beat off the challenge of Sunderland for his signature. He was immediately installed as the Magpies' new captain.

England captain Jack Hill joined the Magpies for a record fee from Burnley.

Also to join the playing staff were full-back Bob Thomson, another Scottish international who was part of a swop deal that took Bob McKay to Sunderland. United's vast Scottish contingent now numbered 14 professionals. In a 3-2 victory over Leeds United, Newcastle fielded an entire line-up without an Englishman in the ranks, a rarity in the Football League. Ten Scots and reserve Welshman, centre-half Ed Wood took the field.

Changes at St James Park brought results and the Tyneside club recovered in the remaining months of the season to finish in 10th position, although they were knocked out of the FA Cup by Third Division Swindon Town. Newcastle embarked on a European tour during the close season of 1929 visiting Italy, Czechoslovakia, Hungary and Austria, but with it entered a hornet's nest of trouble. United won their first game, 1-0 with the Ambrosiana club of Milan, but it was an experience they wanted to quickly forget. The Italians resorted to rugby style tactics and United's players limped off the field with Tommy Lang, hardly ever to lose his cool, being sent off. He was given his marching orders along with his opposing full-back and had to suffer a nasty set of bite marks on his neck. Newcastle did not give an exhibition display to say the least. They mixed it too and a brawl was the outcome. The crowd did not like it and afterwards a mob gathered around the club's motor coach. Stones and bottles whizzed through the windows and skipper Hill, together with Fairhurst and reserve goalkeeper Micky Burns were all injured. There was more trouble at the team's hotel, United's players having to barricade themselves in their bedrooms. Hughie Gallacher noted in his memoirs, "Frankly I was scared stiff and never more glad to see cops in my life".

RESERVE BID

In season 1929/30 United, desperate to obtain better football for their reserve combination, attempted to gain entry to the Central League and were initially successful winning eleven votes. However, after an appeal by Stockport County who had been thrown out in the Magpies' favour, Newcastle's entry was rejected because the club had offered "prejudicial inducements" to visiting teams. They took an undertaking to pay return fares from Leeds and overnight expenses of £20 for trips to Tyneside. United had to go back to the North Eastern League cap in hand and plead for a re-entry into the competition they had resigned from a few weeks earlier.

The tour turned sour after that opening. Against WAC Vienna in another rowdy 90 minutes, United lost 2-0 and then came an embarrassing 8-1 defeat at the hands of Slovak Czechoslovakia when the Geordies were accused of not trying by Czech officials. That controversy behind them, United travelled to Budapest to meet a Hungarian select - a match that blew up almost into an international incident. The match was another rough contest and Gallacher said of continental football he experienced for the first time, "Their skill was at an absolute minimum and the only way they could stop us was by the crudest tactics imaginable". Newcastle lost 4-1 and both Gallacher and Alf Maitland were sent-off following punch-ups. Newcastle had to be escorted through a seething crowd by armed soldiers so much ill feeling had been aroused. Hungarian officials were incensed and withheld part of United's appearance fee of £165, whilst at the same time made a formal complaint to the Football Association as to Newcastle's performance and attitude to the so called exhibition game. They also accused United's players of being drunk on the field and back on British soil a Football Association

Newcastle on tour during the summer of 1929, pictured with the Milan team. Notice Gallacher, bottom right, in friendly pose with the opposing goalkeeper. The match was no friendly matter and ended in a nasty confrontation.

Inquiry criticised the club's handling of the tour. As to the drinking....Alf Maitland recorded that, "It was a boiling hot day so we rinsed our mouths out with a drop of Scotch and water"!

The 1929/30 season about to commence was to be Hughie Gallacher's last with Newcastle United. The player-director conflict had not been healed and just before the new term's kick-off in August he asked for a transfer, being linked with both Arsenal and Tottenham. A week before, United had purchased another Scot, Duncan Hutchison from Dundee United, a centre- forward with a good reputation north of the Cheviots and who had just crashed 40 goals in one season for the Tay club. Gallacher saw the signing as his replacement, especially when it was suggested the new man would be handed the centre-forward's role with Gallacher being pushed inside. Fierce debate raged on the subject. Gallacher was still King of Tyneside and many said the club would dare not transfer him. They were right in the short term. Differences were again patched up, Hughie signing another year's contract. However the rift between club and player was broader. It was not to be healed.

In spite of the transfer speculation Gallacher started on top of his game, as if to show Newcastle officials what they would miss. And the Magpies went off like a bomb. Gallacher scored three goals on the first Saturday of the season against Manchester United in a 4-1 victory and then they hit Blackburn Rovers for five. Gallacher netted eleven goals in the first ten games, it was just like old times. His scoring prowess though, could not stop the Gallowgate club sliding to 21st place. It was to be a relegation threatened season for United, and Gallacher, with his goals - he grabbed 34 - saved the Novocastrians from the drop.

No-one played with more skill and heart for the black'n'whites that season. His commitment was unquestioned. Hughie's loyalty to his club got him into more confrontation though when the Scottish Football Association wanted him to play for his country on the same day as an important relegation clash with Arsenal. He chose United's cause and fell out of favour with the Scots.

Newcastle's fight to avoid the drop lasted to the very last day of the season and a game with West Ham United during May. It was to be Gallacher's last game in a Newcastle shirt, although nobody, except perhaps a few club directors, knew it then. A 50,000 crowd saw a dramatic 63rd minute Joe Devine goal ensure First Division survival. Devine was a desperate £5,575 buy from Burnley and his lifeline goal was worth the heavy outlay. It was a match United had to win, a draw would have sent them tumbling into Division Two. United were lucky over the 90 minutes as Vic Watson, the League's leading scorer had an off day for the Hammers and, "missed a bag of goals".

Newcastle finished in 19th position and skipped the trapdoor by a point. It was their worst recorded position in the First Division while the Magpies also registered 16 away defeats in the season, the poorest in the club's past. Team spirit had been at an all time low with dressing-room discontent and argument. The supporters didn't like it and Tommy Urwin was the unlucky individual to suffer the fans' wrath culminating in a transfer to neighbours Sunderland.

In the FA Cup Newcastle found rather better luck, a year the media speculated that Hughie Gallacher was to pick up a winner's medal. They reached the quarter-finals and played lowly opposition in each tie. York City, Clapton Orient and Brighton were all from the Third Division and all disposed of, but without a lot of conviction. York, in their first year as a League side, held United at St James Park after a thrill a minute tie in a snowstorm. They grabbed a deserved equaliser once Gallacher had nodded United in front. At Fulfordgate, Newcastle won 2-1 after the home side had gone in front before a record crowd. Over 700 Magpie fans were locked out.

Hull City were no strangers to United in the 6th Round. Managed by Bill McCracken, his struggling Second Division line-up arrived on Tyneside and attracted a huge 63,486 attendance and at one stage the crowd was so packed together that the barriers gave way. They drew 1-1 and the Tigers went on to win the replay 1-0 at their Anlaby Road ground. Another record crowd turned up for the game which saw both sides' fortunes ebb and flow from one end to another.

Alf Maitland, born in Leith, but who appeared for the Football League XI.

Star striker Duncan Hutchison arrived at Gallowgate in August 1929 and was nicknamed 'Hurricane Hutch'.

Again many new faces were tried in the senior team during the season. Following Devine and Hutchison, big fees were paid for winger Jackie Cape from Carlisle United and locally born full-back David Fairhurst, then at Walsall. England keeper Albert McInroy made the short trip from Roker Park for £2,750 and Dave Davidson was picked up for £4,000 from Liverpool. The most important purchase of all though was Sammy Weaver, who was secured from McCracken's club, Hull City, for £2,500 as a player with a "promising future".

Youngsters were also tried. Wing-half George Mathison from Walker, and the two Richardsons, full-back Joe and forward Jimmy, both from Blyth Spartans earned a place. The intense transfer activity however, showed that United's bold policy of introducing a junior set up in the twenties had yet to pay off. The Newcastle Swifts had been born a few years earlier and competed in the Tyneside League. Headed by Colin Veitch, it was noted by a club official that, "our object is to find stars in the rough and give the local lads a chance". It was to take many years before kids came flooding through the system.

More rows had continued between Gallacher and club officials and reports circulated that he had been offered to arch rivals, Sunderland in a record deal. Denials were swift and profuse, but the local paper which released the story stuck by its headline. Gallacher was amazed at Newcastle United's attitude. He had actually signed a new contract for the 1930/31 season, yet within a few hours was apparently being offered to the Roker Park club. Hughie was vexed and said, "No-one has ever shown the door to Hughie Gallacher twice. I am not a pawn to be transferred willy-nilly".

The majority of Newcastle's board, as well as boss Cunningham, now wanted rid of the player. Gallacher admitted that he was never on the best of terms with United's tall Glaswegian manager. He said to a friend, "Once Cunningham arrived as boss I knew my days were numbered at Newcastle United". Nothing came of the Sunderland transaction, nor of an approach, apparently by a London club. That club turned out to be Chelsea. Hughie though made it clear he did not wish to leave St James Park and was being pushed out the door. He was proud to be a Newcastle player and had a fondness for Tyneside. United fans still

United's players out for a round of golf. Hughie Gallacher, front right, provides the camera with a casual pose complete with cigarette in his mouth.

worshipped him and petitions, letters and irate callers flooded the club. On no account did they want Gallacher to be transferred.

The end of season incident died down with Gallacher officially a United player for another year. Immediately on the old season's close he travelled with the Scottish international party to meet France in Paris. While he was impressing the French public and sightseeing in the capital, negotiations on Tyneside were taking place behind his back to make him a Chelsea player. This after five years as Newcastle United's top scorer and with over 140 goals behind him in a black'n'white shirt. Gallacher wasn't happy, but he soon reluctantly signed for the Londoners. He felt betrayed and said later, "Why Newcastle wanted to let me go I never found out. But with such an attitude I was bound to leave the club. Better sooner than later".

Albert McInroy joined United from Sunderland after winning an England cap.

Newcastle received a massive £10,000 fee, only a few hundred pounds short of David Jack's transfer record when he moved from Bolton to Arsenal a year before. It was cash United needed. After many good years financially the club was now feeling the pinch with the twenties depression reaching the St James Park coffers. Crowds were still good, an average of almost 37,000, but poor transfer dealings had cost the club dearly.

The departure of Gallacher and his magic feet, marked the end of an era at St James Park. The stars of both the 1924 and 1927 trophy winning sides had disappeared to various parts of the country. The twenties was a decade that had seen penicillin and television invented, that saw women given full voting parity and which welcomed the first solo flight across the Atlantic. Live theatre and music-hall comedy thrived, silent cinema and Valentino had been at their peak and talkies were on their way. Slim young things danced the fast moving Charleston and fashions saw women's hair boyishly short and skirts barely to the knee. The Tyne Bridge had been opened, Newcastle Brown Ale launched and the vast North East Coast Exhibition took place on the Town Moor.

The twenties had brought Newcastle both the FA Cup and League Championship. It also saw United try, unsuccessfully, to comprehensively develop St James Park into a super-stadium while the era also brought Hughie Gallacher to Tyneside. With baggy shorts, a thick flapping jersey and clumsy looking football boots, the wee Scot had certainly made an impression. But now Newcastle's supporters had lost their hero - not for the first or last time. His magic was soon to return to St James Park and create more news, albeit in the blue of Chelsea.

SUPPORTERS' CLUB FORMED

During February 1930 the first Newcastle United Supporter's Club was formed with an annual subscription of 1s 0d per season.

How one cartoonist saw Hughie Gallacher's departure from Tyneside in the summer of 1930.

Centenary Profile 9

The Model Professional

"the type that never gives his manager a moment of anxiety"

Topical Times, 1921

FRANK HUDSPETH WAS ONE OF THOSE model professionals who rarely made the back-page news or caught the eye on the field in the way more flamboyant individuals did. He was the solid, dependable type who settled into his routine game for 90 minutes without fuss or cause for concern.

Every successful team needs two or three unsung heroes to compensate for the stars and headline makers. Tom McDonald was one in United's ranks, Hudspeth was another. Like McDonald, Frank Hudspeth took part in the 1924 FA Cup victory and the 1927 Championship success and was one of the club's many dedicated pro's of the time who played well into their thirties. And Hudspeth was even good enough at that age to be capped by his country for the first time when all of 35 years and six months old - the oldest player up to that point to make his debut in the white shirt of England.

That international appearance against Northern Ireland in Belfast during October 1925 ended in a 0-0 draw and the Newcastle defender had a touch of luck getting into the side to win his only cap. He was called up only on the injury to first choice defenders. Nevertheless it heralded the zenith of the Geordie full-back's career which started some 18 years before kicking a ball about the cobbled streets of Percy Main.

Just as Jackie Rutherford - another from the same Tyneside community - had done a few years earlier, Hudspeth was born and bred on the banks of the river and first caught the eye of United scouts playing for local sides Clara Vale and Scotswood. They kept a note of his progress and when Hudspeth graduated into the ranks of Newburn's eleven and then North Shields Athletic, two strong sides then, Newcastle made their mind up to put him on the payroll. He signed for United in March 1910 for £100 and made his debut in the following season against Bradford City.

It was during a Christmas fixture pile up during the following year that the left-back's shirt became virtually his own property. After a series of outstanding displays Hudspeth became first choice taking over from Tony Whitson and the veteran Jack Carr, another Tynesider who had appeared for England. Frank went on to partner Bill McCracken in defence for almost ten seasons, both serving the Magpies for a record period - 19 years on the club's books. It was a celebrated combination, a mix of the steady Hudspeth and charismatic McCracken.

At 5'9" tall and a bit of a fanatic at physical fitness, Hudspeth went on to to appear in more games than any other United player except goalkeeper Jimmy Lawrence, a total of 472 League and Cup matches. Had it not been for a four year break due to war, Hudspeth would have clocked up an even bigger appearance total. He was among the most durable of outfield players. Frank was 34 when he won an FA Cup medal and 37 when the title came to St James Park. Nicknamed 'Marra' by his colleagues - Geordie for friend - Hudspeth was tough, but with a gentlemanly and fair attitude. It was a rare instance when he lost his temper and Stan Seymour was to say, "He never said a wrong word about anyone", while Topical Times magazine noted, "Frank is the type that never gives his manager a moment of anxiety".

For a full-back, Hudspeth found the net often, scoring 38 goals in his day at St James Park. He was something of a penalty expert and no other player has converted as many spot-kicks for the club, usually stepping back a few places and rocketing the ball into the net. He was skipper at Gallowgate for three years, a

HUDSPETH'S PLAYING RECORD						
	League		FA Cup		Total	
	App	Gls	App	Gls	App	Gls
1910-11	12	0	0	0	12	0
1911-12	17	0	1	0	18	0
1912-13	27	4	8	2	35	6
1913-14	36	4	1	0	37	4
1914-15	36	4	6	0	42	4
1919-20	39	1	2	0	41	1
1920-21	28	1	4	0	32	1
1921-22	41	1	1	0	42	1
1922-23	27	1	2	0	29	1
1923-24	30	2	7	1	37	3
1924-25	34	1	3	0	37	1
1925-26	32	8	3	0	35	8
1926-27	42	3	3	0	45	3
1927-28	23	1	1	0	24	1
1928-29	6	3	0	0	6	3
1918-19 (War time)					10	1
	430	**34**	**42**	**3**	**482**	**38**

Frank Hudspeth

period which included a Wembley victory in 1924 and even being relieved of the captaincy in favour of Hughie Gallacher did nothing to stop his dedication to the club. Before he eventually got into the England side, Hudspeth had been on the fringes of a cap for several years. Frank appeared in trial games and was selected for the unofficial England v Wales Victory International in 1919.

As the 1928/29 season began a 5-0 defeat by Manchester United marked the end of the road for Hudspeth's career in black'n'white colours. Age had finally caught up with him and younger forwards were now able to get the better of the contest - as the Reds very much showed at Old Trafford. When approaching 40 years of age, Hudspeth joined Stockport County in January 1929. He stayed at Edgeley Park only briefly before completing a lengthy playing career with Crook Town as the thirties decade opened.

Afterwards he returned to Tyneside and ran a billiards hall in Newcastle for a while, but football always held an attraction and Frank was involved in the game once more when he became, firstly Rochdale, and then in 1934 Burnley trainer. Among the players Hudspeth helped develop on the path of stardom was legendary centre-forward Tommy Lawton, then a teenager at the Second Division club.

Frank Hudspeth remained at Turf Moor until the end of the Second World War when he left the first class scene. He resided in the Burnley area to his death in February 1963.

Left: Hudspeth meets his rival skipper Charlie Buchan before a Sunderland derby clash. Right: Frank shows off the F.A. Cup at Wembley in 1924.

Centenary Profile 10

The Headline Maker

"The ordinary rules didn't apply to Hughie Gallacher because he was a soccer genius"

Stan Seymour

IT TOOK ONLY FORTY-FIVE MINUTES OF FOOTBALL to convince United fans that they had a good'un in Hughie Gallacher. And yet many were astounded and somewhat concerned when he first ran onto the St James Park pitch. As Gallacher recorded, "The home fans cheered the first few players tremendously. As I ran out the deafening cheers turned to a....Oh! The crowd had just noticed how small I was". But his boyish appearance counted for little once the Scot had the ball at his feet and the goal in sight.

In that game with Everton, Gallacher netted twice. Charlie Spencer said, "Soon after the match began I turned and gave my fellow defenders a thumbs up signal. We knew a real star had joined us". And the fans soon agreed. Gallacher became an instant hero - perhaps United's biggest ever personality.

There have been few players to have made such an impression on the game of football than Gallacher. At 5'5" he was a tough and rough little centre- forward equipped with a full range of skills only a handful of contemporaries can begin to match. His record of 463 goals in 624 senior games speaks for itself. To many who witnessed his quite brilliant all round ability he was simply the best there has been.

Gallacher was the most talked about player during the years between the two wars, and not only because of his footballing skills. The tempestuous Scot seemingly could not keep out of the news whether on or off the pitch. He was a journalist's dream, the biggest headline maker of the era. Gallacher created sensation, controversy and intrigue wherever he went.

Headlines like the day he represented his country in 1925. In many ways a moment that typified his career. Gallacher was in Belfast for an Inter League contest, a game in which he totally destroyed the Irish with a devastating display. He netted five of Scotland's goals in a 7-3 victory. Not only had the Scot repeatedly found the net but he also made the home players and watching fans feel distinctly second-rate - playing irritating tricks with the ball and teasing the opposition almost into a frenzy.

At half-time a note was passed into the Scottish dressing-room from Irish partisans. It was a death threat. Gallacher would be shot if he did not ease up. Hughie of course ignored the threat and continued his scoring and exhibition play until the final whistle. However the extremist home fans were not to be taken lightly. Before the Scotland party sailed for the mainland, Hughie ventured to visit friends in the city. He was warned to be careful, Ireland was no place for strangers then, as now. He grinned, until a bullet splattered on a nearby wall as he walked near Queen's Bridge. Whether it was a real attempt on his life or a grim practical joke will never be known. Gallacher, always a witty character, could see the funny side and afterwards said, "I'll have to extend my stay in Belfast. It seems I still haven't managed to teach the Irish how to shoot straight"!

From early days in the Lanarkshire steel town of Bellshill through a career that spanned all of 20 seasons, Gallacher made a string of remarkable headlines. By the time he was playing for Scottish junior side Bellshill Athletic, he caused the first of many controversial incidents. At barely 17 years of age he was married, a brief and stormy relationship that broke the strong Protestant-Catholic divide. Then, tragically his son died before he was twelve months old.

Gallacher signed for Queen of the South in 1920, played for Scotland's junior ranks and almost died of double pneumonia. Recovering after a long period out of the game his talents were quickly snapped up by Airdrieonians a year later and a century of goals followed in their white shirt. Gallacher made headlines on the sports pages in a big way as the Diamonds challenged the Old Firm of Rangers and Celtic. He was also often in trouble with referees and defenders with his whiplash tongue and ever lit short temper. The more Hughie was seen the more his stature and reputation as a lethal goal-poacher - as well as a stormy terrier - broadened.

In 1924 he won a Scottish Cup winners medal with Airdrie, then became his country's regular centre-forward with scintillating performances in the national blue shirt. His name was thrown into the limelight again when an Irish reporter claimed he shouldn't be playing for the Scots, because it was alleged (wrongly) he was Irish! More controversy.

GALLACHER'S PLAYING RECORD

	League		FA Cup		Total	
	App	Gls	App	Gls	App	Gls
1925-26	19	23	3	2	22	25
1926-27	38	36	3	3	41	39
1927-28	32	21	1	0	33	21
1928-29	33	24	1	0	34	24
1929-30	38	29	6	5	44	34
	160	**133**	**14**	**10**	**174**	**143**

Hughie Gallacher

In his first England versus Scotland game he netted two goals and sent watching scouts rushing south with glowing reports. Newcastle United were determined to secure his signature and amidst fierce competition eventually did. Hughie took to Tyneside immediately and strutted around the area like a Geordie God, always dressing well in tailored suits and trendy headgear. He opened garden parties, graced dances and adored the razzmatazz but was often in trouble of one sort or another. He once appeared in court and was bound over to keep the peace for brawling under the flickering gas lamps of the Tyne's High Level Bridge.

On the field goals continued to flow, almost 150 for Newcastle. He was fast, elusive and difficult to knock off the ball using his short, but stocky frame to good effect. Close to goal Gallacher was sharp and able to take chances with either foot, or head. He was slick with the short pass, able to go past two or three opponents with ease and brilliant at making chances for others. Stan Seymour recorded, "I say without hesitation that he was the greatest centre-forward I have ever seen. The ordinary rules didn't apply to Hughie Gallacher because he was a soccer genius".

Gallacher also taunted opponents with verbal abuse - none quite had a tongue like Hughie - and with niggling pokes and kicks. Sturdy defenders did not like his style one bit and singled him out for special treatment. It produced fireworks on the pitch and more copy for the newsmen. He was suspended and fined by the game's rulers for a succession of incidents and became one of Scotland's legendary Wembley Wizards in 1928 as England were thrashed 5-1. His departure from Gallowgate to Chelsea in 1930 in itself caused uproar and sensation. He didn't want to leave and the fans didn't want to lose him either. But go he did, for a massive £10,000 fee.

A five year stint at Stamford Bridge followed and if anything the headlines he created in London even surpassed those of before. First though he was responsible for St James Park's record attendance when he returned with Chelsea then was involved in player power, rows over money, illegal payments, more suspensions and brushes with the law. In spite of everything a constant supply of goals still came from the Gallacher boot.

His days in the metropolis ended in 1934, the year Hughie also ended up in the Bankruptcy Court due to a prolonged and often publicised divorce. He signed for Derby County, undoubtedly accepting illegal money as part of the transfer, a deal that saw the Rams censored and manager suspended. A productive spell at the Baseball Ground followed, nearly lifting another Championship medal before Gallacher moved on to Notts County and Grimsby Town.

A nostalgic return to Tyneside occurred just before the Second World War when Hughie signed for Gateshead, but the hostilities soon ended his long playing career. Yet away from the field he still managed to create news. As a part-time journalist he was banned from St James Park for being too critical and fell out with the Football Association for refereeing a non-affiliated charity game. He remained very much a personality alongside the Tyne for the rest of his life and created probably the biggest headline of all in 1957, his own sad and dreadful death.

Losing his wife through illness, Gallacher's later years quickly deteriorated. He drank heavily and was charged with the ill treatment of his youngest son and was due to appear in a Gateshead Court on one of the most degrading of charges. Hughie Gallacher never made the appointment. He jumped in front of the York to Edinburgh express train near his home in Gateshead.

His had been an inspiring, and sometimes notorious, life and tragic in its ending. Raich Carter said of Gallacher, "There has never been better", while Tommy Lawton said a few years ago, "If he was around today, then I don't think £2 million would buy him. Players like Hughie Gallacher appear only once in a generation". Hughie Gallacher had made news to the end. The Newcastle Journal's headline was, "Hughie of the Magic Feet is Dead". United fans will never see another remotely like him.

8 THIRTIES DECLINE

1930-1939

• RECORD CROWD WELCOME • WEMBLEY CONTROVERSY • DRAMATIC SLUMP • MANAGERIAL CHANGE • SEYMOUR'S TOUCH •

> *"Persistent ill luck in the matter of injuries and sickness has dragged Newcastle United down"*
>
> *Official Club comment, April 1938*

NEWCASTLE UNITED SUPPORTERS **had plenty to be annoyed about. They had just seen their biggest terrace hero depart to London and had witnessed a Championship winning squad deteriorate into a collection of individuals with little team understanding, fit only for relegation combat. There was much fury in the pubs and clubs of Tyneside and Magpie followers - fervent then just as now - made sure Newcastle's management at least heard their complaints.**

As the thirties decade opened United fared little better with boss Andy Cunningham shuffling and adding to his pack of players in an attempt to come up with the winning combination. The Scot eventually got it right but Newcastle supporters had a frustrating season to endure.

Duncan Lindsay (left) meets Colin Veitch, then a correspondent for the Evening Chronicle, and director John Graham after joining United an May 1930.

The nationwide collapse of trade and industry which brought with it a tide of growing unemployment continued and Tyneside remained as badly affected as anywhere in the country. Strikes, short-term working and lock-outs were common, the Jarrow March occurring in 1936. The working-class found that the decade to come was no better than the decade that had passed. Football, and their heroes in a black'n'white jersey remained the Geordies' outlet. But without Gallacher's influence over the next twelve months Newcastle struggled.

The club tried to solve the problem by paying out £2,700 for Duncan Lindsay, another Scot, this time from Cowdenbeath. Short and sturdy, he boasted a considerable scoring record in the Scottish League albeit at a lower level - 81 goals in 122 league games for his club. He netted six in one Scottish Cup game and Lindsay started off in Gallacher's role but was never in the same class. Duncan Hutchison, fast and furious in style took over, but even together the pair hardly matched up to half a Gallacher. Hutchison's only taste of fortune was in the FA Cup. Known in Scotland as 'Hurricane Hutch', the Fifer netted a superb hat-trick against Nottingham Forest as Newcastle won 4-0, this after Newcastle's ground staff had placed 120 braziers over the Gallowgate pitch to combat a severe frost. Hutchison later became a respected Dundee United director for many years. Cunningham tried veteran England and Derby County forward Harry Bedford too, a £4,000 signing, but United struggled up front all season. Why did United allowed Gallacher to depart was the vexed cry from the terraces.

The fiery Scot was back on Tyneside with his new club Chelsea for the very first game of the season at St James Park and those fans made sure Gallacher - and Newcastle's directors - knew that they still idolised him in spite of his new colours. A huge attendance gathered for the 6.15 evening kick-off. The largest midweek crowd anywhere up to then converged on St James Park and 68,386 turned up. It was a new record gate for United, one that still stands and an estimated 10,000 to 30,000 were locked out. Hundreds sat precariously on the stand roof, others braved tree-top perches along Leazes Terrace.

Fans were crouched right up to the touch-line prompting United winger Jackie Cape to say, "More than once I was forced to scramble my way in and out of spectators". Those supporters who got into the stadium were not necessarily the lucky ones. The crush was, in places, unbearable. One spectator noted that he had put his hands in his pockets before the match started and couldn't get them out again. He claimed to have paid 1s 6d admission, but would have willingly paid £1 0s 6d to get out again!

Chelsea had injury problems and much was expected of Gallacher, skipper on his return. He was up against his former sparring partner once more in Jack Hill. They were to have a real captain's tussle although no major off- the-ball incident occurred. Hughie was greeted with a, "storm of cheering" never witnessed before or since for a visiting player at St James Park. Cloth caps waved and how the Geordies cheered. The hero worship was still evident and Gallacher admitted in later years that the demonstration of sheer adulation from those Newcastle fans had been the most memorable moment of his life.

Twice before half-time the former United centre-forward went close for his new club, but Albert McInroy saved well. Gallacher was in fact a little eager and was caught in the Magpies' offside-trap often. He, as usual, protested at decisions fervently. Newcastle full-back Jimmy Nelson, a new signing from Cardiff City, was carried off after the break, an incident that only spurred the home side on and deadlock was broken with 15 minutes of the match left. Jon Wilkinson lobbed the ball to the far post where Cape rushed in just ahead of Tommy Law to head home. The goal gave Newcastle a 1-0 victory.

Scottish international, Jimmy Nelson, was out of action for several weeks with cartilage trouble after that injury and Newcastle missed his vast experience. Tough and uncompromising, Nelson had been to Wembley twice with the Ninian Park club and was a Wembley Wizard alongside Gallacher in 1928. Although almost 30 years-old, he cost Newcastle a big fee, over £7,000. Jimmy was to recover from injury to skipper the Magpies to their next moment of glory.

Other newcomers were inside-forward Ron Starling who, like Weaver, came with Bill McCracken's blessing from Hull City. Born in Gateshead, he was only just out of his teens when he first pulled on a black'n'white shirt and possessed all the craft to become a top performer. Unfortunately he was frequently in and out of United's line-up and departed for Sheffield Wednesday - only to become an England schemer. Half-back Jimmy Naylor cost £4,000 from Huddersfield Town, but like Starling played his best football in pastures new, at Oldham.

Recent seasons had seen a massive turn-a-round in players but all this new blood still couldn't stop Newcastle again dropping in to Division One's danger zone as the season wore on. United were harshly criticised in certain quarters, non more so than by their former star Colin Veitch, then a correspondent for the Newcastle Chronicle. He annoyed the players so much with his comments that they requested the board to instruct Veitch not to travel with the team, then the custom of journalists. In the coming seasons Veitch became the club's number one critic and relationships broke down especially after a controversial interview with director John Graham which led to the long-standing official's resignation from the board.

After going out of the FA Cup to Leeds United by 4-1 - against a side which included three of the Milburn family and ex United winger Tom Mitchell - Newcastle recovered in time to save their Division

Jack Hill heads the Magpies line-up at the start of the Thirties decade.

Jimmy Nelson, an experienced Scottish international full-back purchased for over £7,000.

DOUBLE RECORD

Newcastle United not only recorded their record attendance of 68,386 against Chelsea in September 1930, but also a new record receipt figure was set up. £4,267 0s 8d was taken at the gate. By comparison if the club had that vast attendance in 1991 something like £350,000 would be collected at the turnstiles. In the same season that United created those two ground records, they also attracted only 10,000 for a league game against Bolton Wanderers.

One place. They played some good football in February and March but deteriorated thereafter not winning a game for the rest of the season which sent alarm bells ringing, although thankfully not to end in disaster.

Two bizarre fixtures took place. The first was at Old Trafford when the Tynesiders won by a 7-4 margin; then against Portsmouth, at Gallowgate, the visitors won by the same remarkable scoreline! Against bottom of the table Manchester United, starlet Ron Starling was the pick of Newcastle's side that rocked a Reds' line-up that had conceded no fewer than 19 goals in the first four games of the season. Newcastle made it an amazing 26 goals in five games and this after Manchester United went 1-0 ahead. On a greasy turf Newcastle hit back, netting three in seven minutes, but the game was all square at 4-4 with half an hour left. Then the Magpies went nap. Signing from Carlisle United, Jackie Cape scored three while Tom Reid grabbed a hat-trick for Manchester United, but still found himself on the losing side.

Portsmouth arrived on Tyneside during November and took part in another extraordinary game. This time the black'n'whites went in front when Lindsay netted, but Pompey flattened United going 4-1 ahead. Newcastle were down to ten men for much of the game when full-back Bob Thomson was forced to hobble on the wing as a passenger. The visitors rallied after a brief United fight back and scored another three to finish 7-4 winners. And it could have been much more with one report noting Newcastle fortunate not to concede into, "double figures".

Henry McMenemy who, as a teenager, made a huge impression in midfield.

Following the Pompey shock - only seven days later - United's fans had to suffer a harrowing 5-0 thrashing on a dark rainy afternoon at Roker Park. And that was not all. Soon after, United's other neighbours, Middlesbrough, arrived on Tyneside and proceeded to hammer the Magpies 5-0 too.

Cunningham had to solve the goalscoring and centre-forward problem for the new season and he did so very effectively by bringing Sheffield Wednesday's bustling leader Jack Allen back north in June 1931. Originally a Prudhoe Castle junior, Allen had joined Leeds United in 1924 and moved on to Hillsborough after a spell at Brentford. In two seasons, as Wednesday lifted the Championship in successive years of 1929 and 1930, Allen had ravaged 74 senior goals. He cost United a bargain £3,500 and proceeded to make a name for himself in Newcastle's annals. He did have spells of mediocrity but as the Northern Echo noted Jack, "led the line with dash and unselfishness".

Allen made all the difference to Newcastle's attack. Boyd and Lang both improved beyond recognition after a spell of poor form and made the wing positions their own. The new striker played a leading role in the development of two gifted young inside-forwards, Jimmy Richardson and Harry McMenemy. They benefited greatly by having an experienced centre-forward to target. Former England schools player Jimmy Richardson had developed quickly from the club's reserve side with an all round ability that was invaluable. He would frequently dash up front on dribbling one man runs that became a feature of his play. The Ashington youngster always grafted too and became something of a workhorse with a magic scoring touch hitting over 50 goals for the Magpies.

Harry McMenemy, not yet 20 years old and from an honoured Scottish footballing family, claimed his place alongside Richardson. He made his debut against Grimsby Town in the third game of the season and impressed so much he became a regular. Only "a strip of a lad" as one reporter noted, his apprenticeship lasted all of two weeks after arriving on Tyneside from Strathclyde Juniors. He wasn't tall, only 5'9", but was cultured and skilful. McMenemy excelled on the ball and possessed a football brain just like his father, 'Nap' McMenemy who had been a famous Celtic and Scotland player. Harry was to be picked for Scotland in the months ahead too, but unluckily was often on the treatment table and on the occasion of his first - and as it turned out - only call up had to withdraw through injury. Ironically his brother John, who appeared successfully for Motherwell, replaced him. Also related to the schemer is Lawrie McMenemy, future Southampton and Sunderland manager and on United's books during the fifties.

Newcastle's league form was much improved after a slow opening. So much so that there was even talk of a Championship bid. United were in

Glasgow born, Jimmy Boyd proved to be a great success on the right flank and consistently scored goals.

NO TO FLYING

As FA Cup winners in 1932 United planned to fly to Paris and Hamburg for exhibition matches. However, boss Andy Cunningham would have none of it. He noted that so far as his precious footballers are concerned, "flying is far too dangerous". Newcastle United were not to fly to a match until another decade, and more, had passed.

3rd place on January 1st, but then efforts were then put into the FA Cup. Cunningham found he was able to choose a settled team, something he had rarely experienced since taking the helm. United went almost three months and ten successive games unchanged - a club record. Yet Newcastle were inconsistent. They could be quite brilliant on occasion, but woefully poor as the 8-1 demolition by Everton at Goodison Park illustrated. The Lancashire club had just gained promotion and were on their way to a noteworthy treble of honours, including the title that year, and had led Newcastle 6-0 at half-time. Another remarkable game was, perhaps surprisingly, a 0-0 draw at Gallowgate with Portsmouth. That 90 minutes of football is thought to be the first game to be played without a corner-kick!

It was, though, in the FA Cup tournament of 1932 that United made the football world sit up and take notice. A 1-1 draw at Blackpool during January started the Magpies' Cup season. In the replay, over 46,000 saw Jimmy Boyd put Newcastle through into the next round with a goal in the 57th minute after majestic work by Lang and Allen. Southport, from the Third Division North, then gave United a rousing but difficult passage in the next tie.

A 50,000 crowd were at St James Park to see the Lancashire club earn a replay after Boyd had put Newcastle ahead in the very first minute. A record gate of 20,010 at Haig Avenue witnessed another 1-1 draw and a Cup-tie high in tension, with Glaswegian Boyd yet again finding the net. It had been a rough tussle and United had to contend with no fewer than ten injuries for the next meeting. The whole senior playing staff was put on alert and travelled to Sheffield, venue of a third meeting. The decisive clash took place at Hillsborough and thoroughly decisive it was. Shortly before the break the score remained at 0-0. Three quarters of an hour later it read, Newcastle United 9 Southport 0! It remains the club's highest ever FA Cup score and, at the time, the best in any competition. Jimmy Richardson, fast becoming a prized front-man soon to earn an England call-up, crashed home three goals and reserve forward, Jackie Cape, two. Boyd, Lang, Weaver and McMenemy concluded the rout.

In the Fifth Round, First Division relegation candidates Leicester City were felled 3-1 after United went a goal behind against the run of play. Newcastle then faced another Third Division side in the quarter-finals, Watford. Just prior to the game though, all at St James Park were stunned at the death of secretary Frank Watt at the age of 77. He had been with Newcastle for 37 years and was a respected name throughout the English and Scottish football scene, possessing great tact and shrewdness. One of several extensive obituaries noted, "his one hobby was Newcastle United and its welfare". His name lived on with Newcastle United when, his son 'Fritz' Watt took over the secretary's chair for nearly two decades.

A minutes silence was observed in Frank Watt's honour before the 6th Round clash with Watford kicked off. St James Park was packed with 57,879 spectators and United gave their past administrator a fitting send-off, sailing into the semi-final with a 5-0 victory. Jack Allen hit a fabulous hat-trick which included a terrific shoulder-high volley that flew into the goal after a choice passing movement from 'keeper to net. Then he capped a marvellous performance with a solo run past three defenders before walking the ball over the line. Newcastle pounded poor Watford for 90 minutes and, additionally, hit the woodwork three times.

That emphatic triumph took Newcastle into a semi-final contest with Chelsea - and with Hughie Gallacher. Jimmy Nelson, now captain, said before the match, "Newcastle United will make a bold bid. We feel it is our year". The Londoners, although having a side packed with internationals including two other Wembley Wizards in Tommy Law and match-winner Alec Jackson, were seldom in the game at Huddersfield. Newcastle won with ease by 2-1 answering several adverse press comments that Chelsea had only to turn up to ensure a Wembley appearance.

Tommy Lang, who complemented Boyd on the opposite flank. Another winger who grabbed his share of goals.

United's F.A. Cup line-up. Left to right: McInroy, Nelson, Fairhurst, McKenzie, Davidson, Weaver, Boyd, Richardson, Allen, McMenemy, Lang, McPherson Jnr (trainer).

United dominated the first half at Leeds Road with piercing attacks at lightning speed. Their pace and incisive football soon had Chelsea reeling. United went ahead after eleven minutes when a Lang free-kick was headed towards goal by Allen. The ball was only half cleared straight back to United's centre-forward who fired low past Chelsea's 'keeper Millington. Newcastle's second goal quickly followed when Boyd went past Law and Ferguson on a brilliant touch-line run. He crossed for little Tommy Lang, only 5'7" tall, to head in from close range. Gallacher responded for Chelsea - as he always did against Newcastle - and forced an error by McKenzie, latching on to a bad back pass before firing past McInroy. Chelsea pressed for an equaliser but Newcastle's defence held

Jack Allen watches the ball enter the net in the F.A. Cup semi-final with Chelsea in 1932.

firm, marshalled by the evergreen Nelson. Newcastle rallied as the final minutes ticked away and McMenemy crashed a header against the bar.

Goalkeeper McInroy displayed much of the ability that won him an England cap back in 1927 and Gallacher was to say, "he was in wonder form". Dave Davidson had proved a good purchase from Liverpool. A rugged rather than cultured defender, the Aberdonian was dependable at the back. Nelson's partner, curly haired David Fairhurst was another of the club's many signings of the period. However, he too was one of the few who were successful. Like Davidson, he was also reliable rather than brilliant and another who hailed from a family of footballers.

Between this stout defence and the enterprising front line were two half-backs - two players who did much to take Newcastle back to Wembley in 1932. Roddie McKenzie was the sole survivor of the Tynesiders' title-winning side of five years earlier and, although over 30 years-old, was a war-horse in the middle of the field. Alongside him was the equally powerful figure of Sammy Weaver who had briskly developed into one of the country's star players and had pushed his way into England's side. Weaver was described in all action terms, one writer of the day noting that he, "heaves like a howitzer, kicks like a mule". Sam's forward bursts created many a goal for United and he was the man who made Newcastle's Cup side tick.

Full-back David Fairhurst, his father and brother both played football.

Ready for the off! Left to right: Davidson, McKenzie, McInroy and Nelson.

ON THE SCREEN

In June 1932 after being largely against the broadcasting of football, United became one of the leaders in attempting to bring about change in the game's somewhat antiquated HQ. However, at a Football League meeting, Newcastle's proposal, "that the ban on League matches should be removed" was heavily defeated. But on the local front the club had a contract with the Gaumont Film Co. to record games for cinema audiences. Also to agree deals were British Movietone, Pathe Pictures and Paramount News.

The Tynesiders had reached their seventh FA Cup final with a side mixed with youth, experience and a never-say-die spirit. Andy Cunningham had at last got his pack of cards right. United's opponents at Wembley were to be Arsenal, overwhelming force throughout the thirties and, in 1932, holders of the League Championship. They were attempting the double that year and Newcastle couldn't hope to match the Gunners player by player. Arsenal's line-up was littered with star internationals; Hulme, Jack, Hapgood and Alex James to name only a few, although Scottish international James missed the final through injury. It was jokingly rumoured in the north east that James had cried off because of the fear of meeting United's hard-man Roddie McKenzie. The pair had clashed violently in the past and earned a hate relationship.

Before making tracks for London, United played in front of the Prince of Wales - a rare Royal visit to St James Park - against Blackpool and then went through the motions in a league fixture at Fratton Park, losing heavily by 6-0. Cup nerves were in the players' minds between the semi-final and final, Newcastle played eight games, lost six and won only once. But nobody cared much about the results. Seven days later it was to be a different story in the surroundings of Wembley Stadium, 90 minutes that have gone done in FA Cup history as one of the most controversial finals ever.

Far left: More Cup training. Roddie McKenzie (left) and Jimmy Nelson on track work around the Gallowgate pitch.

Left: HRH Edward, Prince of Wales chats to Jack Allen and skipper Jimmy Nelson. Trainer Jimmy McPherson looks on.

Below: A pre-Cup final visit to Wembley. United's squad try out the victory steps.

> *"It was a goal all right, the ball was on the line but not over it"*
>
> *Jack Allen, April 1932*

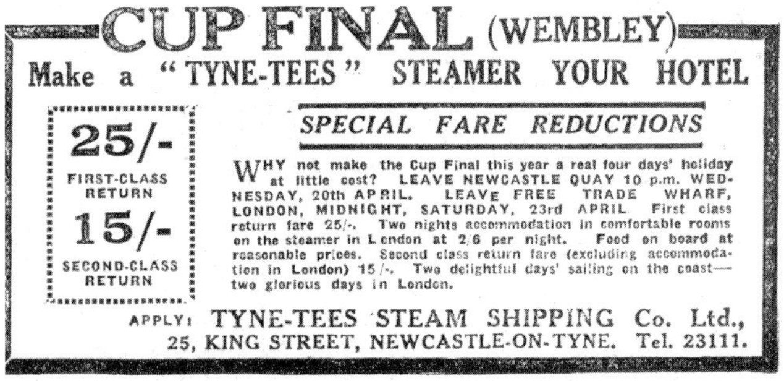

THE YEAR OF 1932 SAW ADOLF HITLER COME TO POWER in Germany. It was a year too that saw Newcastle United lift the FA Cup under the most controversial of circumstances with a goal that perhaps should never have been a goal. It was an incident that created one of the biggest storms in Cup history. Referee Percy Harper was adamant about Newcastle's equaliser though, "It was a goal. As God is my judge the man was in play", he said, and went on, "Whatever the film may appear to show will not make me alter my decision".

Arsenal were 1-0 ahead. Centre-half Dave Davidson intercepted a Hapgood pass and sent a long through-ball for Jimmy Richardson to chase on the right wing. The Newcastle forward's outstretched leg caught the ball just as it was going to cross the goal line. He whipped in a low cross in front of the Gunners' goalmouth and in flashed Jack Allen to bang the ball home with his right foot as Arsenal's defenders hesitated. It was the most controversial goal in the history of the famous old competition, although not the first incident of a similar nature. The 1901 final also featured an 'over the line' goal to debate.

It wasn't until after the game that the arguments started. Press photos from deceiving angles seemed to verify that the ball had crossed the line before Richardson centred. Film from British Movietone News also appeared to support the claim. The Sunday Graphic reported, "Every man must have known what was so clear to onlookers - that the ball had crossed the line". Respected journalist Ivan Sharpe, however, noted in his column, "I attached no importance to the photographs, as I know from experience how the touching up process may, quite unintentionally, alter details". This was a valid point as 'touching up' to photographs in order to highlight the ball or specific players occurred in press rooms around the country right up to the 1960s. The man at the centre of the storm, Jimmy Richardson made the comment, "I was concentrating so hard on reaching the ball, that I couldn't tell you whether it was over the line or not". Goalscorer Jack Allen maintained though, "It was a goal all right, the ball was on the line but not over it". Yet Charlie Buchan from Arsenal's camp was quoted, "I could clearly see the white line, with the ball beyond it". The furore raged for months, indeed years afterwards.

The weather was near perfect for the tie that was to be recorded in history as 'The Over The Line Final'. Almost 15,000 Newcastle fans made the journey, although some reports indicate only 7,500 tickets were available to both sets of supporters. Whatever the number one report highlighted United's boisterous following, "judging by the noise there were many more thousands there". Some fans took advantage of a special trip, organised by the club and Thomas Cook & Son. For 36s 6d they travelled by train to King's Cross with a meal in the dining-car, then toured London and met the United team before heading for Wembley. Jimmy Nelson, who had opposed Arsenal at Wembley with Cardiff in 1927, lost the toss and, as the form book indicated, Arsenal looked the better side early on.

Newcastle supporters continued to enjoy themselves at the Cup final and as always were dressed for the occasion.

McInroy punched clear a Bastin shot and United looked shaky and nervous. The Gunners took the lead after only twelve minutes, following a scramble in their own box which was cleared by Roberts up field to Hulme. The England winger flashed past Fairhurst and crossed to the far post. Outside-left Bob John came in from his flank, McInroy and Nelson misjudged the ball, collided and John had the simplest of tasks of making sure the ball dropped over the line.

Newcastle were not demoralised though. The Magpies hit back and went close on several occasions. In the last quarter of the half Newcastle pressurised the Londoners' defence and then it happened, the goal they all talked about for years and years - United's equaliser seven minutes from half-time. United went

FA CUP RUN				
R3	Blackpool	A	D	1-1
	Blackpool	H	W	1-0
R4	Southport	H	D	1-1
	Southport	A	D	1-1
	Southport	N	W	9-0
R5	Leicester City	H	W	3-1
R6	Watford	H	W	5-0
SF	Chelsea	N	W	2-1
F	Arsenal	N	W	2-1

FACTS & FIGURES	P	W	D	L	F	A
Home	4	3	1	0	10	2
Away	5	3	2	0	15	4
Total	**9**	**6**	**3**	**0**	**25**	**6**

FA Cup Winners 1932

CUP GOALGETTERS
7 Allen, 5 Boyd, 4 Lang, Richardson 2 Cape, Weaver 1 McMenemy

CHAIRMAN: James Lunn
MANAGER: Andy Cunningham
TRAINER-COACH: James McPherson Jnr.
CAPTAIN: Jimmy Nelson

from strength to strength after that controversial moment. Weaver snuffed out David Jack's influence and the black'n'whites matched Arsenal's opening burst.

After the interval Newcastle stepped up a gear to control the game. An almost continual bombardment of their opponents' goal followed, with Lang causing Arsenal's full-back Parker all sorts of problems. Moss made superb full length saves from Boyd and Allen then the Tynesiders took a deserved lead. After 72 minutes Davidson was again involved as he released the ball to Boyd who sent Allen away with a perfect pass. The Magpie leader went past two defenders on a 30 yard goal-bound run and, having a little luck with a rebound to get past centre-half Roberts, smashed a low shot into the net in off a post. It was a great winner. Newcastle almost made it 3-1 near the end when Richardson, or, as some records note, Boyd, drove the ball against the woodwork.

United became the first team at Wembley to lift the FA Cup after going a goal behind. They were noted worthy winners of this North v South challenge in almost every quarter, irrespective of the 'Over The Line' goal. Queen Mary presented the trophy to Jimmy Nelson and off danced Newcastle on their lap of honour.

The public had witnessed a thrilling Cup final after several scrappy affairs. One commentator said it was, "one of the fastest and cleanest exhibitions of first class football ever witnessed". Another reported that Newcastle had produced, "Some of the best football seen so far in a Wembley final". Goal hero Jack Allen had been a pre-match doubt with hernia problems and had played the whole game with a very painful leg. He bravely struggled through and afterwards ended up in hospital as the team continued their celebrations with a break in France and Germany. The other hero of the victory was teenager Harry McMenemy. Showing maturity and composure, 'keeper Albert McInroy said, "He took hold of the forward line majestically".

Following the traditional Cup final dinner - at the Cafe Royal - Newcastle spent a day in Brighton

Wembley Stadium as it looked in 1932 with little cover for spectators.

Jimmy Nelson and Arsenal's Parker lead the teams onto the field.

United are presented to HRH King George V. Left to right: Lang, Allen, Boyd, Richardson, McKenzie, Weaver, Davidson, McInroy, Fairhurst.

Centenary Highlight

Top left: Jimmy Richardson leaps for a high ball in the Gunners' box.

Above: A daring challenge by Jimmy Nelson on England schemer David Jack.

Left: Richardson causes danger again as he gets in a shot on goal watched by Allen and Boyd.

The goal that caused so much controversy. Jack Allen leaps to fire home Richardson's cross. The provider can just be seen extreme left.

FINAL
23 April 1932 at Wembley Stadium
Newcastle United 2 (1) Arsenal 1 (1)

UNITED:
McInroy
Nelson, Fairhurst
McKenzie, Davidson, Weaver
Boyd, Richardson, Allen, McMenemy, Lang

ARSENAL:
Moss
Parker, Hapgood
Jones, Roberts, Male
Hulme, Jack, Lambert, Bastin, John

GOALS: John (12m), Allen (38m), Allen (72m)

ATTENDANCE; 92,298 (£24,688)

Referee; Percy Harper (Stourbridge)
Guest of Honour;
HRH King George V & HRH Queen Mary
Cup HQ; Great Northern Hotel, Kings Cross

FA Cup Winners 1932

before returning north. There was pandemonium on Tyneside on Monday. Crowds estimated at 250,000 welcomed the triumphant side and surpassed any gathering seen in the city. An aeroplane - quite a novelty then - escorted the Cup train from York towards the Tyne, while along the line loud firework explosions echoed to herald the teams arrival. A band played as the side stepped off the train, this after the musicians had been scattered after the Chief Constable's horse fell upon them to the hilarity of the waiting crowd!

Newcastle's party proceeded to the Empire Theatre through the streets in three open topped buses provided by Galleys Coaches. The seething mass of men, women and children hugged the procession with only a few mounted police to retain a semblance of order. From buildings black'n'white streamers were sent fluttering down and many onlookers fainted in the crush. United's FA Cup stars received a bonus of £8 0s 0d each for winning the trophy. The Cup itself was later displayed in several shop windows throughout the region, in Mawson, Swan & Morgan, Fenwicks, British Home Stores and also in the Laing Art Gallery.

Top left: Queen Mary presents Jimmy Nelson with the trophy. Jack Allen is next in line.

Above right: Typical Wembley scenes. Left to right: McMenemy, Richardson, McInroy, Davidson, Allen, Nelson, Weaver, Boyd, Lang, McKenzie, Fairhurst.

Below and left: The F.A. Cup party leaves the Central Station to commence a victory procession.

SEASONS 1932/33 AND 1933/34 WERE to be of marked contrast. As FA Cup winners Newcastle were back as one of the country's major attractions and they looked the part for most of the new season. They started in fine goalscoring form and went into a chase for the title along with Arsenal, Aston Villa and Sheffield Wednesday. With one of the brightest sides in the division, they impressed many judges. United were, as one observer noted, "complete with vigour and dash and abundant craft". They recorded their best ever Christmas holiday period - five wins out of five games played - then toppled Champions to be, Arsenal by 2-1.

Lapses during the latter weeks of the season however, saw United falter and end in 5th position, a long way behind. But for dropping points in uncharacteristic displays during April against Sunderland (0-1), Leeds (1-6) and Blackpool (1-2), Newcastle would have been much closer. That defeat by the Roker men was the decisive reverse. Cunningham said, "The result was a bitter pill. The only satisfying thing about the whole proceedings was the splendid weather". The other major factor was a cartilage injury to Sammy Weaver, the one player United's side depended on most. He missed over half the campaign.

Leeds United knocked the holders out of the 1933 FA Cup competition at the first hurdle. Almost 48,000 shocked Tynesiders saw the Yorkshire side cruise to a 3-0 win, the second such victory in only three years. Leeds centre-forward Arthur Hydes scored a hat-trick in the tie while Newcastle's players had been affected by an influenza bug and several regulars, as well as the manager and secretary, missed the game. New centre-half, Alec Betton played in that match. Long-legged and powerfully built, he came out of the obscurity of non-league Scarborough after good displays in the FA Cup.

ON THE TRACKS

The year of 1937 saw the LNER build several steam locomotives with names of famous football clubs. The Magpies were included.... Number 2858 was christened 'Newcastle United' and the B17 class train ran for several years up and down the east coast route. It was renamed 'The Essex Regiment' and scrapped in the late 1950s.

English v Scottish Cup winners 1932. A contemporary postcard souvenir of the prestigious meeting.

Local lad Jimmy Richardson who deserved his England call-up.

So did Jimmy Murray who had arrived from Scotland, from Cunningham's old club Glasgow Rangers. The Scot was to fill many positions for the Magpies in an unobtrusive way during the coming years. Murray was one who had impressed in the prestige double friendly with the Ibrox club during September. Rangers were then in their finest period of glory and faced United in an English v Scottish Cup winners' challenge. Newcastle won 5-0 with Murray netting twice. McMenemy had a great evening too, while Weaver's display "thrilled the crowd".

However, the Tynesiders did not do so well in the FA Charity Shield. At St James Park, Everton won the impressive looking trophy in an entertaining 5- 3 victory. Newcastle started the goal feast when Harry McMenemy broke free but Everton then went 3-1 up, while Weaver had a penalty saved by Ted Sagar. Dixie Dean went on to score four times in an exhibition display by both teams.

If 1932/33 was to be a season of promise, then the following campaign was one of total disaster. The next six years of United's history were to be the worst on record. Up until then Newcastle United Football Club had been respected as one of the most elite in the country, yet they declined alarmingly, so badly that they went ever so close to beginning life in the Third Division (North).

Ronnie Williams, netted on his debut against Aston Villa in 1933.

On paper, Andy Cunningham appeared to have a decent line up. Included in the available squad of players were no less than six full internationals with two more on the way; Weaver, Fairhurst, Richardson and McInroy of England together with Boyd and Nelson of Scotland. Additionally Harry McMenemy would have played for the Scots but for injury. United's boss was in confident mood as the big kick-off approached, "We are all optimistic. We have a good blend of youth and experience in our make-up" he said.

Yet on the park nothing would go right, especially not in the second half of the season. It was that injury to McMenemy, then an inspirational figure with Weaver, which proved a vital factor. Against Blackburn Rovers, early into the season, the young Scot damaged his knee and was on and off the treatment table for over a year. He was missed and United did little to give their supporters much to cheer about until the festive season arrived. It was, though, worth waiting for.

They had defeated Sunderland 2-1 in a derby full of incident that was marked by two goals from Weaver, but few other performances of note took place. As the holiday matches approached, United were languishing near the bottom of the table with moral at a low ebb. Then, as Christmas drew near, they defeated Liverpool 2-1 at Anfield and, on Boxing Day, took note of the time of the year and a 40,000 Goodison crowd saw United wallop Everton 7- 3. Centre-forward Ronnie Williams, a transfer purchase from Swansea Town in November, at £1,500 another international to the ranks, scored a hat-trick. From Treboath in Wales, Williams was to be capped when out of favour at St James Park and playing for United's Tyneside League side against the Reyrolles Works XI. A few days later he appeared for the Welsh against England. He had replaced Jack Allen, quickly and surprisingly discarded after his Wembley triumph.

The Goodison romp was not the end of the black'n'whites' surge in form. A week later, on New Years Day, Everton's great rivals Liverpool again felt the force of a United side who were clearly better than their league position showed. Newcastle completed a Christmas double over Liverpool as the Reds fell by the remarkable score of 9-2 at St James Park with more hat-tricks coming, this time from Richardson and Weaver. On a heavy and treacherous pitch, United went ahead after only three minutes when Richardson got his first by converting a Lang cross. Liverpool equalised, but Weaver scored a brilliant second for United. A move involving the whole forward line ended with the powerful midfielder crashing the ball home. Before the break however, an own-goal by Betton gave the visitors another equaliser. The pace of the Magpies' game in the second-half was at times unbelievable. Never before had Newcastle scored seven goals in one half and the local press recorded, "United quite overwhelmed the Lancastrians with ingenious and consistent aggressive tactics". Richardson put United 3-2 ahead and it was one-way traffic after that. Boyd, Lang and Williams netted to put all the forwards on the score-sheet.

Tony Leach arrived in the wake of relegation.

Newcastle jumped from 18th to a comfortable 13th placing. All seemed satisfactory and encouraging in the Magpie camp and from that marvellous holiday treat United's fans expected a steady recovery. How wrong they were. There was to be no more smiles for black'n'white followers, just gloom and more gloom. First Wolves sent Newcastle out of the FA Cup, 1-0 at Molineux to a last minute miskick that allowed the Midland side to breakaway and score. Afterwards defeat followed defeat and relegation became a distinct possibility. In the last 14 games of the season from February onwards, Newcastle won just a solitary game and the cheers of the past years turned quickly to howls of derision as supporters, not used to such depressing football, lashed out at the players and boss Cunningham in particular.

The First Division league table was as tight as it could be. Only six points separated eight clubs and a relegation place. Fated injuries hit Cunningham's plans as Weaver missed the crucial run-in at the end of the season, while a long term injury to goalkeeper Albert McInroy at Christmas had an important bearing on United's slump. By Easter, United had ten men in the treatment room.

A final stand was made in the last two games of the season. At home to Wolves, United won 5-1 with United's second international purchase of the season, Bill Imrie netting three goals from his half-back role. Cunningham said, "We are still in the mire, but with a fighting chance of getting clear, but it's going to be a desperate fight". The final game was at the Victoria Ground, Stoke and United had a hopeless task. They were 20th in the table with only Birmingham, who had a vital extra game, below them. Newcastle simply had to win. They didn't. They lost 2-1, while Brum won emphatically - 7-3 at Leicester - and had no need of the game in hand. United finished two points below the St Andrew's club and went down with Sheffield United. After 36 distinguished years in Division One they were back in the second ranks.

Cunningham used 27 players during the season and rarely had a

RESERVES STEP UP

Following a decade of trying, United's reserve eleven were elected to the Central League in place of Stockport County in the summer of 1933. An average crowd approaching 17,000 watched the first season's competition in which United finished in 5th place. Attendances were exceptional then, even the club's third team played in front of 3,000. Six months before being admitted, the Magpies attempted to get their second string into the Scottish League in the place of either Bo'ness or Armadale, two clubs that had been expelled. The Scottish League quickly rejected Newcastle's application.

Bill Imrie, an inspired purchase, but too late to halt United sliding into Division Two.

Three local lads to be given opportunities. Goalkeeper Norman Tapken and full-backs Joe Richardson (left) and Alf Garnham (right).

New centre-forward Jack Smith - an instant success.

Tommy Pearson, another youngster to quickly make headlines.

settled line up. Imrie showed up well at the end of the season but had been signed too late. The ex Blackburn wing-half cost £6,500, was an experienced Scottish international and looked the part for a relegation battle. Red haired, broad shouldered and grim faced, with height and a deadly tackle behind a 14 stone frame. He could play a bit too and became an inspiring individual at St James Park.

In the aftermath of relegation the hue and cry was loud and swift changes were made, with many of the 1932 FA Cup team out of favour. Following Davidson and Allen, out went McInroy, Nelson, McKenzie, Boyd and Lang. Only Fairhurst, McMenemy, Richardson and Weaver remained from that moment of Wembley glory. Beleaguered manager Andy Cunningham splashed out on 31 year-old ex England centre-half Tony Leach from Sheffield Wednesday. An upstanding character and personality of the game at the time, he was appointed captain. A new goalkeeper, Norman Tapken graduated from the local Wallsend Thermal Welfare side and Wilf Bott took over the outside-right position following his arrival from Huddersfield Town. He had a remarkable start in a black'n'white shirt, netting a hat-trick on his debut against Bury at Gallowgate, although afterwards he rarely shined.

Jack Smith, only 19 years-old and who had also arrived from Huddersfield Town, took over the centre-forward's role and was to make a name for himself in the Second Division. A former England schools player, he went straight into the league eleven, scored on his debut and his refreshing appetite in United's attack brought him a stack of goals. Reserve players, Tommy Pearson (ex Murrayfield Amateurs), Billy Leighton (Walker Park) and Joe Wilson (Tanfield Lea) impressed in the senior line-up too. Left winger Pearson did particularly well. The Scot netted 14 goals from the flank in his first full season and was a player of special promise, and one who fulfilled his potential in the coming period. Pearson remained at Gallowgate for 15 years and in all appeared almost 280 times for the black'n'whites. Possessing immaculate ball control he was especially noted for a stunning dummy that left defenders stranded. He scored goals too - 62 for the club. Although his career was interrupted by war, Pearson was to be twice capped for Scotland and, unusually, by England during wartime fixtures.

The gritty Joe Richardson stepped up to take over from past skipper Nelson at full-back. From Bedlington, he was devoted to United's cause for most of his life. As a player in over 200 games, Richardson possessed the traditional tenacity of his local Bedlington terrier, while afterwards Joe was appointed assistant trainer and became a highly jovial and popular back-room figure.

Cunningham was optimistic about United's chances of jumping straight back into Division One. In an interview with the Sunday Sun he noted, "I do not see that there is anything to be scared about. I have faith in our ability". United's boss knew little, though, of Second Division soccer. In spite of the changes, Newcastle did not like their first taste of relegation at all. They suffered a rude shock in Division Two and in the first six games only recorded two points, falling 5-1 to Nottingham Forest on the opening day of the season and 4-1 to Blackpool two days later. They were bottom of the division - the worst start to a season in the club's past.

There were a whole new set of teams to face. Gone were Everton, Arsenal and Sunderland. Now the Magpies faced Plymouth Argyle, Port Vale and Barnsley. To ensure continued support against such clubs United announced massive reductions in entrance money. The 1s 6d entrance fee to the terracing was slashed to 1s 0d. In time though, Newcastle sized up the new requirements of Second Division soccer with their all international half-back line of Imrie, Leach and Weaver looking an imposing trio. United climbed the table steadily, finishing in 6th position just below leaders Bolton Wanderers and Brentford. They even crept into 3rd spot during March, but, when a push was needed, injuries knocked United back. Cunningham was at one point without eight senior players including unlucky

Tom Mather who had the job of trying to regain First Division status.

(left) How cartoonist 'Bos' recorded the F.A. Cup meeting with Arsenal in 1935.

reserve winger Billy Gallantree, out with a broken leg when just beginning to show up well in senior company.

The FA Cup provided little comfort, although it brought a big tie against Tottenham Hotspur and with it a few fireworks. After obtaining a degree of revenge over past adversaries, Hull City - winning 5-1 on Humberside - they met the Londoners at White Hart Lane. Spurs were then struggling to stay in Division One and, in a snowstorm, 61,195 witnessed, literally, a fighting first 45 minutes by United. In a rough match, the Magpies couldn't withstand a second-half Tottenham onslaught and lost 2-0, although the Londoners' tactics were openly questioned. United finished with only eight fit men on the field and Tony Leach sent off. A Football Association Commission followed and looked into the very ill-tempered confrontation.

Harry Ware arrived in the north-east from Mather's old club.

At the end of the season Andy Cunningham called it a day by resigning, a move that stopped United directors from dismissing the Scot. Newcastle had to find a new manager for the first time, but certainly not the last. In the years to follow the club were to hunt for a man to revitalise the Magpies more times than they wanted. Adverts went into the national press and Stoke City boss, Tom Mather was interviewed in London. He landed the job and took control during June 1935 on a three year contract at a salary of £750 per year. An experienced administrator formally with Bolton Wanderers and Southend United, Mather had fashioned Stoke into a useful First Division outfit after winning promotion in 1933. It was hoped he would do the same for United. The Northern Echo made comment on Mather's appointment, "One of the most genial men in football today. He has a good record as a manager and is an outstanding personality in the game".

It was much the same story for 1935/36 as Mather took control - many changes, one of the also-rans in the promotion race and a big Cup game to end in disappointment. The new boss began with the inevitable wheeling and dealing in personnel, although many of the new faces were reserves given their chance by a manager always willing to hand youngsters an opportunity. Jimmy Gordon, Alf Garnham and Albert Harris were three such players to break into the side. Gordon developed quickly and was even tipped for Scotland honours in his first season. He was to become a polished wing-half, a player rarely flustered and, in modern years, the third member of the celebrated Clough-Taylor management team.

With £25,000 to spend in the transfer market - then a vast sum - Mather went back to the Victoria Ground to bring 'play anywhere' man Harry Ware to Tyneside in a £2,400 deal. Ed Connelly, a talented inside-forward from Dumbarton, made his debut when only 19 years of age and impressed many with clever play. Mather also made headline news in an attempt to bring Derby and England forward Sammy Crooks to St James Park, then tried for the legendary Stanley Matthews. Mather had found the wing maestro during his days at the Victoria Ground and said, "I really felt the Stoke City directors would listen". Alas they didn't and no other big name landed on Tyneside that season.

Once again Newcastle couldn't find the added bite and enthusiasm which would have taken them into a challenging position. A poor home record cost the Magpies

WELSH VICTORY

England 1 (Brook) Wales 2 (Mills, Astley)
15 November 1933

For the first time since 1907 a full international was housed at St James Park. The weather was against a large crowd turning up and only 12,000 saw the match. After a 2-1 victory the Welsh claimed the Home International Championship.

England:
Hibbs (Birmingham City)
Goodall (Huddersfield Town)
Hapgood (Arsenal)
Strange (Sheffield Wednesday)
Allen (Portsmouth)
Copping (Leeds United)
Crooks (Derby County)
Grosvenor (Birmingham City)
Bowers (Derby County)
Bastin (Arsenal)
Brook (Manchester City).
WALES:
John (Stoke City)
Lawrence (Swansea Town)
Jones (Leicester City)
Murphy (West Bromwich Albion)
Griffiths (Middlesbrough)
Richards (Wolverhampton Wanderers)
Phillips (Wolverhampton Wanderers)
O'Callaghan (Tottenham Hotspur)
Astley (Aston Villa)
Mills (Clapton Orient)
Evans (Tottenham Hotspur).

dearly, dropping eleven points at St James Park was not promotion form. At their second attempt at getting back into Division One, they were two places lower and almost £4,000 poorer. Not surprisingly gates had dropped from the 30,000 average for First Division fixtures to a little over 20,000. Revenue dipped alarmingly as a consequence. In 1934/35 United collected only £25,120 10s 10d, almost £20,000 down on the 1931/32 figure. In the seasons to follow Newcastle's home attendances were to get even worse. Crowds of 10,000 and less would be recorded. Only 4,000 turned up against Norwich City(1935/36) and Nottingham Forest(1936/37), the worst at Gallowgate since 1900, and the lowest to date. That poor turn-out against Norwich was, in part, also due to a long running 'Pools War', when the Football League withheld fixtures until the morning of the match in a bid to stop Pools companies taking income by unauthorised use of fixture lists. This action had a severe affect at the turnstiles and was swiftly stopped.

It was left to the FA Cup to bring some joy to the terraces, and with it a boost to the club's bank account. Two cracking Fifth Round games against Arsenal were the climax of a run which started at Walsall with a 2-0 success, Smith and Connelly netting the goals. At a time when King George V had just died, United then went face to face with Sheffield Wednesday, led by ex Magpie forward, and now England player, Ron Starling. Fog caused the postponement of the tie at Hillsborough, but once the game did get under way it was Tommy Pearson who earned United a replay with a goal in a 1-1 draw. On Tyneside, Newcastle played with vigour and won comfortably by 3-1. Bott netted twice while Jack Smith - to collect 26 goals that year - hit the other to send United through to meet League Champions Arsenal.

NORWAY CRUSHED

England 4 (Smith 2, Dix, Lawton) Norway 0
9 November 1938
The last full international took place at St James Park when England entertained Norway in a friendly. United's Dougie Wright was capped on that day in front of a healthy crowd of 39,887.
England; Woodley (Chelsea) -
Sproston (Manchester City), Hapgood (Arsenal)
- Willingham (Wolves), Cullis (Wolves),
Wright (Newcastle Utd) - Matthews (Stoke City),
Broome (Aston Villa), Lawton (Everton),
Dix (Derby County), Smith (Millwall).

There was a huge build-up during the week before the tie. At Gallowgate, on the Saturday of the game, crowds were vast - so thick that several of United's players couldn't get through to the dressing-room entrance. All gates were closed two hours before kick-off time with 65,484 - a record Cup gate - inside St James Park and 20,000 locked out. There were 200 casualties with many fans taking perilous vantage points. The crowd was in vociferous mood, perhaps the Gallowgate Roar at its loudest as Tommy Pearson recalled, "It made the hairs on my neck stand on end", while full-back Alf Garnham noted, "That day the crowd was unbelievable, quite unbelievable". And they certainly had plenty to shout about in a stupendous game.

Against their opponents at Wembley back in 1932, a memorable contest took place on a slippery and sand covered pitch. Three times Arsenal took the lead, but three times United fought back to equalise. First Smith's low header equalised Hulme's early opener, then Bowden made it 2-1 against his future club. Harry Ware shook the crossbar then a roar echoed all over the city as Smith levelled for a second time. Immediately Bowden put the Gunners 3-2 ahead with a controversial goal, United claiming the Arsenal inside-forward had blatantly handled the

A United group in civvies during the mid-Thirties - plus-fours and all!

ball. In the final ten minutes Newcastle got their third equaliser. Bott swung the ball across to Pearson who let go a stinging left foot volley from just inside the box into the far corner of the net. The match never rose to great heights of skilful football but, for a stern, sometimes reckless and tense battle, few games have bettered it.

There was another 60,000 plus crowd at Highbury the following Wednesday, but this time the talent of the Gunners was too good for Newcastle in another game of thrills. Arsenal won 3-0, Cliff Bastin striking home two penalties and it was Arsenal's first FA Cup victory over United. Newcastle though had a share of the game and went close with two efforts when only a goal behind. The Londoners went on to win the trophy that year.

RELIGIOUS BAN

During 1938 two United players, big Dominic Kelly, an Irish reserve centre-half and staunch Catholic, squared up to Jock Park, the bustling Protestant outside-right from Lanarkshire. They grappled on the dressing-room floor, Kelly wrapping his hands around Park's throat growling, "Say God Bless the Pope!" Park would have none of it and roared back, "God Bless King Billie!" Harry Clifton managed to pull both players apart and the directors had to maintain a strict religious ban for the rest of the season.

In spite of disappointment at the lack of promotion challenge, Tom Mather was slowly bringing together a side of potential at St James Park and things were beginning to look right. In 1936/37 United almost sustained a big enough push to grab a promotion place, even without the power play of Sam Weaver, lured back to Division One by Chelsea during the summer. On his departure he said, "I am sorry to leave Tyneside, but would not be considering my best interests if I did not accept Chelsea's offer". Comments all to often repeated by other players in years to come.

It was a tantalising season. The Magpies ended it in 4th position in spite of a record six consecutive defeats during January and February. Again, home opportunities were thrown away and by Easter they had just too much to do. No fewer than 17 points were lost at Gallowgate, while away from Tyneside the team did well recording eleven victories. A quick exit in the FA Cup, to eventual finalists Preston North End by 2-0, gave the players only one incentive and they looked good bets for promotion at times. Convincing victories over Doncaster Rovers, 7-0, with four goals from Smith, and 5-1 against both Norwich City and Swansea were the league highlights. At one stage United were playing so well that one correspondent wrote, "Newcastle United's football was so fast that ice-hockey was slow by comparison". Another five goals went past the West Ham United goalkeeper in a game that saw the promising shoot-on-sight talent of Billy Cairns score four. The Hammers' centre-forward Jimmy Martin - making his debut - also got a hat- trick, but ended on the losing side.

Full back Bobby Ancell, to be capped twice in 1937 by Scotland, arrived via St Mirren and became a favourite of the crowd. He was of slight build and always showed a touch of finesse in the art of defending United's goal. Also to head over the Cheviots were Archie Livingstone, Jimmy Denmark and Tom Mooney. Denmark, 6'1" tall, made a big impression playing for his club Third Lanark against United and became a useful centre-half. Mooney was purchased from Airdrie with a reputation as one of the best club players in the Scottish League. He proceeded to become popular too. His terrific shooting power from the left wing earned him several spectacular goals.

Bobby Ancell, a skilful defender from Dumfries.

Welshman Ehud Rogers - known as 'Tim' - was secured from Arsenal, while Jesse Carver cost £2,000 from Blackburn Rovers. Rogers was small in build at only 5'6", but was a potent striker. He was too good for the Gunners' stiffs, indeed he had graduated to the full Welsh side in the Football League Jubilee fixture against Ireland. Centre-half Carver was to become much more famous as a coach on the Continent, later guiding Juventus to the Italian Championship and rebuilding the devastated Torino club following an air crash.

Jimmy Denmark, another Scot who did well for Newcastle.

Persistent injuries disrupted Mather's plans the following year and very nearly sent United tumbling into the Third Division. It was to be the worst in the club's 100 year past. The 1937/38 season started badly before a ball was even kicked. Ancell, Smith, Fairhurst and young striker Billy Cairns, who had shined in the previous twelve months, were all on the injured list. By the beginning of October, Newcastle were lying in the bottom three of the table along with clubs of little pedigree; Fulham, Plymouth, Swansea and Stockport. United had won only one game in the opening ten - a superb 6-0 hammering of Sheffield United.

Bad luck with injuries continued. Ray Bowden, an inspired signing during November to stop the rot, was laid low for a long period with a poisoned elbow. The ex Arsenal and England schemer had cost £5,000 and when on the field proved a revitalising influence. A player full of grace and ability, Bowden had won both Championship and FA Cup medals at Highbury. United also lost Jack Smith, but for reasons of their own making. The Yorkshireman had put the ball in the back of the net on 73 occasions in only three and a half seasons, but was transferred to Manchester United for £6,500. It proved a crucial decision. United struggled for goals and no-one could reach double figures. John Park, from Hamilton Accies, was tried up front, although

Tom Mooney who possessed a ferocious shot.

Centre-half Jesse Carver who later became a respected coach.

showing a lot of robust enthusiasm was never adept in finishing.

Supporters became increasingly despondent as United hovered at the bottom of the table. First Division West Bromwich Albion knocked United out of the FA Cup by a single goal at the Hawthorns and, as the season drew to a close, it was touch and go whether the Magpies would scrape clear of the drop or go through the trapdoor into the unthinkable Third Division(North) - in pre-war days the lowest division in senior football. At the time no other established giant of the game had dropped to that level.

Mather tried a rescue operation by attempting for a second time to lure Stanley Matthews to Tyneside. He returned to Stoke in February and spent three days trying to persuade his former office boy to join United. He was armed with a record five figure package; £5,000 plus former England inside-forward Jimmy Richardson, at a time when only a handful of deals over £10,000 had been completed. Again the deal came nowhere near its conclusion.

Newcastle put a few results together and actually recovered to mid-table but, with the bottom half of the division separated by only a handful of points, United quickly slipped back after a dreadful sequence of six defeats in eight games. A poor Easter programme sent the club into a tense and tortuous climax to the season.

They defeated Chesterfield 3-1 in the last home fixture of the season and then faced three away matches. All were difficult trips - a return with the Spirites and journeys to fellow strugglers, Swansea and Luton. They proceeded to lose the first game and the fear was that, if rivals Nottingham Forest won at Chesterfield and the Magpies didn't have a good day at the Vetch Field, they would be in a dire situation. United's party, travelling home by train via London, were anxious to hear the Forest scoreline - in days when communications were slow, even for football results - so they persuaded a reporter travelling with the side to telephone his London office to find out the score. A group of directors, officials and players huddled nervously around a telephone box in Paddington Station but Chesterfield had won 1-0 and there was jubilation among the party.

AHEAD OF THEIR TIME

An Extraordinary General Meeting of the club in September 1931 saw a resolution passed to allow United to operate a restaurant, act as licensed victuallers, tobacco dealers, advertisers and other non football related activities. Newcastle though, were a half a century ahead of their time. The Football Association rejected the club's plans outright.

Newcastle were in 17th position, with four clubs below them separated by a mere point, as they faced the Hatters on the last day of the season. Newcastle couldn't save their own skin and went down heavily 4-1 and it was left to other results to decide United's fate. Again Nottingham Forest were involved; this time meeting Barnsley, in deep relegation trouble too. Newcastle needed Forest to get a result. They did, holding the Tykes to a 2-2 draw in a highly controversial meeting. Newcastle were safe, Barnsley went down, but only just. In the end Newcastle were saved by one tenth of a goal, finishing four places from the bottom, but with the same points as the Oakwell club. As the club's Annual Report depressingly recorded, "It was the most unsatisfactory playing season in the history of the club". Excuses were not new, the club's summing up noted, "persistent ill luck in the matter of injuries and sickness has dragged Newcastle United down".

Headline signing, Ray Bowden, ex Arsenal and England schemer.

It could have been worse had it not been for a lucky moment in December. United could well have been a point worse off when an away game at Stockport County was abandoned, due to fog, with 15 minutes remaining. The score stood at 2-2 and Newcastle won the replay.

Never had the outlook been so grim, either from a playing or financial point of view at St James Park. Dwindling revenue and massive transfer spending had taken its toll. Over £20,000 was owed to the bank and every board member had to guarantee £2,000 to keep United afloat. The shock at the club's near disaster acted as a catalyst for change. The directors looked closely at Newcastle's situation from every aspect. Chairman James Lunn, at the helm throughout this catastrophic period, had to reverse the club's fortunes. A local councillor, he had been associated with United from the turn of the century, but now came under fire from supporters and rebel shareholders, including William McKeag who had become a foremost critic during the thirties.

During the summer there was much sole searching in the boardroom and one major decision was taken that proved to be a golden move, to set United on the road to another glorious period. The club approached former crowd idol Stan Seymour and invited him to join the board as a new director. After much persuasion Seymour, who had fallen out with Newcastle's management over benefit payments, accepted the position. He said, "What we are out to do now is to put Newcastle back in the place they belong - that is the First Division". He became the third ex player to become a director, the only one though to make a name both on the field and in the boardroom. Previously both Bob Bennie(1930) and John Auld(1897) had taken the route upstairs. The Northern Echo made the comment that Seymour's, "influence and knowledge of the game should prove invaluable".

It was to be the start of a new era in an age on Tyneside that saw prosperity, in comparison to the dismal last ten years, return to the region. Newcastle was transformed with a gigantic Corporation building programme on all sides of the city, the advent of the trolley-bus and the opening of Woolsington Airport with regular flights to London. The club's affairs were completely revitalised and Seymour's magic was passed down to player level as well. Norman Smith was installed as trainer. A past Huddersfield Town star during their marvellous twenties decade, he had trained England and made a name for himself on the Continent. The portly Geordie was to be Stan Seymour's right-hand man for the next 25 years.

In the final season before the Second World War, United performed well and a vast improvement on the previous twelve months took place. Remarkably, a useful side looked to be taking shape, ultimately to be halted in its progress by events nothing to do with football. By the beginning

Ralph Birkett, another star signing and another former Arsenal and England player.

Director James Lunn who, as Chairman throughout the Thirties decade, had many problems to contend with.

of November United had a good basis for a promotion challenge. A near 64,000 crowd gathered for the fixture against leaders Fulham and saw the Magpies triumph by 2-1 and leapfrog over the Londoners into poll position. By the close of the year, they were in 3rd place chasing Blackburn Rovers and confident of promotion.

Again though injuries caused Newcastle to stumble as they had done so often in the decade. This time Clifton(muscle), Gordon(broken fibula), Denmark(cheek bone fracture), Bowden(fractured jaw) and up and coming Scottish kids, left-half from Glasgow, Jimmy Woodburn(cartilage) and Willie Scott(broken leg), were all out for long periods. Although restricted with available players, Newcastle fought on until a promotion make or break battle with Blackburn Rovers at the end of March. United were second, Rovers top with a four point lead.
A 2-2 draw was the outcome and Sheffield United, below the black'n'whites, closed the gap - a very slim one with only four points separating 10th and 2nd place. United slipped and the chance was gone.

Although Tom Mather was still in control, Seymour had a big influence on the purchase of new talent as United spent almost £40,000 on players during the year in spite of debts. The press noted it

HOW ATTITUDES CHANGE

During January 1932 Newcastle played Blackpool in the FA Cup Third Round, a 1-0 victory. However press reports note that the biggest **CHEER** of the afternoon came when it was announced that Sunderland were **BEATING** Southampton 3-0 at Roker Park!

Billy Cairns, a bustling leader who scored over 50 first-class goals for the Magpies.

as, "colossal expenditure", Tom Mather said, "We have spared no expense. If needs be I will spend more". Ralph Birkett, another ex England forward arrived from Middlesbrough for £6,000 and Harry Clifton cost a record £8,500 from Chesterfield. Birkett had been a colleague of Bowden's at Highbury. Inside-left Clifton was born in Newburn and bubbled over with football ability. He was a match-winner and, had war not intervened, could have become a huge star. Full-back Benny Craig joined the staff in November 1938 from FA Cup finalists Huddersfield Town. It was the start of a 44 year association with the Magpies. A shrewd and sound defender, he later became a likeable personality behind the scenes.

SEASON TICKET CHARGES

For the Second Division season of 1935/36, Newcastle's season ticket charges were;

Men	£3 12s 0d
Women	£2 12s 0d
Juniors	£2 2s 0d

Dougie Wright cost £3,250 from Third Division Southend and was rapidly elevated to the top. After four months as a Second Division player, he appeared for England when only 20 years old. His captivating artistry had much to do with Newcastle's resurgence. Billy Cairns took over the mantle of chief goalscorer with 20 in the season. He was a big-hearted, hell-for-leather centre-forward, only 5'9" but with powerful shooting boots. Cairns was to play on with Grimsby Town until he was over 40 years of age. Another noted goal-poacher to be entered the fray too during the 1938/39 season. A tall, lanky youngster by the name of Albert Stubbins made his mark when he replaced the injured Clifton. Combining perfectly with Cairns and Tom Mooney up front, Stubbins impressed so much that one commentator pointed out that he, "has all that suggests he may be an England inside-forward some day". The star of the revival was Ray Bowden who, but for repeated injuries and the coming hostilities, would have also become a huge terrace favourite with his tactical skills and expert placement.

There was an improvement in the FA Cup too. United disposed of bottom of Division One side Brentford 2-0 at Griffen Park, then Third Division Cardiff City went down 4-1 after a replay. In the Fifth Round United received a big draw - Cup holders Preston North End at St James Park. Their team of Scottish stars included such names as Bill Shankly, George Mutch, Robert Beattie and England 'keeper Harry Holdcroft. They were too good for the Geordies and United fell 2-1, but only through two defensive blunders. Nearly 63,000 rolled up for that attractive tie.

The season also saw the Football League celebrate its 50th birthday with local derby matches held around the country, receipts going to a Jubilee Trust Fund for players in difficulty.

Newcastle attracted the second best gate in the country when Gateshead, then a Football League outfit, arrived at Gallowgate. The team from the other side of the Tyne Bridge paraded a new signing in the first of a double meeting. He was non other than Hughie Gallacher, hence the big attendance of 30,500. United won that match by 2-1 but lost the return by the odd goal in five.

At the campaign's close both directors and spectators were well pleased with the revival that had taken place. In the space of twelve months gates were up dramatically. Seymour's influence had added 15,000 on to the St James Park average. The club's accounts however, showed a thumping loss of £16,786. If the actions taken meant the resurgence of Newcastle United over the long term, the investment was well worth the risk as gate receipts would quickly outpace expenditure.

Stan Seymour had made his presence felt. A fresh wind had blown through the Leazes stadium. Seymour - Managing Director in all but name - was to complete his revitalisation of the club, but not until war once again had disrupted the national sport.

Inside-forward Harry Clifton became Newcastle's most expensive purchase at £8,500 from Chesterfield in 1938.

Dougie Wright who rapidly progressed into England's line-up in his first season at St. James Park.

A caricature of wing half Jimmy Gordon

Centenary Profile 11

The Midfield Powerhouse

"The sight of Sammy Weaver in mood is one of the most thrilling things in football"

Anon. Newcastle Utd FC programme, 1934

ASK ANYONE WHO KNOWS A THING OR TWO ABOUT THE GAME of football and Sammy Weaver will be immediately associated with the long throw-in. Weaver was the player who set a pattern for generations of midfield men to follow with a prodigious throw - equal to a corner-kick. He was though, more than just a throw-in expert, - much, much more.

During the Thirties Weaver was a household name, one of the best half-backs around. One journalist of the day aptly wrote of his style, "The sight of Sammy Weaver in mood is one of the most thrilling things in football". His big mop of jet black hair often dominated midfield with power play. He was a thoughtful half-back with vision and was one of the hardest hitters of the ball in the game, always liable to let fly at goal. Ex England star, Charlie Buchan included the United man in his selection of All Time Greats from the inter-war period.

Born in Pilsley near Chesterfield in February 1909, Sam cannot claim to have come from a particularly sporting family like some, although his father was a cricketer of local repute. At school he soon developed a love for soccer and played for his school team at inside-left. He graduated to appear for local sides Pilsley Redrose and Sutton Junction and at the age of 15 Weaver obtained a trial for Sutton Town, a noted side, one step from Football League soccer. They signed the well built 5'9" youngster and Weaver quickly started to impress senior clubs.

Given a chance by Derby County, Sam didn't get on too well but he was spotted by Newcastle's ex full-back, Bill McCracken, then boss at Second Division Hull City. The former Irish international saw much potential in the 19 year-old and Weaver signed for the Humberside club in March 1928 for a £50 fee. He rapidly jumped from the reserve side into the first team during the 1928/29 season. Weaver was soon building up a reputation as a future star. So much so that within a year and a half of his debut he was heading for the First Division.

McCracken was to give his old club first refusal on Weaver's signature and United paid out £2,500 to acquire the 20 year-old left-half come inside-forward. Weaver joined the Gallowgate staff in November 1929 at a time when the Magpies were in crisis near the foot of the table. He went immediately into the senior ranks as part of a rebuilding process and made a pleasing first appearance for his new club against Arsenal at Highbury. Newcastle unexpectedly won 1-0 and Weaver finished off a highly satisfactory display by scoring the winning goal.

He was perhaps the perfect midfielder. Powerful and strong in the tackle, Weaver was good in the air too, but it was when he was able to slip into an attacking role that Sam was at his best. His first game in front of the home crowd was against Aston Villa and he again scored a goal in a 2-2 draw. Weaver started off on Tyneside with the fans very much behind him and quickly became the crowd's favourite. He was one of the few successes that season as United avoided relegation by a slim margin.

By the time boss Andy Cunningham had put together the 1932 FA Cup side, Weaver was the country's outstanding young player. International honours came

WEAVER'S PLAYING RECORD	League		FA Cup		Total	
	App	Gls	App	Gls	App	Gls
1929-30	15	5	6	0	21	5
1930-31	34	1	2	0	36	1
1931-32	40	6	9	2	49	8
1932-33	19	3	0	0	19	3
1933-34	32	14	1	0	33	14
1934-35	33	6	2	0	35	6
1935-36	31	6	5	0	36	6
	204	**41**	**25**	**2**	**229**	**43**

Sammy Weaver

Weaver in England's eleven for the international with Scotland in 1933. Also in the team is Ron Starling, a former colleague at St. James Park. Left to right, back: Strange, Hart, Hibbs, Cooper, Sammy Weaver, Arnold. Front: Hulme, Hunt, Blenkinsop, Starling, Pickering.

his way when he was chosen to play for his country against the Scots at Wembley, the first of three caps for England. Weaver played exceptionally well in front of a new record Wembley crowd as Scotland were beaten 3-0. His long stride and forceful attacking play was one of the features of the game. One report observed that, "A new star is born".

Only two weeks later Weaver found himself back at Wembley, this time for the FA Cup final. To crown a marvellous personal year he produced another grand display, but then was sidelined by a cartilage injury and had to battle for fitness. In spite of United's decline and demotion into Division Two, Weaver remained one of the game's foremost players. Most knew the midfield general was far too good a player to be stranded in a second grade of football, so a quick return into Division One by United was essential if he was to remain with the black'n'whites.

It didn't happen and although Weaver remained loyal to United for two seasons - being top scorer in 1933/34 - the inevitable occurred. No-one expected him to reject a move to Chelsea when the approach was made. He didn't and by the start of the following season was installed at Stamford Bridge after seven seasons with the Magpies in which he made 229 League and Cup appearances and scored 43 goals. Chelsea manager Leslie Knighton paid £4,166 and Weaver again had an immediate impact with his new club. He netted twice this time on his debut and was quickly appointed captain of the Blues.

When war broke out in 1939 Weaver joined the Metropolitan Police for the early part of the hostilities, turning out for Chelsea in wartime fixtures. He signed up for the Army and during his service life was still able to play football, guesting for several clubs as he travelled the country. Derby County, Mansfield Town, Notts County and West Ham saw Weaver's influence. So too did Southampton, Wrexham, Stockport County, Leeds United and Fulham. When demobbed in 1945 he again joined Stockport on a free transfer and stayed in Lancashire before, at 38 years old, Sam called it a day in the summer of 1947.

It was the end of a long and memorable playing career, and the end of the Weaver throw that had thrilled football for over a decade. He was the champion of all time. As a youngster Sam watched Tottenham's Arthur Grimsdell, the only player to make some use of the tactic, albeit limited. Weaver saw its advantages and practised the technique assiduously from his early days at Sutton. He could throw without difficulty from the touch-line to the far goalpost and on one occasion, in a match with Huddersfield Town at St James Park, threw the ball so far that it bounced out of play on the opposite flank without anyone touching it! The distance, afterwards measured by United groundsman Sandy Mutch, was recorded as over 48 yards. And remember this was achieved with the heavy, laced ball, a totally different proposition to the lightweight match-balls of today. United, and later Chelsea, found they had a match-winner in the Weaver throw. Countless goals resulted from his formidable throw to the near or far post.

Weaver's other love apart from football, was cricket. Having been a fine medium fast and spin bowler in the Yorkshire League, he moved onto the Derbyshire ground staff for several years and then played two County Championship matches for Somerset in 1939. But for concentrating on football, and then war, Weaver would have probably achieved stardom in this sport too. Later he became Derbyshire's masseur and resident trainer at Trent Bridge for Test Match fixtures.

After hanging up his football boots, Sam joined the training staff at Leeds United then moved south to Millwall in June 1949. Bromley was his next call before a long association started with Mansfield Town in 1956. Appointed at first as coach, he later became boss(1958-1960), resumed coaching then became physio and scout as well as caretaker manager.

After well over 50 years in football he retired completely in 1980, yet Weaver could never totally be far from the game he loved. Into his seventieth year, Sam was still to be seen helping out frequently at the Field Mill Ground - right up to his death in April 1985.

9 FORTIES RESURGENCE

1939-1950

• WARTIME PLAN • RECORD SCORELINE • ATTENDANCE BOOM • TRANSFER HEADLINES • FA CUP STORM • PROMOTION BID • TITLE CHALLENGE •

"You weren't footballers when you played for Newcastle United in those days....you were Gods"

Jack Fairbrother, November 1990

STAN SEYMOUR'S MASTER PLAN IN THE **revival of Newcastle United came to an abrupt halt with only three games of the new campaign over. Adolf Hitler, Germany's corporal-turned-chancellor, made sure of that. For months suspense mounted and fears grew that Hitler's war machine was going to push Europe - and possibly the rest of the globe - into a Second World War.**

As Seymour and boss Tom Mather put together their team line-up for the opening fixture of the season with Millwall, Prime Minister Neville Chamberlain was involved in concentrated diplomatic activity that would hopefully stop a conflict. But Germany had intensified action against Poland and many newspapers were predicting the new football season wouldn't last long.

The summer of tension had put a halt to big swoops into the transfer market. However, United travelled to London to face Millwall with two new faces in the party - outside right Dave Hamilton, signed from Scots junior eleven Shawfield and who was to display a cool and skilful talent, together with centre-forward Willie Scott, another youngster who had arrived from Aberdeen a year before, but had been out of action with a broken leg. Hamilton showed up well in the opening games, but was most unlucky. Not only did war halt his progress, but he, too, was unfortunate to break a leg virtually ending his career before it had really began.

United didn't perform well in the capital. On a hot and sultry day they fell 3-0 at the Den and were criticised for both a lack of authority in defence and penetration up front. Newcastle old boy, Jimmy Richardson scored two of the Londoners' goals. It was the first season that League football saw the now familiar numbering from 1 to 11 on the back of the players' shirts. Newcastle's first official No 9 was Billy Cairns.

The black'n'whites did little better against Nottingham Forest four days later at the City Ground. They lost again, this time by 2-0. Ominously though, the following day Prime Minister Chamberlain had issued his ultimatum to Hitler after bombing raids on Crakow and Warsaw and the subsequent invasion of Poland. The following Saturday it was to be football as usual - or at least as normal as one could expect with the country on the brink of war. For the first viewing at St James Park, the Magpies hit form in the most remarkable way considering what was to dramatically happen 24 hours later. But, as Newcastle's programme notes read, "One feels a certain futility in discussing the immediate future of football". Everyone knew war was barely hours away. United signed off in sparkling style.

Swansea Town faced a United team in destructive mood. Newcastle's forwards at last found their touch up front and walloped the Welshman 8-1 with six goals after the half-time break. Ray Bowden in particular performed brilliantly. Not only did the elegant schemer strike three goals, but he prompted and probed all afternoon and assisted Pearson, Cairns and the two youngsters, Hamilton and Scott, finding the net. Bowden concluded his fine career with a hat-trick on that day, although not one to be included in the official record books as all three results of that season were scratched from the Football League annals.

Only 14,000 saw the game, the last before the conflict put a stop to it all. People clearly had other priorities to cope with. There was a mass evacuation of 75,000 children from industrial Tyneside to relative safety in the countryside of Northumberland and Durham. The King made an emergency visit to Downing Street to discuss events with the Prime Minister. Thousands of potential blood donors were being registered, while Parliamentary Bills were waiting to be rushed through The Commons including the call-up of all men between the ages of 18 and 41.

The following morning, Sunday 3rd September 1939, war was declared. Unlike the First World

War, football's authorities almost immediately called a halt to the season with a government ban on the assembly of crowds and an order to close places of entertainment giving them little option. Newcastle's players found their contracts cancelled within a fortnight and out of work footballers were faced with either enlisting, taking on essential war work or waiting for their call-up papers.

In the place of the Football League programme friendlies took place, but only with the permission of the local police who controlled the gathering of public crowds. United faced Leeds United, then Barnsley and Middlesbrough. Newcastle United continued to operate throughout the hostilities, unlike the 1914-18 conflict, although neighbours Sunderland did close down for a period.

A Regional League of eleven clubs was set up by mid October consisting of teams from Tyneside to the Yorkshire Pennines. United started this programme with a 2-1 victory over Hartlepool United and the black'n'whites did well in the coming months, facing local teams such as York City and Darlington and more sturdy opposition like Huddersfield Town and Bradford Park Avenue. Newcastle were top of the table alongside Leeds United as 1940 opened and, with a 3-0 victory over the Elland Road side, went out in front. But they fell out of the race at the last gasp and ended Runners-up to Huddersfield Town.

A knock-out tournament was arranged too and in the first War Cup Newcastle reached the semi-final by disposing of Bradford Park Avenue and Middlesbrough on a home and away basis, then Bristol Rovers and Blackpool in a one match contest. The south-west country club had a tedious journey travelling some 350 miles north in wartime Britain, then lost to a Billy Cairns goal and had to make the long return. Blackburn Rovers were the Tynesiders' opponents in the semi-final and were handed home advantage to Newcastle's annoyance. The Lancashire club won by a single goal after a slip by 'keeper Tom Swinburne following Nobby Clarke's header on target. It was a costly mistake and robbed United of a Wembley appearance. The Ewood club went on to lose to West Ham United in the final. Swinburne, from County Durham, was capped by England in 1940, his sons later had notable careers in the game too.

Goalkeeper Tom Swinburne in action against Burnley.

As war escalated, football faced mounting difficulties. Players were hard to locate, so too were adequate referees. Travelling became increasingly awkward and United found at times they had to play two games on the same day to avoid fixture pile ups. In June 1940, and with two different teams, they won at Leeds 3-1 and then lost 4-3 at Bradford City.

Shortages of almost every commodity affected life. Clothing coupons hindered the club, change in kit was virtually impossible and Newcastle often turned out in a very washed out looking black'n'white attire. Petrol was limited and not surprisingly sport was never given priority. Indeed, a game with Sheffield United on Tyneside in 1940 was postponed because the Blades couldn't arrange transport. The corresponding fixture at Bramall Lane was also cancelled, this time because German bombs had devastated the pitch. On Tyneside the Luftwaffe carried out missions as well, although St James Park was left largely unscathed with only shrapnel damage to the Leazes roofing taking place. Roker Park was not so lucky, it was bombed in 1943.

Len Duns, the Sunderland forward who was one of many 'guest players' for United during the war.

Crowds dropped to as low as 2,000. By government decree St James Park could not hold more than 15,000 except by sanction while gas masks became a common sight on the Gallowgate terraces. Players started to join the forces. Benny Craig signed up for the Artillery, Dougie Wright joined the Tyneside Scottish Regiment - The Black Watch - along with colleagues Willie Scott and Dave Hamilton. Scott was one of the 30,000 who did not get away from Dunkirk and was captured. Hamilton was lucky, he did. England wing-half, Wright later took part in the Normandy landings and was seriously wounded, afterwards to be told he would never play again, although he did manage to resurrect a career with Lincoln City. Full-back Craig served in the Middle East and won bravery medals as well as skippering the Combined Services soccer team.

Others were engaged on essential work, down the pit or in giant munitions factories like Vickers - Armstrong or the Royal Ordnance Works at Birtley. They still were able to retain a part-time association with St James Park. Albert Stubbins was engaged in the shipyards on Wearside as a draughtsman, Charlie Wayman - one of the club's young finds - was a miner who also had a spell in the Royal Navy.

Newcastle United's management found it difficult to pick a settled line-up with so many players having other priorities. With transfers abandoned, United reverted to the new guest system which allowed any registered footballer to appear for any club. Had it not been for this scheme wartime football of a senior grade would have collapsed. In the early years of the war, United's guests included Len Duns from Sunderland's thirties Cup and Championship side. Once a Newcastle amateur, he performed successfully in a rival black'n'white shirt. So did Leeds United wing-half John Short.

Ray Westwood, one of two famous Bolton players to wear the black'n'white shirt.

Gateshead born, he was big, blond and forceful and netted regularly for the Magpies, 35 goals in only 43 appearances. Bolton Wanderers forwards Ray Westwood and Donald Howe wore the United shirt too, and in a game with York scored eight goals between them. Westwood had been capped six times for England.

Manchester City's Alex Herd, father of David Herd, turned out as well. Harry Eastham, the Liverpool forward, did likewise and was from a noted family too. His father was an international and his younger brother was to join Newcastle - and eventually play for his country also. Jackie Robinson of Sheffield Wednesday, an eye catching inside-right was an England player and Shiremoor born. Liverpool's captain Phil Taylor was to become another England international after the war, as was inside-forward Stan Pearson of Manchester United. All played for the Magpies and many more guests were to follow, including several more famous names. Conversely United's stars appeared for other clubs too. Tommy Pearson pulled on Aston Villa's claret and blue and Albert Stubbins even turned out for Sunderland - appearing in the War Cup final of 1942.

With such selection problems United searched the area for budding footballers and used the five war years as a period for nurturing promising youngsters in readiness for an official go-ahead once more. It worked a treat. When peace was restored the club was to be ideally placed for a surge back into Division One with a batch of youngsters eager to become stars. Opportunities for teenagers were never better. They now went straight into the first team and usually stayed there. Newcastle canvassed widely for local kids. Trial matches were organised and they could answer adverts in the press. A whole batch of eager talent flocked to St James Park. Jackie Milburn was one, so too were Charlie Wayman, Bobby Cowell, Tommy Walker, Ernie Taylor and Charlie Crowe to name a few of many.

League competition expanded following the transitional period in 1939/40. Regional competitions were thrown together into enormous tables with complicated procedures and staged qualifications for War Cup entry. Football was hardly of a standard spectators were used to, but the aim was to entertain the war-torn population and entertain they certainly did. Games usually saw a hatful of goals. In season 1942/43 Newcastle scored 113 times and in 1944/45 122 goals went into the net. United thrashed Middlesbrough and Bradford City 11-0 in the same season. Hull City went down 7-0, Middlesbrough again, this time by 8-2, while Leeds United were trounced 9-0. An amazing 6-6 draw with Gateshead took place in 1942. It was the norm for virtually every game to see four or five goals at least. In that thrashing of Bradford City the opposition included four amateurs and a young half-back by the name of Joe Harvey, a player to shortly lead United to triumph. Those 11-0 victories are Newcastle's second highest competitive scoreline. Eddie Carr netted six times against Leeds, another one of the black'n'whites guest players to impress. Stubbins collected five goals in the mauling of Boro.

It was not uncommon for visiting sides short of a player to ask for a volunteer from the crowd. Even United had difficulties and the Magpies often didn't know who would be available until an hour before the kick-off. But it created interesting conditions for football. In season 1942/43 United met Leeds on six occasions with the games featuring an incredible 47 goals, the Tynesiders netting 28 of those. In the final match of the sequence at Gallowgate, Newcastle were leading by four clear goals with 20 minutes left then Leeds scored five to claim victory!

Newcastle were also beaten heavily on occasion, and by teams not usually associated with such results. The guest system was used efficiently by several sides in the north east and Gateshead and Darlington were two such clubs to inflict big wins over the Magpies. The Quakers crushed United 8-2 and Gateshead won convincingly 4-0. They fielded pre-war stars, many stationed in nearby garrisons like Catterick.

The War Cup became the competition to win. A knock-out tournament continued, later to be split north and south with a national final. Apart from the first year's competition, United also threatened

United and Middlesbrough line up before the start of a Tyne v Tees derby contest in May 1945.

to reach Wembley in 1940/41 when again they battled to the semi-final, all matches being decided after a home and away aggregate result. Having eliminated Rochdale and York City, United faced Middlesbrough and recorded a 4-0 victory. Crowds nearing 13,000 assembled alongside Tyne and Tees, big gates for the early years of the war. Sheffield United proved tougher opposition and, after going down 2-0 to the Tykes at Bramall Lane, Newcastle struck four second-half goals to secure a semi-final place. Preston North End faced the Magpies, one of the pre-war elite. At Deepdale the Lilywhites won 2-0, but then before an extraordinary 29,931 crowd that roared encouragement for the whole 90 minutes, Newcastle couldn't break down the North End defence. The game ended goalless and for the second year running Tyneside's hopes fell at the semi-final. Preston's goalkeeper, Jack Fairbrother, impressed Seymour in that tie - a performance Newcastle's leader would remember. For the remaining seasons of the War Cup, United did not progress far in the tournament.

They did, however, lift the local Tyne Wear Tees Cup in 1944 and in novel circumstances. Having reached the final to play Darlington over two legs, the second meeting remained stalemate at the end of extra-time, 0-1 on the night and 3-3 on aggregate. To settle the tie it was decided to play on until the first team scored! That was United through Jackie Milburn 32 minutes over the extra-time whistle. Darlington incidentally fielded no fewer than seven guest players in that game.

Although not winning any silverware of note, United could boast the country's most potent goalscorer, Albert Stubbins. Now at centre-forward, he had developed quickly during the early years of the war. Born in Wallsend, but brought up in the United States, Stubbins became a top class striker. He was tall with long legs which he used to good effect, enabling him to control awkward balls. He was extremely fast and wore size eleven boots which packed a fearsome shot. Stubbins did much to lift the shadows of war with an astonishing display of goalscoring. He scored goals by the dozen; in threes, fours and fives, time and time again. The Tynesider netted more than an average of a goal a game over seven wartime seasons, a total of 232 goals in only 188 games.

He hit 40 goals in four of those seasons showing tremendous consistency. In one noteworthy spell as 1941 opened the lithe centre-forward bagged four consecutive hat-tricks and then almost made it five by getting two goals in his next match. Stubbins had netted 15 goals in five successive games. It was an amazing strike-rate. He was to appear for England in 1945, against Wales at the Hawthorns and later went on to win League Championship and FA Cup medals with Liverpool. Just what sort of record Stubbins would have set, had first-class soccer continued uninterrupted is one of the game's imponderables.

Other names to establish themselves as war raged were left-back Bobby Corbett from Throckley who was to go on to partner another youngster in defence, Bobby Cowell, at Wembley in 1951. Tom Smith hailed from Horden and appeared on many occasions in the half-back line. Goalkeeper Cam Theaker rivalled Tom Swinburne and guest Dave Cumming for the No 1 jersey. Signed from Grimsby Town just before the war, Theaker spent almost a decade on the St James Park payroll. The position was one of intense rivalry over the coming years with two further capable goalkeepers vying for the role, Eric Garbutt and Jerry Lowery. Norman Dodgin and Doug Graham were two more local products to force their way into the team. Dodgin, from Sheriff Hill was one of the grafters of the side at left-half, while Ashington born Graham was a stylish defender who had been converted from centre-forward.

Future England superstars of the fifties, Tom Finney and Stan Mortensen both guested for the black'n'whites in 1942/43. Finney, to be capped 76 times for England, in fact scored a hat-trick for United against Gateshead. The electrifying Mortensen, a Tynesider from South Shields, was to become, like Finney and Milburn, one of the game's personalities when at Blackpool.

Another future England player to turn out for the club was Jimmy Mullen of Wolves, also a

Goal-king Albert Stubbins. The majority of his football career was taken up by the war.

GOAL POWER

Albert Stubbins crashed home no fewer than 29 hat-tricks during wartime years for United as he was accumulating a massive 232 goals.

1939/40 20 app 10 goals
1940/41 19 app 21 goals
1941/42 26 app 33 goals
1942/43 29 app 42 goals
1943/44 32 app 43 goals
1944/45 31 app 43 goals
1945/46 33 app 40 goals

5 Goal strikes.....5
4 Goal strikes.....6
3 Goal strikes....18
Additionally Stubbins found the net on 21 occasions in friendlies too.

The Magpies as war ended in 1945. Included in the line-up are Albert Stubbins and several new young hopefuls, including Jackie Milburn and Charlie Wayman.

Jerry Lowery, one of several 'keepers on the staff.

Left half Norman Dodgin who became a regular in the promotion side.

Future England star, Stan Mortensen, appeared for United in 1943.

Geordie by birth. Other notable guests were Eddie Carr, an Arsenal starlet just before war who was unlucky to badly damage a knee at Highbury. From County Durham, he played for United on 70 occasions and knocked 56 goals into the net for the club being the ideal foil to Stubbins. Future Spurs boss, Bill Nicholson appeared 19 times while Middlesbrough's 'keeper David Cumming was a regular in 1943/44 and 1944/45. He had been capped by Scotland.

There were several north-easterners who appeared for the club in wartime, but who didn't get into United's side once normality returned. Most made a name for themselves elsewhere. Johnny McNichol was one. He became a regular at both Brighton and Chelsea, one of the Stamford Bridge heroes in their title victory of 1955. John Dixon was another to win honours, he skippered Aston Villa to FA Cup victory in 1957 and appeared over 400 times for the Midland side. Goalkeeper Ray King, with brother George King also on the books, hailed from Amble in Northumberland. Ray was later picked for the England B team in 1954 when appearing with Port Vale, the year the Third Division side almost reached Wembley in the FA Cup. In one match for the Magpies he saved a penalty and badly damaged both wrists stopping a stinging drive. Despite pain he played on for some 15 matches before X-rays confirmed they were broken!

Centre-half Ron Sales appeared on 42 occasions for the club before serving Leyton Orient and Hartlepool. George Moses and Laurie Nevins were to end up at the Victoria Ground too. Charles Woolett was a regular for the Magpies for four seasons before joining Bradford City for the start of peace-time football. Alan Gilholme battled effectively up front and later appeared for Bishop Auckland at Wembley, while Eddie Copeland was another who served Hartlepool after 1945.

By the middle of the 1944/45 season there was a small trickle of players leaving the forces and returning to Tyneside. News also filtered back to the region of their footballing heroes. Tim Rogers was entertaining the troops by playing services' football in Egypt while Jimmy Gordon was fighting the Nazis in France after 'D' Day. Willie Scott was still a prisoner of war and Benny Craig had fought at Anzio. Some were not so lucky. Like Dougie Wright several United players were wounded, some even killed. Pre-war star Bill Imrie was a war fatality while young inside-forward, Colin Seymour, son of United's director Stan Seymour, was tragically killed in a RAF crash near Perth. He had made three appearances in the forward line for the Magpies.

During April 1945 signs that football was fast returning to something like normal was witnessed with an exciting War Cup tie with Bolton Wanderers. There was a big crowd of 43,453 for the deciding home leg to see if Newcastle could score the four goals they needed to erase the Wanderers' 3-0 first leg advantage - two of the goals given away by defensive blunders. A sensational hat-trick by Stubbins put Newcastle level but in extra-time, although scoring another, United conceded two also and went out. Bolton, with Nat Lofthouse in the side, reached the final.

United's bench as peace-time football resumed. Tommy Pearson is in the centre, director William McKeag second from left.

In August 1945, the month of the dreadful Hiroshima bombing and with war all but over, Football League competition was just about back to normal. For the new season regional leagues remained, streamlined into north and south and a 42 match programme was reinstated. It was to be a final rehearsal before a return to normal football. Attendance restrictions were lifted and the turnstiles at St James Park clicked more than anywhere else in the country with several of United's home matches topping the 50,000 mark and over 60,000 turning up for the FA Cup meeting with Barnsley.

Newcastle's directors caricatured by 'Bos' in November 1945.

Tom Mather by this time had returned to the Potteries and United's directors had no immediate plans to appoint a successor. Stan Seymour remained at the forefront of playing policy heading a selection committee of A.G.Stableforth, William McKeag and Wilf Taylor, the latter two directors, like Seymour, to become powerful masters of Newcastle United. Norman Smith was again the chief trainer.

Benny Craig, played for the Magpies both before and after the war.

Most of United's pre-war stars of 1939 never resumed where they had left off. Quality players like Bowden, Ancell and Birkett had all but retired. Clifton and Pearson returned, so did Gordon, Wright and Craig, although all were now into, or approaching, their thirties and had missed the best years of their careers. Only Craig and Wright were part of United's eleven that opened peacetime football again in twelve month's time.

Newcastle finished the 1945/46 season in 6th place. Only League Champions Sheffield United scored more goals than United, Stubbins again proving a prolific scorer, the Northern Section's top goalgetter. Milburn and Wayman developed well too - they grabbed 14 goals each. Stubbins led the way in a 9-1 victory over Stoke City, the highlight of the season. The red haired Geordie netted five times and ran stand-in centre-half Cowden ragged. Stanley Matthews, in Stoke's line-up, was not only impressed with Stubbins, but also by a raw 21 year-old by the name of Milburn. The master winger said to Jackie after the game, "I think you have a bright future if you continue to play like that". He was certainly right. United also demolished Blackburn Rovers by 8-1 and Stubbins again found the net five times. They handed Sunderland a four goal hiding, a game in which United netted their 100th goal of the season. All told the black'n'whites scored 110 times that year.

The FA Cup returned in all its glory and replaced the War Cup. With it came a stirring tie with Barnsley who included in their ranks an up and coming forward called George Robledo, as well as ex Magpie Joe Wilson who had appeared for Newcastle way back in 1929. Over two legs - the only time the FA Cup has been decided on aggregate - United lost 5-4. In the deciding match at Oakwell, United should have cruised home after taking a two goal advantage south. But the Reds put up a terrific display, with Wilson in particular playing the game of his life.

War had changed the balance of football power and many sides at the top during the late thirties were not the same force. New clubs replaced them

Above:: Jackie Milburn, soon to become a Tyneside hero.

including Newcastle United. Seymour brought his batch of youngsters through to form part of a nucleus to re-embark on the promotion target. With the addition of several impeccable buys they created quite an impact in the coming 1946/47 season. Seymour had enticed Joe Harvey from Bradford City for £4,250 and during May 1946 Frank Brennan arrived for £7,500 from Airdrie. The backbone to the next great United eleven had arrived. Also to join the Tyneside ranks was inside-forward Roy Bentley, as a goalmaker to replace Clifton. He cost United £8,500 from Bristol City and was unorthodox, cool headed and able to score and create goals. Later joining Chelsea, Bentley scored 9 goals in only 12 games for England.

The club headed for Norway and Sweden during the close season in an attempt to further blend and forge the side in readiness for the big re-start and a promotion bid in August. While most of the friendlies were typical strolls, United came up against IFK Norrkoping, a team to give the Magpies a 5-0 hiding. They were one of the Continent's top sides boasting Gunner Nordahl as their star. The Swedes were to appear at St James Park the following November and win again, this time taking part in a terrific 3-2 contest watched by an enthralled 47,124 crowd. The Swedish champions showed that European football was now developing rapidly, following an impressive tour by Moscow Dynamo that had captivated the UK.

The 1946/47 season kicked off against Millwall - a repeat of the aborted 1939/40 programme - and 39,187 saw United romp to a 4-1 victory. Jackie Milburn opened the scoring while the costly Bentley

Top: Newcastle and Bolton line up in March 1946 for a minute's silence in rememberance of the Burnden Park disaster.
Below: Chairman G. Rutherford and Joe Harvey (behind) lead United out with their counterparts from Bolton.

How one cartoonist saw United inside-forward Roy Bentley.

was outstanding. Attendances continued to boom now hostilities were over as Tyneside experienced a new atmosphere. United's average home gate for this first peace-time season was an amazing 49,435, by far the best supported club in the country in spite of Second Division status. People wanted to enjoy themselves and they especially wanted football more than anything else. The region's enthusiasts were given plenty to keep them talking as the Magpies went through a very eventful return to first class football - and as ever continued to be controversial with it.

One of Newcastle's expensive buys Albert Sibley, nicknamed 'Joe', who cost £6,500 from Southend.

Newcastle challenged well for promotion being Second Division leaders up to the festive games, but then lost three in a row. Every match was like a Cup-tie, a big crowd charged with atmosphere. United were almost everyone's favourite for promotion especially after a massive spending spree brought plenty of stars to Gallowgate. Joining Harvey, Brennan and Bentley was Joe Sibley from Southend United while George Stobbart arrived from Middlesbrough to take the place of Albert Stubbins who had departed for a post-war record £13,000 fee to Liverpool. Newcastle used the money only a matter of weeks later to sign Bradford Park Avenue's matchwinner Len Shackleton. A long term target of Seymour's, United had tried to sign the inside-forward in the previous season, but were given a firm rebuff. Yet United's director persisted and landed the 23 year-old who had scored over 170 goals for Bradford. The Yorkshire club wanted to top the fee Liverpool paid for Stubbins the previous month and once bargaining reached £13,000, Newcastle director Wilf Taylor created a new national record by handing over an extra 3d piece.

What a debut awaited Shackleton and United's fans three days later. Against struggling Newport County, United equalled the Football League's highest ever score, smashed the Second Division record and Shackleton scored no fewer than six goals on his first appearance - and in the very first minute Newcastle missed a penalty! At the end of the

UNITED'S 13 GOALS

Newcastle United equalled the Football League scoring record against Newport County in 1946 sharing the 13-0 scoreline with Stockport County's victory over Halifax Town in 1933/34.

1-0 (5m) Shackleton to the far post, Wayman heads in
2-0 (7m) Shack beats three men, crosses, collects a return and scores
3-0 (28m) Shack to Wayman who fires into the net
4-0 (30m) Shack to Pearson, onto Wayman who shoots home
5-0 (31m) Wayman to Shack who scores his third
6-0 (35m) Shack is back again and rams another into the net
7-0 (36m) Shack completes his third goal in a five minute spell
8-0 (53m) Shack resumes his scoring feast by crashing another past Turner
9-0 (66m) Shack to Pearson to Milburn who scores
10-0 (69m) Harvey finds Milburn who bulges the net
11-0 (73m) A Shack pass gives Wayman the chance, a rebound off the 'keeper
12-0 (82m) Pearson puts in Bentley who finds the net
13-0 (87m) Shack claims his sixth off full-back Wookey's shoulder

Len Shackleton. A record purchase and six goals on his debut made headlines in 1946.

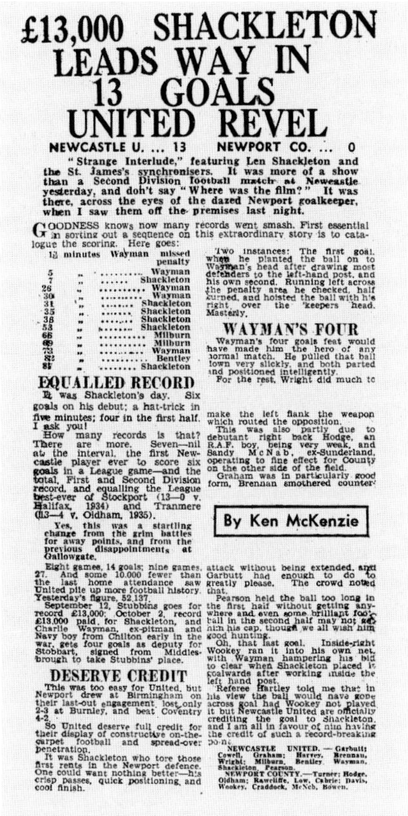

£13,000 SHACKLETON LEADS WAY IN 13 GOALS UNITED REVEL

NEWCASTLE U. ... 13 NEWPORT CO. ... 0

"Strange Interlude," featuring Len Shackleton and the St. James's synchronisers. It was more of a show than a Second Division football match at Newcastle yesterday, and don't say "Where was the film?" It was there, across the eyes of the dazed Newport goalkeeper, when I saw them off the premises last night.

GOODNESS knows now many records went smash. First essential in sorting out a sequence on this extraordinary story is to catalogue the scoring. Here goes:

1½	minutes	Wayman missed penalty
5	"	Wayman
7	"	Shackleton
26	"	Wayman
30	"	Wayman
31	"	Shackleton
35	"	Shackleton
38	"	Shackleton
53	"	Shackleton
66	"	Milburn
69	"	Milburn
73	"	Wayman
82	"	Bentley
87	"	Shackleton

EQUALLED RECORD

It was Shackleton's day. Six goals on his debut; a hat-trick in five minutes; four in the first half. I ask you!

How many records is that? There are more. Seven—nil at the interval, the first Newcastle player ever to score six goals in a League game—and the total, First and Second Division record, and equalling the League best-ever of Stockport (13—0 v. Halifax, 1934) and Tranmere (13—4 v. Oldham, 1935).

Yes, this was a startling change from the grim battles for away points, and from the previous disappointments at Gallowgate.

Eight games, 14 goals; nine games, 27. And some 10.000 fewer than the last home attendance saw United pile up more football history. Yesterday's figure, 52,137.

September 12, Stubbins goes for record £13,000; October 2, record £13,000 paid for Shackleton, and Charlie Wayman, ex-pitman and Navy boy from Chilton early in the war, gets four goals as deputy for Stobbart, signed from Middlesbrough to take Stubbins' place.

DESERVE CREDIT

This was too easy for United, but Newport drew at Birmingham on their last-out engagement, lost only 2-3 at Burnley, and beat Coventry 4-2.

So United deserve full credit for their display of constructive on-the-carpet football and spread-over penetration.

It was Shackleton who tore those first rents in the Newport defence. One could want nothing better—his crisp passes, quick positioning and cool finish.

Two instances: The first goal, when he planted the ball on to Wayman's head after drawing most defenders to the left-hand post, and his own second. Running left across the penalty area he checked, half turned, and hoisted the ball with his right over the 'keepers head. Masterly.

WAYMAN'S FOUR

Wayman's four goals feat would have made him the hero of any normal match. He pulled that ball down very slickly, and both parted and positioned intelligently.

For the rest, Wright did much to make the left flank the weapon which routed the opposition.

This was also partly due to debutant right back Hodge, an R.A.F. boy, being very weak, and Sandy McNab, ex-Sunderland, operating to fine effect for County on the other side of the field.

Graham was in particularly good form, Brennan smothered counter-attack without being extended, and Garbutt had enough to do to greatly please. The crowd noted that.

By Ken McKenzie

Pearson held the ball too long in the first half without getting anywhere and even some brilliant football in the second half may not get him his cap, though we all wish him good hunting.

Oh, that last goal. Inside-right Wookey ran it into his own net, with Wayman hampering his bid to clear when Shackleton placed it goalwards after working inside the left hand post.

Referee Hartley told me that in his view the ball would have gone across goal had Wookey not played it but Newcastle United are officially crediting the goal to Shackleton, and I am all in favour of him having the credit of such a record-breaking point.

NEWCASTLE UNITED.—Garbutt; Cowell, Graham; Harvey, Brennan, Wright; Milburn, Bentley, Wayman, Shackleton, Pearson.

NEWPORT COUNTY.—Turner; Hodge, Oldham; Rawcliffe, Low, Cabrie; Davis, Wookey, Craddock, McNeb, Bowen.

Action v Newport County. Shackleton scoring one of his six goals.

quite sensational match the scoreline read - Newcastle United 13 Newport County 0 - and a 52,137 crowd couldn't believe their eyes. Everything the magical feet of Newcastle's new inside-forward did that afternoon went right and everything the poor Welshmen did went wrong.

As the game started United immediately forced the pace and surged towards the opposition's goal. In the opening seconds Pearson crossed, defender Hodge handled - a penalty. Up stepped Wayman, but 'keeper Turner saw the ball onto the woodwork. What a start considering what was to follow. After that set-back Newcastle, and Shackleton, hardly missed the target again. Within six minutes of that spot-kick United were 2-0 ahead, then they rattled in another five in the ten minutes before half-time. Shackleton scored four of those goals including an astonishing three in only five minutes on the half-hour.

Included in County's side was Norman Low, son of United's Edwardian international Wilf Low, but the Welshmen were completely and utterly overwhelmed by a display of "on the carpet football" as the Sunday Sun reported. The second half was a total walk-over with the forward line, as Shack recorded, "blended into a force of shattering, world beating quality". Charlie Wayman, playing at centre-forward for the first time, scored four and quickly warmed to the position and Shackleton - the only United player to score six goals in a senior game - said of the match, "Everything went perfect. My passes found their men, I beat opponents with ease, my feints worked beautifully. I sensed when passes were about to be sent my way". In summary he noted, "The gods were with me". Many supporters simply lost count of the scoreline, one inked 14-0 into his copy of the programme, while another had to dash home to check the result on Sports Report. He was a young Peter Mallinger, present-day Vice Chairman of the club. It was the first game he had attended!

Shackleton was a complete showman who possessed skill and tricks on the ball like no other footballer before or since. It is doubtful if the game has seen a more entertaining player, although at times he was infuriating to watch with spasms of inconsistency. But for an unwillingness to conform to rigid patterns he would have won many more than the five England caps he did pick up. However, following several displays of magic from Shackleton relations turned sour between club and player. He was to describe his stay at St James Park as, "My stormy couple of seasons with Newcastle United". There were several petty matters of difference and the future England schemer rarely had a good word to say about the way the club was run. Very quickly relationships deteriorated. He was offered to Blackpool ten months before his eventual departure as part of an exchange deal to bring Stan Mortensen to his native Tyneside.

Nevertheless, to start with United's forward-line of Milburn, Bentley, Wayman, Shackleton and veteran Pearson, became quite a force. All bar Wayman, who went on to score 200 goals, were either already, or shortly to become, internationals. Newcastle's name was making national headlines with the transfer activity and buzz of St James Park. Their line up cost a staggering sum then - almost £50,000. Big money

SERVICE MATCHES

St James Park was used for many servicemen's fixtures to entertain the public and to give the military relaxation during the war. Among games that took place were England v Army, RAF v Army and 2nd Battlion Herefordshire Regiment v 53rd Searchlight Regiment RA. Those games featured many top footballers and were in aid of war charities including the Red Cross, Wings for Victory and Spitfire Fund. Even the servicemen of the United States staged a game - the US Army playing the US Navy at baseball in 1944.

stars they may have been, but Newcastle's footballers were still very much part-timers. Many still had jobs out of football, both Milburn and Shackleton worked at the pit-head at Hazlerigg and Roy Bentley related that, "Some players did a lot of training, others hardly any". There was little actual coaching. Football was still a long way from the sophisticated game of today.

Newcastle should have strolled to promotion success, but it was the FA Cup that brought their downfall. A Cup run into the semi-final distracted the side and their main aim of elevation to the First Division was lost. There was no shock this time when Third Division Crystal Palace returned to the north east in the Third Round. United gained a convincing 6-2 victory with three goals in all of four minutes just before half-time rocking the Londoners. The win saw United face Southampton in the next round and the Saints included a young full-back making his debut in the Football League that season, Alf Ramsey. The future England boss received a roasting though, along with his colleagues. Charlie Wayman grabbed a hat-trick to give Newcastle some measure of revenge over their bogey team of past years before a 55,878 crowd at Gallowgate. The St James Park turnstiles were closed and it was the Saints who actually went in front before Wayman took control.

Top: Charlie Wayman proved to be a potent leader of the attack.

Bottom: Wayman striking home a goal against Plymouth.

Following a week of weather watching due to an awful winter(United had six matches in a row cancelled), Leicester City arrived on Tyneside on a bitterly cold and snowy day. The game was almost called off, but 300 Newcastle fans cleared the pitch of its carpet of snow and Leicester proceeded to hold the Geordies to a 1-1 draw in spite of the Magpies' dominance. In the replay on another snow-covered pitch at a packed Filbert Street, Roy Bentley clinched the winner after a goalmouth mistake and after City had taken an early lead with a penalty.

Top First Division outfit Sheffield United, the FA Cup favourites provided Newcastle with their 6th Round opposition. It was to be a difficult tie before a crowd of 46,911 at Bramall Lane. United though - the Newport thrashing apart - produced their best performance of the season to win 2-0 and put the club into another semi-final. Roy Bentley was on the mark again, this time from the penalty spot after an innocuous tackle gave United the important advantage, while Jackie Milburn found the net too. Newcastle's first half performance was exceptional. As one report noted, "United's star studded forward line dazzled Sheffield". They were brilliant on the day with Dougie Wright and Len Shackleton controlling the match from midfield and providing their front men with precision passes. Wright was unluckily injured before the season's close and lost his place at the club when sidelined with cartilage trouble. In the closing stages of the match, United annoyed the home fans by wasting time, kicking the ball far into the adjoining cricket field at Bramall Lane. Covered in deep snow it took a minute or so to retrieve the ball on each occasion.

United should have been on top of the world after that. Through to the semi-final, and still in the hunt for promotion. Yet there was discord in the camp. Newcastle lost home fixtures against Southampton and Fulham then during the side's Cup training at Seahouses trouble flared up when Shackleton and Harvey went on strike after blowing their top in a row over club houses which had been promised, but had taken some time to be sorted out. Both were later suspended by United's directors. Then more controversy when Charlie Wayman, top scorer who ended the season as the division's leading marksman with 30 goals, was dropped for the semi-final clash. This after a supposed row with trainer Norman Smith - although to this day United's centre-forward does not know the exact reason why he was left out. The slightly built leader, he was only 5'6", was to move quickly afterwards, to Southampton for £10,000, a club who had been impressed with his skilful play in the previous FA Cup meeting. One director, Lord Westwood, father of the later Chairman, came out in the local press stating that little Charlie deserved better treatment

Right: Len Shackleton (No. 10) turns away after slotting home a goal at a wintery St. James Park.

and should never have been dropped. This unrest was to clearly affect the side as they made a bid for a Wembley appearance, and afterwards a Division One place. Team morale was shattered.

In the semi-final with Charlton Athletic, then in Division One and FA Cup finalists the year before, Newcastle flopped sensationally. The Magpies had been clear favourites to win at Elland Road, but in front of 47,821 onlookers the Londoners swept Newcastle aside in a more than convincing manner. On a dreary, damp afternoon they strolled to a 4-0 success and this after a pre-match attack of foot poisoning damaged the Cockneys' preparations. The tie was won well before half-time, although United started like a bomb having two shots kicked off the line. Had one of those efforts entered the net it may have been a different outcome. Charlton skipper Don Welsh netted twice in an opening counter burst and just on half-time Athletic made it 3-0. Charlton - managed by north easterner Jimmy Seed - went on to win the Cup.

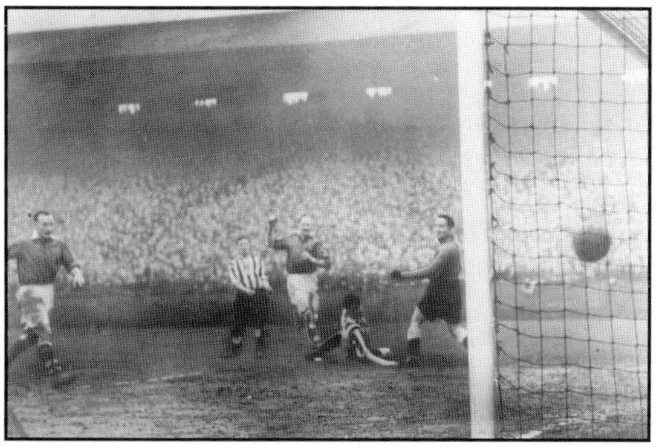

One of Charlton's four goals that demolished United in the 1947 F.A. Cup semi-final. Goalkeeper Swinburne looks back in anguish.

Full-backs Bobby Corbett (left) and Bobby Cowell (right) combine to stop the ball from entering the net.

United still had a chance of promotion after that shock. They started in the right manner by giving Luton Town a 7-2 hiding, the Magpies netting four goals in the space of seven minutes as the Hatters caught a Magpie backlash. But relationships between management and players were not settled and United dropped to a final 5th place. It was a sad and sour end to what otherwise was an exciting return to football.

Out of the mire came the decision to appoint a new team manager in an effort to improve harmony with the playing staff. It was a wise move and Stan Seymour laid down the qualifications he would demand from Newcastle's next boss, "He must be an ex footballer with the tact of a diplomat, the wisdom of Solomon and a general's strength of character". A short list of two candidates was decided upon. Charlton Athletic's Don Welsh - the man who destroyed United in the semi-final - and George Martin, Luton Town's manager. It was Martin who got the three year contract, by a slender margin of one vote, sources noting that Luton's brilliant 4-3 victory over United in the season just closed after being 3-0 down, had proved he was a first class motivator. Martin had played as a forward for Hull City, Middlesbrough, Everton and Luton, at Goodison Park appearing alongside Dixie Dean for a while. He was a man of sober character and of many talents. Martin was also a sculptor and singer of renown, a direct-speaking personality and he made an immediate impact on United's players. Most important of all though, he possessed organising ability and a football brain. His salary was quoted as £1,250 a year with a £250 bonus if he guided the club to promotion. The Scot was given full responsibility for selection of the team - the first time United's board had relinquished control of the line-up, although Stan Seymour worked very much hand in hand with the new boss.

MATCH OFF

In December 1945 United's away fixture at Bradford was cancelled because of the breakdown of the side's train at Northallerton. Another more embarrassing incident occurred during season 1946/47 when West Ham United were due at Gallowgate. However the match was postponed due to frost and snow, but United's administrators slipped up and forgot to inform the Londoners. They spent £77 travelling to St James Park only to find the place deserted with 'Match Off' notices on the turnstiles!

George Martin, United's new manager from Luton Town.

Martin took time to sort out United's internal feuding. It was a stormy period and during the first half of the 1947/48 season there was much coming and going. Courageously - for the plan could have easily back-fired - out went several big names; Bentley(Chelsea), Pearson(Aberdeen), Shackleton(Sunderland) and Wayman(Southampton). All left for big fees, Shackleton's transfer creating a new record of £20,050 when no fewer than twelve clubs were lined up for an auction, Sunderland just topping Bolton's bid by £50. All were to proceed, like Wayman, to have first class careers elsewhere. Bentley was to lead Chelsea to the Championship in 1955 and Pearson to stay at Pittodrie for many a year, later as manager.

With over £40,000 collected in transfer fees, new faces arrived at St James Park with 'keeper Jack Fairbrother and George Lowrie the big name signings. Fairbrother arrived from Preston for

£18,500 George Lowrie, at the time the club's biggest ever purchase.

£6,500 while Lowrie cost £18,500, United's biggest transfer then and again very nearly a record. A Welshman, Lowrie made a name for himself with Coventry and Wales. Unfortunately he was dogged by knee trouble after impressing the Tyneside public with three goals in a match and a quarter. He was out of action for many months and eventually moved to Bristol City for half United's massive transfer fee. Willie McCall, an ultra-direct winger arrived from Aberdeen as part of the Pearson deal, but didn't stay south long. Wartime products Norman Dodgin and Doug Graham were given chances. Nicknamed 'The Duke', Graham was dubbed the best dressed man in the north east!

It was an astute piece of management by Martin, one of the best spells of wheeling and dealing in the club's past. Yet the manager was at first criticised heavily, especially at the sale of Shackleton and after adverse comments were made about the club's style of management. Fans at the giant Vickers factory were so incensed that they staged a "Keep Shack" protest meeting. However, United's manager was confident the changes would succeed.

Joe Harvey (second from left) leads this group of United players in training.

Supporters rolled up in their droves. The club received almost 15,000 applications for the meagre 1,500 season-tickets and attendances surpassed anything before or since. Fans queued for two to three hours to get inside St James Park for every game. Even gates of 20,000 turned up for the Stripes v Whites practice match! The Geordie fans created a national record that season with a truly amazing average of 56,299 seeing Newcastle's 21 home games. It was a record until Manchester United passed it by a small margin in 1968. Finances were in turn given an even bigger boost. From struggling to cope during the hostilities with annual revenue of around £12,000 and an overdraft approaching £28,000 as war began, United's coffers jumped, receiving gross income through the turnstile of £126,059 0s 8d in 1946/47 and a massive £151,319 7s 8d in 1947/48. Admission was 1s 6d and with wages still minimal at £10 per week the overdraft quickly disappeared. United became a cash rich club, one of the most affluent in Britain. They could now afford the luxury of even investing part of their fortune - over £50,000 was lodged with various building societies. They were also to spend £30,000 on ground improvements, another £30,000 on modern accommodation for players. It was a remarkable transformation.

That massive following was a huge boost to the team. They gave the Magpies a goal start in every home fixture with an intimidating roar of encouragement. United were to win 18 of their home fixtures. The fans helped in other ways too being quick to respond to a plea for clothing coupons to enable the club to acquire new kit. The war was still having an effect on the way of life with rationing of certain commodities lasting until 1949. Days of cars and televisions for all were still a long way off.

Newcastle began with a winning start, defeating Plymouth Argyle 6-1 on the opening day of the season. But United had to learn that they had to battle their way out of Division Two as well as continue to play classical football. One of the last occasions before Martin's sweeping changes took place was a 4-1 victory over Cardiff City during November. Several correspondents of the day recorded that United's forward display even surpassed the Newport highpoint of twelve months earlier. It was another Shackleton exhibition - reckoned by many to be his finest. The Sunday Express wrote, "It was a day full of magnificent dribbles. A day too of crafty passes. Cardiff were bedazzled, bewildered and finally bewitched by Shackleton's genius". Jack Fairbrother, in goal, said afterwards that United's forwards were "an unforgettable sight". The game also included a ten second goal by Jackie Milburn, now to be flung into the limelight as the crowd's favourite.

By Christmas, Newcastle were in a challenging position, but never guaranteed of success. They were a bit of a Jekyll and Hyde outfit, winning brilliantly one week, but failing the next. However, following the club's exit from the FA Cup, once more by Charlton, they pushed on relying on their impeccable home record.

SUNDERLAND'S HOME

Three times during the war Sunderland played 'home' matches at St James Park when Newcastle United were not in opposition. Firstly in April 1940 they faced Darlington in a War Cup tie, their own stadium being closed at the time because of the hostilities. They drew 1-1, won on aggregate, and then met Leeds United, again at Gallowgate and once more they ended level with the visitors. Five years later in 1945, the Wearsiders met Gateshead in the final of the Tyne Wear Tees Cup and fell 6-3. Ex United striker Billy Cairns netted twice for the Redheugh Park club.

Martin installed discipline and determination - to the omission of attacking flair. Some didn't like it, but his plan worked.

At Easter United were still in the hunt lying in 2nd position behind Birmingham City and closely followed by Sheffield Wednesday and Charlie Wayman's Southampton. Inspired by Harvey and balding full-back from pre-war days, Benny Craig, United clicked into overdrive and this in spite of injury problems at the crucial stage of the season. Newcastle did well against Barnsley, Doncaster and Nottingham Forest,then gained a full haul opposing Bradford. One week in April clinched United's promotion back to Division One starting with the visit of Fulham to the north east for a midweek fixture. A dramatic George Stobbart penalty produced two more precious points in a thrilling game that wasn't concluded until the very last moments of the match. There were just four minutes left when Newcastle were awarded a penalty after Milburn had been tripped - outside the box claimed Fulham. With the tension unbearable Stobbart was entrusted with the spot-kick and, in a silence in which you could have heard the proverbial pin drop, the ball was placed on the spot. The stocky forward from Pegswood advanced, took a couple of steps and the ball thudded into the net. 54,061 roared their heads off.

Three days later it was promotion rival Sheffield Wednesday's turn to feel the white hot atmosphere of St James Park. It was a decisive game, a match that proved to be a battle royal. If the Magpies picked up a victory they would be four points ahead of the Yorkshire club with only two games left. The Owls had stayed at Tynemouth all week and watched United's performance over Fulham so they knew exactly what was needed. In front of another charged crowd of 66,483, Wednesday shocked Newcastle and their vast following in no uncertain manner.

United had won ten games on the trot at Gallowgate while no visiting team had scored a goal in three months. Yet within ten minutes, the Yorkshiremen were ahead through a penalty. Benny Craig handled on the line and Whitcomb silenced the masses by netting the spot-kick. And they were worth their lead, having two shots kicked off the line. George Stobbart equalised with a superb goal after being put through and the Magpies went storming into the lead immediately after the interval. Joe Harvey rose to head home one of his rare goals from a Tommy Walker corner.

Wednesday, though, were far from being toppled. They rallied and seized a deserved equaliser nine minutes from time when Marriott scored. The game looked a certain 2-2 draw. Then enter hero-to-be Frank Houghton, a reserve half-back playing on the wing. With three minutes to go, he put United 3-2 in front following a goalmouth melee, Houghton finishing up with Jimmy Woodburn flat out on top of him. Amazingly, within two minutes he had done it again. Milburn slipped a through ball in his path and Houghton was off in another valiant

George Stobbart arrived from Middlesbrough and scored nine precious goals in the promotion year.

charge. He crashed into the Sheffield 'keeper McIntosh, but at the same time poked the ball into the net. In the process he broke his right arm and horribly gashed a leg. Houghton slumped to the ground as the crowd erupted. Meanwhile, United were 4-2 ahead and just about back in the First Division.

Man of the moment Houghton, a £5,500 signing from Ballymena in January, never had a better 90 minutes football. Born in Lancashire, he was to be a most unfortunate player not to build on his 1948 success due to a series of mishaps. He later not only broke his leg, but suffered badly from tuberculosis spending several years out of action.

ADMISSION 1945/46

Season-tickets	Adults	£5 guineas	
	Under 14	£3 guineas	
Match-day	Ground	1s	6d
	Boys & Forces		9d
	Wing Stands	2s	6d
	Paddocks	2s	6d
	Centre Pavilion	3s	6d

Those supporters who held a season-ticket for the aborted 1939/40 season were granted free admission.

The following week Newcastle collected the point required to be certain of promotion at Tottenham. They got it with a 1-1 draw on FA Cup final day, Sibley hitting the vital goal. United went up with Birmingham City after 13 years out of the First Division. The final game of the season - at home to Millwall - saw a mass of rosette clad fans waving banners and rattles fill the stadium, just as future generations of Tynesiders would do in 1965 and 1984 on promotion being achieved.

Much of the success went down to skipper Joe Harvey and centre-half Frank Brennan who instilled determination in the rest of the side. Harvey just missed an England cap, appearing for the Football League against the Scots during March. The pair

Wing half Frank Houghton who netted two late goals to ensure victory over Sheffield Wednesday in the promotion decider.

WARTIME INTERNATIONAL

England 2 (Clifton, Lawton) Scotland 1(Dodds)
2 December 1939

The first wartime Red Cross international took place at St James Park before a 15,000 crowd. Tommy Pearson was capped by England - the only Scot ever to play for the English - in place of Eric Brook who was injured in a pre-match car accident at Dishforth. Joe Richardson also came into the side for Sam Barkas also involved in the crash. Richardson's full-back partner in United's line-up, Bobby Ancell was in Scotland's eleven, while Harry Clifton and a fifth Newcastle player, Tom Swinburne, were also capped. Clifton headed England's winning goal - a spectacular full length diving header - after a cross from man-of-the-match Stanley Matthews. It was the first of several wartime representative games at Gallowgate. Ralph Birkett and Albert Stubbins were to be capped in future matches.

ENGLAND:
Swinburne (Newcastle United)
Richardson (Newcastle United)
Greenhalgh (Everton)
Goslin (Bolton Wanderers)
Harper (Barnsley)
Mercer (Everton)
Matthews (Stoke City)
Carter (Sunderland)
Lawton (Everton)
Clifton (Newcastle United)
Pearson (Newcastle United).

SCOTLAND:
Dawson (Rangers)
Carabine (Third Lanark)
Ancell (Newcastle United)
Pinkerton (Falkirk)
Baxter (Middlesbrough)
Brown (Hearts)
Finan (Blackpool)
Walker (Hearts)
Dodds (Blackpool)
Napier (Sheffield Wednesday)
Caskie (Everton).

kept the opposition goalless in 20 league games. The Magpies' team spirit was much in evidence. It was a major factor to stay with the side for the next decade. Top scorer was Jackie Milburn, who during the season reluctantly switched from outside-right to centre-forward replacing Wayman. In his first game wearing the famous Number 9 shirt against Bury, he scored three goals. Scot Bob Fraser, an emergency signing from Hibernians as cover for the defence, performed well too.

The first eleven were not the only successful Magpie side either. The Central League team walked away with the Championship for the first, and up to now, only time when they finished ahead of Manchester United. Crowds were even amazing at this level of football. 19,824 saw the clash with Bolton Reserves and the average was almost 13,000. Captain Tot Smith was the mainstay along with Benwell lad Andy Donaldson. He netted 33 goals in only 30 appearances. Donaldson was unlucky to have, first Wayman, then Milburn as rivals for the centre-forward's role. In fact, at one stage United's management were undecided whether to keep Milburn or Donaldson when Middlesbrough made an approach for the pair. United picked Milburn and his team-mate headed for Ayresome Park for £17,500.

Local products Ron Batty, Charlie Crowe and Ernie Taylor were regulars too and were to have their glory in the senior side in the months to follow. Other youngsters graduated from the club's prospering youth policy including Tommy Thompson, a goalscoring schemer with a delicate touch who later shined for Preston and Villa, and for England. Andy Graver created goal records in the lower divisions, while 5'4" George Hair sped down the flank in a perky and elusive fashion.

Apart from the Central League side, the club also ran a Junior set up. In a further development to Colin Veitch's pioneering Swifts, United had three kids' teams by 1950 - 15 year olds, 16 year olds and 17 year olds - all under the banner of the NNNN's,

the Northumberland, North Durham and Newcastle Nursery. This was a separate organisation to the football club, although funded by them and later to become part of the St James Park regime as simply, the N's. One United director said, "The N's may be the making of Newcastle United in the not too distant future". The club also financed Throckley FC as a nursery. While United always found players from this considerable set up, they always relied on the transfer market first and foremost.

During the successful 1947/48 season, United's supporters created another attendance record when First Division Champions, Liverpool, along with past hero, Albert Stubbins, attracted 44,830 for a friendly game on a vacant FA Cup Saturday. It was the highest gathering for a non competitive match between two English clubs. Big attraction Stubbins missed a penalty as Liverpool won 3-0. It had been quite a season all round.

THE CROWD'S GOAL

Newcastle scored one of the strangest goals seen at St James Park against Chesterfield in September 1947. The visitor's 'keeper Ray Middleton on hearing a whistle - from the crowd - put the ball down and backed away to take what he believed to be a free-kick for offside. Jackie Milburn promptly ran up and banged the ball into the net and the referee gave a goal! Chesterfield, however had the the last laugh. They won 3-2.

Houghton is helped to his feet in some agony after grabbing one of his two goals against Sheffield Wednesday. Jackie Milburn has a breather on the ground.

Jack Fairbrother in training on the St. James Park pitch.

Centenary Highlight

Top left: Newcastle mascot of the 1940's, Jimmy Nicholl.

Above: George Stobbart (left), watched by Andy Donaldson fires towards goal..

Left: Frank Brennan and Doug Graham join forces to stop this opposition forward.

Promotion 1948

DIVISION TWO PROMOTION 1947-1948	P	W	D	L	F	A	Pts
Birmingham City	42	22	15	5	55	24	59
Newcastle United	**42**	**24**	**8**	**10**	**72**	**41**	**56**
Southampton	42	21	10	11	71	53	52
Sheffield Wednesday	42	20	11	11	66	53	51
Cardiff City	42	18	11	13	61	58	47
West Ham United	42	16	14	12	55	53	46
West Bromwich Albion	42	18	9	15	63	58	45
Tottenham Hotspur	42	15	14	13	56	43	44
Leicester City	42	16	11	15	60	57	43
Coventry City	42	14	13	15	59	52	41
Fulham	42	15	10	17	47	46	40
Barnsley	42	15	10	17	62	64	40
Luton Town	42	14	12	16	56	59	40
Bradford Park Avenue	42	16	8	18	68	72	40
Brentford	42	13	14	15	44	61	40
Chesterfield	42	16	7	19	54	55	39
Plymouth Argyle	42	9	20	13	40	58	38
Leeds United	42	14	8	20	62	72	36
Nottingham Forest	42	12	11	19	54	60	35
Bury	42	9	16	17	58	68	34
Doncaster Rovers	42	9	11	22	40	66	29
Millwall	42	9	11	22	44	74	29

REGULAR SIDE

Fairbrother
Cowell or Fraser - Craig
Harvey - Brennan - Dodgin
Sibley - Stobbart - Milburn - Shackleton - Pearson

CHAIRMAN: George F Rutherford
MANAGER: George Martin
TRAINER-COACH: Norman Smith
CAPTAIN: Joe Harvey

RESULTS	Home	Away
Plymouth Argyle	W 6-1	L 0-3
Chesterfield	L 2-3	W 1-0
Luton Town	W 4-1	L 1-2
Brentford	W 1-0	L 0-1
Birmingham City	W 1-0	D 0-0
Leicester City	W 2-0	D 2-2
Leeds United	W 4-2	L 1-3
Fulham	W 1-0	L 0-3
Coventry City	D 0-0	D 1-1
West Ham United	W 1-0	W 2-0
Bury	W 1-0	W 5-3
Southampton	W 5-0	L 2-4
Doncaster Rovers	W 2-0	W 3-0
Nottingham Forest	L 0-2	D 0-0
Bradford Park Ave	W 2-0	W 3-0
Cardiff City	W 4-1	D 1-1
Sheffield Wednesday	W 4-2	L 0-1
Tottenham Hotspur	W 1-0	D 1-1
Millwall	W 1-0	L 1-2
West Bromwich Albion	W 3-1	W 1-0
Barnsley	W 1-0	D 1-1

LARGEST VICTORY;
6-1 v Plymouth Argyle(H)

HEAVIEST DEFEAT;
0-3 v Fulham(A) & Plymouth Argyle(A)

AVERAGE HOME ATTENDANCE:
56,299

TOP GATE:
66,483 v Sheffield Wednesday

LEAGUE APPEARANCES
42 Brennan, 39 Milburn, 37 Harvey, 26 Stobbart, Dodgin, Craig, 25 Fairbrother, Shackleton, 21 Pearson, 20 Fraser, 19 Cowell, 18 Sibley, 17 Garbutt, Woodburn, 16 Graham, 15 McCall, 13 Houghton, 12 Bentley, 8 Walker, Taylor, 6 Wayman, Hair, 5 Lowrie, Donaldson, 4 Thompson, Corbett, 2 Crowe.

LEAGUE GOALS
20 Milburn, 9 Stobbart, 7 Shackleton, 4 McCall, Sibley, 3 Bentley, Harvey, Pearson, Walker, own-goal, 2 Wayman, Woodburn, Thompson, Houghton, Hair, 1 Dodgin, Donaldson, Lowrie.

Defender Bob Fraser who filled in at right-back during the season.

United's line-up in 1948. Left to right, back: Houghton, Craig, Brennan, Garbutt, Fraser, Woodburn. Front: Sibley, Harvey, Donaldson, Milburn, McCall.

NO IMPETUS WAS LOST FROM THE promotion charge as United took the First Division by storm. They pushed strongly for the Championship in 1948/49 and reinstated the club's high standing in football. A 1-0 win over Everton just before Christmas took Newcastle to the head of the table, one point in front of Portsmouth. Ernie Taylor, now fully established in the side, scored the goal and was the outstanding player on the field. His control and eye for the open space made him an expert link man. Totally unselfish and only 5'4" tall, Taylor was to be highly respected in the coming decade, appearing for England and reaching three Wembley finals with three different clubs.

Newcastle continued to be a big attraction. The largest crowd United have played in front of - excluding Cup finals - turned up for another game in the same month. Against Manchester United 70,787 saw 90 minutes of football, played unusually at Maine Road due to Old Trafford's redevelopment after major bomb damage. At the halfway stage of the season only three defeats had been recorded and it became clear that the title was going to Tyneside or to the south coast at Fratton Park, Portsmouth.

A First Division outfit once more. Left to right, back: Cowell, Harvey, Fairbrother, Smith, McMichael, Crowe. Front: Mitchell, Walker, Taylor, Milburn, Robledo.

There was no FA Cup to distract Newcastle either. After several days of wondering if the Third Round tie with Second Division Bradford Park Avenue would go ahead because of the weather, the Magpies fell 2-0 on Tyneside causing one of the season's upsets - but not the biggest, that was reserved for Yeovil's demolition of Sunderland. After this setback United continued on the heels of Pompey winning well at Gallowgate, but dropping valuable away points.

In a Tyne-Wear derby clash, United won 2-1 with Milburn, pushing for an England place, and new signing from Barnsley, George Robledo scoring the goals. Chilean Robledo arrived in a double swoop along with his younger brother Ted for £26,500. Another famous name entered the fray as well. Bobby Mitchell made his league debut in that Sunderland match after being secured for £16,000.

New purchase George Robledo makes a spectacular leap for the ball against Chelsea's Medhurst.

This after United had failed with a bid to land Blackburn's international winger Bobby Langton. Money was no problem to United. They were prepared to break the bank in an attempt to bring Hibernians and Scotland ace Gordon Smith to the north east. They chased the Scot unsuccessfully for all of four years and were said to have offered as much as £30,000, then by far a national record.

The crucial game with Portsmouth took place at St James Park during April. United simply had to win to give themselves any chance of reducing the three point lead Pompey held. A 60,611 gate were stunned at the outcome. Portsmouth most definitely showed who was going to win the Championship by smashing United's challenge with a five goal strike. Left winger Jack Froggatt scored a hat-trick and his opposite partner on the right, Peter Harris netted twice in a 5-0 hammering. Remarkably all the goals were headers. The game was played at a terrific pace and Portsmouth trotted off the field virtual First Division Champions in their jubilee year. Future United skipper, Jimmy Scoular was one of those happy Pompey stars.

Newcastle then disappointed their fans further by slipping down the table. They had been five points clear of 3rd placed Derby County, but lacking conviction fell to 4th position when they should have finished as Runners-up. Still, it had been a most successful return to the First Division and an average gate of 53,702 was again the best in the country. Newcastle's travelling support was even then immense too. For a game at Blackpool, almost 10,000 made the journey over the Pennines. Local fans complained that the Geordies, "made so much noise that they couldn't hear the band"! Supporters continued to watch the reserve team and a record Central League attendance of 21,721 saw Burnley Reserves in September 1948.

SAFE IN THE SOCK

When United journeyed to away fixtures during the late 1940s, secretary Frank Watt had a novel way of securing the club's travelling expenses. Instead of keeping the cash in the hotel safe, he simply stuffed it down his socks. He maintained that no would-be thief would ever think of looking there!

Jackie Milburn watches his effort creep past the opposition's goalkeeper.

Below: Newcastle v Derby County 1949. Action at the Leazes End of the ground.

In spite of such a buoyant atmosphere there was much unrest in the dressing-room. George Martin had not cured the problems totally and at one stage no fewer than 16 players asked for transfers. There was a strong undercurrent of discontent amidst a large staff of almost 40 professionals. Among those to try to depart were Bobby Cowell, Jackie Milburn and Ernie Taylor. It was not the first occasion future idol Milburn had tried to get away from Gallowgate. Back in May 1947 a written request was considered by United's board. Surprisingly perhaps, directors Rutherford and Seymour suggested that he be granted a transfer - thankfully though the decision was made for the manager to speak to the player. Martin persuaded Jackie to stay, but he was to try to leave again, because, as the club's minutes record, "he did not desire to play centre-forward".

Ron Batty appeared at full-back for most of the season. From West Stanley he played in 181 games for United at left-back, one of the side's unsung heroes of the era. Jackie Milburn remembered him as a defender who, "could cut wingers in two with his tackling". Another local discovery was Tommy Walker. Extremely versatile, he had recovered from

DEBUT PAYMENT

Charlie Crowe made his first team debut for United in a 9-1 victory over Stoke City in 1945. The professionals in United's side received £2 10s in wages, Crowe, still an amateur had to claim expenses. He received 1s 6d tea money and 1s 0d travelling expenses. As the player said, "At the time I thought it was a bit unfair"!

a broken arm and had switched from outside-left to outside-right to accommodate Bobby Mitchell's talents. Fair haired Colin Gibson was another big money buy at the start of the campaign from Cardiff City, yet never got into the groove in United's forward line. He was quickly to move on for £17,500 to Aston Villa only six months later. Gibson went on to display his best football in the claret and blue.

Colin Gibson, another big forward signing but one to be dogged by injury.

A major tour of North America took place in the summer. United's party of 16 players and six officials crossed the Atlantic on board the Queen Mary for a six week spell of football and sightseeing. They were insured for £1 million, unthinkable money in 1950. The tour started off badly with a minor player revolt when United's stars found out they were only booked into tourist class rooms. An outcry followed, especially when they found out the Scottish FA party were in first class berths, and a player deputation declared, "Better accommodation or else we don't play"! The squad was quickly upgraded to the upper decks.

Newcastle played ten games, won them all scoring a massive 79 goals. Included was a 16-2 victory over Alberta with Milburn and Robledo hitting the net no fewer than eleven occasions between them. It is the club's biggest ever scoreline. United also reached double figures against Saskatchewan(13-2) and Washington State(11-1), while the American press were often intrigued at the British sportsmen. They puzzled at how they could

Outside-right Tommy Walker, fast and direct, he netted 40 goals for the Magpies.

Advertisement carried by one of Ontario's local newspapers for the exhibition visit of United during their tour of North America.

earn only around £600 per year at most when in comparison centre-fielders of the New York Yankee baseball team received all of $90,000. They called British football the, "poverty sport".

Jackie Milburn collected 31 goals on the tour adding to the 19 he netted in the First Division. Having made his debut for England against Northern Ireland - when he scored in a 6-2 victory - Milburn was now hailed as 'Wor Jackie' less than a few months after the sleek Ashington forward wanted to be away. He was now said to be worth £30,000, Derby County offering close to that figure in the following season. After being unsure of his future at St James Park, the board now said bluntly, "the player was not for transfer".

Newcastle die-hards wanted a trophy brought to St James Park. United's fans thought that following the slip-up at the end of last season, the Magpies would make amends in 1949/50. And why not - Newcastle had put together an imposing side. Marshalled supremely by Harvey, in defence they were solid around the towering figure of Frank Brennan with locals Bobby Cowell and Bobby Corbett - soon to be replaced by new signing Alf McMichael - very effective. Up front they could be dynamite with Milburn and Robledo forming a deadly duo while Walker and Mitchell were a perfect mix of the straightforward and unorthodox on the flanks. Scot, Mitchell was at this time building up a huge following with dazzling displays. Ernie Taylor and another newcomer, George Hannah, who arrived with McMichael from Ireland, were rivals for the delicate schemers' role.

Yet the new season was a big let down. Newcastle started off badly missing Joe Harvey with an early season injury and they slipped as far down as 17th position. At the mid point of the campaign there was no chance of silverware ending up at St James Park, not in the league or FA Cup. Two defeats by Middlesbrough before bumper Christmas crowds - 53,596 still a record at Ayresome Park - took United into a Cup-tie with Oldham Athletic, and while they won comfortably by 7-2, Newcastle fell in the next round. Roy Bentley's club, Chelsea convincingly stopped Newcastle in their Wembley tracks and were full value for their 3-0 victory. Almost 65,000 were at Stamford Bridge for that game.

From the FA Cup exit the black'n'whites made a good league recovery moving into the top five. The side's composure and gritty play re-emerged and they created another north east record crowd on the way. This time 68,004 at Roker Park saw the local derby during March. United held title-chasing Sunderland 2-2 with Frank Houghton and Ernie Taylor scoring and Frank Brennan the commanding influence.

Seymour's two young recruits from Linfield, McMichael and Hannah, impressed many observers. Alf McMichael was to stay on the staff for another 14 years while George Hannah graced the turf on many occasions with his subtle touch on the ball. Jackie Milburn and George Robledo both turned out in the 1950 World Cup tournament in Brazil during the summer, for England and Chile respectively. Milburn wasn't in his country's first choice line-up initially, but after the shock 1-0 defeat by USA at Belo Horizonte, eventually got his chance.

United may not have won any trophies as Tyneside so much wanted, but the side to take many of the headlines during the fifties was almost in place. Newcastle supporters did not have to wait long for success as the new decade burst into a period of triumph.

Above: Bobby Corbett, from Throckley, a fine attacking left-back.

PREMATCH TACTICS

George Martin's typical dressing-room talk during the late forties as related by Charlie Crowe consisted of;
Fairbrother (Goalkeeper)...."Jack the penalty area - make it your own. You are the boss".
Cowell & Corbett (full-backs)...."Now the two Bobs; these two wingers - put a rope around their necks".
Harvey (captain and half-back)...."Joe - keep them going".
Brennan (centre-half)...."Frank - put him in your pocket".
Crowe (half-back)...."Charlie - give them the usual" (Smashing his right fist into his left palm).
Walker (right-wing) & Milburn (centre-forward)...."Tom and Jackie - show them your backside".
Taylor (inside-forward)....Ruffling Ernie's hair, "Aha, Aha - the little man", nodding as to emphasise some point.
Robledo (inside-forward)...."George - the far post".
Mitchell (winger)...."Mitch - that extra man - don't overdo it".

Left: Possessing abundant craft on the ball, George Hannah became a big favourite.

Centenary Profile 12

Black 'n' white through & through

"Joe was a gem - a man's man. He knew how to treat players and get the best out of them"

Malcolm Macdonald, February 1989

JOE HARVEY SAW IT ALL HAPPEN IN OVER 50 YEARS in the game - the majority at St James Park. Cup incidents by the hatful....three successful finals, another as Runners-up, the embarrassment too as victim of the minnow. Promotion success, European glory, and relegation. Harvey was a devoted servant and few worked as hard for United's cause. He was a barnstorming skipper, an influential manager and later knowledgeable backstage aid. He was simply black'n'white through and through.

Joe Harvey was born in Edlington, a pit village near Doncaster. Being a Yorkshireman by birth he was blessed with that region's traditional grit. He started adult life as an apprentice machinist in the colliery brass foundry and played football for the local team, Edlington Rangers. A forward then, Joe had the chance to join Wolves in November 1936 when 16 years old. He jumped at the opportunity, but the Molineux club were not too impressed and within a year packed him off to Bournemouth, their nursery team. Harvey didn't last long on the south coast either, but he did find a good home with Bradford City. Following an unsuccessful trial with Hull City, he joined the Valley Parade set-up in the summer of 1938.

Harvey established himself as a reserve at Bradford before the outbreak of war and during the troubled years acted as a PT Instructor in the Royal Artillery, graduating to the rank of Company Sergeant Major. He played football whenever he could and guested for several clubs scattered around the country including, Aberdeen, Hartlepool and Aldershot. Joe was also once stationed at Tynemouth Castle.

Newcastle United became interested in his ability during the autumn of 1945. Stan Seymour was on the look out for a half-back and Harvey was recommended. By this time he was a first-team regular at Valley Parade, a versatile player too, turning out at inside-forward, centre-forward and even outside-right as well as his customary half-back position. He could find the net, being City's top scorer in 1943/44 with 17 goals - grabbing two against United. At 6'0" he showed little frills, but was full of determination. Although wanted by Middlesbrough too, Harvey signed for the Magpies at a Darlington public-house in October 1945. He cost United £4,250, money quickly repaid. Joe's first appearance in a black'n'white jersey was against Blackpool, a 2-2 draw in the wartime Northern League. In the very next game he was appointed captain and went on to skipper the side more than any other player, leading United out for eight years.

Harvey was Stan Seymour's first big signing. United's director-manager went on to build a marvellous side round Joe's tough and rugged defensive qualities. Now operating regularly at right-half, he was at his best when the contest was at its most fierce. Hating to lose, he always pushed to the limit and made sure his colleagues did the same. Harvey was a character in the camp, a formidable leader who always stood up to be counted, yet in days when football was very different, he often had a couple of pints of Guinness on a Saturday lunchtime before a game. And Joe always had a smoke at half-time too, like many of his team-mates!

Promotion and Wembley victories in 1951 and 1952 saw Joe Harvey become United's figurehead. His personality affected the whole club. Direct and honest, with a great sense of humour, he kept the players in check and if they slackened gave them a mighty growl. He was recognised at representative level, being picked for the Football League side on three occasions, skippering the team in 1951. It was one step from a full cap.

During the close season of 1953 when approaching 35 years of age, he became player-coach witnessing another FA Cup triumph in 1955 from the sidelines. Harvey then had a brief spell with Crook Town before trying management with struggling Barrow and Workington. He had nearly entered that sphere back in 1951, applying for the vacant Carlisle job, but Newcastle would not release him. Now the opportunity was there and Joe had a tough seven year managerial education at Borough Park and Holker Street. Arriving at Barrow for his first day as boss he found that he had only five players and his club missed having to apply for re-election only by goal average in 1955/56. Workington initially struggled too, but Harvey's influence gradually saw the Reds reach the promotion fringes.

Joe Harvey

HARVEY'S PLAYING RECORD	League		FA Cup		Total	
	App	Gls	App	Gls	App	Gls
1946-47	34	3	4	0	38	3
1947-48	37	3	1	0	38	3
1948-49	38	2	1	0	39	2
1949-50	22	1	0	0	22	1
1950-51	36	1	8	0	44	1
1951-52	37	1	7	0	44	1
1952-53	20	1	0	0	20	1
1945-46 (War time & Cup)					35	1
	224	**12**	**23**	**0**	**280**	**13**

He applied for the vacant Newcastle United job firstly in 1958, but lost out to Charlie Mitten. Joe though was soon to return to Gallowgate, but not until he almost quit the game to concentrate on a newsagency business he had opened in the west end of Newcastle. In the summer of 1962 he tried for the United post again and this time succeeded, initially on a twelve month trial. His stay in charge lasted all of 13 years!

Director Stan Seymour remarked to the press, "With Joe Harvey in charge of the players, we have laid the foundation for a fighting bid for a quick return to the top class". Joe revitalised his former club and put the Magpies back in Division One within three years. He went on to fashion United into an attractive side capable of winning trophies. He didn't flinch at paying big money for players and didn't waver when criticism was thrown the manager's way. Harvey preached entertaining football with stars who thrilled the fans. He once noted though, "You have got to have a mixture of big names and home grown talent. Finance necessitates that". Harvey always had both; Macdonald, Smith and Green the big buys; Moncur, Craig and Robson the juniors made good.

Harvey took United into Europe, to a Fairs Cup victory on his birthday and then on to the FA Cup final in 1974. His greatest ambition was to win at Wembley as a manager and the side's performance against Liverpool distressed him for years. Joe was never going to become the best manager in the game, but he was a dogged fighter and very much admired by the players around him. He left tactics largely to his coach and relied on inspiration to get the best out of his men. Malcolm Macdonald said, "He was more than a manager - he treated the Newcastle players like his sons", the centre-forward added, "Joe was a gem - a man's man. He knew how to treat players and get the best out of them". David Craig noted, "I would have walked through a brick wall for Joe".

At the end of the 1974/75 season he resigned after mounting pressure from supporters, frustrated that his side had not reached the very top. A couple of years later those same fans were shouting for him to return after a dismal slump in results. Harvey remained in the backrooms of St James Park as assistant manager and chief scout and was awarded a merited testimonial in 1977. He took an active interest in the club to his last day.

Joe Harvey died suddenly of a heart attack in February 1989 when still on the payroll of Newcastle United. He was 70 years old and for 37 of those years had been serving the club. Joe, with his craggy and warm personality will still be part of Newcastle United for a long time to come yet.

Centenary Profile 13

The Rock of Tyneside

"No centre-half in my time ever dominated the middle more completely than Frank"

Jackie Milburn

IT IS UNUSUAL TO FIND A CENTRE-HALF BECOMING the idol of the fans. That feat is more often than not reserved for a goalscorer or midfield entertainer. But Frank Brennan, big and tough at the heart of United's defence, equalled his colleagues in the popularity stakes at the time, namely Jackie Milburn and Bobby Mitchell. A few will say he even surpassed them.

Built like a colossus, his long legs and massive frame dominated the Newcastle penalty area for almost ten years and no centre-forward relished the thought of a tussle with Brennan. He became the foundation of United's magnificent defence, a pivot who rarely seemed flustered and who never panicked when opponents threatened. He was often a complete defence in himself.

Brennan hailed from Annathill on the outskirts of Glasgow and was born in 1924. He soon became an outstanding schools' player. Bigger and stronger than his class-mates he signed for junior club Coatbridge St Patricks and quickly began to develop into a footballer. His incisive kicking and tackling brought the attention of local Scottish League sides, and also of English club Wolves. A move to the Midlands fell through, as did a contract with Albion Rovers, but Frank signed for Airdrieonians in February 1941. He was still a part-timer working at the local pit and brick works and appeared for the Broomfield Park club throughout the war years. Brennan's qualities were noticed by Scotland's selectors and he was picked for the prestige Victory International with England at Hampden Park in 1946. The Scot had just turned 21 years of age and many top managers and scouts in the vast 139,468 crowd saw Frank effectively sit upon England leader Tommy Lawton throughout the game. Lawton hardly got a kick and immediately Newcastle United made a move for the centre-half.

United had tried to purchase Willie Woodburn of Rangers, but had little chance of prising him from Ibrox and now turned their attention to Brennan. The 6'3" and 14 stone defender was seen by the Magpies as the ideal man to partner Joe Harvey in their master plan. With Brennan commanding the defence and Harvey midfield, they would possess a formidable backbone to a new side. In May 1946 United beat off a challenge from Sunderland and Preston North End to bring Brennan to Tyneside with £7,500 going to Airdrie for his services.

Newcastle pushed hard for promotion the following season and just missed out, partly due to Brennan's absence for almost a dozen games. Two Scotland caps came his way, but his popularity back in his native country was never as great as it was in England. All told Frank only won seven full caps over an eight year period. In 1947/48 he was outstanding as United returned to the First Division. An ever-present, his powerful heading ability and firm tackles gave confidence to the whole side. Frank was a player's player with a simple motto of, "Get the ball away and let the others play the football". Joe Harvey remarked that he was the perfect example of "Constructive destruction", that is, he would win the ball and set up an attack with a simple ball to the nearest colleague. The Scot was by now a huge favourite at St James Park and could do little wrong. Even a rare sliced clearance into the crowd went unabused. Brennan possessed a good burst of speed for such a big man, but he always aimed to stop his opponent before the forward could get past and test Frank in a chase. Wearing size 12 boots, his feet gave the ball a mighty wallop when clearing his lines was the order of the day.

His stopper's game at the back was rated the best in the Football League by many top judges. By the start of the 1950/51 season he had missed only two games for United in three years. That 1951 season ended in Wembley triumph and credit went to Brennan for his FA Cup final performance against the brilliant talents of Stan Mortensen. One match report noted, "Brennan sealed up the centre of the field like a cork in a bottle". In the following year's victory much praise was again given to the Scot as he held together an off-form United eleven. Many reporters noted United would have lost but for his display. The Journal commented, "Brennan was striding like a giant to chop off dangerous Arsenal thrusts", while the Sunday Sun noted, "Only the exceptional power of Brennan averted a possible sensation".

Frank Brennan

BRENNAN'S PLAYING RECORD	League		FA Cup		Total	
	App	Gls	App	Gls	App	Gls
1946-47	31	0	5	0	36	0
1947-48	42	0	1	0	43	0
1948-49	41	0	1	0	42	0
1949-50	41	0	2	0	43	0
1950-51	32	1	6	0	38	1
1951-52	38	1	7	0	45	1
1952-53	38	1	2	0	40	1
1953-54	39	0	5	0	44	0
1954-55	6	0	0	0	6	0
1955-56	10	0	0	0	10	0
	318	**3**	**29**	**0**	**347**	**3**

Brennan, a formidable figure in United's line-up. Left to right, back: Robledo, Graham, Fairbrother, Batty, Hannah, Crowe. Front: Walker, Houghton, Brennan, Graver, Mitchell.

The granite centre-half was at his peak, a box office attraction in his own right. Quite a humorous character too, he once only took a single toothbrush with him on a ten week tour of South Africa, while his enormous eating habits were a legend on Tyneside during the fifties. By the time United reached Wembley for a third time in 1955, Brennan was reaching the end of his playing career. Now 31 years old, he had a couple of years ahead of him, but instead of going out in style, a series of controversial bust-ups with United's directors ended a marvellous association with a bitter taste.

Trouble had started when he opened a sport's outfitters shop in Gallowgate which rivalled Stan Seymour's business, although no-one ever officially admitted that was a reason for the rift. Frank then had to suffer a £7 per week drop in wages - then nearly half his income. The media latched on to the affair and rumours, predictably so, pointed fingers at Newcastle's directors. Brennan refused to accept the salary cut and was put on the transfer list, and eventually got no wages at all. The Players' Union got involved and the affair was blown into an ugly controversy. Brennan won a lot of sympathy with his popular support and United's hierarchy took a battering.

Union chief, Jimmy Guthrie even took Brennan's case to the TUC and made a passionate speech. He said, "I stand as a representative of the last bonded men in Britain, the professional footballers". The ex Portsmouth and Crystal Palace player went on, "We seek your help to smash a system in which in this year of 1955 human beings are being bought and sold like cattle, a system which in feudal times ties men to one master or, if they rebel, stops them from getting another job. Frank Brennan is such a man". The TUC passed an unanimous resolution which expressed concern at "the continued denial to professional footballers of proper and reasonable conditions of employment".

A massive campaign was launched to reinstate Frank. The local press backed him and well-supported public meetings were called. It was to no avail though. Brennan's career at St James Park was over. In March 1956 he was transferred to North Shields as player-coach, this after 347 appearances for the Magpies. Controversy raged on as to why he was allowed to drift into non-league obscurity and why the massive rift between the club and one of its top players was allowed to deteriorate to such an extent.

Brennan did a fine job at Appleby Park for the next six years putting North Shields on the football map. He then coached in Singapore and several other countries for the British Council before returning once more to North Shields. His charisma and know-how took them to Wembley in 1969, guiding an FA Amateur Cup victory over Sutton United. He once noted the triumph even surpassed the thrills of 1951 and 1952. A period at Darlington followed as both coach and manager, but he resigned during the 1971/72 season to return to the non-league scene with South Shields this time. Shortly afterwards he quit the game for good and concentrated on his sports business a goal-kick from St James Park.

Residing in Whitley Bay, Frank Brennan remains the best centre-half to wear the black'n'white shirt in one hundred years. As Jackie Milburn said, "No centre-half in my time ever dominated the middle more completely than Frank".

10 WEMBLEY TREBLE

1950-1955

• WOR JACKIE'S YEAR • ROBLEDO'S WINNER • FLOODLIGHTS UNVEILED • RECORD PURCHASE • HAT-TRICK TRIUMPH •

> *"The first side had the lot and I'm convinced we were good enough to have won the double"*
>
> *Bobby Cowell, August 1985*

THREE TIMES IN FIVE YEARS THE ROAR of the Blaydon Races rang out over Wembley Stadium as Newcastle United reached the pinnacle of their 100 year history. The club's Edwardian mastery may have been more rewarding in terms of pure football, but the FA Cup triumphs of this era gave the Magpies much prestige at a time when the mass media was becoming increasingly powerful - television and all. Everyone the nation over talked about United first as the black'n'whites developed into a terrific combination, especially in the cut and thrust of Cup football and United's supporters found themselves in a period of intense fervour not matched since.

There was practically no transfer activity during the summer months of 1950. George Martin and his directors were content with the staff as it stood, the squad turning out to be near perfect. Although the league campaigns of 1950/51 and 1951/52 were very much overshadowed by FA Cup action, the Magpies' First Division performances were good, especially in the first of those years when they went close to eventual Champions Spurs.

Newcastle climbed to top position by mid September with a 3-1 home victory over Chelsea, this only three days after a 6-0 romp against Huddersfield Town. Facing Arsenal later in the same month, United created a new club record by going ten games without defeat from the opening fixture. They toppled the Gunners 2-1 through goals from Taylor and Milburn before almost 67,000, then made it eleven unbeaten with a draw at Sheffield Wednesday. United slipped from the head of the table after that, but still hung close to leaders Arsenal with Robledo showing power up front - he grabbed hat-tricks in successive weeks against Liverpool and Blackpool.

Tottenham took over at the top from their London rivals and gave a mighty hiding to United in the process. A crowd of 70,000 saw the newly promoted Spurs flash seven goals past Jack Fairbrother in a performance to rank as perhaps their best ever at White Hart Lane. They gave a superb display of one-touch football on a sodden park. Tottenham were in the middle of a run of eight successive wins and in the two preceding games at their North London home had scored eleven goals! Newcastle were handicapped when McMichael was carried off, but they had already conceded five by then. And the fact was that United didn't play badly with a line-up almost identical to that which lifted the Cup six months later.

At the turn of the year United were in 5th place, five points behind Tottenham, but with a game in hand. There was still an outside chance that Newcastle could take Spurs close, however the FA Cup interrupted league action and put an abrupt end to that idea. The Magpies only won three of their last 13 fixtures after the semi-final and ended in 4th position. Players still qualified for Talent Money - a legally paid bonus for finishing in the top places. A total of £220 was paid out among the squad with ever-presents Fairbrother, Cowell and Walker receiving the full £20 each. At the other end of the scale, reserve Tommy Paterson who had appeared once, received 9s 6d.

Manager George Martin left in December, lured to Aston Villa. One of the reasons for his departure was the strong influence Seymour held over team affairs. As Bobby Mitchell remembered, "Stan Seymour was undisputed boss". The side hardly missed Martin as they progressed on their Cup charge. A new secretary was appointed that year too, Ted Hall replacing Frank Watt Junior who died in October to end a 55 year family association with United. Hall had been on the staff since the early weeks of 1927.

The following year of 1951/52 saw the Magpies complete the season in 8th place, and as the First Division's top goalscorers, netting 98 times, 113 including FA Cup games, the club's best. United glowed with confidence and exuberance and they got off to a spectacular start to the new season, again the best in their history. A 6-0 home thrashing of

George Robledo who formed such a productive strike-force with Jackie Milburn.

Stoke City, with Milburn getting a hat-trick and fellow striker Robledo on the scoresheet, sent the fans home in raptures. That partnership of Milburn and Robledo - a sort of double centre-forward role - was to be the country's most feared combination. By the end of April, Robledo had claimed 39 goals while Milburn had 28.

George Robledo was proving a marvellous buy. From the inside-left position his goals equalled Hughie Gallacher's 1927 record, a total yet to be passed by any striker since. Robledo was solidly built at 5'9" tall and possessed film star looks. He revelled in a confrontation with a big defender and took a lot of weight off Milburn. He could pass the ball accurately, had a good first touch and most of all he was an opportunist of the finest quality. Nicknamed 'Pancho' by his team-mates, he used to blast them in from all angles, and even from a few yards out would give the ball a terrific whack. In a four and a half year stay, George registered 91 goals in 164 games, a devastating strike-rate. He was though, to soon return to Chile and remained in his native country up to his death in 1989.

Plenty of those goals were seen in the first half of the season with United storming into 4th spot by Christmas. A 7-2 revenge win over League Champions Tottenham was well received on the first day of September, a game in which Bobby Mitchell had Spurs full-back Alf Ramsey chasing his shadow all afternoon. Within four minutes Mitch had gone past the defender, dribbled up to 'keeper Ted Ditchburn and netted a marvellous solo effort. United's other winger, Tommy Walker then scored the second and Robledo registered a close-in third. Before half-time Mitchell grabbed his second after a dream pass from schemer Hannah. Spurs came back into the game after the resumption to make it 4-2, but in the final quarter of the match, Mitchell stepped up a gear and United rallied. Robledo completed his hat-trick and Ernie Taylor scored United's seventh in the closing stages. If that goal feast wasn't enough only a fortnight later - United's next home game - another seven goals were scored! This time Burnley were on the receiving end of a 7-1 hammering. In four matches Robledo netted all of eleven times.

Tottenham made amends for that heavy reverse - a highly embarrassing one for the title holders - by taking the Charity Shield with a 2-1 win after another fine open game at White Hart Lane. But the Tynesiders were to have the last say in a series of mouth watering confrontations with the Londoners.

Newcastle in change colours. Left to right, players only, back: Harvey, Crowe, Fairbrother, Brennan, McMichael. Front: Walker, Cowell, Taylor, Milburn, Robledo, Mitchell. Manager Martin (left) and trainer Smith (right) are also in the group.

Newcastle's double FA Cup triumph started in January 1951 without the talent of international centre-half Frank Brennan because of a tonsils operation, nevertheless Second Division Bury were beaten easily, 4-1 on a waterlogged pitch at St James Park. Bolton Wanderers proved a much harder task in a contest that The Journal noted as, "a game so swamped in thrills as almost to defy analysis". With home advantage United went in front after only three minutes when Bobby Mitchell found the net. It was a game full of anxiety and thrills as the Wanderers fought back to take a 2-1 interval lead with both goals coming from Willie Moir. Then Jackie Milburn stamped his presence on the tie and

'Wor Jackie' advertising his own brand of football boots, at 63 shillings a pair.

George Robledo drives the ball past the Stoke 'keeper in the 1951 F.A. Cup tie.

became in the second half, not for the first or last occasion, United's hero. Firstly he netted a terrific equaliser one minute after the restart, swinging round with little room to hit a 20 yarder into the corner of the net. Then the Ashington flier latched onto a Taylor through ball, sprinted clear of the offside line to glide the ball home for the winner, although Bolton will always insist that he was well offside, a point agreed by many correspondents at the match. The 67,596 crowd - the biggest at St James Park for any Cup tie - were sent home exalted. Sadly, due to the crush, two 60 year old fans were killed, while the club's electric apparatus for limiting the gate broke down and many supporters were allowed entry over the permitted safety level. Matt McNeil, at 6'3", a tough reserve stopper in for Brennan, played England leader Nat Lofthouse well and could be satisfied with his performance in spite of an injury which saw him led away before time.

Cup training for Tommy Walker (left), Ernie Taylor (centre) and Charlie Crowe (right).

The Fifth Round saw United travel to meet Stoke City who were never a match for the Magpies. They had already been defeated in league meetings and with a backing of some 12,000 travelling followers, George Robledo hit the net twice in a 4-2 win, two "dashes out of the blue" as they were recorded. The Victoria Ground also witnessed the return of Brennan to stiffen the defence. There was a possibility of a Tyne and Wear clash in the next tie, the quarter-final, but fate kept the two rivals apart and brought United face to face with a team from the Third Division (South) that cost only £350, Bristol Rovers.

A packed Gallowgate saw the west country outfit play well above themselves to earn a replay at Eastville. It was a magnificent performance from the underdogs. They were the first team to deny the black'n'whites a goal at St James Park and their goalkeeper was rarely troubled by a United side forced into an uncharacteristic display. Rovers trooped off the field to a sporting ovation and to rapturous press acclaim.

However, there was no second chance for Bristol in the replay. In a rousing quarter of an hour, Rovers took the lead then United struck decisively with three goals. Taylor, Crowe and Milburn netted on an Eastville mudheap and sent Newcastle into a semi-final to meet Wolves, 3-1 victors over Sunderland.

Charlie Crowe, who scored a fine goal in that victory over Rovers was having his best season in the team. Installed at left-half, he was a good club man to Newcastle, as one profile of the day noted, "a tireless worker and a real Geordie grafter". Later he was to become a proficient FA Coach, one of England supremo, Walter Winterbottom's "Twelve Disciples" as they were to be known.

Against the Wolverhampton Wanderers at Hillsborough, a thrilling game resulted despite the 0-0 scoreline. The referee disallowed two goals inside the first five minutes, one for each side, as the game got off to an amazing start. But over 90 minutes Wolves were a lucky side to have another chance of reaching Wembley. There was little argument about that. Throughout the game United's Fairbrother hadn't a real shot to save, which was just as well as United's 'keeper had picked up a knock, whereas his counterpart, England's Bert Williams saved effort after effort including two sensational stops to thwart Mitchell and Milburn. An equally absorbing encounter was witnessed four days later at Huddersfield.

Incessant rain had left the Leeds Road pitch flooded and the replay only went ahead after the local fire brigade had drained the surface. Two goals by United in about 40 seconds, with Wolves leading and threatening to run Newcastle off their feet, put the Magpies into their eighth Cup final. It had been another highly charged and competitive game and Newcastle just about deserved their victory after Wolves had opened the scoring on 17 minutes through a good goal by inside-forward John Walker. Bobby Mitchell then missed a sitter after having mesmerised the Wolves defence on his own. On a run in which he went past four men and faced only

Jack Fairbrother ends up with the ball as Wolves attack United's goal in the 1951 semi-final. Other Newcastle players are, left to right: Corbett, Cowell, Brennan and Harvey.

The goals that sent United to Wembley. Left, Jackie Milburn cracks the ball past Bert Williams. Below: Mitchell (left), drills home Newcastle's second.

the 'keeper, United's winger, in his own words, "trod on the ball and fell over"! And that wasn't all. The ball ran free to Taylor who fired towards the net, but it hit Mitchell on his back as he was climbing up and bounced to safety. Many United fans thought it was going to be one of those days, but on the half-hour United were level. Ernie Taylor evaded three tackles and placed the ball for Milburn in a position that he couldn't miss. Less than a minute later Milburn was again involved as he dispossessed centre-half Shorthouse with one of his famed slide tackles and crossed for Mitchell, running in, to make amends and give United a Wembley ticket.

Ernie Taylor had dominated midfield in the game and was an influential figure that year. Although barely nine stone, 5'4" in height and pulling on size 4 boots, he was quick and thoughtful, the brain of the attack. Unselfish and delicate in his football, he was a somewhat impertinent player too - in the mould of the great Alex James, a cheeky genius. Taylor though, always had difficulty holding a regular place in United's eleven and soon moved on to the team he conquered in the forthcoming Cup final, Blackpool, for a £25,000 fee. This in spite of player deputations to Seymour not to sell him. Joe Harvey pleaded, "Don't give the Little Fella a transfer. Transfer me, anybody, but keep Ernie. He makes everyone play". Taylor later returned to Wembley with his new side, and with Manchester United. He also won an England cap in 1954.

The long two month wait for FA Cup final day to arrive saw injuries cause concern. Brennan broke a bone in his hand, Joe Harvey suffered from Achilles heel trouble and full-back Alf McMichael fractured a wrist in a car-park training session with Bobby Cowell. McMichael, who appeared for Ireland during the year, was unluckily not fit for the final and was replaced by Bobby Corbett, his rival all season.

Cartoonist Dudley Hallwood's view of the United and Wolves semi-final meeting in 1951.

Newcastle relax before the F.A. Cup final with Blackpool. Left to right: Cowell, Corbett, Crowe, Walker, Taylor, Stokoe, Mitchell, Brennan, Harvey, Robledo and Milburn.

Centenary Highlight

> *"That second goal of Jackie Milburn's finished things. It was the sort of goal you dream about"*
>
> *Stanley Matthews, April 1951*

THE PRESS CLAIMED UNITED'S VICTORY A ONE man show by Jackie Milburn. However, as the man of the moment said, "It was anything but that. It had been a good all round performance, but I must admit I enjoyed scoring those two goals". And they were two of the finest goals seen at Wembley Stadium. As an added feat Jackie had scored in every round of the competition that year.

First Division Blackpool were United's opponents. In their second final in four years and including the nation's darling, Stanley Matthews. United though, were to put a stop to his dream of lifting a winners' medal. Blackpool decided to play an offside game and on several occasions during the first half the lightning quick Milburn almost caught them dead. Within ten minutes of the restart he did. Following a Matthews raid for Blackpool, Robledo cleared his lines and interchanged with Milburn. Collecting a long pass down the middle, United's centre-forward went past centre-half Hayward on the half-way line and set off on a long, lonely run for goal down the centre of the vast Wembley pitch. For about 40 yards he galloped and as goalkeeper George Farm advanced, he sent a perfect low shot into the net. That goal was good enough to win any match, the one that followed was arguably classed as Wembley's best ever.

Ernie Taylor, who had been intelligently prompting throughout the game, collected the ball from Walker just outside the Blackpool box after the winger had gone past two men. He stopped the ball with his right foot before casually backheeling it into the path of Milburn who hit a left foot pile-driver from 25 yards into the top corner of the net. Jackie noted, "I hit it harder than I can ever before remember hitting a football". A tremendous goal which rounded off an unbeatable personal performance. Blackpool's England maestro Stanley Matthews said, "That second goal of Jackie Milburn's finished things. It was the sort of goal you dream about".

Those two gems were the only moments worth remembering about the game in which Blackpool, with Matthews and Mortensen their big hopes, played well below form and dragged United into a frustrating offside contest. Yet it still had been an absorbing match with United's defence holding firm, very much a grim rather than stylish final. Crowe and Corbett did a good job on Matthews while Brennan subdued the threat of Mortensen. Charlie Crowe was singled out for particular praise by many observers, "a colossal nuisance to everything tangerine" noted the Sunday Sun, while legendary centre-forward Hughie Gallacher, reporting for a local paper, wrote, "Crowe had a great game and I thought that he was the outstanding half-back on the field".

Early in the match Slater had grazed the crossbar for Blackpool and Cowell had cleared off the line, a marvellous leap

Eric Thompson's

CUP FINAL LINE-UP

They can reach the heights

NO two players in the Cup final between Blackpool and Newcastle United will watch each other more warily than Hayward and Milburn. This is the big test of vigilance in a match of all-star variety.

Jack Milburn, Newcastle United centre forward, moves from stop to top speed with the acceleration of a rocket. "His burst of speed is a wonderful asset," says his big-match pal Mortensen. Another asset is the Milburn snap shot taken at any angle. Highly dangerous. Born at Ashington, one of the Milburn Soccer clan. Wrote for United trial and signed in 1943. Winger, and now an England leader. Former pit-worker. Fond of cricket.

Eric Hayward, Blackpool centre half, will also rocket, if it means soaring for a danger-laden ball. His tackling is resolute and his concentration grimly unwavering. In one match as a schoolboy centre forward he scored 13 goals. Playing cricket when Port Vale went to see him, and they had to wait until he had hit 66. Signed Port Vale 1934 at 17; joined Blackpool 1937. Finalist 1948. Played for Combined Services in India. Assists Blackpool Cricket Club.

Jackie Milburn's duel with Blackpool's Eric Hayward was to be a crucial factor in the final.

to stop a Mortensen header reaching the top corner with Fairbrother beaten. The United 'keeper noted, "It was 0-0 at that stage and a very important clearance". Milburn had the ball in the net, but was pulled up for handball - although for years later Jackie reckoned there was nothing wrong with that effort. He also had a chance of a special Wembley hat-trick when Robledo again sent him clean through late on. This time Milburn delayed his shot and Hayward made a desperate tackle with a certain goal beckoning.

Queen Elizabeth handed over the FA Cup and winners' medals, while each member of the team received a strong handshake from King George VI to a chorus of the Blaydon Races and the clatter of bells and rattles from United's 12,000 travelling fans. A few supporters had paid over the odds for tickets - touts had arrived and a 3s 0d ticket went for £3 10s. Some Tynesiders made the trip by aeroplane, progress from their last journey to Wembley all of 19 years ago when steamers down the North Sea was one mode of transport.

United's 1951 side was perhaps the best of the treble of Wembley triumphs during the fifties. Jackie Milburn and Bobby Mitchell said so, and Bobby Cowell did likewise, "The first side had the lot and I'm convinced we were good enough to have won the double" said the full-back. They were solid at the back

FA Cup Winners 1951

FA CUP RUN

R3	Bury	H	W	4-1
R4	Bolton Wanderers	H	W	3-2
R5	Stoke City	A	W	4-2
R6	Bristol Rovers	H	D	0-0
	Bristol Rovers	A	W	3-1
SF	Wolverhampton Wanderers	N	D	0-0
	Wolverhampton Wanderers	N	W	2-1
F	Blackpool	N	W	2-0

FACTS & FIGURES

	P	W	D	L	F	A
Home	3	2	1	0	7	3
Away	5	4	1	0	11	4
Total	**8**	**6**	**2**	**0**	**18**	**7**

FINAL

28 April 1951 at Wembley Stadium

Newcastle United 2(0) Blackpool 0(0)

UNITED:
Fairbrother
Cowell, Corbett
Harvey, Brennan, Crowe
Walker, Taylor, Milburn, Robledo(G), Mitchell.

BLACKPOOL:
Farm
Shimwell, Garrett
Johnston, Hayward, Kelly
Matthews, Mudie, Mortensen, Slater, Perry.

GOALS;
Milburn(50m), Milburn(55m)

ATTENDANCE;
100,000 (£39,336)

Referee; W.Ling (Cambridgeshire)
Guest of Honour;
HRH King George VI & Queen Elizabeth
Cup HQ; Oatlands Park Hotel, Weybridge

CUP GOALGETTERS
8 Milburn, 3 Mitchell, Robledo, 2 Taylor, 1 Walker, Crowe.

CHAIRMAN: John W. Lee
MANAGER: Stan Seymour
TRAINER-COACH: Norman Smith
CAPTAIN: Joe Harvey

Tynesiders gather around Nelson's Column on a sightseeing tour before the 1951 final.

HRH King George VI is introduced to Bobby Mitchell by skipper Harvey. Charlie Crowe is next in line.

and could be quite dazzling going forward with a punch that proved formidable. They possessed a fabulous team spirit with few jealousies, although they did have their altercations like any side - a row taking place on the very eve of the final over ticket allocation. Acting manager Stan Seymour was an influential man in charge. He had now played for United and managed the club to a Cup victory. Seymour, donning a fedora on his head had led United out with Joe Harvey behind. His pre-match talk comprised only a few words, "I'm not going to tell you how to play, that's your job. You wouldn't be playing for Newcastle today if you weren't good enough. Go out and do your stuff".

Prior to the homecoming a reserve fixture was staged at St James Park and almost 60,000 crowded into the ground in readiness for the Cup victors' arrival at Barrack Road. They were heralded through the streets in three open-topped coaches of the Thames Tees Tyne service by 200,000 people. A huge banner awaited them, "Welcome Hyem Canny Lads"! Skipper Joe Harvey said, "We knew we would get a terrific reception, but I never imagined it would be like this. It was wonderful". Welcome Home indeed.

Jackie Milburn's magnificent double strike.
Top: United's centre-forward coolly slots the ball past George Farm.
Bottom: Farm has no chance with Jackie's 25 yard rocket.

Above left: Joe Harvey receives the trophy from the King watched by Stanley Rous and Jack Fairbrother.

Left: United's Cup winners. Left to right, back: Cowell, Milburn, Fairbrother, Robledo, Corbett, Crowe. Front: Walker, Taylor, Seymour (director-manager), Harvey, Smith (trainer), Brennan, Mitchell.

The Magpies drive in triumphant procession through the streets of the city.
Inset: Joe Harvey brings the F.A. Cup back to St. James Park
followed by Milburn and Crowe.

UNITED'S SECOND GLORY TRAIL IN 1952 started just as the Magpies' form peaked. They had a difficult Third Round tie with Aston Villa who included both Colin Gibson and Tommy Thompson in their line-up, two ex Magpies. Having won 4-1 at Roker Park on Christmas Day and 3-0 against Preston, United were in confident mood when Villa trotted onto the St James Park turf to a packed audience of 56,897. However, for the majority of the game nothing went right for the Tynesiders. After only 13 minutes the crowd was silenced as Villa charged to a 2-0 lead with another former Newcastle player, John Dixon, grabbing both goals. Newcastle though, were always at their most dangerous in this era with their backs to the wall and so it proved again.

Villa held a 2-1 lead until eight minutes from time, then Bobby Mitchell took over when all seemed lost. The Scot scored twice with cracking shots in the space of seconds to put United 3-2 in front. Bobby Cowell swung a pass across the field to Mitchell on the corner of the penalty area. The winger caught a glimpse of the goal and walloped the ball with terrific power. It flew into the net. Then straight from the kick-off he was back again. The ball found its way to Mitchell once more. And again he let fly to give United the lead. Bobby recalled, "I'll remember the look of disbelief on those Villa defenders' faces until my dying day". Yet he wasn't finished. Mitchell skipped away, found Robledo who made it 4-2 a minute later with the Villa players completely dazed and United's fans wild with delight.

ROKER'S BLACK'N'WHITE DAY

During season 1950/51 neighbours Sunderland discarded their traditional red and white strip in favour of United's black'n'white. Sunderland, at home to Southampton in the FA Cup 4th Round on January 27th had to change and they borrowed a set of Newcastle's colours. It gave them United's FA Cup luck too - they won 2-0! Berwick Rangers also loaned a set of United's Cup shirts in February 1952 - they won too, defeating Alloa 4-1.

That superb win put United through to meet Tottenham Hotspur once more, and United had to travel - the toughest draw in the hat. It was to be the fourth memorable meeting of the season and there was a huge build-up to the game. Stan Seymour said, "The team that wins this one will win the Cup". With the gates closed and 69,009 in White Hart Lane, the clash of League Champions against Cup holders went Newcastle's way. The Magpies destroyed Spurs 3-0 in appalling muddy conditions by using the correct tactics of playing to the grassy wings. Mitchell was once more outstanding giving Ramsey another roasting. The victory was highly praised by the national press as Newcastle produced bursts of intense football they were renowned for. No team could live with them on this form, not even the celebrated Spurs eleven. Ken McKenzie in The Journal wrote, "In a ruthless display of brilliant efficiency Newcastle United completely outmatched Tottenham Hotspur." Two goals from Robledo and a thunderbolt by Mitchell from 20 yards settled the issue and sent the 15,000 Geordie following back to Tyneside with a Wembley visit on their minds

United v Spurs F.A. Cup tie in 1952. Billy Foulkes sends a diving header to test Ditchburn.

again. The game had been televised back in the north east, and the handful that could afford a set watched a treat - in black and white of course. Newcastle's display had been one of the finest team efforts in the club's history, yet that performance was to be surpassed in a matter of five weeks when the club made another Cup journey south.

Former Third Lanark goalkeeper Ronnie Simpson had by now taken over from Jack Fairbrother who had broken his collar bone. It was an unlucky mishap for United's 'keeper as he never reclaimed his position. Fairbrother had been a popular servant to United, a witty personality never at a loss for words. He was a 'keeper who relied on positioning, making a great study of angles rather than diving round his box. Simpson cost the club £8,750 and was in contrast the opposite in style to his predecessor. He was small and acrobatic and had a truly remarkable career in the game. Starting as a 14 year old with Queen's Park, he was not to retire until after he had won a Scottish cap, European

New signing Ronnie Simpson, an agile and spectacular goalkeeper.

Cup medal and a bagful of Scottish domestic honours with Celtic when 40 years of age. Simpson's father had also played for Scotland during the thirties.

On the left touch-line, Tommy Walker performed to his peak without headlines and was the other match-winner at White Hart Lane. While he never rivalled Bobby Mitchell in the popularity stakes, Walker's more direct route to goal was highly effective. He could find the net too, like Mitchell, and scored 38 goals in 204 appearances for the black'n'whites.

In the Fifth Round, United had another long trip, this time to Swansea. The Magpies were hard pushed by the tough tackling Welshmen and by Ivor Allchurch's more subtle skills in particular. Newcastle much fancied the influential midfielder and had a bid of £25,000 for the youngster turned down. They were however, to get their man some six years later. United managed to clinch the grim tussle with another important goal from Mitchell following a Walker corner. Once more a difficult hurdle faced United in the quarter-final, having to travel again to high-riding Portsmouth, League Champions in 1949 and 1950, a club which had won five of the last seven games against the black'n'whites.

Jackie Milburn slides in to score one of his hat-trick of goals in the F.A. Cup tie with Portsmouth.

Simpson dives to stop an Ivor Allchurch effort in the Fifth Round tie at Swansea.

With a 6-2 win over Huddersfield Town as a boost, United lined up against Pompey facing a stern challenge. There was high expectation of a furious battle on the south coast and that's exactly what happened. The 45,000 crowd who left Fratton Park that afternoon believed they had just witnessed one of the greatest games of football the era had produced. Writer Geoffrey Green noted, "Here was a grey afternoon touched by glory". United won 4-2 after 90 minutes of top class soccer packed with incident and which swayed back and forth in dramatic style.

After only a matter of three minutes, Portsmouth were one up with a header fit to win the match scored by Belgian winger Marcel Gaillard. Newcastle clawed themselves back into the game and equalised in the 39th minute with the ever dangerous Milburn scrambling in a goalmouth chance, sweeping the ball home from six yards. On the hour Robledo netted, but was adjudged offside, however two minutes later Milburn struck once more. Taking a ball from Foulkes he volleyed goalwards. The ball struck the angle and dropped dead in the back of the net. United were in front 2-1, then it was Pompey's turn to hit back and equalise through Dougie Reid after Simpson's parry left the ball at his feet. The thrills continued as Cowell cleared off the line and Milburn concluded a memorable hat-trick. Forced to veer left in a run at goal, he took three Portsmouth defenders with him. Faced by Froggatt, Ferrier and Dickinson, Jackie fired an acute 30 yard shot that flew past a bemused Ernie Butler in the home goal and into the netting. It was a marvellous strike and one

LOST TROPHY

When it came to returning the FA Cup to Lancaster Gate in 1952 there were a lot of red faces at St James Park. After searching high and low, no-one could find the valuable trophy! More frantic searches took place until, as one report noted, they found it in a cupboard, "under piles of old newspapers and abandoned brooms, brushes and buckets"! Looking worse for wear, officials quickly gave it an overhaul at the local silversmith and made sure the trophy got back to the FA's headquarters in one piece.

ADMISSION 1951/52

Season-tickets

Centre Pavilion	£6 guineas
Wing Stand	£5 guineas

Match-day

Ground adults	1s 6d
Stand adults	4s 0d

to finish Pompey. George Robledo sealed the terrific victory near the end.

Jackie Milburn reckoned that afternoon was his finest hour and the last goal, his best. Ronnie Simpson said, "It's simply the greatest goal I ever saw in my life. I've never seen a ball hit so hard and so accurately from such an impossible position". One newspaper called Milburn's performance, "a dazzling display, rarely has a centre-forward been so deadly in the face of stern opposition". The victory at Fratton Park even surpassed United's brilliant football against Aston Villa and Tottenham.

So to another semi-final at Hillsborough. Blackburn Rovers had earned the right to face United, a Second Division side, but torrid Cup fighters to the end. For the 20,000 travelling support it was a disappointing trip to Sheffield as United displayed anything but their true form. Both goalkeepers made the headlines, Simpson making a brilliant stop near to the final whistle. He saved a Nightingdale blockbuster from only four yards with a spectacular leap. Yet Blackburn had bolted their chance and showed their best was only equal to United's worst. Most were confident that Newcastle wouldn't play so badly in the replay at Leeds.

In a Cup-tie that had everything, Newcastle should have been three up before half-time, however the whistle went all square. Midway through the second period a Brennan clearance found Milburn who crossed perfectly. George Robledo was on the other end of the centre and the Chilean outjumped two players and headed home to put United 1-0 up. However, Rovers rallied with great spirit and returned the compliment ten minutes from time. Ronnie Clayton, then only 17 years old, started the move that ended in Eddie Quigley firing in a left foot equaliser. Then the game moved into a dramatic conclusion when Newcastle were awarded a penalty with only four minutes left.

A Robledo header was handled by Campbell on the line and a spot-kick immediately awarded. But United's next problem was that no-one wanted what was going to be a tense, pulse-quickening moment! Normal penalty expert, Jackie Milburn had taken a knock and George Robledo said no. Skipper Joe Harvey looked frantically for someone and nonchalantly Bobby Mitchell took the ball. Several United players couldn't look - one kick and United would be either, at Wembley, or still locked in a furious struggle. On the touch-line Stan Seymour hid his head in his hands. Up stepped Mitchell, a few paces and....Whack....the ball bulged the rigging and Elland Road erupted. United were through to another Wembley final. Mitchell said, "I just looked at a spot in the net and hit the ball as hard as I could". It flew only a yard of 'keeper Elvy, but he hardly saw it. It had been Mitchell's first ever penalty in English football and he couldn't have picked a more nerve racking and vital moment to take it. United's star winger didn't score a more important goal.

Incidentally Blackburn's account of the incident claimed that a United forward had fouled their 'keeper as Robledo headed the ball towards the goal. It was noted that Elvy was, "checked by a blatant and vicious elbow to the ribs". The referee though, never saw it and the penalty award stood. It had been quite a game. As Stan Seymour said afterwards, "It was the toughest semi-final imaginable", while Joe Harvey noted, "I've never been in a harder struggle".

Newcastle were back at Wembley and what a performance they had dished up getting there. They hadn't faced an easy game - the Magpies had disposed of three clubs from the top six in Division One and had only one home tie. And they were to overcome another feared side in the final, one that had finished third in the table.

United fielded several reserves and youngsters during the period up to their Wembley appointment. Scot Hugh Cameron, locals George Lackenby and Ken Prior, as well as £9,000 Welsh signing from Southend United, Reg Davies, all played a handful of games. At inside-right, Davies was to show lovely touches at times and his tally of 50 goals in 170 games was better than most at St James Park. United took it easy for their run-in to Wembley. They lost four, drew one and only won three, including however, a 6-1 triumph over Aston Villa in the fixture before travelling to the capital.

Inside-right Billy Foulkes also came into the side that season. Signed from Chester during October 1951 for £11,500, his rise to stardom was nothing but sensational. With only a single First Division game to his credit, Foulkes entered international football in a headline-making fashion. Playing for Wales against England, he netted after only four minutes pouncing on to a free-kick - it was his first kick of the match! Then he grabbed the United shirt taking over from Taylor and became an FA Cup winner inside six months. Foulkes went on to win eleven caps at Gallowgate before moving to Southampton.

Right: George Robledo opens the scoring in the F.A. Cup semi-final with Blackburn.

Below: Mitchell's winning spot-kick in the dying moments of the match.

Welshman Billy Foulkes, a new acquisition up front.

YOUTH CUP ENTRY

In season 1952/53 the Magpies first took part in the FA's new Youth Cup. United's results in that inaugural season were;

R1	Scarborough	W	9-0
R2	Billingham Synth	W	8-3
R3	Sunderland	W	3-2
R4	Barnsley	L	1-2

Ron Harbertson, signed from Seghill and who later played for a string of lower division sides, netted six goals against Scarborough, a marvellous way to kick off the competition. Bill Curry surpassed Harbertson's effort when he scored eight times against Silksworth in the following season's tournament. For many years to follow United were usually eliminated in the early rounds and it was not until 1961/62 that Newcastle's kids won the trophy.

"I nearly passed out as the ball hit the post and went into the net"

George Robledo, May 1952

SOUTH GRAND STAND

ENTER AT TURNSTILES K (See Plan on back)

ENTRANCE (LEFT) 43

Row 8 Seat 29

Empire Stadium, Wembley

THE FOOTBALL ASSOCIATION CUP COMPETITION

FINAL TIE

SATURDAY, MAY 3rd, 1952

Kick-off 3 p.m.

Price 21/- (Including Tax)

CHAIRMAN AND MANAGING DIRECTOR, Wembley Stadium Limited

THIS PORTION TO BE RETAINED (See Conditions on back)

A photograph that needs little explanation. Newcastle's party arrive back on Tyneside for another victory parade.

THE 1952 FA CUP FINAL WAS A SHOWDOWN between the north and south superpowers - Newcastle United and Arsenal - winners of the trophy between them for the last two seasons. It was a repeat of Newcastle's 1932 Wembley visit and again the Gunners were aiming for the double - again they lost on both counts.

The final though, was sadly a match of no greatness with United playing below standard and most of the glory going to Arsenal who were deprived of the injured Wally Barnes for most of the game. Yet what is often forgotten is that Jackie Milburn was a passenger for a long period once Roper had slowed him up with a tackle. Following United's magnificent journey through an arduous Cup programme they maybe deserved a slice of luck in the last hurdle. That fortune was that Arsenal had an off day too.

On a slippery pitch, the morning rain was ideally suited to Newcastle's quick-passing forwards, but it was Arsenal who made an enterprising start playing fast, slick football and for 15 minutes were in complete command. Lishman went close and the United goal had the narrowest of escapes when Cox closed in and sent the ball rolling across goal for Logie to just fail to connect. Then they lost Barnes, damaging a knee attempting to tackle Milburn after only 18 minutes and Newcastle gradually took control as the game advanced. United's centre-forward had a back-header kicked off the line and a Mitchell cross ran along the crossbar.

In the second half United played better against the ten man Gunners and, following countless chances that went for a burton, it appeared that they just couldn't put the ball away. Missed opportunities were almost costly as Arsenal nearly sneaked a goal when a Lishman header struck the crossbar. It was left until six minutes from time before Newcastle settled the tie. At a point in the match when the Londoners had two men down injured - Holton and Roper - Ted Robledo found Bobby Mitchell, the one man who looked as though he could win the game for United. He sent a dangerous left-footed cross looping over the Arsenal defenders to the far post for George Robledo to head into the net off the woodwork. It had been decided at half-time to get the ball to Mitchell who would in turn hit deep crosses for the twin centre-forward thrust of Robledo and Milburn to claim. The plan worked, George Robledo said, "I nearly passed out as the ball hit the post and went into the net".

The FA Cup was heading for Tyneside again, although Arsenal still had time to rap the bar through Forbes. Newcastle made football history. They equalled Blackburn's record in 1891 of winning the trophy in successive seasons. It was not one of Newcastle's most inspired performances. Mitchell took the honours up front, the only forward to do himself justice and once went, "past three Arsenal defenders on a sixpence". Brennan was the pick of a good display by the defence with Bobby Cowell coming a close second after a fine game of perfect distribution and crisp tackles. Once more United's fighting spirt saw them through, as the Weekly Chronicle noted, "It is this that will be remembered rather than any vast superiority in technical skill".

Arsenal boss, Tom Whittaker, brought up in Byker and who had played for Newcastle Swifts, could only look at the heavens and curse his ill fortune. The Gunners' ten men had performed heroics and as one report confirmed, "could have stolen a goal near the close". Seymour said afterwards to Arsenal's squad, "We've won the Cup, but you've won the honours".

Back in Newcastle, in every home, on every street corner and in every public-house, the north east only knew eleven heroes, and they were in black'n'white. Everywhere the toast was, "Newcastle United"! The population of Tyneside was again out in force for the homecoming, a carbon copy of twelve months earlier. The region's heroes had a lucrative year. The player's Cup bonus for the season mounted to £63 10s 0d a man plus a £50 share of the Cup pool. Newcastle, remarkably, fielded the same eleven players in every game to Wembley.

FA Cup Winners 1952

FA CUP RUN

R3	Aston Villa	H	W	4-2
R4	Tottenham Hotspur	A	W	3-0
R5	Swansea Town	A	W	1-0
R6	Portsmouth	A	W	4-2
SF	Blackburn Rovers	N	D	0-0
	Blackburn Rovers	N	W	2-1
F	Arsenal	N	W	1-0

FACTS & FIGURES

	P	W	D	L	F	A
Home	1	1	0	0	4	2
Away	6	5	1	0	11	3
Total	**7**	**6**	**1**	**0**	**15**	**5**

CUP GOALGETTERS
6 Robledo(G), 5 Mitchell, 3 Milburn, 1 Foulkes.

CHAIRMAN: Robert Rutherford
MANAGER: Stan Seymour
TRAINER-COACH: Norman Smith
CAPTAIN: Joe Harvey

FINAL

3 May 1952 at Wembley Stadium
Newcastle United 1(0) Arsenal 0 (0)

UNITED;
Simpson
Cowell, McMichael
Harvey, Brennan, Robledo(E)
Walker, Foulkes, Milburn, Robledo(G), Mitchell.
ARSENAL;
Swindin
Barnes, Smith
Forbes, Daniel, Mercer
Cox, Logie, Holton, Lishman, Roper.

GOALS;
Robledo(G)(84m)

ATTENDANCE;
100,000 (£39,351)

Referee; A.E.Ellis (Halifax)
Guest of Honour; RH Winston Churchill
Cup HQ; Royal Albion Hotel, Brighton

Another Cup winning eleven. Left to right, back: Hall (secretary), Cowell, Harvey, Simpson, Brennan, McMichael, Robledo E., Smith (trainer). Front: Walker, Foulkes, Seymour (director-manager), Milburn, Robledo G., Mitchell.

Stan Seymour leads his United team on to the Wembley turf. Harvey follows with Cowell, Foulkes, Milburn, Mitchell, Robledo and Walker.

Above: The goal that clinched the F.A. Cup for Tyneside for a second successive year. George Robledo watches his header strike the post and enter the net.

Right: Prime Minister Winston Churchill hands the trophy to Joe Harvey; Milburn looks on.

FA Cup Winners 1952

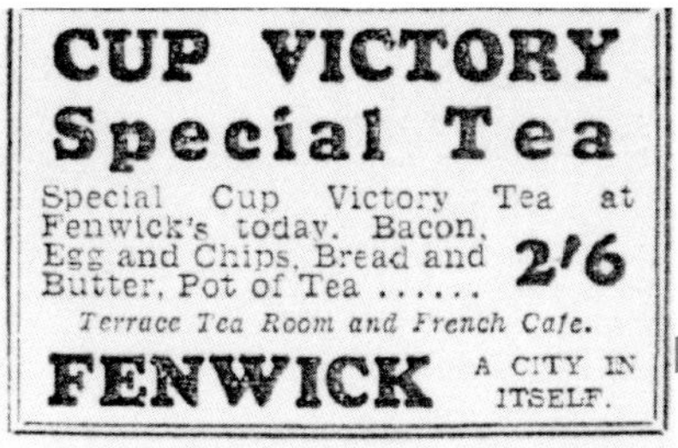

Cup final humour. The Journal's cartoonist portrays events at Wembley.

United show off the F.A. Cup in the streets of Newcastle.

Dressing-room champagne. Left to right, back: Robledo E., Mutch (physio), Seymour (director-manager), Harvey, Brennan, Robledo G., Smith (trainer), Mitchell. Front: Cowell, Walker, Foulkes, McMichael, Milburn.

A FORTNIGHT AFTER THEIR 1952 SUCCESS, United set off for a long, enjoyable, yet somewhat gruelling 70 day tour of South Africa. The FA Cup went with them, United having to apply for an Export Licence from the Board of Trade and the famous trophy was valued at all of £200. Charlie Crowe recorded that the lengthy flight from London was anything but a pleasant experience, indeed at times a terrifying one when one of the plane's engines broke down in flight! The party had two stopovers - in Tripoli and Kano, which as Crowe recorded was, "the worst place on earth". However the return was much better, on board one of the first Comet flights with only a single touchdown.

Half-time in the first Test Match with South Africa during the tour of 1952. Frank Brennan dips the ball in a bucket of water while Foulkes, McMichael and Milburn discuss tactics with Seymour.

Advertisement from one of the tour programmes in South Africa.

Homeward bound! Newcastle's party about to board a Comet aircraft back to England. Left to right: Stokoe, Smith (trainer), Brennan, Milburn, Hannah, McMichael, Batty, Crowe, Robledo.

In South Africa, United's players were hailed as heroes wherever they went and returned loaded with gifts. Frank Brennan brought back a spear and leopard skin while Stan Seymour became so concerned at the excessive hospitality that he asked his hosts to cancel cocktail parties on the day before a match. United played 16 games and netted no fewer than 73 goals. The highlights of the tour were Test Matches against the South African national XI. Newcastle won 3-0 in Durban, but lost 5-3 in a return match in Johannesburg before crowds approaching 25,000. The Magpies reached double figures once, planting ten goals past the Border Province 'keeper with Robledo hitting the net seven times - the best by an individual player in any United game. In another fixture, against Lourenco Marques, a young negro watched United's 5-0 victory. He was non other than Eusebio, a future world star.

The strenuous trip, on top of an equally straining home campaign had its effect when the new season rolled up in August 1952. United's play, especially up front, where they were described as, "desperate" at times, never reached the heights of the previous two years. The side rarely appeared to be settled with several players absent. They were weary and jaded and probably the African tour did deaden their play. Milburn, who underwent a cartilage operation, and Harvey, with his foot in plaster, missed many matches and the loss of such key men was damaging. Milburn in fact only netted five goals, his sharpness and authority up front were hugely missed. Brennan was not as commanding and no-one suitably replaced Ernie Taylor's influence; he had departed by then to Bloomfield Road.

The league campaign did not produce many headlines, although the Geordies' first win of the season occurred in rousing fashion. Behind 3-2 to Preston North End with only ten minutes remaining, George Robledo hammered two goals within 50 seconds and United triumphed 4-3, while the 2-0 victory over Sunderland at Roker Park was a good early win. They reached 8th spot as Christmas approached, but fell away drastically after New Year not recording a victory for eleven games. United slid down the table into the relegation zone and a 5-1 reverse at Portsmouth prompted Seymour to say, "It should have been 10-1!" The Magpies then crucially lost at home to Bolton Wanderers - to a Lofthouse hat-trick - and in a very tight relegation struggle, rivals Stoke City lost at Derby and Newcastle found

CORONATION CUP

Queen Elizabeth II was crowned in 1953 and to celebrate the event football staged a Coronation Cup tournament held in Glasgow. Eight top clubs were invited to take part and Newcastle were there along with Tottenham Hotspur, Manchester United, Arsenal, Aberdeen, Hibernians and the Old Firm of Rangers and Celtic. After defeating the Dons 4-0 at Ibrox before 16,000, United faced Hibs and their 'Famous Five' forward line in the semi-final. Three of those strikers - Turnbull, Johnstone and Reilly - netted in a 4-0 victory for the Edinburgh side. A crowd of 48,876 saw that tie, again at Ibrox. Celtic won the trophy.

themselves safe. Yet it had been a desperately close thing for the FA Cup holders. They ended the season in 16th place.

Manchester United won the Charity Shield contest, while the cherished FA Cup gave Newcastle's faithful no cause for joy that year either. After two such glorious runs, United's defeat at home by Second Division promotion contenders Rotherham United was hard to stomach. They had played anything but well to beat another Division Two club, Swansea Town after a postponement because of fog inside eight minutes had sent a 63,499 Gallowgate crowd home annoyed. Newcastle's party had returned to Tyneside from their Alnmouth Cup headquarters to find St James Park engulfed in a fast-descending mist. As the game kicked-off the fog worsened and within minutes was so thick that the referee had no alternative but to call a halt to play. On that same evening, Gateshead, playing less than a mile away, defeated Liverpool despite the fog!

Quite incredibly that huge crowd returned, almost to a man, three days later. This time 61,064 went through the turnstiles to see if United could start on a hat-trick of FA Cup runs. In spite of a lack-lustre performance, Newcastle won 3-0 and went on to meet Rotherham in the next tie.

United had no excuses for their 3-1 defeat by the Yorkshire club who were managed by former Tyneside favourite Andy Smailes. The Magpies gave a poor display in a howling gale. Jack Grainger, the Miller's star winger, netted twice after Vic Keeble had put United in front. Newcastle tried to sign the England 'B' player after the Cup-tie, but the deal fell through and United purchased another Rotherham player, Len White, instead.

That season saw the appearance of floodlit football at St James Park, Newcastle being the third First Division side to switch on the bright lights. On 25th February 1953, Glasgow Celtic, who included Jock Stein and Bobby Collins, in their line-up, lost 2-0 beneath the lights, this a return challenge after a marvellous 3-3 draw before 61,000 plus at Parkhead two years earlier. Then mounted on the top of the West Stand and on several telegraph poles along Leazes Terrace, the 80 lights were of poor quality by modern standards and created many shadows. At half-time they were actually switched off plunging the big crowd into total darkness. All that could be seen was a mass of lighted cigarette lighters and matches - an eerie sight. But the game was still an enormous success, proved by the 41,888 fans

Above: With fog descending Newcastle and Swansea players leave the pitch after barely eight minutes of play.

NEWCASTLE UNITED FOOTBALL COMPANY, LIMITED.

PROFIT AND LOSS ACCOUNT

For the Year ended 31st July, 1952.

BALANCE SHEET

As at 31st July, 1952.

Left: The club's balance sheet for season 1951/52 showing income through the gate of £157,794 15s 3d.

A North v South challenge between United and Glasgow Celtic. The game ended all level at 3-3.

who turned up to see the new innovation. George Robledo, United's top scorer, hit both goals, while the cost of electricity used for that game was no more than £2! Other floodlit friendlies were arranged, with Airdrie and East Fife. It was the start of a new era for football.

Charlie Crowe and George Robledo indulge in a game of cards on their way to a fixture.

Tommy Casey arrived early in the proceedings that season, a £7,000 signing from Bournemouth. The Irishman was to graduate to play for his country on 12 occasions and showed a gritty determination at left-half. The close-season was one of change. Joe Harvey retired and concentrated on coaching while the Robledo brothers were lured back to Chile. Several South American clubs had tried to poach George since he started to make headlines with United. In February 1951, Universidad Catolica of Santiago wanted him and even the resident Chilean ambassador tried to persuade the player to return home. That deal - worth a massive £30,000 to United - fell through, but another Chilean club, Colo Colo succeeded and paid a big fee to take the pair back to South America in May 1953. The powerful elder of the two brothers, George, was to be missed. He had knocked home another 18 goals in the season just completed.

New faces were to arrive during the summer months, while young players already at the club were to push for a regular chance. Vic Keeble was one, another was Bob Stokoe. Signed from Colchester United, Keeble took over the No 9 shirt deputising for Milburn. Stokoe had been on the Gallowgate pay-roll since 1947 and was a play anywhere half-back, actually making his debut - and scoring - at centre-forward. For years he was deputy to Harvey, then moved to centre-half and found himself reserve to Brennan. With competition for places so fierce, Stokoe actually made three transfer requests before he at last got a permanent first team place in 1953/54. Stokoe was strong in the tackle and went on to skipper the club. He later became one of the game's longest serving managers being in charge of a string of clubs, notably Blackpool, Sunderland and Carlisle United, taking the Roker men to FA Cup triumph in 1973. In spite of his many travels Stokoe never lost his fondness for the black'n'whites and helped out behind the scenes as the club's Centenary approached.

RECORD TRANSFER BID

Towards the end of the 1952/53 season with United's side in need of an injection of fresh talent, the club tried to tempt Fulham to part with three of their highly acclaimed stars - Bobby Robson, Bedford Jezzard and Johnny Haynes. Fulham wanted a massive £60,000 and after much deliberation Seymour and Co felt that was too high and pulled out of the deal. As it turned out the amount may well have been a good price. All three went on to appear on aggregate a total of 78 occasions for England.

The selection committee also experimented with reserves Tommy Mulgrew, George Brander and Tommy Cahill. They also splashed out heavily on two recognised international players. With new record signing from Portsmouth, Scottish international Jimmy Scoular an influential addition to United's team, the club started the season in new spirits. With a reputation as a fearsome personality, £22,250 Scoular took over from Harvey as both right-half and captain, although for a spell he handed the skipper's job to Crowe, Stokoe and McMichael when results didn't go well. From Livingston, Scoular had little respect for anyone when it came to football. He was tough as any rival, yet displayed dainty skills and could hit a 40 yard pass to precision. He was one of the game's characters and opposing fans loved to have a go at him.

Jimmy Scoular arrived to take over from Harvey as both captain and right-half.

An opening 2-1 victory over Sunderland at St James Park put Tyneside's fans on top of the world. United started comfortably, but were handicapped by an injury to Scoular on his debut, a knock that kept him out for a month. United's other big purchase, England schemer Ivor Broadis was secured at the same time as forward Alan Monkhouse. Broadis cost another substantial fee, £17,500 and had shined during the 1954 World Cup in Switzerland over the summer. After a run of impressive displays the ex Manchester City inside-forward never fitted into the Gallowgate set-up. He became something of a rebel and suffered for it, later being omitted from the 1955 FA Cup final side, although he had played in several earlier rounds. Centre-forward Monkhouse landed on Tyneside from Millwall for £11,500 and while he never became a household name gave good service to the club, scoring eleven goals in only 23 appearances.

Expensive signing, England schemer Ivor Broadis, in action against Huddersfield Town.

However, with all this new blood, United couldn't click and by the end of 1953 were in urgent need of points at the bottom of the table along with other north eastern clubs, Middlesbrough and Sunderland. The very near FA Cup elimination by Lancashire Combination leaders Wigan Athletic did not help confidence. Largely composed of elder, experienced Football League players, Wigan took United to a replay after a 2-2 draw on Tyneside. It was the Latics' finest hour and they almost pulled off a shock victory in front of a near 53,000 crowd. They actually led 2-1 and it was left to Jackie Milburn to, "save the Magpies from the utter humiliation of defeat". United's forward evaded three tackles and drove home an 18 yard shot for a glorious equaliser.

United won narrowly 3-2 at a packed Springfield Park, with Broadis, Keeble and White scoring, but it had been another tense affair full of near misses at both ends of the ground - a typical David and Goliath meeting. It had also been a controversial visit to Lancashire with United's officials complaining bitterly about the facilities. With Wigan's stand having recently been burnt down, the temporary changing rooms had only one light bulb - which was connected to a car battery - and one bath! Seymour would have none of it and was so appalled that he arranged to, firstly, change at the club's Southport hotel and then later at Wigan's Corporation Baths. United's party afterwards snubbed their host's post-match reception.

In the next round Burnley were defeated 1-0 through a Bobby Mitchell penalty in another replay. This was after the Scot had missed from the spot on a snow covered pitch at Turf Moor. It was a better performance by Newcastle and some of the old fighting spirit was slowly returning. League leaders, West Bromwich Albion, were United's Fifth Round opponents at the Hawthorns. They had already crushed the black'n'whites 7-3 back in September on Tyneside, and in another classic and thrilling match Albion won 3-2, Ronnie Allen grabbing a hat-trick. They had dominated in the first half and United in the second.

Now that FA Cup interest had disappeared, the Tynesiders had to seriously concentrate on winning league points. They were down to 18th place at one stage, but a 4-3 win over Manchester City early in April, followed by two convincing home victories over Sheffield Wednesday and Arsenal, made sure of their First Division place. They finished in 15th position and their form was both perplexing and frustrating. They were good away from home, but dreadful at St James Park where, in the years after World War Two, the side had the capacity to give their visitors a goal start and still win. United lost ten matches on their own soil, including an incredible record six in a row early on. Perhaps the crowd asked too much of the side after such a successful period. They were quick to criticise if things went wrong, which they did. The press were also swift to pass a stinging rebuke. One report made the comment that, "Newcastle were just a rabble playing a blend of plucky third class soccer and a weary apology for the top class game".

Although much criticised again early into the 1954/55 season with performances that seemed to quickly turn from brilliantly purple patches to indifference that was rubbish, United gave their fans another FA Cup run to remember. However, as one journalist observed, they needed, "the luck of four leprechauns and three gremlins" to battle through to Wembley.

RECORD SEQUENCE

United's FA Cup success during 1950 to 1953 created a record unbeaten run of 16 games. From a 4-1 victory over Bury in the 3rd Round of 1951 to the 3-1 defeat by Rotherham United in 1953, United won 13 of the 16 games, including of course two finals. This stood as a record until Tottenham Hotspur recorded 18 games in a run from 1980 to 1983.

Ronnie Simpson leaps to push a Ronnie Allen shot to safety in the F.A. Cup tie with WBA in 1954.

The new campaign couldn't have opened better with a brilliant 3-1 victory against Arsenal before over 65,000 at Highbury. This was quickly followed four days later by a 3-0 win over Cup holders West Bromwich. Len White then crashed home a hat-trick of headed masterpieces against Aston Villa - a hint of things to come from the Yorkshireman - but from then on Newcastle flopped and in a testimonial match with Doncaster Rovers the majority of the first team were beaten 7-2. Youngsters were drafted in, goalkeeper John Thompson and centre-forward Bill Curry, who was soon to play for the newly formed England Under 23 side.

A December revival took Newcastle away from the bottom placings following good wins over Sheffield Wednesday, Portsmouth and Arsenal. However, the team still hadn't mastered their inconsistency, for they lost 6-2 to Sheffield United, conceding four goals in the first eight minutes. It was hardly the right way to prepare for the Third Round FA Cup-tie at Plymouth seven days later.

Manager Doug Livingstone arrived just as the Magpies set off on a F.A. Cup trail.

Just before that defeat at Bramall Lane, Newcastle's board appointed another manager. With league results continuing to be far from satisfactory the club dispensed with the old directors' committee and Seymour gave way to Scot Duggie Livingstone, although the new manager's duties would be confined to primarily coaching while his team selection, together with any transfers, had to be sanctioned by the board. An unflappable character, Livingstone possessed a good pedigree in management having recently led Belgium's national side to the World Cup finals where his team competed in the same group as England. He had been involved in management at Exeter and at both Sheffield clubs. As a player, the Scot appeared prominently at full-back for Celtic and Everton and was regarded as a model professional. On New Year's Day 1955 he moved into the hot-seat at St James Park and in his first game in charge saw United crash in that tussle with Sheffield United, one of his old sides. Livingstone had barely time to get to know the players before the long trip to the west country was upon him.

It looked an easy tie against a struggling Second Division club, but as so often happens it proved an uphill task. Ronnie Simpson was United's saviour as the Magpies played second fiddle on an icy pitch. But Vic Keeble pinched the only goal of the game - a low drive in spite of the attentions of two tackles. That victory took Newcastle into the draw for the next round and a tie with Brentford, another lowly club, resulted.

At St James Park it should have been a walk-over for the black'n'whites, but the FA Cup showed again what a great leveller the competition is. Pitch conditions were once more difficult, United winning narrowly 3-2 with Brentford displaying tremendous spirit, pushing the Tynesiders close in a fighting finish. Newcastle were also to show that spirit in the next tie, an epic with Nottingham Forest.

United v Forest Cup action. Alan Monkhouse scores one of his two goals.

During a spell of football from 19th February to 2nd March, Magpie supporters witnessed a feast of dramatic football. Three exhilarating tussles with Forest - 330 minutes of fevered challenge - and a derby with Sunderland in between. The contest with the Trent club was as Ron Batty said, "the hardest part of our Cup journey". The weather caused problems again and on a hard, snow covered park, Second Division Forest were dominant in the first game at the City Ground. There were only a few minutes left when Peter Small gave the home side the lead - he had been brought back from hospital after going off earlier following a bad fall. Most thought the game to be over. United's exit from the competition looked a cert, but Jackie Milburn was one who didn't consider the game to be dead and within two minutes had equalised - a disputed goal - Jackie squeezing the ball inside the post from an acute angle. Before the replay, United met Sunderland in the 78th derby confrontation and confidence was shattered when the Reds took both points in a 2-1 home defeat. United had to pick themselves up to face Forest again.

The first replay was postponed because of the continuing severe winter, but 100 workers cleared the pitch of 15 inches of snow to allow the next attempt to go ahead. The replay went into extra-time with Forest putting up a great fight after Bobby Mitchell's beauty and a close-in conversion by Keeble had given United a 2-0 lead. They pulled the game back to 2-2 and a second replay. The two clubs spun a coin for the next venue and decisively

BIG CROWDS

Over 40,000 were at St James Park to see Third Division Gateshead take on the might of West Bromwich Albion in the 4th Round of the FA Cup in February 1952. WBA won 2-0 and Ronnie Allen scored both goals. Another big crowd turned up when top local side Bishop Auckland appeared at the stadium for an important FA Amateur Cup game. In March 1954 a gate of 54,210 saw the semi-final victory over Briggs Sports, while in the replayed final a month later, 56,008 saw Bishops draw 2-2 with Crook Town. That was the biggest crowd for an amateur game away from Wembley.

United won home advantage. Alan Monkhouse, a reserve in the main, and one who enjoyed these heavy pitches, came into the side for the injured Keeble. Once more the match went the full distance and the former Millwall striker hit United's two goals, although the winner came only two minutes from a fourth meeting. His first was a stinging low drive, the other a glorious running header. Monkhouse wasn't the star though, that honour went to the sparkling Milburn who ran himself into the Gallowgate mud in spite of a painful stomach muscle injury which went on to affect the rest of his career.

HILLSBOROUGH, SHEFFIELD

FOOTBALL ASSOCIATION CUP—SEMI-FINAL

York City

versus

Huddersfield or Newcastle

SATURDAY, 26th MARCH, 1955

Kick-off 3.0 p.m.

South Stand Enclosure 6/-

1529

Secretary and Manager

Huddersfield Town stood between United and a semi-final place and it took two more games to get past this strong First Division outfit who included Bill McGarry at right-half. United carried the luck as in previous rounds and also showed that never-say-die spirit for the umpteenth time. Once the Terriers had taken the lead after half-time, the black'n'whites left it ever so late to grab an equaliser and only three minutes remained when Len White earned United a replay, this after a narrow escape in their own box. Glazzard appeared to have been clearly brought down, yet no penalty resulted and the ball broke for Newcastle to rush up field. Mitchell went on a mazy run and swept a perfect cross to the far post where White crashed the ball into the net. It was dramatic stuff. In that tie at Leeds Road, Bobby Mitchell was on song and tormented England full-back Ron Staniforth all afternoon. Ronnie Simpson recorded, "Mitch took Staniforth for everything but his wallet". Bobby really dazzled during both games and was the player to see United into the semi-final. Newcastle's star winger was to say, "It was the best game I ever had in a black'n'white shirt".

In the replay United again had their share of Dame Fortune. All was stalemate at 90 minutes, but in extra-time a left foot special from Mitchell and a scrambled goal from the on-form Keeble took United through to a match with giant-killers York City. The minnows' scalps that year had included the mighty Spurs and Blackpool, they very nearly added the name of Newcastle United too. York were on a tremendous run at the time and bidding for promotion with star forward Arthur Bottom crashing in goals left, right and centre - form that prompted United to buy him. Luck was also on the Magpies side in the Hillsborough tussle on a day pouring with rain. The game ended 1-1, Keeble again scoring in a goalmouth melee, but not until City had scared the pants off Newcastle. The black'n'whites fell way below form and almost caused a sensation by allowing Third Division York the honour of reaching Wembley. Bottom equalised with a great 30 yard run and shot and they piled on the pressure in the closing stages. At one stage a Bottom header almost gave City the Wembley ticket. In a scramble, the ball - as York players maintained - crossed the line, but the referee didn't agree and the game ended in a draw. At Roker Park, United found better form and won comfortably 2-0. They left the killer goal though, to the dying minutes when Keeble, with a typical header, clinched the game. This effort added to White's early picture goal following a perfect build-up and cross by Milburn.

F.A Cup mania. United fans stand in line waiting for tickets for the Sixth Round clash with Huddersfield Town.

TICKET SCANDAL

United's players were involved in a FA Cup final ticket scandal in 1952 after they had received up to 100 tickets each. Afterwards the Football Association ruled that in future, clubs in the final would receive only 12 tickets per player, to a maximum of 15 players. In 1955 United's men were not happy at this allocation, but the club - fearful of another outcry - were determined to obey the rules. They threatened to field their reserve side at Wembley if the first team did not toe the line.

Vic Keeble rises to send the ball against the bar in the semi-final clash with York City at Hillsborough.

Throughout the Cup run United dished up an assortment of football and they hadn't fielded a settled side. Jackie Milburn had been switched around the forward line and was not guaranteed a place. He noted, "I never for one moment thought we were good enough to get to Wembley". But get there they did. Before the final, United went through a fixture pile-up. At one stage they had eight games in the space of three weeks, seven of which were at home! Recovering league form, Newcastle finished in a respectable 8th position only losing two of their last twelve games. Bobby Mitchell was top scorer with 23 goals, Milburn closely followed with 21. Work started on ground improvements at the programme's conclusion. The Leazes End was altered, a gym in the car park built, and plans for an impressive main entrance and reception area went ahead, to become one of the most modern entrance-halls to any ground in the country at the time. Jutting out from the back of the old and unsightly brick and corrugated iron structure was to be a pillared building gleaming with polished wood and plate glass.

Wembley Stadium beckoned for a third time in only five years. Manchester City had won through to meet United in the FA Cup final. They had beaten Sunderland at Villa Park in the other semi-final and ended the north east's dream of a Tyne-Wear final. No-one had to tell United what arrangements had to be made. They had reached the final on this occasion out of 504 entries for the competition, but during the preceding weeks went through several moments of crisis. Simmering in the background throughout was the squabble between Frank Brennan and the club that had put United's name into headlines for the wrong reasons, while Welshman Reg Davies dropped out with flu. So did Charlie Crowe, straining ankle ligaments only seven days before at Tottenham. Davies was to be most unlucky. He had been 12th man in 1952 and was to miss out again. Jackie Milburn was in bed with laryngitis while Ron Batty had fractured his wrist, but was able to continue with a soft covering. In for the injured McMichael, who had missed most of the season, Batty had been with the club since 1945, a loyal club player despite being stuck in the Central League many times. The ex pit-man was respected by many and several colleagues were to say he was the best left-back on the St James Park staff. Len White and Tommy Casey came into the side, while George Hannah secured a place too. Only 9 stones, but with skills that made him a most attractive

PISTON BREAKDOWN

During March 1954 United's party had a lucky escape on their way to play Huddersfield Town. They were involved in a train crash when the locomotive's engine's piston rod broke. Travelling at 70 mph they were fortunate that no injuries occurred and had to hire a bus to take them the remaining 14 miles to Leeds Road. They arrived at the ground at 3.00 pm and the game kicked-off 22 minutes late.

player, Hannah was to play an important role in the final. After eight years on Tyneside George was to have another long spell at Manchester City where he was just as popular.

Duggie Livingstone had other problems too, not least having to persuade the board to accept his Cup final line-up. When he took his team-sheet to the directors' meeting at the County Hotel he came out and told the awaiting players, "This is the team, but I didn't want it"! United's directors had changed it when Livingstone astonishingly planned to leave Jackie Milburn out of the line-up. Stan Seymour exploded and shouted, "What! Wembley without Milburn. Nonsense!" Wor Jackie was promptly put back in and the manager told in no uncertain terms which side would line up at Wembley.

LUCKY PENNY

United's FA Cup win in 1955 marked an amazing record for the club's lucky Victorian penny. Sent to Frank Watt by an Australian Newcastle supporter, it was first carried by Neil Harris when he scored one of the goals that gave the Magpies Cup victory in 1924. The coin was then carried by United's centre-forward in 1932 and Jack Allen netted twice. In 1951 it was taken onto the pitch by Jackie Milburn who also found the net with two beauties and in 1952 Milburn had the lucky charm once more, while in 1955 it was Vic Keeble's turn to carry the memento and see United through to victory.

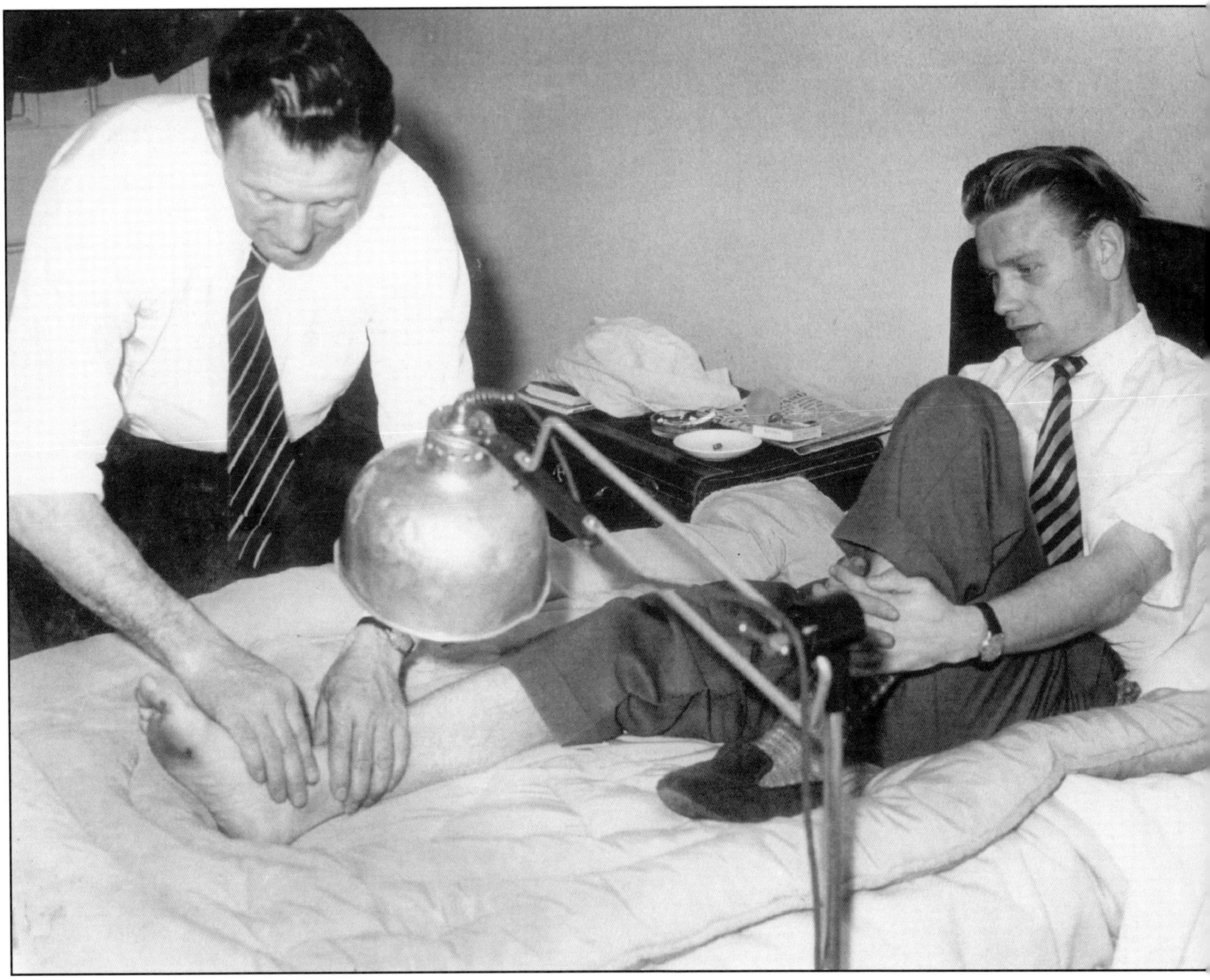

Charlie Crowe receives treatment in a frantic bid to get the half-back ready for Wembley. The unlucky Tynesider missed the game with Manchester City.

Centenary Highlight

> *"They are the chosen, the darlings. They walk in company with the gods"*
>
> *Bob Ferrier, May 1955*

REFEREE REG LEAFE BLEW HIS WHISTLE, Don Revie kicked-off and the 1955 FA Cup final was under way. City attacked but the ball quickly fell into United's possession and Scoular sent his forwards towards Trautmann's box. Milburn hit a pass to White who flicked a return inside for Jackie to force a corner. White took the kick and, with City's defenders crowding round the aerial menace of Vic Keeble, the ball fell right for the unmarked Jackie Milburn. Jackie was never noted for his heading ability, but on this occasion sent the ball crashing into the roof of the net from twelve yards. Only 45 seconds were on the clock - the fastest Cup final goal at Wembley.

It was a sensational start on a perfect day for football. Around 40,000 Newcastle fans couldn't believe their eyes - but cheered themselves hoarse nevertheless. Manchester City though were not to be subdued. Favourites at the outset, they had finished 7th in the First Division, just above United, and had displayed some sleek and accomplished soccer that season with the innovative 'Revie Plan' - a deep lying centre-forward - proving effective. They hit back after that shock opening but, like Arsenal before them, had a player injured early into the game. After 20 minutes Jimmy Meadows fell trying to stop the twisting and turning run of Mitchell and had to be led away with torn ligaments. Ironically it was almost on the same spot as Wally Barnes' injury three years before.

City's deserved equaliser came on the stroke of half-time when Hayes crossed and Bobby Johnstone dived to head high into Simpson's top corner for a splendid goal. After that though, Newcastle took command through the efforts of Scoular and Hannah. German 'keeper Bert Trautmann made the first of several brilliant stops and with more fortune United could well have run up a cricket score.

Within eight minutes of the restart Newcastle took the lead again. White clipped a ball to the far post which found his opposite winger, Mitchell near the City box. Controlling the ball, the Scot went past Spurdle and struck a low drive from within a foot of the 'keeper's by-line just inside the post, deceiving Trautmann into expecting a cross. It was a cheeky yet brilliant goal.

United pushed forward testing the City defence with searching play. Delightful long ball service from Jimmy Scoular gave the forwards several chances while Bobby Mitchell ran amok. Trautmann thwarted United's attacks until Hannah crowned a great individual display by finishing off a glorious move. Scoular hit a 40 yard pass for Mitchell to cut in and feed Hannah who volleyed through a ruck of players into the net from twelve yards. Although there was still half an hour left, the game was over. A weary ten man City were never going to come back from being 3-1 behind. United strolled through the final period as if it was a training session.

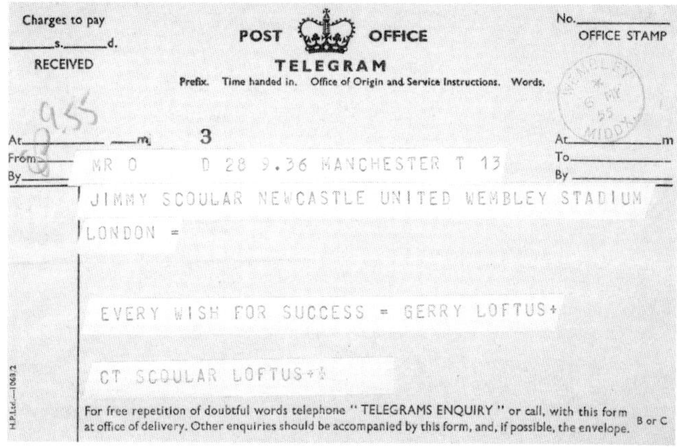
POST OFFICE TELEGRAM

3

MR O D 28 9.36 MANCHESTER T 13

JIMMY SCOULAR NEWCASTLE UNITED WEMBLEY STADIUM LONDON =

EVERY WISH FOR SUCCESS = GERRY LOFTUS+

CT SCOULAR LOFTUS+

For free repetition of doubtful words telephone "TELEGRAMS ENQUIRY" or call, with this form at office of delivery. Other enquiries should be accompanied by this form, and, if possible, the envelope.

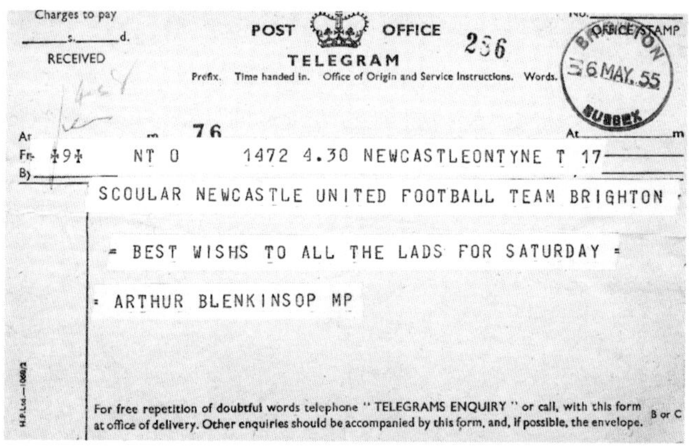
POST OFFICE TELEGRAM

76

NT O 1472 4.30 NEWCASTLEONTYNE T 17

SCOULAR NEWCASTLE UNITED FOOTBALL TEAM BRIGHTON

= BEST WISHES TO ALL THE LADS FOR SATURDAY =

= ARTHUR BLENKINSOP MP

For free repetition of doubtful words telephone "TELEGRAMS ENQUIRY" or call, with this form at office of delivery. Other enquiries should be accompanied by this form, and, if possible, the envelope.

Cup final good wishes sent to skipper Jimmy Scoular before the 1955 Wembley meeting with Manchester City.

NORTH GRAND STAND

ENTER AT TURNSTILES (See Plan and Conditions on back) F

ENTRANCE 79

Row 25 Seat 7

EMPIRE STADIUM, WEMBLEY

The Football Association Cup Competition

FINAL TIE

SATURDAY, MAY 7th, 1955

Kick-off 3 p.m.

Price 15/- (Including Tax)

CHAIRMAN AND MANAGING DIRECTOR, Wembley Stadium Limited

THIS PORTION TO BE RETAINED

This Ticket is issued on the condition that it is not re-sold for more than its face value.

It was United's Cup yet again, although the convincing triumph was slightly overshadowed by the injury to full-back Meadows. The Magpies had their own casualties in the second half though, both White(ankle) and Milburn(muscle) were at only half pace. Several of United's players maintained they would have been a match for an eleven man City on the day in any event. Scoular, Mitchell and Hannah were the stars, but it had been a fine all round performance with Bob Stokoe outstanding at centre-half. Scoular's contribution though, was singled out for high praise. The rugged Scot commanded the middle of the field and totally snuffed out the danger of the much vaunted Don Revie. From start to finish his iron-grip was evident.

FA CUP RUN

R3	Plymouth Argyle	A	W	1-0
R4	Brentford	H	W	3-2
R5	Nottingham Forest	A	D	1-1
	Nottingham Forest	H	D	2-2
	Nottingham Forest	H	W	2-1
R6	Huddersfield Town	A	D	1-1
	Huddersfield Town	H	W	2-0
SF	York City	N	D	1-1
	York City	N	W	2-0
F	Manchester City	N	W	3-1

FACTS & FIGURES

	P	W	D	L	F	A
Home	4	3	1	0	9	5
Away	6	3	3	0	9	4
Total	**10**	**6**	**4**	**0**	**18**	**9**

FA Cup Winners 1955

CUP GOALGETTERS

5 Keeble, 4 Mitchell, 2 White, Monkhouse, Milburn, Hannah, 1 Curry

CHAIRMAN: Stan Seymour
MANAGER: Duggie Livingstone
TRAINER-COACH: Norman Smith
CAPTAIN: Jimmy Scoular

Above: Newcastle's 1955 squad of players. Left to right, back: Scoular, Casey, Foulkes, Simpson, Milburn, Stokoe, Batty, Crowe. Front: Livingstone (manager), White, Davies, Keeble, Broadis, Hannah, Mitchell, Smith (trainer).

Left: To the roar of 100,000 spectators the Magpies take the field. Scoular leads the side followed by Cowell, Batty, Milburn and Mitchell.

Centenary Highlight

Jackie Milburn's 45 second strike.
Left: Len White sends the ball to Milburn's head (3rd from left), and below: Wor Jackie does the rest - a wonderful leap and the ball flies into the net. Notice Vic Keeble, surrounded by three City defenders, leaving Milburn unmarked.

Left: A marvellous action study of centre-forward Vic Keeble. In typical style he attempts a brave header despite the attention of a City defender.

Right: Scoular leads his team down the Wembley steps followed by Ron Batty.

Left: HRH Queen Elizabeth greets Jimmy Scoular and is about to present the trophy. Bobby Cowell is next in line, while Stan Seymour looks a contented man in the background.

FINAL
7 May 1955 at Wembley Stadium
Newcastle United 3 (1) Manchester City 1(1)

UNITED;
Simpson
Cowell, Batty
Scoular, Stokoe, Casey
White, Milburn, Keeble, Hannah, Mitchell.
MANCHESTER CITY;
Trautmann
Meadows, Little
Barnes, Ewing, Paul
Spurdle, Hayes, Revie, Johnstone, Fagan.

GOALS;
Milburn(45 secs), Johnstone(44m),
Mitchell(53m), Hannah(58m).

ATTENDANCE;
100,000 (£49,881)

Referee; R.J.Leafe (Nottingham)
Guest of Honour; HRH Queen Elizabeth II
Cup HQ; Royal Albion Hotel, Brighton

FA Cup Winners 1955

Above: Familiar dressing-room jubilation. Left to right: Seymour (director), Simpson, Cowell, Keeble, Batty, Hannah, Scoular, Stokoe (behind), Casey, Livingstone, Smith (trainer) and Crowe.

Celebrations were in the Savoy again, then a relaxing evening on Sunday at the London Palladium where entertainer Max Bygraves held the FA Cup aloft! Monday arrived and it was back to Tyneside for the well rehearsed homecoming. Three Cup victories in five years was an outstanding achievement in any era of football. No other club has equalled the feat since and it has only been matched in the very earliest days of the tournament. Newcastle also created a new Cup record by appearing in ten finals and equalled the Blackburn and Aston Villa record of six wins each.

Three players took part in each triumph, Milburn, Mitchell and Bobby Cowell. Newcastle were perhaps not in the truly classic mould of League Champions of that era, Manchester United or Tottenham Hotspur, but when it came to the FA Cup, the Magpies were an inspired eleven - almost touched with magic. Bob Ferrier wrote, “They are the chosen, the darlings. They walk in company with the gods”. Bobby Mitchell was to write in his memoirs, “I give full credit to Stan Seymour. He built up an atmosphere that was truly remarkable. Everyone, from the stars to trainees was imbued with the tradition of Newcastle United”.

Above: Captain Scoular with the F.A. Cup, having a quick shave in the Wembley dressing-room.

Right: The unlucky Charlie Crowe - an injury victim - joins in the victory celebrations with Simpson (left) and Batty (right).

Left: Directors Wilf Taylor (left) and Stan Seymour (right) show off the F.A. Cup with Jimmy

Centenary Highlight

United's Cup heroes pay a visit to Newcastle Breweries.
Left to right, back: Davies, Smith (trainer), Casey, Milburn, Stokoe, Batty, Cowell, Simpson. Front: White, Hannah, Livingstone (manager), Scoular, Keeble, Mitchell.

Newcastle's triumph as seen through the eyes of cartoonist Dudley Hallwood.

In an open-topped Armstrong omnibus, Newcastle's party leave the Central Station. Left to right: Scoular, Keeble, Cowell, Casey, Hannah, Stokoe, Batty.

FA Cup Winners 1955

The F.A. Cup arrives back at St. James Park for the third time in five years. Jimmy Scoular and Tommy Casey enter the stadium followed by manager Livingstone.

Centenary Profile 14

The Modest Hero

"He was the most exciting thing I have ever seen on a football field"

Bob Stokoe, 1989

HE WAS CHRISTENED JOHN EDWARD THOMPSON - JET - and surely no other footballer had such an appropriate set of initials to embark on a career in the game. When Jackie Milburn walked into St James Park, boots in a brown paper parcel, in August 1943 there started a special association not only between player and club, but also between player and the whole of the north east region. One that remains strong as ever, several years after his death in 1988.

Milburn - modest and likeable - formed a bond with his fellow Geordies like no other. They adored him and he adored them back. To a wider audience the name of Milburn became very quickly synonymous with Newcastle United and with Tyneside, even to people who had only a passing interest in the game. He became the club's foremost ambassador.

From established football stock in Ashington, Milburn was born only a few days after United had lifted the FA Cup at Wembley in 1924. His family were all soccer mad and he is a member of what is perhaps the greatest footballing clan in Britain. The first Jack Milburn played in goal for Shankhouse and Northumberland during the pioneer days of the game. Then there was 'Warhorse' Milburn, a famed local player. He had 13 children and several played football. Tanner Milburn appeared for Ashington during their Football League days and the family grew even further when this particular Milburn had four sons, as well as three daughters. The boys of course took to kicking a ball around.

Tanner's brother, Alec also played for Ashington after turning down a chance with Spurs and he produced Wor Jackie, while Tanner's offspring turned out in league football too; George, Stan, Jim and Jack. All played for Leeds United except Stan, who appeared for Chesterfield and Leicester City, as well as the Football League side. All were tough and noted performers. Additionally Jimmy Potts, the Leeds 'keeper, married into the Milburns too. It was quite a family which becomes further entangled as Tanner's daughter, Cissie, is of course mother to Jackie and Bobby Charlton. And it was Newcastle's Jackie Milburn who really put the family name into the headlines when he became an England international during the 1948/49 season.

Jackie had left school in 1938 when aged 14. Instead of going down the pit, the young Milburn took a job in Dorking as a pantry boy, far flung from his future success. Home sickness soon brought him back north though, where he started his football career assisting Hirst East Old Boys and later Ashington YMCA. War in 1939 saw Milburn try to join the Navy but, lacking height, he was rejected. Twelve months later he had shot up to 5'10" and had become an apprentice fitter at the local colliery. His football progress was outstanding. He appeared for the local ATC and for the county side and was soon at St James Park making an impression in a trial match.

In his first game he scored two goals, then really caught the eye the following weekend - all with a borrowed pair of boots. His performance could have been picked from Roy of the Rovers. Playing inside-left for the Stripes against the first team Blues, his side were 3-0 behind and Jackie had been a flop. But in the second half, after an inspired talking to by trainer Joe Richardson, Milburn rattled six goals into the net. Jackie was on his way to becoming a Newcastle United legend.

A week later Stan Seymour signed Milburn for the statutory £10 registration fee and United's boss was convinced that he had found a gem. The youngster immediately made his debut in a wartime fixture at Valley Parade, home of Bradford City. United went down 2-1, but as Jackie recalled it was, "The most memorable moment of my career, even those Wembley victories can't match it. To pull on the black'n'white jersey for the first time was something special".

The following game was his home debut, a return meeting with the Yorkshire club and it took Milburn only two minutes to show the Geordie public what was to follow - the first of nearly 250 goals scored for United - and it was achieved with his first kick too. He continued at inside-forward during those mid forties, a position that many judges, including Charlie Buchan, reckoned was his best. He also played on the flank and showed the swiftness of foot that was to create many goals from the centre-forward position. That important change occurred in October 1947 and his first game in the famed Number 9 shirt resulted in a hat-trick. He was a reluctant centre-forward, but George Martin persuaded him to stick it out, maintaining he had all the assets to become a great leader.

Jackie Milburn

MILBURN'S PLAYING RECORD

	League App	League Gls	FA Cup App	FA Cup Gls	FL Cup App	FL Cup Gls	Total App	Total Gls
1946-47	24	7	3	1	0	0	27	8
1947-48	39	20	1	0	0	0	40	20
1948-49	34	19	1	0	0	0	35	19
1949-50	30	18	2	3	0	0	32	21
1950-51	31	17	8	8	0	0	39	25
1951-52	32	25	7	3	0	0	39	28
1952-53	16	5	0	0	0	0	16	5
1953-54	39	16	5	2	0	0	44	18
1954-55	38	19	10	2	0	0	48	21
1955-56	38	19	4	2	0	0	42	21
1956-57	32	12	1	0	0	0	33	12
1943-46 (Wartime)			2	2			97	40
	353	**177**	**44**	**23**	**95**	**38**	**492**	**238**

Milburn in action at Wembley in the 1951 F.A. Cup final - the day he netted two memorable goals against Blackpool.

Milburn topped the scoring list as United were promoted and in Division One he went off like a bomb. Defences had no answer and he was soon representing England, scoring on his debut. He went on to play 13 times for his country, scoring nine goals including a hat-trick against Wales. To many it was a dozen appearances too few. Milburn became a Geordie legend - the pit-man turned hero. He was a versatile player, operating over the seasons in all forward positions for United. He worked hard at his game, once saying, "I would kick a ball against a wall for hours". Jackie was not the selfish or ruthless type of leader. He looked casual at times and would always consider passing when perhaps he should have had a crack at goal himself. He hated heading the ball too, due to a fibrositis complaint. But he was still a radiant player. Milburn had the ability to hit the ball, using either foot, with tremendous power and Charlie Crowe said, "He was the most natural striker of a ball I've ever seen". And could he run, devastatingly fast. When in full flight he was breathtaking and once ran 100 yards in 9.7 seconds. He possessed flair for a special finish and was noted for scoring from what seemed impossible angles, and also on the run where his control of the ball was nigh perfect. Milburn's famous trick of sliding on one knee to tackle a defender, hooking the ball and then sprinting away is one that surprised many a centre-half. Bob Stokoe was to remark, "He was the most exciting thing I have ever seen on a football field".

By the turn of the decade Milburn was the spearhead to United's double FA Cup triumph in 1951 and 1952. It was in the first of those finals that Jackie was elevated to superstar status with a double strike worthy of any Goal of the Season award. Another final followed in 1955, and another memorable goal. Milburn remained at Gallowgate until the summer of 1957 when he moved to Linfield as player-manager. He was 33 years old and was offered a lucrative deal....£25 per week, £1,000 signing-on fee and a club house. After a basic £17 wage packet at St James Park it was heaven.

Milburn turned out in the early days of the European Cup - scoring two goals - and helped win League and Cup honours in Ireland. He was named Ulster Footballer-of-the-Year in 1958 and was equally as popular at Windsor Park, netting some 150 goals. In January 1963 he tried senior management with Ipswich Town after a spell coaching with non-league Yiewsley and Carmel College. He succeeded Alf Ramsey who took charge of the England side but, at Portman Road, Milburn had a rough passage. Inheriting an ageing squad, he had to rebuild and Ipswich were relegated. He noted, "the pressure was unbelievable". He was too nice a guy to wander in that managerial jungle and left East Anglia to return north a year and a half later.

Entering the newspaper world, Milburn remained for over 20 years covering north eastern football from the press-box. Given the Freedom of the City - and few hold that honour - Jackie Milburn remained a gentlemanly and modest individual to his final day. When chatting about his belated testimonial match in 1967 he said, "I was worried to death that no-one would turn up. Ten years is a long time. People forget". Jack, modest as ever should have known better. Geordies do not forget heroes and Jackie Milburn was their biggest. Almost 46,000 crowded into St James Park for the midweek spectacular.

No other player has scored more senior goals for Newcastle United and it is doubtful if anyone in the future will approach the popularity which the name of Milburn still holds in the north east of England.

Centenary Profile 15

The Wizard of the Wing

"A supreme entertainer, able to thrill the crowd with ten minutes magic to brighten even the dullest game"

Ivor Broadis

JACKIE MILBURN WAS NOT THE ONLY UNITED player who hogged the newspaper headlines during the club's marvellous fifties era. There was another huge personality in the ranks, every bit a match-winner as was Wor Jackie. He was Bobby Mitchell, Bobby Dazzler to all. On the touch-line few were his equal. Even contemporaries like Matthews, Finney or Liddell couldn't surpass Mitch when he was on song. To see him taunting his full-back was simply magic.

Mitchell though, was not just a trickster and ball-player who flitted in and out of the match and pleased the fans, he was very much a key figure in United's team plan netting crucial goals and providing telling crosses for Milburn or Robledo to crash into the net. United owe much of their FA Cup success to his brand of left-wing play.

A native of Glasgow, Bobby started football in the cobbled back streets after taking part in little-organised soccer at school level. He noted he played with, "a rag-ball, a tin-can, or on really lucky days, an old tennis ball". On leaving school he joined the Market Star junior club and by 1942 was spotted by Third Lanark. Mitchell signed as an amateur when 17 years old, but was soon drafted into the Navy as a telegraphist and posted to destinations such as Malta, the Pacific and Sydney. After war Portsmouth wanted to sign him, but Mitchell preferred to return home to Scotland and back to Third Lanark where he was thrown into the first-team. Thirds were struggling in those days, but it was a good training ground in the Scottish First Division and he started to develop his amazing body swerve and control.

Mitchell quickly climbed to the top, being picked by the Scottish League side in 1946 and becoming Scotland's top scorer a year later with 22 goals. Newcastle United first took notice of the Scot purely by chance. Stan Seymour was covering Partick Thistle players when his eye was fascinated by the opposition and Mitchell's style. His lazy, deceptive stride and casual ease at shooting and crossing the ball had the mark of greatness about it. Firstly, there was no deal on the cards, Lanark would not part. Seymour though was as persistent as ever and, like a good detective, got his man in the end.

The tall, thin and wavy haired Glaswegian signed for United in February 1949, a record fee for a winger at £16,000. Mitchell made his debut in a friendly with Liverpool then followed that with a derby clash against Sunderland. Later he said of his move to Tyneside, "I didn't realise it then, but I was signing a contract which was to bring me some of the greatest happiness it has been anyone's privilege to know in football".

For the next decade and over Magpie fans witnessed many outstanding performances. By the close of the forties, Mitchell had a massive following on the terraces. He liked the ball at his feet and to beat an opponent with his own skill rather than with pace. He was confident - almost impertinent to defenders - and was totally left footed. Like many contemporary ball players he could be infuriating too, longing to hang on to the ball as if it was tied to his foot and tease his full-back, sometimes to breaking point. Joe Harvey once said jokingly,

Bobby Mitchell

MITCHELL'S PLAYING RECORD	League		FA Cup		Total	
	App	Gls	App	Gls	App	Gls
1948-49	13	3	0	0	13	3
1949-50	38	8	2	1	40	9
1950-51	40	7	8	3	48	10
1951-52	30	9	7	5	37	14
1952-53	35	10	2	1	37	11
1953-54	35	14	5	2	40	16
1954-55	40	19	10	4	50	23
1955-56	29	5	4	1	33	6
1956-57	25	2	1	0	26	2
1957-58	36	12	2	1	38	13
1958-59	16	0	0	0	16	0
1959-60	15	0	0	0	15	0
1960-61	15	6	0	0	15	6
	367	**95**	**41**	**18**	**408**	**113**

"He was in the forward line just to give the others a breather"! His biggest asset though, was that he could score goals. He netted 113 from the wing for United and was always capable of getting a vital strike - and in stunning style.

In the FA Cup runs of 1951 and 1952, Mitchell was the dangerman every bit as much as Milburn. Two games illustrate his worth to the team. Firstly in the 3rd Round tie with Aston Villa, United looked dead and buried before he rattled two goals into the net in the space of seconds. Then in the semi-final with Blackburn Rovers his decisive spot-kick in the dying minutes saw United to Wembley. It was typical Mitchell. When the side seemingly needed a boost, he would step up a gear and enter the action.

Mitchell figured strongly in both finals, and also at Wembley for a third time against Manchester City in 1955. Bobby had a field day then, and netted a deserved goal. Scotland honoured Mitchell only twice, unfortunately he was to be second choice to Liverpool's Billy Liddell throughout his career.

After Newcastle's 1955 success the winger entered the veteran stage, however he still managed to remain with United for another six years. Mitchell was in and out of the side during the late fifties and actually put on the transfer list. He agreed terms with Notts County, but the deal fell through and he bounced back to confound critics who said he was, "over the hill". Mitchell showed new boss Charlie Mitten that, even at 34 years old, he could still do a job for United. He appeared from left-half and stayed in the line-up becoming one of United's oldest post-war players - almost 37 when he retired.

He eventually left St James Park during the summer of 1961, joining Berwick Rangers. Bobby returned to Gallowgate though, during October of that year for a testimonial match. The game attracted a massive gate of 40,993 well-wishers, then the biggest in the country for any fixture of its kind, a mark of his popularity. In May 1963, he moved back to Tyneside and joined Gateshead as player-manager, but quickly became disillusioned with football and left the scene soon afterwards.

Residing in Newcastle, Mitchell then became a publican, notably in charge of Jesmond's Cradlewell and The Lochside in Heaton. Surprisingly perhaps, after taking part in 408 contests for the club, Bobby took little interest in the game. A legendary wizard of the wing, Mitchell's mazy runs coupled with a potent goalscoring talent captivated United's faithful for more than a decade. As Ivor Broadis said, he was, "A supreme entertainer, able to thrill the crowd with ten minutes magic to brighten even the dullest game"

Mitchell attacks Manchester City's Meadows and Barnes during the 1955 F.A. Cup final at Wembley. The Scot scored United's second goal in the 3-1 victory.

Centenary Profile 16

Triple Cup Victor

"How he never won an international cap has never ceased to amaze me"

Joe Harvey, August 1984

THREE FOOTBALLING NAMES BECAME ALMOST institutions at St James Park during the last 25 years. Joe Harvey and Jackie Milburn were two. The third is Bobby Cowell, former right-back and holder of a trio of FA Cup winners' medals with United. All three players have rarely been absent from Gallowgate since the Second World War. Harvey was manager and scout, Milburn viewed activities from the press-box and Bobby Cowell has been a devoted fan since retiring in 1956 and is still a popular character in the club's guest-room.

Bobby spent all of twelve seasons with Newcastle United, his full career and it would have been more, but for an injury which cruelly ended his footballing days. Cowell was an accomplished defender and was on the fringe of England recognition on more than one occasion. Joe Harvey said of his colleague, "How he never won an international cap has never ceased to amaze me". Joe went on, "he was a better full-back than Alf Ramsey, then England's choice".

Cowell was born in the village of Trimdon Grange near to the university city of Durham in December 1922. From a mining community, Bobby worked down the pit as a teenager getting £4 a week and often watched his local team play football. His hero wasn't any famous professional of the time, but a larger than life Trimdon character by the name of 'Digger' Dickson. In fact during his teens, Bobby had little time for watching the likes of Newcastle or Sunderland for he was too busy playing himself, for the village team and occasionally for Blackhall Colliery. During war, Cowell turned out for the Home Guard XI and received his first chance at the big-time with Newcastle.

In 1943 he was invited to appear in a trial for United's reserve side against Shotton. Cowell impressed the watching officials and he signed forms in October of that year. His first taste of senior football was against Bradford Park Avenue when United lost 1-0. However, by the time wartime soccer had ended in 1946, Cowell's Football League debut had an altogether different conclusion. The Magpies entertained Newport County in a Second Division match and ran off the field 13-0 victors. Bobby recalled his league baptism, "It was made very easy for me. Newport were never at my end of the field! The Welsh were no world beaters, yet good enough to take revenge later in the season. We went down 4-2".

Cowell had to be content with a reserve place for the early peace-time seasons with seniors Benny Craig, Dick Burke and Bob Fraser all ahead of him for the No 2 shirt. He appeared for the Magpies reserve eleven as they lifted the Central League title and was drafted into the club's promotion side, replacing Fraser, by the end of the season. From then on Cowell became almost an ever-present in Newcastle's line-up. At right-back, he was tremendously quick to make up lost ground and even if a winger jinked past him, Cowell would be back for another go in double quick time. At 5'9" tall, solidly built and brave in a contest, his enthusiasm rubbed off on others. He was always first to be stripped and on many occasions played whilst having injuries that should have kept him on the sidelines. Bobby just hated to miss a game.

Most footballers are content with tasting success in Wembley's unique FA Cup atmosphere once, maybe twice if they are lucky. Bobby Cowell did it three times in five years. With Milburn and Mitchell, he turned out in every single game of those epic Cup runs, all 25 fixtures. He played important roles in several ties including making crucial off-the-line clearances. Jackie Milburn once recalled, "He stopped literally

Cowell greeted by HRH Prince Philip before the 1955 F.A. Cup final at Wembley.

COWELL'S PLAYING RECORD						
	League		FA Cup		Total	
	App	Gls	App	Gls	App	Gls
1946-47	13	0	4	0	17	0
1947-48	19	0	0	0	19	0
1948-49	38	0	1	0	39	0
1949-50	20	0	0	0	20	0
1950-51	42	0	8	0	50	0
1951-52	40	0	7	0	47	0
1952-53	36	0	2	0	38	0
1953-54	41	0	4	0	45	0
1954-55	40	0	10	0	50	0
1943-44 (War time)					18	0
1944-45 (War time)					41	0
1945-46 (War time)					24	0
	289	**0**	**38**	**0**	**408**	**0**

Bobby Cowell

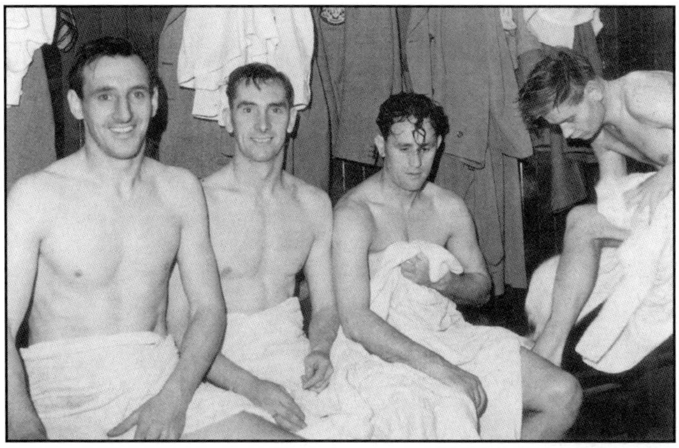

dozens of shots after the goalkeeper had been beaten". Notably at Portsmouth in the 6th Round of 1952 and one famous incident at Wembley against Blackpool when he dramatically catapulted himself upwards to stop a Mortensen effort.

The 1955 FA Cup victory over Manchester City was the last game Cowell played in England. On the summer tour of Europe he was involved in a clash with a German full-back of FC Nurnberg by the name of Uckow. Bobby was left in agony and carried off with knee ligament trouble. Cowell said, "Uckow had been given a hard time by Jimmy Scoular and he took it out on me". The German was sent-off for the foul challenge and had, as it turned out, finished the career of one of United's foremost defenders. In spite of expert attention the injury put Bobby off the pay-roll at St James Park. Cowell was 33 years old and had made, including wartime games, 408 appearances.

He was the first postwar Newcastle player to be awarded a testimonial match and 36,000 supported his benefit game in April 1956. Since then Cowell has been employed on Tyneside in various jobs, from scaffolder to storekeeper, as well as coach to local sides. Residing in Ponteland, Bobby has watched the up and down fortunes of Newcastle United and recalled his days as a spectator with almost as much pleasure as his playing career, noting, "The run to Wembley in 1974 was exceptional. I was jumping up and down when Supermac hit the second against Burnley just like everyone else at Hillsborough".

Bobby Cowell was one of those players who consistently got on with the job at hand in an undramatic way, in many ways like his full-back partner, Alf McMichael. He was a footballer rarely rewarded with headlines but, happily in this case, one who was rewarded with FA Cup medals instead.

Top: Cowell with Brennan, Milburn and Crowe in the St. James Park dressing-room.
Above: Bobby gives the thumbs up sign as the F.A. Cup comes home in 1955.

11 THRILLS AND SPILLS

1955-1961

• TYNE WEAR CONFRONTATION
• MORE CUP DRAMA • ENTERPRISING TRIO
• BOARDROOM RUMPUS
• HIGH COURT WRANGLE
• SECOND DIVISION BECKONS •

"Trying to manage the team and restructure the club was almost impossible"

Charlie Mitten, 1959

IT COULD HAVE BEEN EXPECTED THAT after United's third FA Cup victory in such a short space of time, everything would be rosy at St James Park. For the most part it was, but surprisingly the position of team manager was under review. Duggie Livingstone had only been on Tyneside for barely five months before several questions had been raised as to his ability to manage a club of such standing at the time. His adequate handling of so many stars was in serious doubt.

Newcastle directors and Stan Seymour in particular, were not impressed and several players had clearly not been moved with Livingstone either. Bobby Mitchell was to record, "his methods were somewhat strange to our way of thinking". Charlie Crowe remembered, "He trained us as though we were a bunch of schoolboys and had us climbing ropes and all sorts of circuit exercises", while Jackie Milburn noted, "Frankly, we needed new training like a hole in the head". He even tried to tell United's England centre-forward how to kick properly!

In stepped Stan Seymour and Livingstone's control over playing affairs was severely restricted. He was told to devote his energies to coaching young players and was relegated from the manager's office to the referee's room. His days at Gallowgate were obviously numbered and he moved on quickly, to Fulham. United made the decision to revert back to the old committee system - then almost dead and buried in professional football. It was to be the beginning of a period of decline touched all along the way with controversy. Yet terrific Cup battles continued, goals were scored by the hatful and classy, exciting players were on view right up to the Magpies' relegation in 1961.

Following the 1954 World Cup and national defeats by the Hungarians, English soccer took a hard look at itself in many aspects. Tactics changed, style of dress altered - out went the baggy shorts and in came a more modern looking attire - a lighter ball was used, as were streamlined football boots. Pay was to be increased and European competitions were even talked about. A new age had arrived with the birth of the European Champions Cup and Inter Cities Industrial Fairs Cup, a competition

Front cover from Soccer Star magazine featuring two of the club's most famous personalities, Stan Seymour and Jackie Milburn.

United were later to warm to.

Newcastle entered the modern era as FA Cup holders and with high hopes, but for the first time since the Second World War, United's average home gate dropped to below the 40,000 mark. The missing thousands were part due to United's unpredictable form and part to a gradual decline in football's popularity as other forms of relaxation developed. An increase in admission charges to a minimum of 2s 0d was an added reason.

From a position watching the Second Division trapdoor, the Magpies lifted themselves into 3rd place in the division by Easter and then fell away to mid-table after being knocked out of the FA Cup. 1955/56 was a satisfactory season with the Cup run to the quarter-finals equal to anything before, although the manner of United's exit left a sour taste to the club's supporters.

Vic Keeble who found the net 29 times in 1955/56.

Bobby Cowell's experience was to be missed and no fewer than five players claimed his shirt in the early months of the season. Another long established star had a revitalised campaign though, with 30 year-old Jackie Milburn showing top form, good enough to be called up by England again during October. A 6-2 win at Huddersfield on November 12th started an exciting, but unpredictable five month run that ended on March 3rd and an FA Cup tie with Sunderland. Up front Vic Keeble and Len White joined Milburn playing well, Keeble grabbed eight goals in a four match spell and the side went full speed ahead to a double Tyne-Wear league clash with their eventual FA Cup opponents.

Following a 5-0 victory over Preston North End on Christmas Eve, United faced Sunderland at Roker Park and gave their arch enemies a 6-1 hiding, the biggest by the Magpies in derby meetings. Within two minutes, they were in front when Keeble rocketed a header into the net from a Casey free-kick. Newcastle quickly stormed to a 3-0 lead as Milburn whipped home a left footer and Curry converted a Mitchell cross. Before half-time Keeble was on the mark again and his aerial menace was a constant problem for the home defence as he rose high to head home a Milburn corner.

The second period saw Sunderland, now totally outclassed and routed, fare no better. Milburn registered his second goal with a lovely flick from a Reg Davies lob, then Mitchell crossed again for Curry to get the Tynesiders' sixth goal. It might have been more, however Mitchell was a passenger for the last period of the match. Indeed, but for this

UNDER THE LIGHTS

Floodlit football developed in leaps and bounds during the mid years of the 1950s. FA Cup games were given sanction to use artificial light and the Second Round replay between Carlisle United and Darlington at St James Park in November 1955 was the first between Football League clubs. Newcastle United's first Cup-tie under the lights was the clash with Sheffield Wednesday later into the same season, during January 1956. They were switched on part-way through the game.

The Football League also allowed that postponed games could be played under floodlights if both clubs agreed. The Division One meeting between United and Portsmouth in February 1956 was the very first floodlit League game. The Times correspondent noted, "There is much to recommend it, there is a dramatic, theatrical quality about it". Football had an added dimension. In that game at Fratton Park the lights actually failed an hour before the start and the players were forced to change in candle-light! The match started ten minutes behind schedule and ended in a 2-0 victory.

Above: Bill Curry in action against Everton in October 1959.

United line up before a tour fixture in Madrid. Left to right, back: Stokoe, Simpson, McMichael, Casey, Lackenby. Front: Scoular, White, Davies, Keeble, Curry, Mitchell.

knock United may well have approached the magic figure of nine and erased the memory of that embarrassing defeat by Sunderland 47 years earlier.

To rub salt into the Roker club's wounds, Newcastle again toyed with their foes in the return fixture the following day at St James Park. The result was not so emphatic this time, United winning 3-1 in front of 61,058. Keeble and Milburn added to their Roker tally while Len White was on the scoresheet too. Other players to stand out were Ron Batty, who gave Shackleton an uncomfortable two days, and Bill Paterson, Brennan's replacement at centre-half. He cost the club a hefty £22,500 from Doncaster Rovers and played much like a sweeper yet, this game apart, was rarely a success in the anchor role at the back. United lost heavily on the deal, although the defender did well at Ibrox Park with Rangers.

United's unpredictability continued though. Two defeats followed, including a 3-0 home reverse by West Bromwich Albion in front of a bumper New Year holiday crowd. Then Newcastle met the Second Division's top side, Sheffield Wednesday in their defence of the FA Cup. It was a rousing and sporting tie at Hillsborough with Curry, Milburn and Keeble giving the Magpies an excellent 3-1 victory. Two good wins, 4-0 over Luton Town, and 2-0, at Charlton put Newcastle in fine mood for the next round at Craven Cottage, Fulham.

Top: United v Fulham F.A. Cup. Milburn and White congratulate Vic Keeble after bundling over the home 'keeper to score an important equaliser

Bottom: Jackie Milburn (not in picture) drives the ball into the net at Craven Cottage.

The Londoners, pushing hard for promotion to the First Division too, included previous United targets; Haynes, Robson and Jezzard, as well as Jimmy Hill, later of BBC fame. They were a good attacking side, but suspect at the back, playing the same glory or bust style as United. The game went exactly according to form and United managed to score just one better than Fulham in a match that lived for years. Future England boss, Bobby Robson said that the game was the most memorable he ever played in - against the club he supported as a kid.

Bob Stokoe (right) and Ron Batty rush to take on the great Stanley Matthews in a fixture with Blackpool in 1955.

Newcastle were the more polished side, and they should have sewn the tie up long before the end. Three times in the first half-hour, through Milburn, Stokoe and Casey, United opened the Londoners' defence to score. Casey's effort was a finale to a mesmerizing move, the Irishman sliding through the mud to poke the ball home. Just on half-time Fulham pulled a goal back, but still Newcastle looked easy winners. Bob Stokoe was to say, "We were cocky and confident, then Johnny Haynes began to cut loose". The home side came out after the interval in different mood. With Haynes dominating affairs, they threw everything into attack. The Cottagers scored again making it 3-2, and again, 3-3, with Trevor Chamberlain hitting a hat-trick. The terraces buzzed and Newcastle looked completely deflated. Another goal went past Simpson - from Chamberlain again - but to the crowd's groan it was disallowed by a young linesman called Jack Taylor, who later refereed a World Cup final. Still the Fulham side pressed on and with 15 minutes left got what looked like a deserved winner courtesy of Jimmy Hill to make the score now 4-3. With that goal Fulham eased up and United jumped at the chance to get back into the game.

Bobby Mitchell came more and more into the contest. He crossed a ball for Keeble to charge 'keeper Ian Black - and the ball - into the net. It was a goal....and the equaliser, albeit a highly disputed one. The game turned on that controversial incident. In the dying moments Mitchell stamped his quality on the game again. Another lovely run, a beautiful centre for Keeble to once more lunge forward to head the winner. A stunning victory by 5-4, after being 3-0 ahead, 4-3 behind. What a game.

For the third time a Second Division club opposed Tyneside's FA Cup fighters. Stoke City, with ex Magpie Andy Graver at centre-forward, arrived at Gallowgate for the Fifth Round. Over 61,000 fans, on the Wembley trail they all knew so well, saw Stoke hold superior Newcastle for a long time. However, Mitchell clinched the tie with a wonderful goal near the end and Ronnie Simpson also played his part, saving critically several times when Graver and company threatened.

In the quarter-final the north east giants were drawn together - the first Tyne Wear FA Cup meeting for almost half a century. As one could expect the whole region was even more football daft than normal. With their Christmas double behind them, everything pointed to a United win, and even another final appearance, now only two steps from Wembley. The all ticket match attracted almost 62,000 with record receipts taken of £9,600. It was a pity the stadium did not hold twice the number for the local interest this tie had generated. By kick-off the Leazes Terrace roof was covered with ticketless supporters wanting to see the game. Being United fans, though, they might have wished they had never climbed to their precarious vantage point once Sunderland showed that the form card means nothing in Cup football by winning 2-0.

All fit and raring to go after a training session. Four of United's 1955 F.A. Cup stars, left to right: Casey, Mitchell, Scoular, Keeble.

Unusually, Newcastle were in all white shirts, Sunderland in all red and, with a strong wind blowing over the Leazes Stand, the Wearsiders coped with the difficult conditions far better. United made the mistake of fielding Jimmy Scoular when unfit and they lacked authority in midfield. Sunderland played a tight, close-marking game completely dominating United's attempts to get into the match. For some reason the side's famous battling spirit was missing, as one Sunderland player noted, "They never seemed to fight back". Two goals from Bill Holden sent the Rokerites into the semi-final. It was a bitter reverse. Jackie Milburn said, "We were always the best side in those days and this defeat was almost unthinkable".

Following that demoralising set back United only won one of their ten remaining games and the season ended sourly. Crowds drifted away and gates were down to 20,000. The local press reported that, "United's supporters passed a vote of no confidence in their team". Vic Keeble had a prolific season being top goalscorer with 29 league and Cup goals. Yet Keeble was never too popular with the fans in spite of his success in finding the net. He liked the ball in the air rather than on the floor, and to a high ball he was quite a handful. It was jokingly remarked that Vic would even take a penalty with his head! He moved to West Ham United in 1957 and had a successful stay at Upton Park adding another 50 goals to the 67 he scored for the Magpies.

McMichael and Casey both appeared for the Irish, and Bobby Mitchell, like Milburn, gained a recall for his country. Popular Frank Brennan had gone to North Shields amidst fury that saw Players' Union leader, Jimmy Guthrie brand United as a "slave club".

On the Magpies return from a four match continental tour in which they played Atletico Madrid on the way, United immediately went on the search for new players. Youngsters from Ireland, George Eastham and, shortly afterwards, Dick Keith, both arrived at Gallowgate. They proved to be two of United's choice acquisitions in this period. Eastham hailed from a footballing family. Born in Blackpool, his father had appeared for Bolton and England, while elder brother Harry represented Liverpool - and once for Newcastle during the war. Dubbed the new Peter Doherty, Eastham was a frail looking inside-forward, but who possessed a grace on the ball. He cost £9,000 and was to rapidly show a deft touch in midfield, stroking passes around the field like an experienced master rather than a raw teenager. Stan Seymour made the comment, "George is one of my best ever buys".

Dick Keith stepped into Cowell's boots at right-back against Manchester United and was an immediate success. Indeed, he was honoured as the supporters' Player of the Year at the end of the season. He also cost £9,000 and like Eastham proved a bargain. The 23 year old went on to appear on 223 occasions for United and was soon to be a regular for Northern Ireland alongside his new team-mate Alf McMichael. Tragically he was killed in 1967 following an accident in a builders yard, a couple of years after leaving United for Bournemouth.

Irish international wing-half Tommy Casey.

Ron Batty, a loyal servant to Newcastle United.

Below: Dick Keith about to tackle Manchester City's Fagan. Stokoe and Batty are in attendance.

With the directors trying most of their staff in the new season, including several local youngsters too, United never had a settled team until late in the proceedings. Their away form was poor and early on they went down 5-2, 4-0 and 6-1 in the space of four away matches. They did manage to beat Sunderland in a thunderstorm, 2-1 at Roker Park, a game in which Bob Stokoe had been involved in an off the field bust up with Sunderland players. By Christmas Newcastle were in a relegation position, but Sunderland again eased the Magpies problems. United defeated the Wearsiders, then in a worse situation than Newcastle, by a 6-2 scoreline on a foggy afternoon. United's young lions tore the star studded Roker eleven apart with part-timer Alex Tait scoring a hat-trick.

EURO OPPOSITION

With European opposition starting to attract a lot of interest in Britain, United invited Barcelona to St James Park in August 1960. The game proved to be a classic watched by an enthralled attendance. Ken McKenzie in The Journal wrote that it was, "the finest game I have ever seen". Newcastle were 3-0 up at half-time, but a second half onslaught by the Catalans gave Barcelona a memorable 4-3 victory. Newcastle supporters witnessed a marvellous hat-trick by one of the greats of football - Hungarian Sandor Kocsis. The Spaniards also included international stars Ramellets, Saurez and Czibor. Other clubs to face United in challenge contests included Brazilians Bela Vista, who United thrashed 12-1 - White and Bottom claiming five goals each - TSV Munich and Torpedo Moscow. United's first taste of actual European competition took place when they participated in the Anglo-French-Scottish Friendship Cup in August 1960. They defeated Racing Club de Paris both home and away.

Captain Jimmy Scoular exchanges pennants with the Barcelona skipper before a challenge match in May 1958. The Spaniards won 3-2 before a 50,000 crowd. A return contest was to take place at Gallowgate.

Latter day FA Cup foes and holders of the trophy, Manchester City were United's Third Round opponents during the first week of January. It was a match billed as the "game of the year", a battle of Cup giants. Like United, City were struggling in Division One, but both clubs threw off their league worries to provide supporters with two scintillating games of football. On a blustery afternoon at a rain soaked St James Park and before 58,000, the match ended all square at one goal each. Newcastle were fortunate to have another opportunity, but Ronnie Simpson made several good stops while City's international centre-forward Bill McAdams missed a simple chance at the close. United had grabbed the lead through White's bullet header and Johnstone netted a deserved leveller.

A trip to The Den, home of Millwall, was the prize for the winners of the replay on Wednesday. Newcastle made a surprise team choice with Tait coming in for Milburn and young Bill Punton standing down for Mitchell. United also had a boost with the return to form of Jimmy Scoular and what an inspiration the granite Scot proved to be. The match, again on a heavy, muddy turf and before a big crowd, started with constant City pressure that had United reeling. They scored three goals within 30 minutes, the first a Bob Stokoe own-goal trying to clear over his bar. Johnstone netted with a good header then a minute later Fagan grabbed the third following a glorious through pass by McAdams. It looked as though Newcastle were as good as dead, but the old Cup spirit was soon to pull United back to equalise, and on to victory.

Towards half-time they got into the game for the first time in the match. At the interval though, they were still 3-0 down, but as the whistle went for the restart it took only three minutes for Newcastle to reduce the arrears. Bill Curry was sent sprawling in the box. An obvious penalty and Tommy Casey's rocket shot just went past Trautmann's brave parry. Scoular rallied his team and it was all United, yet minutes were ticking by and they needed another goal. With 16 minutes left Tait did the trick, scoring a goal of a lifetime to give United a chance of saving the game. Just after Dick Keith had hobbled to the dug out, Reg Davies slipped a short ball to the stand-in centre-forward deep inside his own half. Tait began a splendid run beating five City defenders before finally hammering an unstoppable drive into the net from an acute angle. From Bedlington and a former England Youth cap, Tait was highly thought of at St James Park, but as a part-timer - he was training to become a teacher - always found it difficult to retain a place. However, at Maine Road on that evening he was the saviour.

United stormed forward for the equaliser and the pressure on the City goal was now intense. With five minutes left White dribbled towards the box. A ball to Davies who crossed for Curry to flash a header into the net on the run. The score was now 3-3 and in the sporting style of the era, even the City fans applauded the Magpie come-back. That

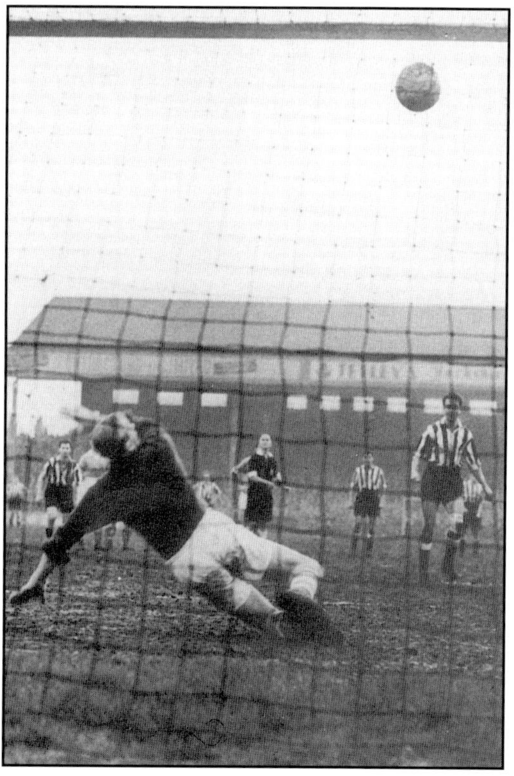

Tommy Casey blasts the ball past Bert Trautmann from the penalty spot in the thrilling Manchester City F.A. Cup replay.

Newcastle v Leicester City 1956. United's defence led by Scoular (right) about to close-in on this City forward. Note the line of old telegraph pole floodlights running along the Popular enclosure.

Below: Reg Davies makes an attempt on goal against Aston Villa. Milburn watches.

was not to be the end of the action in a truly remarkable tie. Extra-time arrived and within only a matter of minutes City were back in front when Bobby Johnstone netted his second of the game. Newcastle had it all to do again, and amazingly they did it.

Davies sent White away down the wing and he cut inside to blast a humming drive past Trautmann from the angle of the box. Two minutes later United's right winger was back again to whack a first time shot just under the bar and give United a 5-4 lead. That's how it remained, although there was still time for Dyson to hit a post for City. It was quite a game, arguably the club's most thrilling encounter. No-one thought that the epic at Fulham could have been bettered, but as Stan Seymour said later, "It was a stupendous tie".

United were caught on the rebound afterwards. They returned to Manchester, to Old Trafford and went down 6-1 to the Busby Babes, but a 3-1 home victory over Arsenal took Newcastle to their Fourth Round clash with Third Division Millwall. A record all-ticket crowd of over 45,000 saw battle commence and over 50 people were injured in the crush. Millwall were tremendous, United mediocre, and the Londoners' Stan Anslow grabbed two goals to end the Magpies season. The unfortunate Malcolm Scott, deputising for centre-half Stokoe, had a day to forget.

The Tynesiders finished in 17th position and had disappointed their fans again. Both Mitchell and Milburn were only a shade of their former selves and it had been a season of indecision on the field. The post-war boom was very much over - the black'n'whites were in decline. Goalscoring was shared between Davies, White and Milburn while the incident that robbed United of George Eastham ended the campaign on a sour note. In a clash with England captain Billy Wright at Molineux, the teenager broke his right leg and was out of action for several months. Albert Franks made his debut that season, a powerful barrel-chested half-back who possessed a mighty throw.

Before the 1957/58 season was under way, players received, at long last, an increase in wages to £17 per week and Jackie Milburn terminated his long stay at St James Park. He departed to become player-manager of Linfield. As the season started it became clear that United had problems. They struggled and were saved from relegation only on goal average with Sunderland going down with the same points. Newcastle's home form was one of the worst in all four divisions of the

Len White and Jimmy Scoular mobbed by autograph hunters.

Arthur Bottom, arrived from Cup oppenents York City.

Football League, and the worst in the club's history, yet they also possessed one of the best away records. They only won six games at St James Park, with the forwards constantly missing chances, and eleven defeats were recorded. Countless games were lost by the odd goal and the directors tried many different team combinations for a second season in a row. They also attempted to bring new talent into the squad going for Celtic's international star Willie Fernie, the outstanding forward in Scotland. United also tried to lure Spurs inside-forward Johnny Brooks, another established international, north. Both approaches failed.

Out of a miserable season however, one player suddenly exploded into action - Len White. While he did not transform United into a major force again, he certainly made a huge personal imprint on the club and its fans. White was handed Jackie Milburn's heralded No 9 shirt, while Vic Keeble by this time had moved to Upton Park. The ex miner had been in and out of the side, but now set forth on a goalscoring blitz that was only ended four years later by a crude tackle at White Hart Lane.

Some new signings were made, though not in a headlining way. Arthur Bottom arrived from York City's FA Cup side after netting 105 goals in 158 games. Irishman Jimmy Hill arrived as part of the Milburn deal, but failed to cause a change in the team's fortunes. Again young locals were drafted in; Jackie Bell (Evenwood), Ken Hale (Blyth), Bill McKinney (Wallsend) and John Nesbitt (South Shields). Gordon Hughes, from Tow Law Town, who had broken his leg last season just when he looked a brilliant find, came back strongly, as did another long term casualty, George Eastham.

Jackie Bell, one of several youngsters to break into the side as the decade closed.

Left-half Bell had a remarkable debut in a black'n'white shirt. Against Luton Town he had just turned 17 years-old and signed professional, then within the opening minutes scored from a corner - his first shot at goal! Bell promised to be a great new star with an urge to go forward at every opportunity. He just missed an England Under 23 cap. Arthur Bottom did well in a short, yet productive stay. His aggressive style and explosive shooting helped United scrape away from the relegation zone. He netted two on his debut and seven goals in only eight games. Teaming up with White, Newcastle scrambled to safety. In a vital game against Manchester City the Magpies rallied to the call and won 4-1. Two goals from Newcastle's centre-forward - one a brilliant solo dribble from his own half - set them on their way.

WORLD CUP HEROES

The World Cup finals of 1958 saw all four home nations qualify for the tournament in Sweden. Surprisingly it was the Irish who took the headlines with United's Alf McMichael, Dick Keith and Tommy Casey in their line-up. They reached the knockout stage eventually losing to France in the quarter-final. Ivor Allchurch was in the Welsh team and they too did well. Newcastle's maestro was an ever-present as Wales also reached the quarter-final, losing to Brazil, the eventual winners.

In the FA Cup, following a 6-1 victory at Plymouth that included a White hat-trick, the Magpies crashed to eventual Third Division (North) champions Scunthorpe United, this less than two weeks before the fateful Munich Air Disaster which stunned football and claimed the life of ex United star, Tom Curry. Scunthorpe thoroughly deserved their 3-1 success at Gallowgate, taken in style on a difficult icy surface. Few in the crowd were sure if the visitors' goal on half-time had counted, it was so close to the whistle. It had, but six minutes after the interval Paterson headed home the equaliser from a Mitchell corner. However Scunthorpe were quick to get back into their groove. Within five minutes a lob into the Tynesiders' goalmouth saw Simpson and McKinney collide and the ball rebounded to Eric Davies who had the simplest of tasks to make it 2-1. It was the killer goal. Newcastle's heads dropped and the Irons grabbed a third.

The 1957/58 season had bluntly been a mess. Many times the directors' team selection had players incensed, and on one occasion the line-up changed at the demand of the senior professionals. It was, not before time, agreed at board level to move with the times and appoint a full-time manager with complete authority for playing affairs. The directors had been busy during the past six months trying to find an adequate man to fill the position after nearly 30 months of committee rule. During the summer several candidates came to the head of the short-list. Swindon's Bert Head declined an offer, as did television commentator and ex Arsenal star, Wally Barnes. Grimsby chief Allenby Chilton and Reading manager Harry Johnston were both linked with the job too. Even then the position was noted as the hottest seat in football. Head made the comment, "You don't know how things would work out up there".

Before the end of June, 37 year-old ex Manchester United winger Charlie Mitten, a controversial character, was appointed by an unanimous board decision, although time was to reveal not all the directors approved of his methods. A first class player, he appeared on 161 occasions for the Old Trafford club scoring 61 goals and winning an FA Cup medal in 1948. Mitten represented England too, but was never one to conform to

Charlie Mitten (left) with director, and later Chairman, Wally Hurford.

traditions and possessed a personality that attracted publicity. And he liked it. He had been involved in the infamous Bogota incident in the summer of 1950 when along with several other star players he flew off to Colombia for a bag of gold worth £200 per week plus a £5,000 signing on fee. Suspended on his return to England, he later became Mansfield Town player-boss and had only a little over two years' experience when he was offered the Newcastle post.

Mitten immediately brought a fresh attitude into St James Park. Very much a tracksuit manager, he was keen on developing new tactics and introducing youngsters. Novel training methods were adopted and a new continental style strip introduced. Gone were the baggy pants and in came a flashy outfit which the fans never took to. Many of his ideas were, at the time revolutionary, but now, formality. He was often to be controversial, complaining bitterly about refereeing decisions. After one incident that incensed him, Mitten noted to the Football League, "I would ask your Committee to consider making referees and linesmen full time members, the officials to report to the nearest League club for training every day at 10.00am. A basic salary could be paid weekly - I would suggest £12 to £15". Perhaps Mitten was a decade ahead of his time.

The new manager realised his staff needed new blood and he searched the country for players. His most important signing was the £28,000 he paid for the Golden Boy of Wales, Ivor Allchurch, who arrived early into the season from Swansea nearly six years after United's first approach for the schemer. He made a great start netting twice on his debut against Leicester City and at once Allchurch became respected as any before him at St James Park. A regular for Wales since 1951 - he collected 68 caps all told - and possessing a complete repertoire of skills, Ivor rarely put a pass astray in midfield and was always a threat from distance, although many of his powerful drives seemed fated to crash against the woodwork. Teaming up with the youthful Eastham, United's midfield had class written all over it. Allchurch played in excess of 700 first class games and netted well over 250 goals. Later he was awarded the MBE for his services to football.

Other notable additions were goalkeeper Brian Harvey from Wisbech Town to replace the injured Simpson, Scottish winger John McGuigan who was once tipped for a full cap, and another flanker in Billy Wright, ex Leicester City. It was however, only Allchurch who stood out as an excellent buy. Mitten also tried for another Welshman in Mel Charles, but lost out to Arsenal.

Following a harrowing beginning for the new boss - a 5-1 home defeat by Blackburn Rovers in front of a large expectant crowd - Mitten's Marvels, as they were to be dubbed, set the Tyne alight with some thrilling, attacking football and home gates rose to over 50,000 again. Inconsistency was the team's drawback though, and after reaching 7th position they slipped to 15th, then rose to final place of 11th. Injuries to Stokoe and White were difficult to cope with, while Mitten was confounded at his side's inability to take penalty kicks. In a run of early season games, six kicks were missed by five different players! White(2), McMichael, Allchurch, McGuigan and 17 year-old John Mitten, the boss's son and an amateur making his debut against West Bromwich Albion, all failed to convert. Two weeks later Newcastle were awarded penalty number seven and Jackie Bell - another teenager - stepped up this time and lashed the ball past the Burnley 'keeper.

Left: Welsh maestro, Ivor Allchurch runs onto the Gallowgate pitch. He won 68 caps for his country.

Below: Charlie Mitten issues instructions before a match. Left to right, back: Whitehead, Greener, Wright, Eastham, McGuigan. Front: Mitchell, Scoular, Curry, Taylor, Allchurch,

Chelsea defeated United 4-1 in the FA Cup at the first hurdle and on Tyneside too. After two postponements because of heavy snow the game went ahead on a thick slime of mud on top of a hard pitch. Within six minutes the Pensioners were 2-0 in front and after the defeat Mitten was reported to the Football Association because of remarks made to referee Arthur Ellis. Chelsea also provided the opposition for one of the most astonishing games in the annals of both clubs.

At Stamford Bridge during September, 90 minutes were played that prompted one journalist to record that the game, "positively hypnotised onlookers". And why not - the match ended 6-5 to Chelsea! It was a football spectacular, a game that saw the lead change no less than five times. At the interval United were a goal down with Chelsea going in 3-2 ahead. It had been an absorbing first half, but nothing compared to the next 45 minutes of drama. Billy Wright got the equaliser, then Albert Franks half hit a 30 yarder to give Newcastle a 4-3 lead. Davies then scored a marvellous solo effort - ending through the keeper's legs - to put United two goals ahead, but then Chelsea hit back as Newcastle slackened. Within 16 minutes the home side fired three goals past Stewart Mitchell in the Magpies' goal, one a terrible blunder by United's Glaswegian 'keeper. Ron Tindall got the winner in this enthralling game, a diving header five minutes from the end, although there was time left for United to miss a sitter at the death. Alf McMichael said of the meeting, "The crowd was going crazy and so was the game". Chelsea also won 2-1 at St James Park in the return league meeting and had proved a thorn in United's side that season.

Events off the field started to make headlines at St James Park with a well publicised disagreement between recent Chairman, Stan Seymour, and new leader, William McKeag. Both were direct and forthright characters and while both hailed from a pit community, they had very different upbringings - one from the working class, the other from a military and college background. They both undoubtedly wished to see Newcastle United remain and prosper as a power, but their ways of achieving that goal were in contrast, and it caused friction and, along the way, several fireworks.

Chairman William McKeag (left) getting in shape for some of his boardroom confrontations. Pictured with boxing star Henry Cooper.

They had differing views on how the club should be run, Seymour wanting to remain as director in charge of team affairs and McKeag wishing to appoint, and support, a young, active manager in the shape of Charlie Mitten. A rivalry simmered in the background during the latter years of the fifties and did little to help the team's performance. One correspondent wrote, "the publicity associated with Newcastle United suggested that St James Park was a storm centre rather than the home of a club of high tradition and peaceful, united endeavour". George Eastham wrote in his autobiography, "When Stan Seymour said black, Alderman William McKeag almost invariably said white". Manager Charlie Mitten had an unenviable position, he was quoted as saying, "Trying to manage the team and restructure the club was almost impossible because of the warring factions on the board". Mitten though had been warned. Before he accepted the appointment old friends, Matt Busby and Bill Shankly advised him about the power politics at St James Park. They both noted the job wouldn't be easy. They were right.

TOWERS ARRIVE

The club's new £40,000 floodlighting system was switched on for the Football League versus Scottish League clash in March 1958. Almost 49,000 turned up for what was a virtual England v Scotland meeting. Derek Kevan scored a hat-trick as the Football League won 4-1. The massive new 150 foot towers, each carrying 45 arc lamps were the highest in the United Kingdom and a Tyneside landmark for the next two decades. ITV covered the second half of the game and paid, what was then, a staggering fee of £2,750 to the Football League. The power of television was slowly edging its way into the game.

McKeag, a local politician, was adventurous in his plans for Newcastle United. On his appointment as Chairman in 1958 he said, "My greatest ambition is to see United get their sights on the European Cup. We have had our share of glory in the FA Cup and League. Let's go ahead to add to our laurels the glamour and glory of the European trophy". Yet McKeag's reign was one of problem after problem. Apart from managerial difficulties, he had to negotiate with the City Council over ground redevelopment when United applied to construct a two tier stand on the Popular terrace, a £250,000 plan which would have increased capacity to 80,000. The council's planners, led by T.Dan Smith, one of McKeag's main political rivals, couldn't accept the club's proposals. It was to be the start of a long and acrimonious saga that would run for over a decade.

William McKeag had been appointed to the board in 1944 after being a fierce critic during the thirties and was a noted figure in the north east. Born in Belmont, one of a large family, he served in the army through two world wars and saw action in several countries including Russia where he was decorated for bravery. McKeag was then elected as a Liberal MP for Durham City and later was Lord Mayor of Newcastle for two periods as well as being a Governor of the Royal Victoria Infirmary and

Royal Grammar School. Always interested in sport, he was at one stage a director of Durham City during their Football League days and also ran at Powderhall as a noted sprinter.

Events in United's boardroom came to a head as the decade drew to a close. A clash in January 1959 saw McKeag offer to resign if Seymour did likewise. As it turned out neither did. Rebel shareholders were to come on to the scene as well. The boardroom unrest, decisions regarding managerial control, not to mention a decline in terms of playing performances, prompted shareholders Alf Hirst and Ernest Pringle to form a pressure group. Others backed the pair including Frank McArdle and Walter Dix. They wanted an end to the bickering and representation on the board through their champion, Lord Westwood, then an outsider. It was the start of another long and unsavory business, this time of shareholder wrangles that lasted on and off for all of thirty years and more. When McKeag ended his stint as Chairman in 1960, he observed it was, "a task of the most thankless and frustrating kind". He continued on the board, and very much an active member, until his death in October 1972.

The close season of 1959 was taken up with a tug of war battle over the services of Charlie Mitten. After only a year in charge speculation mounted that he was on his way to Leeds United. Newcastle's board were, some said, split over his continued appointment and were undecided over the length of any new contract. The Seymour and McKeag camps feuded and eventually came up with a new package....Mitten accepting a three year deal. Jimmy Scoular made the comment, "The players are delighted. We feel that our manager has done something for us". Stan Seymour observed, "I hope this means peace. It is up to us to forget the bickerings of the past and to give the manager our full support".

A catastrophic beginning to the new season was in store for Newcastle for the second time in a row. Tottenham Hotspur ran rings around United's defence with winger Cliff Jones having a field day. They lost 5-1 on the opening day again and then fell at Birmingham and Manchester United. Both were close defeats, 4-3 and 3-2, results which typified United's side then. Mitten did not hesitate at making changes.

Bob Stokoe, to captain the Magpies as a new decade approached.

It worked too, for after November they slowly, but surely climbed to a comforting and respectable 8th position, on the way playing some wonderful thrill a minute football with plenty of goals. White had another exceptional season and, together with schemers Eastham and Allchurch, the Magpies possessed a forward trio the talk of the league. United's two inside-forwards linked perfectly, the experienced old head and the enthusiastic starlet. They provided ammunition for the effervescent White who hit the net from right, left and centre positions. Many United players, and fans, noted the combination as the best they had ever seen. Each complimented the other to provide a dangerous unit.

United had slipped to 18th place when a marvellous 8-2 victory over Everton, two days after Guy Fawkes night, started the revival. Only 23,727 saw that cracking game in which the White-Allchurch-Eastham partnership devastated the Merseysiders. In the first six minutes the Magpies were two up with rasping shots from the edge of the penalty area from wingers George Luke and Gordon Hughes. Five minutes later White sped through to net as Everton appealed for offside. Eastham scored number four from the penalty-spot before half-time. In the 49th minute White grabbed his second and Allchurch gave the home side a 6-0 advantage ten minutes later. United then sat back and allowed Everton's Bobby Collins room to create havoc. The visitors struck with two goals, both from the lively Thomas, but Everton's come-back only served to jerk Newcastle out of their doze. White completed his hat-trick and Welsh star, Allchurch notched his second of the day. Before the close White was near to making the scoresheet 9-2 when his shot crashed against the post.

Winger Gordon Hughes, one of several new forwards tried.

During November and December, United scored 26 goals and in the first game of January hit another seven! Over 57,000 spectators witnessed Newcastle give their fans a great holiday treat by defeating Mitten's old club Manchester United 7-3. White grabbed another hat-trick to take his tally to 17, with only half the season completed. Following on quickly were two classic FA Cup ties with 4th placed Wolves, a club in the middle of a memorable period. A huge Gallowgate crowd of 62,000 saw 90 tense minutes of Cup football. Both clubs had the Wembley look and it was United who stormed off to a flying start. Allchurch hit an angled shot past 'keeper Finlayson without him getting anywhere near it. Wolves, however, were a powerful side and came back scoring twice and it was left to George Eastham to strike a 20 yard equaliser. In the replay under the Molineux lights, United gave two suicidal

ANGLO SCOTTISH LEAGUE

The Anglo Scottish Floodlit League started in 1955/56 after an unsuccessful attempt to start a cross Border League during the previous year. The competition however, was riddled with problems from start to finish with both ruling associations north and south of the Cheviots wanting it to have no place in the game, and to this aim banned competitive matches between the two countries. After three seasons of unofficial tournaments nothing came of the bright idea, then in days before European football had taken hold. The FA wanted the British League idea completely squashed and even threatened to expel clubs - including United - from Football League competition if they continued to take part. In Newcastle's first game, against Hearts during October 1955, Bob Stokoe was substituted by Ken Waugh and, later in the match Frank Brennan went off for Stan Keery - the first substitutes in a 'competitive' match by United.

goals away in the snow and Wolves were value for their 4-2 win.

George Luke, a local lad in his second spell with the club, had a good season on the left wing. Several other youngsters were drafted in. George Heslop appeared at centre-half, but was a player who made a bigger name at pastures new, with Everton and Manchester City. Bill McKinney developed further. Mean and solid at full-back or wing-half, he had a spell of successful penalty kicks which he sent into the net with astonishing power.

The sun soaked months of 1960 saw Gateshead kicked out of the Football League leaving United as Tyneside's sole representative. The coming season marked the beginning of a new era in football as advances in the game continued at a rapid pace. The retain and transfer system was to be altered - with Newcastle United at the heart of it - and the maximum wage rule was at last discarded with Johnny Haynes claiming the first £100 pay packet. It was a year in which Tottenham were to lift the double and when home stars like Greaves and Hitchens ventured to Italy. The modern game had very much arrived. It was a season that saw Newcastle score almost 100 goals, yet also concede 100 too.

Young England star George Eastham. A brilliant midfielder, but one to end up in court with the club.

The Magpies found the net ten times in their two opening games winning 3-2 at Deepdale, Preston through a Len White hat-trick and then Fulham were given a 7-2 hiding four days later on Tyneside. And that's how the season remained - goals, and more goals, but unfortunately the results after this enterprising opening mostly went the wrong way. Newcastle's defence, lacking the services of the experienced Stokoe and Scoular, was totally unable to stop any set of forwards scoring and youngsters Heslop, Thompson and McKinney had a harrowing time. West Bromwich Albion won 6-0, Arsenal 5-0, in the space of a couple of weeks and United inevitably found themselves in arrears before they had even settled down. What was to be a disastrous season could have been a lot worse, but for United's forward play which was as good as the defence was bad.

White scored 29 goals, but he couldn't stop little Colchester United - joint bottom of Division Three - knocking United out of the first Football League Cup tournament. They lost by 4-1 and had been out-skilled and outsmarted. No-one worried too much about that reverse though, as the League Cup was not well supported during its infancy. Indeed several top clubs, including Arsenal and Spurs, boycotted the competition. Newcastle experimented with juniors and reserves and into the side were thrown Heslop, Mitten, Duncan Neale, Charlie Woods and George Dalton.

Thrill a minute action continued. Against West Ham United, the Magpies found themselves 5-2 down with only eleven minutes remaining, yet quite astonishingly Newcastle sent the 20,106 St James Park crowd home breathless with a come-back to clinch a point. McGuigan latched on to a Bobby Mitchell cross, then Bell made it 5-4. It was left to the veteran Mitchell to bulge the back of the net for the equalising goal and earn the biggest cheer of the season. And the game wasn't finished even then. With seconds on the referee's watch remaining, John Lyall kicked off the Hammers' line to deny United the come-back of come-backs. Against Wolves another high scoring draw took place, Newcastle coming from behind again to level the contest 4-4. All eight goals were sizzlers with Mitchell once more having one of his golden days, netting a quite brilliant equaliser eight minutes from the close. End to end football continued all season.

High Court appointment. United's delegation for the Eastham hearing in 1963, left to right: McKeag (director), Hurford (director), Mitten (ex-manager) and Barker (secretary).

There were, however more rumblings within the club. Key playmakers Eastham and Allchurch both asked for transfers and the forthcoming Eastham controversy was to rock the side severely. The schemer had developed into a brilliant young talent. Slightly built, he graduated into England's Under 23 side and was a regular for his country at inside-right. Had he remained at Newcastle, Eastham would have certainly have played for the full national side - which he did eventually do, but not as a Newcastle United player. Relationships between player, manager and the club's officials had deteriorated. Firstly, he had a dispute over a club house, then over wages. Eastham also wanted a job outside football - the club would not grant its permission. Following that, there was a petty argument over match-tickets for his father, then manager of Accrington Stanley. George insisted he warranted seat tickets, while the club's administrators would only hand over a terrace pass. There were other disputes too and boss Charlie Mitten labelled his inside-forward, "The guy with the biggest head, the shortest arms, and the deepest pockets in the business".

A transfer request was lodged - ironically on the same day Allchurch sent one in too, although for very differing reasons, the Welshman wishing to return home to his native country. Eastham was to record, "It became a joke between us to see who would escape first"! The club was adamant he must stay. Eastham was adamant he must go and a further two requests were lodged and two denials given. Stalemate ensued and Eastham appealed to the Football League Management Committee, but it refused to interfere. An added quirk came into the debate too - the very heart of the argument that ended up in the High Court. Eastham had not signed a new contract, but under the existing rules, Newcastle United, if they offered the same terms as before(which they had), could hold onto the player for as long as they wanted. The system was clearly iniquitous, but had survived - until now.

Eastham took his case to the Professional Footballers' Association and Cliff Lloyd and Jimmy Hill, acting as advisers, persuaded the player to take his claims all the way as a Test Case to football's archaic system. On the 13th October 1960 a writ was issued to his employers, Newcastle United, its directors and manager, plus the Football Association and Football League, alleging the club had deprived him of the opportunity to earn his living. For months people within the game speculated that Eastham's dispute would make football history. For the first time in 60 years a new deal for footballers was likely to succeed. Alec Hardaker, the shrewd secretary of the Football League later said, "there had never been any doubt in my mind that the moment one player stepped forward to challenge the legality of the old retain and transfer system its days were numbered".

The case received huge publicity - Newcastle United's name was in the news for the wrong reasons. Most of the public - away from the Gallowgate faithful - were on Eastham's side, while the game itself was split. He had a just cause and football, in the shape of Newcastle United and the game's rules were given a rough ride. Even United's board were not unanimous on their view of the controversy. Director Wilf Taylor, a League Committee member too, wanted the club to release Eastham and get out of what was becoming an ugly mess.

The man at the centre of the storm, Eastham, said to newspapers, "I am being branded as a bad boy because I want the right of every free man, to work for whom I please and when I please". George turned his back on the Magpies going on enforced strike for fully five months. He received no wages and headed south to a family friend, Ernie Clay, later Chairman of Fulham, who offered him a job as a cork salesman in Reigate, while he also did a spot of coaching for Redhill FC.

Before the dispute was brought before the High Court, Eastham was granted his wish, a transfer from Newcastle. The club's board eventually saw no use in holding out to the bitter end and in November 1960 accepted a £47,500 bid from Arsenal. Eastham though, was to carry on with his case, in his own words, "I knew I was right and had to prove it". Legal proceedings were slow and complex. The Court at last heard the case in June 1963 just as Britain was preoccupied with another scandal - the Profumo affair, one that rocked the government just as this one rocked soccer. Wilf Taylor gave evidence on behalf of Newcastle United. A future Vice President of the League, he had the unenviable position of trying to defend the club's position. He was a small, thin man, full of fun and very likeable, but the High Court proceedings were anything but fun for Taylor and for Newcastle United.

CHARITY SHIELD TREBLE

For the third time during the fifties, United lost the FA Charity Shield to the League Champions. In 1951 it had been Tottenham, 1952 Manchester United, and in 1955 Chelsea inflicted a 3-0 defeat at Stamford Bridge. All three games had been entertaining contests and against the Pensioners, Milburn hit both the bar and post. Crowds though failed to turn up for this now prestigious event. At White Hart Lane 27,760 were present, at Old Trafford only 11,381 while 12,802 attended Stamford Bridge.

Len White and Jimmy Scoular in a moment of relaxation playing snooker.

Jimmy Scoular (left) and Ivor Allchurch take a bath following a training session.

During July, Judge Wilberforce delivered his 16,000 word masterpiece that was to change football. He held that the rule which allowed a player to be retained was, under Common Law, illegal, "an undue restraint of trade". The judge however dismissed the player's claim for damages. No club could now hold a player at the end of their contract, although it did not mean total freedom - that came in 1978 - but it heralded a huge step

SIX TEAMS, FIFTY PRO'S

In season 1958/59 United fielded no fewer than six teams in regular competition and had a professional staff approaching 50 players.

First team	Division One
Reserve team	Central League
A Team	Northern Alliance
B Team	Northern Combination
Senior N's	Northern Intermediate League
Junior N's	Newcastle & District Junior League

forward. Eastham had won his crusade and released the so called "soccer slaves". Clubs had now to start dealing with players in a modern, business-like way and to treat them like any other professional employee, whether an accountant, banker or salesman. In summing up Eastham wrote in 1964, "Had Newcastle played fair with me, there would have been no dispute and I would probably have been playing for them now". As it was George deserted what was, in 1960, a sinking ship and Tyneside's fans never forgave him for that. Indeed he was pelted with peanuts and apples on his return with Arsenal. However, his special skills were a big miss. While a rebel during his early days, George became a highly respected player. Capped 19 times for England, he served Stoke City well also and was awarded the OBE in 1973 before emigrating to South Africa.

Albert Scanlon emerges for his United debut in November 1960.

As 1961 opened, and with the Eastham saga taking its course in the background, Newcastle United needed to concentrate on a relegation fight, but instead set off on an FA Cup run with a 5-0 victory over Fulham. That afternoon belonged to 20 year-old Duncan Neale, a wing-half who graduated to the side that season after signing from Ilford in 1959. He scored a hat-trick of finely struck goals when he was supposed to be marking Johnny Haynes out of the match. Stockport County, from the recently formed Fourth Division were United's opponents in the 4th Round, again at Gallowgate. The 4-0 scoreline in United's favour suggests that the game was clear cut. It wasn't and Stockport pushed the Tynesiders close for a long period. Two goals were scored by young Charlie Woods, Mitten's replacement for Eastham.

Before the 5th Round match with Stoke City, the black'n'whites searched in vain for league points. Now 20th in the table luck was not on the club's side. They lost 5-3 at Leicester, a result so typical of the season. In spite of conceding five they had actually deserved to win. After taking a look at Leeds United's defender Jack Charlton, Mitten signed John McGrath from Bury in an attempt to plug the leaking defence. He cost £24,000 plus Bob Stokoe who headed for Gigg Lane to become boss. Capped by England's Under 23 side, McGrath was to take several seasons before he turned into a commanding defender. Other new faces arrived too as Mitten probed for the right blend. Outside-left Albert Scanlon, another England Under 23 player and the manager's nephew, moved from Manchester United where he was still recovering from injuries in the Munich air crash. Another forward, Irish international Liam Tuohy promised much in his opening matches then faded into obscurity. It was over £50,000 worth of talent that flopped for United's boss.

Liam Tuohy arrived on Tyneside from Ireland.

Another helping of FA Cup fortune came United's way as they ended up in the quarter-finals at the expense of Stoke. For the majority of the game, however, City were the better team, but an unfortunate injury to their veteran England forward Dennis Wilshaw, in a clash with centre-half Bill Thompson, swayed the tie United's way. They won 3-1 and Wilshaw was carried off with a suspected broken leg.

A crowd of 54,829 were at Gallowgate for the 6th Round clash with razor sharp Second Division promotion candidates Sheffield United. In the opening quarter of the match Newcastle's dream of another visit to the Twin Towers was systematically destroyed by a fast moving Yorkshire machine. United never got into the game and fell 3-1 thanks to a hat-trick from Billy Russell in the first 18 minutes of play.

With their FA Cup sortie over, United had to knuckle down for First Division survival and scramble clear of the drop in the remaining eleven games. They started well. A 2-1 victory over Aston Villa then a point with Manchester United and two at Tottenham who were marching on to take the title. Mitten had beaten the transfer deadline to bring Jimmy Harrower and Dave Hollins into the battle. He also tried to bolster his side by signing George Herd of Clyde for a record £40,000, but Sunderland nipped in to his annoyance. Former Brighton 'keeper, Hollins saved a Blanchflower penalty on his debut and played like a man inspired in the tussle at White Hart Lane. United became the only side to beat the magical Spurs eleven at home. However, the victory was expensive when an ankle injury to the Magpies main hope of steering clear of relegation, Len White, rocked the club. In a tackle with Dave Mackay, White was left in agony and out for the rest of the season.

Dick Keith immediately followed the centre-forward on the treatment table when he damaged knee ligaments in the rampant 6-1 win by Chelsea at St James Park. Remarkably the score was 0-0 at the interval then Jimmy Greaves struck four goals past Hollins, on his home debut. United looked doomed. They couldn't do anything to halt the slide and went down with Preston North End following a two horse race to beat the drop between United and Blackpool. With four games remaining, the Tynesiders were a point better off than Blackpool, but the Seasiders had a vital extra match. The black'n'whites fell heavily to Everton, 4-0, and in a crucial do-or-die battle with their rivals at Bloomfield Road lost again, 2-1. Blackpool then picked up a draw in their extra game at Manchester City to have a two point advantage over United. Yet the club's destiny continued to the last game of the season. After United scored four against Bolton

IT'S A CORNER

When Newcastle defeated Sunderland 6-2 at St James Park in December 1956, United forced 23 corners to Sunderland's twelve - a total of 35 corners in the game!

Wanderers, their rivals had to lose heavily while the Magpies needed an emphatic win. Newcastle won 4-2 against Blackburn Rovers, but the Seasiders drew 3-3 in a return game with Manchester City and United were a point adrift, which was really two as Blackpool's goal average was far superior. They went down the way they had played all season, with another hatful of goals.

The scoring record speaks for itself. United netted 86 times, one of the highest-scoring teams in the division, but an incredible 109 were conceded, a club record. Perhaps the fact that the side was skippered by no fewer than five different players summed up the sorry campaign.

Newcastle's decline was complete. From FA Cup champions to a relegated side. Attendances dropped too, from a still healthy average of 37,237 in 1959/60 to only 29,000 in the relegation season. It was the first time they had dropped below 30,000 since World War Two. The club was to face financial problems for the first time in over 15 years.

WINGERS DOMINATE

Newcastle United's squad in the 1960/61 season had a familiar ring to it. The playing list included no fewer than six outside-lefts and four outside-rights! They were; Luke, McGuigan, Mitten, Mitchell, Scanlon, Tuohy, Hodgson, Hughes, Marshall and Wilson. On several occasions United fielded four wingers in the forward line with another ex outside-right - Len White - at centre-forward. Certainly Mitten, himself a flanker in his playing days, had a likening for the position.

New goalkeeper, Welsh international Dave Hollins.

Gordon Hughes jumps to send the ball past the visitors' goalkeeper at St. James Park.

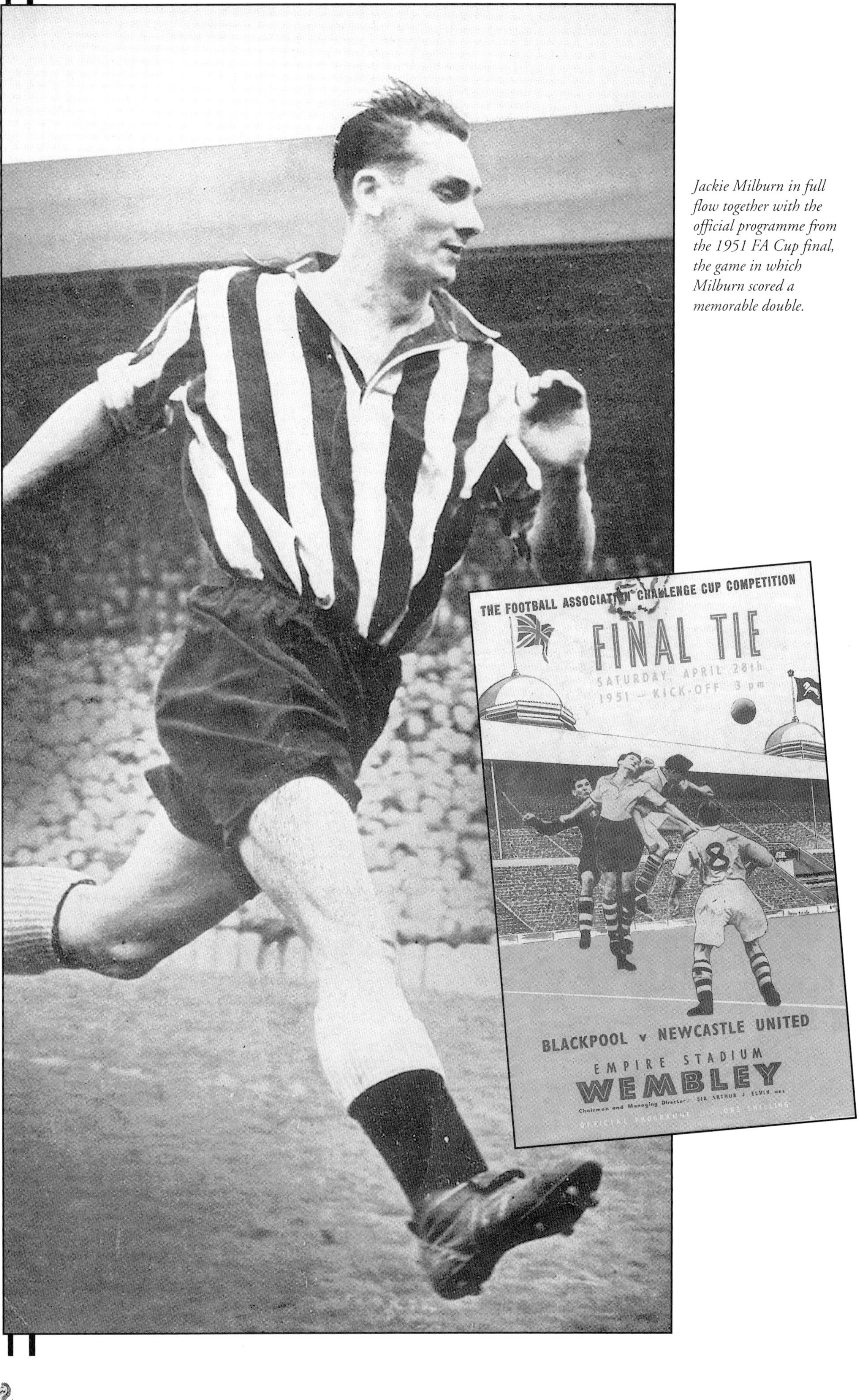

Jackie Milburn in full flow together with the official programme from the 1951 FA Cup final, the game in which Milburn scored a memorable double.

Victorian supporters' card featuring Newcastle East End's Harry Jeffrey and Bob Crielly, two stars of the club's pioneering days. Note that East End's colours were red and white at that time.

Another souvenir from the Victorian era, issued by Sharpe of Bradford who produced several of these cards at the turn of the century.

St. James Park after redevelopment in 1905 with the new West Stand, seating 4,680 spectators, the pride of the North East. The stadium remained as illustrated into the 1930's.

The front cover of a dinner and menu card in celebration of United's League Championship victory in 1907. United saw off the challenge from Bristol City to clinch their second title in three years.

England full-back Frank Hudspeth who holds United's appearance record for an outfield player. The Tynesider played 472 league and Cup fixtures for the Magpies.

Bill McCracken, one of the game's most colourful and noted footballers of all time. At St. James Park for all of 19 years, the Irish international was largely responsible for changing the offside law in 1925.

Centre-forward Neil Harris who was a prolific scorer as Newcastle headed for Wembley Stadium in 1924. Pictured wearing the club's 1920's change colours - a white shirt with black banding.

Souvenirs from United's 1932 F.A. Cup victory, the infamous 'Over The Line' final. Match programme and ticket, together with Roddie McKenzie's winners' medal. All are on display in the Club Museum.

The legendary Hughie Gallacher, the 5'5" Scot who became such a favourite on Tyneside for five years. No other player can better his strike-rate in a black'n'white shirt.

Sammy Weaver who joined the club from Hull City as a youngster and developed into a noted England wing-half. He possessed perhaps the longest ever throw football has seen.

One of Newcastle's many terrace heroes of the immediate post-war years, Bobby Mitchell, who thrilled spectators with amazing runs on the left touchline.

Wembley 1955. Skipper Jimmy Scoular proudly hoists the F.A. Cup on the shoulders of Bobby Mitchell and Bob Stokoe following the 3-1 victory over Manchester City.

Goalkeeper Ronnie Simpson in action. The Scot had a remarkable career, making his debut as a 14 year-old and playing on until he was almost 40.

Following United's second F.A. Cup triumph in successive years in 1952, the club embarked on a tour of South Africa. Illustrated is the Board of Trade Export Licence allowing the trophy to be taken with them. Also pictured is George Robledo's winners' medal from the 1-0 victory over Arsenal.

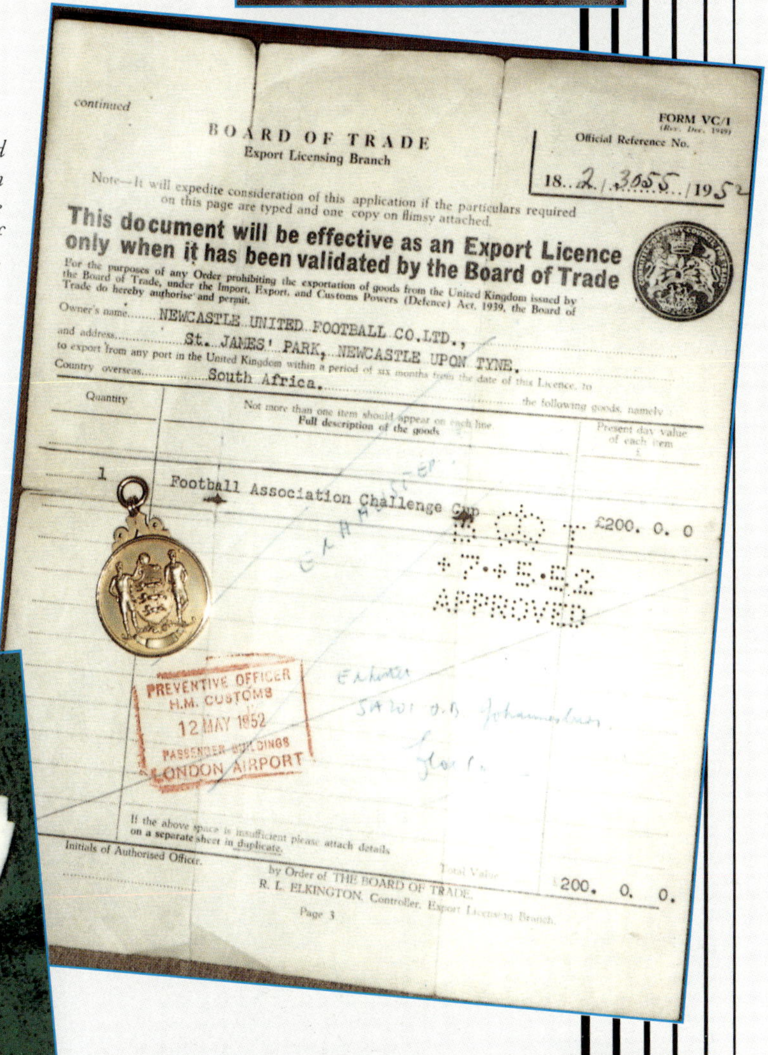

continued

FORM VC/1
(Rev. Dec. 1949)

BOARD OF TRADE
Export Licensing Branch

Official Reference No.
18..2./.3055../1952

Note—It will expedite consideration of this application if the particulars required on this page are typed and one copy on flimsy attached.

This document will be effective as an Export Licence only when it has been validated by the Board of Trade

For the purposes of any Order prohibiting the exportation of goods from the United Kingdom issued by the Board of Trade, under the Import, Export, and Customs Powers (Defence) Act, 1939, the Board of Trade do hereby authorise and permit.

Owner's name........NEWCASTLE UNITED FOOTBALL CO.LTD.,
and address..............St. JAMES' PARK, NEWCASTLE UPON TYNE.
to export from any port in the United Kingdom within a period of six months from the date of this Licence, to
Country overseas..............South Africa.
..............the following goods, namely :

Quantity	Not more than one item should appear on each line Full description of the goods	Present day value of each item £
1	Football Association Challenge Cup	£200. 0. 0

17.5.52
APPROVED

PREVENTIVE OFFICER
H.M. CUSTOMS
12 MAY 1952
PASSENGER BUILDINGS
LONDON AIRPORT

If the above space is insufficient please attach details on a separate sheet in duplicate.

Initials of Authorised Officer. Total Value 200. 0. 0.

by Order of THE BOARD OF TRADE.
R. L. ELKINGTON, Controller, Export Licensing Branch.

Page 3

One of Jackie Milburn's international shirts from his 13 appearances for England. Wor Jackie netted nine goals in those games and many judged he should have won double the number of caps.

Bob Stokoe, on United's staff from 1947 to 1961. He was a grand servant to the Magpies and never lost his fondness for the club in a long career in the game as player and manager.

Newcastle's line-up wearing Charlie Mitten's new continental style strip as the 1950's decade drew to a close. Left to right, back: Neale, McKinney, Stokoe, Garrow, McMichael, Bell. Front: Hughes, Allchurch, White, Mitchell, Scanlon.

Former England wing-half Stan Anderson leading United out at St. James Park shortly after moving from Wear to Tyne in a headline transfer in 1963.

United's half-back line of 1964/65. John McGrath flanked by left, Stan Anderson and right, Jim Iley. They were the cornerstone to the Magpies' successful return to Division One.

Inter Cities Fairs Cup action from the United v Real Zaragoza tie in Spain on New Year's Day 1969. Wyn Davies dives to head one of Newcastle's all important away goals.

Police with dogs struggle to restore order as Rangers fans invade the St. James Park pitch during the semi-final second leg.

The dramatic penalty incident at Ibrox in the Fairs Cup semi-final of 1969. Andy Penman fires the ball towards the United net, but Willie McFaul brings off a brilliant save.

Wyn Davies - another enormously popular centre-forward on Tyneside. Inset: action from August 1970 as 'Wyn the Leap' - seen in typical aerial pose - competes with Crystal Palace defender, Mel Blyth.

CENTENARY
NEWCASTLE UNITED
1892-1992

Bryan Robson developed into one of football's most prolific goalscorers and arguably, the best uncapped striker of his era. Inset: Robson en route for goal against Chelsea at Stamford Bridge.

Newcastle and Scotland captain, Bobby Moncur who marshalled United's defence and led the side to a Fairs Cup victory and Wembley final.

Terry McDermott (right) in airborne semi-final action against Burnley in 1974, while below are the joyous scenes by players and fans alike following one of Malcolm Macdonald's stunning goals in the F.A. Cup semi-final at Hillsborough.

Skipper Bobby Moncur meets his opposite number Emlyn Hughes before the kick-off to the 1974 Cup final against Liverpool.

Moncur's Runners-up medal, together with a match ticket and souvenir card from Wembley.

The Cup heroes return to Tyneside in 1974, alas without a trophy, but still to an amazing reception.

Terry Hibbitt, United's midfield general who was signed for a bargain £30,000 from Leeds United in 1971.

Long serving defender Frank Clark has appeared for United more than anyone in post-war football.

The sad finale to Tony Green's career, carried off following a tackle against Crystal Palace in 1972. The Scottish international was one of the most popular Newcastle players of the modern era.

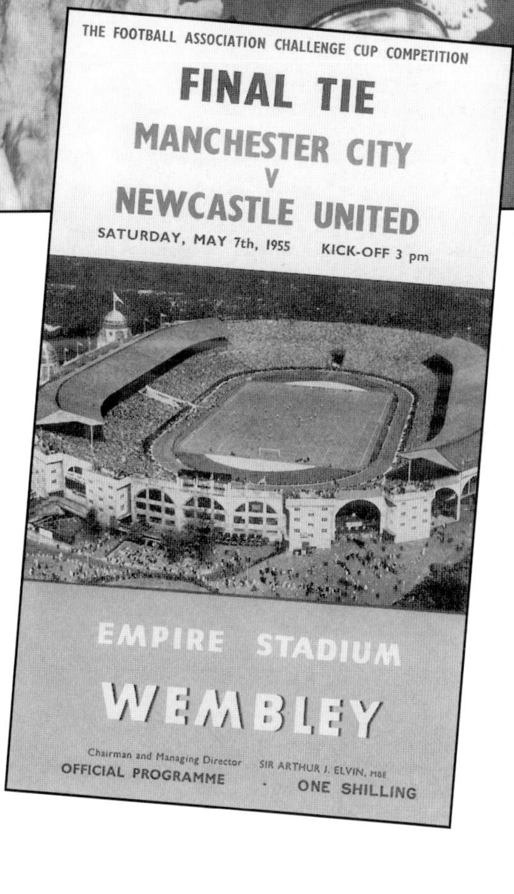

Jimmy Scoular in 1955, just off the train at Newcastle Central Station is greeted by City dignitaries. Programme from the 1955 Cup final against Manchester City.

Centenary Profile 17

As Quick as Lightning

"He just bubbled and buzzed all over the front line"

Charlie Crowe, January 1990

TO BE RATED BY MANY AS AN EQUAL TO Jackie Milburn in the heralded Number 9 shirt, he had to be something special. Len White was a player who transformed an average career into a startling one over the close season of 1957 once his eminent predecessor had crossed the Irish Sea for Belfast. A former Yorkshire miner, White was handed Milburn's shirt by Newcastle's directors in something of a gamble. Previously very much an outside-right and occasional out and out striker who never really showed his potential, White grabbed the opportunity and went on the rampage in the next four seasons. Only Jackie Milburn himself has scored more goals for the club.

White proved a great success and Tyneside warmed quickly to his rip-roaring style. Len liked the ball at his feet and possessed ability to whip past several defenders in one surge forward. He packed a ferocious shot from distance or in the box and was powerful in the air for a small man, with his stocky physique being an advantage when competing with bigger defenders. By the end of 1957/58 Len was strongly tipped for an England place, but an international call never came and White remained one of the best uncapped players of the decade.

Len White was born in 1930 in the small Yorkshire town of Skellow, not far from Doncaster. He was brought up in a working class community and, like most youngsters of his time in Yorkshire, ended down the coal mine, a similar upbringing to many footballers of this era. White started playing amateur football in his teens and his first club of note was the colliery side at Whitwick. He soon had Football League scouts looking at his potential and Leicester City offered the youngster a chance.

Filbert Street's management did not take to Len though, and he returned to pit soccer, this time joining Upton Colliery FC. He again was a hit in that standard of football and soon senior clubs took notice once more. Operating on the wing then, the positional change to centre-forward was some way off, he often hit the net showing tremendous power in his drives at goal. Rotherham United were the club to give him another crack at becoming a professional footballer and he joined the Millmoor staff in May 1948. Close to home, Rotherham suited White perfectly.

He remained a miner and combined hard work in the pit with more hard work on the training ground in his spare time. Without really claiming a regular position in the Millers' team, Len did help in their Third Division promotion side in 1951 and a couple of years later fate brought him to the attention of Newcastle United. Rotherham were drawn to play United in a FA Cup match on the last day of January 1953. White's team provided United with a problem or two and the Magpies were dumped out of the Cup after a famous tussle at St James Park. Following the shock defeat, Stan Seymour took out his cheque book in search of new talent. Rotherham's forwards had looked the part and his first port of call was Millmoor....but not for Len White, Seymour wanted Jack Grainger and once he found a deal was not on the cards, tried for White and got him for a fee of £12,500.

Competition was extremely fierce at Gallowgate then. White had to battle for a place on the right side of the field with Tommy Walker, Bill Foulkes, Tommy Mulgrew, Reg Davies and of course Jackie Milburn, who then operated in several positions. For three years he was in and out of the side. Competition eased a little when both Walker and Foulkes moved on, and in 1954/55 White squeezed into the team on a regular basis alternating from a spell on the wing to a period at centre-forward, changing positions with Jackie Milburn. Although playing seven games of the FA Cup run that year, he was lucky to get into the 1955 Cup final side replacing the injury-stricken Davies at the last moment after being down as 12th man. Yet Len performed well at Wembley laying on

Len White

WHITE'S PLAYING RECORD

	League		FA Cup		FL Cup		Total	
	App	Gls	App	Gls	App	Gls	App	Gls
1952-53	3	0	0	0	0	0	3	0
1953-54	12	2	1	1	0	0	13	3
1954-55	29	14	8	2	0	0	37	16
1955-56	21	7	0	0	0	0	21	7
1956-57	30	10	3	3	0	0	33	13
1957-58	30	22	2	3	0	0	32	25
1958-59	30	25	1	0	0	0	31	25
1959-60	40	28	2	1	0	0	42	29
1960-61	33	28	4	1	1	0	38	29
1961-62	16	6	1	0	2	0	19	6
	244	**142**	**22**	**11**	**3**	**0**	**269**	**153**

Milburn's opening goal in the first minute.

It wasn't until Milburn vacated the centre-forward position that White dramatically entered the limelight. He switched to the leader's role in earnest and piled up the goals for the next four years. At only 5'7" tall, he was still good in the air and quite devastating on the deck. White became a lethal striker with ability that had the terraces roaring with excitement reminiscent of Milburn or Macdonald in full flight. He often looked deep for the action and on many occasions would take the ball past three or four defenders with a change of pace - his biggest asset - and foot trickery in a bee-line for goal. Len hit the ball hard, whether by foot or by head. Colleague Charlie Crowe said, "He just bubbled and buzzed all over the front line and popped up where he was least expected".

Goals were the name of his game all right. In four campaigns he netted 108 times, an average of 27 a season. During 1957/58, White scored twelve times in a ten game sequence and the following season crashed in 15 in a 13 match spell. The call from the St James Park faithful was, "White for England"! They had little doubt that he was the best leader in the country at the time. After he had knocked in a hat-trick for the Football League in the space of eight majestic minutes in 1958, all thought he would lead the national side. The Yorkshireman's display against the Irish at Anfield was stunning, but selection for his country and the forthcoming World Cup in Sweden never came. England chose the ageing Lofthouse or youthful Joe Baker, Brian Clough or Derek Kevan instead. To the fury of Tyneside he was overlooked by England boss Walter Winterbottom.

Apart from his special goalscoring knack, White was also something of a leg-puller in United's camp, as George Eastham recorded, he was the, "club comedian". However there was nothing funny about the way White's skills were lost to the Magpies. An injury in a clash with Spurs at a crucial stage of the 1960/61 season robbed United of their goalgetter. White was six yards from goal and just about to pounce for the ball when Dave Mackay crunched him from behind. It was a reckless tackle, one reporter observed, "Mackay appeared to be in mid air before making contact". It cost the club dearly. Relegation to Division Two quickly followed.

During the vacuum following Mitten's departure, White - now 31 years old - was exchanged in February 1962 for the younger Jimmy Kerray of Huddersfield Town, a move not to please United's fans. While Len's Newcastle career was over, White was far from ready to hang up his boots. At Leeds Road he continued to score regularly, to the envy of Newcastle supporters and helped the Terriers steer clear of relegation to Division Three. He then crossed the Pennines turning out for Stockport County even though he was now very much a veteran.

Approaching 36 years of age, injury started to hamper his appearances and in the summer of 1966 White joined Altrincham. He had concluded a Football League career that had seen four members of his family grace the field. Len was the youngest of four brothers who all played League soccer. Fred made his name with Bradford Park Avenue, Albert with Aldershot and Jack with Bristol City. Len may have ended his senior days in the game, but it wasn't the end of the amazing White dribble altogether. He turned out for Sligo Rovers in Ireland then returned to his native Yorkshire and coached for Bradford. He also played local football into his 50th year and ran a team in Huddersfield as well as working for a tractor manufacturer.

Len White may have been unlucky not to have been at his peak with the black'n'whites at a time of glory, unlike Milburn, Macdonald or Gallacher, yet the picture of his closely cropped head and stocky frame will live for just as long. Many still maintain that if he had played for a London or Lancashire club, instead of the football outpost of Tyneside, he would have walked into the England side.

Len White powers a header towards goal at St. James Park.

Centenary Profile 18

United's most Capped Player

"One of the best full-backs I have ever played against"

Stanley Matthews

ONE OF THE MOST PROMINENT OF NEWCASTLE **United's many fine full-backs over the years is Alf McMichael, captain of both club and country in a spell of 14 seasons at St James Park. Only a handful of players have appeared more for the Magpies and no-one has been capped as often as McMichael. At left-back, this Irishman from Belfast played throughout the fifties for United, yet in an era with so much glory, Alf was rarely given headlines being content to stay in the background as others took the spotlight, just like his full-back partner Bobby Cowell.**

McMichael was born in October 1927 and started playing local soccer with Wolfhill Juniors immediately after the Second World War. He was spotted by Cliftonville and signed for the Belfast side when 15 years-old. Another Belfast club, the country's top side, Linfield picked him up in 1945 and McMichael's game developed quickly after that, winning an Irish Cup medal in 1948 and League representative honours a year later. Talent scouts from England had their eyes on the youngster and he was soon to cross the Irish Sea, but not before he created something of a unique achievement in football. Alf actually managed to get the Linfield versus Cliftonville fixture in 1949 brought forward by 15 minutes so he could dash to catch a train bound for Dublin with his new bride!

United supremo Stan Seymour had witnessed a classy display by McMichael for the Irish League against the Scottish League at Ibrox in spite of an 8-1 defeat for his side. Newcastle's offer was soon heading to Linfield, however the Irish club were not keen to part with the player easily. Seymour haggled for hours with his opposite number, but in the end they agreed a fee of £23,000 which also included another youngster United fancied in the Inter-League contest, George Hannah.

The joint deal went through during September 1949 and within 24 hours, 21 year-old McMichael was immediately plunged into the English First Division against Manchester City. As soon as he got off the Stranraer train he was whisked up to get changed and turned out in front of over 58,000 at St James Park. United won 4-2 and Alf was well pleased with his performance. He later recalled, "What an experience. I had only been part-time training in Ireland and the cross channel pace was much too fast".

Alf quickly adapted to the new conditions having excellent positional sense. McMichael cut out most of the frills and embroidery of the game and concentrated on plain and simple defence. He was a player rarely to take chances and always was dependable - an ideal team man. Copper haired and solidly built at 5'8", he was a decisive tackler and passed the ball accurately. McMichael was first honoured at full level by Northern Ireland in October 1949, a matter of weeks after joining Newcastle. It proved an awful outing for the Irishman as Scotland won 8-2 at Windsor Park. The following month he faced England at Maine Road and suffered again. Ireland this time lost 9-2 and McMichael was dropped for the next fixture. He is recorded as saying, "My entry into international soccer was one of the most miserable events of my life. Grim though as it was I learnt a very valuable lesson". Against the English, Alf was up against Tom Finney at his very best, still, McMichael used the experience well and never again allowed a winger to have such freedom. And afterwards he also tended to raise his game when opposing the top performers or in a special atmosphere. He soon returned to the international stage and became a regular fixture in the Irish line-up. Indeed, his confrontation with Stanley Matthews at national level is part of Irish folklore. They always had a torrid duel and Matthews once

Alf McMichael

	League		FA Cup		FL Cup		Total	
	App	Gls	App	Gls	App	Gls	App	Gls
1949-50	11	0	0	0	0	0	11	0
1950-51	22	0	1	0	0	0	23	0
1951-52	36	0	7	0	0	0	43	0
1952-53	33	0	2	0	0	0	35	0
1953-54	28	0	5	0	0	0	33	0
1954-55	19	1	0	0	0	0	19	1
1955-56	33	0	4	0	0	0	37	0
1956-57	25	0	0	0	0	0	25	0
1957-58	35	0	2	0	0	0	37	0
1958-59	39	0	1	0	0	0	40	0
1959-60	41	0	2	0	0	0	43	0
1960-61	34	0	1	0	1	0	36	0
1961-62	35	0	0	0	2	0	37	0
1962-63	11	0	0	0	1	0	12	0
	402	**1**	**25**	**0**	**4**	**0**	**431**	**1**

Table: **McMICHAEL'S PLAYING RECORD**

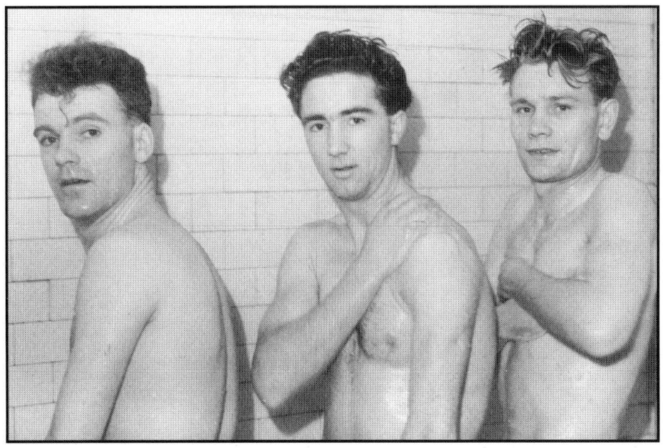

Alf McMichael (left) with Tommy Casey (centre) and Charlie Crowe (right) in the St. James Park showers.

said of the United defender, "One of the best left-backs I have ever played against".

In 1951 the Ulsterman was unlucky to miss United's Wembley success when he slipped in training and broke a wrist. McMichael made the comment, "I visited Wembley as a spectator and it was a bitter experience to be in the stand instead of on the field". Alf was back though a year later and received a winners' medal. However, he again missed out in 1955 when in and out of the side through injury - even turning out on the left wing in a bid to get fit.

The Irishman had skippered his country for the first time three years earlier, before he had even been in charge of United's eleven. He went on to lead his country until Danny Blanchflower took over and was a proud member of their 1958 World Cup giant-killing side. McMichael was also honoured by being picked for the Rest of the UK team to play Wales and was recognised as one of the top defenders in football during the fifties. All told he played on 40 occasions for his country, by far the most capped individual with the club.

The arrival of another former Linfield defender, Dick Keith to the north east in 1956 gave Newcastle a full-back partnership to rival the likes of McCracken and Hudspeth, Craig and Clark, or Kennedy and Nattrass in United's history. Continuing Alf's defensive union with Bobby Cowell, Newcastle were marvellously served in that department during the fifties. Keith was to partner his colleague in international fixtures too.

Ball work on the Newcastle training ground.
Left to right: Cowell, Scoular, Brennan and McMichael.

With well over 400 games behind him - netting a solitary goal against Cardiff City in 1955 - McMichael's stay at St James Park was to be limited once ex team-mate Joe Harvey took over the manager's role at Gallowgate in 1962. Harvey discarded the old hands, and Alf at 35 years-old followed Len White and Bobby Mitchell out of the door. McMichael took the decision to part company like a true pro, even though he so much wanted to create a United appearance record, one of his long-standing ambitions. He was a season short of topping Frank Hudspeth's outfield total.

In June 1963 Alf joined South Shields as player-manager and within a year had a merited testimonial at St James Park. McMichael stayed with the Horsley Hill outfit for six years and turned the non-league side into a FA Cup minnow to be reckoned with. At the start of the seventies decade he returned to Ireland and managed County Down club Bangor for a period. He resided in that town afterwards, working as a brewery rep then in the Harland and Wolff shipyard.

One of Newcastle's most consistent performers, Alf McMichael should be remembered more readily than he has been. He was a loyal club man and a player who earned a gentleman's reputation on and off the field.

12 THE NEW ERA

1961-1968

• JOE HARVEY'S RETURN
• TRANSFER EXTRAVAGANZA
• CUP NIGHTMARE •
• SECOND DIVISION CHAMPIONS
• OWN GOAL LIFELINE • EUROPEAN ENTRY •

"The capacity crowd of 59,000 roared its delight. The sound of bells, bugles and rattles rang out over the city"
Daily Mirror, April 1965

NOT SURPRISINGLY AS NEWCASTLE **United faced Second Division football for the first time since 1947 it was all change within the corridors of St James Park and, as ever, events on and off the field kept United's name in the headlines. The black'n'whites quickly installed a new manager, recovered from relegation and regained their place in Division One, then qualified for European football for the first time. Amidst this resurrection the dispute with the City Council over ground redevelopment escalated in the background, and if anything overshadowed many of the events on the football field.**

The sixties were a period of much economic and social change. A new era dawned which saw attitudes and fashions alter dramatically. The Beatles, The Rolling Stones and the mini skirt became a way of life and a rapid development of Tyneside saw multi-storey flats replace the rows and rows of traditional terraced housing. Motorways started to link cities and United's supporters could very soon travel quickly to follow their heroes.

Charlie Mitten was, surprisingly to many, still in charge for the start of the new season in August 1961. But his stay at St James Park was only to be for a few weeks. To start with Mitten rang the changes, but his new faces were never able to strike a period of sustained success. Fortunately the defence had improved a great deal from their last outing and recorded no substantial defeats. Bill Thompson had an outstanding season at centre-half along with goalkeeper Hollins. Thompson, from Bedlington, a tall and leggy defender would have won an England Under 23 cap but for an unfortunate injury which curtailed his progress. Ivor Allchurch - not allowed to depart as he wished - was appointed captain, although he was later replaced by McKinney after a dispute when the club had refused permission for the schemer to play for Wales. Len White, still not fit and a big miss, was replaced initially by Ken Leek, another Welsh international, who arrived from Leicester City for £25,000. Juniors Alan Suddick and George Dalton looked promising while late season arrivals Jimmy Fell, Billy Day and Jimmy Kerray all appeared too. Leek, with a proven record at Filbert Street, started with a hat-trick in a friendly against Aarhus, but was never a success and was soon to be released. Fell and Kerray were not to impress either. Kerray cost £10,000 - plus Len White - from Huddersfield Town while Fell had been with Everton and although he did much better, never turned United's forward line into a quality combination. Day was valued at £12,000 when he moved to Tyneside from Middlesbrough, but only scored a single goal for the club.

Local product Bill Thompson who impressed at centre-half.

Jimmy Fell, signed from Everton.

Below: One of several forwards tried, Billy Day.

It was an unsettled eleven and included record signing during January, Barrie Thomas, a high scoring centre-forward to replace Leek. He cost £45,000 from Scunthorpe United after netting over 100 goals for the Irons and his previous club, Mansfield Town. Somewhat erratic at finishing and never a football artist, Thomas was the tearaway type and at times very effective. By the end of the season he had topped the Football League's scorers list alongside Liverpool's Roger Hunt. With the 31 goals he grabbed for Scunthorpe, the centre-forward found the net 41 times. But for injury, Thomas could have joined the England squad for training at Lillishall in readiness for the 1962 World Cup in Chile, an unlucky mishap that was typical of his stay on Tyneside. When Thomas was fit and in the team, he was always a threat, registering 50 goals for the Magpies in only 78 games.

Thomas was included in a Scunthorpe line-up that faced United in the League Cup, but he ended on the losing side as the Magpies cruised to a 2-0 victory watched by only 14,372. However, by the time Newcastle faced Sheffield United in the next round they had dropped to 18th position in the

Jimmy Kerray watches the ball go over the line for another goal to United.

Second Division table and speculation mounted regarding the position of manager Charlie Mitten. United lost to the Blades and shortly after the League Cup exit Mitten was sacked. The dressing-room atmosphere had not been good and several players wanted away. United's board decided to terminate his position when Mitten's ally, William McKeag was out of the country and apparently not consulted. McKeag was quoted as saying, "I am shocked beyond measure. How can they do this in my absence". Mitten made the comment about his period in charge of the club, "I think I did a good job. Team performances picked up, the facilities were improved and I left them with a successful youth team".

Barrie Thomas, a centre-forward with a terrific goal record.

Veteran trainer since 1938, 64 year-old Norman Smith was given temporary control and happily the vastly experienced Smith injected some of his fighting spirit to lift United away from the bottom reaches of the division, but not until they had been dismissed from the FA Cup in humiliating fashion.

Peterborough United, elected into the Football League only a year before at the expense of Gateshead, shocked the football world with a 1-0 victory at a misty Gallowgate. A late goal by Terry

Long-serving trainer Norman Smith who was handed the manager's job in 1961.

Bly was enough to dump Newcastle out of the Cup. Nearly 43,000 fans were sent home in total dismay at the depths Newcastle had now reached. However, an even bigger Cup shock was still in store for Magpie supporters.

At the conclusion of the season United were deep in the red at the bank and the famous black'n'whites seemed to have lost all their pride. Angry scenes were commonplace outside the club's offices and shareholders' meetings became increasingly rowdy, at one stage police having to be called to restore order. All was not bad though, as Mitten had noted, United's juniors included several promising youngsters and they carried off the FA Youth Cup defeating Wolves in a two-legged final. The brightest prospect was Alan Suddick, a tall, thin looking winger-come-inside-forward from Chester-le-Street who possessed all the natural skills to become a big star. He had made his debut as a 17 year-old and developed quickly at first, but could never master an inconsistency defect. Suddick was one to shine in Mitten's finale - a 7-2 victory at Bury. He scored in that game and his solo runs had the crowd aroused at the new talent on view. Soon to be elevated to the England Youth and then Under 23 side, he should have gone on to bid for a full cap, but that was not to be. It was other players who in time surpassed the inconsistent genius of Suddick. Bobby Moncur was a slow developer by comparison, as was David Craig. Somewhat shy and still only schoolboys when they headed for Tyneside, it took time for both to push their way into the first team. However, once established they gave the club magnificent service.

The position of permanent manager had occupied the minds of Chairman Wally Hurford and his directors for almost six months. The rocky ride Charlie Mitten received at St James Park didn't help their choice, but on the 1st June 1962 Joe Harvey took control of the club he skippered for eight years. Initially he was installed only on a 12 month trial, with the sack as the price of failure, but Joe went on to remain for 13 years in the manager's office. The Journal disclosed his salary as, "probably £3,000 per year" while Stan Seymour made the comment, "With Harvey in charge of the players we have laid the foundation for a fighting bid for a quick return to the top class". Norman Smith, soon to retire, noted, "it is good to know the reins will be in the hands of a man who has already done much for the club, and burns to do more".

Alan Suddick who became the darling of the crowd.

WAGES ROCKET

Following the removal of the maximum wage rule in 1961, Ivor Allchurch became United's highest paid star. He received a basic £60 per week, three times his previous wage packet. When Ollie Burton signed for United in June 1963 his deal was £35 per week, plus a win and draw bonus and also an extra £1 for every 1,000 spectators that went through the turnstile over a threshold of 30,000. There was additionally a promotion bonus payable too. Incentive schemes had very much arrived.

Harvey inherited a club with morale at a low point and finances in a depressing state. Yet cash was found to enable Harvey to build a new team. Immediately Joe sorted out his players. He brought in Jimmy Greenhalgh as trainer, a tough, inspiring right-hand man. Allchurch got the wish he craved for, a return to Wales with Cardiff City, while long serving Alf McMichael was told he was not required. Out went many faces and in came Harvey's men. He spent £40,000 on Dave Hilley of Third Lanark, who had just missed playing for Scotland's full side. He was greatly admired by Seymour, who reverted to somewhat of an assistant manager to his former fifties ally. Glaswegian, Hilley, stepped into Allchurch's role and became an important signing. With Scottish ball skills to the fore, the slightly built inside-forward could always be relied upon for a goal - scoring 33 for the black'n'whites.

The return of warhorse Joe Harvey resulted in a steady revival at Gallowgate.

Another £17,000 went on Jim Iley, left-half with Nottingham Forest, and like Hilley, it proved a master signing. Thinning on top, but not in stamina or know-how, Iley had also been close to a full cap and was dubbed, "a complete footballer". He possessed control, tremendous shooting ability, was

Harvey's playmaker in midfield, Dave Hilley.

versatile and consistent. The former Under 23 and Football League player was appointed skipper and became the cornerstone to Harvey's promotion bid. Several other players were to arrive in the coming months as Harvey travelled the country for fresh talent.

United finished their second season in the lower division in 7th position. For a while they had a good chance of promotion, but injuries to important players, Barrie Thomas, who had netted 16 goals, and defender Bill Thompson, dashed their hopes. With Thomas a menace in the box, United could at times rustle up quite a firepower. Middlesbrough were sent home with a 6-1 drubbing, while Walsall and Swansea Town also received six goal hammerings. A feature of the season was the further development of young players like Moncur, full-back Colin Clish and Suddick, while new signings Iley and Hilley made a big difference. And in spite of failing to get into the top placings, United could still pack the fans in. Over 60,000 saw each of the two derby encounters with Sunderland who were chasing promotion with Chelsea that year. Both games ended in a draw.

Ex Spurs and Forest wing-half Jim Iley, a player to inspire United back to the First Division.

Leyton Orient, then in the First Division, knocked United from the League Cup after a replay, after a rainstorm and also after a floodlight failure which blacked out the game for five minutes. In the FA Cup, which was crippled by severe December to February snowstorms, the Magpies were eliminated in the 4th Round, 5-0 at Norwich, a game which in fact was not played until mid March. United's 3rd Round tie with Bradford City at Valley Parade - a 6-1 triumph - was postponed an amazing twelve times and didn't get under way until March 7th, two months behind schedule. The 1962/63 season was the worst on record for weather disrupting the game. Newcastle played a solitary fixture between December 23rd and March 1st, at far away and relatively warm Plymouth.

Three of Joe Harvey's new men in training on the St. James Park steps; Burton (left), Marshall (centre) and Taylor (right).

By the season's close Harvey plunged into the transfer market again. Ron McGarry came from Bolton Wanderers for £15,000, a tough, battling leader in every sense of the word and who stood in for the injury prone Thomas. McGarry was to be remembered for a buoyant personality and after flooring Swansea centre-half Johnson and Coventry's Ron Farmer in fist fights on the field was nicknamed 'Cassius'. Inside-left Willie Penman came from Glasgow Rangers, but was often in the physio's room, while shortly afterwards Welsh international Ollie Burton arrived from Norwich City for £37,500 after performing well in the FA Cup defeat at Carrow Road. It was a big amount and the ginger haired defender took quite a time to repay the fee. He was another to be often sidelined with injury.

Walsall's 22 year-old winger Colin Taylor also landed on Tyneside in a surprise £20,000 deal. He had an excellent record at Fellows Park being the Saddlers' top scorer for the last four years. Possessing a thundering shot in his left peg, Taylor was dubbed 'Cannonball'. After trying to tempt Gordon Banks from Leicester City, Gordon Marshall came south from Hearts with a

A Magpie line-up in 1962. Left to right, back: Neale, Thompson, Hollins, McKinney, Dalton, Ferguson. Front: Hilley, Hale, Thomas, Kerray, Fell.

John McGrath runs onto the field - he played an important part in the Magpies' promotion.

reputation of being the best 'keeper north of the border. Although born in deepest England, Marshall had played all his soccer with the Tynecastle club and had tasted success in both league and cup in Scotland. Tall and well built, he was picked for England's Under 23 side in 1960 and proved another good acquisition by the manager. Marshall replaced Dave Hollins following a long running dispute over wages. Harvey was steadily building the squad that would take United back into the First Division, and despite the transfer activity was also gradually decreasing the club's overdraft. United made a modest £4,257 profit on the year.

It was the same story as last time for season 1963/64. Injuries to Penman, Burton, Hilley and once again to Thomas, disrupted the team, but more good signings were made by the astute manager as Trevor Hockey and Bobby Cummings joined the club. Hockey was another up and coming striker, only 20 years-old, his fee of £20,000 from Nottingham Forest was substantial and in short bursts showed match-winning talents from the right-wing in a fast and furious style. Later Hockey was to turn into a marvellous midfield player, characterised by long hair and bushy beard. He was capped nine times for Wales. Ashington born, Bobby Cummings made a return journey to Gallowgate after being kicked out as a youngster in 1956. He had made an impression at centre-forward with Aberdeen and although he was signed as a reserve, was to prove a most useful striker in Newcastle's promotion push.

Joe Harvey's most important signing was ex England wing-half Stan Anderson from Sunderland for £19,000. His sale was sudden and swift and rocked the soon to be promoted Roker scene. Anderson completed the Harvey jigsaw and was to be the man to partner Iley and make the side tick. He in fact replaced the midfielder as captain and arrived when injuries had sent United tumbling to 5th bottom of the division. At 29 years old and having appeared almost 450 times for the Wearsiders, Stan was a first class general with exquisite distribution and formidable shooting power. Anderson was exactly the type of player Harvey was after, someone to organise on the field.

The new skipper observed on his arrival that United's team "was just a shambles". They were in a terrible mess mid season having lost a record six games in a row. Anderson was to make a dramatic impact on the side and Newcastle's new half-back line of Iley, McGrath - now established - and Anderson, was to be the ultimate reason for a revival and subsequent promotion. Although his debut recorded a 4-0 defeat by Cardiff City on Tyneside, United won against Manchester City 3-1 and never looked back, except for one terrible lapse during January.

Following another inglorious exit by a lowly club in the League Cup, this time by Bournemouth, worse was to follow when FA Cup day arrived. Southern League Bedford Town appeared on Tyneside with a good giant-killing record. The blue and white shirts of the bold little part-timers were to be long remembered as they sensationally ran to a 2-0 interval lead. Backed by 2,000 fans, Bedford's teenage centre-forward John Fahy, a 6'1" menace, headed in a cross with McGrath and Marshall nowhere, then just before half-time another centre - low and hard - struck Bill McKinney racing in and the ball crashed past a startled Marshall. While Stan Anderson did pull a goal back, Bedford held out to create the shock result of the season. They were the superior team in every respect. The Sunday Sun reported that United, "were hustled and swept unceremoniously out of the Cup". Newcastle got what they deserved - 'boos' and slow handclaps long before the final whistle. After being FA Cup giants for so long, United found themselves in a period of Cup obscurity, to last for all of a decade.

With only an outside chance of promotion, the last few weeks of the season saw Harvey give youth a chance. Full-backs David Craig and Frank Clark, another junior signed from Crook Town, promised well, as did winger Geoff Allen and wing-half Joe Butler. However, United lost George Dalton with a broken leg when playing at Leeds a side heading for Division One. In an Easter double with the Elland Road club, Dalton clashed with Johnny Giles and was stretchered off, an injury from which he never really recovered. Once tipped for international honours, he was out for over a year and later assisted Coventry City as physio. Dalton joined Alan Suddick in hospital, another injury victim. The brilliant young forward had damaged ligaments and was also out of action for several months.

Having witnessed local rivals Sunderland promoted, United's supporters were desperate for their club to succeed in 1964/65. With so many new faces it was going to take Harvey a little time for his squad to develop together, but optimism prevailed for the new season. One critic observed, "Given freedom from injuries they have more than enough talent to pulverise the entire Second Division". The manager took his squad to Denmark and Germany to prepare for the programme's start and relied heavily on his half-back line. They had quickly forged a superb understanding with Iley and Anderson, the two attack minded wing-halves complimenting each other perfectly - when one ventured up front, the other stayed back. And McGrath, previously something of a ball playing defender, learnt how to be a rugged stopper. With youngsters Craig and Clark installed at the back, Newcastle's defensive formation in front of Gordon Marshall looked first class. They were to keep a clean sheet in 15 league games and conceded only a single goal in another 16 fixtures.

Following a moderate opening with United stuttering against Charlton Athletic, the Magpies got going and by the end of September were top of the division. As Christmas approached they embarked on a tremendous run in which seven games in a row ended in victories, equalling the club's 1909 record. Included were a 6-1 win at Swindon and a 5-0 destruction of promotion rivals

Northampton Town. The Cobblers had gone 17 games without defeat, but three goals in a two minute spell just before the interval saw United steam-roller them. McGarry, who had now displaced Thomas, netted a hat-trick and was proving a dangerous leader. Newcastle turned on a, "pulsating display of pure soccer".

Two holiday fixtures with Middlesbrough brought full points, with Dave Hilley showing sweet skills on the snow covered pitches. United's Scot netted three of the four goals that deflated the Tees-siders' Christmas and over 54,000 saw the game at Gallowgate. At the turn of the year, Newcastle were firm favourites for promotion having a lead at the top of the table over other contenders, Northampton, Norwich and Bolton.

Progress continued to be good, despite an interruption for the FA Cup when United fell at Swansea 1-0. This followed a quick exit in the League Cup by Blackpool, and immediately afterwards United dropped points at Coventry. In that game, Newcastle almost made a remarkable come-back after being 5-1 down. With only 24 minutes remaining they pulled back the deficit to 5-4 - Hilley and McGarry scoring a brace each. In the very last minute they almost clinched a point when Jim Iley flashed a free-kick inches wide.

Another fascinating game occurred in February when Bob Stokoe's Bury were the visitors to the north east. The referee, Mr Windle, added all of eleven minutes to the game and in the dying moments Bury netted the winner to the disgust of the crowd. United not only lost their home record, but also top place in the table. The game also saw Alan Suddick, back to fitness, pull down the shorts of a Bury player to his ankles as he was lining up to take a free-kick! That reverse didn't hinder United at all and a good series of results took them into Easter. Promotion rivals Norwich City were polished off in convincing style and two victories, at Derby 3-0, and on Tyneside against Swindon Town, 1-0, set the scene for the game on Good Friday against fellow promotion challengers Bolton Wanderers. A home victory that afternoon would make sure First Division soccer returned to Tyneside.

Bolton boasted several top players, including Wyn Davies, who in the not to distant future would wear the black'n'white shirt. They also had Francis Lee, Bob Hatton and England players Freddie Hill and Eddie Hopkinson. A crowd of 59,960 crushed into St James Park with youngsters sitting on the cinder track and crouching on the grass verge. The atmosphere was electric, just as it was the last time United were in a similar situation 17 years ago on Good Friday 1948. The first half though, nearly sent the mass of Tynesiders for their tea in anguish as Davies caused havoc in the United defence. But once John McGrath had got to grips with the big Welshman the game turned Newcastle's way. He clattered into Davies on the halfway line and Bolton's leader was never a problem again. Indeed he ended up on crutches for the rest of the season.

Bryan Robson, another youngster to claim a place that season, went on a piercing run, was brought down and from the free-kick Willie Penman knocked the ball home in a crowded goalmouth to give United the goal they so much needed. Jim Iley clinched First Division football with a cracking 20 yard drive, a goal to be remembered for a long time. He recalled, "It was perhaps the finest toe-ender on record". On 57 minutes Iley, Anderson and Hilley moved forward in a clever piece of combination play. Hilley released the ball to Cummings on the edge of the penalty box. The lad from Ashington went past one man and, as he did so, in rushed Iley to hammer the ball past Hopkinson with terrific power.

Very few of the huge attendance went home quickly that afternoon. On the whistle the whole pitch was covered with a leaping, singing mass of black'n'white. The players emerged from the dressing room into the directors' enclosure and threw their shirts to the crowd. Joe Harvey noted that the scenes even surpassed the Wembley homecomings of the fifties. The Daily Mirror recorded, "The capacity crowd of 59,000 roared its delight. The sound of bells, bugles and rattles rang out over the city".

Following the thrill and excitement of the Bolton fixture, United concentrated their efforts on lifting the Second Division championship trophy. They did it with a 0-0 draw against Manchester City on the last Saturday of the season. The success was due to team effort, spirit and character very much in the old Joe Harvey mould. The manager had a settled side and he noted, "The team has done it. Not individuals". It was very much that sort of triumph. They were a solid rather than enterprising V and after several years of trying to put right a perplexing home record, the promotion side showed impeccable form and only lost once, in that controversial game with Bury. They also logged the most points(under the old system) in the club's history. Ron McGarry was top scorer with 16 goals, while Hilley assisted well netting 12 times. Scot Tommy Knox was the only signing during the year, from Chelsea, but the outside-left rarely sparkled.

After four years in charge Joe Harvey had achieved success. He brought back lost pride in the club and ensured that spectators flocked once more to St James Park. When he took over in 1962 United's average gate was down to 27,000. The promotion year saw 35,000 back at Gallowgate on a regular basis. Gate receipts were up to £170,000 and profit on the year amounted to over £46,000. United's outlook was extremely encouraging.

COSTLY HOAX

During March 1964 rumours swept Tyneside before their local derby with Sunderland that the match had been cancelled. A notice was even placed at the Central Station stating that the game was off and coach companies were informed to cancel bookings. All were untrue and the hoax had a dramatic effect on the attendance. Only 27,341 turned up at Gallowgate when a crowd of almost 60,000 could have been expected. With players wages tied to gate receipts it cost United's stars some £30 each, while the club lost around £5,000 in net revenue.

Centenary Highlight

Second Division Champions 1965. Left to right, back: Iley, Burton, Craig, Anderson, Marshall, Clark, Cummings, Thompson, McGrath. Front: Hockey, Hilley, McGarry, Harvey (manager), Penman, Allen, Suddick.

Bolton 'keeper Eddie Hopkinson can do nothing to stop Iley's gem.

SECOND DIVISION CHAMPIONS 1964-65	P	W	D	L	F	A	Pts
Newcastle United	42	24	9	9	81	45	57
Northampton Town	42	20	16	6	66	50	56
Bolton Wanderers	42	20	10	12	80	58	50
Southampton	42	17	14	11	83	63	48
Ipswich Town	42	15	17	10	74	67	47
Norwich City	42	20	7	15	61	57	47
Crystal Palace	42	16	13	13	55	51	45
Huddersfield Town	42	17	10	15	53	51	44
Derby County	42	16	11	15	84	79	43
Coventry City	42	17	9	16	72	70	43
Manchester City	42	16	9	17	63	62	41
Preston North End	42	14	13	15	76	81	41
Cardiff City	42	13	14	15	64	57	40
Rotherham United	42	14	12	16	70	69	40
Plymouth Argyle	42	16	8	18	63	79	40
Bury	42	14	10	18	60	66	38
Middlesbrough	42	13	9	20	70	76	35
Charlton Athletic	42	13	9	20	64	75	35
Layton Orient	42	12	11	19	50	72	35
Portsmouth	42	12	10	20	56	77	34
Swindon Town	42	14	5	23	63	81	33
Swansea Town	42	11	10	21	62	84	32

RESULTS	Home	Away
Charlton Athletic	D 1-1	W 1-0
Southampton	W 2-1	W 1-0
Huddersfield Town	W 2-1	W 1-0
Northampton Town	W 5-0	L 0-1
Coventry City	W 2-0	L 4-5
Plymouth Argyle	W 2-1	L 1-2
Cardiff City	W 2-0	D 1-1
Preston North End	W 5-2	L 0-2
Ipswich Town	D 2-2	L 1-3
Leyton Orient	W 5-0	L 1-2
Manchester City	D 0-0	L 0-3
Bury	L 2-3	W 2-1
Crystal Palace	W 2-0	D 1-1
Norwich City	W 2-0	D 1-1
Rotherham United	W 3-1	D 1-1
Swansea Town	W 3-1	L 1-3
Derby County	D 2-2	W 3-0
Swindon Town	W 1-0	W 6-1
Portsmouth	W 3-0	W 2-1
Middlesbrough	W 2-1	W 2-0
Bolton Wanderers	W 2-0	D 1-1

LARGEST VICTORY;
5-0 v Northampton Town(H), Leyton Orient(H) & 6-1 v Swindon Town(A)

HEAVIEST DEFEAT;
0-3 v Manchester City(A)

AVERAGE HOME ATTENDANCE:
35,659

TOP GATE:
59,960 v Bolton Wanderers (H)

Promotion 1965

REGULAR SIDE
Marshall
Craig, Clark
Anderson, McGrath, Iley
Hockey or Robson, Hilley, McGarry or Cummings, Penman, Suddick.

CHAIRMAN: Lord Westwood
MANAGER: Joe Harvey
TRAINER-COACH: Jimmy Greenhalgh
CAPTAIN: Stan Anderson

Stan Anderson with the Second Division Championship trophy.

LEAGUE APPEARANCES
42 Marshall, Clark, McGrath, 41 Anderson, 40 Craig, 38 Iley, 34 Hilley, 31 McGarry, 24 Cummings, Hockey, 22 Penman, 21 Suddick, 20 Robson, 11 Moncur, 9 Taylor, Knox, 7 Thomas, 2 McKinney, Burton, 1 Allen.

LEAGUE GOALS
16 McGarry, 12 Hilley, 8 Anderson, Cummings, 7 Penman, Robson, 6 Suddick, 5 Iley, 3 Thomas, own-goal, 2 Taylor, Hockey, 1 Knox, Burton.

Captain Stan Anderson throws his shirt to the crowd after the game with Bolton. His colleagues soon follow his lead.

Cheers! - Division One here we come. Left to right, back: Iley, Clark, Hilley, Penman. Front: Cummings, Knox, Craig, Robson, Anderson, McGrath

AS JOE HARVEY AND HIS PLAYERS were preparing for a fresh start in the First Division, United's directors were preoccupied with a long running war of words with the City Council. Ever since the club had submitted for permission to redevelop St James Park as the fifties decade closed, there had been much animosity between landlord and tenant. The announcement that United's stadium, along with Roker Park, was to be a venue for the forthcoming World Cup finals in 1966 pushed the club's hierarchy into planning further development proposals - on the condition of obtaining co-operation and planning permission from the council. Disagreements had simmered in the background before the Football Association's announcement, but now a full scale battle erupted.

The World Cup organising committee insisted on improvements being carried out to St James Park and with no decision having being reached by the council on the club's 1958 proposals, United lodged further plans in April 1963 together with an application for a lengthy extension to their existing lease - ensuring tenure to guarantee the Magpies considerable cash investment for the redevelopment. Drawn out negotiations lasted the rest of the year with the council bringing into the equation the constitutional set-up of Newcastle United. They wanted a major say in not only stadium improvements, but also how the football club was to be run in the future. Councillor Dan Smith, Chairman of the Planning Committee noted, "We are not prepared to leave it to the existing management", while another council member, Arthur Grey said, "While the Corporation will favour securing a lease for Newcastle United they will not be happy to do so for the club as at present constituted and operated". One of The Journal's headlines noted the council's threat as, "Run Newcastle United Football Club our way, or else!" Pressure was being exerted on the club to democratise ownership and United would have none of it. Chairman William McKeag hit back in a rapidly worsening conflict. He said the council, "had thwarted and frustrated United all along the line". They had been, "unco-operative and unhelpful almost at every touch and turn". Newcastle United's proposals got nowhere fast.

Talk of a multi-purpose stadium took place, exactly what the local authority had been looking for since the twenties. A 40,000 capacity "Wembley of the North" was drawn up by the council, but Newcastle wanted no part of it. By April 1964 events became critical. United's lease was due to expire in one and a half years and the FA's deadline on World Cup improvements was even closer. Meetings continued, working parties set-up, claim and counter-claim went back and forward for months, intermingled with a political Labour v Tory council row too. There was even talk of Newcastle United being evicted from St James Park and Alan Hardaker, secretary of the Football League, noted that if United had no ground, "They would be asked to resign".

During the summer, the World Cup committee made the decision that Newcastle United's name would be omitted from their list of centres as the club could not even give an assurance that they would still possess the ground in 1966, never mind have a development plan built. The north east's second venue moved down the coast to Ayresome Park and United missed out on a huge opportunity to be part of the biggest football feast Britain had seen.

Lord Westwood, led the club through a new era and was later President of the Football League.

United's board was furious. McKeag observed bitterly, "It is enough to make angels weep. Not one iota of co-operation or help was given by the City Council". But that was not the end of the affair. For 20 years the battle raged on. A new lease was agreed - albeit only a stopgap five years - and another multi-purpose concept designed, this time with the University and City Council as co-users. Newcastle again didn't want to be a part tenant and took steps to move from their historic home.

In April 1966 first details were revealed of a 35 acre site Newcastle had earmarked in Gosforth, off Sandy Lane, and by August 1968 the club had applied for planning permission. New Chairman Lord Westwood said, "What choice have we? If we don't get planning permission and if we can't make peace with the Council we will be evicted and therefore cease to exist as a football club". He added, "As far back as 1929 the Newcastle United Board submitted a plan for improvements but nothing has ever happened. We have tried and tried, but we are getting nowhere".

Minister for Sport, Dennis Howell was asked to mediate in the vendetta and more confabs took place under the guidance of Lord Lonsdale. Fresh plans were lodged, yet total disagreement remained. The row went through the rest of 1968, through all of 1969 and throughout 1970 too. It went on and on. United even had to drop the City's Coat of Arms from the front of the club programme, relationships were so poor. Newcastle were ready to move to Gosforth, out of the city limit, to Northumberland. A £1 million super stadium was drawn up, approved and all set to go - private boxes, supporters' club, restaurant and all. However, at the last moment in 1971, some semblance of agreement with the council materialised and the plan was scrapped. Lord Westwood said at the time, "I'm the happiest man in Newcastle". A new scheme for the transformation of St James Park was agreed by both parties. It consisted of four new cantilevered stands, yet there was still a long way to go - and many more arguments over the years - before redevelopment started to take shape.

With this storm brewing in the background it was back to the First Division in August 1965 after only four years in the wilderness. United however, found life at the top very difficult and almost made a quick return from whence they came. They had perhaps allowed Stan Anderson to depart too early - he joined Middlesbrough - and there was an urgent need for goalscoring ability with McGarry and Cummings not assessed as First Division material. Newcastle possessed the unwanted distinction of scoring fewest goals on their own ground and eight different centre-forwards were tried, including centre-half Bill Thompson in desperation. All failed and no-one had to tell manager Harvey that a top class striker was a priority.

United were linked with noted goalscorers Ron Davies, Don Rodgers and Albert Bennett and Harvey signed Rotherham's Bennett for £27,500. Born in County Durham, he had just won an England Under 23 cap and was one of the country's up and coming youngsters. Tall, leggy and curly haired, he was, like so many of Joe Harvey's players, dogged with injury, but did have one sustained and successful spell in a black'n'white shirt. United almost got another striker too when during October Harvey plunged for Wyn Davies who had left a deep impression after the promotion battle with

United return to Division One against Nottingham Forest in August 1965. A humorous view of the afternoon's action.

Albert Bennett leaps in glory after scoring against Fulham in 1967.

Youth Cup winners in 1962. Bobby Moncur (front row, 2nd from right), Alan Suddick (front, 2nd from left) and David Craig (left of 'keeper) all took part. Long-serving Benny Craig (extreme right) coached the side.

YOUTH CUP VICTORY

United's seniors may have been in the doldrums at the beginning of the new decade, but the club's youth side lifted the FA Youth Cup for the first time in 1961/62. After trouncing Seaton Delaval 14-0, United's kids eliminated The Corinthians (3-0) and Sunderland (3-1), then favourites Manchester United (2-1) before reaching the semi-final by knocking out North Shields (1-0). Portsmouth faced the Tynesiders and over two legs United reached the final 4-3 on aggregate. They met Wolves - also in a two legged tie - and 13,916 were at Molineux to see United claim a 1-1 draw. At St James Park a 58th minute goal by Bob Moncur in front of 20,588 was enough to win the trophy. He rose to a corner kick and headed home the winner.

UNITED;
Craig (S)
Craig (D), Clish
Chapman, Markie, Turner
Gowlands, Suddick, Watkin, Moncur, O'Neil.

All bar 'keeper Stan Craig, Matti Gowlands and Clive Chapman graduated to league duty with United. Skipper was Colin Clish while Ted Hughes and coach Benny Craig looked after the youngsters.

Bolton Wanderers. However, after agreeing terms with the Lancashire club, Davies demanded too much himself and the deal fell through. United found no-one else and survived on gruelling defence and a late upsurge in form.

The Magpies relied for much of the season on muscle tactics as they battled to stay in Division One and were strongly criticised for it. Bob Lord, Chairman at Burnley declared, "They are the roughest side we have met this season", while Chelsea's boss Tommy Docherty said, "I've seen nothing worse than Newcastle's methods". Joe Harvey defended his side angrily, "It's nonsense to say Newcastle are rough. We are taking the hammerings. But we don't cry".

Peterborough United inflicted a blow on United again, this time knocking the Magpies out of the League Cup by 4-3 after the visitors had been 3-1 up at half-time. It was an entertaining see-saw game for the unbiased few at Gallowgate, but ended in another cup shock for Magpie diehards. Consistency was sadly lacking, clearly seen in the enigma of Alan Suddick. One week he would show international talent, the next be a mere novice. The 21 year-old baffled everyone and went through a terrible patch mid season and almost signed for West

The balding figure of Keith Kettleborough.

Bromwich Albion at a giveaway fee. However, Suddick was to return and become a hero once more. Against Sunderland over New Year, United offered hardly a whimper as the Roker team won 2-0. They were now 19th in the table and something dramatic had to be done. A saviour was needed and he came in the shape of a 30 year-old balding midfielder from Sheffield United.

Keith Kettleborough was signed immediately after that Sunderland fiasco as a short term buy. It turned out to be a red letter day for the club as his experience took hold of midfield and guided United out of trouble. At a cut-price £20,000 he turned a ragged, disjointed unit into a slick moving one. On his debut, Kettleborough inspired United to their first victory in eight matches, a 2-1 win over West Ham. In the next game they grabbed a point at

Sunderland's Martin Harvey and Charlie Hurley are helpless as Alan Suddick drives the ball into the net for a United goal during the derby of 1966.

Tottenham, then on the Welsh border defeated Chester 3-1 in the FA Cup. Two more good league wins followed, but afterwards United slipped from the Cup, defeated 2-1 at home by Sheffield Wednesday, the eventual finalists. This after United had beaten the Yorkshire side the week before.

Kettleborough had an influence on his colleagues. Jim Iley returned to form and a rejuvenated Suddick showed touches of brilliance everyone on Tyneside knew he possessed. Over Easter the youngster sent rivals Sunderland deep into relegation trouble with two cracking goals. At St James Park, he first outpaced both Charlie Hurley and Martin Harvey before driving home a stinging 20 yarder. Then he delightfully interchanged with Hilley on the edge of the box before smashing the ball past Montgomery for a second time. To the joy of Gallowgate's terraces, Suddick totally out-witted Sunderland's expensive Scottish import, Jim Baxter.

United's side lacked nothing in spirit, but was crying out for two quality individuals to add that touch of class needed for Division One football. The close season of 1966 saw a massive search for new talent by the manager and his scouts.

Southampton's Ron Davies was a target again, so too was big John Hughes of Celtic. By the kick-off though, nobody arrived and as the new 4-4-2 and 4-4-3 formations saw the light of day, United went through another worrying and much criticised season. At one stage dissatisfaction among fans led to a group breaking into St James Park, smashing the posts and crossbars and scattering them over the pitch. And after a 3-0 home defeat by Everton a riot broke out with frustrated supporters attacking the club's entrance.

The big signing all Tyneside was waiting for. Wyn Davies, followed by Ron McGarry, appears for the first time in Magpie colours.

The Magpies were lucky to escape relegation in 1966/67 with only the last two home games of the season, against West Ham United and Southampton, giving them the necessary four points for safety. The Tynesiders ended up with the worst goals ratio of all 92 Football League clubs, but still survived and became stronger and stronger after this escape.

Early matches, including a 1-0 League Cup defeat at Leeds, showed where they were failing, in attack again. Supporters were in uproar and blamed the board for not releasing enough cash to the manager and crowd demonstrations - culminating in the Everton incident - were frequent. This prompted Harvey to make a record £100,000 bid for Rodney Marsh and Roger Morgan, Queens Park Rangers' exciting pair, but the offer was rejected. A 6-0 defeat at Blackpool soon followed and this made the manager more determined. He at last got the big signing the whole of Tyneside was waiting for. Joe returned to Bolton and for a second time attempted to buy Wyn Davies. This time he got his man, for £80,000, the biggest amount Newcastle had spent on any individual by far. The 24 year-old was to say, "I was reluctant to move so far from Wales. But as it turned out, it was the best move I ever made".

The Welsh international's debut was to be against Sunderland of all teams. The centre-forward made little difference though as United slumped 3-0. Following that set-back Harvey was desperate for cash to buy again and put the whole playing staff, bar Davies and Suddick, on the transfer list. It was, in fact, Suddick who disappeared first. He joined Blackpool for a club record £60,000 at Christmas. United fans did not like the sale of their favourite, but within hours Harvey used the cash to purchase three players, and undoubtedly saved United from slipping back into Division Two.

Rugged centre-half John McNamee came from Hibs, chunky midfielder Dave Elliott from Sunderland and the spritely winger, Tommy Robson - Gateshead born - from Chelsea. McNamee was to instantly become a character on the pitch. With little finesse, the big Scot revelled in duels with big name centre-forwards and they quickly became a feature of United's play. Dave Elliott displayed an efficient game without taking headlines, while the tip-toe runs of Robson were to give the Magpies a new dimension on the flank.

With Newcastle in bottom position at the end of 1966 there was only one way that the black'n'whites could go - up - and they eventually did that, but very, very slowly. Highlight of the

SUBSTITUTE DEBUT

For the 1965/66 season the Football League allowed the use of substitutes for the first time - but initially only in the case of injured players. Newcastle's first player to wear the number 12 shirt was Albert Bennett against Nottingham Forest on the opening day of the season. He didn't get onto the pitch and it was Ollie Burton who made club history when he appeared for the injured Trevor Hockey against Northampton Town on September 4th. Hockey, as the club's official Football League return notes, had "severe bruising of the right shin and was incapacitated for 72 hours". The first substitute to score was also Burton, netting against Lincoln City in a League Cup tie during September 1967. Newcastle's very first sub is thought to be a player called Beattie who replaced Harry Jeffery in a friendly with Sunderland in January 1895.

Dave Elliott, one of Harvey's signings to save United from the drop.

Big John McNamee who became such a character in defence.

Jim Scott, purchased to provide crosses for big Wyn Davies.

season was a 4-3 FA Cup victory at Coventry, then top of the Second Division. As one reporter noted, it was, "a throbbing, bubbling, cardiac-inducing epic" - a game that brought back memories for many of the fifties glory days. Wyn Davies hit a hat-trick - his only one for United - but the man-of-the-match was Jim Iley who was involved in everything. Three goals found the net in the first five minutes with Davies shooting in from the edge of the box and Pop Robson getting United's second after a flick by Bennett. City pulled a goal back when McNamee deflected a shot into his own net. That rallied the home side and Ian Gibson grabbed an equaliser, but on the half hour Davies slotted the ball past the City 'keeper after Hilley had done all the work. The Welshman scored his third - ramming home Robson's cross to make it 5-3 before Coventry came back again to ensure a nailbiting finish to the tie.

Nottingham Forest proved too good for United in Round Four. They won 3-0 in the Midlands against a makeshift Magpie line-up and it was left for United to concentrate on the relegation battle. Dave Hilley and young reserve striker, Peter Noble, inspired United's last effort to steer clear of the drop. The side's approach work was good at times, and at last they grabbed a little luck which had largely deserted the Magpie camp since getting back to Division One. Almost 40,000 saw West Ham United defender Jack Burkitt, harried by Robson, score a 15 yard own-goal that just about kept United in the First Division. The Magpies made sure by winning 3-1 against fellow strugglers, Southampton in the last home game of the season. For a second year running United were safe.

Tyne v Wear drama. John McNamee hangs on the rigging after netting a late equaliser at Roker Park in 1967.

There was a vast improvement for the 1967/68 campaign. Being doomed in many quarters before they had even started, Newcastle showed that they had built a team to be reckoned with. Indeed, only an exceptional poor away record stopped them making a bid for the title, that was the measure of the revival. United's home form was second to none. They started with a rousing 3-0 victory over Southampton which silenced many of the pre-season doubters and went on not to lose in league matches at St James Park until the very last weeks of the season - 19 games without defeat, a record.

With new forward signing from Hibs, Jimmy Scott adding to the now settled Davies-Bennett combination, goals came a little easier. However, Davies, with only twelve was as high as any individual could reach, while Tommy Robson scored eleven from the wing. Scott was purchased for £40,000 to provide crosses for Davies and Bennett. He showed touches of the exciting ability that had earned him a Scottish cap in 1964. From a footballing family, his father and brother both played the game, Alex, being capped by the Scots too.

It was in cup competitions that United let their fans down though. In the League Cup, Fourth Division Lincoln City, with seven free transfer men in their side, won 2-1 - another shock to swallow. The FA Cup provided an even bigger sensation when Carlisle United arrived at Gallowgate for the 3rd Round tie. With a 56,000 crowd in attendance, Davies was well held by Terry Garbutt and with their big leader mastered, Newcastle were a beaten side. Little Tom Murray knocked home the eventual winner and Ollie Burton had a penalty saved after Davies had been sandwiched in the box. Goalkeeper Alan Ross may have moved before Burton hit the ball, but the Cumbrians deserved their victory nevertheless and had highlighted that the Magpies had very much become dependent on Wyn Davies. If he received the ball in the right place - in the air - and was on form, United ticked. If not they more often than not dramatically faded.

In league football there was plenty to shout about, none more so than the 1-0 defeat of Everton during October, a game packed with incident. United's winner came from the spot after Albert Bennett had been floored by a left-hook from 'keeper Gordon West. The Everton man was sent-off and Jim Iley hit a twice taken penalty past substitute goalie Sandy Brown. It was no classic footballing game, but a tough and physical duel. Ollie Burton was also despatched to the dressing-room, McNamee booked for a flying tackle, Johnny Morrissey carried off and Alex Young sported a massive black eye!

A match that will be remembered for its football rather than brawling was the game with top of the table Sheffield Wednesday. They were hammered 4-0 with Albert Bennett playing his best 90 minutes for the club. It was a victory that confirmed United's problems were over and pointed the way for a European place. Newcastle were powerful up front at last, adding to their grit at the back where Bobby Moncur had flourished. He stepped into Scotland's Under 23 team and developed into a commanding defender. Harvey had put together a side capable of success after two seasons of struggle.

Chelsea went down 5-1 with their centre-half, Colin Waldron, never happy against Davies, being taken for a merry dance by United's number nine - now becoming the crowd's favourite. Over Christmas, Sunderland were toppled 2-1 at Gallowgate in front of almost 60,000 and a John McNamee header in the 88th minute earned a point from the return on Wearside. The 6'0" defender was left climbing the rigging and crossbar of the Fulwell End as he crashed the ball into the net - a picture

MATCH OF THE DAY ARRIVES

Television really took a hold on the game during the sixties and BBC's regular Match of the Day began in 1964/65. United's first showing was in October 1966 when the cameras were at Highbury for the First Division tussle against Arsenal. The Gunners won 2-0 in an eventful match for the TV - Gordon Marshall was carried off after 75 minutes with a damaged cartilage and Dave Hilley took over in goal. Two first half goals by McLintock and Boot were enough for Arsenal to pick up both points.

En route for Europe in 1968. Left to right, back: Burton, Clark, McFaul, McNamee, Gibb, Craig, Davies. Front: Scott, Sinclair, Robson B., Elliott, Robson T.

vivid in supporters' memories for many years after the event. That was a white-hot derby which had enough excitement for the whole season. Two Ollie Burton penalties also flashed past Montgomery in an eventful 3-3 draw.

Even in defeat United's performances were not disheartening. On the last day of the season, Manchester City, needing only a victory to lift the League crown, arrived at Gallowgate. In a glittering match City won 4-3, but the quality of United's football was so good it was hard to say who was running for the Championship at times. And in friendlies Tyneside's fans witnessed a feast of football. During February, European Champions, Glasgow Celtic, including veteran 37 year-old Ronnie Simpson in goal, were visitors to St James Park. He received a tremendous welcome on his return, but his team were beaten through a solitary Jim Scott goal before almost 39,000 fans. It was marvellous stuff and one would have imagined the European Cup itself was at stake for the pace of the game. Jock Stein noted, "This was a great match - one of the best". On the black side, the city saw major hooliganism take place when Celtic's massive following rioted after the contest and virtually every pub showed scars of the new ugly face of soccer. United won at Celtic Park in a return challenge as well, 3-2 in front of 42,000 and completed a super double over Europe's top side. Newcastle proved they could match Europe's best - a poignant double friendly.

Albert Bennett, unluckily injured in the middle of a great run, together with Davies formed a fruitful duo up front. With gates increasing to the 40,000 mark, cash started to pour into St James Park once more and a big signing mid season was Leicester City's top scorer, Jackie Sinclair for £70,000. Another ex Scottish international, Sinclair, however rarely showed his true potential and in the final analysis disappointed many.

It was a satisfying season and although finishing in only 10th place, United qualified for the Inter Cities Fairs Cup - European competition for the very first time. They had squeezed in through the controversial 'one club, one city' rule that was shortly to be scrapped. Newcastle jumped ahead of higher placed clubs, Everton, Spurs and Arsenal, while Manchester United and West Bromwich Albion who finished above them too, opted for the European Cup(as winners) and European Cup Winners Cup(as FA Cup victors). As an added slice of fortune, England was allowed one extra place - from three to four clubs - and in a round-a-bout way United entered the new competition at UEFA's meeting in Copenhagen. Only John Gibson from the Evening Chronicle was present and United's name went into the draw along with other entrants from England; Leeds United, Chelsea and Liverpool. Newcastle would match some of the best sides on the Continent in the coming months. To start with, they drew Dutch giants, SC Feyenoord.

An aerial view of St. James Park during the sixties showing the old West Stand (left), Leazes End (top) and the four massive pylons that dominated the landscape.

A Fairytale Career

"He was completely professional and dedicated in everything he did"

Joe Harvey, August 1985

United were on their way to becoming Europeans.

A COVETED EUROPEAN CUP AND LEAGUE Championship medal, as well as League Cup winners' tankards were the impressive haul Frank Clark won after he left Newcastle United. Discarded when 31 years-old at the end of the Joe Harvey regime, Clark joined Brian Clough's Nottingham Forest and proceeded to have a wonderful twilight to his days in the game. As it was the north easterner had already accomplished much in a 13 year stay at St James Park, winning a Second Division championship medal, a Fairs Cup memento and additionally appearing at Wembley in the FA Cup final. It was something of a fairytale career.

A left-back of sheer consistency for a decade and over with United, only two men have appeared more for the club than Frank Clark - Jimmy Lawrence and Frank Hudspeth. Born in Highfield in 1943, he turned out for his local side in the Northern Alliance at centre-half after appearing for Durham Boys. At 15 years old, Clark had a chance to join West Bromwich Albion and Preston, as well as Newcastle, but aiming to go to college wanted to concentrate on his education. Frank then played for Crook Town as an amateur and reached Wembley in 1961 winning a FA Amateur Cup medal when his side defeated Hounslow Town. He also forced his way into the England amateur and youth line-ups - skipper of the kid's team.

It was success which brought the scouts of Newcastle United to watch the youngster again and the Magpies persuaded Clark to give professional football a go, signing him in October 1962. He had an unlucky beginning when a broken leg against Liverpool Reserves a year later forced him out of action for a long period and put a stop to his development. It was a bad fracture, in two places, but it only postponed the day Clark would claim a first-team place. That occurred for the last two games of the 1963/64 season and he was installed in the number three shirt during United's promotion campaign the following year.

A six footer, Clark was a sound defender and like many of United's full-backs was never spectacular. He took few gambles, jockeying forwards towards the touch-line and tackling when he was ready. Clark was rarely beaten in a chase for the ball possessing a good turn of speed and was a self made footballer rather than a player of natural talents. Although at times not appreciated by sections of the St James Park crowd, Frank was good enough to be selected for the Football League side in 1969 against the Irish and was highly respected in the dressing-room. Joe Harvey said of Clark, "He was completely professional and dedicated in everything he did".

A keen cricketer too - playing regular local cricket in the region - Frank took part in all of United's successful sides of this era and succeeded Bob Moncur as the black'n'whites' captain following the 1974 FA Cup final. However, he then found himself surplus to requirements and Frank perhaps thought a fine career was over when United handed him a free transfer in May 1975. He was to say, "When Newcastle gave me the sack, which was virtually what it was, I nearly went somewhere like Northampton or Doncaster. Then Brian Clough gave me a chance at Forest". Although Cloughies' outfit was then 16th in the Second Division it was the start of five thoroughly wonderful

Frank Clark

CLARK'S PLAYING RECORD

	League		FA Cup		FL Cup		Europe		Total	
	App	Gls	App	Gls	App	Gls	App	Gls	App	Gls
1963-64	2	0	0	0	0	0	0	0	2	0
1964-65	42	0	1	0	1	0	0	0	44	0
1965-66	35/1	0	2	0	1	0	0	0	38/1	0
1966-67	39	0	2	0	1	0	0	0	42	0
1967-68	35	0	1	0	1	0	0	0	37	0
1968-69	38	0	3	0	1	0	12	0	54	0
1969-70	31	0	1	0	1	0	7	0	40	0
1970-71	30	0	2	0	1	0	4	0	37	0
1971-72	40	0	2	0	2	0	0	0	44	0
1972-73	41	0	2	0	2	0	0	0	45	0
1973-74	36	0	10	0	3	1	0	0	49	1
1974-75	19	0	0	0	5	0	0	0	24	0
	388/1	**0**	**26**	**0**	**19**	**1**	**23**	**0**	**456/1**	**1**

years at the City Ground.

Teaming up with another ex United player - veteran Jimmy Gordon, trainer at Forest - Clark was an ever-present as they finished 8th in Division Two and again when they were promoted in 1976/77. Forest went straight to the top of the First Division and became League Champions, and Runners-up the following year. At the same time Clark appeared twice at Wembley in successful League Cup finals as the Reds became a force in the game. Forest defeated Liverpool(after a replay) and Southampton with Clark the ideal squad man, filling in at either full-back or in the centre of the defence, and even once at centre-forward as sub when he scored one of his rare goals.

The highlight of the former United defender's career though, came in May 1979 when Forest, at the first attempt, reached the final of the European Cup. Over 57,000 saw a Trevor Francis goal secure the trophy against Malmo and Frank appeared at centre-half alongside Larry Lloyd. With a side packed with quality players like Francis, Robertson and Peter Shilton, they dominated the match and were worthy Champions of Champions.

Now 36 years old the opportunity to enter management came Clark's way during the summer of that year, at all places, Sunderland. He joined the Roker Park set-up as assistant to Ken Knighton and proceeded to help the Wearsiders into Division One in 1980. Clark was then coach at the City Ground before being appointed second in command - to Knighton again - at Orient in October 1981. That was to be the start of a long and successful stay at Brisbane Road. He became manager in his own right shortly afterwards and was quickly to impress, so much so that Frank was elevated to the boardroom as managing director. With little cash resources, Clark showed he had learnt much from his two former managers, Joe Harvey and Brian Clough, and fashioned a good set-up in London. He eventually saw his club promoted into the Third Division in 1989 in a way that pleased the fans, playing football rather than kicking their way out of the basement.

Frank Clark may now be very much a Cockney resident, but after a total of 457 games for United, he has never lost sight of his roots and affection for the black'n'whites.

Centenary Profile 20

The Quiet Irishman

"He never caused me a problem and was on many occasions the first name I put onto the teamsheet"

Joe Harvey, August 1985

NEWCASTLE UNITED HAS PRODUCED MANY distinguished full-backs over the years. Talent like Carr, Hudspeth, McCracken and Bobby Cowell. Like McMichael, Kennedy, Nattrass, Clark and a name perhaps the finest of the lot, David Craig. A quiet Irishman from Comber, a town a few miles from Belfast, David was the nearest thing to a complete footballer. Silky smooth with consistent distribution of the ball, an attacking flair and firm in the tackle. He gave United 18 years service, clocking up over 400 games in a black'n'white shirt and yet missed many more through injury. If it had not been for a variety of knocks, Craig could well have created a new appearance record. He missed in aggregate almost 100 games due to injury.

A one club man, David played football for his local Boys Brigade team in Ireland and was spotted early by Scunthorpe United. A trial in Lincolnshire followed but, being homesick, Craig was on the boat across the Irish Sea within ten weeks. Back in Comber, he trained as an apprentice engineer before a Newcastle scout took note of his name when he reverted to local football around Belfast. United's officials invited the youngster to Tyneside and, unlike his previous visit to England, this time David settled down quickly in the homely north east. He signed as an apprentice professional in August 1960.

On the St James Park staff at the time were Irish internationals Dick Keith and Alf McMichael, a great full-back partnership for club and country and Craig knew their reputation well. He was lucky to have the late Dick Keith as an early guardian. For a long time Craig lacked confidence, was quiet and reserved, but Keith took him under his wing and helped his young countryman a great deal. David was to eventually replace his mentor in United's side. Coach Jimmy Greenhalgh was another to have a big influence on his early days at St James Park.

At 5'10" tall, Craig turned professional in April 1962 and almost immediately was celebrating by winning the FA Youth Cup. Colleagues in that line-up were Bobby Moncur and Alan Suddick, both to have fine careers too. He soon graduated from junior football in the Northern Intermediate League and a period in the reserves followed alongside experienced heads like Gordon Hughes, John McGrath, as well as on occasion Dick Keith. Within a season and a half Craig was given a chance in United's Second Division side by manager Joe Harvey. Newcastle's boss was impressed with Craig's attitude as well as his skill. Harvey remarked, "If all professionals were as dedicated then the ulcer rate in my line of business would drop alarmingly". He later noted, "He never caused me a problem and was on many occasions the first name I put onto the teamsheet".

Craig's senior debut was at Gallowgate in November 1963 against Cardiff City, coming into the side after a spell of injuries had spoiled Harvey's team selection. He was not yet 20 and Craig took his place alongside other debutants, new signings Stan Anderson and Trevor Hockey. The record book shows it was a disaster day for Newcastle, a 4-0 home thrashing and Craig was dropped with the more experienced Bill McKinney recalled. Craig though, despite the harrowing debut, had showed a great deal of promise and later in the season his chance came again.

David Craig

CRAIG'S PLAYING RECORD

	League		FA Cup		FL Cup		Europe		Total	
	App	Gls	App	Gls	App	Gls	App	Gls	App	Gls
1963-64	13	0	0	0	1	0	0	0	14	0
1964-65	40	0	1	0	1	0	0	0	42	0
1965-66	38	0	2	1	0	0	0	0	40	1
1966-67	25	1	0	0	1	0	0	0	26	1
1967-68	10/1	0	0	0	1	0	0	0	11/1	0
1968-69	26	0	1	1	2	0	9	0	38	1
1969-70	26	1	1	0	0	0	6	0	33	1
1970-71	31	1	2	0	1	0	4	0	38	1
1971-72	36	1	2	0	2	0	0	0	40	1
1972-73	42	3	2	0	2	1	0	0	46	4
1973-74	24/1	0	8	1	2	0	0	0	34/1	1
1974-75	13/2	0	0	0	0	0	0	0	13/2	0
1975-76	14	1	2	0	4	0	0	0	20	1
1976-77	2/1	0	1	0	0/1	0	0	0	3/2	0
1977-78	6	0	0	0	0	0	2	0	8	0
	346/5	**8**	**22**	**3**	**17/1**	**1**	**21**	**0**	**406/6**	**12**

The Irishman took it capably and stayed in the team for the remaining twelve matches - and for just about the next twelve years too.

During the following campaign, Newcastle won the Second Division championship. David missed only two games at right-back and alongside Frank Clark began the full-back combination that was to fill Joe Harvey's defence for the next decade. He won his first representative honour being picked for the Irish Under 23 side against Wales in that season and two years later was in the full side, also against the Welsh when he partnered Alex Elder of Burnley at Windsor Park. David won 25 caps all told, yet that number should have been 35 or even 40, but for those niggling injuries that disrupted his career during the seventies.

Craig became an accomplished First Division defender, the best without doubt said judges on Tyneside - better than rivals Keith Newton, Terry Cooper or Peter Rodrigues - and as Newcastle pushed for a European place he performed to his peak. A regular in the Magpies' entertaining eleven during those years, only injury prevented him becoming an ever-present season after season. In fact a knee ligament problem nearly saw him miss United's Fairs Cup glory, but he recovered in time to take his place in the semi-final with Rangers. He wasn't so lucky in 1974 when a dislocated elbow against Burnley robbed the Irishman of a Wembley appearance. And fate was to be cruel to Craig once more as United returned to the Twin Towers two years later. Then playing at centre-half, he damaged medial ligaments against Liverpool a week before the League Cup final and was forced to cry off. David said, "Yes I was unlucky and very disappointed, but you have to take the rough with the smooth in this business. I unfortunately got more of the rough". Craig did receive some consolation when the FA minted a special medal for him after the 1974 final.

The years following 1976 saw David's appearances in United's side dwindle as younger talent pushed for his place. Now 32 years old, Irving Nattrass took over the number 2 shirt, but Craig still gave the Magpies a couple of years service continuing in the centre-half role. His last season was 1977/78, the year Newcastle dropped into Division Two. He had entered the scene on promotion and left it when relegated 412 games later. Craig had played a noted part in United's 13 year spell in the First Division.

During the summer of 1978 he joined Blyth Spartans for a brief period before concentrating on other interests on Tyneside. He started a milk distribution business then managed a couple of newsagents with partner, Alan Thompson, a past United coach and the man who met Craig off the plane back in 1960. He never fancied football coaching or management, but occasionally still turns up at St James Park in the role of an ordinary spectator.

David Craig didn't cost United anything more than the regulation signing on fee, yet no player could have served the club with greater loyalty. He was never a headline catcher and never controversial, only a consistent performer and a stylist at right-back - one of United's finest home grown talents.

13 EUROPEANS

1968-1971 • MEMORABLE DEBUT • FAIRS CUP TRIUMPH • GLORIOUS EXIT • ITALIAN THUGGERY • PENALTY KICK FINALE •

"We were a team in the best sense of the word. There were no superstars, no world-beaters, just a damned good team"
Jim Scott, March 1991

JETTING THE AIRWAYS OF EUROPE WAS something completely new for the whole north east region. Chairman Lord Westwood remarked at the programme's outset, "Without a shadow of doubt the 1968/69 season will be the most important for Newcastle United for many years". He was ever so right. Thrill and incident followed week after week after week and Tyneside loved every minute of it. Thousands upon thousands of fans packed into St James Park and witnessed three rousing years of gripping football.

United's most eventful season for 13 years started with no new faces except for Scottish Under 23 international, Tommy Gibb, who was signed from Partick Thistle as a £45,000 reserve, but who became an important cog in United's continental machine. Tall and lean, he was quickly given an opportunity due to injury absentees and stayed in the side for the next four years without serious competition. Full of running, often making late dashes into the box, Gibb proved an excellent midfield buy.

Tommy Gibb, a workhorse in the middle of the park.

United had to cope without Bob Moncur, out for two months with knee trouble, while other faces were missing too. Albert Bennett broke down after a similar injury, while Iley, Marshall, Tommy Robson and Jackie Sinclair were all out of favour. Up stepped Willie McFaul to claim the goalkeeper's position having been signed from Linfield two seasons before at a modest £7,000. Like Gibb he wasn't to relinquish the jersey for several years. Geoff Allen entered the action too. Having made his debut back in 1964, the 21 year-old was all set to go places but, unluckily a heavy tackle during October virtually finished the winger's career. He played only one game after that mishap before retiring with ligament problems.

Outside-left Geoff Allen, the man who destroyed Feyenoord.

Having beaten Southport 2-0 in the League Cup, United went into their first European tie with the illustrious SC Feyenoord on Wednesday September 11th. Newcastle had already been eliminated by most observers before even kicking a ball, however, in no uncertain terms, they showed their doubters that this United side was no pushover and not in the competition just to make up the numbers. A crowd of 46,348 at St James Park saw the big names of Dutch football fall completely flat on their faces as United gave them a 4-0 hammering to remember. It was a great team performance of attacking football with the woodwork saving Feyenoord on another three occasions. Allen was the pick of the Magpies' side, having a field day on the left touch-line. Jimmy Scott opened United's European account after Davies picked out Robson and the ball found its way to Allen on the Popular touch-line. The rosy-cheeked winger fired in a low centre across the face of goal and Scott side-footed past Graafland.

Newcastle pounded the opposition all evening and Scott's opener was soon followed by goals from Robson, Gibb and Davies. It was perhaps United's most convincing display of their 28 European games

NEWCASTLE UNITED
FOOTBALL CO. LTD.

Inter-Cities Fairs Cup Competition
First Round—1st Leg

Newcastle Un.
v
Feyenoord

Wednesday, 11th September, 1968
Kick-off 7.30 p.m.

Centre Pavilion

Row F

No. 166

TO BE RETAINED

Tommy Gibb cracks the ball past a helpless Dutch goalkeeper during United's debut in European football in 1968.

to date. The Dutch side were a good team, indeed they went on to win the ultimate prize of the European Cup the following season. Newcastle were cheered off to a standing ovation by their supporters who had been totally absorbed by the new contest.

However, in the return leg it was a different story. With a backing of over 2,000 fans, United learnt their first lesson of European football. The defence and midfield - McNamee apart and still without long term casualty Moncur - were torn apart for much of the game. They didn't play as a unit, kicked anywhere and panicked. But Newcastle survived. Feyenoord only managed two goals and the same mistake was not repeated.

A space of almost seven weeks separated United's next Fairs Cup journey, a trip to Lisbon and a match with the Sporting club. Before this, United fell 4-1 to Southampton in the League Cup when the Channon-Davies partnership destroyed the black'n'whites. The side was then hit by more injuries and young strikers Alan Foggon, Keith Dyson and full-back Ron Guthrie all played well

Alan Foggon, quickly to become a threat up front.

after being thrown into the team. All three were locals. Foggon burst on to the scene and much was expected of the erratic, long-haired kid. At his best when running head on at a defence, Joe Harvey in his typical down to earth manner once introduced Foggon as, "A canny lad. He likes a pint - he'll go far"! Foggon could have made a really big name for himself, but fell well short of the stardom he was tipped to reach. In contrast Keith Dyson was calm and assured on the ball and could expertly hold up play in the striker's role. He scored a good haul of goals for the Magpies - 26 in all competitions - and appeared for England's Under 23 side in 1970.

Wyn Davies heads powerfully into the net against Feyenoord.

Two away four-goal sprees in succession, against Nottingham Forest and Ipswich Town, in which both Foggon and Dyson netted, put United in fine spirit for the Sporting clash. The first leg was held in the majestic Lisbon stadium, a huge concrete bowl with its own hotel complex. As the heavens opened and rain fell in sheets, United went agonisingly close to pulling off a tremendous 1-0 victory. With kids Foggon and reserve centre-half Graham Winstanley in the team, United led until only seconds from the final whistle when a hopeful long range shot by Morais beat Willie McFaul for the equaliser. Jim Scott was the man to give Newcastle an early lead while Moncur - back in the side - was the pick of United's professional display. His organisation in defence was a boost to the team and made sure a repeat of the Feyenoord fiasco did not occur.

Almost 54,000 saw United go through to the next round on a Wednesday evening three weeks later. It was a single goal from now chief scorer Bryan Robson that clinched the game. What a spectacular goal too. After only ten minutes of play, United were awarded a free-kick just outside the Sporting box. Gibb flighted

Another young find, striker Keith Dyson.

'Pop' Robson's spectacular effort against Sporting Lisbon. A rare occasion Newcastle have worn an all-white outfit.

GIBB'S CONSISTENCY

Between August 1968 and October 1972 Tommy Gibb made 171 consecutive appearances for United - a record. He started the run of consistency against Sheffield Wednesday at Hillsborough and went through all of the 1968/69 and 1969/70 seasons, all of the next campaign too, until the 13th game of season 1971/72. For the match at Highbury with Arsenal, Gibb was left out with Irving Nattrass stepping into his role.

the ball to Davies who nodded into the path of Robson above waist height. He jumped to volley a truly superb goal - a plan practised many times on their Hunters Moor training ground. Robson said, "The move worked like a dream". That was United's best created and finished goal of the European era. Newcastle should have converted more chances but 'keeper Damas pulled off a string of fine saves. Robson's gem however, was enough to take the Magpies to meet another noted European side, Real Zaragoza.

There was a further long wait before the next tie during January, a month packed with half a dozen games of outstanding merit. On New Year's Day 1969, United flew out from a snow covered Tyneside and celebrated Hogmanay in the sun of the Spanish city of Zaragoza. It was to be the closest of United's duels, with the black'n'whites playing well on a bone-hard pitch against a fast and highly skilful Spanish line-up. Many of United's players noted that Zaragoza were the best side they were to meet in the cup run. They had twice been Fairs Cup finalists and winners in 1964. United lost 3-2 in Zaragoza, but those two away goals that Davies and Robson scored were crucial and put Newcastle into the next round. In the impressive La Romareda stadium, Davies caused experienced centre-half Santamaria and his colleagues all sorts of problems. They just couldn't handle the Welshman's enormous leaps and physical approach to the game. Davies said in a recent article, "The Continentals couldn't cope with the high ball in the air. It was alien to their style, and I had great freedom". Zaragoza clinched the game with a fabulous winner, created by Martin and completed with venom by Planas.

United v Setubal. Bryan Robson watched by Arthur Horsefield strikes home one of the Magpies five goals.

A flight back to Tyneside and United had to switch their attention to domestic football in the shape of the FA Cup. Against Third Division Reading, managed by Roy Bentley, Newcastle hit form and cruised to a 4-0 victory. United's fourth goal from Jim Scott - a 30 yard screamer - sent the 41,255 crowd home well satisfied. Ten days later and it was the return leg with Real Zaragoza. Record receipts of £20,000 were recorded as over 56,000 packed into St James Park on a frosty night. They saw United triumph 2-1 and go through on away goals after the contest ended 4-4 on aggregate. It was a superb match which prompted VIP Edward Heath, then Leader of the Opposition, to say, "It was a cracking game and I thoroughly enjoyed it". Bryan Robson set the vast crowd alight when he unleashed a drive into the top right hand corner of the Leazes net for the first goal after only 90 seconds. Foggon slipped the ball into Robson's path in midfield. United's leading scorer went past two defenders at inside-right and from 30 yards hit the ball with stunning power. Nieves, in the Spanish goal, could do nothing but pull the ball out of the net. Gibb added another from a corner, diving to bullet home a header and everything looked rosy. But then the Spaniards pulled a goal back and the game remained tense with the crowd knowing that another goal for Zaragoza would take the visitors through. At times United looked second best, yet what they lacked in finesse they made up in effort. Newcastle battled at the back and Zaragoza's goal didn't come. It was United who progressed in the competition to meet another Portuguese side, Vitoria Setubal who had scored 17 goals in the three rounds so far. Also into the quarter-finals went Leeds United and Glasgow Rangers, Britain's other remaining representatives.

The following Saturday, United defeated Arsenal in the mud, another fine match and only seven days later took part in yet another classic encounter. This time Manchester City arrived at Gallowgate in the 4th Round of the FA Cup. The ground was packed with six short of 58,000 for this tie. However United disappointed their noisy followers being unable to score against the League Champions. It was an absorbing game though, with the Blues more polished technique coming out on

Danish international Benny Arentoft who proved his worth in midfield.

top. The 0-0 draw was a fair result with City hitting the woodwork twice. The replay at Maine Road saw an even bigger crowd, 60,844, and the end of FA Cup action for United. They went down 2-0 to complete what was a pulsating January.

Due to a late winter, February was very barren for United and by the time Setubal's players walked onto the Gallowgate turf on March 12th snow persisted. Most of the Portuguese had never seen white flakes before, and undoubtedly the blizzard that occurred on that evening affected their play. Another crowd of 58,000 stood through the atrocious conditions to watch the Magpies gallop to a 5-1 first leg lead. Robson, with two goals, was again a menace for the opposition and it was once more a good all round performance with young full-back John Craggs - in for the injured Craig - playing well. Gibb, Davies and Foggon scored the other goals.

In the return game, switched to the Estadio Jose Alvalade in Lisbon, where United had faced Sporting, the black'n'whites felt their first taste of continental thuggery. With a full scale carnival in progress around the pitch - bands, fireworks and all - the Latin temperament exploded as Setubal found it hard to break United down. The Tynesiders were hacked to the floor, punched and spat on, but Newcastle kept cool heads under difficult conditions to go into the semi-final draw. Davies scored United's goal in a 3-1 defeat. After the physical mauling they received no fewer than eight players received treatment, many for injuries picked up more easily in a boxing ring.

A month and a half elapsed before the long awaited semi-final with Glasgow Rangers took place. By this time Joe Harvey had added Danish international, Benny Arentoft to his squad. He cost only £18,000 from Greenock Morton and proved a bargain purchase. Only 5'7" tall, the Dane marked well, was a tireless worker and had ability on the ball, often underrated by many. Before the big game United turned their attention back to the more mundane task of picking up league points. They slipped into form and lost only two First Division games out of twelve, finally finishing in final 8th position.

Over 12,000 Geordies travelled to Glasgow and a record Fairs Cup attendance of 75,580 gathered at Ibrox Park for the first leg of the semi-final on May 14th. Both sides knew that the winners of the tie would meet crack Hungarians, Ujpesti Dozsa in the final. Classed as favourites by the Scottish press, United performed heroics to keep out Rangers in a 0-0 draw. The Scots were forced to play without three internationals - Mathieson, McKinnon and Johnston - but still sent wave after wave of attacks on the Tynesiders' box. It was 'keeper Willie McFaul who took the headlines. He saved a certain goal from a long range Andy Penman effort, then in a frantic ten minute spell during the first-half, brought down Swedish forward, Persson and referee Adair awarded a penalty. United's Irishman was up to the task though, he dived low to his right and saved Penman's spot-kick brilliantly, pushing the ball round the post. Moncur and McNamee were giants too as Newcastle made a stand in a defensive line across their penalty box. They defied everything Rangers could throw at them and Tyneside couldn't wait for the return seven days later.

ASTROTURF VICTORY

During the summer tour of 1970, United played several games on artificial grass for the first time. On the Astroturf of Seattle they defeated the Seatacs by 2-1 and also earned victories over Chicago, Victoria Royals, Vancouver Spartans and Eintracht Frankfurt. Soon the infamous plastic was to be a part of the domestic scene too. Those wins in North America remain the only occasions the club has won on plastic grass. Back home, in several league and cup games in the future, against Luton, QPR and Oldham, United never won a single match on an artificial surface.

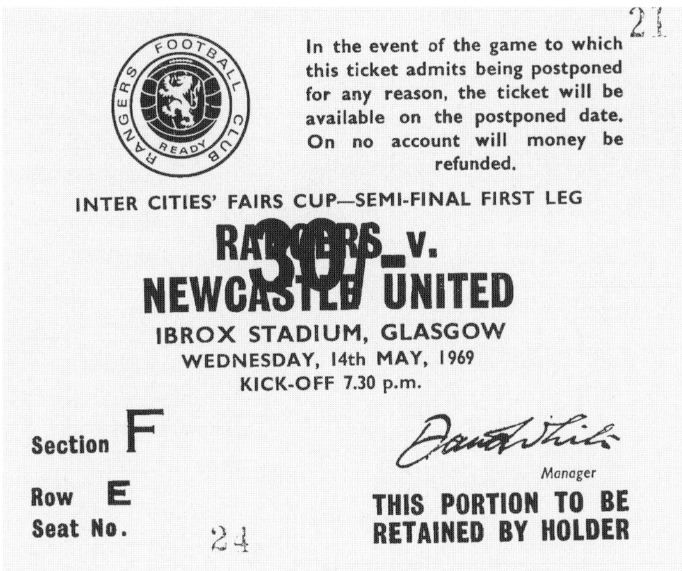

21

RANGERS FOOTBALL CLUB READY

In the event of the game to which this ticket admits being postponed for any reason, the ticket will be available on the postponed date. On no account will money be refunded.

INTER CITIES' FAIRS CUP—SEMI-FINAL FIRST LEG

RANGERS v. NEWCASTLE UNITED

IBROX STADIUM, GLASGOW

WEDNESDAY, 14th MAY, 1969

KICK-OFF 7.30 p.m.

Section F

Row E

Seat No. 24

Manager

THIS PORTION TO BE RETAINED BY HOLDER

Order restored after Rangers' fans' pitch invasion during the Fairs Cup semi-final at St. James Park.

Ollie Burton gets the better of Rangers' centre-forward Colin Stein at St. James Park. Bobby Moncur watches.

The events that occurred in that game, witnessed by an all ticket 60,000 crowd, were certainly worth waiting for - although probably not for the football played. The drama, tension and incident that happened off the field completely overshadowed United's fine 2-0 victory in a very tough, physical game which was more like Bannockburn or Culloden than a Fairs Cup semi-final. When Jackie Sinclair scored United's second goal in the 77th minute all hell let loose. Hoards of drunken Scots went berserk and streamed out of the Gallowgate End and onto the pitch. With bottles and beer cans flying through the air, a massive battle amongst themselves and the police took place. Referee John Gow took the players from the field for fully 17 minutes while police struggled to restore order. A police spokesman said, "If we had enough men we would have arrested the 2,000 fans who were on the park". As it was they had to settle for around 30 and the match was restarted with one continuous line of blue police uniforms from one corner flag to the other. Dogs and horses were in attendance for any hint of more trouble.

By then the game was over. Rangers' players had been shocked by the scale of the incident and Ibrox annals noted, "It was a night of shame, a night when most of us present were ashamed of being Scots". It had been a grim match with lots of tight marking and frequent stoppages. Hard and relentless it was, but United still managed to grab the goals - two magic moments that sent the Magpies into the final. Both came in the second period, the first eight minutes after the interval. The energetic Tommy Gibb hit a wonderful through ball for Scott to chase. He left Mathieson stranded and powered a high angled drive past Neef in the Rangers goal. The second and killer strike started with a long Burton free-kick which was lofted high onto the head of Wyn Davies. In typical fashion he

sent a flick to Sinclair who blasted the ball into the roof of the net.

Remarkably, United's dogged side - criticised in some quarters for lack of finesse - had reached a European final, and at their first attempt. As Jim Scott remarked latterly, "We were a team in the best sense of the word. There were no superstars, no world-beaters, just a dammed good team". Bryan Robson was fast becoming a noted striker though, and was strongly tipped to become an England player after impressing in the Under 23 side. He had scored 30 goals in the season, the first United player to do so since 1952.

United had reached the final on merit eliminating some highly experienced clubs. Zaragoza, Rangers, Sporting and Feyenoord were all regular European competitors, next were Ujpesti Dosza of Hungary who were rated by many as one of the finest sides on the Continent at the time. They had convincingly disposed of League Champions Leeds United. Don Revie, Bill Shankly and Jock Stein all reckoned Newcastle had no chance. No less than six of their players appeared for Hungary in a World Cup match a few weeks before including two famous names, Ferenc Bene and Janos Gorocs.

It had been a long season - the final leg wasn't scheduled until June - it was warm, the talk was of the Test Match series with the West Indies and next season's World Cup finals. Football, or at least the 1968/69 season had closed its door for another summer recess, except that is for one corner of the country - the north east. One columnist noted that, "a miracle on Tyneside had occurred, and it went almost unnoticed". A repeat 60,000 crowd turned up for the Inter Cities Fairs Cup final. They paid by far a record £42,000 receipts to watch the biggest game United had taken part in for almost 15 years. On that evening Gallowgate's pigeons were continually upset as the crowd roared United to victory.

Jack Sinclair volleys the ball past Rangers' 'keeper Neef to make sure United reached their first European final.

Another view of Sinclair's effort. Note the Rangers' supporters on the floodlight pylon.

Centenary Highlight

"Europe's babes emerged man-sized from the banks of the Danube as the new czars of soccer"

Ivor Broadis, June 1969

NEWCASTLE UNITED № 9927
FOOTBALL CO. LTD

Inter-Cities Fairs Cup
FINAL — 1st Leg

(Valid only for First Match at St. James' Park)
For Details see Public Announcements

ADMIT TO

GALLOWGATE ENCLOSURE
(See reverse side for Plan)

Entrance by Turnstiles: STRAWBERRY PLACE
ADJACENT "A" STAND

Secretary

To avoid delays and congestion, it is advisable that Ticket Holders are in position half an hour before Kick-off

TWELVE MONTHS AGO IT WAS ONLY A DREAM, but on a warm evening at St James Park towards the end of May, Newcastle United walked out alongside the white shirts of Ujpesti in the final of the Inter Cities Fairs Cup. For the first 15 minutes of the match United were inspired. They swarmed all over the Hungarians with balls pumped high into the visitors' box looking for the Davies-Robson spearhead. But then the superior technique of Ujpesti started to worry the black'n'whites. McFaul had to save well from Dunai and Bene, then tip a vicious Solymosi free-kick round the post.

The second-half, however, belonged solely to the Tynesiders and after a long wait they eventually broke the deadlock. United's first goal came from a Gibb free-kick on 63 minutes. The Scot chipped a ball over the defence, Davies chested the ball down and fired goalwards. His shot broke off the 'keeper's body for Moncur to drive low into a tiny corner of the net. And it was United's skipper who again was responsible for Newcastle's second eight minutes later. He surged forward from the half-way line, interchanged with Benny Arentoft and, after a lucky break off a Hungarian leg, hit a crisp left foot shot along the ground which just flashed past the 'keeper's outstretched hand. Ahead by 2-0, United were on their way.

The Magyars were flattened and Newcastle had complete superiority. The Journal noted Ujpesti were, "looking far from the greatest side in Europe and were kicking anywhere in front of the full fury of an unstoppable United". Benny Arentoft was very much involved in the third goal which completed a convincing victory. Another one-two movement, this time with Jim Scott, saw United's winger race into the box and just beat Szentmihalyi to the ball and send it over the 'keeper and into the net. Joe Harvey was well pleased, he said, "I think we have got one hand on the cup now".

The victory could have been costly though. Near the end Wyn Davies went up for a ball alongside goal hero Moncur and fractured his cheekbone. To a lesser player it would have meant an immediate operation and of course omission from the second leg. Davies would have none of it. Courageous as ever - he had broken his nose against Rangers - Wyn was to play on until after success was achieved.

The two week wait for June 11th and the second deciding leg was a long one. Yet when the game did get under way on a hot and sticky evening in Budapest, United's small band of travelling fans and most of Tyneside listening on the radio back home, had wished that the day had never arrived. With ceaseless first-half pressure the Magyars swarmed around United's goal.

Skipper Bob Moncur drills home the all important opening goal on Tyneside.

CUP RUN

R1	SC Feyenoord	H	W	4-0	
	SC Feyenoord	A	L	0-2	Agg 4-2
R2	Sporting Lisbon	A	D	1-1	
	Sporting Lisbon	H	W	1-0	Agg 2-1
R3	Real Zaragoza	A	L	2-3	
	Real Zaragoza	H	W	2-1	Agg 4-4
R4	Vitoria Setubal	H	W	5-1	
	Vitoria Setubal	A	L	1-3	Agg 6-4
SF	Glasgow Rangers	A	D	0-0	
	Glasgow Rangers	H	W	2-0	Agg 2-0
F	Ujpesti Dosza	H	W	3-0	
	Ujpesti Dosza	A	W	3-2	Agg 6-2

Inter Cities Fairs Cup Winners 1969

CUP GOALGETTERS

6 Robson, 4 Scott, Davies, 3 Gibb, Moncur, 2 Foggon, 1 Arentoft, Sinclair.

CHAIRMAN: Lord Westwood
MANAGER: Joe Harvey
TRAINER-COACH: Dave Smith
CAPTAIN: Bob Moncur

FACTS & FIGURES

	P	W	D	L	F	A
Home	6	6	0	0	17	2
Away	6	1	2	3	7	11
Total	**12**	**7**	**2**	**3**	**24**	**13**

FINAL

First Leg
29 May 1969 at St James Park
Newcastle United 3 (0) Ujpesti Dosza 0 (0)

UNITED:
McFaul
Craig, Burton, Moncur, Clark
Gibb, Arentoft, Scott
Davies, Robson, Sinclair (Foggon).

UJPESTI:
Szentmihalyi
Kaposzta, Solymosi, Bankuti, Nosko
Dunai(E), Fazekas, Gorocs, Dunai (A)
Bene, Zambo

Goals;
Moncur (63m, 71m), Scott (84m)

ATTENDANCE;
59,234 (£42,415)

Referee; J.Hannet (Brussels)

Moncur jumps high and Davies smiles broadly as the ball hits the back of the net for the Magpies' first goal.

Jim Scott just beats the Ujpesti 'keeper to the ball to score United's third goal at St. James Park.

McFaul made two terrific saves as Newcastle reeled and after half an hour Bene unleashed a terrific shot into the net. United had cracked. Back the Hungarians came and they got another, two minutes from half-time. United's three goal lead looked very small now, but just when they wanted it, that old cup spirit came flooding back.

Joe Harvey's interval talk wasn't a rowdy affair. He clenched his fist, rallied his men and simply told his players to get a goal. He said, "I haven't a clue how you're going to get one...all we need is one goal and Ujpesti will die". It was blunt and straightforward, but it gave his team an uplift. Within a minute of the restart the black'n'whites had got that very goal and their manager's prediction was spot on - the Hungarians collapsed like a pack of cards. Very quickly United were level at 2-2 and then were ahead 3-2. It was United's turn to produce the football skills in an amazing turn-a-round.

Bobby Moncur was the man to set United going. Coming up for a corner, he was in the right place - on the penalty spot - to volley a left foot shot high into the net after Sinclair had floated in a cross. It was a Fairs Cup hat-trick for the man who had not scored a senior competitive goal before. Seven minutes later United equalised and stunned the 34,000 crowd when Arentoft picked up a ballooned clearance following a drive by Scott and scored with another sweet volley. Then Alan Foggon, who had come on for the cramp-affected Scott, streaked away down the middle to a Davies flick-on. The youngster raced clear of Solymosi and Bankuti and hammered a vicious shot that was pushed against the bar. Foggon's reflexes were the quickest and he slid the rebound home to make the scoreline 3-2 after being two behind. Joe Harvey remarked with a broad grin, "I have not seen any cup final or played in one that matched this game for excitement and fighting courage". Ivor Broadis wrote in The Journal, "Europe's babes emerged man-sized from the banks of the Danube as the new czars of soccer".

Sir Stanley Rous handed Moncur the silver trophy - United were Fairs Cup champions. Champagne flowed like water and celebrations went on all evening alongside the picturesque River Danube. Back home the motorcade and St James Park rally was straight out of the fifties glory days. In Tyneside's own little world the event was as big as the monumental landing on the moon by Apollo 11 only a few weeks later.

Teenager Alan Foggon is about to let fly and the ball ends up in the Hungarian net for United's third goal in Budapest.

Jackie Sinclair (No.11) and Jim Scott (No.7) dance away following a Newcastle goal against Ujpesti.

Victory lap of honour in Budapest after an overwhelming 6-2 aggregate scoreline.

FINAL
Second Leg
11 June 1969 at Megyeri Stadion
Ujpesti Dosza 2 (2) Newcastle United 3 (0)

UJPESTI:
Szentmihalyi
Kaposzta, Solymosi, Bankuti, Nosko
Dunai(E), Fazekas, Gorocs, Dunai (A)
Bene, Zambo
UNITED:
McFaul
Craig, Burton, Moncur, Clark
Gibb, Arentoft, Scott (Foggon)
Davies, Robson, Sinclair.
GOALS;
Bene (30m), Gorocs (43m), Moncur (46m),
Arentoft (53m), Foggon (68m)

ATTENDANCE;
34,000

Referee; Mr Haeman (Switzerland)
Guest of Honour; Sir Stanley Rous

Inter Cities Fairs Cup Winners 1969

Fairs Cup Champions. Left to right, back: Burton, Foggon, Smith (coach), Clark, Ross. Middle: McNamee, Craggs, Hope, McFaul, Gibb, Davies. Front: Scott, Sinclair, Moncur, Harvey (Manager), Robson, Craig, Arentoft.

Back on Tyneside – Joe Harvey hoists the Fairs Cup to a packed Gallowgate.

The Inter Cities Fairs Cup on display at St. James Park

THE FAIRS CUP VICTORY WAS A HUGE financial success. Net income was over £44,000 alone and in total the year brought in almost £250,000, while season-tickets for the new season's programme were sold out within days and many were prompted to tip United for domestic honours. Most of the team were on the good side of 30 years old and as a unit could develop further.

The defence of McFaul, full-backs Craig and Clark and Bobby Moncur, with either Ollie Burton or John McNamee at centre-half, was one of the best in the country. Tommy Gibb and Benny Arentoft had been a revelation. Full of workrate, both may have lacked ball technique, yet were still very effective. Curly haired Jim Scott had come into his own, delicate and skilled, he had the knack of finding the net. Up front Wyn Davies and Pop Robson had showed the football world that their partnership was a danger, while at last expensive winger Jackie Sinclair was showing signs of the form that gave him international recognition. And with a batch of youngsters led by the shaggy-haired Alan Foggon, United's potential was unquestioned.

Welshman Ollie Burton, to spend nearly ten years on Tyneside.

With the Fairs Cup on view, the Club's directors get ready for the December 1969 AGM at the County Hotel. L to r: McKenzie, Taylor, Seymour, Barker, Lord Westwood, Rutherford, McKeag, Rush and Braithwaite.

Newcastle, though, couldn't make any progress to claim a home trophy. In the League Cup they went out at the first stage, to Sheffield United when John Tudor, a player soon to be heading for Tyneside, netted for the Blades. And in the FA Cup they also missed the boat, at Southampton, losing 3-0 at the Dell. In league competition they finished in a reasonable 7th position, but at no time did Everton, the eventual Champions, worry about a black'n'white rival. Still, it was the highest placing since 1951 and the Magpies possessed the best defence in Division One, bar the Champions, conceding only 35 goals.

So it was in the Fairs Cup that United gave their fans something to shout about. At first however, a disappointing pairing with Dundee United came out of the bag. That proved a big let down as Tyneside hoped for the like of Juventus or Barcelona, in the hat also. Two goals by Wyn Davies at Tannadice - and he rattled the bar twice as well - were the highlight as United won 3-1 on aggregate.

Having taken care of Sunderland 3-0, with Dyson scoring twice, United found themselves back in Portugal for a tie with FC Porto at the Antas Stadium. Joe Harvey ordered a professional tight display and his side responded with a 0-0 draw. Like Setubal before them, Porto arrived in a frozen north east. The Portuguese didn't take to the frosty climate and a superb goal by Jimmy Scott clinched the tie. Arentoft danced between two defenders to allow the ex Hibs man the opportunity to fire home.

With more visions of Inter Milan, Barcelona or even Ajax being tied with United, another lack-lustre match followed, this time with Southampton, a club to play the Magpies on five occasions that season and three times in as many weeks. Ex Magpie centre-half John McGrath was in the Saints ranks and faced up to Wyn Davies - a repeat of the 1965 promotion confrontation at St James Park. And it proved another tough battle with Davies reaping a little revenge on his opponent by forcing McGrath to leave the field after a clash. Yet the incident had an ironic twist. His replacement, the experienced Jimmy Gabriel went onto play Davies out of the game. And with chances going astray, Southampton held Newcastle to a 0-0 draw and looked favourites to go through with the home leg to be played at the Dell, not a ground to United's liking of late.

As the return game got under way it looked to be another disjointed performance on the south coast. Mick Channon put the Saints ahead and then

100th DERBY

On 27th March 1970 a century of league games with neighbours Sunderland was recorded. At Roker Park, 51,950 saw a 1-1 draw, a match United dominated, but which they couldn't claim a victory. Jimmy Smith fired in a beauty from the edge of the box, however the Wearsiders clawed themselves back into the game with an equaliser. Sunderland were facing relegation that season, while United were 6th in the Division One table. The Roker men slipped into the Second Division a fortnight later.

Ron Davies crashed the ball against McFaul's crossbar while Clark headed off the line. But United held out and with six minutes to go equalised. A delicate chip found the head of Wyn Davies. A nod towards goal and in nipped Pop Robson to lash the ball home. Newcastle won on away goals courtesy of that Robson strike. The victory took United at last to a glamour tie - a quarter-final meeting with RSC Anderlecht, the aristocrats of Belgium.

Against a side full of internationals, including Belgium's captain Paul

Willie McFaul watched by Burton (left) and Craig collects the ball in the second leg tie with Anderlecht.

The goal that knocked the Magpies from Europe. Anderlecht's Nordahl, in background, strikes the ball past McFaul.

Van Himst and an outstanding centre-forward Mulder, the Magpies went down 2-0 in Brussels. They lost both Craig and Clark through injury and Moncur was only a passenger. But for McFaul's impressive handling, Anderlecht may well have rattled up an unbeatable advantage and United knew exactly what was necessary on March 18th - they needed to win by three clear goals. Again Joe Harvey had injury problems, but United received the boost they wanted, a goal within four minutes of the kick-off. Davies leaped for the ball - not for the first or last time - and created havoc in the box. Robson was there to head into the net with Foggon making sure. On 20 minutes Robson was back again taking a pass from Gibb to unleash a scorching drive and put the Magpies 2-0 ahead. They were all square on aggregate and well on their way to completing the job.

The all important third goal took a long time coming, but the 59,000 crowd were joyous to the point of tears when, with only four minutes remaining, Keith Dyson scrambled the ball past 'keeper Trappeniers. United and their injury hit side were through to another semi-final, or so it seemed. Then in the space of seconds, from noise that almost knocked Earl Grey from his high city centre perch, there was complete and utter silence. A Burton clearance rebounded straight to the unmarked Nordahl. A couple of steps forward and he cracked a drive past the bemused McFaul to send Anderlecht, and their brilliant forward-line into the semi-final on the away goals rule. It was a real heartbreaker. The tears were now of agony. Trainer-coach Dave Smith noted it was the side's "finest moment of the season, yet at the same time, the most tragic". It was a glorious exit. United had gone an impressive ten matches in the Fairs Cup without defeat.

That was the season over. United picked up points to secure a European place once more, but only through the help of Derby County, who were banned from competing because of alleged irregularities in their books, and Arsenal, winners of the Fairs Cup in the wake of Newcastle's success. Jimmy Smith

COLOURFUL UNITED

After almost 70 years of wearing a change strip of only white shirts and black shorts, the latter years of the sixties saw United burst into colour. A profusion of different strips were pulled on - royal blue shirts, yellow shirts and black shorts, all white, all blue and all red. There was sky-blue and yellow and latterly silver and black as well as yellow and green stripes. United even turned out in orange shirts against Luton Town. During the twenties, Newcastle did wear an attractive jersey with a V-diamond shape running from the back to front - but only in black'n'white.

LONGEST SEASON

In 1968/69 United played continuous football from 3rd August 1968 to 11th June 1969, a period of 10 months, the longest season in the club's history. The 62 game programme comprised;

Friendlies	3
FL Division One	42
FA Cup	3
Football League Cup	2
Inter Cities Fairs Cup	12

became the Magpies' first £100,000 footballer, signing in July 1969 from Aberdeen. The 22 year-old midfielder was purchased, part in an effort to add skill to the hard running midfield, part to avoid heavy taxation. Nicknamed 'Jinky' and already a Scottish international, he did not have an enjoyable first season in England, often criticised because of a casual approach. But the fans took to his elegance and charm, over 8,000 witnessing his first appearance in a Central League game against Aston Villa Reserves. Smith eventually fitted into the English game despite his enigmatic approach and proved a matchwinner possessing a tantalising right foot able to slip a telling pass to perfection. Bob Moncur was to say, "We have to put up with the bad for the sake of the good. He can win a match on his own".

Jimmy Smith, the club's first £100,000 footballer.

David Ford was another forward capture, another in a long line of attempts to find a consistent winger. He arrived from Sheffield Wednesday in exchange for Sinclair, but like his predecessor never fitted the bill. An extensive tour of North America took place during the summer as the spot-light was on the World Cup in Mexico - Pele, Jairzinho and all.

The 1970/71 season was a virtual carbon copy of the previous year. Knocked out of domestic trophies early on, this time by Third Division Bristol Rovers and then Ipswich Town, the Fairs Cup was once more left to provide some fireworks. And it certainly did that. One of Europe's most famous clubs, the great Internazionale of Milan were United's opponents in the First Round and included in their side were Italian World Cup stars of the summer, Facchetti, Burgnich, Mazzola and Boninsegna. Off-form Newcastle were given little hope of any result in Italy. However United's players rose to the occasion and almost snatched a 1-0 victory in the San Siro stadium with Inter not equalising until the dying minutes. A minute before half-time the menace of Wyn Davies sprinted to a Robson free-kick and sent a diving header into the net through a ruck of boots and studs - a marvellous and brave goal. Davies took a battering from the home defence, but it was nothing compared to what happened a week later on Tyneside.

An all ticket crowd of almost 60,000 poured into St James Park for what was to be a great spectacle of football. What the big gathering actually saw was a severe dose of Italian thuggery. The game commenced in predictable fashion with United - playing unusually in red shirts - storming forward. They tore the Italians apart and after 30 minutes a corner resulted in Moncur powering home a header to give United the lead.

The temperamental Italians disintegrated after that goal. A minute later the balloon went up when Davies feinted to challenge 'keeper Lido Vieri. A fracas followed, and in the melee referee Joseph Minnoy was left on his knees in the box thanks to a lovely left hook by the visiting 'keeper. Police calmed everyone down for a few seconds then the pushing, poking and rhetoric started all over again when Minnoy sent the Italian goalkeeper off the field. What a scene. From that moment the Italians resorted to boxing, wrestling and any other foul tactic to the stop the Magpies, and Davies in particular. At one stage police were almost on the field calming the visitors down. Facchetti - to be dubbed 'Hacchetti' - was the main culprit, but he wasn't far ahead of his colleagues.

Newcastle though, to their credit, didn't retaliate although under severe provocation. They just continued to pile on the pressure with McFaul not required to make a save throughout the game. Frank Clark delightfully skipped a defender to see a powerful drive crash against the crossbar, then Davies incensed the blue shirts of Inter further when he added a second goal to put United into a commanding 2-0 lead. It was a match never to be forgotten for those present.

A trip behind the Iron Curtain provided the Magpies with their next European venture. A return to Hungary, this time to face unknowns Pecsi Dosza. A young, skilful side flew into Tyneside during October and it was again the head of Wyn Davies that caused the visitors all sorts of problems. In front of nearly 51,000 the Pecsi defence couldn't handle the big leader at all. He scored two majestic headers and created many chances that were squandered. Those missed opportunities in the 2-0 success were to be costly.

The return in the town of Pecs, a hundred miles from anywhere, ended in a dramatic penalty shoot-out and United's preparations were anything from

LONG SERVICE

The longest serving member of the playing or training staff in a century at St James Park is Alex Mutch, son of United's goalkeeper of the same name. He joined the club in August 1922 as assistant trainer and was still on the pay-roll as assistant physio to his retirement in 1986, all of 64 years later. His father spent 36 years at St James Park too! Joe Richardson is the longest serving ex player, spending 48 years as full-back and trainer in a span from 1929 to 1977.

Moncur, in an unfamiliar all red strip, heads a goal against Inter Milan.

HOTEL CHANGE

During March 1969 when United played away to Vitoria Setubal, the club were far from happy with the service of their hotel. At dinner the party had to wait 90 minutes - the length of a football match - for the soup course and then another hour for the rest of the meal. Lord Westwood walked out before the main course and decided for the rest of their stay they would dine elsewhere.

ideal. The journey to Pecs, near the Yugoslav border, was a tedious one. The town did not have a hotel big enough for United's party and some of the squad had to share accommodation with the press contingent. The pitch was nothing short of atrocious, bumpy and barren. John Gibson of the Evening Chronicle described it as looking, "more like the Town Moor". Nothing appeared to be going right for the black'n'whites and when the match kicked-off Newcastle quickly found themselves two down, two unfortunate scrappy goals at that - one a debatable spot-kick, the other a lucky deflection. Extra-time came and went, so the tie ended in a penalty lottery. Pecsi opened a spot-kick lead of 3-0 and that was enough. United's penalties were dreadful. Robson hit the bar, Mitchell's was saved and Tommy Gibb's shot came off the 'keeper to crash against the woodwork. It was an inglorious way to go out of the Fairs Cup, but United were out for seven long years.

Newcastle had lost their way somewhat and development on their European victory of 1969 had come to a sudden stop. They finished mid-table and the side started to break up. Scott, Sinclair, Arentoft and Foggon had all left for pastures new. Winger come striker Ian Mitchell was acquired from Dundee United for £50,000 and although a much respected player north of the border, he was a flop in England. Youngster Stuart Barrowclough also joined the staff for £33,000 from Barnsley and the 19 year-old claimed the wide berth in the years ahead. Midfielder Tommy Cassidy, who cost £25,000 from Glentoran, found a place too. It was to take the Irishman several seasons to become a regular, but eventually he showed neat skills and the expert ability to thread a telling pass through the opposition's defence. He went on to appear 24 times for his country.

Half-back turned striker John Tudor arrived late in the season from Sheffield United and at the end of the campaign Harvey decided on a major change in strategy. Bryan Robson had departed to West Ham United after controversial statements about the club, and Davies, so long the major force behind United's European success, fell out of favour and within months was to move as well. Just before the 1971 FA Cup final the manager forked out £180,000 for the 21 year-old, Second Division goalscoring machine, Malcolm Macdonald. Brash and arrogant, he arrived on Tyneside in a blaze of publicity. With supporters frustrated at the lack of domestic success it was vital that Macdonald was successful.

'The Battle of St. James's

How one United supporter recorded United's fiery meeting with the Italians from Milan.

To the tune of 'Blaydon Races'

*Aa went doon to St. James's
To see Inter Milan,
There was me and sixty thousand there
Afore the game began,
Aa took me tea and sandwiches,
Me muffler an' me rattle,
But Aa should've took me boxing gloves
To help them win the battle.*

*CHORUS
Oh me Lads,
Yer should've seen the fightin,
They were thumpin, they were kickin,
They were scratchin, they were bitin,
Aam glad that Aa was there meself
It made me feel quite famous,
The night the Lads beat Inter
At the Battle of St. James's.*

*The first half went along quite nice,
Joe Harvey wore a grin,
The lyties, well they weren't too bad,
But they couldn't hold wor Wyn,
The goalie thumped the referee
And got his marching order,
And then it went from bad to worse,
And from worse to bloody morder!*

*CHORUS repeat
Oh me Lads,*

*But never mind, the Lads got through,
Into the second roond,
They've drawn a team from Hungary,
They'll beat them oot the groond,
Joe Harvey's just signed two new men,
They must have cost a stack,
He's got Henry Cooper on the wing . . .
And Cassius Clay right-back!*

*CHORUS repeat
Oh me Lads,*

Centenary Profile 21

The Welsh Flier

"If you could screw studs into his head he would be another George Best"

Ivor Broadis,, September 1969

WYN DAVIES MAY NOT HAVE BEEN A PROLIFIC goalscorer in the true tradition of United's Number 9 Heroes, and he almost received as much criticism as praise, but the big Welshman was an exceptional personality and King of St James Park for five years. He joined Newcastle in a headline transfer deal during October 1966, costing United £80,000, almost doubling the club's record fee. It was a successful conclusion of a long chase by manager Joe Harvey for the player who had netted 74 goals in 170 games for Bolton Wanderers.

After missing relegation narrowly, United's boss had to strengthen his team and Harvey almost clinched the deal for Davies a year earlier in 1965, but the transfer was called off. As negotiations opened for a second time, Joe was determined to get the big fella. Competition was fierce as Davies was linked with a stream of First Division clubs including Sheffield Wednesday, Sunderland and Arsenal. Wyn had netted 12 goals in the first 12 games of the new 1966/67 season and was in demand. Joe Harvey met the Welshman at a secret hide-out in Bolton and this time all was agreed, United increasing their previous terms and persuading Davies to head north to Tyneside.

The Magpies were fortunate as events turned out, because once Davies had signed the transfer form Joe Mercer's Manchester City arrived on the scene with a late bid and it was quite probable that Wyn would have chosen Maine Road - a closer home to Bolton and Wales. But he was now a Newcastle player and there was much excitement on Tyneside at the club's centre-forward acquisition.

He arrived at St James Park sporting a crew cut, donning a fur coat and carrying his boots. Quite a reception greeted him. Pressmen galore, TV crews and hundreds of school kids all clamouring for interviews and autographs. He was United's first superstar of the modern game, although Davies was something of a reluctant one, being a remote character and a puzzle to many of his team-mates. He was a loner in United's camp, unlike most of Newcastle's centre-forward idols.

Twenty-four hours after landing on Tyneside, Davies made his debut against Sunderland, this after a kidnap attempt by University ragweek students was foiled - Wyn being hidden away for a day by club officials in Heaton. He immediately sampled the white hot Geordie atmosphere as well as his new club's problems, then 20th in the First Division. Davies though, gradually made a difference. The type of forward who caused havoc in the opponents box, at 6'1" and 12 stone, he was powerfully built and was never afraid to put himself around. His aerial menace was rarely matched by any defender, Davies having the gift to appear to hang in the air and soar above his rivals. And while he was never a genius on the deck, Wyn held the ball up well and controlled the forward line. He could also expertly kill the ball dead on his chest - a much admired part of his repertoire.

Gradually United's team plan figured around 'Wyn the Leap' as he was to be called. The high ball game suited Davies and the dominance he possessed in the air created chances for others with subtle flicks, lay-offs and defender's panic-making space and openings for, first Albert Bennett, then Bryan Robson. The Welshman was very much a provider of chances, the target man up front and was never lethal in front of goal himself. He grabbed his share of course, many with huge jumps and powerful headers that found the net.

As United surged into European competition, Davies

Wyn Davies

DAVIES' PLAYING RECORD

	League		FA Cup		FL Cup		Europe		Total	
	App	Gls	App	Gls	App	Gls	App	Gls	App	Gls
1966-67	29	6	1	3	0	0	0	0	30	9
1967-68	41	12	1	0	1	0	0	0	43	12
1968-69	37	11	3	0	0	0	12	4	52	15
1969-70	40	9	1	0	1	0	8	2	50	11
1970-71	34	2	2	0	1	0	4	4	41	6
	181	**40**	**8**	**3**	**3**	**0**	**24**	**10**	**216**	**53**

became the dangerman, the one continental defenders feared the most. A whole succession of experienced international talent could not shackle the Welshman as Bryan Robson related when Zaragoza's Santamaria first challenged United's leader, "Wyn climbed right above him - I still remember the look of astonishment on the Spaniard's face". Chairman Lord Westwood noted, "I can say that without Wyn Davies United would never have won the Inter Cities Fairs Cup". He netted ten goals in the 24 European games United played and took a fearful battering as well - bruises, stitches, a fractured cheekbone, a broken nose and severely gashed leg were some of his rewards. He was punched, poked and kicked by defenders who couldn't handle his physical approach. But Wyn was always a courageous individual and kept on playing, although he frequently pleaded to officials for protection - and often was ignored.

Once Newcastle had been eliminated from Europe in 1970, manager Joe Harvey dispensed with Wyn's style of play and, following an injury, he found it difficult to get back into the side, even appearing once in the unaccustomed position of outside-right. The Welshman's days at St James Park were over. During the close-season the 29 year-old was off to Maine Road to team up with his long-standing admirer Joe Mercer in a £52,500 deal. The flame-haired leader had clocked up 216 appearances for United and scored 53 times. Not many goals, but look at the goalscoring record of his partners Bennett and Robson. Together they hit almost 100.

A fervently proud Welshman, born in Caernarfon in 1942, Wyn was a regular for his country for a decade, graduating from both Youth and Under 23 sides and appearing on 34 occasions for Wales. Once back in Lancashire he continued on what was a much travelled career. Davies had started in the Football League with Wrexham in 1960 after appearing for local sides Llanberis and Caernarfon Town. He was tracked down by scouts of Manchester United and Aston Villa, but following trials it was back to the Welsh leagues for the one time apprentice plumber and quarry worker. At the Racecourse Ground, Wrexham, he quickly made his mark in Division Four and still a teenager joined Bolton in March 1962, then in the First Division, albeit struggling to avoid the drop.

After his successful periods at Burnden Park and on Tyneside with United, he remained only briefly at Maine Road before moving across Manchester to Old Trafford. Another short stay followed before he joined Blackpool in the summer of 1973. Then Davies - now 31 years old - headed south pulling on the shirt of Crystal Palace for an equally brief stint. Stockport County signed him in August 1975 before the Welsh flier ended his long career with Crewe Alexandra. Davies retired from senior football in the summer of 1978. He had almost 700 appearances and over 200 goals to his name.

Wyn did continue playing, with Northern Premier side Bangor City and also in South Africa's National Football League, for Pretoria club, Arcadia Shepherds. He returned to England and settled in Bolton working as a baker - an occupation which was a far cry from the superstar status he experienced on Tyneside.

Wyn Davies may not have been the best footballer in the world, yet he left a deep impression on United's supporters with his whole-hearted attitude. As thousands of them roared, "You've not seen nothing like the Mighty Wyn"!

A 300 Goal Machine

"The best uncapped striker in the business"
Jimmy Greaves, 1981

A FAIRLY SIMPLE GOAL MARKED THE START OF A prolific career as a goalscorer for Bryan Robson. Barrie Thomas crossed the ball and Robson was on hand in the six yard box to side foot the ball into the net. Over a period of 20 years from that day at Charlton in September 1964, to the time he retired in 1984, Robson smashed 300 goals past some of the best defences in the country - and in Europe too. It was an outstanding record.

Born in Sunderland, but bred in Prudhoe alongside the Tyne, Robson was one of United's many junior products of the early sixties coming into the ranks alongside Bob Moncur, Alan Suddick and full-backs Craig and Clark. After periods at both Leicester City and Northampton Town, he signed amateur forms for the Magpies from Clara Vale Juniors and turned professional in November 1962. Having made his debut when still a teenager at The Valley, it took Robson a while to fully establish himself. But his manager always knew he had potential saying, "We are going to see a lot more of this boy"

The 5'8" tall striker was in and out of the line-up in the club's promotion season of 1964/65, but ended as a regular, although never the consistent goalscorer he was to become. Given the nickname of 'Popeye' at school - to be shortened to 'Pop' - the days of First Division struggle saw Robson in United's attack, but along with other forwards he found it hard to put the ball in the net. Although out of favour for a year, he was learning all the time and was ready to answer his manager's frantic plea for a goalscorer at the start of the 1968/69 season. Wyn Davies' partner up front, Albert Bennett, was crocked and in stepped Robson to form a unity with the big Welshman which Joe Harvey must have dreamed of.

The little and large duo of Davies and Robson knitted together perfectly. The tall centre-forward provided the target and Robson capitalised on the space and chaos he created. It worked a treat and Robson's career flourished to become one of England's most deadly strikers. Every bit an opportunist poacher in the Greaves mould, Bryan was also able to score the spectacular effort too. Goals like the 35 yarder against Sporting Lisbon that screamed into the top corner, the stunning first timer that Setubal's 'keeper never saw, or the side volley against West Ham United at Upton Park in 1970 that earned the Goal of the Season award.

He scored 30 goals in 1968/69 including six in the triumphant Fairs Cup run. England's manager was suitably impressed and called United's forward into the Under 23 side. Then a year later he was included in the Football League's team to meet the League of Ireland at Barnsley. But that was as far as Robson got in the international reckoning. Jimmy Greaves noted that he was, "The best uncapped striker in the business who had time and time again revealed his goal snatching skill in an era dominated by defences". Yet England's full set-up ignored him.

With Newcastle going through a sticky patch following their exit from European football in 1970, Robson and Harvey had an unsavoury bust up and he was off to West Ham United in a £120,000 transfer during February 1971 - a record transaction for both clubs. Robson was at the peak of his career - 25 years

Bryan Robson

ROBSON'S PLAYING RECORD

	League		FA Cup		FL Cup		Europe		Total	
	App	Gls	App	Gls	App	Gls	App	Gls	App	Gls
1964-65	20	7	0	0	0	0	0	0	20	7
1965-66	23	9	2	1	0	0	0	0	25	10
1966-67	37	10	2	1	0	0	0	0	39	11
1967-68	12/1	4	0	0	0	0	0	0	12/1	4
1968-69	42	21	3	1	2	2	12	6	59	30
1969-70	42	22	1	0	1	0	8	3	52	25
1970-71	29	9	2	1	1	0	4	0	36	10
	205/1	**82**	**10**	**4**	**4**	**2**	**24**	**9**	**243/1**	**97**

old and had registered nearly 100 goals for the Magpies.

In the Hammers' fluent and attractive style of football, a total contrast to United's high ball game, Robson continued to be a respected goalpoacher. Alongside the likes of Billy Bonds and Trevor Brooking, he netted a further 104 times during the next seven seasons and was the Football League's top scorer in 1972/73 with 28 goals. During the latter days of his long career - he didn't stop playing until he was 40 years old - the Wearsider trekked back and forth from south to north of the country. He joined Sunderland, the team he supported as a kid, in 1974, aided them to promotion then returned to Upton Park less than two years later. He went back to Roker Park again in the summer of 1979 then onto Carlisle as player-coach in March 1981. At Brunton Park, Robson helped another successful promotion campaign then had a brief spell at Chelsea, in a similar capacity, before having a third spell with Sunderland. He returned to Carlisle next, as a player, then as manager in August 1985. But that was a brief sojourn into the managerial world - all of 49 days - before heading for the the non-league circuit.

Robson looked after a newsagency in Gateshead and occasionally turned out for the town's Northern Premier League club as well as Newcastle Blue Star. He returned to senior football in the shape of Hartlepool in 1988 as assistant boss. However it was another short appointment before concentrating on coaching and scouting for Manchester United.

Bryan Robson possesses a formidable strike record for a player who never reached the England side - and who didn't turn out for the regular trophy winning clubs - much like one of his predecessors at Gallowgate, Len White. After playing almost 750 senior matches, the height of his career was to be those three wonderful years touring Europe with the Magpies - and with it a series of spectacular goals that set Tyneside alight.

14 HAWAY THE LADS!

1971-1975 • SUPERMAC ARRIVES • CUP NIGHTMARE II • UNPREDICTABLE TAG • WEMBLEY DISAPPOINTMENT • HARVEY BOWS OUT •

"It all started to work for us at West Bromwich....the best team performance I have been involved with"

Malcolm Macdonald, December 1990

THE SEVENTIES WAS THE ERA OF ENTRY into the Common Market, holiday trips abroad and fast food became the norm, while £ s d vanished in favour of decimalisation. Computers started to take the country into a high-tech age, sponsorship entered the world of football and skinhead gangs raged from ground to ground. At St James Park there were changes too as Newcastle United became the game's biggest spenders fashioning an attractive, but highly unpredictable team.

The next few years saw United give their supporters plenty to shout about, although all was not to their liking. They possessed a team capable of great things at times, yet very much an inconsistent and frustrating line-up. This period belonged largely to one man - Supermac. Malcolm Macdonald had arrived on Tyneside and was to immediately claim the adulation of the crowd.

The unveiling of the £180,000 Cockney took place in the French town of St Etienne and he found the net with a scorching knee-high volley. Then at St James Park he took a back seat to Eusebio who graced the field with his Benfica line-up. United were without Moncur and Smith, both laid down with nagging injuries, and Harvey saw his new signing have a quiet game which ended in a 1-0 victory for the Magpies thanks to a Tommy Gibb goal. Macdonald was soon to explode though, and the roar of 'Supermac! Supermac!' was heard for the first time as he formed a bond with the Gallowgate faithful inside a mere 60 minutes.

Following two games in London, United's opening league match of the 1971/72 season was against the power of Liverpool. Newcastle won 3-2 and Macdonald couldn't have wished for a better home debut hitting a hat-trick to remember. It was a dream start, even though he was later carried off after a collision with Ray Clemence going for a fourth. Three times the explosive boot crushed a Liverpool side intent on winning the game. His first was a thundering spot-kick, his second pure genius.

Newcastle's first team pool in 1971. Left to right, back: Craig, Mitchell, Barrowclough, Burkinshaw (coach), Burleigh, Cassidy, Nattrass, Gibb. Middle: Davies, Dyson, McNamee, Macdonald, Tudor, Clark, Smith, Burton. Front: Young, Craggs, Moncur, Harvey (Manager), Foggon, Arentoft, Guthrie.

Macdonald dragged a ball on in the box, making time and space for himself, then - thump - the ball flew into the top corner. The third was another roaring drive across Clemence and low into the net.

Macdonald commented on his debut success, "It gave me confidence, showed me that I could score regularly in the First Division - as I had been doing in the Second and Third. Most importantly the hat-trick answered some questions in the minds of the fans who hadn't seen me play". It certainly did that. Magpie supporters were astonished at his devastating finish and one-way-to-goal approach. With new signing from Leeds United, Terry Hibbitt looking dominating in midfield, there was much expectation for the new season. Hibbitt was a virtual unknown, having spent almost eight seasons in Don Revie's squad without hitting the headlines. But the little Yorkshireman was to team up with Macdonald to provide plenty of action.

However, results did not go as planned. By the end of October United were rock bottom of the division. They suffered a record six defeats in a row and in the process registered two four-goal hammerings in the space of a week by Arsenal - a League Cup knock-out included. Moncur was the influence that was missing, his absence was a crucial factor while midfield lacked a partner for Hibbitt. Harvey had to do something. He did, signing Scottish international Tony Green from Blackpool and what a buy he proved to be. On his home debut, the sparkling link-man inspired United to a 5-1 Texaco Cup win against Coventry City, then a 3-1 success over Southampton. He was immediately taken to heart by the skill-admiring Geordies and Newcastle gradually improved.

At first United couldn't agree terms with the Bloomfield Road club for Green, but after a few weeks of hard negotiation a fee of £150,000 was agreed with Keith Dyson going west as part of the deal. It was the highest transfer paid for any Scot at the time. A diminutive figure at only 5'7", almost schoolboyish in appearance, Green possessed amazing close skills that could get him out of a tangle of legs. He had a devastating turn of speed to take him clear of defenders and often into the box on mini-runs that caused chaos. Added to a ferocious shot, he was quite an addition. Stan Mortensen, Blackpool's former boss said of Green's special talents, "He is one of the most natural ballplayers I have ever seen in my life".

The unlucky Scot, Tony Green, played only a handful of games due to injury.

FIVE GOAL STRIKE

Malcolm Macdonald made his debut for England against World Champions West Germany and netted in a 2-0 victory. But that was nothing compared to his record five goal strike against Cyprus in the European Championships a month later during April 1975. Newcastle's centre-forward hit all of England's goals and he remains the only player to grab five at Wembley, while Malcolm also equalled his country's all time scoring record. The Daily Mirror wrote that Macdonald was, "incredible, unstoppable". The spree made up somewhat for his Wembley disappointment with United in 1974.

From the moment the little Scot started to wear a black'n'white shirt United slowly climbed clear of the relegation area. Green and Hibbitt combined well in midfield and Macdonald was the force in attack. United changed from a shambles to a side with tremendous promise, displaying an entertaining and vibrant style of football.

Even with United on a good run they, however, still managed to cause one mighty sensation in the Third Round of the FA Cup. Newcastle were drawn against Hereford United, top club in the Southern League and with a good reputation as giant-killers. They arrived on Tyneside for a meeting that was to develop into one of United's biggest nightmares - the blackest chapter in the side's modern history. After torrential rain and snow for a week, the first attempt at the tie was postponed, but on a Tuesday evening the game went ahead before 39,381 fans. Hereford never allowed United to control the game producing tenacious tackling and lots of skilful football too. And they were handed a start to give them a massive boost in confidence. Within all of 17 seconds the non-leaguers were in front and the three other goals in the 2-2 draw were all scored in a frenzied first-half too.

Centre-half Pat Howard, signed from Barnsley for a bargain £23,000, hesitated chasing a long punt and Hereford's Owen rifled the ball home. Newcastle equalised within three minutes when Macdonald was up-ended in the box and relief flooded back to United's ranks when the centre-forward lashed home the spot-kick. Tudor then put the Tynesiders ahead, but Hereford hit back quickly with a superbly struck 20 yarder from Colin Addison, the former Arsenal star.

Weather again caused postponements to the replay at Edgar Street - four of them - and weary journeyies for the travelling United team and fans. The game went ahead on Saturday February 5th with the BBC Match of the Day cameras in attendance. They were waiting for a shock and they got one. With Moncur back after injury, United at first dominated the game. The opening 45 minutes were theirs with Green buzzing in midfield. United should have scored three or four goals by the interval, but did go deservedly into the lead after half-time when 22 goal Macdonald headed in a curling cross by on loan striking partner Viv Busby.

Pat Howard, a bargain signing by Joe Harvey.

United were almost home and dry then, with only four minutes to go, Ron Radford blazed an incredible 35 yard shot into the top right hand corner of McFaul's net - for years and years recorded as a goal of extra special merit. Hereford came alive and Newcastle wilted in the Cup atmosphere. In extra-time Ricky George got a goal from close in that crept inside the post. United were out of the FA Cup and the whole nation saw it on television. It was the first time a non-league side had toppled First Division opposition for 23 years. Newcastle were cruelly the laughing stock of the game. They hadn't played badly, but had paid for not converting their first-half dominance into goals. Fate was on Hereford's side. A few months later the Welsh border club was elected to the Football League, due mainly to their giant-killing act over the Magpies, and almost a repeat performance against West Ham United.

Newcastle, although deflated, bounced back in style, so typical of their Jekyll and Hyde character in the seventies. They triumphed 2-0 at Old Trafford the following weekend and reclaimed a slice of pride. Green was, as usual, man-of-the-match outshining all Manchester United's array of stars, Charlton, Law and Best included. He set up both Newcastle goals and went on to claim the Player-of-the-Season award. No player deserved it more. United finished the campaign in 11th place, the Hereford reverse apart, it had been a satisfying year. Macdonald represented both the Football League and Under 23 side - and scored a 25 yard special in his country's jersey. He netted 30 goals in all games for United in his first season. Malcolm was the new hero and had very much answered his doubters.

The Popular enclosure on Leazes Terrace closed during the season allowing work on a new East Stand to at last commence. Finally, after many years of haggling with the City Council, Gallowgate was to see a redevelopment plan actually start. A year later the £420,000 stand was opened, but even then it appeared to be jinxed and was some months late due to a lengthy builders' strike. United, though, had now 3,400 precious seats and the considerable revenue they brought in season-ticket sales, at the time a complete sell-out.

Newcastle's side developed a stage further over the following twelve months. They often looked a very good team with Macdonald, Hibbitt and back to fitness Jimmy Smith in fine form. United's unpredictable tag was hard to dispose of though, and an injury to Green against Crystal Palace early into the season disrupted the side. In a tackle with tough defender Mel Blyth, the Scot's right knee was shattered, an injury which eventually forced the dazzling player out of football. It was a heart-breaking ending. Joe Harvey was almost in tears, "It was the saddest day of my life", he said, and went on, "He was my very best buy. I could watch him all day and every day". So could United's fans, but Tony Green was another name added to a growing list of injury victims during this period. Geoff Allen, Ollie Burton and soon, another magical player, Jimmy Smith were all forced to retire. Green only played 35 games, but will be remembered as if he had appeared over 350 times for the black'n'whites.

Other injuries, to Macdonald and to Moncur again, also had their effect, but in spasms of brilliant football United could turn in scintillating displays. Against Leeds United, dominant force in the early seventies, United won 3-2 with the winning goal on that afternoon rated as one of the best scored in the whole country that season. Gibb made a strong run down the right wing and fired in a hard, low cross. Barrowclough superbly dummied the ball on the penalty spot to leave two Leeds defenders for dead. The ball was met by the onrushing

Lord Westwood (left) entertains Prime Minister Ted Heath at St. James Park in 1973.

Malcolm Macdonald and Supermac did the rest - a first time, low right foot shot into the corner of the net. As one report noted, Newcastle's "decisive build-up tore open one of the best cemented defences in Europe".

At one stage in the season Joe Harvey was voted the First Division's Manager of the Month and the Magpies finished in 8th position. They were however, knocked out of both cup competitions early on. After defeating Port Vale, at the time managed by Gordon Lee - to soon be heading for St James Park - they were sent tumbling out of the League Cup by the Magpie old boys of Blackpool. Bob Stokoe was in charge and Alan Suddick returned to Gallowgate to inspire his team to a 3-0 upset. Both Micky Burns and John Burridge were also in Blackpool's line-up. The FA Cup saw Bournemouth come to Tyneside for the first time and a Supermac goal helped United to a 2-0 win giving the black'n'whites a Fourth Round home tie with Second Division Luton Town. Macdonald's former club shocked a 42,276 gate by coasting to a 2-0 success with both goals coming in the first-half from winger John Aston. Their side included another ex Newcastle player in Gordon Hindson.

United did well in two other competitions, albeit fairly meaningless and held for those clubs who didn't qualify for Europe. In the Texaco Cup tournament they reached the semi-final before losing to Ipswich Town and in the Anglo-Italian Cup, United went one stage further and lifted the trophy. It was though, to many, a tournament that the club could have done without. Matches against Italian clubs AS Roma, Bologna, Como and Torino turned out in many instances to be fiery affairs. All told six players were sent off - Macdonald included - four in one explosive game against Torino at St James Park. In Rome, Newcastle's party had to be escorted from enraged home supporters by armed police after winning 2-0 in the Italian capital.

In the final during June, they defeated AC Fiorentina by 2-1 in Florence. David Craig and an own-goal by goalkeeper Superchi registered the goals before a 45,000 crowd. This was achieved too without Supermac, by now elevated into the full England side and on the overseas tour. Irving Nattrass played several times during the season - he was another of the club's fine full-back developments. Alan Kennedy and Gordon Hodgson were two further local juniors who stepped up for senior baptism.

The 1973/74 season was to be one of the most memorable to a generation of Magpie fans - ranked alongside the epic Fairs Cup victory. When United were good, they were brilliant, indeed devastating, yet when they were bad, they were depressingly poor. The lack of consistency remained and thwarted any chance of really striking for the title, but in the different game of cup football, United became a feared side, especially with the spearhead of Macdonald up front who had forged a fruitful partnership with John Tudor.

The season opened with a new three up, three down system and Newcastle, through Macdonald, got off to a flying start at West Ham. He scored both goals in a 2-1 win and by the end of September United were in a healthy position just behind the leading clubs. Newcastle at last laid their League Cup bogey with a 6-0 victory over Doncaster Rovers. Macdonald scored more goals, this time three, and young Keith Robson, a tall and powerful striker from a group of emerging juniors, grabbed two. But the man to steal the show was Frank Clark. He scored his first ever goal taking a pass from Smith and striking a low shot home.

PELE'S GENIUS

United embarked on a long tour of the Far East in the summer of 1972 and met up with Brazilians Santos in an exhibition match in Hong Kong. United led 2-1 at half-time and were looking comfortable until 15 minutes of pure genius from the world's greatest player - Pele - changed the game dramatically. He netted three goals and Santos won 4-2. Yet it was Tony Green who scored the goal of the game - a stunning drive from 35 yards that left the Brazilian keeper stranded.

Macdonald stormed on. He found the net with his 100th league goal in the victory over Manchester City and was the division's leading scorer. Then tragedy struck. He suffered knee problems and underwent a cartilage operation early into November and was out of action for six weeks. United then went through a damaging and bruising series of games with Birmingham City. Playing them in three competitions, a vendetta started in the Texaco Cup tie after City full-back Tony Want broke a leg in a clash with Jimmy Smith at Gallowgate. Smith was sent off after only 53 seconds of the match - one of the fastest dismissals of all time - and relationships between the two sets of players, officials and fans deteriorated rapidly. United came out of the series of matches minus Nattrass, just capped by the Under 23 side, Frank Clark, both cruelly hacked down in a grudge match at St Andrews, and Smith, suspended. And they were knocked out of the League Cup by a Trevor Francis penalty.

Purchased for a small fee from Bury, Terry McDermott developed into the perfect midfield link.

With Macdonald recovering quickly from his operation, attention then switched completely thereafter to the FA Cup which overshadowed everything else in the north east. Isthmian League club Hendon were United's Third Round opponents and they gave Newcastle a mighty fright on Tyneside. It took the Magpies until three minutes to the interval before they broke through the amateurs' resolute defence when Pat Howard latched onto a long Macdonald throw-in. But the second half belonged to the visitors and on 68 minutes they grabbed a deserved leveller from veteran England amateur international Rod Haider - an insurance broker - who whacked the ball past McFaul.

In the replay on Watford's ground the television cameras were there again, in an attempt to catch

United stumbling once more. However, they made no mistake this time winning 4-0, all started by a solo goal from Supermac. Hibbitt, McDermott, a signing from Bury to replace Gibb, and Tudor scored the other goals. That game kicked off on a Wednesday afternoon just after midday because of a political crisis at that time. With a miners' strike and three day week crippling the country, floodlights had been banned to save energy.

United had to dispose of Scunthorpe United in the next tie to be in the Fifth Round draw for the first time in 13 years. Scunthorpe, from Division Four, were no strangers to Tyneside and, as in the 1961 League Cup meeting, many recollected their famous victory over the black'n'whites back in 1958. Without Hibbitt, who was under suspension, the side again fumbled at the hands of the lesser club. An early blunder by teenager Alan Kennedy allowed the visitors to take the lead, but a fierce drive by McDermott from 25 yards earned United a replay. McDermott proved a marvellous find. At £25,000 he was another of Joe Harvey's bargains. He would run all afternoon like his predecessor Gibb, but McDermott added more skill to the side and was soon in England's Under 23 team. As in the previous round, Newcastle made no mistake at the second attempt. They played much better and won 3-0, Macdonald netting twice at the Old Show Ground.

John Tudor, became the ideal foil for Macdonald in attack.

Tudor's header completed a delightful move for United's third goal against West Bromwich Albion.

That victory took the Magpies to The Hawthorns and a stiff tie with West Bromwich Albion, near the top of Division Two and managed then by Don Howe. It was almost 20 years to the day that the clubs had last met in the FA Cup, and in the Fifth Round too. West Bromwich won that game in 1953 and went on to the final. Newcastle won this tie and also reached Wembley.

It turned out a marvellous afternoon for the thousands upon thousands of travelling Geordies who literally took over Albion's ground. And how United turned on the style. In a change strip of the light blue and yellow of the mighty Brazil, they played like world beaters and triumphed 3-0, this after losing Hibbitt through injury with only 18 minutes of play gone. On came Jimmy Smith to dictate the game in his own brilliant way. Len Shackleton noted in The People, "Jinking Jim's brand of magic lifts Newcastle". He laid on the first goal with a perfect cross for Macdonald to head home, then after the interval was again involved as Barrowclough netted from a clever Tudor dummy. Seconds later, from a lightning attack, Tudor's spectacular header made it 3-0. It could, and should have been 4-0 when Macdonald broke through and scored a beauty in spite of a foul challenge by centre-half John Wile. However, the referee brought back play for the infringement to the annoyance of the Newcastle camp. The same was to happen in the coming semi-final six weeks later, but then referee Gordon Hill had the intelligence to wave play on giving Supermac the advantage.

Macdonald noted the Hawthorn's victory as, "the best performance I have ever been involved with". Joe Harvey said, "That will frighten a few". United had come to the boil at the right moment. Newcastle's boss had put together an exciting team. Up front Tudor and Macdonald were dynamite while Moncur and Howard formed a good defence. Craig and Clark had the healthy challenge from the

FIVE SECOND STRIKE

A pre-season friendly at Muirton Park in Perth, home of St Johnstone during July 1972 provided football with perhaps its fastest ever goal. From the kick-off, Tudor tapped the ball to Malcolm Macdonald who blasted it long and hard from just over the half-way line - some 55 yards. The ball sailed over the home keeper's head and into the net. The timing - unofficially between four and five seconds! Macdonald noted, "I don't think anyone will ever score a goal faster than that"! Newcastle won the game 7-3 with the Magpies' twin strikers hitting a hat-trick each.

young talent of Nattrass and Kennedy to keep them on their toes and McFaul was safe, and at times spectacular. In midfield Hibbitt and McDermott were potential England players while Jim Smith was, perhaps - Macdonald apart - United's key player. If the dazzling Scot was in the mood Newcastle became a potent force. Bob Stokoe was to say of Smith, "His touch and pace of pass equals anything I've seen". The slim midfielder was recalled to the Scotland side that year, while Tommy Cassidy emerged as a useful schemer that season too. After being on the transfer list, the Irishman staked a claim to a permanent place.

The talk on Tyneside was of Wembley and speculation mounted when the Sixth Round draw was made. United were paired with another Second Division outfit, Nottingham Forest, and held home advantage. An all ticket crowd of 54,500 saw the first of a series of games to be talked about the country over. United started off as an unrecognisable unit compared to the one that had destroyed Albion so convincingly. After only 90 seconds they were behind. Bowyer chased a long pass, met it before McFaul and the ball lodged in the back of the Leazes net. Forest fought hard and were quicker to the ball than a weary-looking Magpie eleven. Duncan McKenzie was showing immaculate control and caused United increasing problems. Newcastle took a long time to recover, but following a corner they grabbed an equaliser when David Craig stabbed the ball home for one of his rare goals. The jubilation was short-lived though. Just before half-time O'Kane fired a 20 yarder past the diving McFaul and Forest were back in front at 2-1. United looked a defeated team and, when Lyall drove a penalty into the net after the interval when Craig brought down the dangerous McKenzie, they appeared finished.

Then it happened, the incident that caused so much controversy for weeks. United fans, incensed by the penalty kick incident and dismissal of Pat Howard for disputing the decision, invaded the pitch and the match was brought to a halt for eight minutes. On the resumption there was an amazing turnabout. Forest were clearly affected by the break, but had agreed to carry on. Newcastle were a different team with the packed house coming to life. Backed by ear-piercing support, the inspired ten man United battered the Forest defence. They pulled a goal back when 'keeper Jim Barron pushed Macdonald and foolishly gave away the second penalty of the tie. McDermott stroked the spot-kick and reduced the arrears to 3-2. With 22 minutes remaining Forest panicked and United got the equaliser. A Hibbitt cross, low and hard, was met bang on by Tudor who dived full length to crash a great header into the net. United were not finished either. With a matter of seconds remaining they got the winner. Tudor crossed and Macdonald headed back for Moncur to volley into the roof of the net. An incredible 4-3 victory after being 3-1 behind. It took a while for the streets to clear of celebrating fans that evening.

Newcastle fans swarm across the Gallowgate pitch against Nottingham Forest. Referee Gordon Kew took the players off the field.

With the whole of Tyneside talking about the forthcoming semi-final with Burnley, Forest appealed to the Football Association claiming that the pitch invasion had caused a change in the course of the match. After an agonising wait for an FA Committee to deliver its verdict, the region erupted with the news that the FA had annulled the game. "Diabolical", said Joe Harvey, "My reaction is one of disgust", howled Malcolm Macdonald. A replay would go ahead the following week at Goodison Park, Liverpool. There was nothing that anyone could do. United had to start all over again a week Monday and prove they could defeat Forest fair and square.

John Tudor dives to head a spectacular equaliser in the Sixth Round epic at St. James Park.

Bob Moncur volleys the ball past the Forest 'keeper to complete a remarkable come-back. McDermott looks on.

The majority of the 41,000 crowd on Merseyside belonged to the north east and what support United received. A fine match resulted despite being scoreless. The Magpies played at a frantic pace and should have left no room for

The joy of an F.A. Cup goal. Bob Moncur receives the congratulations against Forest.

argument for they were far the better side this time. They hit the woodwork three times, but just couldn't put the ball in the net. Another replay at Everton took place on Thursday, the FA strangely not allowing a game to be staged at the City Ground. Again United's travelling masses made the trip and gave the team rousing support. It was a nailbiting 90 minutes of action full of anxiety and tension, but Newcastle finally cracked Forest through a characteristic goal from Macdonald. A Barron goalkick was headed strongly back towards the Forest goal by Smith. Macdonald was away like an Olympic sprinter. Despite having centre-half Serella hanging round his neck in an attempt to pull him back, he hit a low drive beneath the goalkeeper sending the Magpies once more to meet Burnley - this time without argument. The Geordie drone of 'Haway The Lads' echoed non-stop over Goodison Park as it had done on every ground since its television debut at The Hawthorns in Round Five.

First Division Burnley included in their side ex United forward Peter Noble and future skipper Geoff Nulty. They were a polished team in the top half of the table, but non outside Lancashire fancied their chances. Newcastle had the Cup glitter, yet as the game progressed it was clear that it needed something special to defeat the young Turf Moor outfit. They were the better team for an hour, outplaying Newcastle with an assured display. Nulty hit the bar with a looping header and McFaul had to be in good form to keep Burnley at bay. Then two moments of Supermac's pace and power took Newcastle to Wembley in spectacular fashion.

A long clearance out of defence sent United's centre-forward chasing the ball down the middle from the halfway line with Colin Waldron in pursuit. Macdonald shrugged off the foul challenge of the Burnley centre-half who was trying to haul him to the ground and hammered a shot against the oncoming 'keeper. From the rebound Mac drove the ball right footed between the posts. His arms went up, fists clenched and Hillsborough erupted with 30,000 Geordies echoing the now famous cry of 'Supermac! Supermac!'

Almost immediately McFaul made brilliant saves from Collins and James as Burnley attempted to grab a quick equaliser. They were crucial stops that earned Newcastle's Wembley place just as much as Macdonald's goals. A few minutes later the game was wrapped up. Burnley were caught out again when Hibbitt first-timed a tremendous diagonal 50 yard through-ball for Supermac to once again gallop after. He ran half the length of the field before drawing the 'keeper and slotting the ball into the net. That goal brought the house down to scenes of overwhelming emotions on the terraces. Joe Harvey was as excited as the fans. He remarked on his goalscoring hero, "If anybody was wondering why they call him Supermac, then they will be in no doubt now". United were through to a record breaking 11th FA Cup final.

Before that day arrived, Newcastle had to pick up league points to make certain that a Wembley appearance did not coincide with a relegation fight. They had slipped from 2nd position in November down to 18th place winning only two league fixtures in three months. With games in hand over other strugglers, the black'n'whites managed to lift themselves to a comfortable 15th place. They also defeated Burnley again, this time in the final of the Texaco Cup, then headed south for a much more important meeting at Wembley Stadium.

Supermac in full flight. Macdonald drives the ball into the Burnley net at Hillsborough.

> *"May 4th 1974 will haunt me forever. I felt sick and embarrassed. We never got started and I can't understand it"*
>
> *Joe Harvey, 1976*

TYNESIDE'S HEROES FACED LIVERPOOL IN THE FA Cup final, probably the most feared side in the country at the time. But if Newcastle clicked - if Supermac clicked, if Smith clicked - they could beat anyone, including Shankly's men from Anfield. Newcastle also had a proud record to maintain having played five, and won five finals at Wembley, three of course with Joe Harvey very much involved as player, then coach.

United relied on the power of Macdonald who had scored in every round, but sadly the final, as far as Newcastle was concerned, ended as a super-flop. Liverpool were ruthlessly efficient, especially during the second half when Kevin Keegan was outstanding. Newcastle never got going and rarely did Macdonald receive any service from his schemers. Only Pat Howard and 19 year-old Alan Kennedy, in for the injured Craig, played to standard. The four man midfield was totally out of touch. Hibbitt worked hard, but didn't get far, finding the Liverpool machine overwhelming, as he said, "You beat one man and there's another, and then another". Smith was in one of his languid moods, while Cassidy never matched Liverpool's workrate. Only McDermott was remotely effective, so impressive that Liverpool signed him within six months.

Newcastle were over confident, nervous and never mentally right. Kevin Keegan noted in his biography that there was a huge difference between the sides, "As the teams walked out, Joe Harvey was drawn and pale. Shanks was waving at everybody. Bobby Moncur looked pensive. Emlyn Hughes looked as if he was enjoying himself". He added, "Newcastle looked a little afraid". United played poorly in the first half, but held Liverpool and many reckoned they couldn't play as bad in the second 45 minutes. They could - were in fact even worse - and Liverpool stepped up a gear. Player of the Year, Ian Callaghan controlled midfield and Keegan ran amok. Alec Lindsay had a good looking goal disallowed for offside by a fraction, then future Newcastle star Keegan struck twice, both clinically executed goals and Heighway found the net with another.

United's display was one of the poorest in an FA Cup final in recent years and it was the most one sided final since Wolves toppled Blackburn Rovers in 1960. The Magpies could only create a few half chances and a solitary corner. Two strikes by Macdonald - which would usually have tested the 'keeper - ended wide into the crowd. The only thing Newcastle won at Wembley on that day was the pre-match invitation race. Over 3000 metres, Tyneside athlete Brendan Foster, donning a black'n'white vest, scorched the rest of the field. It should have been a good omen.

Newcastle didn't win any friends and their 35,000 followers were a demoralised lot. A dejected Malcolm Macdonald said in the dressing room, "I'm just sorry we let them down". Joe Harvey recorded that, "May 4th 1974 will haunt me forever. I felt sick and embarrassed. We never got started and I can't understand it". Bob Moncur was equally as depressed. He said to a Sunday Sun reporter, "There are no excuses for us and I'm not going to make any".

It was an undignified conclusion to United's swashbuckling and dramatic ten game Cup run. Despite a disappointing end, the season had been an exhilarating one. Financially it had been terrific. From the FA Cup final alone United grossed £55,707. United's supporters did not easily forget the Wembley debacle, but they turned up in their thousands to welcome the team home nevertheless. It takes little effort to applaud victors, even a team that had been defeated with honour. But the scenes to welcome Newcastle's side - so humiliated - were amazing and a credit to Tyneside's loyal fans. Many of the players ended in tears. No other city could have swallowed such a defeat with so much honour.

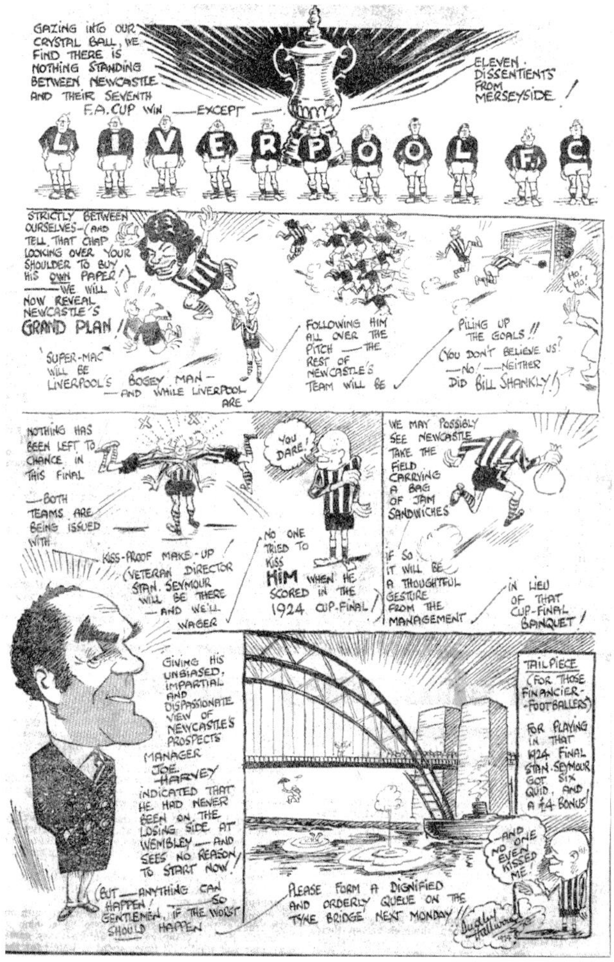

Dudley Hallwood's view of the black'n'whites' visit to London.

FA CUP RUN				
R3	Hendon	H	D	1-1
	Hendon	A	W	4-0
R4	Scunthorpe United	H	D	1-1
	Scunthorpe United	A	W	3-0
R5	West Bromwich Albion	A	W	3-0
R6	Nottingham Forest	H	W	*4-3
	Nottingham Forest	N	D	0-0
	Nottingham Forest	N	W	1-0
SF	Burnley	N	W	2-0
F	Liverpool	N	L	0-3

*R6 *Match result annulled, replay ordered by FA*

FACTS & FIGURES	P	W	D	L	F	A
Home	3	1	2	0	6	5
Away	7	5	1	1	13	3
Total	**10**	**6**	**3**	**1**	**19**	**8**

FA Cup Finalists 1974

CUP GOALGETTERS

7 Macdonald, 3 Tudor, McDermott, 2 Barrowclough, 1 Moncur, Howard, Hibbitt, Craig

CHAIRMAN: Lord Westwood
MANAGER: Joe Harvey
TRAINER-COACH: Keith Burkinshaw
CAPTAIN: Bobby Moncur

United's Wembley squad. Left to right, back: Burleigh, Barrowclough, Gibb, Nattrass, McFaul. Middle: Harvey (manager), Craig, Hodgson, Cassidy, Howard, Smith, McDermott, Burkinshaw (coach). Front: Macdonald, Moncur, Clark, Tudor, Green, Hibbitt.

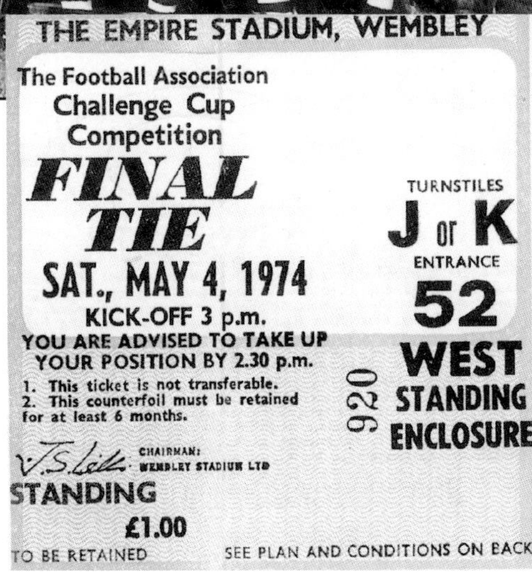

Centenary Highlight

Right: A marvellous picture of Willie McFaul in action, diving to tip this Liverpool free-kick to safety.

Below: McFaul can only look towards his net, while a delighted Kevin Keegan begins to celebrate a Liverpool goal.

FA Cup Finalists 1974

FINAL
4 May 1974 at Wembley Stadium
Newcastle United 0 (0) Liverpool 3 (0)

UNITED;
McFaul
Clark, Howard, Moncur, Kennedy
Smith (Gibb), McDermott, Cassidy, Hibbitt
Tudor, Macdonald
LIVERPOOL;
Clemence
Smith, Thompson, Hughes, Lindsay
Cormack, Hall, Callaghan
Heighway, Toshack, Keegan
sub Boersma

GOALS;
Keegan (58m), Heighway (75m), Keegan (88m)

ATTENDANCE;
100,000 (£212,650)

Referee; G.C.Kew (Amersham)
Guest of Honour; HRH Princess Anne
Cup HQ; Selsdon Park Hotel, North London

The welcome United's defeated side received when they returned to St. James Park.

THE FOLLOWING YEAR SAW UNITED give another exciting season's football, although added to the smiles were more than a few moments of apprehension. There was plenty of action at both ends of the field with Macdonald and Tudor continuing to form a lethal duo up front. They netted 50 goals all told with United's leader ending the season the First Division's top marksman.

In defence, however, the side was not as proficient. Discarding skipper and general at the back, Bobby Moncur, who joined Sunderland, they missed a commanding figure and young Glen Keeley, signed from Ipswich Town after a mere five league outings, had a rough time. Newcastle finished mid-table with the highlight of the league campaign a 5-0 drubbing of Chelsea during November. Alan Kennedy, playing in midfield and who gained a great unity with the crowd during the season, together with the promptings of Jimmy Smith, took the Londoners apart that wet afternoon. Supermac grabbed two goals and Kennedy, Barrowclough and youngster, Paul Cannell recorded the other strikes. However, inconsistency remained. United fell 5-2 at home to Spurs and 5-4 on a visit to Ipswich.

IN THE DOCK

Relationships between Football Club and City Council have never been too harmonious and degenerated to a low point in 1974 when the Council sued United over the actions of their supporters. Queues for tickets to watch the FA Cup semi-final with Burnley were immense and started forming through the night. On a bitterly cold evening United's fans had ripped down part of the fencing to Leazes Park to build fires and the Council held Newcastle United responsible for the damage. However, the judge ruled in the club's favour, that they could not be held responsible for actions of the public outside St James Park.

Alan Kennedy graduated into the England reckoning in double-quick time.

Kennedy's progress was astonishing. The Sunderland born full-back loved to attack down the left flank and created many a goalmouth opportunity. He was picked for the England squad to meet West Germany in March, but unluckily the youngster had to withdraw because of injury. As it turned out he would have found himself in the team too and Kennedy had to wait almost a decade before he received another chance, although he did win England Under 23 and B honours. His partner at full-back was another junior development, Irving Nattrass who had by now also claimed a regular place. Showing the same cultured football brain as his predecessor David Craig, Nattrass was also quickly in the England reckoning winning an Under 23 cap. Many thought the black'n'whites had the best full-back pair in the country - and both players were just into their twenties.

Newcastle at times oozed skill, flair and confidence. The Football League Cup at last brought a slice of success. United defeated Nottingham Forest again, once more after a replay, but without drama this time. They then followed up with a fabulous 4-0 victory at Queen's Park Rangers with a Macdonald hat-trick the feature of the game. He simply murdered the Cockneys at Loftus Road. Fulham's ageing side fell 3-0 at Gallowgate on a rainy evening, but then along came Fourth Division Chester to halt United's run. It was yet another cup nightmare. At St James Park the 100-1 outsiders held an injury-torn Newcastle side to a 0-0 draw and won the replay at Sealand Road 1-0 to groans from Magpie diehards.

Centre-half Pat Howard receives the Texaco Cup from Sir Alf Ramsey in 1974.

Before the turn of the year Newcastle lifted the Texaco Cup once more, this time defeating Southampton over two legs with £150,000 striker Alex Bruce scoring one of the goals. He arrived from Preston and was capped by Scotland's Under 23 side, but could never break the Tudor-Macdonald partnership. Then came the FA Cup and this season United were forced to play all their games away from home because of the Nottingham Forest affair. So despite coming out of the bag first they had to travel to meet frequent Cup opposition, Manchester City.

Feelings were running high on that January day. Both club and supporters wanted to show football's administrators that the controversial change in venue made no difference. Newcastle shattered their old rivals with two goals inside a minute scored by new signings, Micky Burns and Geoff Nulty. The killer strikes came as Manchester City were starting to put the Magpies under pressure and just as Willie McFaul had made a string of saves which were to earn him the man-of-the-match tag. United's 'keeper had flung himself to stop a certain City goal when Micky Burns latched on to a loose ball and moved quickly out of defence. Macdonald sent a swerving low cross and Nulty mishit a shot only for Burns, following up, to volley the ball into the net. A minute later Supermac was again the goalmaker.

RESERVES TEST

On 1st May 1972, Bury Reserves, needing a point in a Central League game to avoid probable expulsion from the competition, sent their entire first eleven to play United's Reserve team at St James Park. A small band of travelling Bury supporters were there too and witnessed a 2-2 draw. It was enough to keep the Shakers in the Central League.

Alex Bruce, rarely given an opportunity up front because of the Macdonald-Tudor partnership.

He clipped another dangerous cross ball into the box for the galloping Nulty to send a stinging drive past the diving Joe Corrigan.

Burns and Nulty had been purchased from Blackpool and Burnley for big fees and were two players of very differing styles. Small with deceptive pace, Burns was a player for the connoisseur. On his debut against Middlesbrough in a Texaco Cup game, he laid on two early goals then, as Jackie Milburn wrote in the News of the World, "brought the house down with a brilliant piece of magic". The former England amateur player evaded four tackles, walked past the 'keeper and tucked the ball away in style. Burns though, was to clash with Harvey and be an outcast at St James Park until a new regime took over.

Geoff Nulty had impressed the manager in the semi-final meeting with Burnley and, while he lacked the finer skills, was to be a dependable player and another to flourish under a new manager. He replaced Terry McDermott, signed by Liverpool for £170,000 after the player had also fallen out with the boss. Tommy Craig, a midfielder with exquisite touch, was a newcomer too, arriving from Sheffield Wednesday for £110,000. The Scot replaced Hibbitt who had knee trouble. Craig was a similar player to Hibbitt, all left foot precision, but with an added string to his bow - he could score goals, 29 of them for United, many spectacular long range efforts. Craig was to be capped at every level for his country and for a short period he and Smith formed a prominent midfield pairing. They inspired the black'n'whites to a 4-1 revenge win over Liverpool in February. Macdonald and Tudor revelled in the service given by the two Scots and a 38,000 midweek crowd had a night to remember.

However, after a few good performances United slipped up and as in the League Cup, they also fell to a club from the lower divisions in the FA Cup. Walsall were the team, the small, compact Fellows Park the venue. The home side's tactics were better suited to a very heavy pitch in the Midlands. Newcastle couldn't play their normal fluent soccer on the clinging mud, while Walsall's bustling Third Division style suited the conditions perfectly. They won 1-0 and afterwards the season turned sour. It was now the head of Joe Harvey the fans wanted. United only won one of their last eleven games during March and April.

£170,000 signing from Blackpool, Micky Burns.

Loyal and with the good of the club at heart, Harvey went through a disturbing next few weeks. Chants of, 'Haway The Lads!' turned dramatically to 'Harvey Out!'. Coach Keith Burkinshaw was sacked, although much respected by the players and protests continued unabated. It all culminated with Harvey's resignation at the end of the programme after 13 seasons in charge. And forced upon him by public opinion more than anything else. He noted sorrowfully, "There is no pleasure in management now".

Chairman Lord Westwood and manager Joe Harvey. The successful partnership was broken up when Harvey resigned.

BRUMMIE OPPOSITION

In 1973/74 Newcastle met Birmingham City a record seven times - six games taking place in as many weeks. And that was not all. Amazingly, the following season the two clubs met another four times - a total of eleven games in two seasons!

1973/74				
1	Division One	A	L	0-1
2	Division One	H	D	1-1
3	League Cup	A	D	2-2
4	League Cup	H	L	0-1
5	Texaco Cup	A	D	1-1
6	Texaco Cup	H	D	1-1(abandoned)
7	Texaco Cup	H	W	3-1
1974/75				
8	Division One	A	L	0-3
9	Division One	H	L	1-2
10	Texaco Cup	H	D	1-1
11	Texaco Cup	A	W	4-1

UNUSUAL POSTPONEMENTS

Snow and frost have commonly been the prime cause of match postponements at St James Park, however gale force wind was unusually the villain of the cancelled First Division fixture with Liverpool in December 1974. Fears of gales causing damage to United's 70 year-old West Stand were a major concern and therefore the police advised the club to cancel the match. In 1973 another unusual reason forced a game to be brought to an early close. The Texaco Cup fixture in November with Birmingham City ended in darkness due to the government's Emergency Powers at the time banning floodlighting. In extra-time the referee called a halt and the tie was replayed at a later date.

Centenary Profile 23

Captain Courageous

"The supreme sweeper and a most valuable asset both to Newcastle United and Scotland"

Joe Harvey, 1971

BOBBY MONCUR WAS ONE OF UNITED'S FINEST captains. A centre-back with ability to read the game well, and an aggressive, strong-tackling stopper. He was commanding in the air and a great marshal of the side. Moncur will always be remembered first though, for the hat-trick of goals netted in the Inter Cities Fairs Cup final against Ujpesti Dosza in 1969 - his first in almost ten years of taking the field. He led United to victory and recalled those days clearly, "At the time I didn't realise how important Europe was to the fans. It was only afterwards when I looked back at events and thought of the fever it brought to the area. I suppose supporters had been waiting for something to happen for a long time and the Fairs Cup was it".

Moncur had quite a few hiccups at St James Park before those European glory days. He spent his early years in Perth, born in 1945, but later moved to Kirkliston just outside Edinburgh. The son of a policeman, Bob played at centre-forward and left-back for junior sides, captained Scotland schoolboys and whenever possible watched his favourites, Hibernian. He also won Scottish international youth caps and was soon tipped for the full-time game. Preston North End were the first senior club to approach Moncur after he was spotted in Scottish trials at Stenhousemuir. Shortly afterwards Manchester United, Wolves, Burnley and Newcastle all did likewise.

The Magpies were last in line, but after a spell in a black'n'white shirt on approval, he chose St James Park to begin his career in football. Newcastle had a homely atmosphere and he made an impression after scoring four goals against West Wylam in a practise match. Moncur signed apprentice professional in October 1960 and the young Scot started training with the likes of Jimmy Scoular, Ivor Allchurch and Len White, all seasoned campaigners. He operated in various positions during his early days, Moncur's first taste of success was as a teenager in the 1962 Youth Cup run. He scored the winner for United in the final against Wolves and during the following season made his debut in Football League soccer. As an 18 year-old he was plunged into Newcastle's defence for a Division Two clash with Luton Town at the end of March 1963. Bob was up against another budding youngster in the Hatters' line-up - Ron Davies, a player he would face at the highest level in years to come.

Moncur played a handful of games during United's Second Division Championship winning year in 1965, but was something of a slow developer and Joe Harvey almost sold him to Norwich City for a paltry £25,000. However, the Carrow Road club haggled over a few thousand pounds and the deal fell through. Moncur never regretted the breakdown of that transfer. After that upset he was determined to turn an average career as an attack minded wing-half into a great one as an out and out defender. Moncur worked hard at his game and gradually established himself in the No 6 shirt. Manchester United boss, Sir Matt Busby eventually was to rate Moncur the best in the business. Always steady and reliable, he rarely committed himself until he knew the ball was going to be his.

Bobby Moncur

MONCUR'S PLAYING RECORD

	League		FA Cup		FL Cup		Europe		Total	
	App	Gls	App	Gls	App	Gls	App	Gls	App	Gls
1962-63	3	0	0	0	0	0	0	0	3	0
1963-64	3	0	0	0	0	0	0	0	3	0
1964-65	11	0	0	0	1	0	0	0	12	0
1965-66	19/3	0	0	0	1	0	0	0	20/3	0
1966-67	23	0	1	0	1	0	0	0	25	0
1967-68	34	0	1	0	0	0	0	0	35	0
1968-69	30	0	3	0	0	0	10	3	43	3
1969-70	40	0	1	0	1	0	8	0	50	0
1970-71	41	2	2	0	1	0	4	1	48	3
1971-72	21	0	1	0	0	0	0	0	22	0
1972-73	32	0	2	0	2	0	0	0	36	0
1973-74	36	1	7	1	3	0	0	0	46	2
	293/3	**3**	**18**	**1**	**10**	**0**	**22**	**4**	**343/3**	**8**

The 1967/68 season was the turning point in Moncur's career and this after starting as a reserve. He formed a partnership with John McNamee, sweeping up behind the tall centre-half, and showed he was a sure defender. Bob was appointed captain in place of Jim Iley for the first time in February 1968 against Arsenal and United went on to qualify for Europe at the end of the season. Dark haired and powerfully built at 5'10" with thick tree-trunk legs, his progress was also noticed by Scotland and he was picked for their Under 23 side. A fine skipper out of the Harvey mould, Bob handled the responsibility with immense pride and his rich Scots accent could be heard in the stands as he drove the Magpies on. Only his boss, Joe Harvey, has captained United more and together they made a good working team.

A full Scotland cap came his way in May 1968 against Holland in Amsterdam and he was taken to heart by his nation's fans with a rugged performance in the England-Scotland clash of 1970 at Hampden Park. A virtual unknown north of the border, Bob was led off with concussion to a hero's ovation from a massive crowd of 134,000 following a hearty display. After only six appearances Moncur was given the captaincy of his country ahead of John Greig. Bob noted, "Without doubt captaining both Newcastle and Scotland gave me a lot of satisfaction. It was a nice bonus to my career". All told he appeared on 16 occasions for the Scots up to 1972 and was respected throughout the game. He was also an executive of the PFA.

In 1974 he led United to Wembley and the defeat by Liverpool remains Moncur's greatest disappointment like many of the side, "Two teams were out there and only one played." Yet as he remembered, "The homecoming we received I'll never forget....it will stay as my fondest memory". Following that FA Cup final, Moncur never kicked a ball for the club again. He was released by United, too soon thought many, even though at 30 years of age he had started to lack pace in the back four. After 346 games for the Magpies, Moncur joined neighbours Sunderland in the summer for £30,000 and helped the Roker side to the Second Division championship in 1976 - and was voted Player of the Season.

In November of that year he joined Carlisle United as player-manager, but had a struggle at Brunton Park arriving just as they slipped into Division Three and Bob resigned in February 1980. He did have some success in Cumbria though, signing Peter Beardsley for all of a set of strips. Moncur moved back to Edinburgh to take control of Heart of Midlothian, again at a time when his new side needed a revival. This time his winning touch worked as Hearts gained promotion as Division One champions, but then his club tumbled straight back the following year.

Weeks later in June 1981, Moncur was appointed manager of Third Division Plymouth Argyle, replacing Bobby Saxton at Home Park. Yet it was again only a brief stay, the Scot departing early into the 1983/84 season after differences of opinion between manager and directors. He then quit football and concentrated on business out of the game. A natural sportsman, proficient at golf - twice winning the footballers' championship - badminton, tennis and squash, he opened a sports club in Gateshead. He also sailed a great deal having completed the Round Britain Yacht Race inside 35 days, as well as the Fastnet and two Atlantic crossings.

Moncur returned to football as coach with Whitley Bay and was tempted into the Football League management scene again when he took control of ailing Hartlepool in October 1988. However, success was always far from his grasp and he left the game for a second time in December 1989. Newcastle United will do well if they find another skipper with the quality, dedication and spirit of Bob Moncur.

Goalkeeper to Manager

"It is debatable whether there's a better goalkeeper in the country"

Bill Shankly, 1969

ONLY JOE HARVEY CAN BOAST THE KIND OF service that Willie McFaul gave to Newcastle United. The likable Irishman graduated from reserve goalkeeper, to the senior eleven and international choice, then coach to the juniors, to the reserves and first-team. He served under no less than six managers at St James Park then climbed into the hot-seat himself. It was a career that spanned over 20 years on Tyneside, devoted to United's cause since the day he moved to the north east from Linfield as an inexperienced part-timer.

Christened William, although known by many as Iam, he was born in 1943. At school McFaul was a promising right-half and like most teenagers when he first was told to play in goal didn't like it. But he gradually took to the position and was capped at junior and youth level for his country. He had trials at several clubs including Bristol City and Newcastle United too. He played a solitary game for United's juniors before being sent home by Charlie Mitten. McFaul then took up a joinery apprenticeship and played semi-pro for Coleraine before joining Linfield early into the sixties decade where he won Irish league and cup medals and played in European football.

His eventual transfer to Newcastle occurred under remarkable circumstances. During September 1966 United entertained Linfield in a friendly and the Irish club received a thrashing, McFaul seeing no fewer than seven goals flash past him. However, believe it or not, he still had a blinder and Joe Harvey was suitably impressed paying out £7,000 for his signature. McFaul had arrived in the big-time at the relatively late age of 23, and for a second time at St James Park.

Appearances were spasmodic during his first two seasons at Gallowgate and confidence was never one of McFaul's assets at first. But when he pulled on Gordon Marshall's jersey for the game against West Ham on the opening Saturday of the 1968/69 season, McFaul never looked back. Only minor injuries - and they were few - stopped the Irishman holding the position for the next seven years. The blond haired 'keeper was quick and acrobatic. He may not have been one of the tallest in the business, but what he lacked in inches he made up for with instinct and reflex agility. McFaul was a wonderful shot stopper at times, in the mould of Ronnie Simpson. Yet, unlike many spectacular goalies, he invariably hung onto the ball too, not allowing a parry to rebound to an onrushing forward. In football terms he was, 'a safe pair of hands'.

Installed as Joe Harvey's regular choice, McFaul immediately found himself in an action packed era. His first full season saw Newcastle enter Europe and McFaul's performances peaked as United reached the latter stages of the competition. Against Rangers a marvellous penalty save ensured Newcastle were in poll position to go through, while in the final he made a series of fabulous stops against Ujpesti, two worthy of special mention.

At St James Park he flung himself to halt a Solymosi free-kick when the score was still 0-0 and had McFaul not stopped that effort, events could well have turned out so differently. In Budapest another crucial save won the Fairs Cup for United just as much as Bob Moncur's goals. With the Hungarians leading 2-0, Willie dived full length to stop a 25 yard rocket from Dunai entering the top corner of the net. McFaul reckoned it was his best ever save. A 3-0 interval deficit would have sunk the black'n'whites.

McFaul was a consistent performer over the next five years, ranked in the top half dozen 'keepers in the country along with Banks, Clemence, Bonetti and Pat Jennings, his rival at

Willie McFaul

McFAUL'S PLAYING RECORD

	League		FA Cup		FL Cup		Europe		Total	
	App	Gls	App	Gls	App	Gls	App	Gls	App	Gls
1966-67	8	0	0	0	0	0	0	0	8	0
1967-68	3	0	1	0	1	0	0	0	5	0
1968-69	41	0	3	0	2	0	12	0	58	0
1969-70	42	0	1	0	1	0	8	0	52	0
1970-71	41	0	2	0	1	0	4	0	48	0
1971-72	41	0	2	0	2	0	0	0	45	0
1972-73	35	0	2	0	2	0	0	0	39	0
1973-74	40	0	10	0	3	0	0	0	53	0
1974-75	39	0	2	0	6	0	0	0	47	0
	290	**0**	**23**	**0**	**18**	**0**	**24**	**0**	**355**	**0**

international level. Indeed, McFaul's form at one stage prompted the great Bill Shankly to say, "It's debatable whether there's a better goalkeeper in the country". McFaul was unlucky to have such an accomplished contemporary as Jennings, and subsequently never won the haul of caps worthy of his talent. As second choice to the Spurs 'keeper for Northern Ireland he only appeared six times for his country, although he was on the subs' bench on over 40 occasions.

Just as in Newcastle's European success, McFaul played his part during the club's run to Wembley in 1974. Again critical saves in the latter stages made him a hero, but the appointment of Gordon Lee in 1975 marked the end of McFaul's dominance as Newcastle's 'keeper. Now approaching 33 years of age, he called it a day, but certainly did not terminate his stay at St James Park. He was appointed assistant coach in 1975 looking after the juniors, a role which quickly developed through a succession of managers. He was elevated to the reserves, then had a spell as caretaker boss when Richard Dinnis was sacked, before looking after the first-team under Arthur Cox and Jack Charlton. On the resignation of Big Jack in August 1985, McFaul applied for the job himself and landed it, becoming one of a handful of former goalkeepers to have taken charge of a top club. He was the fourth ex Magpie player to hold the position following Cunningham, Seymour and of course Joe Harvey.

Inheriting the nucleus of a good First Division side including superstars to be, Peter Beardsley and Paul Gascoigne, McFaul's term in charge looked at first most encouraging, but the departure of both Beardsley and Gascoigne and a succession of transfer flops saw the amiable Irishman sacked in October 1988. After 22 years as a Newcastle United man, it took a while to adjust to a new life away from St James Park. He scouted for a while, before returning, as manager for the 1990/91 season, to his roots in Coleraine, his birthplace. The Londonderry club were in dire straits and had finished bottom of the Irish League when Willie took control. A complete rebuilding strategy was required of the former United goalkeeper. McFaul's career had gone full circle. He will be remembered on Tyneside as an individual to have given the club complete dedication.

15 REBELS & ROUSERS

1975-1980 • GORDON LEE TAKES OVER • DOUBLE WEMBLEY BID • PLAYER POWER • RETURN TO EUROPE • ALL CHANGE AGAIN • TYNE-WEAR SHOOT-OUT •

"After Gordon Lee arrived as manager the honeymoon for me was well and truly over"

Malcolm Macdonald, August 1976

MALCOLM MACDONALD SAID ON THE arrival of United's new manager, "Gordon Who!" and echoed the sentiments of most on Tyneside. Newcastle's board chose an unknown to replace Joe Harvey, Blackburn Rovers' young boss, Gordon Lee, the son of a miner with a personality that was forthright and dedicated. Tall and angular faced, 40 year-old Lee said on his arrival in a broad Midlands accent, "I consider Newcastle to be the best club in the world". But his appearance brought disappointment and apathy over the appointment. The fans wanted a big name, a Clough or a McMenemy. However, the professional approach that Lee instilled into Newcastle's side gave supporters a pleasant surprise - another Wembley visit and a team that even flirted with League Championship hopes.

Gordon Lee, arrived at St. James Park from Blackburn Rovers.

A full-back with Aston Villa, Lee had won League Cup honours with the Claret and Blues, then fashioned Port Vale into a promotion winning outfit. At Ewood Park, Rovers lifted the Third Division title in 1975 and Lee was that division's Manager of the Year. Blackburn were not happy about losing their manager, claiming United had poached him. They in fact sued the Tynesiders for compensation and a bitter tug-of-war broke out between the two clubs for several weeks.

It was the start of a controversial, yet successful and all too brief, spell in charge of Newcastle United for Lee. He was to split Tyneside over his attitudes to football. Lee admired hard work and dedication, but didn't care too much for superstars and the enigmatic genius. There were public outbursts with Macdonald and rumours that some of the directors didn't like his uncompromising style. Some criticised him for the unattractive tactics employed, others praised him for making United a better all round team. Malcolm Macdonald was to say, "Gordon Lee seemed hell-bent on creating a divided dressing-room", while Jimmy Smith recorded, "He ruined the club". Other factions of the playing staff had other views. Tommy Craig and Geoff Nulty were two of the majority who backed him all the way.

Lee changed many things at St James Park. Bringing his own coach - schoolteacher Richard Dinnis - training was altered and so to was the team's style of play. He installed possession football into the side and a lot of fans, weened on the glory or bust football of Joe Harvey, found the new system slow and boring. Tommy Craig remarked, "He was trying to get us to play like Liverpool and Leeds - and succeeding".

The manager got off to a flying start with a 3-0 victory at Ipswich with Macdonald in devastating form. This good performance was repeated as the League Cup began and at last the black'n'whites made a bid for the trophy for the first and, up to now, only time. A tie with Southport was originally scheduled to be played in Lancashire, but the home club switched the venue to Gallowgate in search of bigger gate receipts. They received those, but also a 6-0 hammering with Lee's new striker from Huddersfield Town, Alan Gowling claiming four goals in an easy romp. By this early point in the season both Macdonald and Gowling - in for the injured Tudor - were riding high in the country's goal scorers' table. United found the net with ease while Tommy Craig prompted brilliantly from midfield and was selected for the Scotland squad.

Gowling, one of the modern Busby Babes at Manchester United, once captained England's Under 23 eleven, but had slipped into the lower reaches of the Football League before Gordon Lee rescued him. Tall and awkward looking, Gowling said of his own style, "I'm not a pretty player, I'm not good to watch. But I like to think I'm honest". He was and proved to be a brilliant scoop grabbing 30 goals in his first season and in only 119 games for the club hit the back of the net 48 times. And all at only £70,000.

Alan Gowling has an attempt at goal against Middlesbrough in August 1976.

Bristol Rovers renewed acquaintances in the next round of the League Cup. United drew at Eastville, but only after a late Gowling equaliser. The Magpies won the replay 2-0 with Craig grabbing a deadlock breaking penalty after Burns had been felled. Last season's rivals Queens Park Rangers, then high flying in the First Division table, were then dispatched at Loftus Road. Newcastle triumphed in great fashion by 3-1 in a match of tremendous pace. Rangers took the lead, but Burns equalised and Macdonald put United ahead. Nulty grabbed a third with a header after ghosting into a good position so characteristic of his play. In the quarter-final United were again given a plum draw, a home game with Second Division Notts County. Newcastle pounded away all evening at the County defence and played a patient waiting game for the breakthrough. That came in a most unusual way when County's 'keeper, Eric McManus sent the Magpies into the semi-final when he fumbled a Macdonald long-throw straight into his own net.

The year turned and United opened 1976 with a thrilling sequence of games that had Tyneside's sporting public completely enthralled with cup action - both in the League Cup and FA Cup - for fully two months. And on top of that, First Division fixtures contained several incident packed games too. It was a spell of football to rival anything in United's past. Newcastle faced up to QPR again, this time in the FA Cup and another memorable duel took place. Stan Bowles made a hash of a penalty in a frantic replay after a scrappy 0-0 draw at Loftus Road, but Tommy Craig didn't miss from the spot to give United the tie by 2-1. Before the Fourth Round meeting with Coventry City, United had an even more important clash, the League Cup semi-final with Tottenham Hotspur.

ADMISSION 1979/80

Season-tickets	
East Stand - centre	£48.00
West Stand - centre	£42.60
Match-day	
East Stand - centre	£3.00
East Stand - wing	£2.50
West Stand - centre	£2.50
Centre Paddock	£2.00
Wing Paddock	£1.70
Gallowgate or Leazes	£1.50
Juveniles & OAP	£0.80

In the first leg at White Hart Lane, Newcastle hung on against a tidal wave of Spurs pressure and survived with only a 1-0 deficit - a good result with a home leg to follow. In fact Craig almost grabbed the equaliser, but a magnificent flying stop from Jennings turned his volley over the bar. The Scot made the comment, "I don't think I've hit a better one. Jennings made an incredible save". Skipper Geoff Nulty said, "If we don't get through now we will have only ourselves to blame". On the 21st January almost

Stuart Barrowclough spent eight seasons in United's squad appearing on 262 occasions.

Dressing-room celebrations after toppling Spurs in the League Cup semi-final.

50,000 saw United reach Wembley Stadium with a convincing 3-1 victory. They pulled out all the stops in an action packed semi-final and got exactly the start they wanted - a goal after only three minutes. Macdonald hit the perfect pass for Alan Gowling who ran past the back four, rounded Jennings and scored. Newcastle were back in the first minute of the second half to destroy the Londoners when a Craig corner was met by Glen Keeley who headed powerfully down and into the net. In the 65th minute the game was over when Cassidy crossed low, Gowling stepped over the ball and Nulty, charging in, blasted past the Spurs 'keeper. Newcastle gave a display of football which always looked like succeeding. As Gordon Lee said, "It was the sort of performance that made me a really proud man". The entire ground became a sea of black'n'white as the near capacity crowd remained in the stadium for a victory lap of honour.

Without having time to think of the coming Wembley trip, United were at Highfield Road for an important FA Cup tie. The Magpies brought Coventry back to Gallowgate with a 1-1 draw and following a 5-0 pounding they gave City in the replay, everyone was targeting a Wembley double. United gained that win with contemptuous ease. Malcolm Macdonald was outstanding, scoring two and making another. United's Number 9 tormented and terrorised the City rearguard all evening. To end a January to remember United took part in another epic - a Division One derby against Middlesbrough on Tees-side. They drew 3-3 with United snatching a point with a double strike in the final two minutes of the game. As a reward for his success, Gordon Lee was voted Manager of the Month, the only occasion a Newcastle boss has received the outright award. As a touch of gratitude to United's fans, Lee had the gallon bottle of Bell's Whisky reduced to miniatures which he handed to the crowd before the forthcoming Cup-tie with Bolton Wanderers.

Into February and an equally exciting period. Another marvellous league clash, a 4-3 victory studded with drama over Derby County took place before United faced Second Division promotion contenders Bolton in the FA Cup Fifth Round. At Burnden Park a truly thrilling 3-3 draw resulted and again Macdonald made headlines scoring two fabulous goals. One a break-away down the middle after a perfect Cassidy through pass, then another, a swinging volley with his right foot from well outside of the box that had BBC's Barry Davies screaming with delight on the television commentary. It was a classic match in which goals don't tell half the story. A totally absorbing non-stop contest that saw Bolton take the lead after only five minutes, then snatch a replay with only minutes remaining on the referee's watch. Tommy Cassidy was quite brilliant on that afternoon, perhaps his best 90 minutes for the club.

The replay before 52,760 on Tyneside ended in stalemate at 0-0, but it was a match that had virtually everything except goals. And it all started again at neutral Elland Road five days later. Without Macdonald and David Craig, United triumphed in grand style. It was another furious match in which Wanderers played well, but guided by goals from Burns and the decisive strike by Gowling, United won 2-1. The Magpies continued on their pursuit of a double Wembley appearance. However, before their FA Cup Sixth Round clash with Derby County they had an appointment in London to keep.

The north east had hoped that Middlesbrough would reach Wembley alongside United, but the Ayresome Park side lost in the other semi-final to Manchester City, whose previous cup meetings with the black'n'whites had been packed with incident. Newcastle's side earned much praise as one of football's entertainers, especially in midfield and up front where Macdonald and Gowling had forged a top class partnership, and Craig and Cassidy were a skilful duo. Mick Mahoney arrived from Torquay United for a bargain fee and took over from the aging McFaul in goal. He showed amazing agility at times, being a wonderful guardian between the posts.

FLOODLIGHTS FAIL

Against Ipswich Town in March 1977 an electricity failure at the power grid in Newburn caused the St James Park floodlights to fail during the First Division fixture. With only part power restored and in dim light, the referee continued proceedings and the game ended 1-1. It is the only occasion to date that lights have failed at Gallowgate.

Irish international Tommy Cassidy, he played 24 times for his

Centenary Highlight

"We are going back to Newcastle with our heads up"

Gordon Lee, February 1976

THE CARDS WERE STACKED VERY MUCH AGAINST United in the 1976 League Cup final. An influenza epidemic had as much to do with United losing the tie as Dennis Tueart's once in a lifetime winning goal. The flu bug hit Newcastle's camp only seven days before the Wembley date and with the side already missing captain, Geoff Nulty with a fractured jaw, and David Craig, knee ligaments, several players were packed off to bed with anti-flu drugs. In addition both Nattrass and Mahoney were doubtful with injuries.

When United travelled south to their Cockfosters HQ they had to leave no fewer than six players behind. Manager Gordon Lee noted to the press, "We have had probably the worst build up any side has had to a final". There was even talk of possible cancellation of the prestige fixture, but that would have caused huge administrative difficulties so United would have to battle on come what may. Glen Keeley and Stuart Barrowclough were drafted into the line-up, while rivals Manchester City had no such problems and in the end their fitness showed.

Being considerably weakened in terms of stamina, United, however, played their part in what was acclaimed the best League Cup final up to that point in the competition's history. It was a good open game with Newcastle looking assured going forward, although their defence was shaky at times and never adequately handled the aerial threat of Royle and Booth - indeed both goals conceded came initially from penalty box headers.

Macdonald had a 25 yarder palmed round the post and the Magpies had most of the early play, but a Keeley foul on Joe Royle proved costly. Hartford's free-kick was headed across the face of goal by the big centre-forward and the youthful Peter Barnes stormed in to fire a half-volley into the net. He was the son of Ken Barnes who had tasted defeat with City against the black'n'whites back in 1955. Newcastle got back in the game though as half-time approached. Cassidy found Macdonald on the right flank. With a burst of pace the England centre-forward approached the edge of the box and fired in a low centre. Gowling, Watson and 'keeper Corrigan went for the ball and it was the long leg of the United striker who met it first. United were level at 1-1.

It was the ideal time to score. United could come out in the second half a lifted side. Yet it was City who claimed all the headlines by scoring within 60 seconds of the restart. And what a goal it was - scored ironically by Newcastle born, Dennis Tueart. Donnachie floated the ball into United's box, Tommy Booth headed across the goalmouth towards the penalty spot and Tueart, back to goal and surrounded by three Newcastle players, produced a clever bicycle kick which sent the ball into Mahoney's bottom right-hand corner. The Blues were back in front 2-1. It proved to be the winning goal, and one worthy of a Wembley final. Skipper for the day, Tommy Craig, made the comment, "It was a marvellous scissor kick. You have to credit the lad, it was a great goal".

Gordon Lee's first team squad. Left to right, back: Mahoney, D. Craig, Smith, Nattrass, Kennedy, Cannell, Barrowclough, Macdonald, T. Craig, Tudor, McFaul. Front: Burns, Nulty, Bruce, Hibbitt, Lee (manager), Cassidy, Howard, Keeley.

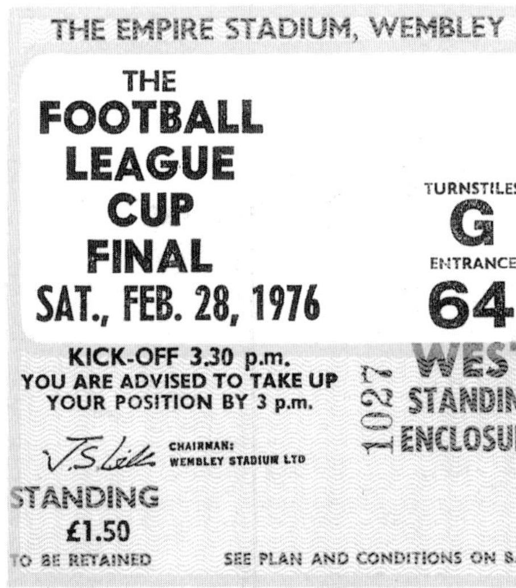

Newcastle had chances to level the match again before the final whistle, especially in a last ditch effort during the final quarter of the match. On 73 minutes Micky Burns found himself with a golden opportunity, but his angled shot was a whisker outside the far post. Then five minutes from time, Corrigan tipped over Gowling's fierce left-footer. United's performance in midfield and attack was a good one with Macdonald turning in a quality display, but the pace of the game, and the energy sapping Wembley turf took its toll. Malcolm Macdonald, one of those affected by flu, said, "My legs were like jelly in the second half and there were at least three others who felt exactly the same". His manager remarked, "We ran out of steam early in the second-half". But as Gordon Lee added, "We are going back to Newcastle with our heads up".

The 30,000 black'n'white partisans at Wembley, and the rest of Tyneside watching on television, were disappointed, yet not disheartened. United may have ended as Runners-up, but they had reclaimed much of the pride lost in 1974.

League Cup Finalists 1976

FL CUP RUN

R2	Southport	H	W	6-0
R3	Bristol Rovers	A	D	1-1
	Bristol Rovers	H	W	2-0
R4	Queens Park Rangers	A	W	3-1
R5	Notts County	H	W	1-0
SF	Tottenham Hotspur	A	L	0-1
	Tottenham Hotspur	H	W	3-1
F	Manchester City	N	L	1-2

FACTS & FIGURES

	P	W	D	L	F	A
Home	4	4	0	0	12	1
Away	4	1	1	2	5	5
Total	**8**	**5**	**1**	**2**	**17**	**6**

CUP GOALGETTERS
7 Gowling, 2 Nulty, Cannell, 1 Burns, Craig(T), Keeley, Macdonald, Nattrass, own-goal.

CHAIRMAN: Lord Westwood
MANAGER: Gordon Lee
TRAINER-COACH: Richard Dinnis
CAPTAIN: Geoff Nulty (Tommy Craig deputising in final)

FINAL

28 February 1976 at Wembley Stadium
Newcastle United 1 (1) Manchester City 2 (1)

UNITED;
Mahoney
Nattrass, Keeley, Howard, Kennedy
Barrowclough, Burns, Cassidy, Craig(T)
Macdonald, Gowling
sub Cannell

MANCESTER CITY;
Corrigan
Keegan, Doyle, Watson, Donnachie
Oakes, Booth, Hartford
Barnes, Royle, Tueart
sub Clements

GOALS;
Barnes (11m), Gowling (35m), Tueart (46m)

ATTENDANCE;
100,000 (£301,000)

Referee; J.K.Taylor (Wolverhampton)
Guest of Honour; Duke of Norfolk
Cup HQ; West Lodge Park, Cockfosters

Peter Barnes opens the scoring at Wembley despite the attentions of Howard, Mahoney, Craig and Keeley.

Newcastle supporters give a chorus of 'Haway the Lads' in Trafalgar Square.

Alan Gowling stabs home United's equaliser just before half-time.

Dennis Tueart's marvellous winner for City. Three Newcastle players can only watch: Burns, Craig and Keeley.

WITH ONE WEMBLEY VISIT DONE AND **dusted, United had to immediately pick themselves up from defeat and continue in their bid for a second and FA Cup appearance at the famous arena. Still very much affected by the flu bug, United sent out a patched-up side to face League Champions, Derby County at the Baseball Ground. Youngsters Eddie Edgar, Ray Blackhall and Rocky Hudson were thrown into the clash and United went down 4-2 and out of the FA Cup. But Newcastle fought well and as Gordon Lee pointed out to the Sunday Express, "We have done football proud, we are the most entertaining side in the country". And he had a point.**

United finished in 15th position after slipping in the league table towards the end of the season, but the year had been a huge success, although honour in defeat was very hard to swallow. Newcastle wrapped the programme up at Tottenham in a game that saw Malcolm Macdonald give Spurs a mauling. Speculation was rife that Supermac had decided to quit St James Park due to the lack of understanding with his manager. As if to show Gordon Lee what he would be missing, Macdonald first struck the bar for Burns to tuck away the rebound, then scored two goals of unquestioned quality himself. The first saw the chunky striker outstrip the Tottenham defence in typical tearaway fashion before unleashing a power shot. Next was an awesome volley which almost ripped the netting from the woodwork.

The club's supporters hoped the inevitable would not happen and that Macdonald and his boss would patch up their differences, but just before the new season opened, Tyneside was rocked by Lee's sale of Supermac - hero of all - to Arsenal for a massive fee, £333.333 and 33p to be precise. The rift between manager and player had widened the longer the 1975/76 season went on. Speculation had been mounting for weeks, everyone knew that Lee did not support the star system and Macdonald on his departure said in a frank interview with the Sunday Mirror, "My first four years with Newcastle were a real honeymoon. I loved every minute of every day. But after Gordon Lee arrived as manager the honeymoon for me was well and truly over".

Now installed in a role he enjoyed, Micky Burns nets at St. James Park. He was United's top scorer for two years in succession.

Lee was to say that he would not have "paid £100,000" for Macdonald and the rhetoric continued between the two parties for many years after. Newcastle's fans, not surprisingly, did not like the decision to sell their idol. Some brought a wreath and delivered it to the club's office, the bereavement card read, "In memory of dear departed Supermac". Terry McDermott was to later say, "Letting Malcolm go was nothing short of a catastrophe". Gordon Lee's comment was that there are no stars at Newcastle, only players who have the honesty and hard work to match their football skills, "I know I did the right thing for the club and the team". Few agreed with him and the majority wanted Supermac very much a United, and not Arsenal, player. Apart from the personality clash there was another underlying reason why United let him go. Some within St James Park reckoned Macdonald had a suspect knee and now was a good time to cash in.

The transfer deal caused local bookies to slash United's odds against being relegated from 25-1 to 4-1. All looked dismal for the new season, but the critics were silenced when Lee and his star-less, dour looking line-up took United into 3rd place by December. Burns and Gowling formed a new strikeforce and a successful one. Burns flourished without Macdonald and the tricky forward went on to become top scorer in the two seasons which followed. Irving Nattrass did well too under Lee's guidance and was in line for a trip with England to South America but, like Alan Kennedy before him, injury forced him to drop out of the tour.

A resounding 4-1 success over Everton put Newcastle within three points of leaders Liverpool and level with Ipswich Town in 2nd place. United tore the Merseyside club apart with the eloquent skills of Tommy Craig controlling the game like a master. There was talk of a serious Championship bid, but then Gordon Lee caused another mighty sensation.

His team had disposed of Sheffield United in the Third Round of the FA Cup and again faced Manchester City in Round Four. City were in contention for the title alongside United and just before the big match with the Maine Road club, rumours flew round Tyneside that Gordon Lee was leaving to take a lucrative £20,000 a year post with Everton - returning to Lancashire where his family were still living. The team was clearly affected and United crashed 3-1 before a 45,300 crowd at Gallowgate with frustrated and annoyed spectators spilling onto the pitch and causing a 12 minute stoppage. Lee was now the public's number one enemy. Within an hour of full-time he was on his way to Goodison Park with 18 months of his contract still to run. He had turned his back on the club that had given him a chance in the big time and few forgave him for that. United had to find a new manager once again - that caused a storm perhaps unparalleled in the club's history.

Coach Richard Dinnis took over as caretaker

Full-back Irving Nattrass gets the better of ex United hero, Malcolm Macdonald now wearing the colours of Arsenal.

boss as Newcastle's board considered who would replace Lee. Several names were linked with the job; ex trainer Dave Smith, Lawrie McMenemy and Wrexham's John Neal. The fans wanted a big name again, especially Brian Clough. Newcastle made an approach for Ian Greaves at Bolton, but their offer was turned down, while the club were also interested in Lincoln's young boss Graham Taylor. Then into the fray stepped a player deputation backing their coach, Richard Dinnis. 35 year old Dinnis did not have much of a footballing background and hardly warranted consideration for one of soccer's biggest jobs. A teetotaller, born in Blackburn, he had not played the game above the level of Blackburn Rovers reserve side and never as a professional. A physical education teacher, United's directors - with due reason - didn't wish to appoint Dinnis as the club's next manager, but the players had a fondness for him and insisted he be put in charge. Events got quickly out of control with a players' revolt, a threatened mass transfer request and even a strike developing.

United's professionals passed a vote of no confidence in the board and rebel shareholders became involved in an increasingly bitter and widely publicised internal row. Malcolm Dix called for Lord Westwood to vacate the Chair, interestingly enough in favour of Gordon McKeag - who Dix, as part of the Magpie Group, would cross swords with in an even bigger rebel challenge some ten years later. United's directors compromised under such player power and Dinnis was reluctantly put in charge of affairs as temporary manager until June. It was an unsavoury affair with the name of Newcastle United in the limelight for all the wrong reasons. And it eventually sent the black'n'whites tumbling back into the Second Division.

Richard Dinnis, led the Magpies to 5th place in Division One.

Gordon Lee's general on the field, Geoff Nulty.

Added to the unhappy business was the transfer purchase of Ralph Callachan, bought from Hearts for £100,000 after Lee had departed, but before a new manager had been selected. Dinnis did not want the talented ball-player and the poor Scot found himself caught in a rift between the manager's office and boardroom. As one director noted, "he was given the cold shoulder by the other players".

Once the February mutiny had died down Dinnis incredibly led United to their highest position in 33 years, and took the side into Europe. He developed the foundations laid by Gordon Lee and many judges still to this day don't know how he did it considering the problems that surrounded the former schoolteacher. Yet the players backed him all the way and Newcastle went on an eleven match unbeaten run and equalled a record of 19 games at St James Park without defeat. A 3-2 victory over Aston Villa lifted the Magpies into a UEFA Cup

Trouble erupts during the Bohemians v Newcastle UEFA Cup tie in Dublin, Mahoney receives attention after being hit by a missile.

place, a return to the European scene for the first time in six years.

In the League Cup, Manchester United inflicted a heavy 7-2 knock-out at Old Trafford after the Tynesiders had disposed of both Gillingham and Stoke City. 'Keeper Mick Mahoney had a nightmare match on that evening. Two local lads, Aiden McCaffery and Paul Cannell, graduated from the Central League side. Both were to do well in the seasons ahead and centre-forward Cannell, a past schools international, was to score several fine goals before he left to sample football in the United States. New club offices were opened in the old gym - now converted - while a purpose built indoor training area was unveiled at United's Benwell practice ground.

During May, Richard Dinnis was handed a two year contract for the good, yet surprising, work he had achieved. However, his relationship with the boardroom was far from satisfactory and it took four months to agree the deal. During the summer months there was a never ending succession of internal problems to sort out, with much grumbling and squabbling over player contracts. Dinnis was never a disciplinarian with his personnel and players broke into factions and cliques that did nothing but rock the St James Park boat. It was an unstable close-season, as director Gordon McKeag related, "an extraordinary period - a desperate state of affairs". There was also a public boardroom row over the manager's position, seemingly the majority wanted rid of Dinnis, but Chairman Lord Westwood backed him all the way.

Tommy Craig, an accomplished midfield player.

With feuding still simmering in St James Park's corridors the 1977/78 season started in a catastrophic manner. After an opening 3-2 win over Leeds United, Newcastle fell to bottom spot following a disastrous sequence of results which saw the Magpies without a victory in ten successive league games. On top of that they also were eliminated from the League Cup by Millwall. United's supporters turned on Dinnis after that. However amongst this misery the black'n'whites returned to European football in the shape of the UEFA Cup, the successor to the Fairs Cup.

Irish club, Bohemians provided the Magpies with an uninspiring tie and at Dalymount Park in Dublin, United drew 0-0 with the part-timers, but not until an uncompromising contest had been fought that saw a terrace battle rage with the players off the field for 14 minutes. This after Mahoney had been struck by a missile. Newcastle won easily in the second leg, by 4-0 with Alan Gowling and Tommy Craig scoring two goals each. The victory sent the club through to an attractive fixture with French side from the island of Corsica, SEC Bastia.

Dinnis made his first transfer signing before the next round when Scottish international defender, John Blackley arrived from Hibernians for £100,000. The cultured looking centre-half though, was not secured in time to face Bastia on the Mediterranean island. Nevertheless the Magpies played very well in the Armand Cesari stadium against a skilful French side who included in their line-up Dutch ace Johnny Rep. United lost 2-1, but very nearly returned home with a draw, Bastia only scrambling the winner in the last minute of the match. It had been a performance totally out of character with their terrible league form and many thought that the side had turned the corner. Alas it wasn't to be.

At St James Park, Newcastle's European dream ended with the magic and class of Rep. He struck two superb goals as his side won at a canter 3-1, and 5-2 on aggregate. Tommy Craig was to say of the World Cup star, "I wasn't impressed at all with him in the first match and I said so. However, in the return leg he rammed my words down my throat". Manager Richard Dinnis remarked honestly, "They gave us a soccer lesson". Bastia were to go on to reach the final of the tournament losing to PSV Eindhoven.

Bastia's Claude Papi pats Tommy Craig on the back after the meeting with the French club in the UEFA Cup.

So with the glamour of Europe quickly over, it was back to the harrowing experience of climbing from the bottom of the First Division. Following the Bastia defeat Dinnis was sacked. That had been on the cards for a long while. He was out after only five months in charge. The players didn't like it and the whole hubbub exploded again. Newcastle United Football Club was in an almighty state. Dinnis said, "It seems to have been just one crisis after another". Tommy Craig summed up the sad chapter by saying later, "Lots of things were said at the time from all quarters that should have been kept within the club". United's midfield general went on, "There was far too much publicity and open speaking".

Willie McFaul took over on a caretaker basis - little did he know the job would be his in years to come - and the usual sprinkling of names were headlined. Lawrie McMenemy again, Fulham's Bobby Campbell, but it was Bill McGarry, ex Wolves boss, who arrived after being second choice of the directors, and not a choice of the fans at all. Frank O'Farrell of Torquay United, not a popular selection either, refused the job and in stepped the tough and uncompromising figure of McGarry. A former Huddersfield Town and England wing-half, he had spent almost a decade in charge of Molineux in the days of Dougan and Bailey. With disciplinarian methods he began to put the pieces of the broken club together - and that was not an easy task. Newcastle were at a post-war low, almost as bad as they were back in 1938. They were bottom of the division, with four of their best players - Gowling, Nulty, Craig and Burns - wanting away and the rest of the playing staff very unsettled.

With McGarry just into his office, his first taste of the black'n'whites' problems was ironically against Supermac's team Arsenal, although the man himself was sidelined through suspension. Macdonald still received an ovation fit for a king from the Gallowgate crowd and after the Gunners had won 2-1, United's former terrace hero remarked, "Newcastle have no chance of staying up". Many of the 23,679 crowd that day were incensed at the whole sorry tale of the previous months. They traced the start of all the problems back to Gordon Lee and chanted repeatedly, "We want our Mac back!"

New boss, Bill McGarry, the former Wolves manager.

An inglorious FA Cup exit didn't help install confidence. They were knocked out by Wrexham at the Racecourse Ground in humiliating fashion by 4-1, when a tie with neighbouring giant-killers Blyth Spartans was on the cards. Newcastle's side was totally ill-equipped for the relegation fight. The fluency of the past successful years' football had disappeared in the midst of argument and anarchy. The players' hearts were not fit for a battle and McGarry had a virtually impossible task to avoid the drop. It was, it appeared, even too hot for the tough figure of Bill McGarry. Within ten weeks of his appointment the ex Ipswich and Wolves manager had seemingly had enough. He was talking to Stoke City about moving to the Victoria Ground. That deal fell through and by the season's end United went down with Leicester City and West Ham United.

Supporters were not pleased as one could expect. They gave their own verdict on the season when only 7,986 turned up for the last home game with Norwich City - the lowest crowd for 40 years. United had created a string of unwanted records; fewest victories in a season(6), most defeats(26), least points(22), fewest number of home wins(4), most home defeats(11). And that was not all; record number of defeats in succession(10), and the most number of games without a victory(21). They used 35 different players - another record - evidence of serious problems. It was a sorry tale.

McGarry tried youngsters and Nigel Walker was one who impressed many. The Gateshead junior was labelled the best home grown talent for years and showed flashes of genius in midfield, but he drifted into obscurity with United's plight not the best of atmospheres to develop a young star. McGarry paid out £250,000 to bring two unknown Scots forwards to Tyneside without even seeing them play - Mark McGhee and Mike Lanarch. Both were inexperienced and expensive flops, although McGhee was to return a decade later as an accomplished international. Chesterfield's England youth player, Steve Hardwick took the place of Mahoney who had lost his confidence in goal. That terrible season saw the end of the Leazes End enclosure too. It was closed to make way for another phase in the

Nigel Walker who displayed flair and skill in midfield.

BLYTH'S BID FOR GLORY

The highlight of a depressing 1977/78 season did not involve United at all, but neighbours from the Northern League, Blyth Spartans. In the FA Cup 5th Round replay - the furthest any non-leaguer has journeyed - they met Wrexham, ironically conquerors of the Magpies, at St James Park. 42,157 turned up to see the contest, astonishingly the biggest crowd at the stadium that season and not surpassed since. The game went into extra time and Wrexham won in the end, 2-1. However the men from Blyth put up a terrific fight and received the acclaim of the whole north east. Included in their line-up were Alan Shoulder and Steve Carney.

New Chairman Bob Rutherford.

redevelopment of St James Park. With its demise the fantastic atmosphere the ground boasted for so long all but vanished. It was indeed a depressing year.

Not surprisingly the season saw changes in the boardroom too. With so much turmoil over the past 24 months it was inevitable. Chairman for the last twelve years, Lord Westwood resigned and Robert Rutherford stepped up to control affairs. The Westwood family had long been associated with United. With a distinguished shipbuilding background, his father was appointed to the board in 1944 and on his death the shareholding passed to his son. Born in Dundee, Bill Westwood, was a charismatic figure. Tall, silvery haired and of course, most noticeable of all he wore a black patch over one eye - a legacy of a car accident. He was an efficient businessman, building up an empire of companies from nothing, as well as guiding Newcastle through an exciting period. Appointed to the League Management Committee, he shook off a challenge from Burnley's Bob Lord, to take the Presidency of the Football League in 1974 - the only United director to hold the post. Lord Westwood was a famous personality, highly respected, yet his big failing was that he was totally divorced from United's masses on the terraces.

Northern League striker turned Magpie hero, Alan Shoulder became an instant crowd favourite.

Bob Rutherford's stock had been even longer linked to the club with two members of the family already having sat in the Chair. Robert Rutherford senior had been club doctor as well as a director. Always dressed in a pin-striped suit and waistcoat, he had served in the trenches of World War One as a surgeon and led the club during the forties. His brother George was Chairman after the Second World War and had been a member of the League Management Committee. The family had purchased shares in the club during the early years of East End's company status. The new Chairman was also a surgeon of respect, as well as an outstanding golfer. However, Rutherford's term of office co-incided with a reversal in the club's fortunes and he was to suffer a reaction from both fans and shareholders.

Record signing Peter Withe; in the end too good for the Second Division.

The most serious challenge to the boardroom to date was instigated by a group of shareholders and supporters led by Malcolm Dix. Fed up with the closed shop ownership of United and tragic decline in the club's fortunes, the Newcastle Supporters' Association was formed essentially as a pressure group for change. The NSA developed quickly in the turmoil of United's relegation and they rapidly became an unwelcome irritation to Rutherford and his directors. They even issued a writ early into 1978 for "suppression of the minority shareholder" and various alleged irregularities in an attempt to overturn the board. The club, though, defended themselves well in the High Court and the rebels were left with heavy costs to bear. Still, they remained a persistent thorn, especially at Annual General Meetings and echoed many supporters' views that change was badly needed within St James Park.

Bill McGarry began the 1978/79 season attempting to bounce straight back into the First Division by completely rebuilding the side. Kennedy left for Liverpool to join McDermott and a career of glory. Craig went to Aston Villa, Alan Gowling joined Bolton while Burns, Mahoney and Barrowclough left too. New faces arrived - they had to and the ill feeling of the last two years was washed clean with new stock. Peter Withe was persuaded to leave Championship club Nottingham Forest, Mick Martin came from West Bromwich Albion, John Brownlie joined his ex team-mate Blackley from Hibs, and many others signed on the dotted line too. Terry Hibbitt returned with John Connolly, Jim Pearson from Gordon Lee's Everton, and Colin Suggett also returned to the north east from Norwich City. A whole string of youngsters pulled on the black'n'white shirt as well. David Barton, Kevin Carr, Jamie Scott and Stuart

One of Bill McGarry's many signings, John Brownlie. He proved a good buy.

Robinson as well as Kenny Wharton and Gary Nicholson were given opportunities, while Blyth Spartans hero, Alan Shoulder came into McGarry's squad too.

Shoulder used to work eight hour shifts night and day at Horden pit and made the big jump from Northern League football to Division Two at the relatively late age of almost 26 years old. But his opportunism and gutsy play up front made him a bargain at £20,000 and something of a local hero. He was a penalty expert as well - striking nine spot-kicks in season 1979/80, the most by any Newcastle player.

Centre-forward Peter Withe was another master signing even at a club record £200,000. Big and strong and much travelled, he was an unselfish leader with a buoyant Scouse personality and filled the supporters' No 9 hero role perfectly. Brownlie and Martin were other good deals. Both cost £100,000 each with John Brownlie showing exciting attacking qualities in the right-back position - the form that earned him seven Scottish caps during the early seventies. Irishman Martin was tall, thin and cool-headed in midfield and was to captain both club and country. Mick eventually played 51 times for Eire following his father's record of 30 appearances for the Republic. John Bird, a Gordon Lee signing from Preston back in 1975, started to show form at centre-half. Often injured, Bird's transfer to the Magpies resulted in North End's boss, the famous Bobby Charlton resigning in protest and turning his back on the managerial game.

Newcastle started another spell in Division Two - their fourth - having ended the previous season with two comprehensive defeats, but McGarry's new line-up of experienced pro's gradually climbed their way up the promotion ladder. United looked good up until a dreadful winter and a long lay-off due to postponements which seemed to knock the rhythm out of the team. They never got going again afterwards, and injuries didn't help either. Pearson, Connolly, Bird, Nattrass and Blackley were all victims and Peter Kelly, a promising young full-back, had just caught the eyes of Scottish selectors before a knee injury put him out of the game.

Third Division Watford - then on the way up - saw United off in the League Cup, while in the FA Cup, McGarry's former club, Wolves won 1-0 at Molineux after United had missed chances on a hard, frosty ground at Gallowgate. The second half of the season ended badly with a 4-1 home defeat by Sunderland, the low point of a terrible run. The Roker men, and Gary Rowell in particular, tore the Tynesiders apart. Rowell was lethal, netting a hat-trick, although United's defence played more like a Sunday pub line-up. 'Keeper Hardwick had a game to haunt him for the rest of his career at St James Park - one from which he never recovered. Thankfully Shoulder and Withe formed a productive partnership in spite of everything and their goals lifted United to a place just below the successful clubs in a very tight Second Division table.

During the summer, full-back Ian Davies was purchased from Norwich City for £150,000 while Stuart Boam arrived from Middlesbrough to command the centre of the defence and take over as captain. He had appeared almost 400 times for the

SECOND RATE CUP

Gordon Lee gained a lot of credit from United's supporters over his stance against second rate tournaments like the Texaco Cup and Anglo Scottish Cup. In September 1976, Newcastle were drawn to play Scottish Premier League club, Ayr United in the latter competition, but Lee was adamant he was going to concentrate on the big prizes of football and wanted nothing to do with the minor trophy. He picked a complete reserve side for the trip to Somerset Park and they lost 3-0. Newcastle were expelled from the competition and fined £4,000. United's boss made the comment, "I did what I thought was best for Newcastle United". Almost every supporter agreed with him.

OWN GOAL SPREE

In the space of two home games in 1975/76, United managed to net three own goals. Against Manchester United during March, Pat Howard headed past his own keeper from a corner, then if that was not bad enough fellow defender John Bird also sent the ball past Roger Jones - a 25 yard lob straight over his head and into the net! In the next home match when Leeds United were on Tyneside, Graham Oates - making his home debut after signing from Blackburn Rovers - netted another 25 yard back-pass after only four minutes. This time the unfortunate keeper was Mick Mahoney. Newcastle lost both fixtures, 4-3 to Manchester United and 3-2 to Leeds!

Tees club and cost United £140,000. Although coming to the end of a fine career, at 6'1" and always composed, he steadied Newcastle's leaky defence. Peter Cartwright was another newcomer, from local club North Shields. Freedom of Contract was an innovation to football and it saw Irving Nattrass move from Gallowgate after nine years, to Ayresome Park. His transfer took a while to sort out, with a Football League Tribunal - another new entry - deciding on a £375,000 fee.

United started off comfortably in the league campaign and without the team playing well. Then, into the season but four short weeks north east fans were given a treat to remember, a two legged League Cup tie between Tyne and Wear. At Roker Park, the Magpies put on a show that had their supporters cheering from start to finish. It was their best performance for a considerable period. Coming back from being two goals behind, the team not only showed character, but also some excellent one touch football. Sunderland's players were flattered by the 2-2 scoreline having been outplayed for long periods of the match. It was United's new buys, Davies and substitute debutant, Cartwright, who scored the goals that put the black'n'whites into the driving seat for the return leg a week later.

Again supporters watched a memorable derby laced with drama and excitement. Newcastle missed chances by the hatful, but Shoulder and Boam headed United into a 2-1 lead with only a few minutes remaining. The Gallowgate crowd was in full song, but then Sunderland grabbed a dramatic equaliser. Boam, otherwise immaculate throughout the evening, lost the ball to Alan Brown just outside the box. The Roker striker hit the ball hard and true to silence the masses. That goal sent the game into extra-time and, with United continuing to squander opportunities, the tie ended 2-2 forcing a nerve racking penalty shoot-out, Russian Roulette style.

Penalty after penalty flew past the respective goalkeeper until Jim Pearson, the unlucky injury stricken Scot, stepped up to take his kick - the 14th of the sequence. Someone had to miss, and it was Pearson who did. He fired his shot weakly at Barry Siddall who made another of his many saves to thwart Newcastle and send the Roker club into the next round. Still, United, despite being toppled, had won back a large slice of honour after last season's humbling by their rivals. Newcastle had won a moral victory. The only depressing facts about those two classic derby encounters were the low attendances at each game. Only 27,746 turned up at Roker Park and 30,533 at Gallowgate. Gates of 50,000 plus for virtually every tussle up to this contest were a thing of the past and showed the decline in football's attraction in a rapidly changing lifestyle.

In Division Two, Newcastle went from strength to strength after their average start. Billy Rafferty arrived for £175,000 from Wolves to bolster the attack, however he never linked too well with Peter Withe. United moved into the top ranking along with Luton Town and Leicester City. Their Filbert Street rivals were defeated 3-2 and the two points collected sent United into the leading position. The Magpies were going well by Christmas then, as all looked good, key midfielder Mick Martin was injured in a top of the table clash with the Hatters and out for the rest of the season. Bill McGarry failed to buy a replacement and paid for a serious miscalculation. A slump followed that knocked the club from pole position to a struggling mid-table placing. Incredibly it all started with an emphatic home victory - a revenge thrashing over Sunderland on New Years Day.

The 3-1 win, after being behind early on, was a convincing performance. Peter Cartwright had equalised the Wearsiders' opener then Tommy Cassidy half volleyed United into the lead from 25 yards, and two minutes later Alan Shoulder scored from the penalty spot. It was the ex non-leaguers 17th goal of the season and he and Withe ran Sunderland's back four ragged. Everyone agreed it was the perfect start to the eighties decade.

Perhaps the side became over confident after that, but there was a huge gap in midfield and had Newcastle signed a quality schemer they would have maintained their promotion push. As it was the rot set in after United were eliminated from the FA Cup on Tyneside by Division Three side, Chester

Scot John Connolly, effective on the wing, but often injured.

on Tyneside. They included in their line-up a young goalscorer by the name of Ian Rush and he showed flashes of the expert striker he was to become with Liverpool. Chester went ahead after only three minutes and Rush made sure of a giant-killing feat by grabbing a second 15 minutes from time.

The promotion clash which followed with Chelsea resulted in a demoralising 4-0 reverse at Stamford Bridge. More defeats followed and boss McGarry tried to turn the tide by introducing £175,000 transfer-deadline signing from Manchester City, Bobby Shinton to the line-up. An improvement was seen and United appeared to be heading in the right direction in a mass scramble for the three promotion places.

Easter proved a make or break period when the group of challengers was cut to just four clubs, alas the name of Newcastle United was not amongst them. A disappointing 2-2 draw with Notts County on Tyneside was followed by another trip to Roker Park. On a warm and sunny Easter Saturday the Reds scored through Stan Cummins, while United failed to cash in on their dominance. Sunderland took the points and accelerated their own promotion run which saw them reach Division One. United's performances afterwards went from poor to dreadful, with the confidence and exuberance of three months ago totally lost. In fact their record in 1980 showed only three victories. Terry Hibbitt noted in the Evening Chronicle, "I don't know what went wrong". But the midfielder did point a finger at his manager as he added, "He put defenders in midfield, and I remember one game where there were seven defenders in ten outfield positions".

Gates had dropped alarmingly over the previous two seasons. Against Wrexham only 7,134 turned up - the lowest at St James Park since the Second World War. United's average was down to a little over 20,000. More than 10,000 supporters had disappeared. Football hooliganism was at its peak of disgusting behaviour and also had an effect on the turnstile figures. Against West Ham United a terrifying petrol bomb was thrown into the visitors' enclosure.

Came the summer break and Tyneside was a pretty disillusioned football community with the much publicised promotion success at Roker Park only adding more heartache to Magpie followers. It was to be a crucial close-season for Bill McGarry. He simply had to find the winning formula.

United's squad as the Eighties decade began. Left to right, back: Connolly, Hardwick, Carr, Manners, Barton. Middle: Brownlie, Nicholson, Cassidy, Suggett, Scott, Mitchell, Pearson, Mulgrove, Robinson, Davies, Shoulder, Bird. Front: Cartwright, Martin, Withe, Walker, McGarry (manager), Hibbitt, Nattrass, Wharton.

Centenary Profile 25

The Goal Machine

"I just know this fellow can be another Jackie Milburn to the supporters"
Joe Harvey, May 1971

THEY CALLED HIM SUPERMAC! THE SEVENTIES belonged to Malcolm Macdonald, no-one could touch him in the goalscoring stakes and on Tyneside crowds flocked to see his exciting one way to goal approach, banging the ball into the net from all distances and angles. Days like the thrilling performance at Highfield Road, Coventry in 1972 when he netted a stunning hat-trick. The first a right foot blaster off the crossbar, the next a scintillating effort with his left from an acute angle, and to round off a trio for the connoisseur, a diving header that left the keeper stranded.

His entertainment value was worth a bomb to United. With a brash and cavalier personality he became a huge crowd puller. Outside Tyneside fans loved to hate him, but at St James Park all that could be heard was the Geordie roar of 'Supermac! Supermac!'. He could do nothing wrong.

The football career of Malcolm Macdonald started on the terraces of Craven Cottage where he watched his Fulham idols, in particular England schemer Johnny Haynes. Macdonald was born in 1950 not far from the ground and played football at school, good enough for both the London and Home Counties junior select team. At 16, the Macdonald family moved to the rural setting of Sussex, to Malcolm's disgust, but his football education didn't stop. As keen as ever he took a long bus journey to play on a regular basis for Knowle Park, a prominent junior club in the Sevenoaks area.

In South London, he first met up with Harry Haslam, the name to put Macdonald firmly on the road to stardom. He was invited to Tonbridge and signed for the non-league side in 1967. Haslam moved to Fulham a couple of years later and Mac followed him to his favourite club without hesitation. However, in his first season with the Cottagers, playing initially at left-back, the Londoners were relegated and the young Macdonald often found it hard to claim a place. He had graduated into the Football League scene, but yet to fully make his mark.

In July 1969 he moved to Luton Town for a £17,500 fee and to Fulham's loss he quickly developed into a devastating goalscorer and flamboyant character, with at times outrageous self confidence. Luton won promotion from the Third Division with Macdonald the spearhead, scoring sensational goals - goals to shortly send the Gallowgate terraces crazy. Many a time he powered his way through packed defences showing a blistering turn of speed ending with a whiplash shot and the ball bulging the net. He was a matchwinner in every sense of the word.

In Division Three he got 27 goals, then up a grade smacked in another 30 and prompted Joe Harvey to risk a record fee for the stocky Londoner to replace the Davies-Robson partnership. United paid out £180,000 - then the second biggest cash transfer in the British game - on the eve of the 1971 FA Cup final for the 21 year-old and Mac took the north east by storm. Arriving for his press-call in a chauffeur driven Rolls Royce, it was typical of his show-biz approach to the game he played. Sceptics said he would be an enormous flop, "He hasn't played in the First Division" and "He's too left sided" they claimed. Macdonald made them eat their words in no uncertain terms.

Joe Harvey said at the time, "I just know this fellow can be another Jackie Milburn to the supporters". He was so right. On his St James Park debut, Malcolm scored a tremendous three goal burst against Liverpool. Tyneside had a new hero. It had been the most dramatic home appearance since Len Shackleton's sensational double hat-trick back in 1946. Ivor Broadis described his three goals in The Journal, the first an equalising penalty, "Macdonald lashed the spot-kick into the roof of the net". The second, to put United in front, "there was tremendous quality in the way Macdonald made something out of nothing, dragging a

MACDONALD'S PLAYING RECORD	League		FA Cup		FL Cup		Total	
	App	Gls	App	Gls	App	Gls	App	Gls
1971-72	42	23	2	2	2	1	46	26
1972-73	35	17	2	1	1	1	38	19
1973-74	29	15	10	7	2	3	41	25
1974-75	42	21	2	0	6	6	50	27
1975-76	39	19	7	4	7	1	53	24
	187	**95**	**23**	**14**	**18**	**12**	**228**	**121**

Malcolm Macdonald

short pass from a challenge to make position and hit a rocket-like cross shot past Clemence with very little to aim at". And the third, "Clark, Hibbitt and Tudor paved the way for Macdonald's third....again with the left foot across Clemence". That was not all, he also cleared off the line and near the end going for a fourth, clashed with the 'keeper and was carried off, legs bent and groggy to a hero's exit. It was Roy of the Rovers stuff. From that moment the supporters adored him. He became perhaps the Hughie Gallacher of the seventies, frequenting expensive restaurants and nightclubs. He drank champagne and smoked fat cigars. He opened his own trendy boutique and was always immaculately dressed.

Goals and more goals followed. He was picked for England's Under 23 side and then for the full eleven in 1973, going onto win 14 caps including an epic evening at Wembley when he netted five goals against Cyprus. United's 1974 FA Cup run allowed the wider football audience to see Macdonald's magic at first hand. He scored in every round bar the final and another trip to Wembley followed in 1976. But his days at Gallowgate were drawing to a close due to a clash with manager Gordon Lee. Macdonald said, "I loved Newcastle until Lee took over". He left Tyneside the way he arrived - in style - by a private jet.

Lee's sale of Supermac to Arsenal before the start of the 1976/77 season was a massive blow to Tyneside's fans.

Controversy raged for months after, and even still does to this day. 121 goals had come by way of Macdonald, a goal every other game. It took the club many years before they found a player with such charisma.

At Highbury, Macdonald continued scoring goals - 29 in his first season - and he reached another Wembley cup final. His record was just as good for the Gunners, 57 in 108 games, although he never reached the pinnacle of crowd adulation achieved on Tyneside. Not long after the 1978/79 season was under way, injury sidelined his talent. A knee injury, not for the first time, troubled him and after a spell recuperating with Swedish club, Djurgarden, he was forced to quit. Not wishing to stay out of the game for long however, Macdonald returned to Craven Cottage and took over commercial activities for Fulham in 1979.

Later he became a thoughtful, articulate team manager and director, building a good Fulham eleven out of nothing. Due to problems out of football, he left the game altogether and settled in Hampshire, although he later had a short period back in the north, running a pub in Berwick. Macdonald had an equally brief spell back in football in charge of Huddersfield Town, but slipped out of the game in 1988 to concentrate on business interests in the south.

Albert Stubbins, himself a great Number 9 noted, "Macdonald was the last of the old fashioned centre-forwards". He was a devastating all round striker, making up for a lack of pure skills with pace and the ability to hit the ball with either foot with awesome power. In the air too he was dangerous, although he wasn't a six footer and, as an added bonus, he possessed a dangerous long throw. Most importantly, Malcolm had a one track mind - for goal - and as his autobiography title noted, he was, "Never Afraid To Miss". Certainly the north east hasn't seen a figure like Mac since and, as with Hughie Gallacher before, will probably not see one quite like him again. Perhaps George Mulhall, Bolton's assistant manager summed up Macdonald's influence on football. He said after witnessing a typical display destroy his side, "He's not Supermac. He is Superman!"

Centenary Profile 26

Provider in Chief

"A marvellous little'un. A wonderful player and a key figure in our line-up during the seventies"

Joe Harvey, August 1985

ONE OF NEWCASTLE UNITED'S FINEST BARGAIN acquisitions in the transfer market was a small, frail looking midfielder signed for a giveaway £30,000 from Leeds United in August 1971. His name was Terry Hibbitt, a player who became a huge favourite on Tyneside in two spells with his non-stop workrate in the United No 11 shirt. Hibbitt developed into Newcastle's midfield general and covered every blade of grass for the Magpies. A partnership with Malcolm Macdonald up front was feared throughout Division One and during four seasons the duo created and scored goals by the proverbial hatful.

Terry was born in Bradford in 1947. His younger brother, Kenny also went on to have a marvellous football career, notably with Wolves. At 13 years of age, Huddersfield Town approached the elder of the two brothers, but it wasn't until some time later that Terry first hit the big time. That was in April 1963 when Leeds United noticed his potential appearing for the Bradford & Yorkshire schoolboys team. Don Revie's scouting network snapped up the youngster and he started to learn the game's basics at Elland Road, just as the Leeds club were en route for a tremendous period of success.

Leeds had a unique set-up in the sixties. They won promotion in 1964 and took a hold on the First Division. Hibbitt made his debut in season 1965/66 and actually scored with his first touch of the ball against Nottingham Forest. However, for the most part he was chiefly a reserve, initially operating at outside-left then as understudy to Johnny Giles and Billy Bremner, two great midfielders. He modelled his own career on that of Giles.

At Elland Road for almost eight years, Hibbitt in fact only played just over 50 games in a white shirt, but did turn out in the 1968 Fairs Cup final against Ferencvaros when only 20, while he also picked up Championship and League Cup medals too. The Yorkshireman proved to other clubs that he was worth a regular first-team place. Having little chance of displacing Bremner or Giles, Hibbitt wasted no time accepting Newcastle's approach at the opening of the 1971/72 season. United boss, Joe Harvey was a good judge of talent and when he wrote out the cheque for £30,000 he knew he had landed a gem. It was the deal of the decade.

Terry first turned out for United at Crystal Palace on the opening day of the new season and played alongside the player he was to form such an exciting and deadly partnership with, Malcolm Macdonald. It was the start of a wonderful period and Hibbitt even outshone Supermac at times, winning two Player of the Year awards ahead of his star team-mate in 1972/73 and 1973/74. Hibbitt's quality left-foot expertly found the surges of Macdonald time and time again. The long precision through ball became a hallmark of United's play and with a centre-forward like Supermac it worked a treat. Terry once said of the partnership, "I always knew where he was. And he always knew when the ball was coming through".

Hibbitt was an incessant talker on the field and a great motivator. A Yorkshireman with traditional grit, he had a short temper and often was caught in flare-ups with opponents and referees. In midfield alongside the likes of Jimmy Smith, Tony Green and Terry McDermott, the Magpies had players of class and football of quality flowed. As Wembley beckoned in 1974 more than one person within the game talked of Newcastle's 5'7" master in terms of an England place. However, his pin-point accuracy and tremendous enthusiasm for the game never saw the international scene, much to the disgust of spectators in the north east. Many reckoned a Hibbitt-Macdonald pairing would have been more profitable than some of England's selections during that era.

Terry Hibbitt

HIBBITT'S PLAYING RECORD	League		FA Cup		FL Cup		Total	
	App	Gls	App	Gls	App	Gls	App	Gls
1971-72	35	3	2	0	2	0	39	3
1972-73	41	3	1	0	2	0	44	3
1973-74	33	1	8	1	3	0	44	2
1974-75	25	0	0	0	4	0	29	0
1975-76	4	0	0	0	0	0	4	0
1978-79	40	0	3	0	1	0	44	0
1979-80	34	2	1	0	2	0	37	2
1980-81	15/1	3	0	0	2	0	17/1	3
	227/1	**12**	**15**	**1**	**16**	**0**	**258/1**	**13**

A bad knee injury against Chelsea halted Terry's glowing career in November 1974 and Harvey had to find a replacement. Tommy Craig arrived at Gallowgate the following month and the deal meant the end of Hibbitt's first spell at the club. Terry did play the odd game before he moved on - even at full back - but a change in manager meant a new port of call. Gordon Lee took over and Terry was off to Birmingham City in September 1975 in a deal that saw United receive a handsome profit, obtaining £100,000 from the Midland side.

Hibbitt spent three excellent seasons at St Andrews, captain of Brum alongside Howard Kendall in midfield. He laid on goals again, this time for Trevor Francis, but he was soon back at St

James Park as a new manager took over at Birmingham - a certain Jim Smith. Terry rejoined United in April 1978 in an exchange deal that saw John Connolly move north too and Stuart Barrowclough head for St Andrews. Appointed club captain, he went on to play for three seasons totalling 259 games and netting 13 goals in his career with the Magpies. His second spell wasn't nearly as productive as his first, yet Terry's displays were still as good as anything the club possessed at the time.

Another injury, this time to a bone in his knee, put him out of football again and it was serious enough to force the pocket sized link-man to quit the scene. Terry hung up his boots in June 1981, but it wasn't the end of the Hibbitt influence on the field altogether. He still played in non-league football for another three years turning out for Gateshead and winning England honours at that level in 1982. He also skippered Gateshead to the Northern Premier League title a year later. He coached and played on and off with a spell at Durham City, until October 1986. Afterwards Hibbitt - like David Craig - concentrated for a while on a newsagency and milk business in Newcastle.

Apart from Terry Hibbitt's obvious footballing skills the player also possessed a bubbling character which rubbed off on the whole team. And in the dressing room he was just as important as out on the field. Joe Harvey described his midfield gem as, "A marvellous little'un. A wonderful player and a key figure in our entertaining line-up during the seventies". Terry Hibbitt became very much one of Tyneside's own, an adopted Geordie, just like his former boss.

16 THE FIRST REVOLUTION

1980-1984

• ARTHUR COX'S BLACK'N'WHITE ARMY • BOARDROOM SHAKE-UP • KEEGAN MANIA • TRIUMPHANT BOMBSHELL •

"It has been my privilege to play all over the world - but I have never played in front of more loyal and caring supporters"

Kevin Keegan, May 1983

THE OPENING OF THE EIGHTIES SAW Newcastle United in deep trouble; a poor team, in a desperate financial situation and with supporters becoming increasingly disillusioned. Yet it was a period of much incident with the first part of the decade seeing the club explode into the limelight once more, then retreat into the shadows. An era that saw no fewer than five personalities occupy the manager's hot seat, while in the boardroom there were even more changes as several directors stood down in a succession of shake-ups. Four men took over the Chairman's role in a testing period culminating in a takeover battle that raged as the eighties came to an end.

At first though, the club needed a complete overhaul....a new manager, new players, new directors and most of all, stars to put Newcastle back on the football map. Supporters got them all as a mini revolution swept through St James Park. And with it came a return to Division One in marvellous style.

Bill McGarry worked hard to keep his best player, Peter Withe on Tyneside during the summer of 1980, but the big striker wanted First Division football and no-one could blame him. His move to Aston Villa for £500,000 marked the beginning of the end for McGarry. Despite intense transfer speculation he never captured any quality player to make United into a promotion winning combination. He tried for Liverpool's Mick Robinson, but couldn't afford the outlay, even toyed with bringing in Finnish international Leo Houtsonan and the experienced, yet fiery Scot, Willie Johnston. Striker Ray Clarke was signed from Brighton for £80,000 in a deal that dragged on for weeks, and Dutch midfielder Frans Koenen arrived from NEC Njimegen for the same amount. Both, however, failed to impress. The close-season did see though, a raw youngster from the Northern League join the Gallowgate staff - Chris Waddle from Tow Law Town. He was quickly to establish himself as a crowd favourite. Long serving Tommy Cassidy left for Turf Moor after all but two months of ten years on Tyneside.

Dutch midfielder Frans Koenen arrived from NEC Njimegen

As well as the signature of Waddle another important deal was clinched during the summer, United's first sponsorship agreement. A £100,000 deal with Scottish & Newcastle Breweries was signed and the famous Tyneside symbol of the Blue Star was to be worn on the equally famous black'n'white jersey. It was the beginning of a close association between the two Barrack Road neighbours.

United kicked off the new season following a tour of Sweden without John Brownlie, injured badly in another friendly with Hearts. They went down to Sheffield Wednesday 2-0, in front of the BBC cameras - the first of a series of terrible showings on television. A 4-0 defeat at Bolton left Newcastle bottom of Division Two, the club's lowest ever placing in the Football League, while in the League Cup, former United captain Jim Iley and his Bury team set the Magpies up for another unhappy exit. It was a splendid cup-tie for the few neutral observers, however United were matched kick by kick by the Fourth Division side. Also in their line-up were Pat Howard and Keith Kennedy, two more ex Gallowgate men. Bury fought well and while they lost the first leg narrowly, 3-2 at St James Park, won the return at Gigg Lane and eliminated United.

Bill McGarry's time was up. He had initially inspired some with his tough brand of management, but then quickly infuriated the majority and alienated many players with his rule of fear. As Tommy Cassidy said, "he fell down badly on man management". Newcastle had won only two league games in the last seven months. Only 9,073 turned up for that League Cup match, one of the club's lowest post-war crowds. The directors had little alternative but to start from scratch once more and events quickly took shape. By the end of August, McGarry was out after less than three years in charge. 62 year-old Joe Harvey was called up to take temporary control and his inspiration took United off the bottom with two victories. Immediately speculation grew as to who would be the new boss. Ian Greaves, former coach Dave Smith and Bob Moncur were named as possibles, as well as the big three north easterners - Bobby Robson, Brian Clough and Lawrie McMenemy. However, it was a virtual unknown who got the job, and quickly too. Within six days, Chesterfield's boss Arthur Cox walked into St James Park as Newcastle United's new manager.

Cox knew the region well having been Sunderland's coach during their FA Cup triumph of 1973 and promotion afterwards. He was highly thought of in the game, indeed United had to fight off the challenge of Leeds for his services. The new manager said on his arrival, "The top flight is where Newcastle belongs and that has to be my target". From the heart of the Midlands, Cox never played senior football due to a bad leg fracture when a junior with Coventry City, but had fashioned a good side at Chesterfield. He had previously been with several clubs in various capacities including Aston Villa, Preston and Blackpool. He boasted a tough, cautious attitude, a non-stop approach to his job and sported a crew-cut hair style. Cox was given a four year contract and the awesome task of revitalising the Magpies.

His first game in charge saw Harvey's revival continue. A 2-1 victory at Queens Park Rangers was recorded and Cox steadily improved the club's position, but as he noted, "There will be no overnight miracles". By the winter holiday period they had climbed the table and were in 14th place. His rebuilding strategy was under way.

In a crazy league table that season, United went on to finish in 11th place. At one stage they were six points from a promotion spot, yet one defeat could have seen them in relegation trouble, such was the scarcity of points separating top from bottom. Some critics noted the season was nothing short of a disaster, but considering what had gone before, progress had been made. United had scored only 30 goals, the side's worst total ever with Bobby Shinton, with seven goals, the most any player could muster.

In the FA Cup, Chris Waddle exploded on to the scene in an all Second Division clash to hit two fine goals against Sheffield Wednesday at St James Park, a match far from a classic, but full of Cup thrills. The youngster led the show, while another kid, Bruce Halliday was superb in defence following an uncomfortable debut at Chelsea a few weeks before. Waddle's first strike was a gem, a sweet left footer from 20 yards - his first senior goal for the Magpies. United received another home tie, against Luton Town, who they had beaten the week before at Kenilworth Road with the help of a Kevin Carr penalty save. The FA Cup meeting turned out to be the match of the season.

Waddle again showed his emerging talent as United gained a two goal advantage with a display which was a revelation. The Magpies flattened Luton with two headed goals from Ray Clarke and Mick Martin - the last superbly made by Waddle after a run and cross down the touch-line. Newcastle wobbled near the end when Ingram pulled a goal back, then Hill crashed a drive against the woodwork with minutes only remaining. The tie brought all the old passion, missing for so long, flooding back to St James Park. United were playing well and Arthur Cox was rewarded with the divisional Manager of the Month award, however just as events were taking a turn for the better, Newcastle created another upset.

They faced lowly Exeter City in Round Five and threw away a chance of reaching the latter stages of the FA Cup. An all ticket crowd of 37,000 - in a vastly reduced St James Park capacity due to redevelopment and safety - saw United's frailty against the minnows. Newcastle blundered their way through 90 minutes of action in which Exeter completely deserved a moral victory after being a goal behind to an Alan Shoulder looping header. The visitors though, equalised with only five minutes to go following a mistake by Halliday.

Continued on page 354

Arthur Cox took over from Bill McGarry and had the job of rebuilding the Magpies.

Republic of Ireland international Mick Martin, to be nicknamed 'Zico' by the fans.

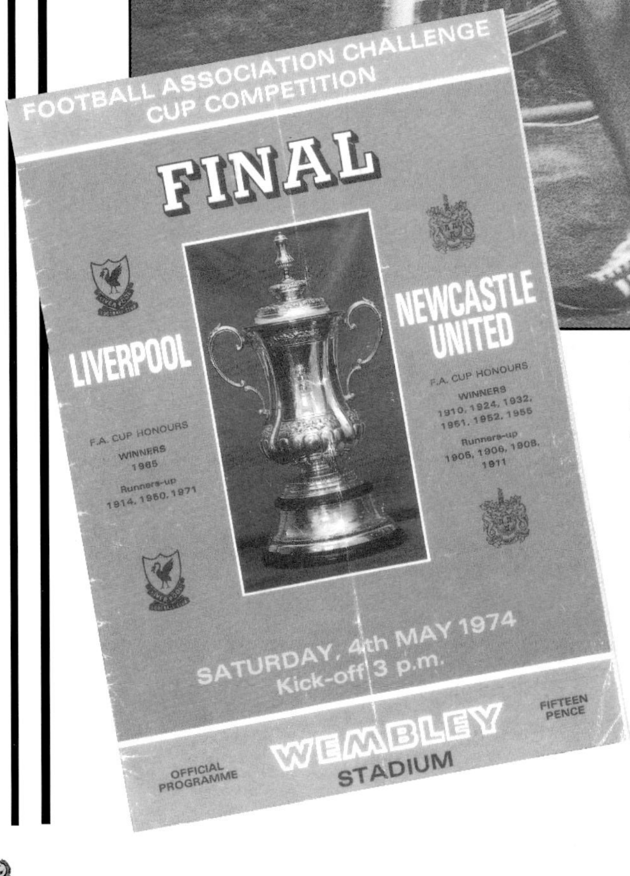

Wembley 1974, Brendan Foster in black'n'white vest takes a lap of honour after winning a pre-match 3,000m race. Programme from the final with Liverpool.

Ialcolm Macdonald who
as idolised during his five
ears of tremendous
oalscoring exploits with
Iewcastle. No other player
f recent years has excited
yneside's fans as much.
nset: the raw power of
upermac' in action against
Vest Ham.

In 1975 Newcastle appointed a new manager in Gordon Lee, a man to transform United's unpredictable eleven into a professional looking outfit, but who also created much controversy during his short stay.

Alan Gowling in action against Coventry City at Highfield Road in 1976 as United advanced towards Wembley on two Cup fronts. The ex-Manchester United striker netted 30 goals during the season.

Celebrations and champagne in the St. James Park dressing room following United's League Cup semi-final victory over Tottenham in 1976.

Alan Gowling is mobbed by his United team mates after scoring in the 1976 League Cup final against Manchester City, but the Blues ran out 2-1 winners.

Gordon Lee's army of supporters at Wembley in 1976. As the banner claims, the Magpies were serious contenders for both the League Cup and FA Cup that year.

Former England skipper Kevin Keegan was the man to lead Newcastle back into the big-time after a period of stagnation. His transfer immediately created an impact as the effervescent Yorkshireman captivated the North East.

United's promotion in 1984 featured some of the best football witnessed at Gallowgate in a century.
Inset above: Kevin Keegan and colleagues receive deserved acclaim from the Geordie support.

Centre-half Jeff Clarke joined United on a free transfer from Sunderland, he proved a commanding defensive figure.

Chris Waddle graduated from Tow Law Town into the England side before heading south to White Hart Lane and then a career on the Continent with Marseilles.

Peter Beardsley, like Chris Waddle, appeared for his country with Newcastle before heading for glory elsewhere. Inset: Beardsley takes on Liverpool's Mark Lawrenson during a First Division clash in August 1985.

A teenage Paul Gascoigne burst onto the scene in 1985/86 with an array of breathtaking skills which promised to match anyone in football. Newcastle though, lost his talents when he moved to Spurs for a record £2.3 million fee.

Mirandinha, the first Brazilian to appear in the Football League. Small, fast and with a potent shot, he cost £575,000,

Centre-forward Mirandinha rounds future United 'keeper Dave Beasant in a match with Wimbledon at St. James Park. In the background is the temporary structure to house season-ticket holders while the Club's new £5 million stand was under construction.

A record fee of £850,000 was spent on goalkeeper Dave Beasant in 1988. The tall Londoner was one of several major transfers around this time. His stay at St James Park lasted for only a brief period.

Long-serving Irish international defender John Anderson joined the black'n'whites on a free transfer from Preston and proceeded to become a popular character at Gallowgate

Jim Smith's Newcastle United line-up as the 1990/91 season was about to get underway. Left to right, Back Row: Dillon, Quinn, Simpson, Robinson, Bradshaw, Anderson. Middle Row: Wright (physio), Clark, Stimson, Kristensen, Wright, Burridge, Scott, O'Brien, McGhee, Saxton (assistant manager). Front Row: Howey, Brock, Sweeney, Askew, Smith (manager), Aitken (captain), Gallacher, Ranson, Sloan.

Black'n'white delight as Mick Quinn congratulates Mark McGhee after his strike partner had converted a penalty against Manchester United in the FA Cup tie during 1990.

Newcastle's youngest ever player, Steve Watson, who made a name for himself in season 1990/91. He still has much to learn but the signs are that he could, with proper nurturing, become the latest in a long line of home grown footballing talent.

Gavin Peacock, United's attack minded midfielder signed from Bournemouth. From a footballing family, his father spent almost 20 years with Charlton.

St. James Park after more than a century of football. The Club's redevelopment plan is now half complete with the Milburn Stand (left) the centre of operations for the Magpies. Further new stands are planned behind each goal.

Ossie Ardiles, the former Argentinian World Cup star, who took charge of United in 1991 when the Magpies were in need of a young and dynamic manager with fresh ideas.

Newcastle United's squad as the Club enters its Centenary Year.
Left to right, Back Row: Roche, Makel, Hunt, Robinson, Elliott, Cole, Sloan, Appleby, Neilson, Heron, Thompson, Watson J.
Middle Row: Galvin (coach), Suggett (coach), Wright, Anderson, Kristensen, Clark, Howey, Watson S., Bradshaw, O'Brien, Srnicek, Fazackerly (coach), Guthrie (kit), Wright (physio).
Front Row: Ranson, Carr, Brock, Quinn, Ardiles (manager), Scott, Stimson, Peacock, Gallacher, Gourlay.

Wembley joy for Malcolm Macdonald and Alan Gowling after United's strikers had carved out Newcastle's equaliser.

Programme from the League Cup final in 1976.

Continued from page 335

Only managing to draw 1-1 at Gallowgate with a club of Exeter's standing was bad enough, but going on to lose 4-0 in the replay at the other St James Park was about as much as some fans could take. To make matters worse television captured it all, move by move, goal by goal, for the nation to see - this after the cameras had already showed United wilting to Chelsea(6-0) and Swansea(4-0). Exeter ran United into the ground. Within 13 minutes they were in front when Carr fumbled a shot, then 6 minutes later it was 2-0 and by half-time 3-0. It took Newcastle all of 56 minutes before the Third Division 'keeper had a shot to save. The Daily Telegraph's reporter observed, "Newcastle clearly were not prepared for the exhilarating football their opponents produced", while Exeter's Tyneside born coach, Malcolm Musgrove made the comment, "Newcastle United are not the Newcastle United of old". The Grecians marched into the quarter finals for the first time in 50 years and to a plum draw with Tottenham Hotspur. Newcastle, their team and supporters, made the long 370 mile trip back to Tyneside with much on which to contemplate.

The defeat showed how low the black'n'whites had stooped. Gates crashed to 17,000 - now 25th in the country's attendance league table, only four years after they were in the top five behind Liverpool, Manchester United and Manchester City with an average of 34,000. The rebuilding process was not going to be instant. With limited cash resources, Cox didn't have the flexibility to buy a complete new team. He did though bring some new faces to Tyneside and in the process broke two transfer records. Defender Peter Johnson cost £60,000 from Middlesbrough, while John Trewick, Bedlington born, returned to his native north east from West Bromwich Albion for a club record of £250,000. Mick Harford cost another record fee, this time for a Fourth Division player. Cox paid £216,000 to Lincoln City, this after the manager had failed to land Andy Ritchie of Manchester United. All three purchases however, were far from satisfactory.

Johnson, after looking the part on his debut, faded to the ordinary. Harford, tall and free-scoring in the lower divisions, was never given the support and the 22 year-old quickly moved on, only to develop into a quality centre-forward winning England honours with Luton Town - United missed a big opportunity with the Sunderland born leader. Trewick, a past schools and youth international, stayed at Gallowgate for three years and hailed from a footballing background, his father and cousin both played for Gateshead in the Football League. But he took a while to stamp his authority on United's midfield.

Off the field, United were in deep financial trouble. The club's Annual Report noted, "The Company is going through a very difficult period and your directors are making stringent economies wherever possible". The club's bankers asked every director to put up £16,000, to guarantee part of a £500,000 overdraft. That was too much for some and during March 1981 boardroom shuffles made the headlines as Lord Westwood and Bob Rutherford, two of the mainstays of the club over the past 20 years, resigned along with David Salkeld. Lord Westwood, 73 years-old, said, "I'm too old to take on the mountainous problems facing Newcastle". Stan Seymour junior, son of the legendary Stan senior, took the Chair after there was talk of a takeover by Ernie Clay - George Eastham's past mentor. Seymour had taken a place on the board in 1976, although for many years before was connected with the club. Stan junior was as dedicated to United's cause as his eminent father. He became a member of the FA Council and was associated with the Northumberland FA for many years, becoming President in 1978. The changes marked the end of an era, the beginning of the new Newcastle United. Seymour remarked, "Never again will we buy old players. We are where we are

Full-back Peter Johnson, manager Arthur Cox's first signing.

Centre-forward Mick Harford, cost a record fee, but stayed at Gallowgate only a few months.

Rock star Bruce Springsteen at St. James Park in one of the club's successful music extravaganzas.

ROCK VENUE

Before the 1982/83 season was unveiled, St James Park was turned into something completely different from a football stadium. During June the goal-posts were taken down and for the first time a stage erected for a prestige rock concert by number one supergroup, The Rolling Stones. Over 30,000 turned up and made the event a huge financial success. Other big names from the music world set up stage at St James Park, notably Bruce Springsteen, Bob Dylan, Queen and Status Quo. All were virtual sell-outs. And Mick Jagger made a return appearance in July 1990 when 25,000 paying £20 a ticket saw another spectacle.

because of our dealings in the transfer market". It was a swinging dig at Bill McGarry and his liking for experienced pro's. The revolution both on the pitch and now off it was in full swing.

Losing Hibbitt, Kelly and Ray Clarke through injuries which ended their careers, Cox had sorted out his staff and listed no fewer than 15 players at the end of the season. The manager had been frantically searching for a striker over the past six months to rectify the team's scoring headache. He looked at a number of players - Ally McCoist and Gary Rowell included - and by the time the new season was under way United fans found a new centre-forward in the No 9 shirt. He was a youngster signed from Everton for £125,000, Imre Varadi, a Cockney born of Hungarian parents. He displaced Mick Harford who went to Bristol City after less than 20 appearances in a United jersey. Varadi proved a popular signing. At 5'9" tall and quicksilver fast, he was always snapping at defenders' heels and bagged plenty of goals for United - 42 in 90 games. He may have missed plenty too, but when Cox sold him after only two seasons there was much anger. The dark haired striker went on to serve a string of top clubs - Sheffield Wednesday, West Bromwich Albion, Manchester City and Leeds - and always scored goals.

Cox also brought in the jovial figure of Tommy Cavanagh as his right hand man, the new season though, started in a poor way. With a new three points for a victory system introduced, a home defeat by Watford started the ball rolling and early signs were of a difficult time. United slipped to bottom spot after losing to QPR on the Londoners' new and controversial Omni-turf and a huge search for talent was undertaken. Before a fresh face arrived though, Malcolm Macdonald, now manager of Fulham, dumped United from the League Cup. The Third Division side had the Magpies on the rack at St James Park and netted two top class efforts reminiscent of Supermac himself. The Cottagers finished off the job alongside the Thames winning 4-1 on aggregate.

Chris Waddle, now a regular, netted United's first goal in almost 900 minutes of away football at Norwich - and at the same time the club's 5,000th league goal - and confidence slowly started to creep through. United moved up the table, but still with little sign of a promotion challenge. The new face Cox brought in was that of Sunderland forward, Alan Brown. A tall bustler, he signed on a loan deal and immediately made a good impact with the razor sharp Varadi up front. Injury however, forced his return to Roker Park in controversial circumstances, most observers asking the question whether United had in fact the money to conclude a deal at £100,000. Cash was still a stumbling block which ever way Newcastle turned. David Mills, the former Middlesbrough striker and who was once the country's most expensive player when he moved from Tees-side, arrived by way of West Bromwich Albion on another loan deal, but like Brown was to return to his previous base. He ended up permanently at St James Park as finances improved a little over twelve months later.

Cox hadn't much alternative but to give youth its chance. Teenagers were brought into the side; Peter Haddock and Wes Saunders in defence, Derek Bell and Kevin Pugh in midfield, while up front Kevin Todd and Paul Ferris were given an opportunity. Ferris, at a few months over 16 years old became the Magpies' youngest debutant. Cox also fielded the club's youngest ever side up to then, against QPR in September 1981 - the average age was just under 23 years old.

In the FA Cup of 1981/82, United were held at home 1-1 on a rain soaked evening by Colchester United, then won 4-3 after extra-time at Layer Road. 120 minutes of tense football saw spectacular goals from Waddle and full-back Wes Saunders and a dogged performance by the Fourth Division side. Colchester scrapped hard all night, but Newcastle just crept through. The Tynesiders met Grimsby Town in the Fourth Round and after a period of atrocious weather - one of the worst in football's history when temperatures dropped to minus 10 degrees centigrade in the north east and much worse elsewhere - Newcastle played the tie in front of a big, expectant crowd. However, in true Newcastle United tradition - the modern version - they let their fans down yet again with another seemingly annual disaster. Newcastle allowed the Mariners a 2-1 victory with the visiting 'keeper, Nigel Batch, raising his game to thwart all the Magpies' efforts. Yet it was a desperate performance against a managerless team of Second Division relegation candidates. Grimsby had taken a two goal lead and even United's effort was an own-goal when all was too late in the dying minutes.

Cox rallied his side after the FA Cup setback and by the final quarter of the season, and as conflict in the Falkland Islands had the nation on the edge of their seats, United climbed to a position just below a promotion pack led by Watford.

SCOTLESS UNITED

With the departure of John Brownlie to Hartlepool in July 1982, United's first team squad were without a Scot in their ranks for the first time ever. Caledonian blood was reinstated when big George Reilly joined the Magpies in February 1985 from Watford.

Former Everton striker Imre Varadi who found the net frequently for United in the Number 9 shirt.

Former England and Liverpool stars, Terry McDermott and Kevin Keegan, now together at St. James Park.

United found a slice of form at the right time. With three points for a win, they leapt up the table recording seven home victories in succession as well as a new defensive record. They had an outside chance of the third promotion place but then, over Easter, only drawing with Leicester City, and losing to Sheffield Wednesday and then Luton, the momentum was lost. The team wasn't quite good enough, finishing in 9th position and all that was left was to relax and watch the World Cup in Spain during the summer.

There was promise for the future though, with talented youngsters like Varadi, who ended up with 20 goals, and Chris Waddle, who was picked for the England Under 21 squad. Newcastle needed two or three top class players to mix with the youngsters - that is, if cash could be found. Within a couple of months the whole of Tyneside was set alight when Arthur Cox magnificently landed one of those very World Cup stars from Spain - a deal that eventually put United back in Division One and saw established names rushing to St James Park to put pen to paper.

United's average home attendance for the period before the 1982/83 season had dropped to the lowest since the war. By the end of the following eventful two campaigns the turnstiles were beginning to approach the 30,000 mark again - in the top five nationally once more, in spite of Second Division status. Only the two Manchester clubs, Liverpool and Tottenham had better gates. One man was responsible for that vast transformation in the club's fortunes....former England captain and number one figure in football, Kevin Keegan who signed for United in a sensational deal during August. It was a master stroke pulled off by Arthur Cox and Chairman Stan Seymour. Cox said, "From the minute I took over as manager here I have longed for the day when the place was buzzing with people wanting to come to the ground. Now that day has arrived".

It was a transfer that shocked football, never mind United's supporters. Negotiations were cloaked in secrecy, then when United were ready they expertly stage-managed the Keegan arrival. He signed for the club amidst the glare of a television and press conference at the Gosforth Park Hotel. Secretary Russell Cushing heralded Keegan's appearance with the words, "We're in heaven. We've got Kevin!" The former Liverpool star had only talked to two clubs - Newcastle United and Manchester United - although dozens were clamouring to sign him. The Magpies thought and acted big, and they paid big too. Backed by sponsors Scottish & Newcastle Breweries whose involvement cannot be understated, he was to be, reputedly, on a wage packet of £3,000 a week linked to the turnstile. It was several times more than the salary of Prime Minister Margaret Thatcher. After his first day on Tyneside Keegan noted, "I can't wait to be playing in front of fans like these". From being a sleeping giant United were back on centre stage, on television week after week, in all the newspapers and magazines and on the lips of football fans the country over. The good old days had returned as Keeganmania hit Tyneside.

At 31 years old, Keegan inspired United's side over the next two years and also attracted other stars to St James Park. Terry McDermott returned to Gallowgate from Liverpool for £100,000, eight years and 25 caps for England after leaving, while Irish international and ex Manchester United product, David McCreery joined him from Tulsa Roughnecks in the States. United were now hot favourites for promotion. Apart from the dramatic Keegan news, other changes occurred at Gallowgate. John Brownlie, Alan Shoulder and Nigel Walker were among those who departed, while arrivals at the ground also included ex Magpie John Craggs from Middlesbrough, Jeff Clarke from Sunderland and John Anderson, who earned a contract on a free transfer from Preston.

Right-back Craggs had been highly respected during his last period at St James Park as a kid, but

Ex Sunderland centre-half Jeff Clarke who proved a bargain signing.

due to the international form of David Craig, had found it impossible to claim a regular place. He moved down the coast to Ayresome Park and proceeded to play 473 games for 'Boro in a polished manner. He was only 17 years-old when he first appeared for United and 33 when he returned. Jeff Clarke was another popular north-east player, and another reaching the end of his career, but while Craggs didn't last the pace, the former Roker centre-half did, and he cost United nothing. From Pontefract, he started his career with Manchester City and bolstered United's rearguard, displaying many a sterling game in a black'n'white shirt until an injury halted his days with United. He later remained associated with the club's junior development programme.

Irishman John Anderson proved another bargain. Having been rejected by Manchester United as a youngster and not being able to hold a place at either West Bromwich or Preston, he arrived at St James Park very much wanting another opportunity. Gutsy and totally committed, he became a firm favourite in double quick time, bouncing back on several occasions when replacements appeared to have terminated his days on Tyneside. Nicknamed 'Ando', he was capped by Eire and was versatile in defence, filling in across the back four. He eventually saw off all his rivals and stayed through five managerial reigns at St James Park to complete ten years as a United player.

The 1982/83 season started in spectacular fashion. Keegan's first game against Queens Park Rangers attracted 35,718 and the television cameras. Not since the days of Supermac had Tyneside seen anything like it. Keegan capped the day by netting the winner in a dramatic comic-strip manner. Linking with Varadi from a throw-in, the England man charged into the box and with a typical piece of cool and clinical finishing slid the ball into the Gallowgate End net past 'keeper Hucker. Arthur Cox noted, "It was pure theatre, if you sat down to write the story, you couldn't have come up with a better ending". One of United's other new faces also had a marvellous debut. Free transfer Jeff Clarke was outstanding at centre-half.

Newcastle United packed in the crowds home and away, but the Magpies stuttered as the new season took shape. Many players found it hard to fit in with the charisma and international standard of Keegan. The youngsters especially found it difficult, they were overcome by the publicity and huge increase in support on the terraces, especially Waddle, who was dropped by the manager only to re-emerge a charged player. Keegan's goalscoring partner in an England shirt, Mick Channon, had a brief spell at St James Park on loan, but still Newcastle found consistency hard to achieve in the first half of the season. Indeed, Malcolm Macdonald's Fulham inflicted another heavy reverse on the Magpies during October.

In the Milk Cup - the renamed and now sponsored League Cup - Leeds United disposed of Newcastle over two legs after a Varadi goal at Elland Road had given the Magpies the advantage. Leeds proceeded to win 4-1 at St James Park. Then Keegan was crucially injured in a testimonial game for John Craggs at Middlesbrough and was out for several games, an injury which in the end was the difference between promotion and failure. Striker Howard Gayle of Liverpool became another loan signing in an effort to plug the Keegan gap, but he hardly filled the former England star's jersey.

With Keegan back in the groove, United struck form and charged into the final games of the season chasing QPR - way out at the top - Wolves, Fulham and Leicester City. From a lowly placing at the half-way stage of the programme, they gave Shrewsbury Town a 4-0 hiding and began a climb to a final 5th position. Goals were registered in quick succession when Keegan, Varadi and Waddle clicked time after time up front. United won at Chelsea, then trounced Rotherham by four goals and followed up with more hatfuls against Charlton and Barnsley. Promotion became a reality, but dropping points to Cambridge United left too much to achieve in the final home fixture of the season against Sheffield Wednesday. Although winning well before a full house, Leicester City just pipped United for the third promotion spot. After the match scenes were reminiscent to that of winning promotion instead of failure. There was intense crowd appreciation of the transformation from a dismal, ordinary side to one bristling with attacking ideas. Keegan was astonished at the demonstration of support from Arthur Cox's black'n'white army. He said, "I swear they won't have to wait more than another twelve months before we have something for them". That something was to be promotion. United had only recorded four defeats in the last 23 league matches - a pointer to the next season's success.

In the FA Cup even the influence of Kevin Keegan could not overcome United's jinx of latter years. Despite earning a fine 1-1 draw at Brighton, then in the First Division, the replay at Gallowgate ended in defeat - a controversial one at that. With the visitors ahead 1-0, referee Trelford Mills ignored what looked a blatant penalty then disallowed two late United efforts that found the net.

F.A. Cup action in 1983. Terry McDermott drives the ball into Brighton's net for Newcastle's goal.

The highlight of a season full of vibrant football occurred early into the programme and surprisingly away from Tyneside, at Millmoor home of Rotherham United. At the beginning of October and with the Match of the Day cameras in attendance Keegan hit the jackpot - four brilliant goals in a rampant 5-1 Newcastle victory. It was a game which could have easily ended 7-5 to United with so much goalmouth action at both ends of the field. And all at a time too when England boss Bobby Robson had announced that Keegan had no role in his new England set up. The ex national skipper showed everyone that he was far too good to be discarded. It mattered little though, as Robson never recalled him to the England team - to many people's annoyance nationwide.

Local lad Neil McDonald who made an immediate impact in the side.

Almost every game had incident, albeit, the good, the bad and sometimes the ugly. Two United players were sent-off at Oldham in a 2-2 draw when both Steve Carney and Terry McDermott were given their marching orders in quick succession as the game erupted in the 67th minute. Debuts were given to juniors Chris Hedworth and 16 year-old Tynesider Neil McDonald, who surpassed Paul Ferris as the club's youngest player. An England youth international, he made 26 appearances in his first season following a £5,000 move from Carlisle United. Varadi and skipper Keegan shared the goals, 43 between them. Waddle, after overcoming the shock of playing with Keegan, started to look a menacing forward and Jeff Clarke was powerful in defence alongside ex Northern League player Steve Carney. He cost United only £1,000 from Blyth Spartans and was an ex colleague of Alan Shoulder. Giving up his electrician's job, Carney started as a utility player, mainly at full-back, but displayed his best qualities in the middle alongside, firstly Clarke and then new signing Glenn Roeder. Much was expected for the following year's football.

United's supporters were eager to see more names added to that of Keegan for the start of the new season. They wanted to make absolutely sure of the outcome the following May with Keegan announcing this would be his last season before retiring. Speculation saw goalpoacher Charlie Nicholas of Celtic linked with United, but manager Arthur Cox spent nearly £350,000 on two full-backs, both of attacking quality with good reputations. England Under 21 player, John Ryan arrived from Oldham Athletic while Huddersfield Town's Malcolm Brown signed on too. Both were highly rated, especially up front, with Ryan, the more expensive of the pair at £225,000, able to give the attack an added matchwinning dimension, although at the expense of his defensive duties. Both players, however never justified the heavy outlay.

The bookies liked United's line-up and made Newcastle favourites to take the Second Division title. But, tragedy struck before the season got under way when Brown injured his Achilles tendon in training and hardly kicked a ball for the rest of the campaign - this after not missing a game for the Terriers for all of 259 consecutive matches. On the face of it more bad news was to follow. Imre Varadi - next to Keegan - the crowd's favourite with 42 goals in two seasons was dramatically sold one week before the big kick-off to Sheffield Wednesday. David Mills returned to Gallowgate as part of the deal and Cox was criticised for the transaction, however, what everyone didn't know was that the cash received, £150,000, was already lined up for a replacement who would virtually seal promotion for United....former Carlisle United man, Peter Beardsley, a forward with pace like Varadi, but who possessed sweet skills that were to link with Keegan almost perfectly.

Malcolm Brown, out with injury immediately after signing for United.

Beardsley, in the North American League with Vancouver Whitecaps, didn't arrive back in his native Tyneside until late September and missed United's opening exchanges. They started well, in a striking new away strip of silver and black, with a victory at Leeds, this after being without a goalkeeper for half the game when Kevin Carr broke an arm - more bad luck for the squad. Welshman Martin Thomas stepped into the action having being signed from Bristol Rovers for £50,000 and started a healthy rivalry for the goalkeeper's position. Kevin Carr, 6'2" tall, had graduated from United's juniors and the Morpeth born 'keeper looked, at one stage, to be heading for a top class career. Thomas eventually won the senior's place though, and went on to appear for his country.

The black'n'whites then fell to unfashionable Shrewsbury Town at home in front of a 30,000 crowd, the first of a dozen such gates at St James Park that season. Chris Waddle was the man to inspire United after that setback with refreshing and skilful performances from the wing. John Wardle in the Sunday Sun noted that he displayed, "true international potential". By the time Beardsley had settled, Newcastle's front three of Keegan, Beardsley and Waddle showed flashes of what was to follow. First signs were against Portsmouth on Tyneside, a 4-2 victory, then promotion rivals Manchester City arrived at Gallowgate during October and the front trio on that afternoon displayed a match winning understanding second to none in the club's past.

Immediately after bowing out of the Milk Cup to the season's giant-killers Oxford United - highlighting United still had a weakness - 33,675 turned up for what was to be the classic of the season with City. Everyone talked of United's performance over those 90 minutes as the best seen in years and years, it was so good. Newcastle won 5-0 while the visitors' agile 'keeper, Alex Williams stopped another five efforts from entering the net. Beardsley scored a hat-trick with Keegan and Waddle netting one apiece. United's style of one-touch football in and around the box thrilled the Geordie crowd.

Kevin Carr who contested the goalkeeper's position with Martin Thomas.

After only eight minutes, Waddle was brought down in the penalty area, but instead of a spot-kick the referee waved play on and Beardsley took the loose ball, side-stepped Caton and netted to open the floodgates. Just before half-time Keegan, who had earlier hit the post, finished off a move started outside the United penalty area and which had class written all over it. John Anderson fed his captain who in turn sent Waddle away. The long-striding winger got to the bye-line, crossed and there was Keegan to bulge the net. After the break the Magpies played exhibition stuff. Wes Saunders had a shot cleared off the City line and on the hour, Waddle met Beardsley's cross and although Williams parried the ball, the ever-alert Beardsley followed up to lash it home. The tricky United striker completed his hat-trick soon afterwards, taking a pass from Waddle and speeding through the defence for the best goal of the day. Near the end, Waddle made it 5-0. Moving onto a McDermott pass, he struck a 20 yard drive low into the corner of the net. United's new striker, Peter Beardsley recorded in his autobiography, "We played as well as I've seen any team play", while his skipper and boss were equally as delighted. Cox called it, "the best performance from any team I have managed", and Keegan, "the sort of game you get only once in years".

JAPAN CUP VICTORY

During the summer break of 1983 the Magpies went on a prestige tour of the Far East travelling almost 20,000 miles. They arrived back with a trophy, the Japan Cup, finishing ahead of Brazilians, Botafogo in a final deciding match — albeit a bruising confrontation before 30,000 in Tokyo. United had played local club Yamaha as well as both the Syrian and Japanese national elevens.

Martin Thomas who was selected for Wales in 1986/87

Two further meetings with other members of the promotion chasing four, Chelsea and Sheffield Wednesday, both away from home, ended in defeat, yet the way United at times took Wednesday apart in a 4-2 reverse still had United's fans cheering and not despondent. Football was fast and entertaining with goals at both ends of the field. Cox though, had to plug his leaky defence. Ryan had been dropped in favour of local lad Kenny Wharton, the side had lost both Carr and Brown and were to soon loose centre-half Jeff Clarke as well. Cox went for Barnsley's Mick McCarthy, but lost out to rivals Manchester City and in his place paid £120,000 for 28 year-old Glenn Roeder, former skipper at QPR and an England B player. While not fully closing the hole at the back, Roeder was the final piece in the Cox jigsaw. He was a steadying and organising influence in defence, a stylish footballer with flair to come forward too. The Londoner possessed a mesmerising double shuffle on the ball which confounded defenders as he moved into attack and which Newcastle's crowd

Newcastle v Manchester City. Peter Beardsley clips the ball past Williams for his hat-trick.

ELECTRONIC AGE

In the 1980/81 season of struggle, United unveiled a new electronic score-board as part of the sponsorship deal with S & N Breweries. The £60,000 worth of gadgetry kept a track of the time, noted the score and teams on the giant screen, gave half-times and a profusion of advertising. And on a goal being scored, up flashed a dancing United player! It was a long way from United's slow manually operated half-time score-board and unreliable tannoy system of the past.

warmed to. He went on to captain United over a four year period once Keegan departed and played 215 times for the Magpies.

January came with United in 3rd spot. They had not been out of the top four since the opening month, but promotion was put on the backseat for a couple of weeks when Newcastle were drawn to face Liverpool in the FA Cup at Anfield - a nostalgic return for Kevin Keegan and Terry McDermott. In true showbiz style the nation captured the romantic side of football as the BBC covered the game live. Liverpool though, spoilt the party for a 15,000 mass of noisy Tyneside fans by crushing United 4-0. It was a typically ruthless Liverpool performance. Newcastle had a long way to go yet and a lot to learn.

It was back to the promotion race and although faltering after the Anfield lesson, Newcastle arrived at the final period of the season in a confident mood. John Trewick came back into the side after languishing in the reserves and reinforced the midfield with his best spell of football for the Magpies. The chasing four; Manchester City, Chelsea, Sheffield Wednesday and United were the teams to beat, although Grimsby Town and Carlisle United were pressing hard. United's promotion run-in started with a 4-1 triumph at Portsmouth and for the umpteenth time that season Kevin Keegan was the crucial factor. He scored two and made two for Beardsley.

An important 2-1 victory at Maine Road followed and boosted confidence. The biggest crowd in the division that season - 41,767 - witnessed that confrontation and saw two classic goals by the Magpies. In the 19th minute Keegan sent a measured header from Waddle's cross into Beardsley's path. On the penalty spot, the Tynesider carried the ball past McCarthy and Bond then whipped a shot high past Williams. Before City could recover, Keegan struck again taking a perfectly weighted pass from McDermott, striding into the box and threading the ball home in style. Keegan reckoned that victory was the turning point in United's season. From then on the side marched towards success with an air of authority.

Despite losing to a negative, but efficient, Sheffield Wednesday on Tyneside, the Magpies bounced back to stop promotion outsiders Carlisle United 5-1 at St James Park with an exhilarating and attacking display, a victory which virtually clinched Division One football. The turning point of the match was a Kevin Carr penalty save after Carney handled in the box. Former United star, Alan Shoulder took the kick and Carr not only stretched to block the shot, but followed up with another stop from the onrushing Poskett. Then,

Right: Glenn Roeder, came to plug the hole in United's defence.

CROWD'S RESPONSE

During the Keegan era gate receipts were broken three times in the 1982/83 season and again the following year. The previous record of £47,974 (v Sunderland) was smashed as Keegan made his first appearance against Queen's Park Rangers. £53,462 was banked and against Brighton in the FA Cup £59,656 was collected. In 1983/84 Keegan's magnetism ensured six gates with over £50,000 taken, topped by the Sheffield Wednesday fixture when £57,998 was recorded. And this was bettered in Keegan's Farewell Match against Liverpool when the figure reached a new peak of £83,000.

from his throw out Waddle screamed away down the wing and the ball ended up at the other end of the field with Keegan finding the net. That goal made the score 3-0 and ended Carlisle's resistance. The 33,458 Easter Monday crowd started singing confidently, "Going Up! Going Up! Going Up!" Apart from Shoulder, the visitors also fielded Tommy Craig and were managed by Bob Stokoe who reinforced the spectator's optimism, he said, "Newcastle are certain to get promotion".

With only a victory all but needed to get back to the First Division, Newcastle went to struggling Cambridge - scene of last season's flop - and again the Magpies were humbled by the Abbey Road side, a club already doomed to Division Three. There was a mass exodus to the peaceful Fen country but, packed into Cambridge's tiny ground, Newcastle's supporters saw a dismal performance. The home side won 1-0 and promotion celebrations were put on ice for another week.

United quickly made amends though. In the side's next home game against another relegation threatened club, Derby County, it was all but over - another great attacking exhibition, another four goals. Keegan started the rout climbing to head in a Waddle run and cross, then the skipper set up Beardsley for a low drive to make it 2-0. Chris Waddle got the third and Beardsley wrapped up the game with a diving header. There could have been several more too as a wretched Derby eleven crumbled in the spring sunshine. Newcastle were just about there. Although mathematically not yet promoted, there was little doubt they would make it, subject to an extraordinary disaster. And there wasn't any. United went to Huddersfield and in spite of being without the injured Keegan and 2-0 behind, spectacular goals from Beardsley - a glorious drive from the edge of the area - and stand-in Mills - a stunning volley - earned the point that won promotion. Arthur Cox had achieved success and his 12,000 strong travelling army of black'n'white fans celebrated in some style.

Those jubilant scenes carried on for another two weeks and against Brighton at St James Park a rapturous pageant occurred as United took acclaim for success - and Keegan in particular. David McCreery noted, "everyone just got carried away on a wave of emotion". The match was of secondary importance. They won 3-1 in front of 36,000 and finished in the third promotion place behind Sheffield Wednesday and Chelsea. Keegan signed off - it was to be his last and 500th league game - in a fitting way. A personal lap of honour, a loudspeaker address to the terraces, and of course with a goal, while he had a hand in the two others as well. He noted, "I couldn't have wished for a more perfect way to end my career". United's skipper added it was, "the greatest atmosphere I ever experienced". And that was quite a statement from a star who has graced the world playing the game.

Keegan's last goal came from a Waddle shot that crashed against the post. Kevin was on hand to slam the rebound past Brighton's veteran 'keeper Joe Corrigan. It wasn't all Keegan though. His two prodigies, Waddle and Beardsley scored as well, and the final goal netted by Peter Beardsley was a gem. He played a one-two with Keegan 30 yards out. Brighton's centre-half got to the ball first, but Beardsley slid in, dragged it from the defender, swivelled and chipped a beauty over Corrigan into the top corner of the Gallowgate net. Keegan remarked, "It was one of the best goals I've ever seen". And it was a marvellous way to end a successful campaign.

Keegan topped the scorers' list with 28 league and cup goals followed by Beardsley on 20 and Waddle with 18. A total of 66 goals between the front three - the undoubted key to promotion. Terry McDermott was as important, his form was outstanding from the beginning of 1984 onwards as he recaptured the international style shown at Liverpool. His distribution and late runs into space dove-tailed perfectly with Keegan. Alongside him, David McCreery was just as valuable in his own way as the defensive anchor. Roeder and Carney formed

Keegan's final league goal. United's skipper takes a rebound and slots the ball past Joe Corrigan.

Chris Waddle nets with a rare header - a strike against Brighton following Keegan's cross.

a much improved rearguard with cost-nothing pair, John Anderson and Kenny Wharton making a nonsense of Cox's expensive transfer splash for Brown and Ryan.

All that was left were the celebrations. Not only to hail promotion, but to mark the departure of Keegan who confirmed his retirement. In his souvenir brochure he noted, "I will never forget the wonderful Geordie fans, and the greatest compliment I can pay them lies in my decision to quit as a Newcastle United player. I have been so warmly received on Tyneside that it would be unthinkable to play for anyone else. The supporters of this club deserve success - and lasting success - more than any other". In a prestige Farewell Match against Liverpool, mounting joy spilled out in waves. A gate of 36,722 saw a 2-2 draw and a spectacular finale. Keegan made his exit from football via a helicopter which swooped onto the Gallowgate turf. Amidst a firework display, he had gone as quickly and as sensationally as he had arrived. Keegan had put Newcastle back in the elite, both on and off the field with two years of thrilling football. United returned to the First Division and as most believed, were on the threshold of a new period of glory. However, in typical Newcastle United tradition of ever being in the news, a bombshell hit the club at the very point of triumph.

Only a matter of days after promotion was achieved United made headlines again when Arthur Cox resigned as manager. It was a surprise to most, but to those with their ears close to the club perhaps not an unlikely event. There had been speculation for weeks that a rift had occurred during contract negotiations and that the board was split over his future. Cox had done his job superbly well, building a side from very little, yet he'd departed in spite of being offered a three year contract worth almost £100,000. And to where - to Third Division Derby County at a much reduced salary. It was a strange decision and one that split Tyneside. Cox resigned over a matter of principle more than anything else. He said to newsmen, "I felt the Board did not appreciate what has been done and were not talking to me in a proper manner". He also wanted a promise of substantial cash resources to buy top-class players - Kevin Sheedy and Mark Wright being linked with St James Park. He wasn't given one and left.

It was back to the managerial merry-go-round. Names were thrown around like confetti - Burkinshaw, Charlton, McMenemy and Malcolm Macdonald, the favourite of many, who had created a live-wire Fulham outfit. At the time when United needed stability for a return to the First Division, the club was thrown into indecision once more. A new appointment was needed - and needed quickly.

KEEGAN'S WORTH

Kevin Keegan was paid a fortune to appear for Newcastle United in an innovative deal linked to increased attendance figures. In his first year he earned more than £80,000 and Chairman Stan Seymour noted, "Every penny is justifiable". In his second, the Yorkshireman received a staggering £215,000 - £4,000 per week, including bonus payments and rake-off from gate receipts. Secretary and General Manager Russell Cushing said, "he was one of the best investments the club has ever made".

A brilliant third goal against Brighton. Peter Beardsley produces a piece of magic.

'Nice one Kev', says Brighton's Joe Corrigan.

Centenary Highlight

Kevin Keegan jumps to head a crucial goal against Derby County.

Keegan - the man who more than anyone ensured United's success.

Peter Beardsley strikes a superb second goal against The Rams.

SECOND DIVISION PROMOTION 1983-84	P	W	D	L	F	A	Pts
Chelsea	42	25	13	4	90	40	88
Sheffield Wednesday	42	26	10	6	72	34	88
Newcastle United	**42**	**24**	**8**	**10**	**85**	**53**	**80**
Manchester City	42	20	10	12	66	48	70
Grimsby Town	42	19	13	10	60	47	70
Blackburn Rovers	42	17	16	9	57	46	67
Carlisle United	42	16	16	10	48	41	64
Shrewsbury Town	42	17	10	15	49	53	61
Brighton	42	17	9	16	69	60	60
Leeds United	42	16	12	14	55	56	60
Fulham	42	15	12	15	60	53	57
Huddersfield Town	42	14	15	13	56	49	57
Charlton Athletic	42	16	9	17	53	64	57
Barnsley	42	15	7	20	57	53	52
Cardiff City	42	15	6	21	53	66	51
Portsmouth	42	14	7	21	73	64	49
Middlesbrough	42	12	13	17	41	47	49
Crystal Palace	42	12	11	19	42	52	47
Oldham Athletic	42	13	8	21	47	73	47
Derby County	42	11	9	22	36	72	42
Swansea City	42	7	8	27	36	85	29
Cambridge United	42	4	12	26	28	77	24

RESULTS	Home	Away
Leeds United	W 1-0	W 1-0
Shrewsbury Town	L 0-1	D 2-2
Oldham Athletic	W 3-0	W 2-1
Middlesbrough	W 3-1	L 2-3
Grimsby Town	L 0-1	D 1-1
Crystal Palace	W 3-1	L 1-3
Barnsley	W 1-0	D 1-1
Portsmouth	W 4-2	W 4-1
Charlton Athletic	W 2-1	W 3-1
Swansea City	W 2-0	W 2-1
Cardiff City	W 3-1	W 2-0
Manchester City	W 5-0	W 2-1
Fulham	W 3-2	D 2-2
Chelsea	D 1-1	L 0-4
Sheffield Wednesday	L 0-1	L 2-4
Cambridge United	W 2-1	L 0-1
Derby County	W 4-0	L 2-3
Huddersfield Town	W 5-2	D 2-2
Brighton	W 3-1	W 1-0
Blackburn Rovers	D 1-1	D 1-1
Carlisle United	W 5-1	L 1-3

LARGEST VICTORY:
5-0 v Manchester City(H)

HEAVIEST DEFEAT:
0-4 v Chelsea(A)

AVERAGE HOME ATTENDANCE:
29,419

TOP GATE:
36,288 v Sheffield Wednesday

Promotion 1984

REGULAR SIDE
Thomas or Carr
Anderson, Carney, Roeder, Ryan or Wharton
McCreery, McDermott, Wharton or Trewick
Beardsley, Keegan, Waddle.

CHAIRMAN: Stan Seymour
MANAGER: Arthur Cox
TRAINER-COACH: Willie McFaul
CAPTAIN: Kevin Keegan

LEAGUE APPEARANCES
Including substitute games
42 Waddle, McDermott, 41 Keegan, Anderson, Wharton, 40 McCreery, 35 Beardsley, 33 Carney, 23 Thomas, Roeder, 22 Ryan, 19 Carr, 16 Saunders, Trewick, Mills, 14 Clarke, 12 McDonald, 3 Haddock.

LEAGUE GOALS
27 Keegan, 20 Beardsley, 18 Waddle, 6 McDermott, 5 Mills, 4 Wharton, 2 Own-goals, 1 Ryan, Anderson, Trewick.

Victory scenes on the Gallowgate pitch. Left to right: Wharton, Beardsley, McCreery, Carr, Keegan, Roeder, Waddle, Carney, McDermott.

Success achieved, Arthur Cox celebrates in the dressing-room. Left to right, back: Carr, McCreery, Waddle, Beardsley, Wharton. Front: Anderson, Carney, Cox, Keegan and trainer McFaul.

Centenary Profile 27

The Charismatic Idol

"No other player in the world could have had such a dramatic effect on the club and its supporters"

Arthur Cox, May 1984

TYNESIDE LITERALLY WENT CRAZY THE DAY **England skipper Kevin Keegan flew into Newcastle Airport to sign for the Magpies. Pressmen, radio and camera crews had a field day. It was a big national story. They chased him all over the north east in a vehicle procession that was more like the Whacky Races. Supporters couldn't believe it. From being in the football wilderness, United were catapulted into the spotlight. His £100,000 transfer from Southampton was a massive scoop and dramatically transformed Arthur Cox's team into a winning formula - one that eventually took the club back to the First Division.**

Keegan made all the difference. His captaincy, skill and charisma turned average players into good ones, indeed in two instances, international ones. He brought other stars to the St James Park camp as well and also turned the despondent spectators into an excited and expectant mass. So much so that queues for season-tickets stretched around the streets of Gallowgate within 24 hours of his arrival. His record in a black'n'white shirt was to be first class. After a marvellous start of three goals in his first three games, Kevin went on to net 49 goals in 85 appearances and importantly had much to do with the rapid development of Chris Waddle and Peter Beardsley as superstars in their own right.

The son of a Geordie miner from Hetton, but brought up near Doncaster, Keegan made a name for himself under the guidance of Bill Shankly at Anfield after being introduced to the Football League by Fourth Division Scunthorpe United during 1968. More a self made player than one with tremendous natural ability, Keegan developed into a 90 minute action man. He was utterly determined with superb positioning and awareness of the ball while his finishing became deadly. Once paired with big John Toshack in the Liverpool side, Kevin was rated the most complete forward of his generation. He won domestic and European honours at Anfield - including an FA Cup winners' medal against Newcastle in 1974, a day when he demolished United. For a player of only 5'8" tall, Keegan was good in the air too using his stocky frame to launch himself in challenges with bigger defenders.

After scoring 100 goals in 321 appearances for the Reds, he took the decision to sample European soccer in June 1977 joining SV Hamburg for £500,000. It was a gamble, but Keegan was a rousing success in the Bundesliga and in the process became English football's first soccer millionaire. Voted European Footballer of the Year in both 1978 and 1979, Keegan also became something of a pop star in Germany and almost qualified for a gold disc for one of his songs.

Tynesider Lawrie McMenemy was the man who landed Keegan once the striker decided to return to the Football League in the summer of 1980 - a surprise move, Keegan joining one of the lesser lights of the game. Kevin was a hit again. He grabbed 37 goals for the Saints over two seasons and saw them reach a high placing in the First Division. He also picked up the PFA Player of the Year award. Appearing 63 times for England, Keegan was the ideal candidate for the national captaincy possessing a friendly, likable personality. He became one of soccer's greatest ambassadors at home and abroad and justly deserved the OBE in 1982 just before heading for Tyneside.

Joining Newcastle in August of that year with the financial backing of sponsors Newcastle Breweries who used the super-star extensively in public relations, the former England player may have pocketed a fortune, but as any United fan will admit, earned every penny of it. The two years he spent as King of Tyneside were something special for supporters of the club - especially a new generation of fans who had not tasted success in any form. There was an aura of excitement in everything to do with Newcastle United. Chairman Stan Seymour said, "The signing of Kevin Keegan is just the impetus Tyneside needed to set local football alight again". And he was just that. By the time Keegan had departed Arthur Cox noted, "No other player in the world could have had such a dramatic effect on the club and its supporters". Importantly Kevin Keegan could communicate with the grassroots and rarely refused an opportunity to meet ordinary fans. He attended hundreds of functions and gatherings during his period in the north east and colleague Jeff Clarke said, "he never lost the common touch and that's what made him great".

Kevin ended his glory-filled 16 year career of more than 700 games and almost 300 goals in a black'n'white shirt immediately after promotion was secured. The 33 year-old said, "My only regret is that I didn't come to Newcastle a little earlier". Afterwards he lived abroad for most of the year - in Marbella on the Costa del Sol - working in various promotional activities. Keegan had come a long way since the days he kicked a ball around for the Peglers Brass Works in Doncaster. For sheer instant and explosive impact, Kevin Keegan was without doubt United's greatest ever signing.

KEEGAN'S PLAYING RECORD

	League		FA Cup		FL Cup		Total	
	App	Gls	App	Gls	App	Gls	App	Gls
1982-83	37	21	2	0	2	0	41	21
1983-84	41	27	1	0	2	1	44	28
	78	**48**	**3**	**0**	**4**	**1**	**85**	**49**

Kevin Keegan

Centenary Profile 28

The Superstar from Gateshead

"He is world class....the most improved player I have ever seen"

Kevin Keegan, 1990

ANYONE WHO FOLLOWED THE DEVELOPMENT OF Chris Waddle from his days as a raw youngster with Tow Law Town, through Newcastle's reserve team into the First Division and subsequent World Cup stage, witnessed a dramatic transformation. It was Alan Oliver of the Evening Chronicle who said of Waddle during his early days in a black'n'white strip, "He didn't impress me at all", this after a reserve game at Consett when he was kicked off the pitch. That comment seems ludicrous with hindsight when such eminent names as Kevin Keegan noted the Tynesider as, "world class....the most improved player I have seen". And when French club, Marseille laid £4 million and more on the table for the services of the Geordie lad who had cost United a mere £1,000.

But in those early days Waddle hardly looked a footballer and many echoed Oliver's view. He appeared a gangly and lumbering player. Yet hidden was a talent that was to reveal a potent striker who could operate on the wing or through the middle. Waddle developed into a forward of exceptional ball skills, deceiving pace, and a wicked cross that goalkeepers hated and centre-forwards loved. Add a vicious curling shot to his repertoire and Waddle became superstar quality.

It was Bill McGarry who gave the signal to bring the Leam Lane youngster to St James Park on a one year contract in the summer of 1980. This was after Waddle had played for Pelaw juniors and Clarke Chapman Works' side and both Coventry and Sunderland had rejected him. Brought up a Reds' supporter, he played once for the Roker reserve side, but Ken Knighton sent him packing. Sunderland in fact had discarded the future England player twice. Jimmy Adamson had also previously shown him the door! United scout Les Common - Jackie Milburn's brother-in-law - liked the look of Waddle, but as he said, "United signed him without too much enthusiasm".

The Magpies sacked their boss within a month of Chris arriving at St James Park and Waddle found Arthur Cox in charge, a personality every bit as tough as his predecessor. And it was Cox who worked harder than anyone to develop those hidden talents. Waddle made an impression in the black'n'whites' Central League side, scoring with either foot from the wing or centre and was quickly in the new manager's first team squad. He made his debut against Shrewsbury Town in October 1980 and really made the headlines in a FA Cup tie with Sheffield Wednesday when he netted two goals. Then Kevin Keegan arrived and Waddle flourished - slowly at first,

then rapidly into one of the game's top front runners. His early inconsistency and self belief was ironed out and from October 1982, Waddle never missed a match for 106 fixtures - one of the best runs in the club's history. In that spell he was ever-present in the Magpies' promotion year of 1983/84 scoring 18 goals.

Tall and quick, although he appeared languid at times, Chris could call on explosive shooting and loved to run at defenders, using feints and foot trickery to whip past opponents. In the First Division, 23 year-old Waddle came into his own, frequently finding the net in his first season. He really made a mark in September 1984 when a first-half hat-trick in 24 minutes shattered QPR at Loftus Road. He went on to make two more goals as well, all in front of England manager Bobby Robson who was in the stand. It was a significant 90 minutes in Waddle's rise to stardom. Peter Beardsley was to say, "He did things that afternoon any player in the world would have been proud of". At the end of the season he had been voted Runner-

Chris Waddle

WADDLE'S PLAYING RECORD

	League		FA Cup		FL Cup		Total	
	App	Gls	App	Gls	App	Gls	App	Gls
1980-81	13	1	4	2	0	0	17	3
1981-82	42	7	3	1	2	0	47	8
1982-83	37	7	2	0	1	0	40	7
1983-84	42	18	1	0	2	0	45	18
1984-85	35/1	13	2	1	4	2	41/1	16
	169/1	**46**	**12**	**4**	**9**	**2**	**190/1**	**52**

up to Mark Hughes in the PFA poll for the Young Player of the Year award.

Chosen for England's Under 21 side and full England squad, he was then elevated to Bobby Robson's team for the international against Eire in 1985. It was the first outing in a career at top level football that has seen Waddle earn over 60 caps for his country - the most by any Tynesider.

Tottenham Hotspur took a fancy to Chris especially after a superb performance at White Hart Lane which included a memorable goal. He picked up a pass from Beardsley, turned inside Roberts and superbly curled a left foot shot across Clemence and into the corner of the net. Waddle was on his way Fed up with Newcastle's and Jack Charlton's long ball game, as Peter Beardsley confirmed in his autobiography, "It was Jack's pattern of play that led to Chris Waddle leaving the club", Newcastle received a handsome profit on their investment. They gained a League Tribunal decided fee of £590,000 in July 1985, although that was short of the £750,000 United valuation. It was a lot of money then, but nothing compared to the amount of cash he generated later - to Newcastle United's loss.

Waddle matured rapidly under Terry Venables and became an England regular as well as a White Hart Lane favourite. However the lure of mega-money from the Continent was too great for both Spurs and the player, and in July 1989 French millionaire club Marseille took him to the Mediterranean coast for a cool £4.25 million. It was then the world's fourth most expensive purchase behind international stars Detari, Maradona and Gullit. It was a deal that stunned the domestic football scene. Chris went on to win French league and cup honours and was elevated to one of Europe's biggest attractions. He appeared in three European Cup runs, a semi-final and final appearance included. Waddle had started on £70 for a week's effort at St James Park, but now picked up a reported £10,000 per week. It was difficult to believe that Chris Waddle was once an ordinary Geordie lad, a sausage seasoner in a Felling factory who had kicked a ball around for fun.

17

A SECOND REVOLUTION

1984-1990

• BIG JACK'S REIGN • GAZZA EMERGES • TAKE-OVER BATTLE • McFAUL OUT, SMITH IN • PLAY-OFF DRAMA •

"The job is bigger and harder than I ever anticipated"

Jim Smith, 1988

JACKIE CHARLTON OBE WAS ONE OF THE north-east's most famous sons. A past World Cup hero in 1966 and a formidable centre-half with Leeds United for 20 years, Charlton had worshipped the Magpies as a child. He was to say, "Newcastle has always been the first result I have looked for". And of course he was from the Milburn clan in Ashington. Ever since the tall, thin Northumbrian entered management with Middlesbrough in 1973, he had been the first choice of many supporters for the Newcastle manager's job.

Possessing a no nonsense approach, he took 'Boro to the Second Division title in 1974, then at Sheffield Wednesday, he again revived the fortunes of an ailing club, guiding the Owls out of the Third Division. He was a first class organiser, a builder of teams from nothing. Now, after his name was linked with the St James Park hot-seat in both 1975 and 1980, the 49 year-old was appointed United's new manager. The fans were happy - although dissatisfied with the way Arthur Cox had departed - and looked forward to a return to the First Division. There was a huge demand for the club's 10,000 season-tickets and the black'n'whites grossed £800,000 in sales before a ball was kicked.

Jack Charlton to start with a popular choice as manager.

Supporters had plenty to be optimistic about. Newcastle had played terrific football on their way out of Division Two and while they may have lost Kevin Keegan, they possessed two players of absolute quality in Chris Waddle and Peter Beardsley. With Roeder, Wharton and McCreery, they had the basis of a decent team. All that was needed were two or three choice signings to bolster the side and replace Keegan's influence and experience.

Big Jack was given limited cash to spend, but never plunged into the transfer market in a headline making way, preferring to first work with the squad he inherited. When he did spend money, it was cautious and uninspiring. His first signing wasn't until six weeks into the season when midfielder Pat Heard arrived in an exchange deal for Ryan from his old club, Sheffield Wednesday. He replaced the international talent of Terry McDermott who left before the season kicked off following a bitter row over money. John Trewick and David Mills had also departed and it was one area of the field where United needed a commanding figure. Heard, a past England youth international never fitted that requirement.

Charlton's tactical pattern which evolved was hardly what Newcastle supporters had been used to over the past two seasons. His style of committed workrate and a high ball game infuriated many of the crowd who wanted the flamboyant United of 1983/84. It also in time frustrated the talent of Waddle and Beardsley, and probably led to both ending up at other clubs. Charlton needed the fans to be patient as he built a side over two or three seasons. They were not and Jack the Saviour quickly turned into Jack the Villain by the end of the season.

Without new blood, United were tipped by many to go straight back into the Second Division. To start with however, Newcastle surprised everyone and by the end of the opening month of the 1984/85 season were top of the world - in fact top of Division One. They started at Leicester and won 3-2, then faced Sheffield Wednesday and won again, 2-1. Aston Villa arrived at St James Park on the first day of September and 31,591 saw Newcastle triumph 3-0 and reach leading position in the table for the first time in 34 years, since September 1950. Chris Waddle was the prime reason for the success. He had been outstanding in all three games and his performance against Villa confirmed he was becoming a player to be considered at the highest level. He scored twice, a

YOUTH CUP SUCCESS

For the second time in the club's history, Newcastle's junior side lifted the FA Youth Cup in 1984/85. They eliminated the holders Everton (6-0), Leeds United (2-0), Manchester City (2-1), then Coventry City (3-0) and in the semi-final, Birmingham City (7-2 agg). United's kids, coached by Colin Suggett, then faced Watford over two legs. Firstly, at St James Park the game ended goal-less and Newcastle were up against it when they travelled to Vicarage Road. Watford took the lead, but Paul Gascoigne and Joe Allon shared four goals to give United victory by 4-1. United; Kelly, Dickinson, Tinnion, Nesbit, Scott, Kilford, Hayton, Gascoigne, Allon, Forster, Wrightson. Sub Stephenson.

Gascoigne and Allon were the stars - they had scored 19 goals between them. Other players from the squad to progress to Football League status were Gary Kelly, Brain Tinnion, Tony Nesbit, Kevin Scott, Jeff Wrightson and Paul Stephenson.

Top left: United's successful F.A. Youth Cup squad in 1985, led by coach Colin Suggett (extreme left) and captain Paul Gascoigne (front, right of ball).

lovely right foot shot, then a left foot drive past Mervyn Day. And he created another for his partner, Peter Beardsley with a brilliant dummy. He was tipped for an England place and was elevated to Bobby Robson's squad following two more eye catching performances in London, at QPR, where he scored a hat-trick, and later at Tottenham.

At Loftus Road a bizarre 90 minutes took place that saw United 4-0 in front at half-time - Newcastle's biggest interval lead - courtesy of a stunning display by Waddle. Yet the Magpies still did not pick up full points. United were sloppy in defence and allowed Rangers to claw themselves back into the game. One by one, they sent the ball into the United net to reduce the arrears. And even when Waddle set up another Newcastle goal for Wharton, the home side still managed to pinch a point. In the last minute a 20 yarder by Gary Micklewhite flew past Carr to make the scoreline 5-5. Captain Glenn Roeder said of United's second-half performance, "We played like schoolboys".

Following United's bright opening, Charlton's men gradually slid down the table. When they came up against tougher opposition results were altogether different. The Magpies lost to Arsenal, to Manchester United(5-0), and to Everton and Liverpool. They were knocked out of the Milk Cup by Ipswich Town too. By the time the New Year derby meeting with Sunderland took place, United had joined their Wearside rivals at the bottom with the strugglers - slipping from top position to 17th in the table. Charlton had taken Southampton centre-forward Ian Baird on loan, and spent £110,000 on flame haired Gary Megson from Nottingham Forest to increase his options in midfield. Like Heard, though, the manager's new signing was not to be the answer either.

Over 36,000 were at Gallowgate for the Tyne-Wear contest and what a confrontation resulted for the holiday crowd. On a wet New Year's Day an explosive, but highly entertaining clash took place that featured a Peter Beardsley hat-trick. His first goal came after 15 minutes and it was a classic. A left wing corner was knocked out to Beardsley on the edge of the box. He steadied and hit a low drive that flashed past Chris Turner in the Sunderland goal. Half-time arrived with the scoreline still 1-0 and the second period exploded into action as Howard Gayle - once on loan at St James Park - felled Wes Saunders in the box....a penalty. The Sunderland striker did not agree, argued with the referee and was despatched to the dressing-room. Up stepped Beardsley to send Turner the wrong way with a perfect penalty.

Within a further ten minutes the incident was repeated. Wharton jinked his way into the box and this time, Daniel sent him crashing to the floor. Beardsley again faced Turner with the spot-kick, but this time his strike was saved. The pace of the game was fast and furious with tackles becoming fierce and reckless in the mood of a local derby. Sunderland got back into the game when West surprised everybody with a lovely chip, then Saunders saved a certain equaliser with a tackle on the line. But the Roker men had not seen the last of United's future England star Peter Beardsley. It was Megson who set up the quick-silver forward for his hat-trick. He took a pass, moved quickly into the penalty area and with ease drilled the ball past Turner for a third time. And that wasn't the end of the action. With United 3-1 ahead there was still time for more sensation as Saunders was sent sprawling, the victim of a bad tackle by Gary Bennett. The Sunderland defender was also given his marching orders to cap a rip-roaring meeting - a game that also saw six players booked.

One of Jack Charlton's tall target men, Tony Cunningham.

It was an eventful winter on Tyneside with a FA Cup meeting with Nottingham Forest keeping supporters' attention very much focused on the black'n'whites. United did the hard work at the City Ground earning a 1-1 draw, yet in the replay they saw Forest win 3-1 after extra-time. United should have been three up themselves inside the first five minutes of the match, but only managed a single goal by Waddle. It wasn't enough when United failed to last the pace after an hour. Peter Beardsley, hero against Sunderland, had a penalty saved by Hans Segars which proved costly. After equalising, Forest rallied in the extra 30 minutes of play, scored twice and left United a beaten side.

In an attempt to counter the rot, Charlton brought in two players during February and changed the team's pattern dramatically. Firstly he wanted George Reilly from Watford, but Graham Taylor was reluctant to part, so Jack spent £75,000 on Tony Cunningham from Manchester City. Charlton though, still persisted in trying to bring Reilly north and soon after clinched a deal at £200,000. At 6'4", he was the tallest player to wear the black'n'white shirt and at times looked an effective leader - Rambo headband and all. Joining 6'2" Tony Cunningham, who was born in Jamaica, United now possessed an awkward, if not brilliant, forward duo for defenders to handle.

Newcastle now looked to the aerial game more and more with this spearhead, while Waddle and Beardsley were forced to supply crosses and feed off the big strikers on the right and left flanks. The ball was more often than not in the air and Peter Beardsley noted in his biography, "it did not take me long to become disenchanted". He also observed that the manager's tactics were totally at odds with United's fans, "his ideas about football were alien to what the players had been used to and what the supporters wanted to see". United's skilful pair were never on the same wave-length as Charlton to Newcastle's eventual loss. Yet some players likened him to Big Jack. Kenny Wharton noted, "In ten years at St James Park he was by far the manager I admired the most".

Charlton's adjustments to United's pattern worked in part. The Magpies climbed the table, however speculation had increased that 23 year-old Waddle, picked by England in March against Eire, was not going to sign a new contract. He had become the first United player to play for England since Malcolm Macdonald a decade before. Waddle was a player the club very much wanted to keep, as the manager said, "He has been made a very good offer to stay on Tyneside", yet under Freedom of Contract, Waddle refused a new deal and signed for Spurs for £590,000.

Kenny Wharton who, in a long career at St. James Park, appeared at full-back and midfield.

As Waddle headed for White Hart Lane, a new talent emerged from the FA Youth Cup winning side - he was Paul Gascoigne, a chubby looking midfielder from Dunston. Within twelve months he had been tipped as an England star in the making. Kenny Wharton and David McCreery both had good seasons under Charlton's guidance. Wharton, only 5'8" and slightly built, always a terrier and a committed player, blossomed in Jack's team plan. At Newcastle since the days of Bill McGarry back in 1979, he played at full-back or in midfield and was now pushed more in attack, operating just behind the front two. Kenny was to complete ten years service at St James Park. David McCreery was another gutsy player, a fiery midfielder full of action and stamina. Appearing over 60 times for Northern Ireland, he became something of a terrace favourite, supporters appreciating his simple game of tackling and covering United's playmakers. McCreery played 269 times for the Magpies and was one of the hardiest individuals to wear the shirt.

David McCreery in action against Liverpool in 1985.

It had been a tragic ending to the football season - the Bradford fire, the Hysel disaster - but Newcastle finished their first year back in the First Division in 14th position after easing relegation worries with a victory over West Bromwich Albion and a point with Sunderland at Easter. By the end of the programme there was a desperate need for new faces, especially with Waddle venturing south. Experienced First Division players were required. The fans knew it, so did the media, alas Jack Charlton didn't respond. The summer of 1985 saw no-one arrive in spite of adequate cash resources and during a pre-season friendly with Sheffield United at Gallowgate, the Magpies gave a lack lustre performance and disgruntled supporters turned on Big Jack. The cry was, "Sack Charlton" and "Charlton Out". He was given a rough ride and as

£5 MILLION STAND

In the close-season of 1986, United demolished their 80 year-old West Stand and commenced work on an impressive looking £5 million structure that in many ways appeared more like a five-star hotel than a mere facility to house football supporters. Within its impressive walls were conference and function rooms, club offices, executive clubs, a restaurant, more private boxes and later a museum, as well as 6,607 seats. To be named the Milburn Stand as a lasting tribute to Wor Jackie, it was opened during the 1987/88 season and was to be the focal point of the modern Newcastle United.

Chairman Stan Seymour with new manager Willie McFaul who first joined the club back in 1966.

forthright as ever, sensationally quit immediately after the game. He said, "the crowd want rid of Jack Charlton, so now they are rid of Jack Charlton". Chairman Stan Seymour noted, "Newcastle United has suffered set-backs in the past, too many to think of perhaps. But life has to go on".

Coach Willie McFaul stepped into the breach as the club's sixth boss in only ten years. He was given the manager's role on a caretaker basis, but after a few weeks had been offered a contract and within twelve months had a three year deal secured. McFaul's influence did wonders for United's shattered confidence. He abandoned Charlton's long ball game and United reverted back to a fluent style of precise football. Peter Beardsley remarked, "He knew what the lads wanted and what the fans wanted - we started to play football again". Newcastle picked up eight points from their first four games. Liverpool were defeated 1-0 in the process, through what the manager declared as, "a terrific team performance". George Reilly grabbed the winner from close range, but it was Beardsley who was the man on song. He revelled in the new freedom and scored 19 goals that year, many as usual in a magical fashion. He was included in England's team, alongside his past colleague, Waddle.

McFaul strengthened the squad by paying £150,000 for Irish international winger Ian Stewart from QPR, although it was a deal set up before Charlton departed. He also brought Everton's England B defender John Bailey to Tyneside for £80,000, while another international, Manchester United's Welshman Alan Davies arrived too. Only Scouser, Bailey remotely showed qualities good enough for the black'n'white shirt and as it happened they were all overshadowed by local teenager Paul Gascoigne. The 18 year-old flourished in McFaul's team and against Liverpool he had matched the Reds' powerful midfield of Whelan, Nicol, Molby and Johnston. Gascoigne had problems at first - sent off for striking an opponent against Birmingham and later at QPR and Derby - but was quickly to reach the fringes of England's Under 21 side. He netted nine goals in his first full season.

Winger Paul Stephenson, from the Youth Cup side as well, made his Football League debut, while another youngster emerged strongly too and was called up for England's Under 21 squad. Neil McDonald had made his debut as a 16 year-old after just two Central League and three Junior games for the Magpies. The former Wallsend Boys' Club player, became another terrific prospect in midfield or full-back and won five caps at Under 21 level. McFaul changed centre-forwards before 1985 was out, allowing Reilly to depart and bringing in Hull City's Billy Whitehurst for £232,000. Chased by several clubs, the manager said of his new signing, "He's a big lad with a very big heart". Whitehurst though, like his predecessor, was never a First Division player and did not stay long on Tyneside either.

In the FA Cup, Second Division promotion contenders, Brighton shocked a large St James Park crowd for the second time in four years. They took the lead after only 50 seconds and United's Cup hopes vanished as seen all too often in this era. It was a similar story in the Milk Cup. After defeating Barnsley over two legs, Newcastle fell to Oxford United, another club to have inflicted a recent knock-out on the Tynesiders. In the league though, United continued in a confident way. During February and March they chalked up a fabulous run of five successive victories, taking care of Coventry, Forest, Arsenal and Ipswich, as well as a small degree of revenge over Oxford United. They finished the season in a creditable 11th place and, but for some out of character home lapses, might have ended in the top five.

McFaul's new centre-forward purchase, Billy Whitehurst.

The season ended on an extraordinary note when West Ham United thrashed the Magpies 8-1 at Upton Park. It was a remarkable game which saw three different players wear United's goalkeeper's jersey. Before the match, McFaul had 'keeper problems. Martin Thomas and, on-loan Dave McKeller, were both injured, yet with no-one else available Thomas turned out despite a painful shoulder.

TOP TEN STATUS

In 1987 the club's status in English football was highlighted, not by the Football League or Football Association, but by the new power in the game - the television companies. When bidding astronomical sums for the rights to screen the English game, they split football into three sections; a top five, a second five - together known as the 'Superleague' - and the rest. United came in the second category and received substantial cash benefits.
Top five; Liverpool, Everton, Manchester United, Arsenal, Tottenham Hotspur.
Second five; Aston Villa, Newcastle United, Nottingham Forest, Sheffield Wednesday, West Ham United.
Importantly all were First Division clubs. Newcastle had to retain their place to hold on to their 'Superleague' status.
This they could not do.

The inevitable happened as he damaged it after only a few minutes and Newcastle quickly found themselves 4-0 in arrears with the Welshman a passenger. Substitute Chris Hedworth then took over in goal and amazingly was hurt in a charge for the ball and had to leave the field too. United ended up with Peter Beardsley between the posts and eight goals flying into the net!

The 1986/87 season saw new sponsors installed at St James Park as Lancashire brewer, Greenalls, took over from Scottish & Newcastle after six years of support and McFaul saw his team have a dreadful start. They were given a lesson by Champions Liverpool on the opening day - a 2-0 home defeat - and went six matches without victory, collecting only two points out of a possible 18. Beardsley and Roeder were often absent injured or forced to play when unfit, and the manager had little in reserve. Youngsters Kevin Scott and Joe Allon were thrown into the fray and while both scored on their debut against Sheffield Wednesday, were dropped for the next game. Injuries continued to ravage McFaul's squad with Gascoigne a long term casualty and Newcastle were lodged at the bottom of the division. Yet on occasion United could still play some attractive football and against West Ham United they showed a vast television audience that they were in a false position.

Paul Goddard, an expert front runner who was also an instant hit with Newcastle's fans.

Scheduled to meet the Hammers in a live broadcast, the game looked to be heading for a flop for the watching millions. However, United appeared anything but relegation candidates as they roared to a 4-0 victory. England boss Bobby Robson, at the meeting, said, "Newcastle certainly did not look like a side at the bottom of the First Division". Peter Beardsley had one of his magical 90 minutes Geordie fans loved and the opposition hate. It was a performance of flair and ingenuity with new signing Andy Thomas scoring twice. At £100,000 from Oxford United, he looked a snip.

Centre-half Peter Jackson, quickly to become a terrace favourite.

The West Ham victory apart though, there was not too much to cheer United's faithful as 1986 was played out. Beardsley suffered from a niggling injury all season and this on top of mounting transfer speculation deadened his play. He scored only five times in the year. McFaul needed an experienced front man and during November 1986 spent a club record £415,000 on West Ham's 27 year-old striker Paul Goddard. It was a master stroke of business by the Irishman. Goddard's natural control and love of the ball played to feet, dovetailed beautifully with Beardsley. The former England player led United's line brilliantly and although he didn't find the net regularly for some time, made up for it with a late season burst scoring goals in each of seven successive games. Andy Thomas also settled to add to the striking choice, but after another personal goal feast fell into obscurity. The manager also strengthened the defence paying £250,000 for Bradford City's skipper Peter Jackson. At 6'1", the Yorkshireman quickly became a popular character in the centre of United's back four. However, after an exceptional beginning to the season, he also fell out of favour and returned to Valley Parade.

After being noted as relegation certainties at the end of February, a late rally saw Newcastle climb from the foot of the table. Paul Goddard, backed by a fit Gascoigne and Beardsley, inspired the recovery. They went nine games without defeat in an impressive run which began with a victory over fellow strugglers Aston Villa in the first week of March - United's first win in ten league games. They defeated Southampton 2-0 to move off the bottom, recorded two more victories, then an encouraging 1-0 success at Arsenal and took care of Manchester United 2-1 in front of 32,706. Facing Chelsea in a crucial contest at St James Park, Goddard and Gascoigne linked together in the 71st minute and United picked up the three points required for safety. Goddard's goal was his eighth in nine games - a lifesaving strike-rate for the Magpies and a club record.

For the first time in several years the Magpies at last progressed in one of the cup competitions. After being eliminated by Second Division Bradford City in the Littlewoods Cup, Newcastle disposed of Northampton Town in the Third Round of the FA Cup during January. Thomas and Goddard were on the mark to take the black'n'whites into a tie with Preston North End. Ex Magpie centre-half, John McGrath brought his Fourth Division side to Tyneside and before 30,495 United strolled into the last 16 for the first time in six years with a 2-0 victory. In Round Five, Newcastle faced Tottenham Hotspur - and Chris Waddle - at White Hart Lane, and a crowd of 38,033, including 10,000 from Tyneside, saw a close 90 minutes of action. United were knocked out by a dubious penalty decision converted by Clive Allen in the 21st minute.

Included in the side was Darren Jackson, a young Scot purchased from Meadowbank Thistle during October. He developed quickly appearing up front and in midfield, as well as later at full-back. He figured in McFaul's team plan for most of the season and was destined for a bright future. But a change in management saw the slightly built player leave for Dundee United at £200,000. His departure may have shown a healthy profit, but it was a big mistake as Jackson turned into a prolific scorer at Tannadice.

Signed from Meadowbank Thistle, Darren Jackson established himself in the side.

As the season drew to a close everyone connected with the club were resigned to the fact that Peter Beardsley, their biggest asset at the time, was on his way out of Gallowgate. Now a regular in the England squad, the ex Carlisle striker, turned his back on United like his former team-mate Chris Waddle and negotiated a deal with Liverpool in a British record £1.9 million move to Anfield. He departed with some bitterness after a wrangle over money and said, "I was upset and angry at Newcastle's attitude". The club and player could not agree on a new contract, although being offered a substantial deal, and when it became apparent the rift could not be healed, Newcastle cashed in before a League Tribunal fixed a fee. As with Waddle, Newcastle United's terms were exceptional, but the player saw the glitter of trophies at Anfield and was off.

United's directors and manager had to stem a growing wave of criticism aimed at the club following the sale of Waddle, and now Beardsley. McFaul needed an eye-catching deal and at the end of August 1987 splashed out £575,000 on a Brazilian international, Mirandinha. The 28 year-old centre-forward arrived on Tyneside after a 23 hour journey from South America along with three agents. The dusky Brazilian said, "All I want to do is score goals for Newcastle United". Mira, as he was to be nicknamed, had recently got onto the scoresheet for his country at Wembley against England, and landed on Tyneside with a reputation of having plundered almost 300 goals in South America. He was small, quick and possessed a stinging shot. McFaul was to say honestly, "Some may see it as my biggest gamble". A gamble it was - and one not to pay off, although the little Brazilian did show flashes of genius and for a while limited the flak targeted towards the club. McFaul also spent heavily on bringing Welsh international Glyn Hodges north from Wimbledon for £300,000, but the midfielder could never settle and only spent 86 days at St James Park before returning south to Watford.

Season 1987/88 was not only a difficult twelve months for the Magpies, but also for the game in general as football came into direct conflict with Prime Minister Margaret Thatcher. Hooliganism had escalated over the past decade, becoming an horrendous problem, and the government was determined to stamp it out, no matter how. Compulsory membership schemes, all-seater stadia and restrictions on away support were all discussed, and even threatened to be installed as law. There was much fury at the way soccer was being forced to change. Most top clubs - Newcastle United included - didn't support the various ideas and in time they were all scrapped, except the concept of all seater accommodation, this once the fateful Hillsborough disaster had taken its course.

Brazilian Mirandinha, he never adapted to an English relegation struggle.

With Gary Kelly, the son of a former Preston and Eire goalkeeper, installed as Newcastle's first choice 'keeper, United kicked off with two away fixtures at Tottenham and Sheffield Wednesday. After losing to Spurs, then winning in Yorkshire, McFaul's side had another dreadful start to the season. They won only twice more in the next 13 games and suffered another football lesson from Liverpool at Gallowgate. On top of this they were knocked out of the Littlewoods Cup by Wimbledon - a club to prove a thorn in the Magpies' flesh that season.

Irish youngster Michael O'Neill who ended up as United's top scorer in 1988/89.

On the bright side however, Mirandinha looked the part at times. He netted twice in a 2-2 draw at Old Trafford and by December had started to make the sceptics change their tune on continental players. The Brazilian netted in four games in a row as the black'n'whites steadily improved and climbed the table to 12th place. Paul Gascoigne led the charge. Newcastle saw off Manchester United, won 2-0 at Nottingham Forest on New Year's Day and then took care of Crystal Palace in the FA Cup. Another good victory - 2-0 over Spurs, with Gazza striking twice - saw the Magpies to a Fourth Round tie with Swindon Town at St James Park. Almost 29,000 witnessed United romp home by 5-0 and on this form there was even talk of a run all the way to Wembley. Gascoigne again scored two goals and controlled the show. Irish youngster Michael O'Neill also impressed in that FA Cup victory. Brought over from Coleraine, one of McFaul's former clubs, the part-timer quickly progressed to his country's forward line and went on to appear on ten occasions at international level whilst at St James Park.

With home advantage, Newcastle then met up once more with Wimbledon, a side against which United just could not play. The Londoners' tough methods and high ball game completely spoiled McFaul's smooth running style of football. With a much publicised contest between Vinny Jones and Paul Gascoigne taking place as a side-show, the Dons won 3-1 and dispelled any dreams of a Wembley visit. United played the new First Division force of Wimbledon four times that year and picked up a solitary 0-0 draw.

A teenage Paul Gascoigne driving forward and leaving a defender in his wake.

From that setback though, Newcastle stormed up the Division One table to finish in 8th position and on the way O'Neill blossomed scoring an incredible eight goals in five successive fixtures, including a hat-trick against Luton Town. He ended as the season's top scorer and the tricky forward was even dubbed, "the new George Best". But instead of developing further, the Irishman dramatically faded from the scene. Struck by illness, injury and loss of sparkle, he was to be a one season wonder and joined Darren Jackson at Dundee United.

Hearts striker John Robertson moved from Edinburgh in a new record signing. McFaul paid out £750,000 before the end of the season for the player who had a marvellous scoring record in Scotland - 147 goals at Tynecastle, including 31 in the Premier Division that year. Small and alert, Robertson had an unhappy and brief stay on Tyneside, but was to eventually reach the Scotland side and continue his goals feast back with Hearts - to United's loss. Full-backs John Cornwell and Brian Tinnion were also regular squad players that year. Cornwell was purchased from McFaul's former colleague, Frank Clark at Orient for £50,000, while Tinnion, locally born, had progressed from the junior ranks. He graduated to England's Under 21 squad, but unluckily had to withdraw from a tour of Brazil due to injury.

For the third time in almost as many years the season ended on a sour note with the Magpies losing their most prized asset. Protracted negotiations with Paul Gascoigne had started to take place as early as January in an attempt to conclude a long term contract with the youngster who had been tipped as a cert for an England place. The same pattern had developed for first Waddle, and then Beardsley. Newcastle supporters feared the worst. Another star was to move on.

Gascoigne rejected United's five year £1 million deal - itself a huge package and before Freedom of Contract came into force the Magpies decided to release him, although Gordon McKeag noted, "We desperately wanted him to stay". Tottenham Hotspur made an approach for the 21 year-old and during the summer he deserted the black'n'whites for £2.3 million, another British record fee. Neil McDonald followed Gascoigne from his native Tyneside - he joined Everton in a £525,000 transfer.

With Gascoigne's departure coming quickly on the heels of the loss of United's two other big names, fans became, not surprisingly, more and more frustrated. Losing all three players - and all were of special international quality - was a devastating blow. Political in-fighting commenced behind the scenes with dissatisfied shareholders once again having their say. This time though, they did more than become a nuisance as they mounted a full scale hostile takeover.

Chairman Stan Seymour had moved aside in June 1988, allowing Gordon McKeag to take control. The son of past director Alderman McKeag and a Gosforth solicitor, he was to move unwittingly into a cauldron of trouble. Appointed to the board in November 1972, McKeag had been raised with Newcastle United in his blood through his father's great enthusiasm for the Magpies. Highly respected in football's inner circle, he became a member of the Football League Management Committee and was just pipped as President of the League. McKeag was also appointed to the Football Association's Executive Committee and held a substantial say in the corridors of power.

It was left to McKeag to lead a traumatic fight against the takeover, mounted by a powerful consortium led by property developer millionaire, John Hall and backed by shareholder Malcolm Dix together with the old NSA. Formed into the Magpie Group, their aims were to rid United of the traditional closed-shop ownership and to fully democratise the club to the wider public. They were supported by several Tyneside personalities and businessmen, as well as by the region's major local newspaper, The Evening Chronicle, whose substantial media power gave them unparalleled coverage. With considerable financial clout, the Magpie Group started an aggressive campaign to purchase the limited shares in the club and a savage attack on United's management at all levels. Seemingly everyone got in on the act of club-bashing. Ex players had their say, Terry McDermott noting that United have, "never been in such a shambles as they are now". Kevin Keegan remarked, "This club should be buying players like Gascoigne and Beardsley, not selling them". McKeag received hate-mail and obscene and threatening phone calls, yet, to his credit, stood up to it all.

Hall started his bid for power at St James Park by offering £500 for each 50p share, then rapidly increased the amount to £1,000. Money appeared no object as the share value rose sensationally as one side and the other bartered for control of the company's holding. At one stage values had escalated to a figure of £7,000 a share! A Dutch Auction resulted and in many instances nothing short of madness prevailed. Hall and Dix managed to persuade McKeag's colleagues in the boardroom - and major shareholders - George Dickson and Ron McKenzie, to sell out for substantial six figure amounts. Then they pulled in the shares of ex Chairman Lord Westwood. But McKeag was a dogged and shrewd fighter. A man of high integrity and devoted to Newcastle United's cause, he brought in wealthy businessmen Peter Mallinger and Bob Young to the boardroom and later elevated General Manager, Russell Cushing to director. United also won a High Court action over voting rights of a portion of defector, Dickson's shares. It was a contest that captivated the north east for months and months.

By the end of the confrontation as 1990 opened - and more than £2 million later - Hall still hadn't acquired sufficient shareholding to take control of the club and oust McKeag. With around 40% equity, he was though, a powerful adversary and a period of stalemate followed. The Chairman observed that the power struggle, "was very damaging for the club". And without doubt it had affected the team as well. United's fans, whipped up by the debate, became highly critical and, as compared to the past, less generous and supportive of the players on the field. In fact they were on occasion downright hostile - and at a time when the side needed a strong positive backing. Fringe groups sprouted up on the back of the Magpie Group and many home matches became more like a left-wing political rally than a football match. Local Metro Radio disc jockey, Alan Robson, even launched a record supporting the rebels - entitled of course, "Sack The Board!" - the chant that had replaced the rousing roars of support in the past. The furore that went on in the background reached both the players and manager. The playing staff were concerned about their own position if major changes occurred in the boardroom. Several new signings noted privately that they would never have agreed to join the Magpies had they known the extent of political fury at St James Park.

All friends and smiling faces. The players in the share battle that rocked the club. Left John Hall (later Sir John), Malcolm Dix (centre) and United Chairman, Gordon McKeag.

With all this corporate brawling starting in the background, Willie McFaul had to buy, and buy well, to not only replace Gascoigne, but also to try to halt mounting criticism from supporters. With a safe full of cash, the manager went on a massive multi-million spending spree in the summer of 1988. Following the purchase of Robertson, he created not only a new club record, but also a British record fee for a goalkeeper when 29 year-old Dave Beasant arrived from FA Cup winners Wimbledon for £850,000. The Londoner had just made headlines by saving a penalty at Wembley and then lifting the FA Cup as skipper. He had been an important part of the Dons rise to the top during the eighties. Beasant, who stood 6'4", went on to appear for the England B side and eventually won a full cap.

McFaul then paid the same amount for Beasant's Plough Lane colleague, centre-half Andy Thorn, who had played five times for England's Under 21 team during the previous season. Scot John Hendrie cost £500,000 from Bradford City with a reputation as a matchwinning winger. Fellow north countryman, Archie Gourlay, from Morton and Lee Payne from non-league Barnet, were two expensive reserves. They both flopped, along with another signing, Albert Craig, who arrived via

RAPID OWN-GOAL

During October 1984, Ipswich Town were visitors to St James Park and within 20 seconds of the game starting, had scored a bizarre own-goal! Neil McDonald took a Waddle flick and crossed a long ball aimed for Peter Beardsley. The ball fell for Scottish international full-back George Burley and he blasted the ball past his own 'keeper Paul Cooper to give United a 1-0 lead. It was perhaps the quickest own-goal ever recorded in football.

Record purchase at £850,000, goalkeeper Dave Beasant. He was one of several signings to wear United's colours for only a brief period.

Dumbarton. It was almost £300,000 of cash wasted.

The manager's new look Magpies embarked on the 1988/89 season in a mood of renewed optimism. However, from the earliest games it became evident that the abundance of new faces were finding it difficult to blend together, in spite of lots of quality on paper. McFaul's £4 million team made their debut at Goodison Park and crashed 4-0 in a horrifying display. Indeed it took only 34 seconds for Everton to find the net! For the third season in a row, Newcastle started badly, but unlike previous campaigns they were not to recover. United didn't register their first victory of the season until the sixth fixture, yet that was one of the black'n'whites' best performances in a decade. United travelled to Anfield and claimed full points for the first time since November 1950 with a 2-1 triumph. Then 19th in the table, no-one gave the Tynesiders a hope against League Champions, Liverpool, but a lovely goal from John Hendrie - a low and accurate drive - and a Mirandinha penalty, after the winger had caused trouble again, gave United the points.

However, it was only a brief respite. They scored in only one of the following nine matches and were locked at the bottom of the table with West Ham, Middlesbrough, Aston Villa and Luton Town. As autumn drew near, United were still struggling in 19th position, had been eliminated by then Third Division Sheffield United in the Littlewoods Cup, and Newcastle's board now had a double headache - the mounting takeover battle as well as a managerial and team crisis. Decisive action was taken when Willie McFaul was sacked in October, but then

Centre-half Andy Thorn who arrived from Wimbledon after appearing for England's Under-21 side.

John Hendrie was added to the forward line in a big deal from Bradford City.

United's beleaguered hierarchy had a major problem trying to find a new boss - an appointment that took almost two months to fill. They tried for Arthur Cox, David Hay and Howard Kendall, with the Tynesider and former Everton favourite being the preferred choice. But all turned down the job. With youth coach Colin Suggett being handed temporary control of team affairs in a partnership with Mick Martin, United simply had to find a new boss quickly. He came in the shape of Yorkshireman Jim Smith of Queen's Park Rangers, who accepted the post in December. United had tried to land the same manager back in 1984 and he possessed a fine track record. An enthusiastic lower division wing-half during his playing career with prominently Aldershot, Halifax Town and Lincoln City, Smith had tasted promotion success in charge of Colchester United, Birmingham City and Blackburn Rovers. He moved to Oxford United in 1982 and proceeded to build a first class set-up at the Manor Ground with successive promotion campaigns and frequent cup giant-killing feats - including victory over Newcastle. And at Loftus Road he reached Wembley in the Milk Cup.

48 years-old, Jim Smith's reign was to be similar in many ways to that of Bill McGarry's a decade before. He arrived as United were destined for the Second Division and couldn't put a stop to the slide. Then he embarked on a spending spree bringing many experienced players north, just failed

to get promotion and then ended leaving in failure. Smith was to say shortly after arriving, "The job is bigger and harder than I ever anticipated". He later added, "If I had known in advance of the two years of heartache I faced, I would not have taken it".

Smith immediately swung into action. To generate cash to build his own team, out went big names - Beasant(Chelsea), Robertson(Hearts) and later Thorn(Crystal Palace), Mirandinha(Palmeiras) and Hendrie(Leeds). In came full-backs, former England defender Kenny Sansom and ex Manchester City star, Ray Ranson, while from his old haunt at Loftus Road, Kevin Brock arrived to bolster the midfield for £300,000. Brock had followed his manager from Oxford to London and had reached the England B side. Cultured on the ball, he was to become United's midfield playmaker over the next few years. Former Manchester United schemer, Liam O'Brien had been installed by caretaker boss Suggett and Robbie McDonald had been purchased from Holland, only to have a harrowing time in the striker's role at St James Park.

More new faces joined the staff in the coming weeks too. Frans Pingel and Bjorn Kristensen crossed the North Sea from Denmark, striker or midfield man Gary Brazil from Preston North End, and full-back Paul Sweeney headed over the border from Raith Rovers, all for an aggregate sum of nearly £800,000. There were to be more comings and goings too - a remarkable piece of transfer dealing. In a short space of time Smith wheeled and dealed his way through more than 40 players.

To have a short stay at Gallowgate, former England full-back Kenny Sansom.

However, the manager's transfer plunge was all too late. He couldn't stop the slide. Smith noted in his biography, "I got caught up in the tension at the club and possibly over reacted in the transfer market". He tried to fashion a new team in a few months, a task that needed two or three years. A brief period of hope occurred in March when the inconsistent Mirandinha hit a patch of goalscoring form and United defeated Everton and Norwich City, but then the Magpies didn't win another game, losing seven out of the nine fixtures remaining. The low point came with a 4-0 defeat by Wimbledon at tiny Plough Lane before a paltry 5,206. It was astonishing to consider that lowly crowd at a First Division match and the once proud and mighty Newcastle United humbled by a club only recently fit for Isthmian and Southern League soccer. Yet the Dons pulverised a feeble looking United side.

Manager Jim Smith just missed taking The Magpies back into the First Division.

Newcastle finished propping up the First Division with a mere 31 points and only three wins at St James Park in the entire season - the worst in the club's history. United had scored a miserable 32 goals with only 19 at Gallowgate. They had gone down without a fight and used no fewer than 35 different players - more than any other club in the four divisions.

Midfielder Kevin Brock followed from Loftus Road.

Some reckoned that an FA Cup Third Round marathon with Watford had much to do with Newcastle's inability to climb from the bottom. They were locked into a record breaking tie with the Vicarage Road club that lasted four games and 450 minutes of football - longer than United's epic with Derby County back in 1924. At St James Park, Watford held the Tynesiders and took Newcastle south after a 0-0 draw. In the replay, United fell behind after only two minutes and without even touching the ball, but then the Magpies dominated the rest of the half and Kevin Brock netted a deserved equaliser. Mirandinha drilled home a penalty before another spot-kick gave Watford a lifeline.

In the second replay over 28,000 returned to Gallowgate, but witnessed their second goal-less encounter and it was all back to Vicarage Road two days later for the deciding match. The game went into extra-time for the third occasion and as a fifth meeting looked likely Watford gained the advantage with a lucky

FOREIGN IMPORTS

Following on from the successful purchase of George and Ted Robledo, together with Benny Arentoft, United fielded several players from overseas countries, especially so in the eighties. To arrive were Mirandinha(Brazil), Kristensen(Denmark), Pingel(Denmark), Koenen(Holland) and Srnicek(Czechoslovakia). Since the 1960s, United also offered trials to a considerable number of foreign imports, and most were internationals. Few though were to remain at St James Park for one reason or another. Included were;
Teoman Arika (Turkey), Ray Xuereb (Malta),
Victor Nogueira (Portugal),
George Christouplos (Australia),
Leo Houtsanan (Finland), Shalom Tikva (Israel),
Chris Zoricich (New Zealand),
Jan Eriksson (Sweden),
Thomas Hubcheck (Germany),
Ove Hansen (Denmark), John Doyle (USA).

Scottish international Mark McGhee who, in his second spell at the club, formed such a fruitful partnership with Mick Quinn.

break. Glenn Roeder, who had been outstanding in each match, deflected a harmless looking shot and totally wrong-footed Tommy Wright in United's goal to give the Hornets victory. Wright, from Ireland, had taken over from Beasant and Kelly as the Magpies' 'keeper and went on to wear his country's jersey at full international level.

Despite a new period in the Second Division, season 1989/90 was to be an action packed year. It opened with a bang and closed with a bang as Smith was determined to make a quick return to Division One at the first attempt. With the experienced Bobby Saxton installed as his assistant, Smith spent a frenzied summer remodelling his team in a period of continued activity in the transfer market. Portsmouth centre-forward Mick Quinn and Celtic's veteran striker Mark McGhee were paired up front and proceeded to become the Football League's most feared partnership. Unknown full-back Mark Stimson cost £150,000 from Spurs and another £75,000 was paid to Falkirk for youngster John Gallacher. Midfielder Kevin Dillon returned to his native north-east on a free transfer, also from Portsmouth, while play-anywhere defender Darren Bradshaw came from York City. Goalkeeper John Burridge, at well over 30 years of age, signed from Southampton for a small fee, and winger Wayne Fereday joined the ranks from Smith's former club Queen's Park Rangers. With a complete change in staff, the manager made the comment, "It has been the craziest year of my life". All McFaul's expensive signings had by now been discarded. With such an altered line-up most supporters were optimistic yet, as ever with the Magpies' unpredictable fortunes, still knew that anything could happen.

For Mark McGhee his return to St James Park was a chance to show Tyneside that he had come a long way since his younger days at the club under Bill McGarry. Having a fine track record with Aberdeen, SV Hamburg and Celtic, McGhee had won several domestic and European honours as well as playing for Scotland since leaving Tyneside. At 32 years-old, the Scot showed exquisite close control and became an ideal partner for Quinn, who developed into a goalpoacher as good as any before him in a black'n'white shirt.

The opening day of the season brought another big spending club - Leeds United - to St James Park. Newcastle fielded five debutants and Mick Quinn instantly became a terrace hero by striking home four goals as Newcastle won a rousing tussle by 5-2. John Gallacher was the other new face to impress. Signed as a youngster who hopefully would develop in the coming years, the Scot immediately showed he possessed matchwinning talents on the flank and was worth a place in the side.

Quinn continued to plunder the Second Division defences as United moved up into 3rd position. Then his partner McGhee got in on the act with eight goals in only ten games, including a strike that helped eliminate Reading in the Littlewoods Cup. It was a prolific attack with the Scots more finite skills blending perfectly with Quinn's poaching instincts. However, West Bromwich Albion managed to prevent the pair from scoring in the Third Round of the Littlewoods Cup on Tyneside. A single goal by Chris Whyte was enough to knock United out - only for the Magpies to visit the Hawthorns a week later and promptly thrash Albion 5-1 in a Second Division game. Their place in the front-runners was reinforced following a 2-0 victory over rivals, and leaders, Sheffield United at St James Park. It was United's best performance

John Gallacher arrived on Tyneside and quickly became a threat up front.

Newcastle's new skipper, Celtic and Scotland favourite, Roy Aitken.

of the season in front of a crowd of 27,170. Newcastle matched the Tykes' aggressive tactics, but also displayed sweet moments which ripped apart the visitors. Mick Quinn said, "We played some great stuff, and they had no answer to it". Gallacher and Quinn netted the goals that prompted many United fans to boast - dangerously - that they were certainties for promotion.

December was a bad month for the black'n'whites, they didn't win a game and started the New Year with another defeat - a ruthless 4-1 home reverse by Wolves, courtesy of England striker Steve Bull. He netted all four goals, including a hat-trick in the space of only nine minutes at the start of the second half, to leave Newcastle demoralised. They had slipped dramatically in the promotion race - now down to 7th in the table. Manager Jim Smith had to instil confidence again. He did so by dipping into the bank account once more and Scotland's World Cup captain, Roy Aitken became a headline addition from Celtic. Aitken, one of several in the side past 30 years of age, cost £500,000 and was immediately appointed skipper. At Parkhead all his career, he had won no fewer than six Scottish Championship and five Scottish Cup medals in over 600 games for Celtic. And he was picked over 50 times for his country. His experience and driving enthusiasm from midfield or the back, returned Newcastle to the promotion race. They remained unbeaten for ten games with Aitken the inspiration.

The Magpies' new captain made his first appearance against Leicester City at St James Park and what a debut awaited the rugged Scot. The match opened sensationally with Aitken surging forward to send Fereday clear and McGhee headed in a cross after only five minutes. Leicester though, hit back with United's sloppy defence giving Wright a chance to equalise. Then, in an end-to-end encounter, City 'keeper Hodge pulled down Dillon in the box and went on to save John Anderson's spot-kick. It was a costly miss as the visitors went 2-1 in front when Burridge missed a centre and Walsh pounced from close range, but the Magpies fought back to level at 2-2 just on half-time. Stimson crossed and Quinn made space and found the net with a rocket finish.

The second period was just as pulsating. Gary McAllister rifled in a superb goal for City then set up Campbell to make it 4-2 and it looked as though Roy Aitken's initial taste of English football was to be an occasion to forget. However, the dramatic climax to this thrilling match was still to come. First, substitute John Gallacher latched onto a McGhee flick after a delightful move and United had pulled the score back to 4-3 with ten minutes remaining. Aitken, an influence throughout, led Newcastle forward for the equaliser. Brock floated in a corner, O'Brien flicked the ball on and Quinn was in the right place to send the ball into the net. Leicester were stunned, yet United were not finished. They stormed into attack in the dying minutes. McGhee received the ball on the edge of the box and with magical close control, pivoted to fire home an 88th minute winner into the corner of the City goal. Three goals in 13 minutes. United had won 5-4 and Aitken punched the air in jubilation.

OWN-GOAL DOUBLE

Centre-half Peter Jackson remarkably netted two own-goals in the match with Manchester United in 1986/87 - one in each half. After only four minutes he headed past a bemused Martin Thomas when trying to clear the bar, then a Whiteside shot was helped on its way into the net by the unhappy Jackson. United crashed 4-1 at Old Trafford.

Scotland's captain certainly gave the side an added boost, and in time for an FA Cup challenge too. After taking care of Hull City at Boothferry Road the Tynesiders met Reading - the team United had already disposed of in the Littlewoods Cup. Newcastle had to travel again in Round Four and roared into the lead at Elm Park when Quinn headed into the net, however their advantage lasted only two minutes when the home side equalised. McGhee then made it 2-1, but Trevor Senior put Reading on equal terms again. Mark McGhee was on the target for a second time in the 71st minute, a goal that appeared to have sealed the tie. Newcastle then committed suicide when a dreadful Gallacher backpass in injury time landed straight at the feet of Michael Gilkes. He beat the stranded Burridge and made the final score 3-3.

A gate of 26,658 was recorded for the replay and they saw United saunter into the Fifth Round with a convincing 4-1 victory. McGhee and Quinn were once more on the scoresheet, assisted by young David Robinson, a reserve striker from Walkergate. That triumph took Newcastle into a prestige battle

1986 WORLD CUP

Newcastle United Football Club was well represented one way or another in the 1986 World Cup held in Mexico. England, who reached the quarter-finals, included Peter Beardsley in their line-up as well as the recently departed Chris Waddle. Northern Ireland fielded two Magpie players in Ian Stewart and David McCreery. Future St James Park star, Kenny Sansom was also in England's team, while Roy Aitken appeared for Scotland. Additionally England's party possessed three past Newcastle supporter's in their ranks - boss Bobby Robson, skipper Bryan Robson and midfielder Trevor Steven!

with Manchester United on Tyneside - a tie elevated to national and overseas coverage by live television. And the vast audience certainly received entertainment value as a thrilling game took place which produced five goals and some of the most remarkable action of the season. A debatable strike by Mark Robins put the visitors in front following a first-half corner, although Ranson had appeared to clear off the line. The match remained that way until Mark McGhee slotted home an equalising penalty in the 51st minute after another contentious refereeing decision. Danny Wallace though, restored Manchester United's lead on the hour before Newcastle immediately hit back. Kevin Scott rose to a corner and headed powerfully past Jim Leighton. Incredibly it was the third goal that ended in fruitless debate with the referee - the 'keeper having been impeded by Quinn. United's goal was all to no avail when Brian McClair completed a stunning move to clinch the game for the Reds by 3-2. Nearly 32,000 saw that tie.

Back to Second Division action and United recovered to regain 3rd position behind Leeds United and Sheffield United. Smith tried to give his side another boost by bringing Hull City's Geordie midfielder Billy Askew back home for £150,000, but that deal was not to be a success. It didn't matter though, as United ran up six straight wins. In an important home meeting with Swindon Town - also in the hunt for a First Division place - Newcastle dropped vital points in a 0-0 draw with a fast moving, attractive Robins outfit managed by Ossie Ardiles. Swindon's 'keeper Fraser Digby saved brilliantly from Benny Kristensen to foil United in the second half - it was a turning point in United's season. The points lost could well have made all the difference between returning to the First Division, or not. At the time Leeds had only a two point advantage, while the Blades were ahead by one. Had Newcastle won, they would have gone top of the table and the season may have ended all so differently with United out in front.

On the final day of the season, United travelled to Middlesbrough with promotion still in reach, but only if Leeds or Sheffield United lost. A victory was needed to stand any chance of claiming one of the two automatic promotion slots, but their Tees-side rivals thrashed Newcastle 4-1 after an inept display by the Magpies. A restricted crowd of 18,484 were at Ayresome Park, while another 14,000 saw the game transmitted to Gallowgate on a giant screen - the first such relay at St James Park. As it turned out, Yorkshire clubs Leeds and Sheffield United both won emphatically and marched into the First Division in style. United finished in 3rd place - six points clear of 4th placed Swindon Town, but missed automatic promotion. Instead, Newcastle had to compete in the Football League's recent innovation of a Play-off contest for a final promotion spot - something of a blast from the past, and a similar end of season tournament to the Test Matches which were last competed for over 90 years ago.

Bitter disappointment and frustration were in store for the club and supporters. United faced a two-legged derby clash - with Sunderland of all teams - with the prize a one-off game at Wembley for a place in Division One. It was the biggest Tyne-Wear derby since the glorious Edwardian era, and after the season's other two meetings had ended all level, the contest was eagerly, if nervously, awaited by both camps. Newcastle earned a 0-0 draw at Roker Park before 26,641 in the first leg, just what was needed. And a furious contest it was. In an ill tempered clash, referee Vic Callow booked six players and sent-off one in a dramatic climax to the

A crucial penalty save by John Burridge in the first leg of the Play-off with Sunderland. It gave United the advantage, alas to be wasted in the return game.

game. In the dying seconds of injury time, Mark Stimson was harshly adjudged to have brought down the bustling Gabbiadini in the box - a penalty. But after arguments had raged, John Burridge flung himself to stop Hardyman's drive and then was himself kicked by the Sunderland player who was dismissed amidst uproar.

On May 16th a near capacity 32,216 turned up at Gallowgate to see - as most expected - United march into a Wembley final. Sunderland had other ideas as veteran Eric Gates fired the Wearsiders into an early lead and Gabbiadini wrapped the game up with a second. Newcastle never got going, although had McGhee's early shot found the net instead of the woodwork, a different outcome may well have been recorded. After a gruelling 48 match programme United were leap-frogged by a side six points worse off and who finished three places below the Magpies in the final analysis - and by Sunderland, the old enemy - a cruel way to end the season. It was all too much for many ardent Geordie fans. A mini pitch invasion halted the game for nearly 20 minutes as teenage supporters showed their disgust.

In the end, perhaps the long season dragged United down at the last hurdle. Crucially, Quinn and McGhee looked tired as May began. The deadly finishing that had ravaged 61 goals in all competitions had withered. The price of failure was to be high. First Division football had been an absolute must for Newcastle United. Against Sunderland record receipts of £157,153 were taken and revenue of that order was guaranteed with better quality opposition in Division One. United now had to face another season of mediocre visitors and with it lower crowds and less cash income. With that defeat at the hands of Sunderland, they said goodbye to well over £1 million extra revenue.

Newcastle also paid for a series of inexplicable lapses which had thrown several goals away in the final moments of fixtures - and in the process dropped almost a dozen points. They drew 14 games, when at least four or five of those should have been clear victories. United could have walked away with the title had their attitude been more professional in defence. That apart, centre-half Kevin Scott emerged strongly that season. From Easington, the 6'2" defender had joined the staff in December 1984 and had played alongside Paul Gascoigne in the junior's FA Youth Cup victory a year later. Positive, and proud to wear the black'n'white shirt, he was shortly to lead the club into their Centenary Year as captain.

Although Newcastle United missed promotion by a whisker and the Sunderland debacle left a bitter taste, the fortunes of the club were looking up. Jim Smith appeared to have gathered a good squad of players while boardroom politics had by now taken an turn for the better. Following a period of stalemate between the warring factions, Gordon McKeag and John Hall made peace. In April 1990 a seat on the board was offered to the Tyneside entrepreneur, while at the same time an agreement to democratise the club was made. A public Share Issue was to be drawn up soon as possible. The Second Revolution was almost in place. Yet, in true United tradition, everything was again turned upside-down within twelve months.

Tempers rise in the United v Sunderland Play-off at Roker Park. The referee steps in between Gordon Armstrong, Mark McGhee and Roy Aitken.

Centenary Profile 29

A Genius with the Ball

"Peter Beardsley has the potential to become the greatest player in English football for the next decade"

Kevin Keegan, 1990

KEVIN KEEGAN TOOK A THROW-IN TO HIS striking partner Peter Beardsley. A first time lay-off back for Keegan who hit a precision return pass into the box. Beardsley anticipated the move and skipped into the danger area to collect the ball. A jink one way, a feint the other and he went past a defender and the out-rushing 'keeper. Another defender arrived with a tackle, another dummy sent him diving the wrong way and the Newcastle striker tapped the ball over the line. It was a goal which had quality stamped all over it and typified Peter Beardsley's art at finding the net with brilliant efforts, many of them in spectacular fashion which had fans roaring with delight.

That gem was against Portsmouth in February 1984 as United were moving into overdrive for a promotion push. One of the major reasons for the club's success that year was the acquisition of Beardsley during the previous September. Manager Arthur Cox sold centre-forward Imre Varadi and set up Beardsley as his replacement. 5'8" tall, the quick and skilful forward gave United an added dimension. Teaming up with Keegan, the duo made a dynamic pairing. Beardsley possessed all the ball skills to dovetail the intelligent play of Keegan and he revelled next to the former England captain. First time passing, quick one-twos, Beardsley's trickery complimented Keegan's vision and, when added to the talent of Chris Waddle on the flank, Newcastle strikeforce was perhaps the best to wear a black'n'white shirt since the days of Milburn, Robledo and Mitchell.

Peter Beardsley had in fact been at Gallowgate several years before he joined the staff for a £120,000 fee in September 1983. Born on Tyneside, in Longbenton, he was one of Wallsend Boys' Club's many young finds and he had had a week's trial with United's junior side, but Bill McGarry hesitated and it took many a mile before Beardsley returned to his home-town club. He had been rejected by Gillingham, Cambridge United and Burnley, however while Peter was at St James Park as just another budding kid, Carlisle United manager, ex Magpie skipper, Bob Moncur nipped in and took him to Third Division Brunton Park. Moncur was quickly hooked by the Tynesider's exciting potential and after signing for the Cumbrians in 1979 Peter quickly became a favourite.

He was lured to Canada two years later by Johnny Giles, then in charge of Vancouver Whitecaps. Beardsley joined a host of ex Football League players in America for a £275,000 fee and played alongside the likes of Peter Lorimer, Dave Thomas and Terry Yorath. In the giant stadiums and on the plastic grass, Beardsley was a hit, at a time when the North American Soccer League boomed. Playing all the year round - Peter returned to Carlisle out of season - English clubs noted his exciting displays and Manchester United offered the Geordie the chance to return to the Football League in September 1982. He was at Old Trafford on an extensive loan-come-trial for almost six months, and although he managed only a single game - a Milk Cup tie against Bournemouth, and that only 80 minutes - boss Ron Atkinson wanted to take him on, but as skipper Bryan Robson noted, "We couldn't afford to sign him". Manchester United's loss was Newcastle's gain and within six months Arthur Cox had pushed ahead with the deal that brought Beardsley full circle back to his native Tyneside.

United's boss had been linked with the quicksilver striker as early as February 1981 and he was determined to follow up his interest. Cox knew, without doubt, that Beardsley was something special. He was right of course and Peter went on to

Peter Beardsley

BEARDSLEY'S PLAYING RECORD

	League		FA Cup		FL Cup		Total	
	App	Gls	App	Gls	App	Gls	App	Gls
1983-84	34/1	20	1	0	2	0	37/1	20
1984-85	38	17	2	0	4	0	44	17
1985-86	42	19	1	0	2	0	45	19
1986-87	32	5	2	0	2	0	36	5
	146/1	**61**	**6**	**0**	**10**	**0**	**162/1**	**61**

score 20 times in United's promotion success - the majority of his strikes, goals of sheer genius. But with Cox departing and Jack Charlton installed as boss, Beardsley found his football philosophy was never on the same channel as Big Jack's. Yet Peter still quickly imposed his silky style on the First Division and followed Chris Waddle into the England side, making his debut against Egypt late in January 1986 when he came on as substitute and immediately set up a goal.

That was the start of a fine career in an England shirt. He began the next international in Israel then clinched a place in the forthcoming World Cup by buzzing in a fixture with the USSR. He burst into the limelight as Gary Lineker's partner and England did well during the Mexico World Cup. He went on to appear 49 times for his country, 15 as a United player - the most appearances by any Newcastle man. He also skippered England on one occasion, in another match against Israel in Tel Aviv.

By the time the 1986/87 season was half completed he was lured from Tyneside by the considerable pull of Anfield and in the close-season Liverpool paid a British record fee of £1.9 million for his skills. Qualities that prompted Kevin Keegan to say, "Peter Beardsley has the potential to become the greatest player in English football in the next decade".

Beardsley left in search of trophies and he duly got them - a League Championship medal in 1987/88 and 1989/90, as well as both FA Cup runners-up and winners' medals together with a League Cup final appearance.

Although still a matchwinner at Anfield, he found himself on the sidelines on several occasions and following Kenny Dalglish's resignation, the arrival of Graeme Souness and the subsequent purchase of Dean Saunders, 30 year-old Beardsley was on his way. He joined neighbours Everton during August 1991 in a £1 million deal and proceeded to become - as he had done at all his clubs - another instant hit at Goodison Park.

Beardsley's stay at Gallowgate - like both Waddle's and Gascoigne's - was all too short, only four years. His talents should have graced the turf for twice that period. Supporters can only imagine what may have been achieved if all three stars could have performed together over a sustained period.

Centenary Profile 30

The Second Clown Prince

"The most exciting British talent since George Best"

Trevor Francis

CHRIS WADDLE AND PAUL GASCOIGNE BOTH hailed from working class estates in Gateshead and while Waddle may have made the big time when he moved from Tyneside, it was nothing compared to the impression Paul Gascoigne made on the football scene - and at the same time wider society too. The lad from the other side of Gateshead town to Waddle, joined him at Tottenham and within weeks had become the country's biggest personality.

Gazzamania had arrived. His face was everywhere; on the back pages of every newspaper, on the inside pages and often on the front page too; in magazines from Match Weekly to Radio Times. He was on television advertising products, notably taking over the Brut role from Henry Cooper, appearing with Wogan and even cutting a re-make of Fog on the Tyne with Lindisfarne. He became BBC's Sports Personality of the Year in 1990 and earned himself a place in Madame Tussards. There were Gascoigne pens, Gascoigne games and even Gascoigne dolls! In such a short space of time, after arriving in London's metropolis, he became the mass media's hottest property.

Everyone on Tyneside admired his success, as they did Waddle's, indeed were proud he was a Geordie. But there was a deep anger that he had to leave St James Park to find wider super-stardom. Gascoigne was Newcastle United's biggest ever discovery. Nurtured from a 16 year-old apprentice, he developed his precocious talent and showbiz personality so quickly that he out paced the gradual improvement in the club's own resurgence.

Dunston born, Gascoigne first signed for United on the 25th June 1983 on a wage of £25 per week. He had appeared for Redheugh Boys Club and turned professional in May 1985. Anyone who saw the FA Youth Cup run of 1985 would agree that one player stood out miles above the other teenagers - Paul Gascoigne. His talent was on such a different level that he appeared like a Brazilian World Cup star in a Sunday pub game at Low Fell. He simply waltzed around opponents in that age group and quickly skipped the Central League side altogether. Jack Charlton had the chubby youngster in the first team squad as substitute for the derby game at Roker Park. He appeared in the next fixture, replacing George Reilly against QPR, and then went into action for his full debut against Southampton as McFaul took over the manager's chair in August 1985.

Gascoigne had much to learn, but his potential was phenomenal. Once during his early outings he literally went in and out of six defenders in an attempt to walk the ball into the net. He ended up a yard out of the Leazes goal, was tackled and the chance went begging. He should have passed or blasted the ball home and colleagues were visibly annoyed. Inexperience told, but that was Gascoigne. He was infuriating, yet brilliant at the same time. Like all teenagers though, Paul learnt and by the time England manager Bobby Robson had put him into his Under 21 side against Morocco and noted he would soon be in the full squad, his performances were increasingly mature for such a youngster.

At 19 years old, Gascoigne began to control United's play and made headlines whenever he appeared, filling the mantle of the departed Waddle and Beardsley. One match in particular signalled Paul's growing maturity. Against Manchester United, the Magpies took three points with the midfielder outstanding, and in Glenn Roeder's words, Gazza, "ran Bryan Robson ragged". A natural footballer if there was ever one born, he had every ball skill and more. Gascoigne could go past opponents with ease, hit short or 40 yard passes to feet and display the vision to create a matchwinning opportunity. He packed a shot of power and found the net with spectacular long range efforts or skilful curling free-kicks as good as anyone on the world stage. He also would ghost into the box and find the net too.

Additionally Gazza possessed workrate and no little

GASCOIGNE'S PLAYING RECORD

	League		FA Cup		FL Cup		Total	
	App	Gls	App	Gls	App	Gls	App	Gls
1984-85	2	0	0	0	0	0	2	0
1985-86	31	9	1	0	3	0	35	9
1986-87	24	5	0	0	2	0	26	5
1987-88	35	7	3	3	3	1	41	11
	92	**21**	**4**	**3**	**8**	**1**	**104**	**25**

Paul Gascoigne

aggression, always tackling and bustling for the ball - albeit at times rather recklessly. In essence, he was almost the perfect footballer with only a fiery temperament his one defect. Former England star Trevor Francis was one of many who was impressed, "The most exciting British talent since George Best", he noted. Gascoigne was the new Clown Prince of Soccer. In the same mould as Len Shackleton, he possessed all the craft and entertainment value of United's former inside-forward. Gazza worked hard at his game, but also liked to have a laugh on the field - and the fans loved it. No game was dull if Gascoigne was on the park, whether he was caught in conflict with a defender, debating with officials or joking with the crowd.

He became the game's most sought after player and receiving the PFA's Young Player of the Year award in 1988 served to boost his reputation even further. Manchester United fancied him, so did Tottenham and Liverpool. And Newcastle tried desperately hard to keep the youngster. Willie McFaul was prepared to offer a lucrative five year contract, but Terry Venables swooped and handed over a cheque for £2.3 million - the biggest fee between British clubs and Gazzamania took over. He made his debut for England shortly afterwards and the World Cup in Italy during the summer of 1990 elevated Paul to an even higher stage.

Rich Italian clubs soon had their eyes on him. Lazio of Rome were impressed and tabled a massive £8.5 million to Spurs. There followed a protracted and much publicised set of negotiations, but in the end the deal was scuppered due to a mixture of circumstances which included a bad knee injury which Gascoigne unluckily picked up in the 1991 FA Cup final. The transfer was though, to be resurrected and put into mothballs until the summer of 1992 at a reduced £5.5 million and subject to the star's fitness.

United may have received over £2 million, plus a share of any subsequent transfer - wisely negotiated on his sale - but undoubtedly his departure led to the club's decline and eventual relegation. A formidable team could have been built around his genius that would have seen the Magpies go up, instead of down. Newcastle United and their supporters were very much the losers as Gascoigne is seemingly destined to become one of Europe's biggest superstars.

18

TOWARDS A NEW CENTURY

1990-1992

• SHARE EMBARRASSMENT • PROMOTION LET-DOWN • OSSIE'S IN CHARGE • YOUTHFUL BIRTHDAY •

"There is only one place for Newcastle and that is in the First Division. The sooner we are there the better"

Ossie Ardiles, April 1991

IN THE HISTORY OF NEWCASTLE UNITED events at St James Park have rarely been dull, and so it remained in the years leading towards a new century. While the fresh season was to be a huge disappointment, although as ever newsworthy, activity away from the dressing-room was intense as the club made an adventurous bid to raise millions in a public share issue.

The Football League added an extra promotion place to the Second Division for the 1990/91 season, so Newcastle United had an even better chance of returning to Division One. There were to be three automatic promotion slots and another after a play-off between four clubs. Surely United could claim one of the top positions everyone asked, never mind finishing as low as 7th to qualify for the play-off. After last season's near-miss they were one of the favourites for promotion. Surely they should have made it, but the black'n'whites confounded everybody. They finished in their worst position in the Football League since the miserably poor showing of 1938.

Mick Quinn instantly became the crowd's new Number 9 hero by striking four goals on his debut.

Jim Smith was content to keep largely the same squad as the new season kicked off. He had little option as finances were in a critical state with a vast sum owed in loans. A deepening recession and rising interest rates hit the club hard with a long term mortgage on the Milburn Stand increasing as the country's economy worsened. The manager therefore had to be both prudent and wise in his transfer activity. However, the funds he was given - over £1 million during the season - were not put to good use. Firstly, Aberdeen's Scottish international Neil Simpson joined the midfield ranks for over £180,000. With a box full of medals in Scotland, he was another player approaching 30 years of age, Newcastle's eighth in the squad. Jim Smith noted that, "I'm expecting him to make an impact". Simpson only played five times for the Magpies - and never a complete game! Scott Sloan, Tyneside born, cost £65,000 from Berwick Rangers after netting 18 goals in Scottish football, very much as a forward to be groomed for the future.

Both players failed to catch the eye and Smith's later dealings were also to largely disappoint when a signing of inspiration was desperately needed. The manager wasn't backed by his existing squad either as last season's promising team-work deteriorated alarmingly. Alan Oliver wrote in The Pink, "he was let down by players' legs which had gone and players' hearts which just were not in the job". Only Mick Quinn - who grabbed another 20 goals - Kristensen, Ranson and 'keeper John Burridge could say they had played well. The much travelled Burridge, who became the club's oldest post-war player at 39 years-old, went on to become Player of the Season before being handed a free transfer.

Injuries were a major factor and physio Derek Wright was never as busy as during the 1990/91 season. He had to

John Burridge arrived as a veteran, yet performed well enough to pick up the Player of the Year award in 1990/91.

cope with an incredible run of bad luck with a whole team queuing up for treatment. Influential players Brock, Aitken, Ranson, Kristensen and McGhee were all missing for long periods, while no fewer than ten of the staff needed surgery of one degree or another. On top of that both Quinn and Kristensen - again - were missing through suspension as United had five players sent-off during the year.

To start with though, Newcastle began well and looked set to live up to expectations winning three of the first four fixtures. But signs of deep problems ahead were evident when Charlton Athletic arrived on Tyneside and took United apart. They won at a canter by 3-1 and more bad news was to follow. Drawn to face north-east rivals Middlesbrough in the Rumbelows League Cup over two legs, few were confident of the outcome remembering the Magpies poor showing against 'Boro the previous season. It had been 25 years since Newcastle last won at Ayresome Park, and the Tees-siders continued their recent dominance over Newcastle by winning comfortably 2-0. In the return leg, United couldn't pull back the difference, managing only a single goal by John Anderson. They were not helped when star striker Quinn was dismissed following a clash with visiting 'keeper Stephen Pears. By November, United had gone seven successive matches without victory and dropped as low as 19th position. Instead of a sustained promotion push the season looked to be heading nowhere.

Away from Jim Smith's mounting problems, United's directors announced plans for a new phased development of St James Park - the umpteenth over the last 25 years. The ground was now to be completed by constructing new stands at the Leazes and Gallowgate ends, as well as altering the East and Milburn Stands, all at a cost of £16.5 million. On completion, capacity would increase from 31,000 to 41,262. The club's aim was to have a new super-stadium ready as one of the twelve "Regional Stadia" for any possible European Nations' Cup in 1996, or even the World Cup of 1998. The stumbling block was of course cash and, as Chairman Gordon McKeag said, "The full co-operation of the City Council and the Freemen", words echoed by his father almost 30 years before. But relationships were much more harmonious with their landlords now and progress was made in reaching a satisfactory agreement.

Funds were to be raised in part by a bold, yet somewhat risky, public share issue which was launched at the end of October 1990. With the aim also to democratise the club, as heralded by the Magpie Group, a lavish prospectus was issued nationwide with the intention of generating interest and cash in a new company - Newcastle United plc - that "should be one of the foremost clubs in the First Division, playing in one of the best stadia in the country, and should make a successful return to European football". It was hoped that in the long term, eight million ordinary shares worth over £7 million after expenses would be sold, while the short term target was to raise £2.5 million. The club's statement to prospective funders read, "You would not be buying a financial proposition so much as a part of the Tyneside heritage". It added, "The Newcastle United share certificate will be something many people will cherish along with their memories of the past glories of the Club and their hopes for a bright future for football in Newcastle".

The share issue, as required by law, gave a remarkable insight to the financial position of the club. At the close of business on 5th October 1990, Newcastle had a turnover of £4 million, but were in debt to over £4 million too, plus another £732,167 liability in respect of player signing-on and transfer fees. Against that, the market value of the playing staff was, "approx £6.8 million", while United also held the freehold property of 16.45 acres at Benwell. United had 29 Registered players, two Non-contract and 15 Trainees under a Youth Training programme. Not so long ago Newcastle employed 50 professionals alone.

Also highlighted was the considerable revenue taken from ancillary income, from both corporate and individual customers. With 58 Executive Boxes - one of the biggest set-ups in the UK - a restaurant and function suite, numerous sponsors' lounges, executive clubs and club merchandise, the money generated from this side of the business had become a lifeline. It was one of the largest hospitality organisations in football.

Following a slick advertising campaign the share issue closed at the end of November, however before that date it was clear that it was not going to be a success. The minimum subscription of £2.5 million was not reached and therefore the share issue was abandoned. Only £1.2 was pledged in support which included over £0.5million from Newcastle Breweries making a mediocre £700,000 from other businesses and supporters at large. The reasons for its failure were many, but a worsening recession and spectator disenchantment were the main factors, together with a major misjudgment at support from local enterprise. After all the flag-waving from the Magpie Group of the past two years, their call for democracy fell totally flat. Supporters - the silent majority - were not bothered, while several of the high profile backers of John Hall's cause did not come up with cash at the crunch. And to make matters worse, the black'n'whites had spent £550,000 on the launch of the share issue - money wasted which they could ill afford.

In the wake of this embarrassment Gordon McKeag honourably stepped down from the Chair in December 1990 and Scotsman George Forbes took over. The new

Front cover from the Club's Share Issue Prospectus document.

ADMISSION 1991/92

Season-tickets	
Milburn or East Stand	£165 - £245
East Paddock seats	£130
Family enclosure seat	£100
Milburn Paddock	
& Gallowgate End	£115
Executive tickets	
Boardroom Club	£2,000
Centenary Club	£1,100
Executive Club (plus season-ticket)	£200
Private Box (to seat eight) (average)	£8,500
Match-day	
Milburn or East Stand	£8 - £12.50
Standing areas	£6
Juveniles	£3

Gavin Peacock whose all action play in midfield made him one of United's key players.

'Benny' Kristensen, continued to play for Denmark when on Tyneside.

Former England Under-21 skipper, Ray Ranson.

Chairman noted on his appointment, "What the club needs now is a period of stability". Forbes took over as United looked to be heading for ruin. There was still a potentially volatile boardroom, a huge overdraft to contend with, an ageing team that appeared to have little enthusiasm for the game and thousands of disillusioned fans. Forbes though, set about his monumental task in a quiet, but authoritative way, maintaining he would be his own man and noting, "This club will be successful again - I'm dedicated to that". Within twelve months his leadership of the Second Revolution was to be well under way at St James Park, just as a much bigger transformation swept across eastern Europe and the Soviet Union. Although, just as in those former communist states, Forbes still had much to do, especially to radically improve the club's financial position.

John Hall, gutted at the share fiasco, left the board completely taking a post of Vice President and leaving his son, Douglas Hall, as the Magpie Group's sole representative. But that wasn't to last long. He too departed, in May 1991, a decision that was a perplexing one in the eyes of many of the Magpie Group's supporters. Following a near three year battle to win a say in the affairs of the club - if not control - the Halls made an exit from the scene when they had reached a position of influence. Many of their supporters at grassroots level were left bewildered. While their campaign did, without doubt, bring about change in the boardroom, the confrontation proved disastrous for the club. Many fans begged the question, "Was it all worth it?" The answer from many was a firm "No!" Nevertheless the Hall camp still remain the club's major shareholders, and would soon return to the board.

In the midst of this despondency United did receive a boost when Newcastle Breweries took over from their rivals, Greenalls and were installed in a £1.1 million three year deal as the Magpies main

Eire international defender John Anderson who completed ten years' service with the club in United's Centenary Year.

sponsor for a second time. Also to help the financial situation were substantial loans from John Hall and new Associate Director, Trevor Bennett, which jointly saw another £1 million plus injected into the club.

Jim Smith needed to reinforce his ravaged team with new blood if they were to get back into the promotion race. Money was found and with Aitken and new signing Simpson having a nightmare season, midfield was strengthened by the introduction of £350,000 Gavin Peacock who arrived at Gallowgate from Bournemouth in a deal that saw Wayne Fereday move south. The son of Keith Peacock, who had a long and distinguished career with Charlton Athletic, the 23 year-old proved to be one of the manager's few successful additions during his time in charge of the Magpies. A former England schoolboy and youth international, his attacking, all-action game gave the team a new dimension and supporters quickly warmed to his enthusiasm and ability to find the net in some style.

Smith also tried to bolster his flagging attack by bringing a succession of players on loan. 6'1" Dave Mitchell, an Australian international born in Scotland, came from Chelsea, Paul Moran from Spurs and Tommy Gaynor by way of Nottingham Forest. Gaynor and, to a lesser degree, Mitchell performed well, but were not strikers of the high quality that United needed and all three returned to their previous homes. However, it was not all gloom as Bjorn Kristensen and Ray Ranson came into their own. While Kristensen's Danish colleague, striker Frank Pingel quickly returned to Scandinavia, the tall, slim defender showed Tyneside's public he was very much an assured player - one with a First Division look. Versatile in midfield or at the back, he was cool-headed and at his best when moving forward. Nicknamed Benny, he had cost £260,000 from AGF Aarhus and had an international pedigree, having won 17 caps for his country and also competed in European competition. He displayed the sort of ability that fans had come to enjoy from Danish players of recent years and was recalled to the international scene during the season when he appeared for his country against Bulgaria. Ranson, almost 30 years of age, and who suffered at the hands of the Gallowgate boo-boys during his early days on Tyneside, eventually won over the fans during the season with some accomplished displays at right-back. The St Helens born player appeared over 200 times for Manchester City, winning several Under 21 caps as well as a single appearance for the England B side.

Another amazing game with Leicester City took place during winter, less than twelve months after the stunning contest at St James Park. United found themselves 2-1 behind at Filbert Street as the half-time whistle went, this after an opening burst that should have seen them four goals ahead! Leicester made the Magpies pay for squandering those opportunities by scoring two more and running to a 4-1 lead by the 67th minute. But then came a fight back. Quinn reduced the arrears in superb fashion, dummying a defender then lobbing Hooper into the top of the net from 30 yards. O'Brien headed another and United were now only 4-3 behind and all thought it was going to be a repeat of last season's epic. City's David Kelly got another - his hat-trick - to make sure it wasn't, but Newcastle still didn't give up. They stormed to the other end at every opportunity. Quinn completed his own hat-trick and the game ended in an absorbing 5-4 home victory, although manager Smith commented in frustration, "We were so clearly the better team".

Following a stirring 2-0 victory over First Division strugglers Derby County in the opening round of the FA Cup, Nottingham Forest were United's visitors in Round Four and reinforced their record of being the Magpies' most frequent Cup opposition. United played Forest two more times to take the total meetings to 17 games. Brian Clough's men journeyed to Tyneside for a much delayed, but what was to be a rousing tie. Jim Smith asked for, "pride to be a powerful factor tonight" and the Magpies responded. They were fired-up and raced to a 2-0 advantage within the first 12 minutes of play, Quinn and McGhee setting United on their way to what looked like becoming a convincing win. But then, after Newcastle missed chances to wrap up the game, the First Division club slowly came back into the match and when Stuart Pearce grabbed a goal back United started to feel the strain. Nevertheless, Forest's equaliser didn't come until the dying seconds when Nigel Clough lashed the ball into the net. The following Monday, Forest won easily in the end, by 3-0, however the game was much closer than the scoreline suggests and Newcastle's performance gave some hope for the rest of the season.

United were now languishing in a mid-table position. Smith's last ditch gamble to rescue the season was another plunge into the transfer pool. With only a limited sum of just over £500,000 available his purchase had to be right. He needed someone to inspire and transform the side, just as Aitken had done last season, albeit in the short term. However that man never arrived. First Smith spent £170,000 on Kettering Town's 20 year-old centre-forward Andy Hunt, a tall, gangly looking front-runner, then another £350,000 on giant Czech Under 21 'keeper Pavel Srnicek from Banik Ostrava - with QPR's Stejskal and West Ham's Miklosko, the third 'keeper in the Football League from that country. Both were untried youngsters, and while both looked good buys for the future, they were to do nothing to help United get back into the promotion frame.

Czech goalkeeper Pavel Srnicek who, after a critical start, won over the public.

MATCH RECEIPTS

Match revenue climbed dramatically during the latter years of the eighties decade, in spite of Second Division football.

1985/86	Division One	£1.654 million
1986/87	Division One	£1.878 million
1987/88	Division One	£1.738 million
1988/89	Division One	£2.355 million
1989/90	Division Two	£2.648 million

Income to the club will reach almost £3 million as United enter their Centenary Year of 1992. A hundred years ago it didn't even contribute £2,000!

As early as November speculation had mounted that Smith's job was on the line with a succession of names being linked with Newcastle United - including Kevin Keegan and England skipper, Bryan Robson. By the spring, Newcastle were still struggling to make even the play-offs never mind an automatic promotion place and, at the end of March 1991, Jim Smith resigned with eleven matches still to be decided. It was a surprise only in timing with most observers acknowledging United would need a new boss, one way or another, at the season's close. The departing manager was quoted as saying, "I just felt I'd had enough. If you make a mistake here, it's not just a mistake - it's a disaster". Chairman George Forbes noted, "I am determined to find a manager who wants to come here and turn all our promise and potential into solid achievement". United's Chairman didn't take long. There was none of the many weeks of agony and embarrassing refusals as in the past. Forbes got his man first go and in double quick time - he was Swindon Town's up and coming young manager, former World Cup star, Ossie Ardiles.

The former Tottenham midfielder was appointed in time for the game with Bristol Rovers at the beginning of April. He said on agreeing to the move, "I was immediately excited by the challenge". Very much an introvert character unlike his predecessor, Ardiles added, "I did not hesitate for a moment". In an interview in The People, he went on, "I wanted this job because I know I can do it. I have the greatest confidence in myself". On the club and the task in front of him, "I knew it was big. But when you arrive you realise it's even bigger". United had to fork out £160,000 in compensation to Swindon, but George Forbes said, "I hope it is the start of a new era. We have got the man we wanted and we will give him all the support we can".

Ardiles brought in his ex Spurs team-mate Tony Galvin as assistant. It was a young managerial pairing - Ardiles was 38 years old and Yorkshireman,

Former World Cup star, Ossie Ardiles shortly after joining The Magpies as manager.

Galvin aged 34 - yet they possessed a wealth of experience at top level behind them. Galvin, a midfielder come outside-left who had played ten seasons with Spurs, appeared 29 times for Eire and picked up FA Cup medals with Tottenham in 1981 and 1982 as well as a UEFA Cup success two years later. It was a highly educated partnership too - Ardiles had nearly become a lawyer, while Galvin holds a degree in Russian Studies!

Against Bristol Rovers, Ardiles received a rapturous welcome at St James Park as he strolled onto the pitch, arms in the air and black'n'white scarf round his neck. But it wasn't to be a fairytale beginning for the South American. United lost 2-0 and slipped further away from play-off qualification. He was honest enough to declare that Newcastle's promotion hopes were non-existent, "We have too much of a gap to make up, and we do not have the team to do it".

From the start the new manager imposed his own style, that of steadied build-up in possession and with the ball on the ground rather than six feet above it. And immediately Ardiles looked to the future. He raised more than a few eyebrows as he axed United's ageing players one by one. Dillon, Aitken, McGhee, Askew, Simpson and later Burridge found they had no place in his plans. In their place a batch of youngsters were given opportunities to impress - and they certainly did that. From an average age of around 28 when Smith was in charge, the line-up changed to a youthful 22. Indeed, very quickly Ardiles sent out the youngest ever side Newcastle have fielded. Against Barnsley at Oakwell, no fewer than six teenagers were in the team, and they earned a point in a 1-1 draw.

Newcastle's new star find, former England Schools' captain, Lee Clark.

Lee Clark, from Wallsend and much heralded as a star of the future, but who had been ignored by Smith, was introduced in midfield. A regular for England's junior sides he skippered his country through Under-15 to Under-18 levels and collected 25 youth caps. Clark was to prosper as the new season began and stand out as the most accomplished and mature of his young colleagues. Ex Wallsend Boys' Club player David Roche and faired haired Lee Makel, from Washington, joined him in midfield, while John Watson was given an outing too.

MANAGEMENT COMMITTEE

When Gordon McKeag was elevated to the Football League's Management Committee in 1988, the appointment continued United's fine tradition of serving in the top echelons of the game. Along with Everton, WBA, Birmingham City and Arsenal, the Magpies have provided most members on the League's ruling body with Lord Westwood becoming President, a post McKeag just missed out on.

J.Cameron	1907-1916
J.P.Oliver	1917-1928
G.F.Rutherford	1938-1942
W.B.Taylor	1956-1970
Lord Westwood	1970-1981
W.G.McKeag	1988-date

Robbie Elliott, another from Wallsend Boy's Club, Alan Neilson, born in Germany, and Teessider Matty Appleby were given opportunities in defence. Up front Steve Howey and David Robinson - both blooded by Smith - were also given a chance.

The pick of the bunch though, was 16 year-old Wallsend lad, Steve Watson, who started the season on a trainee scheme and finished it with 27 senior appearances to his name. He had appeared for Northumberland Boys in three different age groups and was another to have been developed through the Wallsend Boys' Club set-up which had already seen Peter Beardsley and Neil McDonald make the grade at St James Park. Watson was the new United find and, whilst he had a lot to learn, possessed heaps of confidence and all the natural talent to become a star, as well as an unique and spectacular 50 yard throw-in in which he performed a somersault before releasing the ball! Watson became Newcastle's youngest ever player when he made his debut as substitute against Wolves, aged 16 years 223 days. Settling at right-back, although he preferred midfield, he showed a match-winning urge to move forward. Within weeks he was elevated to the England youth side and tipped as a future superstar - one that the club was not to let slip away this time. Kevin Scott was appointed captain in

Right: Steve Watson who became United's youngest ever player when he appeared against Wolves in 1990.

Kevin Scott, took over from Aitken as the black'n'whites' captain.

place of Roy Aitken and with so many local kids in the new United line-up, enthusiasm and pride in wearing Tyneside's famous black'n'white kit returned.

Yet, as a whole, the season was nothing short of a disaster. United rarely fielded a settled side and they used no fewer than 36 different players in the programme, a new club record. They finished in 11th position in the table which equalled their worst post-war placing, while they averaged only 17,267 at the turnstile. Nevertheless the potential for pulling in the fans was still evident - as shown when almost 30,000 saw the Nottingham Forest FA Cup-tie and over 25,000 arrived to see a Second Division fixture with West Ham United when the season's optimism had not been overtaken by despondency. And the arrival of Ardiles saw the season end on a high note. By the time his introductory six week period at Gallowgate was over and the programme completed, the new boss had already won over the support of Tyneside. It had been a refreshing change in the type of football being offered - attractive and youthful. The manager noted, "I'm very encouraged by the performances of the team with all the new youngsters". And so were supporters, although the Magpies still had a long way to go in order to turn their refined football into a winning formula.

Former Nottingham Forest winger, Franz Carr, to show much potential up front.

FULL BACK PAIRING

At West Ham in April 1991, United fielded what is thought to be the youngest ever full back pairing in the Football League. Steve Watson, at 17 years 23 days, and Robbie Elliott, aged 17 years and 120 days, faced up to the Hammers' attack and were outstanding in a 1-1 draw. Newcastle now remarkably held not only the youngest record, but also the oldest! Back in February 1923 against Cardiff City, Billy Hampson and Bill McCracken were both past 40 - again thought to be the oldest defensive partnership in history! They didn't do as well as their younger counterparts as United went down 5-0 at Ninian Park and didn't play together again.

As United prepared for the 1991/92 season - and moved into the year the club was to record its Centenary - there was a mood of renewed hope. Smith's failure was quickly forgotten and season-ticket sales were up to previous First Division levels topping £1 million. Ardiles had given fans much to look forward to, but severely restricted finances did not allow for sweeping transfer deals and players had to be off-loaded to boost funds, as well as to reduce a heavy wage bill - a legacy of the previous regime. Dillon, Burridge and McGhee were all given free transfers. Simpson joined Motherwell and Aitken, St Mirren, both for fees way below their purchase price.

Ardiles, backed all the way by his directors, turned down a £1.5 million bid for Steve Watson which could have funded two or three deals. Vice-Chairman Peter Mallinger said adamantly, "There is no way we will let Steve Watson go. It would be like selling a young Paul Gascoigne again. The days of Newcastle United releasing their best players are now over". The manager had to be content with bringing Nottingham Forest's coloured winger Franz Carr to St James Park for £250,000. Born in Preston, Carr had, over the past five years, showed flashes of genius and a scorching turn of speed in the Football League. Capped at England schools, youth and Under-21 levels, he instantly became a crowd favourite giving United's attack some much needed pace and flair.

Dublin born Liam O'Brien was lodged in the anchor role of Ardiles' celebrated diamond midfield formation and was to prove a good choice. After recovering from a broken leg, the Irish international looked a composed and elegant schemer at times, but was bedecked with inconsistency which stopped him becoming a really great player. Mick Quinn was very much the key man. He signed a new three year contract, but it was clear that he couldn't do it by himself. Even with Carr in the side, two or three of the youngsters had to really break through if Newcastle were to mount a promotion challenge.

At the start of the season, the Magpies were installed as favourites, along with Sunderland, in a Second Division that looked on paper to be very ordinary. Ardiles though, did not have a happy start. Before a ball was kicked in anger he lost

Liam O'Brien fitted into Ardiles' key midfield anchor role.

Kristensen(knee) and Ranson(Achilles tendon), both injured in pre-season warm up fixtures. On top of that John Gallacher broke down once more with a persistent shin problem. To the Magpies' annoyance, United's opening game with Charlton Athletic even had to be switched to a Sunday and played at Upton Park, home of West Ham, because the Cockneys' return to The Valley was several weeks behind schedule.

In that fixture, which Charlton won 2-1, Newcastle rarely threatened and offered little to suggest that they were going to be a force in the coming season. The bad start continued as Watford stole a point at St James Park, then Middlesbrough steam-rollered the Magpies again - by 3-0 - the first of four scheduled derby meetings of the season. More poor results followed, with defensive mistakes the root cause, as Pavel Srnicek and his back four looked far from a solid combination. Missed chances compounded the errors as, up front, Quinn and Carr had plenty of opportunities. Carr though, looked a snip at £250,000 and his piercing runs, often against two or three defenders, had the crowd roaring their heads off but time and time again his crosses were wasted. Most of Ardiles' kids found the strain too much and were promptly dropped, including Watson. All that is except Lee Clark who flourished, displaying the talent that had been evident in junior ranks over the past few years. Small and slightly built, he was assured on the ball in midfield, possessing the awareness and vision to create an opening as well as being able to find the net. As a reward Lee was elevated to England's Under-21 squad.

OPEN DAY

In November 1990 United organised their first Open Day in 98 years at St James Park and an amazing 20,000 men, women and children passed through the club's Milburn Stand. They viewed the inner corridors of St James Park, met players, directors and officials. Mick Quinn was astonished at the turn-out, he noted, "I couldn't believe my eyes". And all this after 24 hours earlier 15,000 had suffered a miserable 0-0 draw with Barnsley at Gallowgate.

With such a raw line-up, success was not going to be instant and more than one respected voice in the game pleaded with United's supporters to have patience. They included Jack Charlton - himself a victim of the fans' wrath.

Looking back to when both Joe Harvey and Arthur Cox inherited a struggling Second Division side near the bottom of the table, United took three and four years respectively to get back into Division One. Ardiles, laden with the club's present day problems may take just as long - and no-one should criticise him for it.

Football was open and entertaining, albeit littered with mistakes. A terrific end-to-end tussle took place in the Rumbelows Cup as United faced up to Fourth Division Crewe Alexandra. Noted for a rampant goalscoring front line, Crewe stunned the Magpies at Gresty Road by going three goals up by the 22nd minute, and each could be counted as a defensive error. Ardiles' fortunes looked to be taking an even worse turn, but at last Newcastle learned to battle on the pitch as well as try to play cultured football - and as a result finished victors in a remarkable come-back.

First Andy Hunt pulled a goal back, then enter Gavin Peacock who turned what looked to be another embarrassing defeat by a minnow into triumph by scoring a magnificent hat-trick. It was some match - Crewe also struck the woodwork three times! In the second leg United went through without a goal feast this time, but comfortably enough after a late Steve Howey goal.

Another fascinating game took place a few days later in a Zenith Data Systems Cup fixture covered live by Sky television. Once again Newcastle were tremendous going forward, but the defence was nothing short of a shambles at times. By full-time the score was 3-3 after 90 minutes of attack-minded football, yet the contest was just beginning. In extra time Rovers surged forward and went 5-3 in front, then Newcastle hit back to equalise and with a Mick Quinn penalty - his hat-trick - went into the lead by 6-5! In was an astonishing match, and one even then not over. In injury time John Aldridge went down in the box and a harsh looking spot-kick was given. The former Liverpool striker drilled home the equaliser and the final whistle went all square at 6-6.

UJPESTI REVISIT

Hungarian's Ujpesti Dosza made a sentimental re-visit to St James Park just before the start of the 1991/92 season for a pre-season friendly. Led by Ferenc Bene, who had starred for the side in the Inter Cities Fairs Cup final of 1969, their visit brought back many memories of that triumphant European year. A Mick Quinn hat-trick - including two penalties - ensured the same scoreline as that marvellous day over 20 years before. United won 3-0, but this time in front of a much reduced crowd of only 10,000.

So to penalties and it was the Magpies, not Tranmere, who made a mess of their quota and lost the unforgettable twelve goal spree.

United's defence needed experience and organisation. Ironically the one man who could have given that to the Magpies - Roy Aitken - was recalled to the Scotland pool as a central defender after good displays for his new club, St Mirren. Perhaps Ardiles was too hasty in letting the vastly experienced Scot depart. Newcastle persisted in giving goals away and found themselves without a victory at St James Park until eliminating Crewe in the Rumbelows Cup - a new club record. Bad luck continued to hamper the manager's plans as Carr was injured then worse followed. Against Portsmouth, Mick Quinn crashed against a post and badly damaged his knee as he netted in the 3-1 defeat. United's goal king was off to hospital and out of action for the rest of the year at least. Following that reverse Newcastle slumped to bottom of the table for only the fourth time in their history. Skipper Kevin Scott said, "We can't blame anybody but ourselves". Events could not get much worse.

Ardiles has to instil confidence as well as grit and steel into his ravaged line-up to have any chance of stopping Newcastle United tumbling into Division Three in their Centenary Year. What a disaster that would be, yet it could easily occur. Just ask giants of the game Aston Villa, Wolves, both Sheffield clubs, neighbours Sunderland and presently West Bromwich Albion. But for once the manager may receive backing from all on Tyneside instead of a constant stream of criticism from almost every quarter which seemingly has been the norm over the past decade. If Newcastle United is to thrive then everyone needs to pull in one direction - the club itself, as well as supporters and the media.

As the club's Centenary Year of 1992 arrives and United enter their next one hundred years, the Magpies are slowly improving after a shock start. As ever, the potential for success is there. They have an enterprising and youthful outlook; stability of sorts - as compared to the last rocky 15 years - has returned to St James Park and with it a new regime in both the boardroom and manager's office. There have been many changes behind the scenes to prepare Newcastle United for the challenge of the 1990s and 21st century. The stadium is well on the way to becoming one of the best in the country. Great strides have taken place in marketing and promoting the club, while the commercial activities are more than a match for most and are just awaiting a return to the money-spinning First Division, or now-destined Super-League. And that is a must, the pre-requisite for lasting success and prosperity. With better opposition, and even European football, cash would flow into United's coffers with gates approaching 30,000 on a regular basis. It would be revenue that would, in turn, finance player acquisitions and further ground improvements. It remains to be seen if Ossie Ardiles can transform the playing staff into a successful eleven who can achieve that goal.

Perhaps in the not too distant future the famous black'n'whites will reclaim their position as one of football's most respected clubs and will once again be recognised as a power in the game - just as they were in those noble days of Edwardian England when Colin Veitch and Peter McWilliam were masters of the field. Or when Stan Seymour, Hughie Gallacher and Sammy Weaver pulled on the black'n'white shirt with honour, along with the many larger-than-life characters during those fabulous fifties - an era when Jackie Milburn and Bobby Mitchell captivated a nation. And in the recent past, when such names as Bobby Moncur, Malcolm Macdonald, the especially charismatic Kevin Keegan and the superstar trio of Waddle, Beardsley and Gascoigne have entertained in thrilling style on the St James Park turf. Time only will reveal.

No doubt though, the next century will have its fair share of the incident, controversy - and no little glory - that has been so very much a feature of Newcastle United Football Club's
FIRST 100 YEARS.

Pointing the way forward to a new century! United's centre-forward Mick Quinn.

THE MEN IN CHARGE AS UNITED HEAD TOWARDS A NEW CENTURY

GEORGE FORBES
Chairman

A 47 year-old Scot from the borders, George Forbes was for over 20 years just an ordinary United supporter like thousands of others before being appointed to the Board in 1983 in place of Fenton Braithewaite. Raised in Coldstream, his favourite player was Jimmy Smith while his uncle, John Johnston was on United's books during the thirties. Forbes himself played local amateur football and was also proficient in car rallying, taking part in international competition. Managing Director of an auctioneer's business in Wooler and Newcastle, he worked hard behind the scenes to find the middle ground during the Magpie Group's take-over attempt and following the collapse of the share issue in December 1990 was propelled into the Chairman's job.

PETER MALLINGER
Vice Chairman

Born in Tynemouth and brought up in Jesmond before emigrating to Canada, Peter Mallinger has been a diehard Newcastle United supporter since the immediate post-war years, even though for the majority of the time he has lived in Leicestershire. Roy Bentley was his early hero and he has followed the Magpies through thick and thin ever since. Appointed to the directorate in February 1989, Peter said on his elevation to the Board, "It is a lifetime dream come true". A workaholic to United's cause and a director of several companies, he made his name in the retail and textile business. 55 years old, he looks after all of the club's commercial interests from hospitality and sponsorship, to the Club Shop and Museum, and makes an invaluable contribution to United's off the field income. Was once a right-half on Leicester City's 'A' books and had trials with Derby and Coventry.

RUSSELL CUSHING
Secretary & General Manager

From East Anglia and United's Company Secretary. With a background in accountancy, Russell Cushing joined United as Assistant Secretary in June 1971 after a period at Carrow Road, home of Norwich City, and has since lived through some of the most incident packed times that could be imagined. Within a couple of years of settling on Tyneside he became the youngest Secretary in the First Division and has since been at the forefront of Newcastle's affairs - many controversial and testing problems to overcome on the way. After 20 years service for the club - one fifth of the time United has existed - he was appointed a director in November 1989 and manages the considerable administration that makes United tick from day to day. Aged 44, Russell is considered to be one of the top senior executives in the game. He stepped down from the boardroom in a November 1991 re-shuffle.

GORDON McKEAG
Honorary Life Vice President

Football League Management Committee, FA Council, FA Executive Committee, FA Challenge Cup Committee.

Aged 64, son of past Chairman and twice Lord Mayor of Newcastle, Gordon McKeag is a prominent local figure, a solicitor and a valued official of both the Football Association and Football League. He was Chairman of the club from 1988 to 1990, when he stepped down after the share issue. During that volatile two year ordeal, McKeag made a courageous stance against what seemed overwhelming odds. It could be said that he won the day and at the same time enhanced his reputation as a man of integrity. Articulate and extremely humorous at times, he has watched the Magpies since the 1930's and was raised on the goal skills of Albert Stubbins. A keen all round sportsman, Gordon played rugby and squash for Northumberland, cricket for Tynemouth and is Chairman of Jesmond Lawn Tennis Club, while he also sits on the regional golf association too. Was a director of the club from 1972 to 1991 when he resigned in a board restructuring process.

BOB YOUNG
Director

A former colliery worker who now heads his own mining empire based in Consett, Bob Young joined the Newcastle United board in June 1989 on Chairman Gordon McKeag's invitation. That was at the height of the share war with the Magpie Group and Young stepped into the firing ground as a replacement for George Dickson who had defected the cause. Aged 45, he went on to play a major peacemaking role in bringing the two factions together, and was appointed Vice Chairman before standing aside in May 1991 because of his world-wide business commitments. Born in Broompark, near Durham City.

STAN SEYMOUR
Honorary Life President

Northumberland FA President, FA Council, FA Challenge Cup Committee, FA Match & Grounds Committee.

Took the place of his famous father in the boardroom in 1976, Stan junior himself has been connected with Newcastle United for more than 50 years and is passionately committed to the Magpies since being hooked on the great Hughie Gallacher, a colleague of his father's at St James Park. He also has strong links with local football being not only President of the NFA, but also the Northern Alliance. Chairman of the club from 1981 to 1988, and now aged 74, Stan Seymour had much to do with landing the deal that brought Kevin Keegan to Tyneside. In his younger days played football and rugby, while he later refereed in the region. Managed his father's sports retail business for many years before putting all his energies into Newcastle United's activities.

TREVOR BENNETT
Associate Director

Trevor Bennett was appointed to a new post of Associate Director in January 1991 and has a wealth of experience on which Newcastle United can call. From the South Wales mining community of Blaina, he moved to Leicester before the Second World War and set up a window manufacturing business which developed into a highly successful nationwide operation. Serving with the Royal Artillery in North Africa, Italy and Greece during the hostilities, he has always been interested in sport, boxing for the army and turning out as a trialist for the Welsh schoolboys at rugby. A past magistrate, Trevor avidly supported Leicester City for over 50 years becoming Club President in 1984. He is also very much involved in the fortunes of Leicestershire Cricket Club and is a Vice President and Trustee at Grace Road, while golf is another sport he follows with much enthusiasm too. Trevor Bennett, at 70 years old, keeps a very active life and now has an affinity to Newcastle United as well.

JAMES RUSH
Vice President

Newcastle United's longest serving official, James Rush was appointed to the Board in April 1967 in place of Wally Hurford. Born in Longbenton, now a retired businessman who owned a major glass manufacturing concern, he also had many other interests. His hobbies included greyhound racing, music, arts and literature - he is a Fellow of the Royal Society of Arts - as well as being an author and lecturer. He also is associated with the scout movement and before the war learned to fly and piloted the Royal Mail from the Continent to London. During war service as a squadron leader in the RAF, he was decorated with the AFC and saw action in the Battle of Britain as well as Europe, India and Africa. He afterwards took up air racing - including becoming British Champion in 1963 and once flew in and out of the skyscrapers of New York. Mr Rush has always been a Newcastle United supporter at heart and now remains associated with the Club as Vice-President.

SIR JOHN HALL
Vice President

Mastermind of the highly successful MetroCentre in Gateshead, 58 year old John Hall is Chairman of Cameron Hall Developments Ltd and has, over the last decade, become one of Tyneside's leading entrepreneurs. Born in North Seaton, the son of a Northumberland miner, he started his career in 1949 as a surveyor with the National Coal Board. He led the Magpie Group's take-over attempt in 1988 and by April 1990 had a seat on the Board, albeit for only a short period. Following the share issue that fell foul of the region's public Sir John resigned, but remained connected to the Club as Vice President. Dedicated to the north east's prosperity, he was honoured with a knighthood in the Queen's Honour's List and remains the major shareholder in Newcastle United.

DEREK McVICKERS
Director

Born and bred in Consett, Derek McVickers was appointed to the board in November 1991 after being a supporter since the glory days of the 1940's and 1950's. A prominent businessman in Derwentside, he is Managing Director of an electrical contracting company as well as a sports outfitters business, while he sits on several committees in the region. He is also a District Councillor, a post held for the past 16 years. A keen sporting enthusiast, Derek appeared for England YMCA at cross-country running and has competed in the Great North Run, Walk and Ride, being a noted cyclist. President of both Consett football and rugby clubs, he has been in the crowd at every one of United's six cup finals since the war. Resides in his home town of Consett.

DOUGLAS HALL
Director

Son of Sir John Hall and Managing Director of Cameron Hall Developments, Douglas rejoined the club's management in November 1991's restructuring. Aged 33, he was initially appointed a director following the two year takeover attempt by the Magpie Group, in which he was a leading player alongside his father. His first stay in the boardroom was all too brief - only 191 days - resigning due to business commitments. However, Douglas returned to give the club his considerable experience from the world of corporate dealing. His company, Cameron Hall Developments, are involved in several sporting activities in the north east, including the funding of Newcastle United's Centre of Excellence. A supporter of the Magpies' cause since the sixties, Douglas resides in Gateshead.

FREDDIE SHEPHERD
Director

Born in Gilsland on the Northumberland-Cumbria border, Freddie Shepherd was schooled in Australia for a few years, then brought up in the east end of Newcastle upon Tyne. He worked for BP Marine before joining the family business, Shepherd Offshore. Now Managing Director of that successful company, he was appointed a director of United in November 1991. A Newcastle supporter since the days of his hero, Jackie Milburn, he also is keen on sailing and is President of Newcastle Yacht Club. Additionally he is dedicated to helping local football, his own Shepherd Offshore FC operating in Tyneside's Sunday League. Living in Jesmond and 50 years of age, Freddie is committed in guiding Newcastle United back to the First Division and once again witnessing success at St James Park.

A Worthy No.9 Hero

"I have never known a player with more hunger for scoring goals"

Ossie Ardiles, August 1991

THE FANS SANG OUT IN FULL VOICE, "MICKY QUINN, Micky Quinn, Micky Quinn". United's newest Number 9 had arrived and had become an instant hero after a debut bettered only by Len Shackleton's amazing day back in 1946. Against Leeds United and in front of a 24,396 St James Park crowd, Quinn rammed four goals past Mervyn Day to crown a great performance in front of his new fans. Apart from Shackleton only three pre-war stars can claim to have netted hat-tricks on their first appearance - Wilf Bott, Bob McKay and Harry Brown.

Quinn's first hit the net after 18 minutes with a right foot penalty, then he headed home Brock's crossball just after half-time. The centre-forward was on the mark again when he converted a dangerous centre by Gallacher and his last was the best of the lot - showing composure as he raced from the half-way line to a Dillon through pass to slot the ball into the net again.

It was the start of a prolific season for Quinn. He scored nine goals in the opening five matches and the striker proceeded to almost equal Hughie Gallacher's long-standing goals record. The Scouser went on to net 36 senior goals(32 in the league) and had it not been for a late dip in form could have toppled that 62 year old record. As it was he was the Football League's leading scorer winning the coveted Adidas Boot and only the fourth player in United's history to top 30 league goals. Gallacher and Robledo are the only men to have scored more in a single season.

And believe it or not, manager Jim Smith had misgivings about the size of the fee Portsmouth were asking. The Fratton Park club wanted over £800,000 for the 27 year-old striker, Smith offered £450,000. For once Freedom of Contract and the League Tribunal worked in United's favour - they had to pay more than they wanted at £680,000, however, as events turned out Quinn was cheap at the price when he joined the Magpies in June 1989. Indeed within 12 months United had turned down a £1.2 million bid from Wimbledon.

A bubbling personality from Liverpool having supported the Reds from Anfield as a teenager, Quinn went through life in the lower divisions before establishing himself as a quality leader. He started with Tranmere Rovers as a schoolboy then Derby County as an apprentice. Mick had a spell with Wigan Athletic before joining Stockport County in July 1982 where he claimed 40 goals in a season and a half. That prompted a move up a grade and it was at Oldham Athletic that Quinn began to make an impression under the guidance of up and coming young boss, Joe Royle, himself a noted centre-forward. Mick cost £52,000 when he moved across Manchester in January 1984 and he totalled 34 goals in 80 appearances for the Boundary Park outfit before joining Portsmouth in March 1986. With Pompey, he just missed out on promotion to Division One, but succeeded the next time round as runners-up to Derby County when Mick's 22 goals made him the Second Division's leading marksman.

Quinn is not a highly skilled type of front-runner or a picture of an athlete, yet he knows the centre-forward's business inside-out. At 5'10", he hustles and bustles and most importantly senses where the goal is. A natural goal-poacher,

QUINN'S PLAYING RECORD								
	League		**FA Cup**		**FL Cup**		**Total**	
	App	Gls	App	Gls	App	Gls	App	Gls
1989-90	47	32	4	2	2	0	53	34
1990-91	43	18	3	2	2	0	48	20
	90	**50**	**7**	**4**	**4**	**0**	**101**	**54**

Mick Quinn

razor sharp in the box, if Mick receives a half-chance, the ball is invariably tucked away. Rarely to score with a spectacular effort - in the mould of say, Macdonald or Beardsley - Quinn often grabs his goals with close-in sharp-shooting and headers in the six yard box. At his most dangerous with his back to goal, he is quick to turn and leave defenders rooted to the spot as the striker fires the ball towards the net.

Nicknamed 'The Mighty Quinn', he is a predator to rank with the best and will always guarantee his manager goals, so far finding the net almost 250 times in twelve years, including over 50 for United in his first two seasons. His past manager Joe Royle was to say, "He'll shoot and he'll keep shooting until he scores", while his current boss Ossie Ardiles remarked, "I have never known a player with more hunger for scoring goals".

Mick Quinn possesses the ideal make-up - goalscoring ability, coupled with a buoyant character - to become one of United's biggest Number 9 heroes. Certainly a worthy successor to so many past stars in the celebrated shirt.

Centenary Profile 31

The Little Argentinian

"I won't tolerate anything except total pride in the Newcastle shirt"

Ossie Ardiles, April 1991

CHAIRMAN GEORGE FORBES KNEW EXACTLY WHO he wanted to lead Newcastle United into the next Century following the resignation of Jim Smith as manager. He didn't hesitate in seeking out 38 year-old Osvaldo Ardiles, the former Tottenham and Argentinian World Cup star who was then in charge of Swindon Town. By coincidence, United played his club in a Second Division fixture only days after Smith's departure. Negotiations didn't take long. There was a lot of common ground and a deal was concluded within 24 hours.

Ardiles had proved to the football world that he had the potential to become a top boss. The way he fashioned the Robins into a quick moving, attractive line-up impressed everyone - including Newcastle supporters who sampled his soccer first-hand in an entertaining display towards the end of the 1989/90 season. Swindon were many people's top Second Division side that year, better than promoted clubs Leeds United and Sheffield United. And the little Argentinian had initially achieved success too, when Swindon defeated Sunderland in the play-off at Wembley, but then faced the wrath of football's authorities for irregularities which took place before Ardiles was installed in the manager's office. The aftermath rocked the Home Counties club and Ossie was ready for a fresh start - and the much bigger challenge to put Newcastle United back in the limelight was one he could not refuse. Although he knew little about the Magpies, ex colleague Chris Waddle, as well as former boss, Keith Burkinshaw, gave a glowing testimony of the club's traditions and potential. Ardiles noted, "It's a club to rank with Tottenham, Liverpool and Arsenal".

Osvaldo Cesar Ardiles was born in Cordoba, Argentina's second city, in 1952, one of four sons of a lawyer. He began the road to the world stage at 17 years of age with Instituto Cordoba after appearing for boys' club side Red Star. Ossie joined the big time when he signed for Buenos Aires club, and one of the best teams in the Argentine, Huracan when he was 22. He developed rapidly after that, winning the First Division championship in 1973 and breaking into the national side twelve months later. Then it was across the ocean to England, and in a twelve year playing career in the Football League, Ardiles built up a reputation as a thoughtful and elegant midfielder.

He joined Burkinshaw's Tottenham Hotspur in the summer of 1978, immediately after his country's impressive World Cup victory over Holland on his native soil. Ossie was a regular for Argentina's successful side alongside Passarella, Tarantini, Luque and Kempes. Ardiles appeared in six of the seven games and was so important to manager Cesar Menotti's plans that he was picked for the final even though he was struggling with a broken toe. All told the slightly built midfield man appeared on 42 occasions for his country, including taking part in the next World Cup, in Spain in 1982.

Spurs paid £325,000 for the 5'6" schemer and he arrived in London in a joint deal with his international colleague Ricci Villa. It was a bit of a gamble for Burkinshaw and more than one cynic doubted the wisdom of the move. But it was a deal that paid off handsomely for both club and player. At White Hart Lane, Ardiles entered the action in a blaze of publicity. Seasons 1978/79 and 1979/80 were periods of consolidation for the North London club as Burkinshaw fashioned an entertaining eleven in true Spurs traditions. They lifted the FA Cup in 1981 with Ossie in the side, then reached the semi-final of the European Cup Winners Cup and lost in the final of the Milk Cup. In 1984 he was part of the squad that lifted the UEFA Cup and during that time Ardiles had become the darling of the Spurs crowd with attractive displays.

At the time of the Falklands crisis, the Argentinian spent nine months on loan to Paris St Germain to avoid the mounting feeling towards his home country. He returned to Spurs though, and was honoured with a testimonial against Inter Milan in May 1986. In total he turned out over ten seasons for Tottenham and made 311 appearances. After spells with QPR and Blackburn Rovers, Ossie joined Swindon Town in July 1989 as player-boss. He only appeared twice on the field - as sub - and he made the transition from player to manager very smoothly and very quickly. His entertaining playing style mirrored the way of his managerial methods. He liked quick passing in possession and plenty of running off the ball. And if his team lost, it would go down playing football.

Installed at St James Park on a six figure three year contract, - the biggest United have paid for any manager - he at once sorted out the playing staff. Immediately the side began to display the Ardiles' attractive style of football. An educated and sober character - he spent almost five years at law school - Ossie Ardiles has the appetite to succeed and reach the top as a manager just as he did as a player. Quoted in The Journal, he said, "If we get the foundation of the club right we are going to be able to keep the new Gascoignes, new Beardsleys, new Waddles". And as he noted in another interview shortly after joining United, "I won't tolerate anything except total pride in the Newcastle shirt". It was the kind of response every Newcastle fan wanted to hear.

Ossie Ardiles

CENTENARY ANALYSIS

		LEAGUE HOME						LEAGUE AWAY														TOP	AVERAGE
SEASON	DIV	P	W	D	L	F	A	P	W	D	L	F	A	Pts	Pos	FAC	FLC	EUR	CHAIRMAN	MANAGER	CAPTAIN	SCORER	ATTEND
1892-93	NL	5	3	1	1	16	6	5	2	0	3	15	1	11	2	R1	-	-	A. Turnbull	Committee	W. Graham	8-Sorley	3,417
1893-94	Two	14	12	1	1	44	10	14	3	5	6	22	29	36	4	R2	-	-	A. Turnbull	Committee	W. Graham	17-Wallace	4,075
1894-95	Two	15	11	1	3	50	27	15	1	2	12	22	57	27	10	R2	-	-	D. McPherson	Committee	W. Graham	18-Thompson	4,469
1895-96	Two	15	14	0	1	57	14	15	2	2	11	16	36	34	5	R2	-	-	W. Neasham	Committee	R. Foyers	20-Wardrope	7,014
1896-97	Two	15	13	1	1	42	13	15	4	0	11	14	39	35	5	R1	-	-	W. Neasham	Committee	J. Stott	15-Smellie	8,399
1897-98	Two	15	14	0	1	43	10	15	7	3	5	21	22	45	2P	R2	-	-	W. Neasham	Committee	J. Stott	18-Peddie	11,905
1898-99	One	17	9	3	5	33	18	17	2	5	10	16	30	30	13	R2	-	-	W. Neasham	Committee	J. Ostler	20-Peddie	16,706
1899-00	One	17	10	5	2	34	15	17	3	5	9	19	28	36	5	R2	-	-	W. Neasham	Committee	A. Aitken	16-Peddie	15,891
1900-01	One	17	10	5	2	27	13	17	4	5	8	15	24	38	6	R1	-	-	W. Neasham	Committee	A. Aitken	16-Peddie	15,439
1901-02	One	17	11	3	3	41	14	17	3	6	8	7	20	37	3	R3	-	-	J. Telford	Committee	A. Aitken	12-Roberts	15,000
1902-03	One	17	12	1	4	31	11	17	2	3	12	10	40	32	14	R1	-	-	J. Telford	Committee	A. Aitken	10-McColl	18,147
1903-04	One	17	12	3	2	31	13	17	6	3	8	27	32	42	4	R1	-	-	J. Telford	Committee	A. Aitken	16-Appleyard	18,749
1904-05	One	17	14	1	2	41	12	17	9	1	7	31	21	48	**CH**	F	-	-	J. Cameron	Committee	A. Aitken	18-Howie	22,411
1905-06	One	19	12	4	3	49	23	19	6	3	10	25	25	43	4	F	-	-	J. Cameron	Committee	A. Gardner	21-Orr	24,954
1906-07	One	19	18	1	0	51	12	19	4	6	9	23	34	51	**CH**	R1	-	-	J. Cameron	Committee	A. Gardner	17-Appleyard	33,319
1907-08	One	19	11	4	4	41	24	19	4	8	7	24	30	42	4	F	-	-	J. Cameron	Committee	A. Gardner	22-Appleyard	30,900
1908-09	One	19	14	1	4	32	20	19	10	4	5	33	21	53	**CH**	SF	-	-	J. Bell	Committee	C. Veitch	15-Shepherd	31,508
1909-10	One	19	11	3	5	33	22	19	8	4	7	37	34	45	4	**W**	-	-	J. Lunn	Committee	C. Veitch	31-Shepherd	28,249
1910-11	One	19	8	7	4	37	18	19	7	3	9	24	25	40	8	F	-	-	J. Lunn	Committee	C. Veitch	33-Shepherd	29,037
1911-12	One	19	10	4	5	37	25	19	8	4	7	27	25	44	3	R1	-	-	G.T. Milne	Committee	W. McCracken	14-Hibbert & Stewart	25,211
1912-13	One	19	8	5	6	30	23	19	5	3	11	17	24	34	14	R4	-	-	G.T. Milne	Committee	W. McCracken	9-Stewart	28,237
1913-14	One	19	9	6	4	27	18	19	4	5	10	12	30	37	11	R1	-	-	G.G. Archibald	Committee	J. Hay	10-Shepherd	27,020
1914-15	One	19	8	4	7	29	23	19	3	6	10	17	25	32	15	R4	-	-	G.G. Archibald	Committee	J. Hay	16-Hibbert	17,999
1915-19	**NO COMPETITION DUE TO WORLD WAR ONE - LOCAL LEAGUE ONLY**																		J. Graham	-	-	-	-
1919-20	One	21	11	5	5	31	13	21	6	4	11	13	26	43	8	R2	-	-	J.P. Oliver	Committee	W. McCracken	10-Smailes	37,401
1920-21	One	21	14	3	4	43	18	21	6	7	8	23	27	50	5	R3	-	-	J.P. Oliver	Committee	W. Low	19-Harris	41,921
1921-22	One	21	11	5	5	36	19	21	7	5	9	23	26	46	7	R2	-	-	J.P. Oliver	Committee	W. Low	23-Harris	34,799
1922-23	One	21	13	6	2	31	11	21	5	6	10	14	26	48	4	R1	-	-	J.P. Oliver	Committee	W. Low	15-McDonald	26,815
1923-24	One	21	13	5	3	40	21	21	4	5	12	20	33	44	9	**W**	-	-	J.P. Oliver	Committee	F. Hudspeth	23-Harris	28,543
1924-25	One	21	11	6	4	43	18	21	5	10	6	18	24	48	6	R2	-	-	J.P. Oliver	Committee	F. Hudspeth	20-Harris	27,885
1925-26	One	21	13	3	5	59	33	21	3	7	11	25	42	42	10	R5	-	-	J.P. Oliver	Committee	F. Hudspeth	25-Gallacher	30,862
1926-27	One	21	19	1	1	64	20	21	6	5	10	32	38	56	**CH**	R5	-	-	J.P. Oliver	Committee	H. Gallacher	39-Gallacher	35,061
1927-28	One	21	9	7	5	49	41	21	6	6	9	30	40	43	9	R3	-	-	J.P. Oliver	Committee	H. Gallacher	21-Gallacher	28,810
1928-29	One	21	15	2	4	48	29	21	4	4	13	22	43	44	10	R3	-	-	D. Crawford	Committee	J. Hill	24-Gallacher	33,014
1929-30	One	21	13	4	4	52	32	21	2	3	16	19	60	37	19	R6	-	-	J. Lunn	Committee	J. Hill	34-Gallacher	36,831
1930-31	One	21	9	2	10	41	45	21	6	4	11	37	42	36	17	R4	-	-	J. Lunn	A. Cunningham	J. Hill	14-Hutchison	29,392
1931-32	One	21	13	5	3	52	31	21	5	1	15	28	56	42	11	**W**	-	-	J. Lunn	A. Cunningham	J. Nelson	23-Boyd	34,220
1932-33	One	21	15	2	4	44	24	21	7	3	11	27	39	49	5	R3	-	-	J. Lunn	A. Cunningham	J. Nelson	19-Allen	27,548
1933-34	One	21	6	11	4	42	29	21	4	3	14	26	48	34	21R	R3	-	-	J. Lunn	A. Cunningham	J. Nelson	14-Weaver	25,104
1934-35	Two	21	14	2	5	55	25	21	8	2	11	34	43	48	6	R4	-	-	J. Lunn	A. Cunningham	J. Nelson	16-Smith	20,429
1935-36	Two	21	13	5	3	56	27	21	7	1	13	32	52	46	8	R5	-	-	J. Lunn	T. Mather	A. Leach	26-Smith	22,094
1936-37	Two	21	11	3	7	45	23	21	11	2	8	35	33	49	4	R3	-	-	J. Lunn	T. Mather	W. Imrie	24-Smith	24,548
1937-38	Two	21	12	4	5	38	18	21	2	4	15	13	40	36	19	R3	-	-	J. Lunn	T. Mather	W. Imrie	9-Imrie & Park	20,625
1938-39	Two	21	13	3	5	44	21	21	5	7	9	17	27	46	9	R5	-	-	J. Lunn	T. Mather	J. Denmark	20-Cairns	35,339
1939-40	WL	10	6	0	4	38	20	10	6	0	4	20	19	24	2	SF	-	-	J. Lunn	S. Seymour	-	14-Cairns	6,972
1940-41	WL	13	11	0	2	39	14	10	1	0	9	10	27	24	10	SF	-	-	G.F. Rutherford	S. Seymour	-	21-Stubbins	6,828
1941-42	WL	19	10	5	4	53	42	16	2	7	7	26	37	36	37	-	-	-	G.F. Rutherford	S. Seymour	-	33-Stubbins	8,228
1942-43	WL	18	9	4	5	59	43	17	6	3	8	51	47	37	14	R1	-	-	G.F. Rutherford	S. Seymour	-	42-Stubbins	10,617
1943-44	WL	16	10	2	4	41	24	16	5	2	9	27	38	34	11	R3	-	-	G.F. Rutherford	S. Seymour	-	43-Stubbins	17,461
1944-45	WL	18	11	0	7	64	27	17	6	2	9	42	41	46	5	R3	-	-	G.F. Rutherford	S. Seymour	H. Clifton	43-Stubbins	19,168
1945-46	WL	22	13	4	4	68	27	22	8	1	12	38	43	47	6	R3	-	-	G.F. Rutherford	S. Seymour	J. Harvey	39-Stubbins	39,616
1946-47	Two	21	11	4	6	60	32	21	8	6	7	35	30	48	5	SF	-	-	G.F. Rutherford	S. Seymour	J. Harvey	34-Wayman	49,435
1947-48	Two	21	18	1	2	46	13	21	6	7	8	26	28	56	2P	R3	-	-	G.F. Rutherford	G. Martin	J. Harvey	20-Milburn	56,299

CENTENARY ANALYSIS

		LEAGUE HOME						LEAGUE AWAY														TOP	AVERAGE
SEASON	DIV	P	W	D	L	F	A	P	W	D	L	F	A	Pts	Pos	FAC	FLC	EUR	CHAIRMAN	MANAGER	CAPTAIN	SCORER	ATTEND
1948-49	One	21	12	5	4	35	29	21	8	7	6	35	27	52	4	R3	-	-	G.F. Rutherford	G. Martin	J. Harvey	19-Milburn	53,702
1949-50	One	21	14	4	3	49	23	21	5	8	8	28	32	50	5	R4	-	-	J.W. Lee	G. Martin	J. Harvey	21-Milburn	46,456
1950-51	One	21	10	6	5	36	22	21	8	7	6	26	31	49	4	**W**	-	-	J.W. Lee	S. Seymour	J. Harvey	25-Milburn	47,693
1951-52	One	21	12	4	5	62	28	21	6	5	10	36	45	45	8	**W**	-	-	R. Rutherford	S. Seymour	J. Harvey	39-Robledo	50,766
1952-53	One	21	9	5	7	34	33	21	5	4	12	25	37	37	16	R4	-	-	R. Rutherford	S. Seymour	J. Harvey	18-Robledo	45,669
1953-54	One	21	9	2	10	43	40	21	5	8	8	29	37	38	15	R5	-	-	S. Seymour	S. Seymour	J. Scoular	18-Milburn	45,815
1954-55	One	21	12	5	4	53	27	21	5	4	12	36	50	43	8	**W**	-	-	S. Seymour	D. Livingstone	J. Scoular	23-Mitchell	42,987
1955-56	One	21	12	4	5	49	24	21	5	3	13	36	46	41	11	R6	-	-	W.B. Taylor	D. Livingstone	J. Scoular	29-Keeble	39,740
1956-57	One	21	10	5	6	43	31	21	4	3	14	24	56	36	17	R4	-	-	W.B. Taylor	Committee	J. Scoular	13-Davies & White	36,235
1957-58	One	21	6	4	11	38	42	21	6	4	11	35	39	32	19	R4	-	-	W.McKeag	Committee	R. Stokoe	25-White	36,382
1958-59	One	21	11	3	7	40	29	21	6	4	11	40	51	41	11	R3	-	-	W.McKeag	C. Mitten	R. Stokoe	25-White	40,280
1959-60	One	21	10	5	6	42	32	21	8	3	10	40	46	44	8	R3	-	-	W.E. Hurford	C. Mitten	R. Stokoe	29-White	37,237
1960-61	One	21	7	7	7	51	49	21	4	3	14	35	60	32	21R	R6	R1	-	W.E. Hurford	C. Mitten	I. Allchurch	29-White	29,694
1961-62	Two	21	10	5	6	40	27	21	5	4	12	24	31	39	11	R3	R2	-	W.E. Hurford	N. Smith	W. McKinney	11-Allchurch	27,359
1962-63	Two	21	11	8	2	48	23	21	7	3	11	31	36	47	7	R4	R2	-	W.E. Hurford	J. Harvey	R. Keith	16-Fell & Thomas	31,209
1963-64	Two	21	14	2	5	49	26	21	6	3	12	25	43	45	8	R3	R3	-	W.E. Hurford	J. Harvey	S. Anderson	21-Thomas	29,028
1964-65	Two	21	16	4	1	50	16	21	8	5	8	31	29	57	**CH**	R3	R2	-	Ld. Westwood	J. Harvey	S. Anderson	16-McGarry	35,659
1965-66	One	21	10	5	6	26	20	21	4	4	13	24	43	37	15	R4	R2	-	Ld. Westwood	J. Harvey	J. Iley	15-Suddick	33,273
1966-67	One	21	9	5	7	24	27	21	3	4	14	15	54	33	20	R4	R2	-	Ld. Westwood	J. Harvey	J. Iley	11-Robson	32,085
1967-68	One	21	12	7	2	38	20	21	1	8	12	16	47	41	10	R3	R2	-	Ld. Westwood	J. Harvey	R. Moncur	12-Davies	38,118
1968-69	One	21	12	7	2	40	20	21	3	7	11	21	35	44	9	R4	R3	**W**	Ld. Westwood	J. Harvey	R. Moncur	30-Robson	39,296
1969-70	One	21	14	2	5	42	16	21	3	11	7	15	19	47	7	R3	R2	R4	Ld. Westwood	J. Harvey	R. Moncur	25-Robson	38,718
1970-71	One	21	9	9	3	27	16	21	5	4	12	17	30	41	12	R3	R2	R2	Ld. Westwood	J. Harvey	R. Moncur	10-Robson	31,842
1971-72	One	21	10	6	5	30	18	21	5	5	11	19	34	41	11	R3	R3	-	Ld. Westwood	J. Harvey	R. Moncur	26-Macdonald	32,398
1972-73	One	21	12	6	3	35	19	21	4	7	10	25	32	45	8	R4	R3	-	Ld. Westwood	J. Harvey	R. Moncur	19-Macdonald	28,308
1973-74	One	21	9	6	6	28	21	21	4	6	11	21	27	38	15	F	R3	-	Ld. Westwood	J. Harvey	R. Moncur	25-Macdonald	32,791
1974-75	One	21	12	4	5	39	23	21	3	5	13	20	49	39	15	R4	R5	-	Ld. Westwood	J. Harvey	F. Clark	27-Macdonald	33,690
1975-76	One	21	11	4	6	51	26	21	4	5	12	20	36	39	15	R6	F	-	Ld. Westwood	G. Lee	G. Nulty	30-Gowling	34,269
1976-77	One	21	14	6	1	40	15	21	4	7	10	24	34	49	5	R4	R4	-	Ld. Westwood	R. Dinnis	G. Nulty	17-Burns	33,934
1977-78	One	21	4	6	11	26	37	21	2	4	15	16	41	22	21R	R4	R2	R2	R.J. Rutherford	W. McGarry	G. Nulty	16-Burns	25,037
1978-79	Two	21	13	3	5	35	24	21	4	5	12	16	31	42	8	R4	R2	-	R.J. Rutherford	W. McGarry	T. Hibbitt	16-Withe	20,926
1979-80	Two	21	13	6	2	35	19	21	2	8	11	18	30	44	9	R3	R2	-	R.J. Rutherford	W. McGarry	M. Martin	21-Shoulder	23,711
1980-81	Two	21	11	7	3	22	13	21	3	7	11	8	32	42	11	R5	R2	-	R.J. Rutherford	A. Cox	M. Martin	7-Shinton	17,350
1981-82	Two	21	14	4	3	30	14	21	4	4	13	22	36	62	9	R4	R2	-	S. Seymour	A. Cox	M. Martin	20-Varadi	17,736
1982-83	Two	21	13	6	2	43	21	21	5	7	9	32	32	67	5	R3	R2	-	S. Seymour	A. Cox	K. Keegan	22-Varadi	24,573
1983-84	Two	21	16	2	3	51	18	21	8	6	7	34	35	80	3P	R3	R2	-	S. Seymour	A. Cox	K. Keegan	28-Keegan	29,419
1984-85	One	21	11	4	6	33	26	21	2	9	10	22	44	52	14	R3	R3	-	S. Seymour	J. Charlton	G. Roeder	17-Beardsley	25,810
1985-86	One	21	12	5	4	46	31	21	5	7	9	21	41	63	11	R3	R3	-	S. Seymour	W. McFaul	G. Roeder	19-Beardsley	23,307
1986-87	One	21	10	4	7	33	29	21	2	7	12	14	36	47	17	R5	R2	-	S. Seymour	W. McFaul	G. Roeder	13-Goddard	24,554
1987-88	One	20	9	6	5	32	23	20	5	8	7	23	30	56	8	R5	R3	-	S. Seymour	W. McFaul	G. Roeder	13-O'Neill	21,656
1988-89	One	19	3	6	10	19	28	19	4	4	11	13	35	31	20R	R3	R2	-	G. McKeag	J. Smith	A. Thorn	11-Mirandinha	22,839
1989-90	Two	23	17	4	2	51	26	23	5	10	8	29	29	80	3	R5	R3	-	G. McKeag	J. Smith	R. Aitken	34-Quinn	22,325
1990-91	Two	23	8	10	5	24	22	23	6	7	10	25	34	59	11	R4	R2	-	G. Forbes	J. Smith	R. Aitken	20-Quinn	17,267

Notes

Test Matches, Play-offs not included in League totals.

Consolidated record for 1939-40 includes aborted League fixtures.
Top goalscorers and average attendance figures include Cup fixtures.

CH = Champions
SF = Cup semi-finalists
NL = Northern League
W = Cup Winners
P = Promoted
WL = Wartime League
F = Cup finalists
R = Relegated

FACTS & FIGURES

CLUB HONOURS

First team

Football League Champions:	1904/05, 1906/07, 1908/09, 1926/27
Division Two Champions:	1964/65
Division Two promotion:	1897/98, 1947/48, 1983/84
FA Cup winners:	1910, 1924, 1932, 1951, 1952, 1955
FA Cup runners-up:	1905, 1906, 1908, 1911, 1974
FA Cup semi-finalists:	as above plus 1909, 1947
Football League Cup runners-up:	1976
Inter-Cities Fairs Cup winners:	1969
FA Charity Shield winners:	1909
FA Charity Shield runners-up:	1933, 1952, 1953, 1956
Sheriff of London Charity Shield winners:	1907
Football League War Cup semi-finalists:	1940, 1941
Texaco Cup winners:	1974, 1975
Anglo-Italian Cup winners:	1973
Japan Cup winners:	1983
Tyne-Tees Cup winners:	1944
Cumberland Cup winners:	1947, 1951
Shields Ingham Cup winners:	1923
Norfolk & Norwich Charity Cup winners:	1911
Northampton Hospital Charity Shield winners:	1912
Newcastle & Sunderland Hospital Cup winners:	1912

CLUB RECORDS

Top home attendance:
68,386 v Chelsea 3rd Sept 1930 (Div One)
Best average attendance:
56,299 1947/48 (Div Two)
Record receipts: £157,153 v Sunderland
16th May 1990 (Div Two play-off)
Record victory:
13-0 v Newport County (H) 5th October 1946 (Div Two)
Record defeat:
0-9 v Burton Wanderers (A) 15th April 1895 (Div Two)
Most league & cup goals in a season:
39 by H. Gallacher 1926/27
&
G. Robledo 1951/52
Most goals in a match:
6 by L. Shackleton v Newport County (H)
5th October 1946 (Div Two)
Youngest player: S. Watson
16 years 223 days (November 1990 v Wolves)
Oldest player: W. Hampson
44 years 225 days (April 1927 v Birmingham C)
Longest serving player:
W. McCracken (1904-23) **&** F. Hudspeth (1910-29)
19 years each

Longest serving individual:
J. Richardson (player & trainer 1929-77) 48 years
&
A. Mutch(physio & trainer 1922-86) 64 years
Record transfer fee received:
£2,300,000 for Paul Gascoigne 1988
Record transfer fee paid:
£850,000 for D. Beasant & A. Thorn both 1988

CENTENARY SUMMARY

In 100 years and 88 seasons of senior football from 1892 to 1992, the club's record of first team matches played, together with a performance analysis can be categorised as follows:

Competition	**No. of games**
Football League Division One	2544
Football League Division Two	1000
Football League Test Matches & Play-offs	6
FA Cup	294
Football League Cup	74
European competition	28
Wartime League & Cup	270
Anglo-Italian Cup	7
Texaco Cup	28
Anglo-Scottish Cup	7
Anglo-Scottish League	14
Simod Cup	3
Full Members Cup	1
Mercantile Trophy	4
Zenith Data Systems Cup	5
Charity Shield	6
Other Invitation competitions	33
Football League Jubilee	3
Festival of Britain	1
Northern League	10
North Eastern League	1
NE Counties Cup	2
Tours abroad	191
Other friendlies	513
Total	**5045**

Division One	63 seasons	72%
Division Two	25 seasons	28%
Glory Years	15 seasons	17%
Near Misses	7 seasons	8%
Above Average	36 seasons	41%
Below Average	24 seasons	27%
Disaster Years	6 seasons	7%

Number of Managers 16
Number of Players 878 (competitive fixtures only)

Note:
League statistics to end of season 1991/92, cup and friendly figures to November 1991.

MOST GAMES

League & Cup fixtures

PLAYER	POSITION	SEASONS	APPS
1. JIMMY LAWRENCE	Goalkeeper	1904-22	496
2. FRANK HUDSPETH	Left-back	1910-29	472
3. FRANK CLARK	Left-back	1962-75	457
4. BILL McCRACKEN	Right-back	1904-23	432
5. ALF McMICHAEL	Left-back	1949-63	431
6. DAVID CRAIG	Right-back	1962-78	412
7. BOBBY MITCHELL	Outside-left	1949-61	408
8. JACKIE MILBURN	Centre-forward	1946-57	397
9. WILF LOW	Half-back	1909-24	367
10 TOM McDONALD	Inside-left	1921-31	367

MOST GOALS

League & Cup fixtures

PLAYER	POSITION	SEASONS	GOALS
1. JACKIE MILBURN	Centre-forward	1946-57	200
2. LEN WHITE	Centre-forward	1953-62	153
3. HUGHIE GALLACHER	Centre-forward	1925-30	143
4. MALCOLM MACDONALD	Centre-forward	1971-76	121
5. BOBBY MITCHELL	Outside-left	1949-61	113
6. TOM McDONALD	Inside-left	1921-31	113
7. NEIL HARRIS	Centre-forward	1920-25	101
8. BRYAN ROBSON	Inside-forward	1962-71	97
9. JACKIE RUTHERFORD	Outside-right	1902-13	92
10 ALBERT SHEPHERD	Centre-forward	1908-14	92

STRIKE-RATE

League & Cup fixtures (50 or over goals scored)

PLAYER	SEASONS	No.of goals & games	%
1. HUGHIE GALLACHER			
Centre-forward	1925-1930	143 in 174 games	82%
2. ALBERT SHEPHERD			
Centre-forward	1908-1914	92 in 123 games	75%
3. JACK SMITH			
Centre-forward	1934-1938	73 in 112 games	65%
4. BARRIE THOMAS			
Centre-forward	1962-1964	50 in 78 games	64%
5. BILL APPLEYARD			
Centre-forward	1903-1908	87 in 145 games	60%
6. BILLY CAIRNS			
Centre-forward	1933-1944	53 in 90 games	59%
7. JOCK PEDDIE			
Centre-forward	1897-1902	78 in 135 games	58%
8. LEN WHITE			
Centre-forward	1953-1962	153 in 269 games	57%
9. VIC KEEBLE			
Centre-forward	1952-1957	67 in 120 games	56%
10 GEORGE ROBLEDO			
Inside-forward	1949-1953	91 in 164 games	55%

*up to c.s. 1991

MOST CAPPED PLAYERS

Including substitute appearances

PLAYER/TEAM	SEASONS	APPS
1. ALF McMICHAEL		
Left-back for Northern Ireland	1950-60	40
2. DAVID CRAIG		
Right-back for Northern Ireland	1967-75	25
3. DICK KEITH		
Right-back for Northern Ireland	1957-62	23
4. MICK MARTIN		
Midfield for Eire	1978-83	22
5. TOMMY CASSIDY		
Midfield for Northern Ireland	1970-80	20
6. DAVID McCREERY		
Midfield for Northern Ireland	1983-89	19
7. BOBBY MONCUR		
Defender for Scotland	1968-72	16
8. PETER BEARDSLEY		
Striker for England	1986-88	15
9. MALCOLM MACDONALD		
Centre-forward for England	1971-76	14
10 IVOR ALLCHURCH		
Inside-forward for Wales	1958-62	14

CLUB OFFICIALS OVER THE CENTURY

Directors

Archibald GG
Auld JR
Bates SF
Bell J
Bell JW
Bennie RB
Bennett T
Black J
Bowman G Sir
Bramwell W
Braithwaite F
Cameron D
Cameron John
Cameron James
Carmichael M
Catesby WP
Cowan J
Crawford D
Cushing R
Davis H
Dickson HH
Dickson GR
Dougan J
Dunn E
Forbes GR
Forster GR
Fox A
Good W
Graham J
Hall D
Hall J Sir
Henderson R
Hudson WR
Hurford WE
Johnson R
Lee JW
Lewis J
Lilburn W
Lunn J
Mallinger PC
Matthews GR
Milne GT
Molineux W
McConachie G
McKeag W
McKeag WG
McKenzie R
McKenzie RR
McKenzie RW
McVickers D
MacPherson D
Neasham W
Nevin RW
Neylon J
Oliver JP
Oliver R
Oliver T
Peel JE
Rush J
Rutherford GF
Rutherford R
Rutherford RJ
Salkeld DV
Sanderson WJ
Seymour GS
Seymour S
Shepherd F
Simpson RW
Stableforth AG
Strother Stewart R
Taylor WB
Telford J
Turnbull A
Westwood Lord Snr
Westwood Lord Jnr
Young R
Zollner L

Presidents

Braithwaite F
Seymour S
Westwood Lord junior

Vice Presidents

Hall J Sir
Rush J
Seymour GS
McKeag WG

Secretaries

Barker JD
Cushing R
Ferguson JS
Hall E
Golding WH
Hoole MG
Neylon J
Watt FG senior
Watt FG junior

Note:
For Chairmen, managers and captains of the club over the century see Centenary Analysis chart.

CONGRATULATIONS

THE FOOTBALL ASSOCIATION

I am delighted to add the congratulations of myself and my colleagues at Lancaster Gate to all those received by Newcastle United Football Club as this great old club celebrates its Centenary.

Newcastle United is a majestic club steeped in tradition, a club of mighty achievements both in the Football League and the FA Challenge Cup. The club has appeared in eleven FA Cup finals and has lifted the famous trophy on no fewer than six occasions. Four times the First Division championship pennant has fluttered proudly over St James Park. And the Magpies have tasted the exciting world of European soccer, winning the Fairs Cup in 1969.

United have faded from the honours list in recent seasons and this has not been easy for North East fans to accept. But there is cause for optimism now - where would football be without it - as a new manager with a new outlook attempts to bring the good times back to one of the greatest hotbeds of English soccer.

Graham Kelly
Chief Executive

SUNDERLAND

We at Roker Park offer our sincere congratulations on your club's achievement of its Centenary Year. Newcastle United has a proud and distinguished tradition and history, and without doubt is very much in the hearts and minds of the many people who have supported the club through many decades. We trust that your centenary celebrations prove both successful and memorable.

RS Murray
Chairman

THE FOOTBALL LEAGUE

On behalf of The Football League it is a pleasure to send congratulations to Newcastle United in their Centenary Year. On a personal note I have only happy memories of my many visits starting in the post-war years.

Whilst it is accepted that supporters are generally only interested in the present, it is at times such as these that we can look back and reminisce. Few clubs can boast more success than The Magpies. What a wealth of talent has graced the turf of St James Park - Len Shackleton, Albert Stubbins, Jackie Milburn, Len White, Ivor Allchurch, Bobby Mitchell, Chris Waddle, Peter Beardsley, Paul Gascoigne - and I've only just started, they are only the forwards! I mustn't forget the part the supporters have played - over the years they rate the best.

Thanks for the first hundred years. Best wishes for the second hundred.

David Dent
Secretary

RANGERS

On behalf of Rangers Football Club, I would like to congratulate you on your success over the past one hundred years and I look forward to renewing acquaintances sometime throughout the next century!

Kind regards from everyone at Rangers Football Club.

RC Ogilvie
Secretary-Director

WIMBLEDON

Congratulations and best wishes to you in this your Centenary Year - we hope promotion comes up in this your 100 break.

BLACKBURN ROVERS

Blackburn Rovers FC send Newcastle United FC all their best wishes in celebrating their Centenary Year in 1992.

SHEFFIELD WEDNESDAY

In the history of football certain clubs are prominent, amongst this elite is Newcastle United. Throughout the world its famous black and white colours are known even by those who have only a passing interest in the game.

Their support is always tremendous, bordering on the fanatical. Last season here at Hillsborough in a mid-week game between two clubs in the Second Division, the atmosphere was electric and the crowd exceeded 32,000, showing that no matter what division the club are in, the magic of Newcastle United remains.

WEST HAM UNITED

On the occasion of Newcastle United's Centenary Year it is a pleasure to recall the association of our clubs during the past. Only two clubs have faced the Hammers in more Football League matches and several have been memorable and high scoring encounters. And we have acquired two splendid goalscorers from St James Park in Vic Keeble and Bryan Robson. Our ways have parted at present, but when we meet again it will assuredly be in an atmosphere of bonhomie, good friendship and memories that can never fade.

CELTIC

It gives me great pleasure to extend the congratulations of Celtic Football Club to the chairman, directors, players, staff and supporters of Newcastle United on the occasion of their Centenary.

I have personal memories of games between our two clubs over the years and particularly an encounter at Celtic Park in September 1951 which brought together the winners of the Scottish and English Cups of that year. Fittingly enough the match ended with honours even in a 3-3 draw watched by 65,000.

On behalf of everyone at Celtic Football Club, I wish all at Newcastle a most successful Centenary Year both on and off the football field.

JC McGinn
Chairman

HARTLEPOOL UNITED

We express our congratulations on Newcastle United reaching its Centenary in 1992. Your club has for many years been the pride of the North East, and long may this continue.

KD Green
Chief Executive

LINFIELD

On behalf of my club I congratulate Newcastle United FC on reaching its Centenary. The links between our two clubs go back many years to the time that both Dick Keith and Alf McMichael joined your club from Linfield to be followed by George Hannah and Iam McFaul. More recently Tommy Wright was transferred from Linfield too. In addition each of those players gained international recognition with Northern Ireland.

And of course it was not all one way traffic because in the late fifties one of Newcastle United's most famous sons, Jack Milburn, was transferred to this club as Player Manager and set Northern Ireland football alight with his skills and scoring ability. We were very honoured to be associated with the statue which has been erected in Newcastle Upon Tyne to honour this great man.

D Campbell
Chairman

WATFORD

May I extend to you our sincere congratulations for your club's Centenary throughout 1992. We hope you have a most enjoyable time and celebrate by achieving promotion to the top flight.

Eddie Plumley
Chief Executive

PORTSMOUTH

Portsmouth Football Club wish to extend its sincere best wishes to Newcastle United in their Centenary Year, and may this great club prosper.

LEICESTER CITY

United and Leicester City go back a long time together - an opening win for the Magpies on 29th September 1894 provided the first Football League encounter between the clubs, followed three weeks later by - surprise, surprise - a high scoring 4-4 draw at Filbert Street.

Those high scores are still traditional of United and City clashes - no United fan will forget their fightback at St James Park in January 1990 to win 5-4 from a 4-2 deficit with ten minutes to go, or Leicester's revenge at Filbert Street by the same score in December of the same year!

Let's hope that 1992 sees more games of the traditional style, with both clubs celebrating anniversaries - it's a hundred years at Filbert Street for Leicester - with promotion back to the First Division.

YORK CITY

Although York City's and Newcastle United's paths have not crossed in League football they have been involved in memorable FA Cup matches. In 1929/30 the clubs met in the Third Round at St James Park and on a snow covered pitch City gave a magnificent display and held their famous First Division opponents to a l-l draw. In the replay, after another tremendous battle, United ran out 2-1 winners.

Twenty-five years later in March 1955 the sides met in the semi-final at Hillsborough as City were bidding to become the first Third Division club to reach Wembley. An epic tussle ended 1-1 and the replay was staged at Roker Park where 58,000 saw the Magpies triumph 2-0 and so end our dream. Twelve months later City signed Newcastle centre-forward Alan Monkhouse, while City's scoring hero Arthur Bottom moved to St James Park.

Newcastle officially opened the floodlights at Bootham Crescent in 1959, United giving a 'dazzling' display to win 8-2. And in City's history three of our managers were former Newcastle players; Tom Mitchell, Charles Spencer and recent boss, John Bird. We offer our congratulations to Newcastle United's Centenary.

MANCHESTER CITY

Newcastle versus Manchester City....the fixture conjures up memories of great encounters in both League football and Cup competitions. The Magpies 3-1 FA Cup triumph in 1955, the incredible Third Round replay two years later when City surrendered a 3-0 half-time lead to eventually lose 5-4 in extra-time. The amazing scene at St James Park when Joe Mercer's men clinched the Championship in 1968 and the League Cup final of 1976 which saw City gain revenge for that earlier Wembley defeat. Great games all, and many more besides....your friends at Maine Road look forward to our next meeting.

HULL CITY

Hull City has always found that relationships with Newcastle United have been amongst the friendliest we have come across. An example of this was the last match of the 1990/91 season, when we already knew we were relegated to the Third Division and played our last game at St James Park. The courtesy and friendship shown by the directors to our directors, was noticeable, but not surprising. Although we won the match, there was no animosity amongst the crowd and indeed our players were shown and given friendly reception from a naturally partisan Newcastle crowd. We wish you well in the future and congratulate you on your Centenary.

MW Fish
Chairman

WOLVERHAMPTON WANDERERS

On being asked about Newcastle United, my thoughts went back to season 1950/51. Both clubs were in their halcyon days. Newcastle defeated Wolves in the FA Cup semi-final at the second attempt and then I was lucky enough to see the final at Wembley when 'Wor Jackie' scored his two memorable goals. In a League match the following Wednesday, Newcastle again beat us and they also paraded the FA Cup which they subsequently won on a further two occasions in a five year spell. Great days for your club, may they soon return.

JA Harris
Chairman

CARDIFF CITY

The Bluebirds are pleased to offer sincere congratulations to The Magpies upon reaching their Centenary. As a club whose history is also entwined in FA Cup triumph, we readily recognise the contribution made to our great game by the men of Tyne and look forward to renewing acquaintances in the First Division! Congratulations from the men of the Taff - here's to the next 100!

NOTTS COUNTY

Notts County Football Club wishes to congratulate Newcastle United in their Centenary Year. The Magpies of Nottingham hope that the Magpies of Newcastle continue flying high for another 100 years.

NE Hook
Chief Executive

LEEDS UNITED

The Directors. Management, Players and Staff of Leeds United send their warmest congratulations to Newcastle United on its Centenary. And we look forward to welcoming the Magpies back where they belong in Division One very soon.

CRYSTAL PALACE

Crystal Palace Football Club would like to offer Newcastle United their heartiest congratulations on reaching their Centenary Year.

RG Noades
Chairman

IPSWICH TOWN

Newcastle United are one of the greatest names in British football. Those famous black and white stripes have been worn by some tremendous players over the years including Kevin Keegan, Malcolm Macdonald, Chris Waddle and Paul Gascoigne.

My own club's links with Newcastle take us back to our first Football League manager Scott Duncan and the late great Jackie Milburn, someone who has a special place in the history of both clubs. I wish you warmest congratulations on your Centenary and, in true Ipswich tradition, toast to your success in the future.

J Kerr
Chairman

OLDHAM ATHLETIC

Oldham Athletic extend their warmest congratulations to Newcastle United in their Centenary Year. A club of great tradition and history, Newcastle United have played their full part in promoting our great game and deserve our applause.

BOLTON WANDERERS

It is difficult to believe that Newcastle United Football Club is only 100 years old this year. Such has been the club's impact on the history and traditions of football and the wealth of great players and characters that have come out of Tyneside, it's hard to imagine The League before The Magpies.

The club's proud record in the last century speaks for itself. Well over half those hundred years have been spent in Division One. As a player I used to love competing at St James Park in front of that fantastic crowd of Geordies. Their knowledge of the game is equalled by that of the Lancastrian or Yorkshireman and I can think of no greater praise than that.

There have been many stirring encounters between Bolton Wanderers and Newcastle United over the years and, for our part, we look forward to more in the future.

On behalf of the Directors, Management and Staff at Burnden Park I offer our congratulations on the first hundred years, long may you continue to be a credit to the game.

Nat Lofthouse
President

WEST BROMWICH ALBION

Congratulations from all at The Hawthorns on qualifying for a telegram from the Queen! West Bromwich Albion have always regarded matches against Newcastle United as being particularly special events, and look forward to renewing them for a further hundred years.

EVERTON

My congratulations to Newcastle United Football Club on achieving it's Centenary Year.

The club has been in the forefront of English football throughout its existence and over the years its Chairmen and Directors have played a prominent part in the running of the League. On behalf of the Board of Everton Football Club I wish you every success in the future.

Sir Philip Carter
Chairman

PRESTON NORTH END

In your Centenary Year best wishes and congratulations to the Magpies from all at Deepdale. Since we first met in an FA Cup tie in January 1898 followed by our first meeting in the League in October of that year, there have been many memorable games between the Clubs.

United have, deservedly so, by their footballing deeds assured themselves of a notable place in the history of the game, an achievement for which they can justifiably feel proud. Long may your valuable contribution to football continue.

CHELSEA

Congratulations on your Centenary. Newcastle United is part of the fabric and tradition of English football, and we wish you well for the future and hope that during your Centenary Year you reclaim your rightful place in the First Division.

C Hutchinson
Managing Director

OXFORD UTD

Oxford United would like to congratulate Newcastle United on its Centenary and wish the club and its supporters every success in the future. While our two clubs have only met on relatively few occasions, one of those will stand out forever - the Cup match at The Manor on 30th October 1985. The significance to Oxford United supporters was that we went on to Wembley that year - our only major Cup success. Treasure and be proud of your history.

SWINDON TOWN

From The Robins to The Magpies, many congratulations on your Centenary. Every success in the next hundred.

MILLWALL

Millwall Football Club congratulates Newcastle United Football Club on their Centenary and wishes them every success for the next 100 years.

SCUNTHORPE UTD

The Directors, Management and Staff of Scunthorpe United Football Club would like to express their congratulations on the Centenary of Newcastle United and trust that the celebrations in this respect will be a great success.

BARNSLEY

Newcastle United Football Club has a rich and proud history streching back for 100 years. My club has enjoyed an excellent relationship with this great club and I am pleased to be able to contribute to this Centenary Publication. I should like to congratulate Newcastle United Football Club on reaching its Centenary and extend my sincere good wishes for the future.

JA Dennis
Chairman

NORTHUMBERLAND FA

Northumberland Football Association congratulate Newcastle United Football Club in reaching their Centenary Year in 1992. We wish the Directors, Staff and Team success in future years to come.

DURHAM COUNTY FA

Durham County Football Association congratulate Newcastle United Football Club on its Centenary. Although there is tense rivalry between our senior clubs, we are aware of the amount of work that the club has done over the years for many lesser teams on both sides of the Tyne and which is appreciated. We hope that the highlights of the first century, notably the 1950's, will soon be repeated and the club once more will gain the promotion it so richly deserves.

ARSENAL

On behalf of Arsenal Football Club may I offer the Directors, Staff, Players and Supporters of Newcastle United, our most cordial congratulations on your Club Centenary.

Arsenal Football Club is proud of its longstanding associations with one of the great English Football Clubs. We believe that there exists a shared tradition of values which demand a continuing commitment to excellence both on and off the field of play. We wish you a successful Centenary Year and another century of achievement.

PD Hill-Wood
Chairman

MANCHESTER UNITED

Everyone at Manchester United Football Club, Directors, Management, Players, Staff and Supporters extend their very best wishes to all at Newcastle United on the occasion of your club's Centenary.

Our paths have crossed many times in both League and Cup. Games of high-scoring and equally high drama have been numerous.

Perhaps the most important meeting was back in 1909 when we were paired together in the F.A. Cup semi-final.

Newcastle United had appeared in three of the previous four finals, so it was quite an achievement when we won 1-0 at Bramall Lane to take our place in the F.A. Cup final for the first time.

St James Park has always been, and will no doubt remain, one of the most formidable grounds which any club must visit. Geordie support for their club is legend and any victory gained at Gallowgate is one to be valued.

Manchester United is honoured and proud to have been associated with their namesakes for the best part of a century. Long may it continue.

BIBLIOGRAPHY

Newcastle United Literature

Aitken : Feed The Bear (p Mainstream)
Appleton : Hotbed of Soccer (p Hart Davis)
Beardsley : Peter Beardsley, An Autobiography (p Stanley Paul)
Beardsley, Hardisty : Proud To Be A Geordie (p Knight Fletcher)
Bell : Born To Soccer
Bentley : Going For Goal (p Museum Press)
Charlton : Cissie (p Bridge Studios)
Charlton : For Leeds And England (p Stanley Paul)
Eastham : Determined To Win (p Stanley Paul)
Edminson : Newcastle Utd, A Portrait in Old Picture Postcards
Gibson : The Newcastle Utd Story (parts 1, 2, 3) (p Pelham)
Gibson : Newcastle Utd, A Pictorial History (p Archive)
Gibson : Kevin Keegan, Portrait of a Superstar (p Comet)
Gibson : Wor Jackie, The Jackie Milburn Story (p Sportsprint)
Gowling : Football Inside Out (p Souvenir Press)
Hardisty : Auf Wiedersehen Kev, Tribute to a Superstar (p Newcastle Utd)
Harvey : The Joe Harvey Story (p Newcastle Utd)
Joannou : Newcastle Utd, A Complete Record (p Breedon)
Joannou : The Hughie Gallacher Story (p Breedon)
Joannou : The History of Newcastle Utd (p Newcastle Utd Supporters Club)
Joannou : A Complete Who's Who of Newcastle Utd (p Newcastle Utd Supp Club)
Keegan : Kevin Keegan (p Arthur Barker)
Macdonald : Win! (p Pelham)
Macdonald, Woolnough : Never Afraid To Miss (p Cassell)
Milburn : Golden Goals (p Soccer Book Club)
Milburn : Jackie Milburn's Newcastle Utd Scrapbook (p Souvenir Press)
Moncur : United We Stand (p Pelham)
Rippon : Great Soccer Clubs of the North East (p Moorland)
Shackleton : Clown Prince of Soccer (p Kaye)
Simpson : Sure It's A Grand Old Team To Play For (p Souvenir Press)
Smith, Dawson : Bald Eagle (p Mainstream)
Stein : Chris Waddle, The Authorised Biography (p Cockerel)
Wilson, Editor : Football Under The Skin (p Tyne Wear Museums Service)

Official Club Documents

Minutes of Board Meetings 1882-1960
Match-day programmes, home & away 1890-date
'United' Official Club newspaper 1986-date
Shareholders Newsletters 1980-date
Share Ledgers 1890-1920
Player Transfer Records 1892-date
Match Records 1892-date
Various scrapbooks and cuttings 1900-date
Annual Reports 1893-date
Various Club handbooks, booklets.

Newspapers

Many different titles have been used in research from The Illustrated London News to The Scotsman and The Daily Herald. However, the main source of newspaper reseach has been the local Newcastle Evening Chronicle, The Journal and Tyneside's football edition, The Pink, together with their previous titles from 1880 to date. Specific articles, many life-story serialisations, which have been of great help include;

Bobby Mitchell : My Life In Soccer, Sunday Sun 1961
Colin Veitch : My Life Story, Sunday Sun 1931
Colin Veitch : My Football Reminiscences, Thomson's Weekly News 1927
Peter McWilliam : My Story, Weekly Record 1927
Tom Hall : The History of Newcastle Utd, Weekly Chronicle 1952
Alf McMichael : Alf McMichael Looks At Soccer, The Journal 1958
Hughie Gallacher : Ups and Downs of My Football Life, Sunday Post 1931
Hughie Gallacher : Hughie Gallacher Tells All, Weekly Chronicle 1950
Dick Kirkup : The Hughie Gallacher Story, 1974
Various : North East's 100 Greatest Footballers, The Journal 1972
Hereward : History of Newcastle Utd, NUFC Official Programmes 1932/33
Paul Tully : The All Time Great Matches, Evening Chronicle 1991
Paul Tully : The All Time Greats, Evening Chronicle 1991

Annuals, Magazines

Many such documents have been used, including Gamages, Athletic News, News of the World, Playfair, Northern Echo and Rothmans yearbooks from 1890 to date. Magazines used in research include Charles Buchan's Football Monthly, Soccer Star, Northern Football, The Footballer and The Mag. Many miscellaneous articles from other issues have also been used throughout the research.

Books

Literally hundreds of books on the game of football have been utilised in the compilation of this history. Most important of all has been the Complete Record series of club histories, published by Breedon Books. Now covering almost 40 clubs nationwide, the series has become a cornerstone to historical research.

SUBSCRIBERS

1 Newcastle United Football Club
2 Newcastle United Football Club
3 Newcastle United Football Club
4 Newcastle United Football Club
5 Newcastle United Football Club
6 GEORGE FORBES, Chairman, Newcastle United FC
7 The Lord Mayor of Newcastle upon Tyne, Councillor THOMAS J. MARR
8 The Football Association, Lancaster Gate, London
9 The Football League, Lytham St. Annes
10 PETER C. MALLINGER, Vice Chairman, Newcastle Utd FC
11 RUSSELL CUSHING, Secretary & General Manager, Newcastle Utd FC
13 W. GORDON McKEAG, Honorary Life Vice President, Newcastle Utd FC
14 STAN SEYMOUR, Honorary Life President, Newcastle Utd FC
15 DOUGLAS HALL, Director, Newcastle Utd FC
16 DEREK McVICKERS, Director, Newcastle Utd FC
17 FREDDIE SHEPHERD, Director, Newcastle Utd FC
18 BOB YOUNG, Director, Newcastle Utd FC
19 TREVOR L. BENNETT, Associate Director, Newcastle Utd FC
20 Sir JOHN HALL, Vice President, Newcastle Utd FC
21 JAMES RUSH AFC, Vice President, Newcastle Utd FC
22 JEREMY BEECHAM, Leader of the Council, Newcastle upon Tyne
23 KEVIN KEEGAN OBE
24 HAYDN BIDDLE, Managing Director, Newcastle Breweries Ltd
25 OSSIE ARDILES, Manager, Newcastle Utd FC
26 PAUL JOANNOU, Stockbridge, Edinburgh

27 NORMAN GREENOP, Gamblesby, Penrith, Cumbria
28 JANICE M. HEIGHWAY, Thurmaston, Leicester
29 RAYMOND HEIGHWAY, Low Fell, Gateshead, Tyne & Wear
30 PHILIP SCOTT, Pegswood, Morpeth, Northumberland
31 MICHAEL A. CRAGGS, Watford, Hertfordshire
32 CHRISTOPHER SCOTT HENZELL, Killingworth Village, Newcastle upon Tyne
33 PETER J. FINKILL, Jarrow, Tyne & Wear
34 STEPHEN WILLIAM RODEN, Newsham, Blyth, Northumberland
35 GEORGE R. DICKSON, Newcastle upon Tyne
36 PAUL TOLAND, Hadrian Park, Wallsend
37 STEPHEN JOHN BLAND, South Church, Bishop Auckland, County Durham
38 DAVID HUGHES, Godden Green, Sevenoaks, Kent
39 RICHARD HUGHES, Godden Green, Sevenoaks, Kent
40 MELVYN HUGHES, Godden Green, Sevenoaks, Kent
41 CHARLES LEWIS, Edinburgh
42 MICHAEL HALL, Fenham, Newcastle upon Tyne
43 JOHN ALDER, Gateshead, Tyne & Wear
44 GARETH KING, Wednesbury, West Midlands
45 JONATHAN ROBERT HOPE, Benwell, Newcastle upon Tyne
46 KEITH HATELY, Fellside Park, Whickham, Newcastle upon Tyne
47 JEFF BURTLE, Fenham, Newcastle upon Tyne
48 DAVID HOGG, Whitburn, Tyne & Wear
49 MARK NOBLE, Jarrow, Tyne & Wear
50 DEAN CHRISTOPHER, Lincoln
51 GARY THOMPSON, Wallsend, Tyne & Wear
52 WALLACE WILSON, West Moor, Newcastle upon Tyne
53 STEPHEN A. LAMB, Harrow, Middlesex
54 JEFFREY THOMSON, Westerhope, Newcastle upon Tyne
55 JAMES YOUNG, Shieldfield, Newcastle upon Tyne
56 BRENDAN OSWALD, Wake Green Park, Moseley, Birmingham
57 M. DOWLING, Brookfield, Middlesbrough, Cleveland
58 ANTHONY NEIL GILLESPIE, Newton, Derbyshire
59 ARTHUR HUMBY, Leicester
60 BRIAN ALLAN, Newcastle upon Tyne
61 STEPHEN DAVID HANDY, Windy Nook, Tyne & Wear
62 PHILIP JAMES MYERS, Westerhope, Newcastle upon Tyne
63 JARED & LINDA ROBINSON, Ardwick Le Street, Doncaster, South Yorkshire
64 WILLIAM MARSH, Doncaster, South Yorkshire
65 ROBERT ALAN LEE, Trimdon Grange, County Durham
66 KEBVIN F. HILL, Newcastle upon Tyne
67 SHAUN CASSIDY, Arthur's Hill, Newcastle upon Tyne
68 KELLY SMITH, York
69 Mr & Mrs W. CRIPWELL, Westerhope, Newcastle upon Tyne
70 DAVID G. BROWNLOW, Newcastle upon Tyne
71 MICHAEL IAN BURNIE, Heaton, Newcastle upon Tyne
72 JULIE ELIZABETH DIXON, Lambton, Washington, Tyne & Wear
73 JOHN JAMES MOWBRAY, Birtley, County Durham
74 E. SCHOLES, Gosforth, Newcastle upon Tyne
75 MARGARET PETRIE, Dene Grange, Newcastle upon Tyne
76 TONY NOBLE, Newcastle upon Tyne
77 NEIL MURRAY, Newcastle upon Tyne
78 MALCOLM LAX, Rugby, Warwickshire
79 NICHOLAS CHARLES VINCE, Foxton, Leics
80 NEIL McQUEEN, Forest Hall, Newcastle upon Tyne
81 GAVIN HAIGH, Newton Hall, Durham
82 IAN STRAUGHAN, Sedgefield, County Durham
83 ROBERT TONES, Kelloe, County Durham
84 MALCOLM WOODHALL, Hexham, Northumberland
85 STEVEN THOMSON, North Shields, Tyne & Wear
86 JOHN EDMINSON, Newcastle upon Tyne
87 ALAN E. WILLIAMSON, Gateshead, Tyne & Wear
88 RAYMOND DUNN, Kirkby Stephen, Cumbria
89 ALLAN SCOTT, West Jesmond, Newcastle upon Tyne
90 IAN WILSON, Cramlington, Northumberland
91 MICHAEL PESCOD, London W11
92 T.E. PESCOD, Mickleton, Chipping Camden, Gloucestershire
93 PAUL EVANS, Chapel House, Newcastle upon Tyne
94 JANE & CRAIG SINCLAIR, Sompting, Lancing, West Sussex
95 GREG ANTONY PHILLIPS, Berwick upon Tweed, Northumberland
96 ROBERT GRAHAM LOWES, Highfield, Rowlands Gill, Tyne & Wear
97 PAUL ROWE, Newton Hall, Durham
98 GEOFFREY P. PINCHEN, Low Fell, Gateshead, Tyne & Wear
99 ANTONI GADOMSKI, Red House Farm, Newcastle upon Tyne
100 MALCOLM SCOTT, Tweedmouth, Berwick upon Tweed, Northumberland
101 DAVID STEEL, Washington, Tyne & Wear
102 MICHAEL BURTLE, Denton Burn, Newcastle upon Tyne
103 DAVE GREAVES, West Hallam, Derbyshire
104 J.D.J. McMORROW, Heaton, Newcastle upon Tyne
105 SPRINGFIELD COMPREHENSIVE SCHOOL, Jarrow, Tyne & Wear
106 ROGER TALBOT, New Penshaw, Houghton-le-Spring, Tyne & Wear
107 J.T. MOODY, Usworth Village, Washington, Tyne & Wear
108 DAVID GRAY, Hebburn, Tyne & Wear
109 DEREK EDWARD FAIRLESS, Allendale, Hexham, Northumberland
110 IAN CANT, Pontefract, West Yorkshire
111 BRIAN WELSH, Blue Bridge, Milton Keynes, Buckinghamshire
112 ERIC HOGG, Fairfield, Stockton-on-Tees, Cleveland
113 ROBERT POLLARD, Blaydon on Tyne, Tyne & Wear
114 PETER ROBSON, Friars Cliff, Christchurch, Dorset
115 DOROTHY M. ROBSON, Friars Cliff, Christchurch, Dorset
116 PAUL & BOBBY McKEOWN, Ferryhill, County Durham
117 DEREK ORTON, Coxhoe, Durham
118 A.J. STOCKDALE, Ford Village, Berwick upon Tweed, Northumberland
119 DAVID & IAN THIRLAWAY, High Howdon, Wallsend, Tyne & Wear
120 STEWART GILLSTROM, Edinburgh
121 DAVID PATRICK McKENNA, Barwell, Leicestershire
122 PAUL GOWANS, Ashington, Northumberland
123 MALCOLM A. McKENNA, Aycliffe Village, County Durham
124 STEVE LITTLE, Sherwood Rise, Nottingham
125 R.L. BORTHWICK, Oadby, Leicester
126 KEVIN McDONALD, North Shields, Tyne & Wear
127 SUSAN ELIZABETH GRANT, Dore, Sheffield, South Yorkshire
128 DENIS WRIGHT, Washington, Tyne & Wear
129 DALE LANG, St. Albans, Hertfordshire
130 ROGER TAMES, Newcastle upon Tyne
131 JOHN CUTTING, Ipswich, Suffolk
132 T.P. KELLS, Bispham, Blackpool, Lancashire
133 GARY JAMES PATRICK FINLAYSON, Dundee, Scotland
134 GEORGE W. BLAIR, Alnwick, Northumberland
135 JOHN WILSON, Blackpool, Lancashire
136 FIONA M. BENNETT, Bedlington, Northumberland
137 DAVID MOY, Seaton Delaval, Whitley Bay, Northumberland
138 WOODENTOP BULLIVANT, Newcastle upon Tyne
139 STEVE ATKINSON, West Boldon, Tyne & Wear
140 MICHAEL GRANT, Dore, Sheffield, South Yorkshire
141 ALAN SUDDES, Kilburn, Derbyshire
142 PAUL HEALEY, Kingston Park, Newcastle upon Tyne
143 DAVID HALL, Deckham, Gateshead, Tyne & Wear
144 JOHN WATSON, Duston, Northampton
145 PATRICK J. BIRNIE, Prestonpans, East Lothian
146 PAUL DENNIS ATKINSON, St. Johns, Newcastle upon Tyne
147 ALAN J. ROBSON, Hett, Durham
148 IAN BLENKINSOP, Hartlepool, Cleveland
149 HAROLD J. TAYROGES, Newcastle upon Tyne
150 IAN & ANDREA GLEN, Pyrford, Woking, Surrey
151 DANIEL WALKER, Gateshead, Tyne & Wear
152 LES RUFFELL, Little Haywood, Stafford
153 ROBERT KEITH GREY, Cleadon Village, Sunderland, Tyne & Wear
154 G.E. SHEPHERD, Woodlands Park, Wideopen, Newcastle upon Tyne
155 J. McMULLEN, Walker, Newcastle upon Tyne
156 CHRISTOPHER HARRISON, Whitley Bay

157 MICHAEL J.P. GAFF, New Herrington, Houghton-le-Spring, Tyne & Wear
158 RICHARD WAUGH, Seghill, Cramlington, Northumberland
159 R.W. CLARKE, Farnham, Surrey
160 DAVID SIMPSON, Ashington, Northumberland
161 DAVID ANDREW ROBINSON, Bowburn, Durham
162 SHAWN JAGGER, Ayton, Washington, Tyne & Wear
163 ANTHONY PORTER, North Shields, Tyne & Wear
164 STEVEN RICHARD GEORGE STOKER, High Heaton, Newcastle upon Tyne
165 H.W. GOLDING, Porthmadog, Gwynedd, North Wales
166 SIMON COX, South Shields, Tyne & Wear
167 R.T. COLLINSON, Carlisle, Cumbria
168 WES GARGETT, Coxhoe, County Durham
169 THOMAS WILLIAM ARKLEY, Selby, North Yorkshire
170 MICHAEL ANTHONY O'DONNELL, Bermondsey, London SE16
171 MICHAEL CONNOR, South Stanley, County Durham
172 IAN GRIFFITHS, Esless Park, Wrexham, Clwyd
173 STEVEN McINTOSH, Cleadon, Sunderland, Tyne & Wear
174 BILL WELSH, Killingworth Township, Newcastle upon Tyne
175 LOUIS AZZOPARDI, Mtarfa, Rabat, Malta
176 JULIE STANFORD, Glasson, Carlisle, Cumbria
177 ROSS DOUGLAS BAILEY, Colney Heath, St. Albans, Herts
178 PETER CLARK, Blyth, Northumberland
179 DAVID JACK, Burnopfield, Newcastle upon Tyne
180 JASON WILKES, Jarrow, Tyne & Wear
181 ANDY WOOD, Prudhoe, Northumberland
182 JACK WOOD, Totnes, Devon
183 RICHARD STOCKEN, Holmes Chapel, Crewe, Cheshire
184 LEON BRUNT, Witham, Essex
185 DEREK, NICHOLAS & PAUL MOONEY, Rothwell, Northamptonshire
186 KENNETH MOONEY, North Shields, Newcastle upon Tyne
187 PAUL YOUNGER, Tynemouth
188 YVONNE JEWELS, North Shields
189 COLIN WHEATLEY, Hartburn, Stockton-on-Tees, Cleveland
190 DAVID N. DURNIE, Colburn, Catterick Garrison, North Yorkshire
191 RICHARD O'SHEA, Colburn, Catterick Garrison, North Yorkshire
192 GEOFFREY KNOWLES, Coundon, Bishop Auckland, Co. Durham
193 KARL WILLIAM CLASPER, Walker-Dene, Newcastle upon Tyne
194 GEORGE VICKERS, Wallsend, North Tyneside
195 STEPHEN DEREK BROWN, Strood, Rochester, Kent
196 TY BROWNE, Denton Burn, Newcastle upon Tyne
197 ROBERT & ANNMARIE ROBSON, Watford, Herts
198 DAVEY SMITHSON, Lumley, Chester-le-Street, Co. Durham
199 ALAN DORMER, Consett, County Durham
200 STAN MOORHOUSE, Smarden, Kent
201 IAN SHANKS, Amble, Morpeth, Northumberland
202 SIMON HILDREY, Worcester Park, Surrey
203 JOHN LANGAN, Brampton Bierlow, Rotherham, South Yorkshire
204 J.M. ARMSTRONG, Blyth, Northumberland
205 T. STODDART, Woodham, Newton Aycliffe, Co Durham
206 WILF McGREGOR, Deworth, Windsor, Berkshire
207 ROGER PHILLIP IAN BLAIR, Guildford, Surrey
208 ANTHONY LANG, Newcastle upon Tyne
209 HARRY DEFTY, Boldon Colliery, Tyne & Wear
210 KEVIN DIAPER, Whickham, Newcastle upon Tyne
211 DEREK RICHARDSON, Walker, Newcastle upon Tyne
212 DEREK HANSON, Farnborough, Kent
213 KEVIN BEWICK, North Shields, Tyne & Wear
214 LESLIE USHER, Clavering Park, Whickham, Newcastle upon Tyne
215 MICHAEL PATRICK MULLIGAN, Chirton, North Shields, Tyne & Wear
216 ANDREW MORGAN, Godden Green, Sevenoaks, Kent
217 DEREK GRAHAM, Whickham, Newcastle upon Tyne
218 DAVID LUMB, Bromley Cross, Bolton, Lancashire
219 JOHN W. BRADLEY, Holton le Clay, Grimsby, South Humberside
220 DAVID KEATS, Thornton Heath, Surrey
221 MICHAEL C. KNIFTON, Yarm, Cleveland
222 JOHN DEREK WHEATCROFT, Lenton, Nottingham
223 NEIL DEVINE, Harlington Hayes, Middlesex
224 PAUL BISHOP, Stalybridge, Cheshire
225 R.W. MARWICK, Coatbridge, Lanarkshire
226 Mrs. J.A. MOTSON, St. Albans, Hertfordshire
227 J.A. HARRIS, Enfield, Middlesex
228 DAVID DYER, Heaton, Newcastle upon Tyne
229 PETER SMITH, Weybridge, Surrey
230 FREDERICK JOHN LEE, Ford, Plymouth, Devon
231 GEOFFREY WRIGHT, Ware, Hertfordshire
232 ANTHONY TAYLOR, Moorside, Sunderland, Tyne & Wear
233 CRAIG DULLER, Totnes, Devon
234 ULRICH MATHEJA, Nurnberg, Germany
235 S. JOBSON, St. Johns, Worcester
236 IAN SMITH, Honley, Huddersfield, West Yorkshire
237 L.A. ZAMMIT, Fareham, Hampshire
238 GARY JAMES, Denton, Manchester
239 KAREN MEWS, London WC1
240 G.S. McIVER, Gosforth, Newcastle upon Tyne
241 R.G. McIVER, Colliers Wood, London
242 WILLIAM CANTWELL, Llandudno, Gwynedd, North Wales
243 DAVE RIDLEY, Greenacres, Heanor, Derbyshire
244 EDWARD LESLIE RIDLEY, Oadby, Leicester
245 KEN SIMPSON, Teddington, Middlesex
246 DAVID NG, Ponteland, Newcastle upon Tyne
247 JOHN CHAPMAN, Luton, Bedfordshire
248 RALPH MORTIMER, London NW4
249 JOHN A. TURNER, High Etherley, Bishop Auckland, Co. Durham
250 ALAN H. TURNER, High Etherley, Bishop Auckland, Co. Durham
251 J. RINGROSE, Romford, Essex
252 COLIN SMITH, Rise Park, Romford, Essex
253 PAUL EDEN, Newport, Shropshire
254 DAVID MANKELOW, Chorlton, Manchester
255 TERJE KVICKSSON, Bergen, Norway
256 STEPHEN BRENNAN, Byker, Newcastle upon Tyne
257 ANDREW KIRKHAM, Wokingham, Berkshire
258 TONY RYMER, Gosforth, Newcastle upon Tyne
259 RAYMOND S. PERCY, Leeds, West Yorkshire
260 STEPHEN W. PURVES, Grantown on Spey, Morayshire
261 GARY DAVID STAWARD, Hebburn on Tyne, Tyne & Wear
262 DAVID LYEN, Twickenham, Middlesex
263 MICHAEL JOHN LITTLE, Kingston Park, Newcastle upon Tyne
264 ROBERT NEIL JOHNSON, Cherry Tree Hill, Chaddesden, Derbyshire
265 NIGEL G. MADDISON, Broomhill, Sheffield, South Yorkshire
266 MARK WADDELL, Lowestoft, Suffolk
267 IAN SMAILE, Ealing, London
268 ALLAN GALLI, Walworth, London
269 STEWART FELL, Radcliffe, Manchester
270 TONY VAUGHAN, Ashford, Middlesex
271 COMUS ELLIOTT, Weavering, Maidstone, Kent
272 CHARLES LEONARD ELLIOTT, London S.E.19
273 DAVID K. JAMESON, Whitley Bay, Tyne & Wear
274 COLIN A. MIDDLETON, Harrogate, North Yorkshire
275 M.A. STEIN, Southgate, London
276 GRAEME & PATRICIA ROBINSON, Dudley, West Midlands
277 THOMAS GORDON, Brentwood, Essex
278 DUNCAN K.M. GRAHAM, Loundsley Green, Chesterfield, Derbyshire
279 STEPHEN BROOKE, Newbury, Berkshire
280 PHILIP GOULDBOURNE, Maidstone, Kent
281 BARRY BARKES, Harestock, Winchester, Hampshire
282 RAYMOND ANDREW McDERMOTT, Detmold, Germany
283 K.P. TURNER, Fleet Marston, Aylesbury, Bucks
284 ROGER M. DOUGLASS, Richmond, Surrey
285 JOHN L. DOUGLASS, Jindalee, Queensland, Australia
286 PHILIP HOGARTH, London SW1
287 MARK TURNER, West Denton, Newcastle upon Tyne
288 ANDREW BARR, Bow Brickhill, Milton Keynes, Bucks
289 ANDY WAIT, Denton Burn, Newcastle upon Tyne
290 JEREMY PARWANI, Gillingham, Kent
291 BILL DODDS, Eastbourne, East Sussex
292 STEPHEN CARR, Woodford Hollow, Tipton, Staffs
293 A.J. ANDERSON, Hitchin, Herts
294 CYRIL GEORGE, Aberfan, Merthyr Tydfil, Mid-Glamorgan
295 GEOFFREY TARN, Basingstoke, Hampshire
296 MICHAEL PILCH, Watton, Thetford, Norfolk
297 CENTRAL LIBRARY, Newcastle upon Tyne
298 HAZEL THOMPSON, Stranmills, Belfast, Northern Ireland
299 DEREK LUKE, High Wycombe, Bucks
300 GARY LUKE, High Wycombe, Bucks
301 DAVID A. ELLIOTT, Rosehill, Wallsend, Tyne & Wear
302 FRANK EVANS, Sundorne Grove Farm, Shrewsbury, Salop
303 PAUL S. KIERAN, Mossley, Ashton under Lyne, Lancashire
304 PAUL DAGLISH, Detmold, Germany
305 E.R. CRAWFORD, Leicester
306 J. STEPHEN RUDDICK, Croydon, Surrey
307 TONY & MICHAEL RODGERS, Hounslow, Middlesex
308 GLENN WILLIAM CARVER, Highbury, London
309 BOGDAN TOMICZEK, Cieszyn, Poland
310 IAN W. RUDDICK, Ascot, Berkshire
311 SURTEES SCOTT TABERHAM, Wollaton, Nottingham
312 ANDY MALEY, Oadby, Leicester
313 DAVID TAIT, South Croydon, Surrey
314 JOSEPH TAYLOR, Ryton, Tyne & Wear
315 JOHN JAMES CLARKE, Pinxton, Nottinghamshire
316 PAUL MANN, Westfield, Woking, Surrey
317 TONY & KAREN HUNTER, Cheriton, Folkestone, Kent
318 C.A. STEWART, Bognor Regis, West Sussex
319 STEPHEN CARNEY, Monkseaton, Whitley Bay, Tyne & Wear
320 STEVE RAILTON, Woodside, London SE25
321 ROBERT GREENLAND, Fulham, London, SW6
322 ANTHONY BRITTON, Braintree, Essex
323 JEFF DAVIDSON, Streatham, London SW16
324 ROSS ALEXANDER BOWMAN, Newcastle upon Tyne

325 JOHN VINTON WILKINSON, Newcastle upon Tyne
326 CHRISTOPHER ROY ANNAN, Newcastle upon Tyne
327 ALEX JOE HUMBLE, Washington, Tyne & Wear
328 LOU J. PHEMISTER, Lincoln, Nebraska, U.S.A.
329 JAMES H. EXLEY, West Drayton, Middlesex
330 STEPHEN TANSEY, Farndon, Nottinghamshire
331 BRYN LLEWELLYN, Bradford, West Yorkshire
332 A.N. BROWN, Menston, Ilkley, West Yorkshire
333 LIAM LAVELLE, Whitley Bay, Tyne & Wear
334 JOHN B. CLARK, Whitley Bay, Tyne & Wear
335 ALAN YOUNGER, North Shields, Tyne & Wear
336 STEPHEN YOUNGER, Uxbridge, Middlesex
337 GARRY COSGROVE, North Shields, Tyne & Wear
338 ANDREW ABBEY, Woodhouse, Leeds, West Yorkshire
339 Dr. KEITH BEVERIDGE, Sedgefield, Co. Durham
340 ALAN COLEMAN, Leigh-0n-Sea, Essex
341 STEVE FOUKES, Syston, Leicester
342 KEITH DOUGLAS, Gosforth, Newcastle upon Tyne
343 PETER LEE, Houghton-le-Spring, Tyne & Wear
344 DARRELL HAWKSWORTH, Marsh, Huddersfield, West Yorks
345 S.R. CHAMPION, Belmont, Durham
346 STEPHEN KANE, Haltwhistle, Northumberland
347 LARS-OLOF WENDLER, Hoganas, Sweden
348 CHRISTOPHER AHERNE, York, North Yorkshire
349 PHILIP C. RICE, York, North Yorkshire
350 KARL ERIK STRODL, Peterlee, County Durham
351 GEORGE EASTON-KYLE, Windsor, Berkshire
352 STEPHEN McMULLEN, Newcastle upon Tyne
353 SANDRA HUZZARD, North Shields, Tyne & Wear
354 TERRY BENHAM, Colden Common, Twyford, Winchester
355 JOHN AYRE, Fenham, Newcastle upon Tyne
356 A.H. HUTCHINSON, Hilton, Inverness
357 KEVIN WHITBY, Royston, Hertfordshire
358 ADAM GORDON, Ravenshead, Nottingham
359 BRIAN CRAWFORD, Hatfield, Hertfordshire
360 MARK FIELD, Preston, Lancashire
361 JULIAN FIELD, London E3
362 HUGH COLLINGWOOD, East Molesey, Surrey
363 STUART MATHER, Morpeth, Northumberland
364 CHARLES ALFRED SCHOLEY, Great Barr, Birmingham
365 JACK H. PINDER, St. James, Barbados
366 MICHAEL G. HUDSON, Jarrow, Tyne & Wear
367 JOHN CLOUSTON, West Wickham, Kent
368 DAVID W. TEASDALE, Abu Dhabi
369 DAVID PEASE, Norwich, Norfolk
370 W. McCARTHY, Woodley, Reading
371 J.E. TINDLE, Alvechurch, Worcestershire
372 NEIL MAGEAN, Harrington, Workington, Cumbria
373 JONATHAN ROSS SMITH, Bishopthorpe, York
374 ROBERT JAMES MOORE, Binley, Coventry
375 DAVID TAYLOR, Sunderland, Tyne & Wear
376 WILLIAM THOMAS COLE, Witham, Essex
377 ARRAN P. TOWERS, Eltham, London
378 R.B. JOHNSON, Lancashire
379 ROBERT JOHN SYRETT, Kidderminster, Worcs
380 G. TAYLOR, Little Aston, Sutton Coldfield
381 JAMES THOMPSON, Regents Park, London
382 DEAN SCOTT THOMPSON, Hampton Hill, Middlesex
383 COLIN CAMPBELL, Nunthorpe, Middlesbrough
384 PHILIP HENRY BROWN, Darlington, Co. Durham
385 KEITH ROBERT BROWN, York, North Yorkshire
386 DEREK FORSTER, Westerhope, Newcastle upon Tyne
387 DAVID DODD, Felling, Tyne & Wear
388 PAULINE MORRALLEE, Prudhoe, Northumberland
389 MARK WORTH, Caterham, Surrey
390 GEORGE MICHAEL STEPHENSON, Rock, Alnwick, Northumberland
391 CATHERINE MAIR, Blaydon, Tyne & Wear
392 MICHAEL HARLE, Prestbury, Cheshire
393 MIKE LANCASTER, Bush Hill Park, Enfield, Middlesex
394 JAMES ROBERT GROUNSELL, High Heaton, Newcastle upon Tyne
395 KEITH ANGLES, High Heworth, Gateshead, Tyne & Wear
396 JAMES WILLIAM HOGG, Great Birtley, Chester-le-Street, Co Durham
397 P. SIMPSON, Bensham, Gateshead, Tyne & Wear
398 THOMAS KEITH PARKER, Lincoln
399 ANTHONY B. HILL, Darras Hall, Ponteland, Northumberland
400 ANDREW GLASSE, Crawcrook, Ryton, Tyne & Wear
401 PAUL ALAN BROWN, Melton Park, Newcastle upon Tyne
402 RONALD GIBSON, Headingley, Leeds, West Yorkshire
403 PHILIP JOBSON, Ryton, Tyne & Wear
404 DAVID PETER EMMERSON, Walkerville, Newcastle upon Tyne
405 TONY ADAMSON, Chaplin, Newcastle upon Tyne
406 RAYMOND WALTON, Cockermouth, Cumbria
407 RONALD BOWER, Wilmslow, Cheshire
408 STEPHEN ALAN STONES, Darlington, County Durham
409 MICHAEL JONES, Birtley, Chester-le-Street, Co Durham
410 ALAN BROWNLESS, Peterlee, County Durham
411 B.S. CARTER, Hadrian Park, Wallsend, Tyne & Wear
412 J.A. WATSON, Benton, Newcastle upon Tyne
413 P.T.FULLERTON, Leeds, West Yorkshire
414 R.R. TYERMAN, Edmundbyers, Consett, Co Durham
415 KEITH GIBBISON, Bishopstone, Swindon, Wiltshire
416 ERNIE WILSON, Whitby, North Yorkshire
417 IAN MUDIE, Whickham, Newcastle upon Tyne
418 S.H. COLE, North Kensington, London
419 PHILIP KING, Darlington. County Durham
420 JON MICHAEL TURNBULL, Kingstown, Carlise, Cumbria
421 G. SOWERBY, Didcot, Oxon
422 JONATHAN HALL, Henleaze, Bristol
423 GERAINT JONES, Shooters Hill, Woolwich, London
424 STEVE SMITH, Cheadle Hulme, Cheshire
425 DAVID PETER McCRUDEN, Newcastle upon Tyne
426 J.M. WOOD, Caversham, Berkshire
427 DAVID OSWALD NEWTON, Felling-on-Tyne, Gateshead
428 WILLIAM BELL, Sutton-in-Ashfield, Nottinghamshire
429 GLEN D. MARSHALL, Sutton-in-Ashfield, Nottinghamshire
430 T.D. REDPATH, Wooler, Northumberland
431 S.D. REDPATH, Churchdown, Gloucester
432 K.M. SLATTER, Churchdown, Gloucester
433 ROGER STEPHEN MEARA, Darras Hall, Ponteland
434 M. BLAKEY, Felpham, Bognor Regis, West Sussex
435 WILLIAM B. KILMURRAY, Victoria, London
436 WILLIAM B. KILMURRAY, Victoria, London
437 ALAN DAVIES, Worcester
438 DAVID WADE, Darlington, County Durham
439 A. JONES, Eton Wick, Windsor, Berkshire
440 PETER S. BLACK, Boxmoor, Hemel Hempstead, Herts
441 M. BAYLEY, Bourne, Lincolnshire
442 TONY GALVIN, Asst. Manager, Newcastle Utd FC
443 DEREK FAZACKERLEY, Coach, Newcastle Utd FC
444 COLIN SUGGETT, Coach, Newcastle Utd FC
445 DEREK WRIGHT, Physiotherapist, Newcastle Utd FC
446 PETER KIRKLEY, Youth Development Officer, NUFC
447 Dr. KEITH BEVERIDGE, Club Doctor, Newcastle Utd FC
448 JEFF CLARKE, PFA Football in the Community Officer, NUFC
449 KEVIN SCOTT, Captain, Newcastle Utd FC
450 PAVEL SRNICEK, Newcastle Utd FC
451 TOMMY WRIGHT, Newcastle Utd FC
452 JOHN ANDERSON, Newcastle Utd FC
453 MATTHEW APPLEBY, Newcastle Utd FC
454 DARREN BRADSHAW, Newcastle Utd FC
455 ROBBIE ELLIOTT, Newcastle Utd FC
456 BJORN KRISTENSEN, Newcastle Utd FC
457 ALAN NEILSON, Newcastle Utd FC
458 RAY RANSON, Newcastle Utd FC
459 MARK STIMSON, Newcastle Utd FC
460 STEVE WATSON, Newcastle Utd FC
461 BILLY ASKEW, Newcastle Utd FC
462 KEVIN BROCK, Newcastle Utd FC
463 LEE CLARK, Newcastle Utd FC
464 ARCHIE GOURLAY, Newcastle Utd FC
465 LEE MAKEL, Newcastle Utd FC
466 LIAM O'BRIEN, Newcastle Utd FC
467 GAVIN PEACOCK, Newcastle Utd FC
468 JOHN WATSON, Newcastle Utd FC
469 JOHN GALLACHER, Newcastle Utd FC
470 STEVE HOWEY, Newcastle Utd FC
471 ANDY HUNT, Newcastle Utd FC
472 MICK QUINN, Newcastle Utd FC
473 DAVID ROBINSON, Newcastle Utd FC
474 FRANZ CARR, Newcastle Utd FC
475 ALAN THOMPSON, Newcastle Utd FC
476 DAVID ROCHE, Newcastle Utd FC
477 GRAHAME McDONNELL, Newcastle Utd FC
478 KEN SLATER, Newcastle Utd FC
479 TONY TOWARD, Newcastle Utd FC
480 E. JOANNOU, West Benwell, Newcastle upon Tyne
481 DAVID COXON, St. Leonards on Sea, Hastings, E. Sussex
482 ALAN CANDLISH, West Denton, Newcastle upon Tyne
483 ANTHONY JOHN FIDDES, Chapel Park, Newcastle upon Tyne
484 JOE ANTHONY FIDDES, Chapel Park, Newcastle upon Tyne
485 ALAN LODGE, Stockbridge, Edinburgh
486 PAUL TULLY, Denton Burn, Newcastle upon Tyne
487 DOUGLAS MILLIKEN, Duddingston, Edinburgh
488 CHARLIE CROWE, Longbenton, Newcastle upon Tyne
489 ANTHONY G. ROSSA, Anstey, Leicester
490 GERALD C.O. TOON, Scraptoft, Leicester
481 EAMON C. HEIGHWAY, Thurmaston, Leicester
492 JULIAN BASKCOMB